Photoshop® CS Artistry

Mastering the Digital Image

▼▼▼▼▼▼▼▼▼▼▼▼▼▼

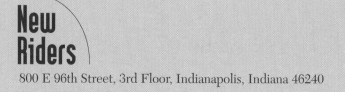

New Riders

800 E 96th Street, 3rd Floor, Indianapolis, Indiana 46240

Barry Haynes

Wendy Crumpler

Seán Duggan

Photoshop® CS Artistry

Mastering the Digital Image

By Barry Haynes and Wendy Crumpler

Published by: New Riders Publishing
                  800 E 96th Street, 3rd Floor
                  Indianapolis, IN 46240 USA

International Standard Book Number: 0-7357-1374-X

Library of Congress Catalog Card Number: 2003111992

Printed in the United States of America   1 2 3 4 5 6 7 8 9 0

First Printing: January 2004

TRADEMARKS

All terms mentioned in this book that are known to be trademarks or service marks have been appropriately capitalized. New Riders cannot attest to the accuracy of this information. Use of a term in this book should not be regarded as affecting the validity of any trademark or service mark.

Adobe Photoshop CS is a registered trademark of Adobe Systems, Incorporated.

WARNING AND DISCLAIMER

Every effort has been made to make this book as complete and as accurate as possible, but no warranty of fitness is implied. The information provided is on an "as is" basis. The authors and the publisher shall have neither liability or responsibility to any person or entity with respect to any loss or damages arising from the information contained in this book or from the use of the CD or programs accompanying it.

PUBLISHER
Stephanie Wall

PRODUCTION MANAGER
Gina Kanouse

PROJECT EDITOR
Michael Thurston

INDEXER
Cheryl Lenser

TECHNICAL EDITORS
Seán Duggan
Tim Gray

MEDIA DEVELOPER
Jay Payne

COVER DESIGN
Wendy Crumpler and
Barry Haynes

COVER PRODUCTION
Barry Haynes and
Wendy Crumpler

COVER PHOTO
Barry Haynes

BOOK DESIGN AND PRODUCTION
Wendy Crumpler and
Barry Haynes

MANUFACTURING COORIDINATOR
Dan Uhrig

MARKETING
Scott Cowlin
Tammy Detrich

PUBLICITY MANAGER
Susan Nixon

A MESSAGE FROM NEW RIDERS

Every so often in the world of publishing, a book comes along that stands taller and stronger than the rest. *Photoshop CS Artistry* is that book. This is the sixth edition that New Riders has had the honor to publish. Barry Haynes and Wendy Crumpler have given us, and all of you, a gift: quite possibly the best Photoshop book on the market. Rarely have we seen a book so embraced by its readers. Rarely do we see the type of anticipation for a new edition that *Photoshop CS Artistry* inevitably receives. New Riders takes pride in producing great books and building great relationships with our readers and authors. To put it simply, *Photoshop CS Artistry* is why we publish books.

We have worked with Barry and Wendy for many years now. They are great authors and great people. Their knowledge and passion have inspired hundreds of thousands of readers and a great many editors who have had the fortune to work with them. Their dedication to their readers and this book is something special. Thank you Barry and Wendy.

This is a different kind of Photoshop book, and it is for a different type of Photoshop user. This is for the perfectionist, someone not satisfied with getting close, but only satisfied with getting it right. This book will show you how to do that. This book doesn't simply teach you how to use Photoshop; it shows you how to master it. We feel that no other Photoshop book better addresses the needs of the photographer, artist, and serious student. Please let us know how you use this book and how it works for you. Because as Photoshop and its users evolve, so must this book. Thanks...

HOW TO CONTACT US

As the reader of this book, you are our most important critic and commentator. We value your opinion and want to know what we're doing right, what we could do better, in what areas you'd like to see us publish, and any other words of wisdom you're willing to pass our way.

As Publisher at New Riders, I welcome your comments. You can fax, email, or write me directly to let me know what you did or didn't like about this book as well as what we can do to make our books better. When you write, please be sure to include this book's title, ISBN, and author, as well as your name and phone or fax number. I will carefully review your comments and share them with the authors and editors who worked on the book.

Please note that I cannot help you with technical problems related to the topic of this book, and that due to the high volume of email I receive, I might not be able to reply to every message. Thanks.

Fax: 317-428-3280
Email: stephanie.wall@peachpit.com
Mail: Stephanie Wall
Publisher
New Riders Publishing
800 E 96th Street, 3rd Floor
Indianapolis, IN 46240 USA

VISIT OUR WEB SITE: www.newriders.com

On our Web site, you'll find information about our other books, the authors we partner with, book updates and file downloads, promotions, discussion boards for online interaction with other users and with technology experts, and a calendar of trade shows and other professional events with which we'll be involved. We hope to see you around.

Email Us from Our Web Site

Go to www.newriders.com and click on the Contact Us link if you
- Have comments or questions about this book.
- Want to report errors that you have found in this book.
- Have a book proposal or are interested in writing for New Riders.
- Would like us to send you one of our author kits.
- Are an expert in a computer topic or technology and are interested in being a reviewer or technical editor.
- Want to find a distributor for our titles in your area.
- Are an educator/instructor who wants to preview New Riders books for classroom use. In the body/comments area, include your name, school, department, address, phone number, office days/hours, text currently in use, and enrollment in your department, along with your request for either desk/examination copies or additional information.

ABOUT THE AUTHORS

Barry Haynes has been involved with photography since he was 14 using a Kodak Instamatic 104 on a trip to England. He later became a U.S. Navy photographer and attended most of the Navy's advanced photography courses. After getting his BA in computer science from University of California, San Diego, Barry spent 10 years, from 1980 to 1990, doing software development and research at Apple. It was a great time to be at Apple, and Barry was able to be a part of Apple's growth from 500 employees to over 10,000. He took a leave of absence from Apple in 1990 to set up a darkroom and get back to his photography. He soon found himself teaching Photoshop workshops and the notes for those evolved into Barry's advanced Photoshop Artistry book series, the latest of these being this *Photoshop CS Artistry: Mastering the Digital Image* from New Riders. His books are very popular with photographers and artists who are using Photoshop to create their final artwork.

He also teaches in-depth digital printmaking workshops from his studio in Corvallis, Oregon. Barry enjoys using his Photoshop darkroom techniques to print, show, and sell his own photography using Epson 4000 and 7600 printers. Check his image gallery at www.barryhaynes.com. He is currently working on a new training DVD and/or book entitled *Making the Digital Print,* which will cover all aspects of making the best art quality digital prints. Barry has given talks and workshops for Palm Beach Photographic Center, Santa Fe Workshops, Anderson Ranch, International Center of Photography, the Photoshop Conference, Seybold Seminars, MacWorld, the Center for Creative Imaging, advertising agencies, design firms, photography stores, and other organizations. His articles appear in *Communication Arts*, *Camera Arts*, and other photography magazines.

Wendy Crumpler has been in advertising and design since 1980. She has worked in print, television, CD-Interactive, interactive television, and computer-based training. Prior to her discovery of the computer in 1981 and the Macintosh in 1986, she was an actress and teacher. She is the author of two versions of her popular *Photoshop, Painter, and Illustrator Side-by-Side* book from Sybex and also *Gateway: A Spiritual Journey on the Andean Path*. She has done production, illustration, design, and training for a variety of clients using many applications. She has worked for Angotti Thomas Hedge, Boardroom Reports, Deutsch Advertising, J. Walter Thompson, TBWA Advertising, Wechsler Design, Wells Rich Greene, Canon, Parke Davis, and AT&T.

Seán Duggan is a photographer and digital artist who combines a traditional fine art photographic background with extensive real world experience in the field of digital imaging. He is a co-author of *Real World Digital Photography* (Peachpit Press, 2003) and is an Adobe Certified Photoshop Expert. His Photoshop tutorial column can be seen regularly in *MacDesign* magazine and he also writes articles on Photoshop and digital imaging for *PCPhoto, Outdoor Photographer*, and *Digital Photo Pro* magazines. His photographs have been exhibited at the Monterey Peninsula Museum of Art, the Center for Photographic Art in Carmel, California. He is an instructor in the photography department at University of California, Santa Cruz Extension, where he teaches regular classes on Digital Photography and Digital Imaging for Photographers. Seán provides Photoshop and imaging consulting services for photographers and companies and also teaches custom and private workshops at his studio. Visit his Web site at www.seanduggan.com.

LET US KNOW WHAT YOU THINK

There's been a lot of student and reader involvement in the shaping of this book. Listening to people who use these techniques helps us to refine and dig deeper to find solutions to our clients' and students' problems. And, we get smarter in the process. We love what we do and invite you to become part of the digital revolution with us. Let us know what you think of the book, what was helpful, what confused you. We are committed to empowering people to use their minds and spirits, computers, and software to advance their own artistic abilities and to make a difference on this planet.

TAKE ONE OF OUR IN-DEPTH WORKSHOPS

We live in Corvallis, Oregon, an arts-oriented college town where we teach week-long, hands-on workshops for up to six students at a time. These classes are tailored to meet the individual needs of those students. Barry's next DVD/book project is *Making the Digital Print*, an in-depth guide for those who are making digital art prints. For more info on this as it progresses, check out Barry's Web site at www.barryhaynes.com. We welcome your ideas and thoughts for this book and our other projects including Wendy's *Gateway* book. Check for the latest information about the details, times, and locations for our digital imaging courses, as well as book updates, scanning and printing tips, and other useful information on our Web site, www.barryhaynes.com.

WE LOOK FORWARD TO HEARING FROM YOU!

Barry Haynes Photography, Maxart
2222 NW Brownly Heights Drive
Corvallis, OR 97330
541-754-2219
email: Barry@maxart.com, or Wendy@maxart.com

Please check our Web site: http://www.barryhaynes.com

DEDICATION

Imagine all the people
Living life in peace...

You may say I'm a dreamer
But I'm not the only one
I hope someday you'll join us
And the world will be as one

John Lennon (1940-1980)

This book is dedicated to the probability of peace on Earth. As we become more connected to our brothers and sisters across this planet it is increasingly apparent that we, the people, want this. If we imagine it, we can make it happen, and leave it to our children as our greatest gift.

Do your part. Make art. Make peace. Heal the world through who you are and the acts you do. Be brave, speak up, challenge injustice, greed, and the status quo. Be kind and compassionate with those you do not understand. Love the land, the creatures that inhabit it, and one another. Each of us has an important role in bringing peace. When we reach critical mass, peace will not be stopped no matter who believes they hold the reigns of power.

ACKNOWLEDGMENTS

Each time we go through the amazing process of putting a book together, we worry. How will it be this time? Will we get the support we need, will people be competent, will they be fun? It's a difficult and daunting task to put so much effort into a book that will need to be updated again in a very short time. But, each time we write, we're blessed with people who ease the way, straighten us out, keep us going, and make us laugh.

So thank-yous to:

Seán Duggan, for updating chapters 36 & 37, for being a great instructor using *Photoshop Artistry*, and for being a great Dad! Your tech edit comments were really superlative—you know your stuff and you know the audience!

Michael Thurston, for being the chillest person we know (don't change that) and for sending great comments. That really helps! Thanks for being a fabulous editor. We thought about dedicating this book to the comma!

Stephanie Wall, for going out of her way to make things work for us and for doing great things to sell and promote this book. A person who bathes her dog in her own bathtub has to be a good person! Max asks if we like our publisher. We say "Yes."

Stacey Beheler, for helping us out with a variety of things from royalties to plane tickets and especially for being there to send a message to Stephanie when we need to talk to her.

Tim Gray, who helped us make sure that PC users would feel at home with *Artistry*.

Jay Payne, for burning the final CD so it works and looks right on Mac and PC and for being easy and friendly to work with.

Cheryl Lenser, for our fabulous index. We think it's the best of any Photoshop book and makes *Artistry* a truly great resource.

Brad Bunnin, minister, attorney, friend. We continue to rely on your advice and knowledge—you are such a gift. We're looking forward to reading your political sermon.

Jim Rich, for all your help with color and calibration, for your friendship; it's great to call up and ask "Hey Jim, what do you think of this?".

Mark Reid and Dave McIntire for feeding our photography art group and for being inspirational as well as good friends. All the members of the Corvallis Photo Arts guild for being a group of artists and friends I go to on Thursday nights, a welcome night off from writing.

Bill Atkinson, a generous and creative human being, whose fire to know and share and learn pulls us in and pushes us forward.

Charlie Cramer, a gifted artist, whose work always inspires us. Thank you so much for sharing your knowledge, friendship, and music. You, Bill, and the Bruces are my photography mentors and great friends!

Bruce Ashley for his calm spirit and wonderful images, and for his help and advice, particularly with digital cameras.

Bruce Hodge, who is not only a wonderful photographer, but the kind of friend who would drive your station wagon all night to your new home and then hop a flight so's not to miss his daughter's recital. Was there ever better?

Adobe's Julieanne Kost, Russell Brown, Chris Cox, Marc Pawliger, and many others, thanks for detailed information during the beta testing, a great new Photoshop CS, and for using our book.

Garth at Cross Roads Camera here in Corvallis, Pro Photo in Portland, Jack Saik, Thomas Bach, Bruce Ashley, the Photo Arts Guild digital group, and others for help with digital camera files and questions.

Bruce Fraser, Joseph Holmes, Dan Margulis, and Jeff Schewe who continue to dig deeper into the possibilities of accurate color.

Pauline Osborn and all the dancers in the NIA group. Through movement we find health of all kinds.

Our friends, David and Loretta, Denise and Wolf, Greg and Jennifer, Tina and Jack, and many others for helping us through this process and their kids Jackson, Justin, Zack, Chase, and Cody for playing with Max when we were busier than we wanted to be. Al and Mary, Bruce and Liz, Roger and Jane, all the McNamaras, Diane, Luke, Karen, Peter, and Marcella you are always there for us even though we are separated by too many miles these days.

Denise Ross, who makes great hand colored prints, for inspiring me to spend more time doing my art.

Maria Ferrari for her flower images and beautiful Native American black-and-whites on Scala film.

All of the fabulous teachers and caregivers who help Max grow more fantastic every day.

Denise Haynes, a great grandma and a terrific person.

Our son, Max, who continues to lead us, inspire us, teach us, and make us laugh.

Our readers, who give meaning to our work.

From Barry to Wendy

I look forward to spending some vacation time with you, now that this book is done! Thanks for updating so many chapters and writing lots of the new material in this edition. You are a great partner and artist, we do this together!

From Wendy to Barry

Ten years! I think we might actually have something, here. Thanks for your support and encouragement, I continue to learn so much from you. Swimming in the sea of life together, I've become a much better swimmer.

Finally, and most importantly, our thanks to the Divine Creator for the bounty of this life and for giving us a chance to contribute in what we hope is a positive way.

TABLE OF CONTENTS

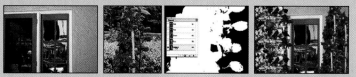

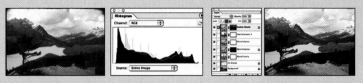

The first things you do to a normal image after scanning it in either 8-bit or 16-bit per channel color: Using a Levels 16-bit adjustment layer for overall color correction to set highlights and shadows, overall brightness, and to correct for color casts; using a Curves Adjustment layer to adjust contrast; using a Hue/Saturation Adjustment layer to saturate overall and adjust specific colors; and using Curves for tweaking certain color and brightness ranges. This chapter includes a complete introduction to Levels and Curves. Fine-tuning the Banff Lake image using adjustment layers with masks and Curves, and the Color Sampler to darken and enhance the sky and remove spots and scratches. Saving your Master RGB layered image, then resampling and sharpening it separately for RGB or CMYK printer output and for a Web image.

Overall color correction using Levels, Hue/Saturation, and Curves Adjustment layers on a problem image that has unbalanced colors and lacks a good highlight position. Using the Photoshop CS selective Hue/Saturation features along with Color Samplers to more accurately measure and adjust colors. Make final improvements to specific off-color and dark areas using manual and Levels mask selections, Adjustment layers, and Hue/Saturation tricks; dealing with out-of-gamut colors when converting to CMYK or a printer space; and the details of using the Unsharp Mask filter to sharpen an image.

Using Color Range and Replace Color to easily isolate all the yellow flowers and change their colors. Using Selective Color to fine-tune those colors after RGB to CMYK conversion. Moving Replace Color or Color Range results into an adjustment layer's layer mask to soften or edit the mask, as well as change the color as many times as you like without degrading the image.

Using Hue/Saturation, Levels, and Selective Color along with the Color palette and Color Samplers to make sure the colors, tones, and moods match between several photos of the same object(s) on a multipage spread. How to make a series of studio photos match even if they start out as different colors.

SECTION 4: ADVANCED COLOR CORRECTION AND RESTORATION TECHNIQUES   266

This section shows you a variety of advanced color correction techniques. We discuss Duotones and their use to enhance the tonality of black-and-white images, as well as to create beautiful color images in publications using fewer than four colors. We show you several difficult retouching examples that use the Photoshop CS Healing Brush to fix damaged film and restore old photographs. We also show you how to combine several different scans of bracketed photographs to get a better final result. There is also a discussion of using Lab color versus RGB for your Overall Color Correction process.

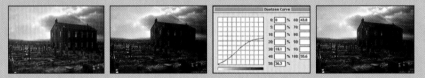

Using the Photoshop CS Duotone features with custom curves, looking at separate duotone and tritone channels, printing duotones as EPS, and converting duotones and tritones to RGB and CMYK for final output. Duotones are a great way to get a sepia or other toned effect even when working with Epson and other digital RGB printers.

Doing overall and final color correction and retouching of an image that has serious saturation and color problems in facial shadows, using one good channel and a Channel Mixer Adjustment layer to fix the others. Retouching using the new Healing brush and comparing that to using the Clone Stamp tool, sharpening, and final spotting.

Scanning old, faded, and damaged photographic prints using a flatbed scanner, then using 16-bit grayscale Levels histograms and Curves to bring back the original contrast and details. Converting to 8-bit grayscale, then adding local contrast enhancement Curves with masks to bring out details within the shadows and also improve flat areas. Retouching using the new Healing brush along with the Clone Stamp tool to remove scratches, damaged areas, and blemishes. Converting to RGB, then adding masked Hue/Saturation adjustment layers with Colorize on to add color to a black-and-white original. Creating and adding a sky where the original was completely white.

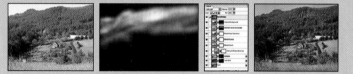

Using layers and layer masks to seamlessly combine three 16-bit per channel bracketed digital captures of the same scene shot with the Canon digital Rebel on a tripod. All images are first processed with Photoshop CS Camera Raw, then combined using aligned 16-bit layers to get highlights from the underexposed version, shadows from the overexposed version, and the rest of the image from the normal exposure. Learn how to line up the three captures (also how to line up bracketed scans), create masks to separate the parts you want from each, and how to use grouped adjustment layers to color correct each image separately while looking at the combined results. The final touches are applied as you burn and dodge, then sharpen the combined image using my Sharpen Only Edges BH action script from the ArtistKeys action set.

Working with an image in the Lab color space involves a different perspective as we use some of the same, and also some new, color correction tools and techniques. Lab, Threshold, many more layers, adjustment layers, and layer masks are used to combine Red, Green, and Highlight Bryce Stone Woman areas, creating a final image with a great red canyon as well as wonderful green bushes and trees. This example has been refined and enhanced several times to produce a very impressive final image.

The examples in this section use Blend modes, filters, bitmaps, calculations, layer styles, shape layers, layers, and other effects and techniques in combination with each other to achieve a variety of special effects, including motion simulation, drop shadows, pattern creation, glowing text, text with shadows, building an exciting CD cover with effects, using the Photoshop CS painting brushes and options, and many others. Magenta highlighted chapter names in the table of contents are essential chapters for everyone to read.

Detailed explanations and examples of using the Blend modes in all the tools (painting tools, the Fill command, Layers, Layer Styles, Calculations, and Apply Image); the many variations and uses of the Apply Image and Calculations commands demonstrated and demystified. We've added some new images and reorganized this chapter to better explain the new Blend modes and Blend Mode palette organizations that were added in Photoshop 7 and are there for CS.

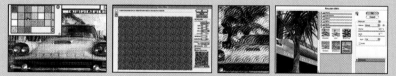

Using the Photoshop CS Shape Layers, Vector Masks, and Layer Style effects. Modifying a shape using Add, Subtract, Intersect, Exclude, and Combine. Creating and editing Custom Shapes and Shape Libraries, importing shapes from Illustrator, understanding the various Layer Effects, and creating your own Layer Styles. This chapter is in the format of an Adobe Acrobat PDF file in the Chapter 32 folder on the *Photoshop CS Artistry* CD. It can be read using the free Adobe Acrobat reader, which comes on the Adobe Photoshop CS installation CDs.

Creating texture and pattern effects using pattern overlays, pattern fill layers, diffusion dither bitmaps, the Texturizer filter, Lighting Effects, and the Photoshop CS Pattern Maker. This chapter shows you the layer blending techniques that allow the possibility of creating thousands of other custom and original layer effects.

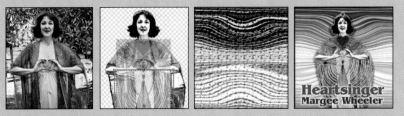

Creating an actual CD cover using Photoshop's filters, layer masks, layer effects, Blend modes, and advanced blending. Use the Extract command to make a knock-out. Use shape layer, text layer, and fill layer capabilities to create effects. Use Layer Sets to organize your work. Explore the uses of filters and the Liquify command.

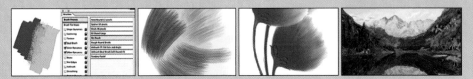

An exploration of Photoshop CS's brushes and Brush Options palette, building custom brushes, saving brush presets and tool presets, setting up digital painting files for maximum flexibility, creating a digital acrylic painting, using the Clone Stamp for painterly effects, and creating a quick digital portrait. This chapter works best with a pressure sensitive tablet. Photoshop CS's brushes are also compared to Painter's to determine which appliction and set of features is really best for those who want to paint digitally.

SECTION 7: IMAGES FOR THE WEB AND MULTIMEDIA 396

Using the newest Photoshop CS features to create and customize your own Web Photo Galleries, Contact Sheets, and Picture Packages. Using Photoshop CS with its 4-Up Web Optimization dialogs as well as other Web features to create the highest quality 8- and 24-bit GIF, transparent GIF, PNG, and JPEG images and HTML pages for Web sites and multimedia projects. Understanding 8-bit and smaller Color palettes and creating small, fast images that look good on both the Mac and PC. Magenta highlighted chapter names in the table of contents are essential chapters for everyone to read.

Using the Photoshop CS 4-Up dialogs or just using Photoshop CS to create GIF, JPEG, and PNG files. Understanding Web file naming conventions. Creating and comparing GIF, JPEG, and PNG files and seeing how they look on 8-bit versus 24-bit systems. Understanding all the JPEG options (Optimized, Progressive, ICC Profile, Blur, and Matte) and the GIF Options (Lossy, Color Reduction Algorithm, Dither, Transparency, Interlaced, Matte, and Web Snap), and also the Photoshop CS weighted options using text and vector shape layers, as well as Batch options for Droplets.

Using the greatly improved Photoshop CS File/Automate/Web Photo Gallery options to create your own great-looking and customized Web Photo Galleries. Use Actions to improve gallery image sharpness, learn how to get better titles and also how to automatically create the HTML code for these galleries so you can place them directly into your own Web site. We also discuss creating Photoshop CS's improved automated Contact Sheets and Picture Packages, which are very useful for photographers. See how to create your own custom Picture Package layouts.

Chart of Print Display Longevity and Access Info for Wilhelm Research

(To get this very useful latest information about the longevity of a variety of digital prints on many different papers used with the latest digital printers, go to www.wilhelm-research.com.)

FOREWORD BY BARRY & WENDY

Photoshop CS Artistry AND HOW IT WORKS

Photoshop CS Artistry is the seventh edition of the Photoshop Artistry series, which has sold over 150,000 copies. You'll discover that you can learn a lot from this book. The examples in *Artistry* teach you how to use Photoshop CS by working with typical situations that you encounter as a photographer, artist, or production artist. This is Photoshop for creating fine images that are sometimes high-quality reproductions of reality and sometimes fine renditions of composites and effects. Here we'll tell you a little bit about our philosophy in writing this book and the improvements we've made in this edition. We hope this will help you to decide if *Artistry* is the book for you.

If you have a previous edition of *Artistry* or are trying to decide which edition to purchase, I'd get this CS edition if you are using to planning to use Photoshop CS with OS X or Windows XP, especially if you recently acquired a digital camera, as we've added great info about digital cameras and Photoshop Camera Raw. See more info later in the Forward for previous Artistry readers.

THE DESIGN OF PHOTOSHOP CS ARTISTRY

Sections One and Two of *Photoshop CS Artistry* are reference sections that contain 17 chapters explaining the different parts of photoshop and its tools as well as the concepts you need to understand to work with those tools as well as artisticly and efficiently color correct in a calibrated environment containing scanners, digital cameras, calibrated monitors and printers. Sections Three through Seven contain 20 hands-on step-by-step chapters that guide you through initially more fundamental but eventually quite complex examples as you learn to use Photoshop in a variety of color correction, compositing and image enhancement situations. All the images required to do these examples are on the Photoshop CS Artistry CD. If you finish all these examples and truly understand them and all the Artistry captions, you'll end up being an expert Photoshop user.

If you're a photographer, an artist or anyone who likes to create beautiful images, this book will help you do that using Photoshop! If you need to do it quickly and efficiently, we'll help you with that too. Understanding what you are doing and why you are doing it will turn you into a more powerful and creative Photoshop artist. If you are a beginner to Photoshop, reading this book more or less in order is the way to go. We try to introduce new ideas and explain them before we assume you already know them. If you are an intermediate or advanced user, you may learn more by reading the sections and doing the exercises in the areas of your most important interests and needs. You should also check www.barryhaynes.com for the latest tips about using new scanners and printers, useful links, our workshop schedule, and also for new techniques and examples that didn't get on the *Photoshop CS Artistry* CD.

THE MASTER IMAGE CONCEPT

We give you a strategy for managing your digital images by creating a "Master Image" for each photograph that contains the original scan or capture along with many Adjustment layers and masks that turn that image into what you envision. This

Master Image is developed within a known color space that you can then convert using Photoshop and ICC profiles for each of your color inkjet, color laser, or dye-sub printers as well as color transparency output or compressed images for your Web sites. These same Master Images can also be used to create custom CMYK files for each of your printing situations. You only have to color correct the Master Image once, you then use color management and calibration, along with sharpening Action scripts, to generate a color compatible file for each type of output.

Understanding and developing good workflow habits is one key to becoming proficeint with Photoshop. The steps to create a master image are the foundation of digital imaging. Learn them well an your work will consistently be above the crowd.

NOT JUST RECIPES BUT UNDERSTANDING

In addition to student tested, step-by-step instructions, *Photoshop CS Artistry* includes explanations of concepts like color correction, calibration, 16- and 8-bit file formats and compression, duotones, selections, masking, layers, layer masks, adjustment layers, fill layers, shapes, layer styles, blending options, histograms, history, and channels, so you really understand what you are doing and are not just blindly following directions. Understanding allows you to expand the ideas in this book as you apply them to your own situations and creations.

STEP-BY-STEP EXERCISES

For each exercise, we spell out the detailed, step-by-step process and include all the steps you'll need at that point in the book. You can practice the technique yourself because the original images, masks, and progress steps, as well as the final images for each example, are all on the *Photoshop CS Artistry* CD included with the book. We have taught these or similar examples over the past fourteen years to thousands of students across the country and the world. Their feedback has helped us refine the exercises to make them easy to understand, concise, and full of special tips for more advanced users. **For example, based on reader requests, *Photoshop 6, 7 and CS Artistry* show the actual steps the reader should perform in bold.** The explanations for the steps are in normal text. This will help you more quickly go back and practice examples over again.

We start with simple examples like cropping and color correcting a photograph. We cover color correction in great depth, and then move on to things that you normally would do in the darkroom, like changing contrast, burning and dodging, removing spots and scratches, and making a nice photographic print. Before we get into compositing and special effects, we talk about the importance of having absolute control over the colors in your photographs—which you can do with ease and understanding now using the latest Photoshop CS color management features.

The masters of color photography have used contrast reduction masks, shadow, highlight and color masks in the darkroom to make very fine Ilfochrome, C, and dye transfer art prints. Using these techniques, you can make specific colors pop by increasing their saturation and changing their relationship to the rest of the photograph. Now most of them have switched to digital techniques and are making Light-Jet 5000 or Epson 4000, 7600 and 9600 inkjet prints. *Photoshop CS Artistry* shows you how to do all these things digitally using 8 or 16 bit adjustment layers, layer masks, and multiple layers of the same image, and how to generate art-quality out-

Ansel Adams, discussing the decision to make his original negatives available for future photographers to print, wrote in his autobiography that

"Photographers are, in a sense, composers and the negatives are their scores. ...In the electronic age, I am sure that scanning techniques will be developed to achieve prints of extraordinary subtlety from the original negative scores. If I could return in twenty years or so I would hope to see astounding interpretations of my most expressive images. It is true no one could print my negatives as I did, but they might well get more out of them by electronic means. Image quality is not the product of a machine, but of the person who directs the machine, and there are no limits to imagination and expression."

Ansel Adams had a good vision for the future that we are now living. We hope this book will help you experience that vision in your photographic work.

put to the LightJet 5000, Epson 1280, 2200, 4000, 7600 & 9600, Fujix Pictrography, and other printers, and very importantly, to the Web. We also talk about output to separations for printing on a press. We show you how to use the above techniques along with custom sharpening actions to get great quality prints from digital captures, digital Camera Raw files, Kodak Photo CD and Pro Photo CD scans as well as scans from the better desktop film scanners including the Nikon 4000, 8000, Imacon, Polaroid Sprintscan 120 and Epson 2450 and 3200.

COMPOSITING, BLEND MODES, FILTERS AND EFFECTS

After we explain how to make a fine color print using Photoshop, we make extensive use of layers, layer masks, and image compositing techniques. You can do commercial compositing techniques easily using Photoshop, and we present step-by-step examples for some simple compositing jobs and then move on to some more complex examples that involve using hard- and soft-edge masks, as well as a variety of shadow effects and the features of layers, adjustment layers, and layer masks. The Apply Image and Calculations commands, the Blend mode variations and layer styles are explained in detail along with examples of where to use them. *Photoshop CS Artistry* also includes many tips and techniques on getting the most from the Photoshop filters and the Photoshop CS brushes. We also get into creating duotones and bitmaps, adding textures to images, and other fun things.

IF YOU HAVE AN EARLIER EDITION OF PHOTOSHOP ARTISTRY

If you are a photographer or artist currently using Photoshop 7, read the Chapter "Overview of New Photoshop CS Features," at the beginning of this book, to decide if the new features Adobe added for version CS make this useful for you. If you decide to upgrade to Photoshop CS, then get *Photoshop CS Artistry*, if you use Photoshop 7 then get *Photoshop 7 Artistry*. *Photoshop CS Artistry* is the first Artistry version to be totally converted from Mac OS 9 to Mac OS X; it will also work fine for Windows XP users. Remember that you need Mac OS X or Windows XP to run Photoshop CS! If you are still using Max OS 9 or an earlier Windows version, an upgrade to CS will involve upgrading your entire system! We upgraded to Mac OS X, are very happy with it and we find that running OS 9 applications usually works fine within the OS X environment. Phew, you don't need to upgrade everything!

In this seventh CS edition, we've added and updated all the information you'll need to use the new Photoshop CS features, especially working with digital captures and the new Photoshop CS Camera Raw filter. We've also added, among other things, new chapters about making selections, 16 bit layers, the History and Layer Comps palettes, combining bracketed photos (from a digital camera this time) and painting in photoshop. We show exactly how to use Epson 2200, 4000, 7600, etc. print dialogs in the OS X environment.

Those of you who already have previous editions of this book will notice that the techniques in all the *Photoshop CS Artistry* examples have been improved to take full advantage of the great features in this new CS version. Since *Photoshop 5 & 5.5 Artistry*, many new examples have also been added to help you learn about the Photoshop CS color calibration and color management techniques as well as making custom monitor and printer profiles, retouching old and damaged photographs, new compositing and effects examples, new color correction images and examples including working with Lab color, digital cameras, the Camera Raw filter, the File Browser and the latest info about creating Web images. You can compare this book to the older Photoshop 4 or 5 versions and quickly see how to use the new features. In the Photoshop 6, 7 and CS versions, we have reorganized the table of contents and the presentation of information to make it flow more logically for people trying to learn Photoshop by reading this book in order. This will also help instructors who are using this as a text book. The CD has an improved ArtistKeys to set up your Actions palette and to give you a great set of function keys and automated sequences for bringing palettes up and down, converting file formats, custom sharpening and large grain removal and doing other useful and repetitive tasks. The CS ArtistKeys has new and improved sharpening scripts as well as a script, called ResUpby10, to resample up in 10% increments for better quality image upsampling.

With this edition of Artistry, we updated the entire book to make it work best with Photoshop CS. We wrote new examples where we felt new information was important. The examples in this edition that were updated from a previous edition are still here because they work well to illustrate a useful technique and they have been tested and improved by myself and thousands of Photoshop students over time. They have been improved for Photoshop CS and will continue to be in our books as long as they are the best examples available to teach photographers and image makers what they need to know.

WHERE WE'RE COMING FROM AND GOING TO

In the *Photoshop 7 Artistry* forward, I told you how I got into writing this book after spending 10 years writing software and doing research at Apple and after doing a variety of photography and photoshop related projects in the 14 years after Apple. This included writing this *Artistry* series since 1994. If you are interested, some of this information is still in the About the Authors page at the beginning of this book. Wendy and I got married in 1994 so we'll have our 10 year anniversary of working with *Artistry*, and each other April 23rd, 2004.

Many people have expressed interest in our future *Making the Digital Print* book. We appreciate that and please keep sending us your requests. Much of the information in that book is taught during the Digital Printmaking for Photographers and other advanced workshops we run at our Oregon studio and at other locations. See the workshops area of www.barryhaynes.com for more info. *Making the Digital Print* will eventually come forth and will probably be in the form of training CD/DVDs first then as a book. The distractions of improving my own photography artwork, updating *Photoshop Artistry*, being concerned about America and the world, keeping my home from leaking and just enjoying life have all taken their toll on the eventual ship date of *Making the Digital Print*. I do believe it will happen but won't predict any more ship dates until something is certain!

We know many of you are artists and we enjoy working with you, many of whom seem to be going though the same transitions we are. There is a lot that we have learned working with Photoshop, digital printing, color correction and calibration over the years. We hope this book passes what we know on to you. Digital Imaging is a constantly changing field and one or two people can only keep up with so much of it. Please contact me at barry@maxart.com or Wendy at wendy@maxart.com when you see something that might interest *Artistry* readers. We get lots of good tips from our readers and pass them on in or Digital Printmaking and Painting workshops, in new book versions and also in the Latest Tips area of www.barryhaynes.com.

We hope *Photoshop CS Artistry* helps you have more fun than ever before with photography and digital imaging.

Barry & Wendy

OVERVIEW OF NEW PHOTOSHOP CS FEATURES

A host of large and small improvements make Photoshop CS a worthwhile upgrade for almost everyone, and especially for photographers.

OUR OVERALL IMPRESSIONS

Photoshop CS (version 8) is one of the largest steps forward for Photoshop, especially for photographers. Support for 16-bit per channel layers and adjustment layers, the new Histogram palette, and the included enhanced Camera Raw filter make the CS version a must-have for photographers, especially those with digital cameras. There are many other new features for photographers including an improved File Browser, Web Photo Gallery, Picture Package, as well as totally new Shadow/Highlight, Photo Filters, Lens Blur, and Match Colors tools. Read on in this chapter for more details!

IMPROVEMENTS PHOTOGRAPHERS WILL LIKE MOST

FULL SUPPORT FOR 16-BIT LAYERS AND ADJUSTMENT LAYERS

This is a great set of features if you want to save all your image detail and keep all your options open. I've recommended doing your scans or digital captures at 16-bits per channel for some time now, then doing at least your initial Levels adjustment with that 16-bit file. To keep all the detailed information in an image, it would be best to leave that image in 16-bit per channel mode, but with Photoshop 7 and earlier versions, you had to convert your file to 8-bits per channel to be able to use Layers, Adjustment Layers, and layer masks. Now with Photoshop CS you can do all your photographic layer work with 16-bits per channel. The filters and tools Photographers need, like Gaussian Blur, Unsharp Mask, Threshold, Find Edges, Minimum, Maximum, etc. all now work in 16-bit. The things that still don't work in 16-bit are the filters like Extract, Liquefy, Artistic, Distort, and Texture, which are used more by designers and effects artists than photographers. Since beginning the Photoshop CS beta testing many months ago,

Here we are working on a 16-bit mulit-layered file. You can see that full Adjustment layer support is there as well as Layer Mask and Vector Mask support. This is great. Time to buy that duel processor G5 with two gigs memory and a large hard disk!

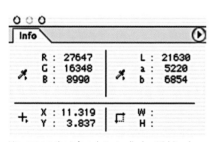

You can set the Info palette to display 16-bit values, which have a range from 0 to 32,768, or you can see your numbers in the 8-bit 0 to 255 range. The 16-bit values are helpful especially for finding the shadow and highlight points using threshold.

The highlighted (darker) filter menus are the ones that work with 16-bit layers. The filters most photographers need for realistic 16-bit imagery now work in Photoshop CS.

I've been creating all my color correction master layers files, along with all my adjustment layers and masks in full 16-bit color. It's great, but the files do end up being more than twice as big this way, so now is the time to get a bigger hard disk and/or a faster computer.

The New Histogram Palette

The Histogram palette allows you to see in real time the effect, on an image's histogram, of the current adjustments you are making to that image using Curves, Hue/Saturation, or any color correction or other adjustment tool. This gives you much better insight into what each adjustment does to the final histogram. If you color correct with the goal of producing a final image having a histogram that is as correct as possible, you'll find the Histogram palette a big help. In previous versions of Photoshop, I've often wanted to see how the histogram looked, and to do this I had to add a temporary Levels Adjustment layer to the top of the layers stack. This is no longer necessary as the Histogram palette always shows me the histogram based on the cumulative effect of all the layers and adjustment layers up to the currently active layer. If the top layer is active, then you see the cumulative histogram of the entire image. This is a feature I've dreamed about for a long time and even put on my wish list for future features from Adobe. Thanks, Adobe, for answering my dreams. What fun to color correct and work using such a great photographic tool. Ansel Adams would love it, I'm sure!

The New Photoshop Camera Raw Filter

When you shoot images with a digital camera, the camera's sensor captures the raw information in the scene, which is sort of like doing a raw scan where you make no use of the scanner's color correction, sharpening, or other tools. If you save the digital camera file in tiff or jpeg format, that raw information is processed before the save by the electronics in the digital camera based on the exposure, white balance, color temperature, and other information and settings the camera had at the time you shot the image. Many digital cameras, especially more expensive ones, allow you to save your digital files in Raw format, which actually saves the unprocessed information from the camera's sensor without processing that information using the camera's electronics. Along with the Raw data, the camera also saves the exposure, white balance, color temperature, and other settings the camera had when you shot the image, but it doesn't use that information to actually process or change the RAW data. Saving your images in Raw format gives you the most options when you process that information later, using the more powerful software and more detailed displays on your computer.

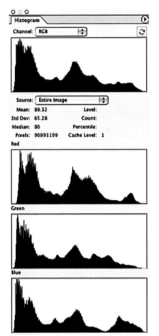

Here we see the full-blown Histogram palette with All Channels View and Show Statistics both on. If you click and drag across a subrange of the histogram, the statistics for just that subrange will show. This can be helpful at times.

Here we see the Histogram palette along with all its options. If you don't have a separate monitor for palettes, then color correcting using the Compact View allows you to see how changes affect the histogram without taking a large amount of screen space.

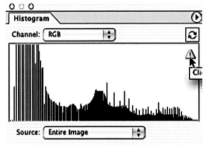

Above we see the Histogram palette with a gappy histogram as it sometimes displays when using the smaller Image Cache to calculate its values. If you click on the yellow exclamation mark in the top right corner, the histogram will recalculate using all the image data and will usually look much better and be more accurate, like the one below. Recalculating with all the image data can take some time when you have a very large file.

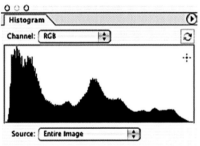

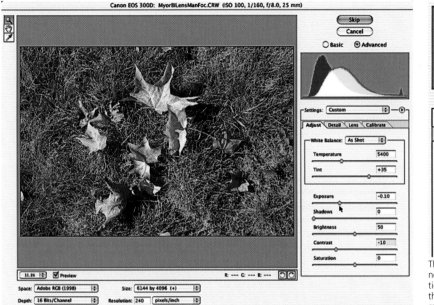

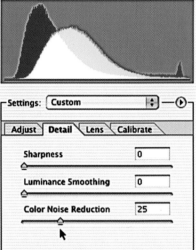

Here we see the main controls on the Photoshop CS Camera Raw filter. When you turn on Advanced at the top-right, the Lens and Calibrate adjustment sections are added. These are not in the Photoshop 7 Camera Raw filter that you can download from Adobe. At the bottom left here, notice that we can choose the color Space, Size, bit Depth, and Resolution of the image as it will open in Photoshop. On the top right we can see that the histogram for this image has been improved, from the one below, to save highlight details by lowering the Exposure setting and shadow details by lowering the Contrast from the Camera Default histogram and Adjust settings shown below. Use the Zoom, Hand, and Eyedropper tools at the top-left to zoom, scroll, and measure the image with the same control keys as you use within Photoshop CS.

The Detail section allows you to change the Sharpness, Luminance Smoothing and Color Noise Reduction settings. I usually change the sharpness from the default of 25 to 0 since I sharpen later after all my color correction is finished. This avoids the typical digital camera sharpening artifacts.

Most digital cameras come with proprietary software you can install on your computer and use to process Raw files after their initial capture. Then you can convert them into a standard format like tiff or jpeg. Different camera types each have their own special features that their proprietary software may process in a special way. Depending on the camera and it's third-party software, that camera software may or may not be as good as the Adobe Camera Raw filter we will talk about here. Each third-party camera software package supports different options and has different levels of efficiency on both the PC or the Mac.

The Photoshop CS Camera Raw filter knows about the Raw camera format and can process these files so you can get more highlight detail, shadow detail, and better color while avoiding sharpening and digital camera artifacts before opening the files into Photoshop. If you need

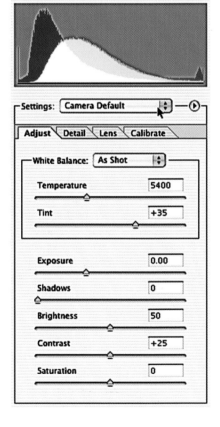

Overview of New Photoshop CS Features

to resample up the files, the Camera Raw filter also does a better job at that than if you were to upsample the files just using Photoshop.

There is a Camera Raw filter that you can download from Adobe for Photoshop 7 but it has fewer features than the Photoshop CS version. The Photoshop CS version has also improved the algorithms that were in the Photoshop 7 download version. I've been quite impressed with the Adobe Photoshop CS Camera Raw filter and what it could do to improve RAW digital images.

When using Adobe Camera Raw, I've found I get better results by setting the Sharpening to 0, no sharpening, in the Detail section. I sharpen my images after doing overall color correction using Unsharp Mask along with my Sharpen Only Edges BH action script, which comes on the *Photoshop CS Artistry* CD. I often lower the Exposure setting in Camera Raw until the highlight values return on the right side of the histogram. If the shadow side of the histogram has a vertical bar, indicating lost shadow detail, this can sometimes be returned by lowering the Contrast setting until the spike is gone from the left side of the histogram. Exposure and Contrast are

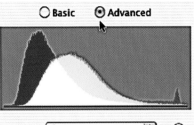

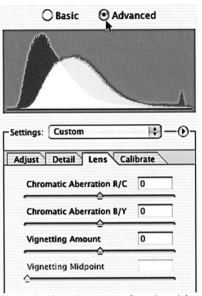

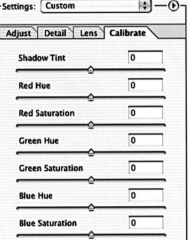

Chromatic Aberration corrects for a lens defect where a lens focuses different colors slightly differently. This is more likely to happen with zoom lenses, and I've also seen it with film cameras. The type of Chromatic Aberration corrected here is where the focus of each color is at a slightly different size as you move away from the center of the image. You'll see this as a red fringe on one side of the image and a green fringe on the other side or a similar problem with blue and yellow. The Chromatic Aberration R/C slider changes the size of the red channel relative to the green channel. The Chromatic Aberration B/Y slider changes the size of the blue channel relative to the green channel. The Vignetting sliders allow you to correct for the Vignetting lens problem where the edges of an image are darker than the center. This is more likely to occur in wide angle lenses.

The Calibrate adjustments allow you to fine-tune the default settings Adobe is using for your type of camera. Your copy of the camera might be different than the default and/or Adobe's settings might not be quite right for your camera. Shadow Tint allows you to compensate for color casts in shadows. Red Hue, Green Hue, Blue Hue, as well as Red, Green & Blue Saturation adjust Photoshop's camera profile for these colors. They should not affect neutral colors. If you are trying to calibrate camera raw for your camera, you might want to adjust these settings with a raw shot of a calibration image lit with controlled lighting. Those adjustments could then be saved and later reloaded for each image.

both in the Adjust section. Setting the Depth to 16-bits per channel allows you to get all the tonal information from your raw camera image and use that while editing in Photoshop CS. If you do need to upsample your image, use the Size pop-up in Camera Raw and you will get cleaner results than if you upsampled using Image Size in Photoshop CS. If your Lens has Vignetting or Chromatic Aberration problems, some of these can be corrected in the Lens area of Camera Raw. You'd use the Calibrate adjustments to compensate for differences between your particular digital camera and the default profiles Adobe has for your type of camera. Camera Raw files are uncompressed so they will be larger than jpegs, if that's what you're used to, but they are smaller than uncompressed tiffs. Photoshop gives you the opportunity to build custom settings for different cameras or lighting, then use those settings whenever you open that type of Camera Raw file, or for batch processing.

For more detailed information on these features and image improvement techniques, see the screen grabs and captions here, or check out the new Digital Camera and Camera Raw chapter.

FILE/AUTOMATE/PHOTOMERGE TO CREATE PANORAMAS

This new Automation utility allows you to specify a group of files to be combined into a panorama image. It automatically opens each file and tries to figure out the correct order; you can easily help it if it makes mistakes. It allows you to tweak

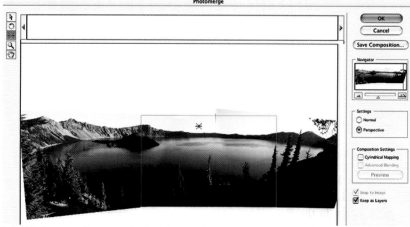

Using File/Automate/Photomerge in Photoshop CS allows one to create panoramas by selecting a folder full of files or groups of files to open. I found that Photomerge was unable to automatically tell the order of the photos in this image of Crater Lake Oregon shot with three 28mm lens exposures on my 35mm camera. It was easy enough for me to use the Arrow tool, top left, to move the images into the correct order and show Photomerge the approximate placement. The Perspective, Advanced Blending, Rotate, and Cylindrical Mapping choices give you some useful options for how you'd like the image to look. If you check Keep in Layers then Photomerge transforms each image, lines up the edges, and gives you a multi-layered Photoshop file where you can easily add layer masks and do final exact blending of the images.

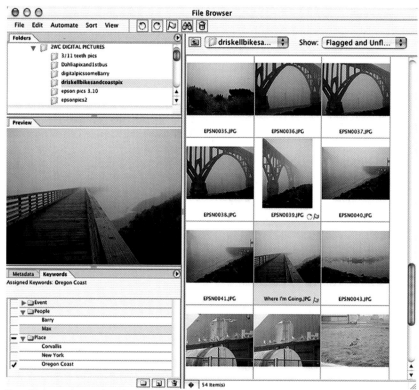

I've added some keywords and tagged this file with the keyword Oregon Coast. If I search using the Binocular button at the top of the window for all the files containing the word Oregon or Coast, this picture will be in the results folder. Notice also the menu bar at the top left. This allows you to create new folders on-the-fly and to run batch processes directly in the browser window.

the file positioning and choose from several methods to automatically combine the file. It also has a Keep in Layers option that allows you to tweak the results after the image arrives in Photoshop with each image being in a separate layer. This seems like a useful new feature, especially for those who use digital cameras and want to combine several images of different parts of a scene to create a more detailed landscape of a large area.

MOVE IMAGES IN FULL SCREEN MODE

Sometimes, it's the little improvements that affect us the most. In the case of being able to move an image with the Hand tool from its centered position while in full screen mode, it was all we could do to keep from jumping up and throwing confetti. It's such a pleasure to zoom in as large as you need to, then be able to move the image to see the edges of the file without having to move all the palettes that you've so carefully arranged on the edges of the desktop. It made taking screenshots for this version of the book so much easier. Truthfully, this one small improvement is worth the price of the upgrade in our opinions because it makes our work easier and faster. We'll pay for that any day.

ENHANCED FILE BROWSER

The File Browser is more robust than Photoshop 7, and in this version, really becomes the organizational tool you've been waiting for. You can now tag your images with keywords, then search for those keywords and move or copy all of those files to a folder that you can create on-the-fly within the Browser. You can flag your files then view only those you've flagged. You can edit information about the file directly in the browser window. In fact, the File Browser has reached a state of such importance that it is always available for you on the Options

Overview of New Photoshop CS Features

bar, no matter which tool you are in. For more information about the File Browser, see Chapter 2: "Navigating in Photoshop."

CUSTOM FILE INFORMATION

For a long time, there has been information embedded in files that you use in Photoshop such as the name of the file and its bit-depth, digital camera info, keywords you entered, and so on. Now, this information is more easily accessible via the File Browser. You can see exactly what's there, much of it is editable, and some of it (the new History Log) can be saved in a separate file. If you plan to use Photoshop to build a Web Gallery, this is where you want to include the title and description of your image that will be part of its webpage. You can input keywords for searches, include AP categories, your copyright and URL, and special instructions for the receiver. If you view this information in the File Browser, any area that has a pencil to the left of it is editable. Much of this appeared in Photoshop 7 as well. What's really new is the capability to create a special template that holds information specific to the type of work you do.

Web Galleries automatically display information from the metadata contained in the File/File Info area.

BETTER WEB GALLERY TEMPLATES

The ability to quickly create a Web Gallery is a feature that more photographers should use. It's quick and Photoshop does all the work for you. If you know just a bit of html or have Adobe GoLive or another Web-creation application, you can modify the pages to suit you exactly after Photoshop has created them. In this version of Photoshop, Adobe has added some improvements that make this feature useful for more than simply displaying your work to the world. There are templates that automatically create an input area for comments on the images. Imagine being able to quickly create a gallery of images for an editorial on begonia gardens of the Northwest, uploading the gallery to the Web and having the editors choose, approve, and comment on the pictures all within a matter of minutes. Seriously, minutes. I had sixty images in a folder and it took about five minutes for Photoshop to open each one and create jpegs for the gallery. Take another five minutes to upload the files (okay, this depends on your ISP connection) and then however long it takes the editor to make her choices. For some of you, work just got a lot easier. And for those of you who have been reluctant to create a Web Gallery, it's time to get your images on the Web. It couldn't be easier, and even if you don't love Adobe's layouts and backgrounds, people are starting to expect that your photos be available to them this way.

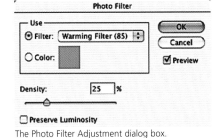
The inclusion of an area for comments and feedback in the Web Gallery feature is just one of the terrific upgrades to Photoshop CS.

APPLY STANDARD PHOTO FILTERS

Warm or cool your image using filters that make sense, or create your own. With Preserve Luminosity checked, this adjustment is very close to simply using a solid color adjustment layer in Color mode at a low opacity. However, when you turn Preserve Luminosity option off, you get something very close to actually shooting through a filter to adjust for exposure problems. And, because Photo Filters can also be found in the Layers palette as adjustment layers, you actually go a traditional filter one better by being able to selectively adjust the effect through a layer mask. It is not, however, a solution for all problems. As our friend, photographer,

The Photo Filter Adjustment dialog box.

and instructor Charles Campbell, says, "…if the viewer can tell that you used a filter, then it was overused."

PICTURE PACKAGE IMPROVEMENTS

Photoshop CS gives you more control over how you print multiple copies of an image or images with its Picture Package automation. You can now customize a layout to suite your specific needs, then save that layout. This means you can choose how many images to print to the sheet, their size, and the amount of space between each one.

LAYER COMPS PALETTE

At the end of the process of building a complex image, you usually need to show several versions to the client. In fact, you generally create several "finals" for yourself with minor adjustments and click among them to decide which one you really like best. You can do this with the History palette, but once you close your file all those changes are gone and you're stuck with the version as it was closed. The Layer Comps Palette solves your dilemma by storing several states of the file that you can return to. The on/off state of the layer's eye icons can be saved as well as the position of the layer in the file's window and the layer effects that are in use at the moment. If you create or delete layers after the creation of a comp state, those changes are not recorded, so this truly is a tool to use at the end of the build process. However, one of the great things about the palette is you can update a comp state if you make some minor adjustment to it, simply with the click of a button. There are also several scripts included with Photoshop CS to export those layer comps to files. The Layer Comps Palette's use is explained more fully in Chapter 7: "Layers, Layer Masks, and Adjustment Layers."

SHADOW/HIGHLIGHT ADJUSTMENT

In a truly remarkable bit of programming, Adobe has given us the Shadow/Highlight adjustment. I think of this as running a curves adjustment through a mask of just the shadow areas all in one fairly easy step. This adjustment is able to bring details out of shadows while maintaining decent contrast. Make sure you open all options in the dialog box by checking Show More Options. Shadow/Highlight is not available as an adjustment layer, so make a copy of your layer before using S/H in case you need the original information later.

Photoshop looks at a range of pixels to determine which areas of the photo are in

Print whatever size suits you with the editing capabilities now in the Picture Package feature.

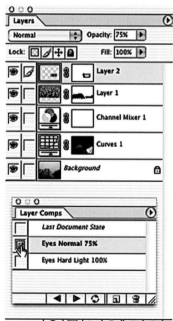
In this version, Layers 2 is in Normal mode at 75%. This state is saved in the Layer Comps palette as Eyes Normal 75%.

In this version of the file, Layer 2 has some layer styles associated with it as well as using a different blend mode and opacity.

The Shadow/Highlight adjustment default settings are for a backlit subject like this man's face.

This is the result using only the Shadow/Highlight adjustment settings shown here.

Here are the settings I used to lighten the man's face in the second picture.

deep shadows as opposed to simply dark areas that are correctly exposed. You set that range yourself via the Radius slider. In experimenting with Shadow/Highlight, I've had the best results by setting this range slider first with both Amount and Tonal Width set at the 50% default. Get the best look you can with Radius and then adjust the Tonal Width slider to select the range of values within your radius setting that are to be adjusted. Finally, tweak the Shadow Amount slider. You may find that you need to move between the Tonal Width and Shadow Amount sliders, adjusting back and forth. Also, one other setting that I found really makes a difference is the Black Clip setting. For the illustration here, I set the clip to 1%, but I've used other photos where I set the amount as high as 5%. The higher this setting, the darker the really deep shadows are. The Highlight sliders work exactly the same, only on the highlight values. In the bottom of the dialog box, the Color Adjustment slider increases the saturation of any area that has been adjusted, and Midtone Contrast is just exactly what it says. I've had better luck using an additional curve after the Shadow/Highlight adjustment to increase contrast rather than using the Midtone Contrast slider.

MATCH COLORS

This new tool is useful for quick color matching of similar images. If you've color corrected one image in a series and you need the same basic color in other similar images, you can pull those colors over by choosing the color corrected version in Match color's Source pop-up. To further refine the colors you are working with, you can use a selection or a layer in either the source or target image. Another useful and fun thing to do with Match color is using the colors from one image to influence the colors in another image as illustrated in the example here.

This is the original Bandon sunset image.

Using Match colors and 25% of the color of this image, I got the result you see below.

SUPPORT FOR LARGE DOCUMENTS

You can now create an image up to 300,000 by 300,000 pixels with as many as 56 channels. You no longer have to piece together files for large displays or go to an outside application to create the size you need.

COLOR REPLACEMENT TOOL FOR RED EYE CORRECTION

In the same bay with the Healing Brush and the Patch tool, you'll find a new tool, the Color Replacement tool. This tool is a bit like painting with the foreground

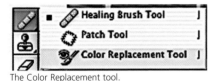

The Color Replacement tool.

color in Color mode, but here you are given the options to sample a particular color in an image and replace only that color and others that fall within the Tolerance value that you set. This works well for replacing red eye, but I haven't found any other exciting uses for it yet. Still, even for a possible one-trick pony, it's good to have a tool that can quickly handle a frequently necessary job.

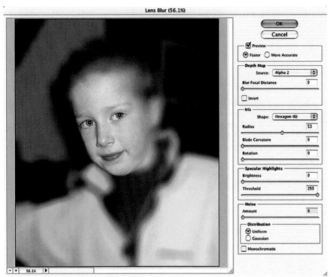

Here, the Lens Blur filter has been run through an alpha channel mask that is black in the area of the face.

LENS BLUR FILTER

When you first hear that Adobe has included a Lens Blur filter, you might be tempted to yawn. "Who cares about another gimmick?" Well, you do. It's so much more than just a blur. You can set the type of iris for your lens and force the highlights to take on that shape, controlling how much of the image is considered highlight. You can change the depth of field of the photo by applying the filter through an alpha channel using a gradient or create a special channel that's white only in the areas that you want the blur to occur. You can even add noise back in simulate film grain. Art photography just got a little bit artier.

CROP AND STRAIGHTEN

If you scan images from prints on a flatbed scanner, you may have run into the situation where simply by closing the top of the scanner, you skew a photo a bit, then either have to rescan or crop and rotate the file once you get it into Photoshop. Now that annoying little task can be handled automatically by using File/Automate/Crop and Straighten. This is true for single images or, more importantly, multiple images that have been included in a single scan. Photoshop CS will look for the edges of the images, then do the best it can to crop each image and rotate it without distortion. It's fast if you have a lot to scan, but it's not perfect. As you can see from the illustration here, it often leaves a bit of an edge. However, if you do a lot of flatbed scanning, it's a great tool for getting started on editing your image.

I've scanned two prints and both are slightly skewed. Crop and Straighten leaves this original scan intact and gives me two cropped images, each in its own file.

Neither image was perfect, though. If you look closely there's a slight white edge on both the upper right and lower left horizontal edges.

IMPROVEMENTS FOR EVERY USER

ADOBE WELCOMES YOU

One of the first things you'll notice when you open Photoshop CS is the new Welcome Screen. If you've used Photoshop before, this screen will lead you to a quick overview of new features. If this is your first foray into digital imaging, Adobe has tried to give you the most important issues you'll face in a nutshell here. Some information is presented in PDF format, some you read through your internet browser, and some must be accessed online. Once you explore the issues that interest you, you'll want to turn off this screen, but you've got to give Adobe credit for working to make a daunting application user-friendly.

The Welcome Screen is a great place to explore the basics and new features of Photoshop CS. If you turn the screen off but later want to access its information, you can also find this under the Help menu.

HISTORY LOG

The History palette was a great addition to Photoshop several versions back, but all of the information it contains vanishes as soon as you close your file—not much help if you want to go back and re-create the steps to a spectacular effect. I used to always suggest keeping a notepad handy to record what steps and settings you used to create your artwork. Now, Adobe does it for you. In General Preferences, you can choose to save a History Log, either in the file you're working on, a separate document, or both. There are three levels of information that you can record: Session only, which logs only the time that you opened and closed a file; Concise, which basically records the same steps that the History palette would record; and Detailed, which remembers all the settings for every adjustment you make. Use Session only if you need the information just for billing purposes and Detailed if you need to follow an exact set of steps to re-create an effect or modify other files based on how you changed the first one. If you are using the Detailed setting, you might want to save the History Log in a separate file only, as lots of detailed information can make your file size larger.

NESTED LAYER SETS

When you create a complex image, you generally keep certain layers in layer sets to help the file stay organized. Photoshop 7 only allowed you to create sets, then either open or close them. There was no way to include one set inside another so they could move together or organize the file a level deeper. Photoshop CS allows you to nest layers up to five levels deep. Those nested layer sets can also be read by Illustrator CS, clearing up another issue that used to be a problem when moving images from one application to another.

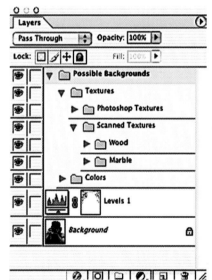

Nested layer sets make organizing a complex file much easier.

IMPROVEMENTS FOR DESIGNERS AND PRODUCTION ARTISTS

FILTER GALLERY

Adobe just made filtering a lot more fun by putting all the artistic filters in a gallery that allows you to try out effects quickly and without having to build a lot of separate layers. The Filter Gallery preview window can be toggled to a very large size, better than any previous version of the application. You can layer different effects and edit the settings for each effect all within one iteration. The different filters can be moved up or down in their layer stacking order so you can see whether you want to Dry Brush the Watercolor version or Watercolor the Dry Brush version. You don't have to say OK until you get exactly the effect you're looking for. Just like older versions of Photoshop, the filtering happens to the currently active layer, so make a copy of it before using Filter Gallery to retain the original layer for later use. The other limitations that I hope will be addressed in future versions are the inability to hit a Save button to save the stacked effect for reuse and the absence of opacity and blend mode sliders. There's still a reason to keep a notebook handy. See the Filter Gallery in use in Chapter 33: "Patterns and Texture."

TEXT ON OR INSIDE A PATH

One of the few remaining reasons to set text in Illustrator rather than Photoshop has been taken care of here. You can now create a flowing line with the Pen tool, then click the line with the Text tool to have your text flow with the Path. If the path is closed, you can choose to either put the text around the path on the outside, or to fill the shape with text. See Chapter 4: "The Tools Palette," for illustrations of the cursor for each instance. Once you have set the type, it can be edited and reformatted the same as regular point or paragraph text with the addition of being able to flip the type on a path or drag it side to side, using the Path Selection tool. This works very similarly to Illustrator, so if you are used to setting type there, you'll feel right at home with this new feature.

PRODUCTION IMPROVEMENTS

No matter what type of work you do, Adobe has ways to help you work faster and more efficiently through keyboard shortcuts, scripts, and help.

CUSTOMIZABLE KEYBOARD SHORTCUTS

Photoshop adds a capability that Illustrator has had for quite some time—Customizable keyboard shortcuts. You can change existing shortcuts that don't work for you (yes, even Command-Z if you want) and input the ones that make sense to you. You can have more than one shortcut for the same command if multiple users have different shortcuts they are used to using or save a keyset for each of them that is easily loaded from the Edit/Keyboard Shortcuts dialog. For those of you familiar with *Photoshop Artistry*, you know that we use the Function Keys via the Actions palette to control many menu items. Keyboard shortcuts for some of the same commands could leave the Function keys free for more complex actions.

Set your new keyboard shortcut simply by holding down the keys you want to use.

A BETTER SCRIPTING ENVIRONMENT

Support for scripting is now built in to Photoshop and does not have to be loaded separately. You can write scripts for Photoshop in many programming languages but the ones spoken of most often are AppleScript for the Mac, VisualBasic for the PC, and JavaScript, which is cross-platform. Scripts that you write can be stored in the Presets/Scripts folder and be available to users via the File/Scripts menu. Several useful scripts (written in JavaScript) are placed there when you install Photoshop. Wendy uses AppleScript a lot because many of the other applications we work with are also scriptable with AppleScript. This way we can automate many of the production tasks involved in creating a book.

BUILD YOUR OWN HELP MENU FILES

If your company has tasks that require specific steps, you can now detail those steps via a Help menu item that you build yourself in a standard html editor. What a boon to on-site training. See the Help menu at the right end of Photoshop's Menu bar and view some of the items Adobe has already placed there. And, yes, there's a Help menu item on how to create a Help menu item.

AND FINALLY

OS X ONLY ON THE MAC

I have to admit, we were a bit concerned about having to switch to OS X to run Photoshop—especially Wendy who works in a lot of different applications. But, after a few starts and stops getting upgrades for software and peripherals, we're both happy with the change. OS X is more stable, better at processing in the background, and is able to keep running if one of your applications crashes. Overall, the organizational structure of the Finder is much better, though there may be a few shortcuts that no longer work for you. If you've been hemming and hawing about upgrading, Photoshop CS gives you ample reason to make the leap. We think you'll be glad you did.

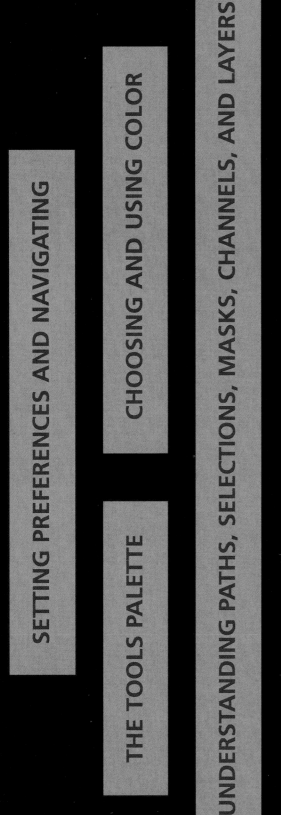

ESSENTIAL PHOTOSHOP TOOLS AND FUNCTIONALITY

SETTING PREFERENCES AND NAVIGATING

CHOOSING AND USING COLOR

THE TOOLS PALETTE

UNDERSTANDING PATHS, SELECTIONS, MASKS, CHANNELS, AND LAYERS

AUTOMATING PHOTOSHOP AND TRANSFORMING IMAGES

THE FILE BROWSER AND HISTORY PALETTE

DIGITAL CAMERAS AND CAMERA RAW FORMAT

Bandon Beach, Oregon, a potential stop on our Advanced Oregon coast workshops. Here we look out to Face Rock, as shot with my trusty old Canon F1 and its 50mm 1.4 lens using Scala film. Scala is a black-and-white positive transparency film which has a wonderful grain pattern and captures great texture and detail. New York photographer Maria Ferrari gave me a roll; it's great!

1 HOW TO USE THIS BOOK AND THE
PHOTOSHOP CS ARTISTRY CD

This chapter gives you a quick preview of what you'll find in this book and some valuable tips on the best way to use it along with the images on the CD, so you can learn from creating the examples.

Photoshop CS Artistry can help both new and advanced Photoshop users. If you read this book from front to back and do the hands-on sessions in order, it is an in-depth, self-paced course in digital imaging. If you're new to Photoshop and digital imaging, going in order may be the best way to proceed. If you are a more advanced Photoshop user and are more interested in learning new techniques, you may want to read the sections and do the hands-on exercises that cover the skills you need to learn. Use the table of contents and index to find the areas you want to reference.

The book has two types of chapters: overview chapters, which contain information that everyone should learn, and hands-on chapters, where you learn by color correcting and creating images. The chapters are ordered beginning with the fundamentals and moving on to more advanced skills. Chapters highlighted with magenta color in the table of contents are essential for everyone to read. All the chapters are in-depth, and we expect most users, even experienced Photoshoppers, to learn something from each chapter. Some of the chapters toward the end of the book are very detailed and assume you already have a lot of Photoshop knowledge. You need to know the foundation skills taught in the earlier chapters before you do the later, more advanced chapters.

The first two sections of this book, "Essential Photoshop Tools and Functionality," and "Color Correction and Calibration to Create a Master Digital Image," present in-depth overview chapters that provide readers with a common base of knowledge. Everyone should read Chapters 3: "Setting System and Photoshop Preferences," 14: "Color Spaces, Device Characterization, and Color Management," and 17: "Steps to Create a Master Image," so you can set up your system and Photoshop correctly, and calibrate your monitor for working with the book and doing color output. The rest of these overview chapters go into a lot of important details. They are not introductory material by any means. If you are anxious to get your hands into the program, though, don't read all of these before you start the hands-on exercises with Chapter 18: "The Colony Composite." You should come back to these earlier chapters later, however, to learn valuable information about the Zone System, picking colors, all the color correction tools, and other important topics. The hands-on chapters generally assume you have read, and have a basic understanding of, Chapters 1 through 17.

The hands-on chapters, and some of the overview chapters, have actual steps where you are expected to do something to one of the images on the CD. These steps are **in a special bold format**. The steps where you are doing something are often mixed in with sentences or paragraphs of extra information that is not always essential to doing the actual steps, but is often very useful information. The first time you read through a chapter, it is best that you read the entire chapter. If you want to go back and redo a step-by-step chapter and you just want to do the actual steps, all you need to do is read and **follow the highlighted sentences**. Many readers asked for a feature allowing them to more quickly go through a chapter a second or third time. The highlighted steps should allow you to do this.

IMPORTANT DIFFERENCES FOR MAC AND WINDOWS USERS

Photoshop users, on both the Mac and the PC, will find this book beneficial. That's because 99.9% of the time everything in Photoshop is exactly the same for Mac and PC users. The contents of each of Photoshop's tool windows and menu bars are the same in a Mac window and a Windows window. Adobe has done an excellent job of making Photoshop cross-platform compatible in every way it can. Mac and PC users both have tested this book, and have found it valuable and easy to use. We have taught in classrooms where some of the computers are Macs and some are PCs and it works out fine.

The following sections discuss the few minor differences between Photoshop on the Mac and on the PC. I also point out any differences within the chapters.

MODIFIER KEYS

References in *Photoshop CS Artistry* to keyboard modifier keys use the Option and Command keys, the main modifier keys on the Mac. **Windows users need to remember that when we mention the Option key, you use the Alt key, and when we mention the Command key, you use the Control key.** In those rare cases where we actually mention the Control key, you also use the Control key on the PC. A Control-click on the Mac to bring up a context-sensitive menu would be a right-mouse click on the PC. To get the Fill dialog, use Shift-Delete on the Mac, but Shift-Backspace on the PC.

FUNCTION KEYS

Most PCs only have 12 function keys on their keyboards, where some Mac extended keyboards have 15. *Photoshop CS Artistry* includes ArtistKeys, a predefined set of function keys that invoke actions that we teach you. We have set these up so the ones used most often are within the first 12 keys. They should work the same for the Mac and the PC. We discuss this further in Chapter 3: "Setting System and Photoshop Preferences." There are a few makers of PCs, specific third-party companies, who have hard wired special functions for certain function keys and certain command keys. Since these are specific to that brand of PC, and not all PCs, you will have to learn how to disable those function keys, if possible, to let Photoshop, and the ArtistKeys, take over their definition and use.

STATUS BAR

Windows users also have a Status bar at the bottom of the Photoshop screen area, which tells you what tool you are using and gives you additional information. This particular help information is not available on the Mac version of Photoshop.

When you insert your *Photoshop CS Artistry* CD on the Mac or Windows systems, the *Photoshop CS Artistry* folder contains the set of Photoshop CS format images for doing the book's exercises. In the Internet and Software Links folder, the *Photoshop CS Artistry* CD contains a link to download demo versions of Adobe Photoshop CS and Adobe ImageReady CS.

The Photoshop CS Layers palette as it appears in Mac OS 10.2.

The Photoshop CS Layers palette as it appears in Windows. This may look slightly different depending on the version of Windows you are using.

WINDOWS AND PALETTES MAY NOT LOOK EXACTLY THE SAME

Because Photoshop CS runs only on OSX on the Mac side and many of our screen grabs came from previous versions of Photoshop, you may find that the windows and palettes on your computer look slightly different from those in the book. If you're working in a Windows environment, you may also notice differences. You'll find, though, that the functionality and pertinent features of each screen grab will match what you are learning and doing in the book and on your computer at any particular time. Wherever Photoshop CS differs from previous versions, we've included new screen shots, but in the interest of time, we've retained older screen shots that are still relevant.

IMAGEREADY NO LONGER INCLUDED

Due to the length of this book and the availability of other books specific to the topic, ImageReady and its uses are no longer covered here. We do, however, still cover all the features of Photoshop that help you create and save images for the Web. For many photographers, this will be all the information you need.

WHAT'S ON THE CD

The *Photoshop CS Artistry* CD that comes with the book includes all the images you need to do the examples in the book. You can use this book and CD as a self-paced course, or you can use it to teach a course at the college or professional level.

When you put the CD in a Mac CD drive, it will come up with the name *Photoshop CS Artistry*, and it will look like a Macintosh directory with folders, files, and icons, as well as Mac format filenames. When you put the CD in a Windows machine, you will see a Windows directory named *Photoshop CS Artistry* that contains files that have the same filenames as in the Mac directory with the three-character suffixes that the PC requires.

Each hands-on chapter's folder contains the images and other information you need to complete that hands-on exercise and a folder called **Extra Info Files**. The Extra Info Files folder contains the authors' intermediate and final versions of the images for that exercise, as well as masks, levels and curves settings, and other helpful information. These allow you to compare your results to the authors'. We have tried to make the images printed in this book look as much like those on the CD as possible. The digital files on the disc, however, are more accurate comparisons of the progress that happens on each creation. To get the best results when viewing any of the CD files, you should calibrate your monitor and system as explained in Chapter 15: "Photoshop Color Preferences, Monitor, Scanner, and Printer Calibration."

TO TEACH A COURSE

We certainly hope that other instructors will use this book to teach Photoshop courses around the world. Since 1990, Barry has used and evolved these examples to teach many Photoshop courses at his Corvallis, Oregon, studio, the Palm Beach Photographic Center, the Santa Fe Photographic Workshops, the International Center of Photography, the Ansel Adams Digital Photography Workshop at Mono Lake, Anderson Ranch, and at many other places. Having a professional course where the students can take home the images and exercises to practice them again later has been a main factor in making Barry's courses so well received. We hope that you can take advantage of his years developing these exercises by using this book as the text for your courses.

If each student purchases the book, they will have copies of all the images and step-by-step exercises. The main images in each chapter folder on the CD are in Photoshop format. Most images open to about 4 megabytes in size and will grow as the exercise progresses. There are several images that are a lot bigger than that, however. For a professional course, I have discovered it works best to use images large enough to see the details students will be working with when they are doing real projects for their art, magazines, film output, and publications. These Photoshop files from the *Photoshop CS Artistry* folder are the easiest to use and give the students the most information for doing the course. If your course machines each have CD-ROM drives, each student should access the images directly from his or her own CD within the *Photoshop CS Artistry* folder.

If you plan to use *Photoshop CS Artistry* to teach a class, please contact the authors at www.barryhaynes.com to find out about school discounts and also to get complete information regarding purchase and distribution of books and images. We also teach our own in-depth workshops, described at www.barryhaynes.com.

USING THE DEMO SOFTWARE ON THE CD

The *Photoshop CS Artistry* CD contains links to download demo versions of Adobe Photoshop CS and Adobe ImageReady CS for both the Mac and PC. You can download these demo versions to try out the examples in the book and learn Photoshop CS, but they don't allow you to save files.

USING THESE IMAGES WITHOUT A COPY OF THE BOOK

We do not mind if teaching institutions or individual users make a copy of the *Photoshop CS Artistry* images on their hard disk or over a network, as long as each user has a copy of the *Photoshop CS Artistry* book. If a school, company, institution, or person gives out copies of these images to any person who has not purchased the book, that's copyright infringement. If a school, company, institution, or person copies the step-by-step instructions, or copies paraphrased step-by-step instructions, and hands either of those out in class, especially when using them with the *Photoshop CS Artistry* images, that too is copyright infringement. Please don't do this! We work hard to create these books and if you don't buy them, we won't be able to afford to continue this kind of effort. Thanks.

IF YOU HAVE PROBLEMS READING YOUR CD

When you get your book, please remove the CD from the holder in the back of the book and immediately transfer it to a solid plastic case for safe storage. The CDs are too easily scratched or made dirty by leaving them in the holder at the back of the book. If you have problems opening a file from the CD, clean your CD with a CD cleaning wipe that you can get from a computer store. This will often solve the problem.

For technical support from New Riders, go to www.newriders.com and click on the Contact Us link.

When you open a folder for one of the hands-on sessions, it contains the images and other files you need for completing the exercise. The Extra Info Files folder will contain things like the intermediate and final versions of the images along with all layers and masks for that exercise, including Levels, Curves, and other settings we used along the way. You can compare these with your results if you have any questions about the way you are doing the exercise.

5

2 NAVIGATING IN PHOTOSHOP CS

*Efficiently using Photoshop's tools, palettes, and windows
makes work go faster. Photoshop 8 has added lots of
features that speed navigation. Even if you're an old hand,
take a look at the changes.*

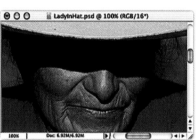

The final number in parenthesis on the title bar in Photoshop CS tells you whether you are working in 8-bit or 16-bit mode. The asterisk after the number means you are previewing in a color space other than the working RGB profile.

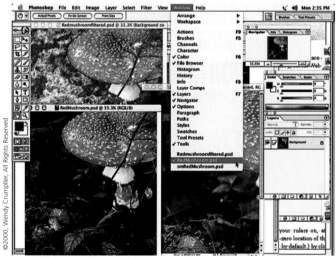

Here we see a Mac Photoshop desktop with three windows open. Notice the Photoshop CS Options bar, which spans the full width of the screen right below the menu bar. The active window is the window in front with its title bar striped. You will see a check mark beside this window's file name at the bottom of the Window menu. You can bring any window to the top, even a hidden one, by choosing it from the bottom part of this menu. In Standard Screen mode, you see open windows for Photoshop and other applications. It's easy to click outside a window and switch inadvertently to the desktop or another application. Your screen also gets cluttered fairly quickly.

Each digital image file you open into Photoshop has its own window. When you first open a file, the window will be a standard Macintosh or PC window with scroll bars and a grow box in the lower-right corner, and all the rest of the standard fare. At the top of the window, in the window's title bar, is the name of the file as it was last saved followed by the zoom factor and the color mode (RGB, CMYK, Lab, etc.) the file is currently using. After a slash, you'll see either the number 8 or 16 to let you know whether the file is 8-bit or 16-bit color. If this number has an asterisk after it, the file has a different profile than the working RGB profile. When you use View/Proof Colors to proof this window to a different color space, the name of that preview space is shown following another slash. In a layered document, the name of the currently active layer is also displayed in the title bar along with the color mode, or Layer Mask if you are working on the mask. If other windows cover the one you want to see, you can find it using the list of open files at the bottom of the Window menu.

THE PHOTOSHOP SCREEN MODES

You can view any of the open files in one of three screen modes, which the icons toward the bottom of the Tools palette denote. The leftmost icon denotes the standard screen mode we talked about above. The middle icon shows the Full Screen mode with menu bar and places the active, top window in the center of the screen, surrounded by a field of gray, which hides other windows from view. The rightmost icon shows the Full Screen mode, without the menu bar.

Working in Full Screen mode with the menu bar offers many advantages. If you are working on a small monitor, Full Screen mode does not waste the space that scroll bars normally take up. One annoyance, not being able to see the corners of your file well in Full Screen mode, has been taken care of in Photoshop CS. You can now use the Hand tool (hold down the Spacebar when in a different tool) to scroll your image around the screen. Accidentally clicking down in the gray area while in Full Screen mode doesn't switch you to the Finder on the Mac,

You can use Option-[or Option-] to scroll to the next lower or higher layer of your file to see that layer's name in the title bar, without the Layers palette on the screen.

or some other application. The gray area is especially useful when making selections that need to include the pixels at the very edge of the document. Using any of the selection tools or the Cropping tool, you can actually start or end the selection in the gray area, which ensures that you have selected all the pixels along that edge. When using a typical Mac or PC window, the cursor often fluctuates between displaying as the tool you are using or the arrow cursor for the scroll bar when you move the mouse ever so slightly while at the edge of the window. Even if you are not using Full Screen mode, if you are making an edit along the edge of the image, you may want to make the window a little bigger than the image. Doing so adds Photoshop gray space between the edge of the file and the window's scroll bars so you can more easily make these edge edits. As you can tell, I am very fond of Full Screen mode. It removes all other distractions from your screen and allows you to focus on your beautiful image surrounded by nondistracting neutral gray. On the PC, Photoshop has this advantage in any screen mode. That is, when the Photoshop screen area is maximized in the Windows user interface, it covers all other programs. On the PC you can use the Window menu to show or hide the status bar, which has additional information

Here we see Photoshop working in Full Screen mode with various palettes around the active window. We can still get to underlying windows by selecting them from the Window/Documents menu or by using Control-Tab to toggle through the windows. A single press on the Tab key removes all these palettes, as shown below, and allows you to use the whole screen for your work. A second Tab press and all the same palettes are back in the same positions. This is a great way to see the big picture. When visible on the PC, the status bar toggles on and off along with the rest of the palettes. Shift-Tab toggles all the palettes except for the Tools palette, shown here on the left side of the image, and the Options palette, right below the menu bar.

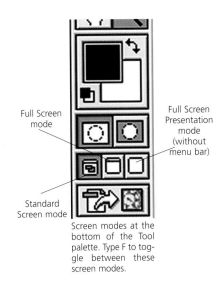

Full Screen mode

Full Screen Presentation mode (without menu bar)

Standard Screen mode

Screen modes at the bottom of the Tool palette. Type F to toggle between these screen modes.

Again in Full Screen mode, here we have used Tab to get rid of our palettes and then Command-0 to fill the screen with the image. View/Fit on Screen (Command-0) will fill the screen with your image, and it fills the entire screen if you first press Tab to remove your palettes. View/Actual Pixels (Command-Option-0) zooms to 100%. Learn to use Command-Spacebar-click to zoom in, Option-Spacebar-click to zoom out, and the Spacebar with a mouse drag for scrolling. Using these shortcut keys is the most efficient way to move around the Photoshop screen, especially in Full Screen mode or when using a dialog box like Levels.

You can now use the Hand tool (or hold down the Spacebar) to move your image around the screen even in Full Screen mode. This is a very useful addition.

about the current file and Photoshop, while in any of the screen modes, although you need to use Alt-W to activate the Window menu if you are in Full Screen Presentation mode. On the Mac, the status bar is at the bottom of the current window and only shows up when a file is in Standard Screen mode. On the PC, the status bar gives you additional hints about how to use the current Photoshop tool. The Mac status bar doesn't have this hint information that can be useful to the beginner.

The rightmost screen mode icon, at the bottom of the Tools palette, gives you a mode similar to Full Screen mode, but with the image surrounded by black instead of gray, and the menu bar removed. We'll call this "Full Screen Presentation Mode." If you are a Photoshop power user, you can work without the menu bar by using command and function keys—but I generally use this mode only for presentations. In this book, we won't be using Full Screen Mode No Menu Bar, so when I refer to Full Screen mode, I'm talking about Full Screen mode with the menu bar.

Here we see two views of the same file. The one on the left is a close-up of the lake shown to the bottom of the more zoomed-out view to the right.

MORE THAN ONE WINDOW PER FILE

You can have more than one window open at a time for the same Photoshop document. To do this, first open a Photoshop file that gives you your first window. Next, go to the Window/Arrange/New Window command to open a second window of the same file. Utilizing this capability, you can, for example, have one window of a section of the file up close and the other window showing the entire file. You can also use this technique to have one window display a particular channel or mask of the file, while another window shows the RGB or CMYK version. There are many uses of this feature and one of the best is to have one window showing how the image will look when printed on one printer, say the Lightjet 5000, and a second window showing you how it will look when printed on the Epson 1280, 2000P, or 7500. To find out exactly how to do this, see Chapter 15: "Photoshop Color Preferences, Monitor, Scanner, and Printer Calibration."

Choose Window/Arrange/Tile, then Window/Arrange/Match Zoom and Location to quickly compare areas of different files.

QUICK REORGANIZATION

Photoshop CS builds on some techniques that have been around for a while when it comes to rearranging the windows on your screen. You can use Window/Arrange/Cascade to stack all the open windows on top of and slightly overlapping each other. You can use Control-Tab or Control-Shift-Tab to scroll through your open windows, and bring each one to the front (use these keys to scroll through open files regardless of their organization or screen mode). Also under Window/Arrange is the Tile command. This will resize all the open windows and arrange them on your screen so you can see at least a portion of every open file—somewhat useful. Here's where Photoshop CS comes in. You now have some additional commands to match the zoom factor or location of the active file, or match both at the same time. This is really useful when you have several versions of the same file open and you want to check how adjustments have affected a particular area. If you're on the Mac, you can also click the yellow Minimize button or double-click the title bar to put your file on the system dock, keeping it handy, but out of the way. On the Windows side, clicking the Minimize button causes the window to be minimized to the bottom of the Photoshop desktop (the gray area withig the Photoshp window) as a small title bar for that window.

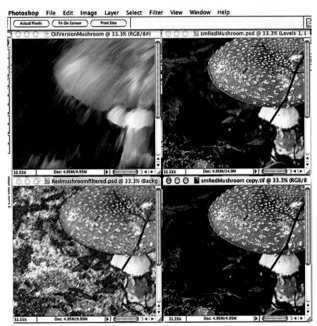

The Zoom and Location are matched to the currently active window. This is very helpful for correction and retouching. And, you can set up a keyboard shortcut for these commands if you use them often.

CONTROL KEYS FOR ZOOMING AND SCROLLING

There are certain keyboard shortcuts that I make everyone learn when I teach Photoshop. IT IS VERY IMPORTANT THAT YOU LEARN THESE THREE SHORTCUT KEYS! Even if you hate keyboard shortcuts and you don't want to be a power user, you have to learn these or you will find working in Photoshop a constant pain. I worked on the Lisa project at Apple. The Lisa was the predecessor to the Mac, and much of the Mac's user interface actually was designed for the Lisa. Larry Tesler, who was head of applications software for the Lisa project, had a license plate on his car that read, "NO MODES." A mode is a place in the user interface of a program where you can't access the tools you normally use. Programs, like Photoshop, that have a lot of modes can be confusing, especially for the beginner. Many tools in Photoshop come up in a modal dialog box; for example, Levels, Curves, Color Balance, and most of the color correction tools. When you use these tools, you are in a mode because you can't go to the Tools palette and switch to, for instance, the Zoom tool. Learning the control keys will help you function even when you're in a mode!

ZOOMING IN AND OUT

If you are inside Levels or Curves and you want to zoom in to see more detail, which I do all the time, you can't select the Zoom tool from the Tools palette the way you usually can. Holding down the Command key and the Spacebar will show you the Zoom icon, which you can then click on to zoom in on your image. Option-Spacebar-click will do a zoom out. When you zoom in and out using the Zoom tool or these control keys, Photoshop zooms by a known amount. If you are at 100%, where you see all the pixels, then you will zoom in to 200% and then 300% and then 400%. You will find that the image is sharper at a factor of 2 from 100%. Fifty percent, 100%, 200%, or 400% are sharper than 66.6%, 33.3%, and so on. You can also use Command-+ and Command-– to zoom in and out. In Standard Screen mode these keys change your window size while zooming, unless you go to Edit/Preferences/General and turn off the default Zoom Resizes Windows. You can use Command-Option-+ or –, which

If you are working in Windows on the PC, use the Alt key where we specify the Option key, and where we specify the Command key, use the Ctrl key.

9

does the opposite to the Zoom Resizes Windows preferences setting. By default, the Spacebar zooming options do not change the window size, unless you type Z for the Zoom tool and then turn on Resize Windows To Fit in the Options bar. With the Zoom tool active, Control-Spacebar-click (right mouse click on the PC) gives you a pop-up menu with various zooming options. Don't forget that you can always zoom so the entire image fits in the screen by pressing Command-0 (zero). If you press Command-Option-0, the image zooms to 100%.

SCROLLING WITH THE HAND ICON AND KEYBOARD

Just holding the Spacebar down brings up the Hand icon, and clicking and dragging this icon scrolls your file. Shift-Spacebar gives you the Hand tool and scrolls all open images at the same time (wonderful when comparing images). Typing an H switches you to the Hand tool. The Hand tool is a good place to be when you are not using another tool because it can't accidentally damage your file and you can then scroll with just a click and drag. You can use the Page Up and Page Down keys on many keyboards to scroll the current image a page worth of pixels up or down. Command-Page Up scrolls to the left and Command-Page Down to the right. Add the Shift key to any of these to scroll 10 pixels at a time. The Home key scrolls to the top left and the End key to the bottom right.

PALETTE MANAGEMENT

Photoshop contains a lot of different palettes, each of which controls a different set of functions. The Tools palette is the main palette. Its functions are discussed in Chapter 4: "The Tools Palette." The different color-picking palettes are discussed in Chapter 5: "Picking and Using Color." The Channels, Layers, Layer Comps, and Paths palettes are discussed in Chapter 6: "Selections, Paths, Masks, and Channels," and Chapter 7: "Layers, Layer Masks, and Adjustment Layers." What we discuss in this chapter is how to most efficiently use all the palettes on the Photoshop screen.

ACCESSING PALETTES

All palettes can be accessed from the Window menu. Any currently open palette will be marked in this menu with a checkmark. You can use this menu to open or close a particular palette even when you are in modal dialog box. You may notice when you click the Window menu that there are keyboard shortcuts that are modifiable already set up for many of the palettes. I recommend using the Actions palette to define function keys to bring up and close the palettes you use most often. I have created a set of function keys for you, called Artistkeys, which I show you how to install in Chapter 3: "Setting System and Photoshop Preferences," and talk more about later in this chapter. The function keys that you use in Actions will override any keyboard shortcuts that you have set.

Pressing the Tab key makes the Tools palette—and all other visible palettes—disappear. Pressing Tab again brings all these palettes up in the same

Clicking the first time on the Zoom button, at the top, resizes the palette so that it just holds the things within it, like the palette directly belowt. In Windows systems the rightmost box closes the palette and the box just to the left of it duplicates the behavior we describe here.

Clicking again in this palette's grow box expands it to the size of the image to the immediate left. The compacted size shown here can be left at the bottom or top of your monitor without taking up much screen real estate until you need it. Double-clicking on the title tab, Channels in this case, collapses the palette down to its smallest size. Double-clicking again on this tab opens the palette so you can see the entire thing. If you hold the Shift key down and drag a palette toward the top or bottom of the screen, it will snap to the edge of the screen, and then neatly open or close to the top or bottom of the screen when you double-click on the tab or click the Grow box.

Clicking the button a second time, or double-clicking the title tab, resizes the palette to show just name tabs, like the palette on the right. Do this when the edge of the palette is on the top or bottom of the screen and the palette will "stick" to the edge of the screen.

locations. Pressing Shift-Tab opens or closes the other palettes without changing the status of the Tools palette and Options bar. You can close any of the palettes, except the Tools palette, by clicking the Close button in the top-left corner of the palette on the Mac or the top-right corner in Windows. If the Tab key does not make the palettes go away and come back, the cursor is probably within a text field on the current tool's Options menu. Just press Return (Enter for Windows) to deactivate that field and the Tab key should hide the palettes again.

PALETTE LOCATIONS

The first time you open Photoshop, most of your palettes will be in groups on the right side of your screen. Click the name tab of any palette to bring it to the front of its group. You can move palette groups or single palettes around on the screen by clicking the title bar at the top and moving the palette to a new location. Photoshop opens the palettes in the same location at which they were last used unless you turn off the Save Palette Locations option within Photoshop's General Preferences. If you find your work goes faster having palettes in particular locations, you can save the locations (and settings) of open palettes using the Window/Workspace/Save Workspace command.

GROUPING AND SEPARATING PALETTES

In Photoshop, you can group several palettes in the same palette window. You then switch between palettes in the group by clicking the name tab of the palette you want or by choosing the palette from the Window menu. If you hide any of the palettes within the group, the whole group gets hidden. Therefore, you are better off grouping only palettes that are used together. Sometimes you want to see two palettes at the same time that are usually used within a group. I do this often with the Layers and Channels palettes. When I'm working on a complicated layer document that has a lot of mask channels, I separate them to see both at the same time. To do this, click the name tab of the palette you want to separate and then drag it out of the group window to a new location by itself. To move more palettes into a group, click the name tab of the palette you want to add and then drag it over the group window. New palettes in a group are added to the right. If you have a small monitor, you may want to group more of your palettes together to save screen space. You can also compact and collapse your palettes by clicking in the green Zoom box at the top left of the Mac window. This box is on the right and has a minus icon on the PC.

THE PALETTE WELL

If your monitor is set to at least 1024 pixels wide, then the Options palette will have a gray area at its right side, called the Palette Well. You can drag palettes and drop them into this docking area. At that point the palette's title tab appears in the docking area and you can access the palette from there by clicking on it. If you have many palettes docked, moving the mouse over the area highlights the names of the palettes without opening one. Click the mouse down on the title of the palette you want to open. The Palette Well keeps occasionally used palettes handy. The good point is that you don't have to go to the Window menu to open or close a palette. The bad point (or sometimes good point) is that the palette closes once you return to your file to work. Any palette that you need to refer on a regular basis, such as the Info palette, should be pulled out of the dock and left open on your desktop. We've put a basic workspace on the *Photoshop CS Artistry* CD to give you an idea of how we arrange our palettes on screen to speed workflow. You can start with that and move palettes around till you find one or more arrangements that work for you. To remove

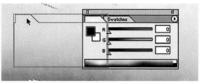

Click a palette's name tab and drag it outside the group window to put that palette within its own window.

Here we see the Color palette after it has been removed from grouping with the Swatches palette. To regroup these palettes, click the name tab of one of them and drag it on top of the window of the other. The palette that is within a group window first has its name tab on the left. New palette tabs are added to the right.

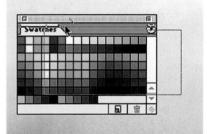

You can also stack palettes vertically. Here we dragged the Color palette on top of the Swatches palette until the gray line shows up in the gray area at the top of the window. Release the mouse at this point and you get the palette arrangement shown below.

By dragging and releasing, you can move palettes into the Palette Well at the top-right of the Options palette. To access one of these palettes, just click on its tab and it will pop open as shown to the right. Use the grow button in variable sized palettes, like Styles, to resize the palette to see all the choices.

Click on the title tab to activate the palette. You can make choices and changes, then as soon as you return to work on your file, the palette will close automatically.

Here we see a typical palette with its Options menu on the top right, accessible by clicking the black triangle icon. Mac palettes have a red Close button on the top left and a green Zoom button for collapsing or opening the palette. The center button, which is yellow on image windows, is the Minimize button. Palette windows cannot be minimized onto the Mac OSX dock. The buttons will show their color when you move your cursor over them. On Windows palettes, Close and Zoom boxes are on the right. The icons at the bottom of the palette are shortcuts for various functions associated with that palette. The name highlighted at the top is the palette's name tab. The names in gray are other palettes that are grouped with the current palette. Below are some standard icons and what they mean depending on the palette they are located within.

a palette from the docking area, just click and drag the palette's title tab to the location you'd like to move it to.

PALETTE OPTIONS

Most palettes have a menu that you can access by clicking the Menu icon at the top right of the palette. The Palette Options show you different ways to display the palette, as well as commands that are often represented by buttons on the bottom of the palette. You should check out the Palette Options on all the palettes that have them. The Dock to Palette Well choice puts that palette in the well at the top right of the Options bar.

CONTEXT-SENSITIVE MENUS

Photoshop has a great feature using the Control key and the mouse (or just the right mouse button on Windows)! At any time, you can hold down the Control key and then press the mouse button (just right-click on Windows) to bring up a set of context-sensitive menus. What shows up in the menu at a particular time depends on the tool you are currently using and the location where you click. If you are in the Marquee tool, for example, you get one menu if there already is a selection and a different one if there is not. If you are in the Move tool, you'll get a menu showing all the layers that currently have pixels at the location where you click. You can then choose the layer you want to access from that menu. There is at least one context-sensitive menu for each tool. These are a great set of time-saving features. To learn

Load Selection from Channel or Path

Save the Selection to a Channel

New Channel, Layer, Path, Action, or Snapshot

Throw away Channel, Layer, Path, Action, or Snapshot

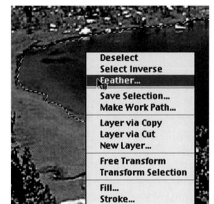

Control-clicking when a selection is active and you are in a selection tool gives you this Context-Sensitive menu, which includes most of the choices you would want involving a selection.

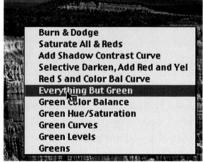

Control-clicking when in the Move tool gives you a menu of layers that have pixels at the location where you clicked. You can then choose the layer you want to make active in the Layers palette.

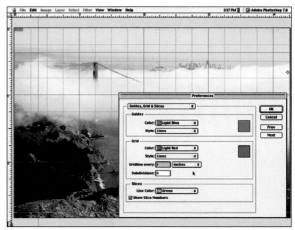

more, see Chapter 4: "The Tools Palette," and also the step-by-step examples throughout this book.

RULERS, GUIDES, AND GRIDS

Photoshop has rulers, guides, and grids, which are very helpful for creating composite images where you need to place objects in exact locations. They are also great for Web and multimedia projects to control the alignment of buttons and action objects. The controls for rulers, guides, and grids are all located on the View menu. As you can see in the diagram on this page, there is a different command key to turn each of the rulers, grids, or guides on and off, but you can also choose to have grids and/or guides removed when you use Command-H, the global hide key. I believe Mark Hamburg, Adobe's lead Photoshop engineer, coined the term "UberHide" for this expanded functionality of Command-H, which before had been used to hide and show selection edges. The UberSnap, Command-Shift-;, can now be used to turn off snapping to the grid and/or guides as well as slices and document bounds. Having snapping on helps you more accurately align items, such as buttons, that need to be exactly vertically or horizontally aligned. You can also use Command-Option-; to lock guides, which will prevent accidentally moving them.

Command-R turns your rulers on, at which point you can set the zero-zero location of the rulers (the top left of the image, by default) by clicking in the top-left ruler box and then dragging to the point in your image that you want to be zero-zero. To return the zero-zero to the top-left position again, just double-click in the top-left corner of the ruler display. You can set up the ruler unit preferences in Photoshop/Preferences/Units and Rulers on the Mac or Edit/Preferences/ Units and Rulers on the PC.

To create a guide, click in the horizontal or vertical ruler and drag the guide to where you want it or use View/New Guide and type in the exact location you want. Clicking the horizontal ruler will drag out a horizontal guide, and clicking the vertical ruler will drag out a vertical guide. You can move a guide, if Lock Guides is not turned on, by using the Move tool (V or the Command key) and just dragging the guide to its new position. Option-dragging a guide toggles it from vertical to horizontal or

Photoshop/Preferences/Guides, Grid & Slices brings up this Preferences dialog box, which allows you to set the color and appearance of your grid, guides, and slices. You can also specify how often you have gridlines and subdivisions. Use Edit/Preferences/Guides, Grid & Slices on the PC.

Using the View menu, you can use Command-R to turn rulers on and off, Command-; to turn Guides on and off, and Command-' to turn the Grid on and off. Using Show Extras Options, a selected number of these, as well as Selection Edges, Slices, Annotations, and Paths, can now be turned on or off using Command-H, the "UberHide" command.

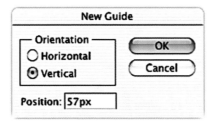

If you need to exactly position a guide, use the View/New Guide command. You can type in any unit of measure regardless of how your preferences are set.

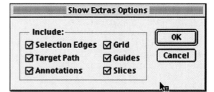

Accessed from View/Show/Show Extras Options, this dialog determines the types of items, if on the screen at the time, that Command-H, the UberHide command, will now remove.

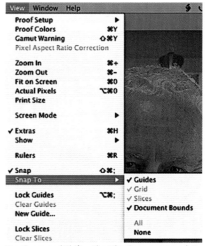

Use Command-Shift-;, the UberSnap command, to Snap To any or all of the Guides, Grid, Slices, or Document Bounds.

vice versa. Another important keyboard option for guides is to hold down the Shift key while dragging out your guides. This forces the guides to even-pixel boundaries, which is critical for multimedia and Web work where precision is paramount. Take a few minutes to play with these options and you will find rulers, grids, and guides easy to learn. You can lock or unlock guides from the View menu and use the Show sub-menu of View to show or hide guides.

When working on projects where I need to measure the sizes and placements, I usually have at least Rulers on. When you are drawing a selection, you can actually see the starting location as well as the current location of the mouse by following the dotted lines that show you the current mouse location along each of the rulers. For faster positioning, turn on the grid as well as Snap To Grid; then you will know that things are exactly placed. To set your own specific locations, create guides anywhere you want. You can then line up objects along these guides. When I am just color correcting a photograph, I usually turn off Rulers, Guides, and Grids and put the image into Full Screen mode so that I can see it unobstructed.

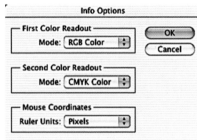

Here we see the Info palette during the Free Transform command. The contents of the right and bottom two sections change to show you information about your transformation.

Check out the many useful display options of the Info palette as accessed from its Palette Options menu.

USING THE INFO PALETTE

The Info palette is one of the most useful tools in Photoshop. Not only does it measure colors like a densitometer (which we will do extensively in the color correction exercises in later chapters in this book), it also gives you important measurements any time you are scaling, rotating, making, or adjusting a selection. The top-right location, the size of the box you are drawing, the degree of rotation, and many other useful measurements are always present in the Info palette. This is a good one to keep up on the screen most of the time. See Chapter 12: "Color Correction Tools," and Chapter 17: "Steps to Create a Master Image," for a discussion of the important Color Sampler part of the Info palette. If you are using the ArtistKeys actions from the book's CD, then function key F9 is used to access this palette. The built-in default Photoshop function keys use F8 for Info and you can even access it with F8 from within a Modal dialog.

THE NAVIGATOR PALETTE

Photoshop has a cool Navigator palette (Window/Navigator or Shift-F2 with ArtistKeys) that allows you to zoom in and out to quickly see where you are in an image and more efficiently move to a particular spot in that image. This palette contains a small thumbnail of your entire image with a red box, called the View box, on top of the thumbnail that shows you the part of the image you can currently see in your window. As you zoom in, you will notice this box getting smaller because you are seeing less and less of the image area. You can click and drag this box, in the Navigator palette, to a new location and then your window will display what's inside the box. This is much faster than doing large scrolls with the Hand tool on the actual image window, because in the Navigator palette you always see the entire image. You do not need to guess where you want to scroll to; just click the red box and move it there. It's even faster if you don't drag the box there, but instead just click down in the Navigator palette where you want the box to be. To change the size and location of the red box, just Command-drag a new box over the area you want to see. You can change the size of the Navigator palette and its thumbnail by clicking and dragging in the Grow box at the bottom-right corner of the palette on the Macintosh, or click and drag on any edge when using Windows. Making the palette bigger gives you more exact positioning within your file using the bigger thumbnail. You can use the

Chapter 2: Navigating in Photoshop

Here is the small, default-size Navigator palette. On the Mac click the green button, on the PC, the top-right Minus button, to return to this size. At 66.67% the entire image is visible on my screen and the red View box tells me I am viewing the whole file. Drag the Grow box on the lower-right corner to make the palette larger.

Navigator palette and red View box when zoomed to 300%. Now only the area in the red View box is visible in the image window.

Dragging on the red View box to change what is visible in the image window.

slider on the bottom right to drag the zoom factor smaller or bigger. You can also click the smaller or bigger icon on either side of the slider to zoom in a similar way to Command-Spacebar-clicking and Option-Spacebar-clicking.

In the bottom left of the Navigator palette is a numeric text box where you can type in the exact zoom factor that you need. If you hold down the Shift key while pressing Enter after typing in a new zoom factor here, you will zoom to the new factor, but the text percentage number remains highlighted so you can enter a new value without having to click the text box again. Again, I have found that images are a little sharper on the screen when zoomed to a multiple of 100% (25%, 50%, 100%, 200%, 400%, and so on). You can change the color of the View box from red to another color by choosing Palette Options from the Navigator palette menu.

Command-dragging a new box to view just the boat and water in the center. When the mouse button is released, we will zoom so this box fills the window.

THE ACTIONS PALETTE

Check out Chapter 3: "Setting System and Photoshop Preferences," to learn how to set up the Actions palette with my ArtistKeys command set to quickly set up function keys to show and hide any palette. You may notice, throughout the book, references like "F11 with ArtistKeys" or just "F11." These show you places where I have created shortcuts for you using the Actions feature. Actions can be used to automate a single menu choice, such as bringing up a palette, or a whole sequence of events, such as complex functions for sharpening and removing noise from an image. Please read Chapter 11: "Automating with Actions," to learn about the wonderful ways you can automate repetitive tasks using actions! Most of the color separations in this book were produced automatically with actions included in the ArtistKeys set and discussed in Chapter 11.

THE BRUSHES PALETTE

Most of the image-editing tools allow you to access the Brushes palette from the Options bar. A few, like the Healing brush, only allow you to make minor changes to their brushes, and some, the Gradient tool for example, do not use the brushes at all. You'll know whether the tool has access to the complete Brushes palette when you see the small Brushes palette icon on the right of the Options bar just to the left of the File Browser icon. To select a particular brush via the Options bar, just click and drag on top of the Brush icon at the left of the Options bar until the cursor is over the brush that you want. If you load BarrysPhotoBrush.abr and open the palette as suggested in Chapter 3 in the "Palettes that You Access Indirectly" section, finding your brush will be easy. When you find the brush you need,

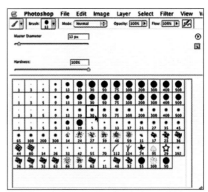

A click and drag on the Brush icon within the Options palette will pop up the Brushes palette, and if you keep the mouse button down, you can move to, and then release on the new brush you want. This allows you to choose a new brush with one click even though the palette is not always up on the screen. If you click once and release on the Brush icon in the Options palette, this leaves the palette open. You can then use the grow box in the palette to change its size, then press Return or Enter to close that pop-up palette. To edit a brush, you use the bigger Brushes palette from the Window menu as shown on the next page.

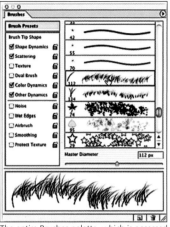

The entire Brushes palette, which is accessed from the Windows menu, has numerous options and views that are explained more fully in Chapter 35, "Digital Paint."

Here is the Tool Presets palette with Current Tool Only checked so all we see is the presets I have made for the Brushes tool, which is the currently selected tool. Clicking on the AirBrush 7% preset picks the 100 pixel soft brush, turns on the AirBrush option, sets the Brush Opacity to 100% and the Flow to 7%, all with just one click.

To create a new tool preset, click on the New Tool Preset icon at the bottom of the Tool Presets palette to the left of the Trash icon. The Include Color checkbox, when checked, includes the color you are painting with the current brush.

release the mouse button and the Brushes palette will disappear and leave you with the new brush selected. This allows you to get a new brush with only one mouse click and also without having the Brushes palette up on the screen all the time. Use Shift-F12 to open the Brushes palette using ArtistKeys, or F5 if you use the default keyboard shortcut. To learn all about the Brush features, check out Chapter 4: "The Tools Palette," and Chapter 35: "Painting in Photoshop."

TOOL PRESETS

The Tool Presets palette (Command-F7) allows you to save the settings for a particular tool, the Brush for example, so with one click you can return to those same settings next time you need them. This is a great time saver since there are many different ways we will be using each tool. An example of this is that I like to use the Paintbrush with the Airbrush mode turned on, using a soft brush and with the Flow of the Airbrush set to 7%. To make a Tool Presets entry for this brush, I just set up my Paintbrush the way I want and then choose the New Tool Preset menu item from the Tool Presets palette and this allows me to save these settings with a name that I choose. Wendy and I prefer to use the Tool Presets palette with the Current Tool Only checkbox checked. Because this removes the clutter of having all presets for all tools displayed, we only see the ones for the tool we are currently working with. If you wanted to use the Tool Presets palette to switch to the tool you want to use, as well as pick its options, then you'd need to work with the Current Tool Only checkbox unchecked. Our predefined set of presets, called ArtistryCSToolPresets.tpl, is in the Preferences folder on the *Photoshop CS Artistry* CD. To load those presets, choose Replace Tool Presets from the pop-up menu at the top right of the Tool Presets palette.

FILE BROWSER

The File Browser is another very useful palette that was added to Photoshop 7 and given some wonderful updates in Photoshop CS. It allows you to look at and organize images and folders on your desktop and hard drives and decide which images to open into Photoshop.

The Photoshop team did a lot of work on the File Browser for this version of Photoshop and it shows. Everything is neatly labeled, and you can do most any organizational task without ever leaving the Browser. Perhaps that's why the Browser icon is now a permanent feature of the Options bar. You may find that you hardly ever need to use the Open command and search for a file again. If you used the File Browser in Photoshop 7 and found it to be slow, you'll be pleasantly surprised by the faster performance of the Photoshop CS Browser.

BASIC ORGANIZATION

The Browser can be divided into five areas—the menu bar on the top, and the four windows in the lower section. The windows can be resized by dragging the dividing lines between the sections, similarly to changing the window size in Excel or other applications. We find it particularly helpful to resize the Preview a bit larger. If you double-click the title tab of any of the left-hand windows, the window will close to make more room for the other palettes or open to display its contents. The palettes in these three windows on the left can be moved to different locations (remaining on the left side) by dragging the title tab to a new location. You can also expand the Thumbnail window to the width of the File Browser by clicking the small

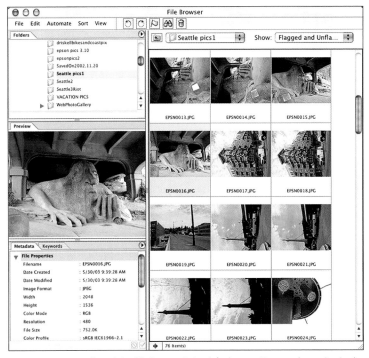

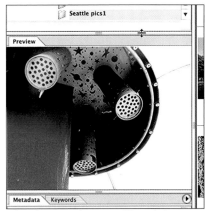

When the cursor changes to this symbol, you can resize the lower windows of the File Browser.

You can move the palettes in the left window up or down to show only the information that you need. Here, the Preview palette is now docked with the Folder palette in the top window.

Here we see an overview of the File Browser in its default state. You can change its size by using the Grow icon in the lower right corner or by clicking the green Grow button on the upper left. The Grow button will open the window to fill the available space. If you want to open and cover your desktop, press Tab first to get rid of all your palettes. When you click on an image, it is shown larger in the Preview window to the left, and information about that image is displayed in the lower left corner. If that image is not rotated correctly, you can rotate its thumbnail using one of the rotate buttons on the top of the palette, then the image will be rotated here and by Photoshop as it is opened. To open any file directly into Photoshop, just Double-click on that particular file, either in the Browser window or the Preview window..

diamond-shaped icon at the bottom of that window. When you find an arrangement that works well for you, save it along with any other open palettes as a workspace using Window/Workspace/Save Workspace from the main Photoshop menu.

The upper-left window holds the Folders palette. This allows you to scroll through your hard drives in a Finder-like way, and similar to Windows Explorer on the PC side. When you click a folder, images and folders that are within will show in the Thumbnail window. Just like Finder or Windows Explorer, you can click the triangle beside a folder to open it and search through subfolders for the items you want.

The bottom-left window contains the Metadata information and Keywords palettes. The Metadata information you see will depend on how and from where your file came, as well as which Metadata Display Options you've turned on via the palette pop-up. If your file was downloaded from a digital camera, you'll get all sorts of information about the camera that was used and its settings, as well as the name of your file, its creation date, and its size. Much of the data was available in Photoshop 7 as well, but now it's organized into sections: File Properties, IPTC information, and Camera Data (EXIF), which show by default; and GPS, Camera RAW, and Edit History, which you turn on via Display Options.

KEYWORDS

The Keywords function is new to Photoshop CS and you're really going to love it. To access the keywords, click the title tab in the lower-left window. Photoshop has

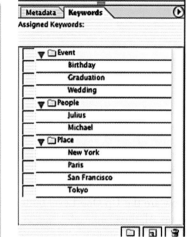

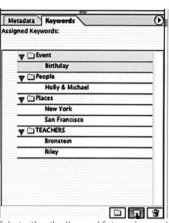

Select either the Keyword Set or a keyword in the set to target that set for the new keyword.

The default keywords may help you, but you'll want to set up your own.

Turn on or off which Metadata information you want displayed in the File Browser by using Edit/Metadata Display Options from the File Browser menu bar.

The Details view of the Thumbnail window. The second file has been highlighted, then flagged by clicking the Flag icon at the top of the window.

already set up a few keywords that you might find useful, but of course, you'll want to create your own keywords to organize your photos. To do this, click the Folder icon at the bottom of the Keyword section to create a new Keyword Set—Landscapes or Animals, for instance—and then type in the name of the new set in the empty box that appears at the top of the window. Next, create individual keywords that belong to the set by clicking the set name or a keyword within the set that you want to target, then click the New Keyword icon (the center one) at the bottom of the window. Once again, you'll get a small blank box where you can type in your keyword. Don't' worry if you inadvertently create a keyword in the wrong category. Simply click down on the keyword, drag it to the correct Keyword Set, and drop it there. If you need to edit the name of the keyword or set, use the pop-up menu or the context-sensitive menu.

To assign a keyword to a photo, click on the photo in the Thumbnail window, and a set of small checkboxes will show up to the left of the keyword and sets. Click the ones that are appropriate for the picture. If you click the Keyword Set checkbox, all keywords in that set are applied to the photo. Once you have applied a keyword to a photo, you can use the Search option to organize the pictures into new folders. Click the Search button on the menu bar (the Binoculars) or use the File/Search menu item and type in the keyword you want. You can also click the keyword in the palette before you click the Search button to automatically fill the input area. All the files marked with that keyword will be gathered into a folder called Search Results (look for it at the bottom of the Browser Folder window) and you can easily move them into the correct folder. I'll talk more about moving and sorting in the section on the Browser Menu bar.

The Thumbnail Window

The Thumbnail window can be viewed several different ways by changing the options in the View menu. You can choose to see Small, Medium, or Large thumbnails for your pictures, or you can choose a custom size for display, the width of which is set in the Preferences/File Browser dialog. The Details option will show you a medium-large thumbnail along with information about the file including its rank, file type, color space, and size. You can rearrange your images using any of the views to make organizing and ranking easier by dragging and dropping the files. This reorganization is saved as a custom sort for this folder. You might need a custom sort for a group of photos if you need to sort out all the ones that show the Chairman of the Board first with those showing only members of the Board next. Once you create the custom sort you switch between it and the regular sort methods.

At the top of the Thumbnail window are the Up One Level button, the Location pop-up, and the Flagged Files pop-up. All three are useful, but it's the ability to quickly flag certain files and show only the ones you want in a folder that I find really exciting. This means if you have a large folder full of waterfall shots, but a client only wants waterfalls in autumn, you can flag just those files, then copy them to a new folder to burn on a CD or send over the Internet. If you then find the client only wants the three that you think are your best shots, unflag the rest and they no longer show up. Later, when the client wants three more to choose from, show both the flagged and unflagged files, then turn on the flags again. It's simple and works great.

The Menu Bar

I've already mentioned a few items that are in the File Browser menu bar, but let's take some time here to look at the incredible navigational power built into this part of Photoshop.

One of the best parts of the new File Browser is the first item in the File menu, New Folder. Take the example I mentioned before, flagging files that you want to copy to burn or send later. Just suppose you forgot to create a folder with the client's name on it before you did your search. Instead of having to go back out to your operating system to create the folder, you can do it right here in the Browser. Before you use the command, click the folder or drive where you want your new folder. When the new folder appears, the name is highlighted and ready for you to rename it. You can now drag files into it from your previous search or from any other folder on your machine. A simple drag will move the files, Option-drag will copy the files if you are on a Mac; Ctrl-drag to copy the files on a PC.

You can open multiple files at once by selecting them and using the Open command, or you can merely double-click on a selected file. To select multiple files, you can Shift-click contiguous images or Command-click images that are not next to each other. You can also open the image or images into ImageReady from this menu, which is great for quickly choosing files for Web processing. If ImageReady is not already running, it will open as well with this command.

The File Info command is the same command found in the main File menu, but here, the file does not have to be open to show you the information. Again, it may not seem like such a big deal, but if you need to look for information a lot, you're going to find this saves you considerable time.

If you have folders that you need to access often, you can put them in your Favorites folder using File/Add Folder to Favorites. You will then be able to access those items from the Location pop-up at the top of the Thumbnail window regardless of whether they have been used recently or not.

The location pop-up navigates you to the most recently used folders as well as your desktop and hard drives.

There's a lot of power built into the Browser's File menu.

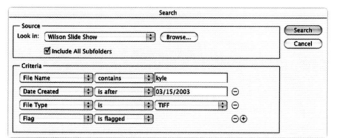

No matter how nit-picky you need to be when you search for files, the Browser's search engine can handle it.

If you need to Rank multiple files all the same way, select them first in the Thumbnail window, then use Edit/Rank. Use this method to clear multiple rankings as well.

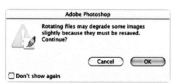

You get this dialog when you choose one of the rotate options from the File Browser. I'd check "Don't show again" once you understand this!

Rotating files may degrade some images slightly because they must be resaved. Continue?

If you choose Apply Rotation from the Edit menu, be sure that you're not resaving jpeg files. You don't get a chance to look at the changes to the file.

The cache holds information about the flags, comments, and thumbnails in a particular folder. You can export that information for any folder, as well as purge the info from a single folder or all folders.

Finally, the File menu (as well as the Binocular button further to the right) is where you'll find the Search command. This is a very sophisticated search engine, allowing you to set up to 13 different criteria. You can even search for the minutiae of Metadata information and call those files into your Search folder. The Browse button at the top of the Search dialog allows you to look over your drive and choose a different folder to search if the one that appears at the top of the window is not what you want.

The Edit menu allows you to select, flag, rank, and rotate your files. The Select All command works no matter what view you use, and you can select all flagged files by using the Thumbnail window pop-up to show only flagged files, then selecting them, as well as by using the command. You can flag the file using the Edit menu command, a keyboard shortcut, or the Flag button to the right of the menu. Select a file or files and use Edit/Rank to apply a number or letter by which to sort files. You can also click beside the word, Rank, if you are using the Large thumbnail view, to key in the rank in an input field. However, the rank is only visible in Large thumbnail view or in Detail view (you can see it in File Info as well).

There are two Rotate buttons to the right of the menu for rotating 90° either clockwise or counterclockwise, but the Edit menu gives you the third choice of rotating 180°. When you first rotate a file a warning dialog will appear telling you that the rotation has only been applied in the Browser, and just like in Photoshop 7, the file will be rotated when it is opened. New to this version is the Edit/Apply Rotation command, which will rotate the files without having them open. Please note that this command cannot be applied to locked files or files in formats that Photoshop does not recognize. Also, remember that if you rotate jpegs this way, they will be resaved as jpegs and the quality will degrade without you having any control over the changes.

At the bottom of the Edit menu are commands dealing with Metadata. As more and more images whiz through space via the Internet, this information becomes increasingly important. Photoshop allows you to save a set of Metadata as a template that can be attached to the files you send with information such as your name, title, and instructions for the image.

The Preferences item under the Browser/Edit menu takes you directly to the Browser preference page.

Most of the commands in the Browser/Automate menu are available from Photoshop's main menu bar File/Automate command. We'll talk more about automation in Chapter 11: "Automating with Actions and Scripts."

The final two menu items, Sort and View, are fairly self-explanatory. If you're upgrading from Photoshop 7, you'll notice a couple of new items in the sort menu (which was at the bottom of the Thumbnail window in PS7), Flag and Custom. Custom sort will be checked if you have manually moved images around in the Thumbnail window. Along with flagging, new items in the View menu are the capabilities of seeing unreadable files, hiding or showing subfolders, custom thumbnail sizes, and showing the location of a file in the Finder.

3 SETTING SYSTEM AND PHOTOSHOP PREFERENCES

Setting up your system and Photoshop's preferences to make Photoshop run more efficiently and make your work easier.

This chapter is essential for everyone to read and follow since it will set up Photoshop in the most effective way for you and also in the way that Photoshop is referenced by the rest of this book. If you are new to computers or Photoshop, some of the discussions and settings here may seem a bit confusing to you. Before going on to the rest of the book, you should read this chapter and set up your preferences as it recommends. Photoshop will run more efficiently and give you better results with your color corrections and separations. Your understanding will grow as you do the exercises and read the rest of the book. Before doing the color correction hands-on chapters, you should also read and set up further preferences as described in Chapter 14: "Color Spaces, Device Characterization, and Color Management;" and Chapter 15: "Photoshop Color Preferences, Monitor, Scanner, and Printer Calibration." Other chapters that are essential for all to read are Chapter 16: "Image Resolution, Scanning Film, and Digital Cameras," and Chapter 17: "Steps to Create a Master Image."

SETTING UP THE PERCENT OF MEMORY PHOTOSHOP USES

You may want to read this section with your Macintosh or PC turned on so you can refer to your screen as you follow the steps outlined here. While running the Macintosh X Finder, choose About This Mac from the Apple menu. An information window opens, giving you the total memory available on your Macintosh. See the caption to the right to find out how much memory is installed on your PC.

Once you know how much memory your computer has, choose Photoshop/Preferences/Memory & Image Cache (Edit/Preferences/Memory & Image Cache on the PC) from Photoshop and notice that the Memory Usage setting is 50% (which is the default). I set Photoshop on my Mac OS X system, which has 1.25 gigs of memory installed, to use 85% of the available RAM. The more memory you have installed on your computer, the higher percentage you can allocate to Photoshop because there will still be enough left for Mac OS X or Windows and several smaller applications to run efficiently. If you don't have much memory, less than 500 megs for example, leave things at the 50% default; if you have lots of memory, give Photoshop a higher percentage. After setting this, click OK in the Memory & Image Cache Preferences dialog box. You need to quit Photoshop and then restart it for these changes to take effect but you don't need to reboot your operating system. When Photoshop starts, it calculates the amount of available RAM in your system. Photoshop measures this RAM (computer memory) by taking the amount of installed RAM and subtracting

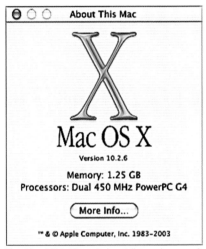

The About This Mac window tells you how much memory is installed in your Macintosh as well as the version of OS X you are running. If you click on More Info, you get other useful information about your computer, its software, and its peripherals.
To find out how much memory your Windows system has installed, right-click on the My Computer icon on the desktop and choose Properties from the context-sensitive menu. This System Properties dialog shows you the amount of memory at the bottom of the General tab that is initially displayed.

Mac OS X added a convention that on each OS X application there would be a menu containing the name of the application and the preferences for that application. This is why Preferences and Color Settings are in the Photoshop menu with OS X but still in the Edit menu with Windows XP.

Here is the Memory Preferences dialog box from my Mac OS X version of Photoshop CS. I've set this Photoshop to use 85% of the available RAM. Here you can see that Photoshop has calculated the available RAM to be 1,156 MB with 85% of that being 982 MB. The dialog box on your PC should look similar and if you have 500 megs or more of memory, you should probably increase the allocation for Photoshop to up to 85%.

These are the different categories of general preferences. You can go to any one of them using this pop-up menu or by clicking the Next and Prev buttons. You can also use Command-1 through Command-9 to get to a particular dialog box. Command-K brings up the General dialog box and Command-Option-K brings up the last preferences dialog box you were working on.

all that is used by software that permanently reserves RAM (including the Mac or Windows OS). Check the Scratch Size and Efficiency box at the bottom-left of your open Mac document, or in the Status Bar on a PC, to see how much RAM is available and how Photoshop is using it. See the "Plug-ins and Scratch Disk" section later in this chapter for more information on Scratch Size and Efficiency.

SETTING UP THE PHOTOSHOP PREFERENCES

You access most Photoshop preferences from the Photoshop/Preferences or Photoshop/Color Settings menus. In this chapter I go through setting the preferences in order and focus on the settings that are important for working efficiently with photographs. I also talk about settings that I believe should be different from Adobe's default settings. For a description of any Photoshop preferences that I don't talk about, see the Photoshop CS manual, online Help, or just hold the cursor over the preference setting and, if you have Tool Tips turned on, a yellow Tool Tips dialog will soon appear and give you a quick explanation of that item. If you are new to Photoshop, prepress. or photography, you may not understand some of the concepts or Photoshop functions mentioned in this chapter. If so, just set the preferences as we recommend for now, and then reread this chapter later after you study the rest of the book.

GENERAL PREFERENCES (COMMAND-K)

COLOR PICKER

You usually want the Adobe Color Picker because it gives you more options than the Apple Color Picker or the Windows System Color Picker. The Adobe Color Picker is the default Color Picker.

INTERPOLATION

Interpolation chooses the algorithm used when making images bigger or smaller. This process is called resampling because you are taking the current image pixels and either adding more pixels or taking some away. Bicubic (better) interpolation is the most accurate way to resample photographs. Smoother is new for upsampling and Sharper for downsampling, but Bicubic is still the most accurate overall. If you are prototyping and speed is more important than image quality, you might try one of the other choices. Nearest Neighbor is the fastest and poorest quality but it does no anti-aliasing, so with screen grabs and line art the sharp edges are not blurred with a size increase. The may be best with screen grabs and line art.

HISTORY STATES

Sets the number of History states Photoshop remembers. This is the number of Undo states you have, and the default setting of 20 is a good place to start. When I am working on a very large file, I'll sometimes set this to 1 to make Photoshop faster because it doesn't have to make the sometimes costly saves of the entire file. When I'm doing retouching with the Rubber Stamp, I often set this to 99 or more with the highest number of Undo states in Photoshop CS being 1,000. See Chapter 8: "History Palette, History Brush, and Snapshots," for more information on this subject.

EXPORT CLIPBOARD

Turn off Export Clipboard to make switching between Photoshop and other applications faster and more efficient on either Mac OS X or Windows XP. You can

Chapter 3: Setting System and Photoshop Preferences

still cut and paste inside Photoshop, just not between Photoshop and other applications. If you need to do inter application cut and paste, you can turn this back on.

SHOW TOOL TIPS

When Tool Tips is on, you get a small yellow line of information that explains what most tools do when the cursor is on top of that tool. Displaying these tips, once you know the program, can slow down Photoshop user response. You can turn Tool Tips off here by unchecking this option. You can use the Tool Tips, for example, to get Photoshop's default explanation of each of these options; try it for the ones I don't mention in this chapter.

ZOOM RESIZES WINDOWS

If this is on, then Command-+ or Command-– in Standard Screen mode will resize your window to fit the new zoom factor as you zoom in or out. Resizing windows for the Zoom tool, including for Command-Spacebar-click and Option-Spacebar-click, is controlled using the Resize Windows to Fit option in the Options palette for the Zoom tool.

BEEP WHEN DONE

Setting Beep When Done is useful if you have a slow computer or are working on exceptionally large files. It lets you go cook dinner while Unsharp Mask finishes up, for example. I used this feature a lot back when I had a slow Mac IIx. With my dual 450 MHz G4, 1.4 gig of memory, and fast hard disk, I don't need the beeps much anymore.

AUTO UPDATE OPEN DOCUMENTS

If Photoshop has a document open and that document is changed by some other application, like ImageReady for example, when returning to Photoshop, Photoshop would automatically read in that document again when this is turned on.

DYNAMIC COLOR SLIDERS

Dynamic Color Sliders allows the Color palette to show you all the possible colors, for future changes, on-the-fly as you are changing one color. It is very useful to have this on when you're color correcting.

SAVE PALETTE LOCATIONS

Save Palette Locations remembers where you had all the palettes last time you shut down and restores them the next time you power up. This is very useful! If you turn it off, then your palettes come up in the default state the next time you start Photoshop.

Tool Tips show up in many places and can help you learn the program and the icons.

These are our recommended settings in the General Preferences dialog box. All we do differently here from the default is turn off Export Clipboard, which can make switching between applications faster. The History Log is the main new option added for Photoshop 8. Check the main text of this chapter to learn more about the History Log.

USE SHIFT KEY FOR TOOL SWITCH

Holding the Shift key down and then typing M, for example, will toggle between the Rectangular and Oval Marquee tools; typing Shift-L will switch between the different Lasso tools. Turning this feature off means that typing M or L without the Shift key down will also toggle through the tool options with that shortcut key. Doing this without the Shift key down can often confuse the unsuspecting user.

RESET ALL WARNING DIALOGS

Various dialogs in Photoshop give you the option of no longer issuing a warning about their particular issue again in the future. Reset All Warning Dialogs will bring all those dialogs up again until you turn them off. The Reset All Tools option returns all tools in the Tools palette to their default states. This may be useful if you have changed a bunch of tools to strange settings, but remember that it may reset some settings you have changed specifically, like the change you'll soon make to the Eyedropper to read a 3-by-3 Average instead of a Point Sample. To do a Reset All Tools in Photoshop 8, you select the Reset All Tools menu item from the pop-up menu in Photoshop 8's Tool Presets palette.

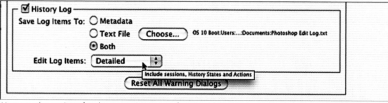

Here are the options for the new History Log feature. Metadata saves the information in the actual photoshop file when you save it. To get this information you use File/File Info then click on the Raw Data choice to the left. Text File saves the info in a file with a name and location that you choose. Both does both. Edit Log Items allows you to choose between Sessions Only, Concise and Detailed logging.

HISTORY LOG

A useful new Photoshop CS feature is the ability to save a history of what you have been doing in photoshop with a particular file and with everything you did. If you don't want your boss to be able to find out every image you opened in Photoshop and exactly what you did with them, then you better turn this off.

Who knows, if you have it on maybe John Ashcroft can even look at your imaging maneuvers over the Internet and tell if your Photoshop has been eyeing something sinful! Be careful with this one. It is actually a useful feature if you want to remember what you did to a file or to a bunch of files over the last week.

The Save Log Items section controls where the log gets saved to. You can save it in the Metadata of each file, which keeps the information about that file with that file. This could help you re-create an effect later even if you forgot to write down what you did. To get the Metadata information, you use File/File Info, then click on the History choice to the left. Text File saves the information about all the files you work on and everything you do in Photoshop in a text file with a name and location that you choose. The Both setting saves the info for a particular file in that file's metadata and it also logs everything to the specified text file.

The Edit Log Items section determines how much log information is saved. The choices are Sessions Only, Concise, and Detailed. Sessions Only just keeps track of when you enter and leave Photoshop. Concise keeps the session info as well as the history of what you did while in Photoshop. Detailed keeps track of all the Concise info as well as whatever Actions you use. I've had my History Log set to Both and Detailed and found that this really gives you a lot of information. Figuring out exactly what this information means is a more difficult exercise, which could be the subject of yet another Photoshop book. Leaving History Log checked will make your files larger and/or continue to grow a file on your disk. I'd only have it on if it's needed.

FILE HANDLING

IMAGE PREVIEWS

If you like to decide whether to save an icon or thumbnail whenever you save a file, then choose the Ask When Saving pop-up choice. You also can choose to Always Save an Icon and/or Thumbnail or Never Save one. Icon refers to the icon picture of your image you see when you are in the Mac Finder. Thumbnail refers to the preview you see in the Open dialog box on a Mac or PC. The Full Size option, mostly a waste of time and space, saves a 72 dpi full-size preview for applications that can use this— not many. In the Windows version of Photoshop, you can create a thumbnail when saving an image, but you don't have the four image preview checkbox

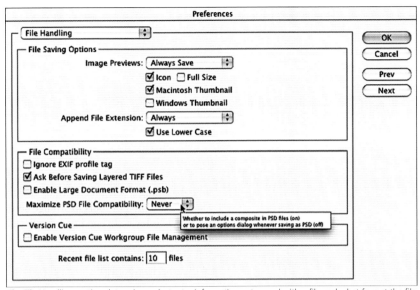

The File Handling section determines what extra information gets saved with a file and what format the file is saved in. It is important that you clearly understand these options.

choices. When you work on files for the Web, it is best to set the Image Preview options to Never Save because any type of preview will increase your file size.

APPEND FILE EXTENSION

If you turn this on (either Always or Ask When Saving), Photoshop appends the correct three-character file extensions to files so they can be understood and opened on any platform. The file extension tells the software the type of file each one is. This is very important especially when you save more obscure files, like the settings from within the Levels tool. Windows systems always save the extension. If you want to make sure your file will be recognized correctly by all the Photoshop tools and on any platform, make sure you turn on Always and the Use Lower Case option.

IGNORE EXIF PROFILE TAG

If you turn this on, then files created with a digital camera that are tagged with the sRGB profile, or some other profile, in their EXIF information will be treated in the same way that files with no profile attached are treated. If your Color Preferences are set up as I recommend later in this chapter, then you will be asked what to do with these files. Generally I recommend that you leave this option off, in which case you will be asked what to do with the sRGB or otherwise tagged digital camera files when you have your Color Prefs set up as I recommend. If the tag from the digital camera is accurate, then you'd leave the image in the tagged space if you were just going to look at it or print it directly. If you were going to color correct the image, then you'd convert it from the tagged space to Adobe RGB upon opening it.

A case where you might want to turn this Ignore EXIF sRGB tag option on would be if your digital camera tags the files with sRGB but you discover that the files actually look, color correct, and print better when tagged with Adobe RGB. You could then turn this Ignore EXIF sRGB tag option on, then these images would be opened and viewed in Adobe RGB when using my default Color Settings. See chapters 14 and 15 for more information on these subjects.

Ask Before Saving Layered TIFF Files

Let's say you open a tiff file created by your scanning software or from a digital camera. When you add a bunch of layers to that file, then save it, Photoshop CS will just save it in tiff format, along with all the layers, because that was the format it started in. Older versions of Photoshop would save files that had layers added to them in Photoshop (psd) format. All the information will be saved in either tiff or psd format, but psd format usually does the saves more quickly and you end up with smaller files. Turning this option on will at least remind you that a layered file is being saved in tiff format so that you have the chance to use File/Save As to save it in psd format.

Enable Large Document Format (.psb)

When you turn this feature on, Photoshop allows you to save very large files in the psb format. These files are not backwards compatible to earlier versions of Photoshop. They can be up to 300,000 pixels in either direction. These large files, with full layer support, can be saved in psb format, tiff format (up to 4 gigs), or Photoshop raw (without layer support) format only. Most people will want to leave this option off unless they need to work with really large files!

Maximize PSD File Compatibility

I recommend most people set this to Never because it makes your saved Photoshop files larger. There is a BIG space cost for having this option on! Every time a file with layers is saved, Photoshop must also save a flattened version of the file in addition to all the layers. Turning off this Maximize psd File Compatibility option saves disk space and time every time you are working on files that have more than one layer. Let's say you open a 500 meg scan of your 6x7 photo, as I often do. If you then add one adjustment layer and resave this file, it will suddenly be a 1 gig file. Adobe would like you to have this option on so Photoshop files open more quickly in InDesign than they do in Quark. Quark 6 may change this situation anyhow. If this option is on, then applications that can't interpret Photoshop layers may still be able to open a Photoshop file because this option saves a flattened version of the file along with all the other layers. For photographers who are mostly using Photoshop, and not using InDesign, this option should be left off.

Recent File List Contains

This controls how many files are listed in the File/Open Recent menu. I usually set this to 10.

The Display & Cursors preferences. These are our recommended settings. Setting the Painting Cursors and Other Cursors settings to Brush Size and Precise is particularly important.

Display and Cursors

Color Channels In Color

Leave Color Channels in Color off—it displays your Red, Green, and Blue, or CMYK, channels with a colored overlay that makes it very hard to see detail. Viewing individual channels in grayscale gives you a more accurate image.

Diffusion Dither

When working on an 8-bit system, the Diffusion Dither option makes smoother transitions on colors that are not in the current palette. I like the Use Diffusion Dither option to display 24-bit images on an 8-bit screen. I recommend leaving this option on if you will be viewing 24-bit images on an 8-bit screen.

PAINTING AND OTHER CURSORS

The Tool Cursors settings are important! If you set Painting Cursors to Brush Size, now the default, you will paint with a circle outline the size of your brush. This setting even takes into account the current zoom factor and is very useful. I recommend this default Brush Size setting. Using the Precise option is like using the Caps Lock key, in that you paint with a cross-hair cursor. Standard uses the standard Photoshop cursors, a different cursor for each tool. I find that the standard cursors usually get in the way of seeing what I am painting. For the Other Cursors option, I recommend the Precise setting, which gives you a very accurate cross-hair for all the non-painting tools.

PLUG-INS AND SCRATCH DISK

The Additional Plug-Ins folder tells Photoshop where to find additional plug-in filters. The default plug-ins that come with Photoshop are already set up when you install Photoshop. In Mac OS X, they are in a folder called Plug-ins, directly inside the Adobe Photoshop CS folder that is normally installed in the Applications folder on your boot drive. In Windows XP, plugs-ins is found at: C/Program Files/Adobe/Photoshop CS. You can always add more plug-ins to that folder and then restart Photoshop. Most often, those plug-ins will appear as their own menu item (such as Flaming Pear) under the main Filter menu. The different filters belonging to a plug-in will be listed under that sub-menu. If you want to get additional plug-ins from another folder that resides outside the Plug-Ins folder mentioned above, then check the Additional Plug-Ins Folder checkbox inside the Plug-Ins and Scratch Disks dialog. When you find the folder that contains the additional plug-ins, you need to click the Choose button at the bottom right of the dialog box. Don't click the Open button at that point, like you would for most other uses of an Open dialog box, or you'll just open the folder to continue the search. On the PC you click OK after clicking on the folder that actually contains the additional plug-ins.

The Scratch Disk preference tells Photoshop where to store temporary files on disk. Even if you give Photoshop plenty of memory, it also stores things on a scratch disk. In fact, Photoshop requires more scratch disk space than the amount of memory you assign to it. Use the largest, fastest disk drive you can afford for your primary (First) scratch disk. If you purchase a computer that has a built-in drive and then later go out and purchase a very large high-performance external drive or a disk array, you probably should specify that disk array as your primary (First) scratch disk because it will be faster than your built-in original drive. You can also specify Second, Third, and Fourth drives on which Photoshop can store temp files when it runs out of space on the First drive. Try to leave at least five to ten times the scratch space for the size of the file you are working on, and certainly leave much more space on the disk than the amount of memory you assign to Photoshop.

Photoshop has a scratch disk efficiency indicator. To access it, select Efficiency in the pop-up menu at the bottom-left of the top window's border when in Standard Screen mode on the Mac. This menu is at the left side of the status bar on the PC. You can bring up the PC status bar from the Window menu. The efficiency rating

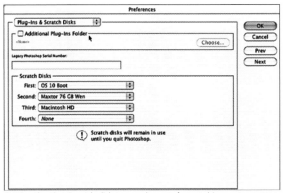

Setting the First Scratch disk to your largest, fastest drive, not necessarily the default boot drive, is very important for Photoshop performance. Also set the Second, Third, and Fourth choice if you have that many drives.

You can put additional Photoshop plug-in filters in a separate folder, so you don't accidentally toss them when you upgrade your Photoshop or reinstall it. This might be a good place to put 3rd-party plug-ins. To do this turn on the Additional Plug-Ins folder option, then click the Choose button when you find the folder containing those plug-ins.

Photoshop CS has a Legacy Photoshop Serial Number text box where you need to add your old Photoshop serial number if you want to use old format plug-in filters that require an old type serial number.

If the Efficiency is at 100%, Photoshop can do all its operations on this file without using the scratch disk. If asynchronous I/O is working with your First scratch disk, you should see the * character to the right of the efficiency percentage, as shown here.

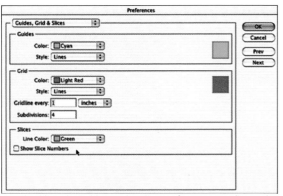

The Document Sizes option in this same pop-up shows you the flattened image size on the left (if you saved the file with no channels or layers) and the actual size including all the channels and layers on the right.

changes depending on the amount of time Photoshop spends swapping image data in and out of RAM from the disk. If your efficiency rating is less than 100% for most operations, you are using the scratch disk instead of RAM. You might want to add more RAM to your system to get better performance.

On the Mac, if the "*" character follows the percent display, your primary (First) scratch disk is operating with asynchronous I/O working. That is good for better performance because async I/O allows the disk to read or write while Photoshop does something else. If you don't see the "*," check the folder within the Applications/Adobe® Photoshop® 8.0/Plug-Ins/Adobe Photoshop Only/Extensions folder called "Enable Async I/O." If this folder *has* the character "~" in front of it, remove that character and restart Photoshop. This turns on asynchronous I/O for Photoshop's primary scratch disk. If you still don't see the "*" character, read the About Enable Async I/O document in the Enable Async I/O folder to learn how to set up the correct disk drivers for async I/O.

The Document Sizes option in this same pop-up shows you the flattened image size on the left (if you saved the file with no channels or layers) and the actual size on the right, while open in Photoshop, including all the channels and layers.

The Scratch Sizes option gives you the amount of image data space Photoshop is using for all open images on the left and the amount of scratch memory space available to Photoshop on the right. If the number on the left exceeds the number on the right, you are using the hard disk for scratch space and likely are slowing Photoshop down. See the ReadMe file that comes with Photoshop for more information about improving Photoshop performance.

The Document Profile option shows you the color profile assigned to this file.

The Document Dimensions option shows you the size the document will print at based on the current dpi settings in the Image/Image Size command.

The Timing option will time how long it took to do the last operation. This can be useful in comparing performance on various machines or with different drives and memory configurations on a particular system.

The Current Tool option just displays the name and info about the current tool selected in the Tools palette. This information can be useful when the Tools palette is not on the screen, although I find that I can usually remember what tool I'm using and would rather have this window set to one of the other settings.

TRANSPARENCY AND GAMUT

The Transparency and Gamut preferences settings allow you to change the way transparent areas of a layer look and also what color is used to display out-of-gamut colors. The default settings work fine for us, but check them out if you want to play around some. You might want to change the settings here for certain types of images; for example, line art work where the line art has similar colors to the transparent grid.

GUIDES, GRID & SLICES

The Guides & Grid preferences allow you to change the way Photoshop guides, grids, and slices appear onscreen. You can change the color as well as the types of lines (you can choose between Lines, Dashed Lines, and Dots). You can also specify how often the gridlines occur and how many subdivisions each major gridline has.

You should set the Guides, Grid & Slices preferences according to the colors of objects in the project files you are currently working on. Above are the colors I use as defaults. I type a 1 (one) into "Gridline every:" so that I get a gridline every 1 inch. This is different from the default value. I also turn off the Show Slice Numbers checkbox at the bottom left.

When working on Web and multimedia projects, I use the grid and guides to help place objects precisely. When you're in the Move tool (V or Command key), you can double-click a guide to bring up the Guides & Grid preferences, then easily change the colors and styles, and view these changes as you make them. Turning off the Show Slices option will remove the irritating colored line that sometimes shows around the edge of your image as well as the slice number in the top-left corner. When you are working on Web projects where you need to divide the image into slices, you'll want to turn Show Slices back on. Most photographers don't need this on all of the time.

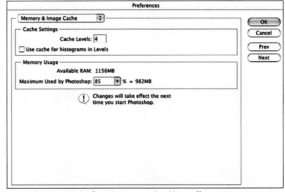

MEMORY & IMAGE CACHE

We discussed setting up Photoshop's memory usage at the beginning of this chapter. The Image Cache increases Photoshop's display efficiency when working with larger files. When Cache Levels is greater than 1, Photoshop makes several internal copies of the file at different sizes and uses the smaller versions to update the screen quickly when zoomed, working with layers, and doing complex tasks. Leaving the Cache set to 4 seems to work quite well for both small and large files. With small files Photoshop will be so fast either way you probably won't notice the difference, and the extra memory overhead for the Cache is minimal. With larger files, you will want the extra screen refresh performance obtained using the Cache. The larger the Image Cache setting, the more RAM and disk space Photoshop uses when you open a file. If you don't have much memory and are working with very large files, you may want to reduce the size of the Image Cache. The largest Image Cache setting is 8, and 1 turns off the Image Cache forcing screen refresh to wait for calculations on the entire file.

We recommend leaving the Use Cache for Histograms setting off; having it on often gives you inaccurate Levels histograms. The histogram you get with Use Cache for Histograms on depends on the current zoom ratio of your file. Leaving it off slows creating a Levels histogram for a large file but ensures that your histograms are always completely accurate and consistent, regardless of your zoom ratio.

Leave the Use Cache for Histograms checkbox off to get accurate Levels histograms. If you turn this on, the smaller cache image will often be used to calculate the histograms. This will not be as accurate because the smaller file has fewer pixels being read. The default of 4 for Cache Levels is good. We discussed setting up the memory usage at the beginning of this chapter. The more memory your computer has, the larger percentage of that memory you can allocate to Photoshop.

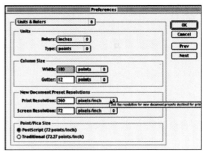

We usually leave the Ruler Units set to inches. When working on Web and multimedia projects, we change it to pixels to get very detailed measurements. The Units setting also controls the dimension display in the Info palette when selecting or drawing rectangles. Photoshop 7 added the New Document Preset Resolutions, which set up the default print and screen resolutions for new documents.

UNITS AND RULERS

The Ruler Units setting in the Units and Rulers Preferences dialog box controls the scale on Photoshop's rulers when you go to View/Show Rulers (Command-R). It also controls the dimension display settings in the Info palette and the initial dimension display when you enter the Canvas Size command. Changing the setting in the Info palette also changes it in Canvas Size. We usually leave it set at inches, but for very detailed measurements as well as for Web and multimedia projects, we change it to pixels. There is also a Percent setting here, which will display your scale and also record your Actions using a percentage of the total size. Turn this on when making Actions where proportional locations and sizes are more important than actual inches or

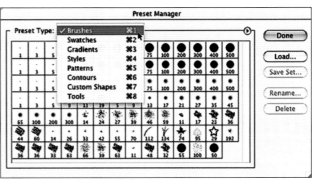

The pop-up menu shows the choices for palettes set up by the Preset Manager. Each of these palettes can have a variety of options chosen from them. Choose Edit/Preset Manager and then choose the Palette Type from the pop-up shown here. Notice another pop-up arrow just to the left of the Done button. This arrow gives you another pop-up menu with the available choices and options for the particular palette you are working with. You can also use the Load button to load a set of items for the palette you are currently working with or to save the items you've already set up for that palette. Here we see BarrysPhotoBrushes.

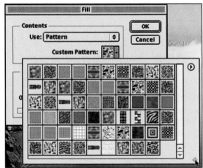

In the Preset Manager, we have chosen the Swatches palette as the Preset Type. The rightmost pop-up allows us to choose a set of colors we want for the Swatches palette, the Web Safe Colors this time. These sets of color choices are also available directly from the Swatches palette menu.

Here we have accessed the Patterns palette from a pop-up inside the Fill command. These pop-up palettes, including the Brushes palette, can be resized by taking one click to open the palette, then a second click and drag to resize the palette so you can see all the options within the shape window you would like. Once you change the size of a pop-up palette, you press Return to close the palette. It will remain this size until you change it again.

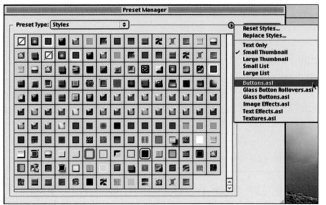

Our AllStyles.asl file contains the original styles plus Buttons, Glass Button Rollovers, Glass Buttons, Image Effects, Text Effects, and Textures. It is fun to load all of these when you are playing around and learning what they do, then you can later use the Style palette pop-up to load the subset you use most often. Keeping all of them loaded all the time makes extra overhead for Photoshop.

pixels. Photoshop 7 added the New Document Preset Resolutions, which set up the default print and screen resolutions for new documents.

THE PRESET MANAGER

Choose Edit/Preset Manager to reach this preferences item (see illustration on previous page). It allows you to set up which items you want to occur in various graphics and effects palettes, such as the Brushes palette, the Styles palette, the Gradients palette, and others. Some of the palettes, the Styles palette for example, give you the choice of replacing the current contents of the palette with the new Styles chosen, or appending those styles onto the list that is already there. By appending all the different Styles one by one and then saving them to a new Style set, we've created a file called AllStyles.asl, which contains all the Styles. When Styles are selected as the Preset Type in the Preset Manager, you can use the Load button to load all the Styles from this file located in the Preferences folder on the *Photoshop CS Artistry* CD. We have also created AllGradients.grd, All Patterns.pat, All-Shapes.csh, and BarrysPhotoBrushes.abr, which you can load from the same folder, provided you have the appropriate Preset Type selected. You can also load these from their respective palettes. **With the Brushes Preset Type selected, use Replace Brushes from the pop-up menu in the Presets dialog now to load BarrysPhotoBrushes from the Preferences folder on the *Photoshop CS Artistry* CD! With the Tools Preset Type selected, use Replace Tool Presets now to load ArtistryCSToolPresets! We use these throughout the book, so it's very important that you load them now!**

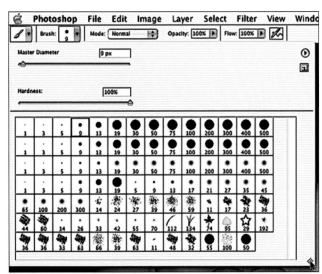

After loading a particular set of items, like BarrysPhotoBrushes here, you can use the grow box in the bottom-right corner of the Preset Manager, the Brushes palette, or the pop-up Brushes Palette to make a window of the size and shape you want. As shown here viewed in Small Thumbnail format, a click and drag in the Brush icon within the Options palette will pop up the Brushes palette, and if you keep the mouse button down, then release on the new brush you want, that allows you to choose a new brush with one click even though the palette is not always up on the screen.

PALETTES THAT YOU ACCESS INDIRECTLY

Some of the items within the Preset Manager don't have palettes that can be accessed from the Window menu directly. The Brushes palette can be accessed from the Window menu, but in Photoshop CS you can also access the Brushes palette from inside the Options bar whenever you are using a painting tool, like the Paintbrush, Airbrush, Clone Stamp tool, and so on. To select a brush from the Brushes palette, just click and drag on top of the Brush icon at the left of the Options bar until the cursor is over the brush that you want. At that point, release the mouse button and the Brushes palette will disappear and leave you with the new brush selected. This allows you to get a new brush with only one mouse click and without having the Brushes palette on the screen all the time. To change the shape of the Brushes palette, click on the Brush icon in the Options palette and immediately release the mouse. That will leave the palette on the screen and allow you to go to the grow box in the bottom-right corner and change the size of the palette. The palette will now remain at this size. You can then choose the brush you want and press Return or Enter to close the palette. The Brushes palette accessed from the Window menu has more options and you can find out how to use them in Chapter 35: "Painting in Photoshop."

The preset palettes that don't actually occur in the Window menu are Gradients, Patterns, Contours, and Custom Shapes. The Gradient palette is accessed from the Gradient Tool Options bar, the Patterns palette is accessed from the Fill command or the Options bar when using the Pattern Stamp or Healing/Patch tools, Contours is accessed from the Quality section of many of the Layer Style options, and Custom Shapes is accessed from the Options bar of the Custom Shape tool. You will learn more about these tools and palettes later; in this chapter you just get to see how you can use the Preset Manager to set up the initial options for them.

COLOR SETTINGS

The Photoshop/Color Settings preferences are the settings that affect how Photoshop displays images on the computer screen, as well as how Photoshop

When you first install Photoshop CS, you will get a message about default color settings. These default settings are what Adobe believes people doing Web development might want. Choose either Yes or No in this dialog, then set your settings as shown in the Color Settings section of this chapter.

When using Mac OS X, there is a standard application menu with the name of the particular application, Photoshop in this case. Within that menu is where you'll find the Color Settings preferences and also the General Preferences, shown above, when using Photoshop on OS X. In windows XP, these are found in the Edit menu!

Use Photoshop/Color Settings to get to this dialog; Edit/Color Setting with Windows XP. Most of the settings here can be obtained directly using either checkboxes or the pop-down menus within this dialog. You need to turn on Advanced Mode, at the top-left, to get the Conversion Options and Advanced Controls shown towards the bottom of the dialog. Putting the cursor over each item will give you a short description of that item within the Description box at the bottom of the dialog. I will tell you a lot more about these in Chapters 14 and 15, more than you need to know right now, so go ahead and set these as you see here. If you don't get excited by using all these pop-ups and checkboxes, you can just click on the Load button and load the entire dialog box using the file called BarrysPS8ColorSettings.csf within the Preferences folder on the *Photoshop CS Artistry* CD.

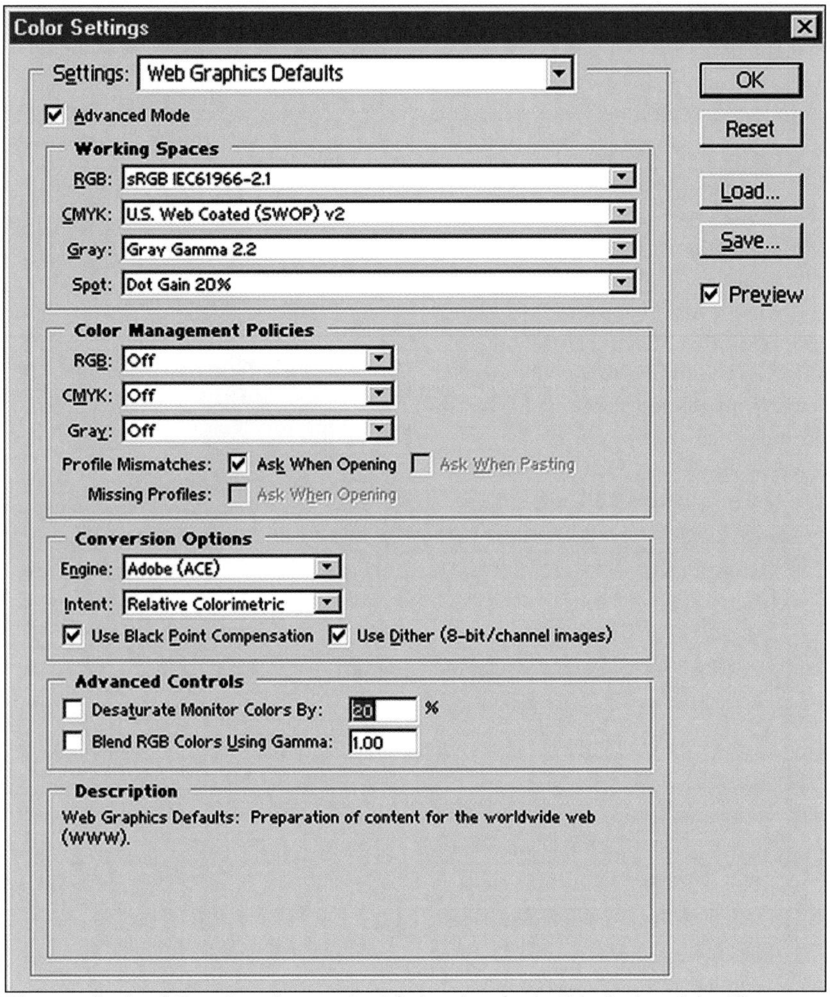

Color Settings

Settings: Web Graphics Defaults

☑ Advanced Mode

Working Spaces
RGB: sRGB IEC61966-2.1
CMYK: U.S. Web Coated (SWOP) v2
Gray: Gray Gamma 2.2
Spot: Dot Gain 20%

Color Management Policies
RGB: Off
CMYK: Off
Gray: Off
Profile Mismatches: ☑ Ask When Opening ☐ Ask When Pasting
Missing Profiles: ☐ Ask When Opening

Conversion Options
Engine: Adobe (ACE)
Intent: Relative Colorimetric
☑ Use Black Point Compensation ☑ Use Dither (8-bit/channel images)

Advanced Controls
☐ Desaturate Monitor Colors By: 20 %
☐ Blend RGB Colors Using Gamma: 1.00

Description
Web Graphics Defaults: Preparation of content for the worldwide web (WWW).

OK
Reset
Load...
Save...
☑ Preview

When you first install Photoshop, these are the default settings for the Color Settings dialog. They are set up to be the least offensive settings for people who don't have critical color requirements and who are probably not going to take the time to read how to set up their color. These are NOT the settings photographers and serious artists want to use. They may be the settings some Web workers want to use, although I imagine color management will soon become important on the Web too, so these may not be the correct settings for Web folks either. To learn more about how to set your Color Settings, see Chapter 14: "Color Spaces, Device Characterization, and Color Management," and Chapter 15: "Photoshop Color Preferences, Monitor, Scanner, and Printer Calibration."

does color separations. Photoshop CS actually lets you proof on the screen in RGB, CMYK, and Lab what your image would look like on any device that has an accurate ICC profile. To use the power of Photoshop CS, you need to set these Color Settings preferences correctly for the type of work you are doing and for the monitors, scanners, and printers you are using. In this chapter we will show you the settings we recommend for working with photographs, but we are not going to explain these settings here because the explanation involves understanding a lot of background material. You should now set your Color Settings to the ones shown here. After doing that, go on and finish the rest of the recommended preference settings in this chapter. To understand the Color Settings recommendations made in this chapter, you need to read Chapter 14: "Color Spaces, Device Characterization, and Color Management," and Chapter 15: "Photoshop Color Preferences, Monitor, Scanner, and Printer Calibration." The settings we give you here are recommended as a starting point, and in Chapters 14 and 15 we will explain how to change them if you want to develop your own custom settings. If you are a beginner, we recommend that you continue to read Chapters 4 through 13 in that order because you will get bogged down in color mania if you go directly to Chapter 14 at this point. More advanced users, especially photographers and heavy color users, may want to read Chapters 14 and 15 after finishing all the preferences settings described in this chapter. In either case, you may have to read Chapters 14 and 15 several times to totally wrap your head around the wonderful ICC color world Photoshop CS supports. By the way, we used the CMYK settings described here to create all the color separations in this book.

OTHER PREFERENCES RELATING TO COLOR

EYEDROPPER TOOL SETUP

Usually when you measure digital photograph values in Photoshop, you want the Eyedropper set to measure a 3-by-3 rectangle of pixels. That gives you a more accurate measurement in a continuous tone image because most colors are made up of groups of different pixels. If you were to measure a Point Sample, the default, you might accidentally measure the single pixel that was much different in color from those around it. Type I to get the Eyedropper tool and set its Sample Size, in the Options bar, to 3-by-3 Average. Setting the Eyedropper to 3-by-3 Average also sets up the Color Sampler to read a 3-by-3 Average, which is what you want.

HIGHLIGHT AND SHADOW PREFERENCES

The last preferences items that you need to set up for color separations are the Highlight and Shadow settings, which you can reach by choosing either Levels or Curves. Here we show you how to get to them from Levels. Open the file named GoldenGate.jpg from the Preferences folder on the *Photoshop CS Artistry* CD. Choose Image/Adjust/Levels, and double-click the Highlight Eyedropper (the right-most one). The Color Picker opens. You should set your RGB highlight settings to 244, 244, 244. The CMYK values that correspond to these RGB settings will depend on your RGB and CMYK workspace settings in the Color Settings preference dialog we just set up. Even if you are using different settings than ours, if your final output space will be RGB, you should make sure your RGB values all equal each other so you get a neutral highlight color when setting the highlight with the Eyedropper in RGB. Click OK in the Color Picker to return to Levels. Double-click the Shadow Eyedropper (the left-most one). Set the RGB shadow values in the Color Picker to 8,8,8, then click OK in Levels. If you get the message "Save new target settings as defaults," click on the Yes choice, which is not the default choice so don't just press Return or these new settings will not be saved. To learn more about these Highlight and Shadow settings and how you use them, turn to Chapter 19: "Overall Color Correction," which takes you through all the basics of color correction.

Usually you want the Eyedropper set to measure a 3-by-3 Average when measuring continuous tone color. Setting either the Eyedropper Options or the Color Sampler Options to 3-by-3 Average will set both of them to the same setting.

ARTISTKEYS TO SET UP YOUR ACTIONS

In the Preferences folder of the *Photoshop CS Artistry* CD, we have given you a predefined set of actions, called ArtistKeysPS8.atn. You should add this set of Actions to your copy of Photoshop since we will be using them a lot in this book.

To save any of your existing actions, choose Window/Actions and then Save Actions from the Actions palette pop-up menu. For Save Actions to work, Button mode needs to be off. You should have also chosen one of the existing Actions sets and have its folder closed and high-

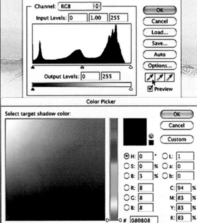

These are the initial Shadow settings we recommend for CMYK coated stock, RGB output to film recorders, digital printers, and general overall color correction of a file. Double-click the Shadow Eyedropper in Levels or Curves to change these settings. Set the RGB values here to 8, 8, 8.

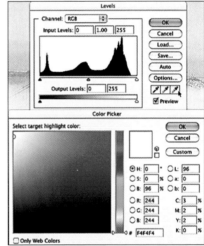

These 244, 244, 244 settings are the Highlight settings we recommend. If we were working on a document using a different RGB profile space, like ColorMatch RGB or sRGB, then the CMYK values for this same RGB setting might change slightly.

lighted. If Default Actions is the only thing there, you don't need to be concerned about saving these, since they are always available from the Actions palette by choosing Replace Actions or Load Actions from the Actions palette menu.

Now choose Load Actions, from the Actions palette menu, and pick the ArtistKeysPS8.atn file from the Preferences folder on the *Photoshop CS Artistry* CD. This will load ArtistKeys and also leave existing actions in place. To replace all actions with ArtistKeys, this is what I did: I chose Replace Actions instead of Load Actions. If you choose Replace Actions you better save any actions, other than the

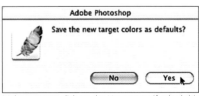

Make sure you click on the Yes answer if asked this question after changing the target color defaults using the dialogs shown above.

Actions	
Tool Palette	F2
Navigator Palette	⇧F2
LevelsAdjLayer	⌘F2
Save For Web	F3
Color Table	⇧F3
CurveAdjLayer	⌘F3
Unsharp Mask	F4
Gaussian Blur	⇧F4
Hue/Sat AdjLayer	⌘F4
Duplicate	F5
Replace Color	⇧F5
Sharpen Only Edges BH	⌘F5
SharpenOnlyEdgesBHBrks	⌘⇧F5
Apply Image	F6
Selective Color	⇧F6
RemoveSkyCrud	⌘F6
Image Size	F7
Threshold	⇧F7
Tool Presets	⌘F7
History Palette	F8
Color Range	⇧F8
Canvas Size	⌘F8
Info Palette	F9
Histogram Palette	⇧F9
Flatten Image	⌘F9
Color Palette	⌘⇧F9
Layers Palette	F10
Channels Palette	⇧F10
Save & Close	⌘F10
Actions Palette	F11
Paths Palette	⇧F11
Horizontal Web	⌘F11
Options Palette	F12
Brushes	⇧F12

The Actions palette with Button mode turned on and ArtistKeys loaded. In Button mode, you can click an action to play it, even if it doesn't have a function key alternative. All the Actions shown here actually have function key alternatives. When loaded on the PC, the Command key functions automatically show up as Control key (Ctrl) functions. The RGB file for this screen grab, named PS8ArtistKeys.tiff, is in the Preferences folder on your CD. You can open it into Photoshop and then print it on a desktop printer at a size allowing you to cut it out and tape it to the plastic on the side of your monitor. This will help you to learn them.

defaults, that you previously had available. What we did to create ArtistKeys is go through all the menu items in Photoshop CS and set up as function keys the ones that you will use most often. For example, F9 through F12 will bring up and close down the palettes you use most often. We tried to do this logically, so F9 is the Info palette and Shift-F9 is the History palette. You need both of these palettes when doing Overall Color correction. F10 is the Layers palette and Shift-F10 is the Channels palette. You often use these together. The Color Palette, which was Shift-F9, has been changed to Command-Shift-F9 because it is used less often than the History palette. I use F2 through F12 to implement single menu items (and we do mention these quite often in the book, so you will find them quick to learn). I mention these keys in context as alternatives, so you don't have to learn them if you would rather not. I consider F1, as well as F13 through F15, optional, so you can use them to reprogram other actions. You can also program many of the Command key Actions, as well as all of the Shift-Command ones.

If ArtistKeys Don't Work

A former student from one of my Printmaking for Photographers workshops called me to complain that his ArtistKeys didn't work when he set them up on his home computer. With Max OS X and Powerbooks or other portables, the leftmost function keys, like F2 for example, are used to control the screen brightness, sound volume and other things. The function keys still do this even within Photoshop with Artistkeys loaded. At the bottom left of the powerbook keyboard is a "fn" key and if you hold this down while pressing a function key then that key will do what it is supposed to do within Photoshop instead of changing the screen brightness or whatever. The "fn" key is how you override these built-in Mac portable function keys. There are many different versions of the Windows OS and many different companies that make PCs. Some of these PC versions have function keys that are pre-assigned for specific tasks on that particular OS or machine. There are too many combinations of PC manufacturers and Windows OS versions to cover every one in this book. If you have problems using Artistkeys on the PC, you will have to look at the manual or help system for your particular version to see how customizing function keys to an application, i.e. Photoshop, works.

I think you'll find the ArtistKeys function key set a valuable asset when working in Photoshop. If you ever want to use one of these function keys for something else, make sure you are not in Button mode and Option-double-click the area to the right of the Action name (In Photoshop CS, double-clicking the name allows you to rename the action). Now set the function key for that action to None, then you can reassign that function key to another action. For more information about Actions, see Chapter 11: "Automating with Actions."

Setting Up Your Palettes and Desktop

When you have set all the preferences described so far, you should then set up your palettes the way you think you will like them. On the next page is one suggested setup, shown on my G4 system. If you have trouble doing this, review Chapter 2, "Navigating in Photoshop," to see how to work with your palettes. When you have all your Photoshop preferences and palettes set up the way you like them, quit from Photoshop, and the next time you start it, Photoshop will come up with all the palettes and preferences as you have left them.

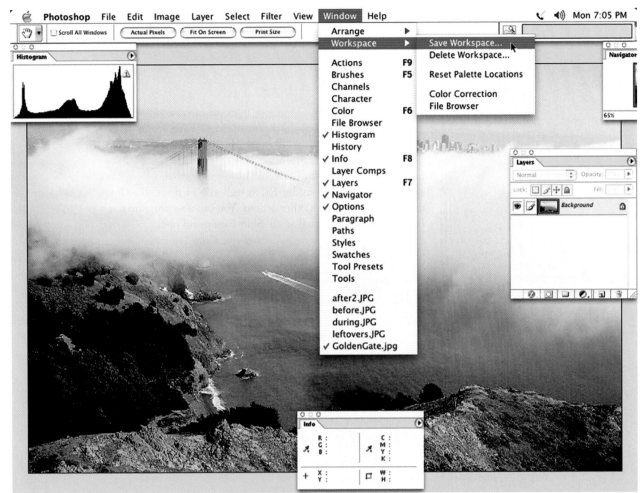

Here we see how I have my palettes set up for Full Screen mode Color Correction on my G4. The setup I use on my PC is similar. First drag each palette to the center of the screen using its Palette tab. That will separate it from any other palettes it is grouped with. Then drag each palette one at a time to the default location you'd like for that palette. Once the palettes are set up the way I want them, I choose Window/Workspace/Save Workspace and name this workspace Color Correction. Notice that I also have a default workspace named File Browser. Each individual palette can be brought up or down using its function key, like F10 for the Layers palette or F9 for the Info palette. The nice thing about learning the ArtistKeys for the palettes is that you don't have to move your mouse cursor or even think about where the palette is (you don't have to use the Window menu); you just press the right function key and the palette appears on the screen wherever you last left it.

SAVING AND STANDARDIZING YOUR PREFERENCES

After you make major changes to your standard Photoshop CS preferences, you should quit from Photoshop immediately. When you leave Photoshop on a Mac with OS 10, the Photoshop Preferences files are updated, then stored on your boot hard drive in a folder with the pathname: Users/YourUserName/Library/Preferences/ Adobe Photoshop CS Settings. On the PC with XP, these files are at: C:\Documents and Settings\YourUserName\Application Data\Adobe\Photoshop\8.0\Adobe Photoshop CS Settings. Quitting at this point ensures that Photoshop saves your preferences changes to these files. If you were to crash before quitting Photoshop, you would lose these latest preferences changes, and Photoshop would revert to the preferences you had when you last successfully quit from Photoshop.

It is a good idea for everyone in your company to standardize on a set of Color Settings and color workspace preferences, especially for the same publication, and vitally important to standardize separation and workspace preferences if you are

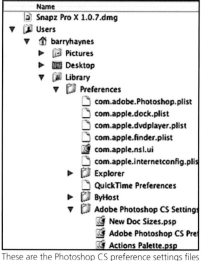

These are the Photoshop CS preference settings files and folders and where they are saved on the Mac with OS X.

doing color corrections and separations. You can copy a standard version of these files to the Photoshop Settings folders on everyone else's machines, or print up a standards document and have your systems administrator make sure that everyone is using the same settings.

FILE BROWSER PREFS

Photoshop CS has added a Preferences setting for the File Browser. If you use the File Browser for large files, you should increase the "Do No Process Files Larger Than" setting so that it is greater than the files you want to browse. You might also want to turn on the Allow Background Processing option so File Browser thumbnails and previews for your larger files can be generated ahead of time. If you do turn on the Allow Background Processing option, be aware that this can slow down other processes on your computer. If you browse a lot of Illustrator or other vector type documents, turning on Render Vector Files will get the File Browser to generate previews for these types of files. Parse XMP Metadata for Non-Image Files should be off for most users. Keep Sidecar Files with Master Files will put a copy of the File Browser previews and thumbnails in folders with your images, so if you move those folders to other computers, the File Browser files will already be generated and available on those computers. It is good to have this on if you copy files from one computer to the other and want to File Browse on the copies.

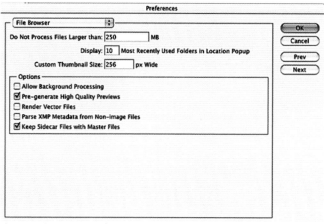

These are the starting preferences I recommend for the File Browser. If you have large files that you wish to browse with the File Browser, you may want to turn on Allow Background Processing so the previews for these files can be generated ahead of time.

Chapter 3: Setting System and Photoshop Preferences

4 THE TOOLS PALETTE

An explanation of each tool in the Tools palette with tips for usage and discussions of helpful, hidden features. General information about Tool presets, selections, cropping, painting tools, and other good stuff!

This is not an exhaustive tour of every tool with all its possibilities and applications. Several other very fine books, including the Photoshop manual, go into more detail. We try to give you all the information that you need for working with photographs. This actually is a lot of fun for us, and we hope you enjoy it and take some time to play with these tools. As you begin to discover how the tools work, you can apply them to the types of images you have been creating and, perhaps, begin to discover new creative impulses.

The tools in the Tools palette are divided into groups that suggest their use. The top section of the palette contains the tools that are used to make selections and slices; move selections, slices, or layers; or crop files. You might think of this grouping as having to do with boundaries or borders.

The second section contains image editing tools used for painting, erasing, sharpening, retouching, and adding effects. If you want to manipulate the actual pixel information of a file or layer, you are probably going to use one of these tools.

The third section contains tools for dealing with vector shapes, whether Bezier curves, custom shapes, or type.

The fourth section holds tools used for viewing the file (Hand and Zoom), making annotations (Notes), and sampling color (Eyedropper).

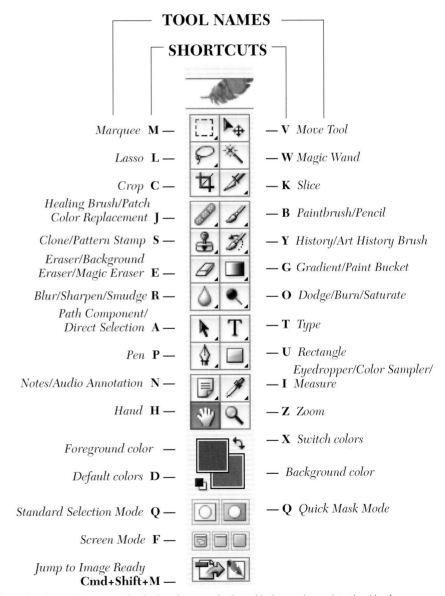

TOOL NAMES
SHORTCUTS

Marquee **M** — — **V** *Move Tool*
Lasso **L** — — **W** *Magic Wand*
Crop **C** — — **K** *Slice*
Healing Brush/Patch Color Replacement **J** — — **B** *Paintbrush/Pencil*
Clone/Pattern Stamp **S** — — **Y** *History/Art History Brush*
Eraser/Background Eraser/Magic Eraser **E** — — **G** *Gradient/Paint Bucket*
Blur/Sharpen/Smudge **R** — — **O** *Dodge/Burn/Saturate*
Path Component/ Direct Selection **A** — — **T** *Type*
Pen **P** — — **U** *Rectangle*
— **I** *Eyedropper/Color Sampler/ Measure*
Notes/Audio Annotation **N** —
Hand **H** — — **Z** *Zoom*
Foreground color — — **X** *Switch colors*
Default colors **D** — — *Background color*
Standard Selection Mode **Q** — — **Q** *Quick Mask Mode*
Screen Mode **F** —
Jump to Image Ready **Cmd+Shift+M** —

The Tools palette with corresponding keyboard commands. Copy this chart and paste it to the side of your monitor for a quick reference.

Some of the tools in the Tools palette have a little arrow in their bottom-right corners. Clicking it and holding down the mouse button shows other tools that you can access from the same icon area. As a default preference, typing Shift plus the keyboard shortcut for that tool will cycle you through the available tools in most cases. I'll note exceptions in the information for specific tools. In the case of the Type tool and the Shapes tool, the different tools available show up on the Tool Options bar.

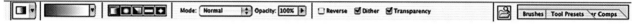

Here's the Photoshop CS Tool Options bar for the Gradient tool. You can see that it streamlines choosing the options you want. There's no extra verbiage here. On the far left is the "title bar" by which you can move the entire palette to a new location. Next is the icon for the tool presets for this tool. The rest of the options available for the tool follow, and on the far right side is a docking bay for frequently used palettes. This keeps them both quickly accessible and out of the way.

THE TOOL OPTIONS BAR

Most of the tools have changeable options you view in the Tool Options bar, which is located by default at the top of your screen. The beauty of the Tool Options bar is its context specificity. It's a very smart palette. If you are performing an action that does not affect an option on the current bar, that option will be grayed out and unavailable. I'll discuss the specifics of the options for each tool in that section.

If you choose a tool by either clicking its icon or using its shortcut character, the options automatically appear in the Tool Options bar if it is present. If not, pressing Return brings up the Tool Options bar. For tools that have brushes, gradients, or patterns associated with them, you'll see an icon on the Tool Options bar with the current swatch. Click the swatch or the associated pop-up arrow to access further options for that brush, pattern, or gradient. When the Tool Options bar is onscreen, pressing Return will take you to the first changeable option, generally an input area, where you can type a value. Hit Tab to move to the next input area, or press Return to accept the values that you just input.

TOOL PRESETS

Tool presets save different options that you've input for that specific tool. Let's say that you often use the Clone Stamp tool with a 9-pixel, soft edge brush in Color Blending mode at 30% Opacity. If for some reason you have to change the settings, it gets tedious to reset all those options again when you need to use those specific settings. Now you can save a Clone Stamp preset that has all of those options, and other presets that have different options that you need on a regular basis. When you

When you save a tool preset, all the current options are saved. You can come back to this tool at any time and choose the preset to quickly reset the options.

have created the presets you need, be sure you save your set with a meaningful name. Using the Presets Manager, you can move tools into and out of sets, and then save very specialized and personalized tools for the way you work. This is particularly handy for use with Photoshop's brushes, where you might create a lot of brushes but want only a subset available for each different type of work you do. You don't have to scroll through millions of brushes to find the one you want.

CONTEXT-SENSITIVE MENUS

Holding down the Control key (right mouse button on Windows) and clicking on the screen opens up a context-sensitive menu of commands you can execute with the current tool and/or options you can set. This is a very powerful feature because the items in this context-sensitive menu may actually come from several different regular menus in Photoshop and are chosen based on Photoshop's state when you Control-click. We point out these context-sensitive menus as you go through this chapter.

This is the menu that comes up when you Control-click the Marquee tool and have no current selection loaded, but you do have selections saved in mask channels.

This is the menu that comes up when you Control-click the Marquee tool and have an active selection. See how the menu changed depending on the context?

THE SELECTION TOOLS

In the first section of the Tools palette are the three primary tools for making selections as well as tools for moving, cropping, and making slices for Web work. In conjunction with items from the Selection menu and the Pen tool (which we discuss later), portions of your image can be isolated for editing by making a selection. Which tool you use depends on the type of image you are using and the type of selection you need. Sometimes, it is not readily apparent which tool will do the best job. We will give you the basics of how they work here, but know that you will need to practice with all of them to understand their use and be able to choose the right tool for the job.

MARQUEE TOOL
KEYBOARD SHORTCUT: Type the letter M. Type Shift-M to toggle between the Rectangular and Elliptical Marquees. Single Row and Single Column Marquees must be chosen from the Tools palette.

You use the Marquee tool to make rectangular or oval selections which you do quite often in digital imaging. Single Row and Single Column you'll probably use less often, but these tools are useful for selecting 1-pixel wide rows or columns of artifacts introduced by scanners or bad media and then deleting or cloning into the selected area.

When you look at the Tool Options bar for the Marquee tool, you see the following areas:

SELECTION INTERACTION: The four icons after the Tool icon in the Tool Options bar control how a selection should interact with any current selection. The default is New Selection; that is, any selection you make will replace the current selection. Next is Add to Selection, which you also can accomplish using the Shift key and making your new selection. (It helps if you begin the new selection outside the old one.) Then Subtract from Selection, which you can do by using this icon or by holding down Option and dragging from within the current selection. Finally, there is Intersect with Current Selection. This takes only the overlapping area of both selections and makes a new selection from it. You also can use Shift-Option-drag to intersect selections. If you use the keyboard shortcuts, you'll see the icons activate as you hold down Shift, Option, or both keys. Pretty cool, if you ask me.

FEATHER: The Feather option allows you to set the amount of blend on the edges of your selection. A larger feather radius gives you more of a vignette effect. The amount of feather is calculated in both directions from your selection border. For example, a 15-pixel feather measures both 15 pixels to the outside of your selection

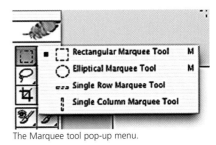

The Marquee tool pop-up menu.

Along with using keyboard shortcuts to control selection interaction, you can choose these icons from the Options bar. From left to right they are New Selection, Add to Selection, Subtract from Selection, and Intersect with Current Selection.

The Options bar also allows you to set the Feather and Anti-aliased features.

39

area and 15 pixels to the inside, giving you a total feather effect of 30 pixels. We rarely set a feather radius on our Marquee tool, preferring to make a selection and then using Select/Feather from the menu bar to set the feather. This way, we can change our radius if we are unhappy with the effect. Also, if you make a selection with the Rectangular Marquee and the feather is zero, you can later choose Image/Crop to crop to that selection. If you set the feather to a non-zero value, on the other hand, Image/Crop is disabled.

ANTI-ALIASED: You may have noticed that the Elliptical Marquee has one other option, Anti-aliased. Anti-aliased subtly blends the edge of your selection with the surrounding area, so you usually want to leave it on. It's also available on the Lasso and Wand tools, but it is grayed out on the Rectangular, Single Row, and Single Column tools, as no smoothing is needed for horizontal and vertical lines. Keep Anti-aliased on when you want your selection edge to blend with the surrounding area. Making selections with Anti-aliased off gives you hard edges that are jagged on diagonal lines and curves.

STYLE: The Style pop-up menu allows you to choose a fixed aspect ratio or a fixed size for either the Rectangular or Elliptical Marquee. You would use a fixed aspect ratio if you were making a selection that you knew needed to have a 4:5 ratio, for example, or a 1:1 ratio for a perfect square or circle. When you choose this option, you cannot input a unit of measure in the Width or Height entry area.

| Style: | Fixed Aspect Ratio | Width: | 3 | | Height: | 2 |

Fixed Aspect Ratio allows you to click and drag until you have a crop that you like while being assured the width to height ratio will be what you need.

| Style: | Fixed Size | Width: | 317 px | | Height: | 256 px |

When you use Fixed Size for the Marquee tool you can input mixed units of measure for Width and Height, such as 3 inches by 400 pixels.

A fixed size is useful when you know exactly the size of the print you want to make and want to crop to that size. Here, if you click with the Marquee tool, you get a rectangular selection of the size that you specified. By keeping the mouse button down while moving the mouse, you can move the selection around the image to find exactly the crop you desire. Of course, you also can use this option simply to select and edit an area of a specific size.

MODIFIER KEYS: Holding down the Shift key while using either of these tools constrains your selection to 1:1; that is, you get a perfect square or a perfect circle. Be sure you release the mouse button before you release the Shift key. However, if you already have a selection, the action is different. The Shift key causes Photoshop to add a new, unconstrained selection to your original selection.

Holding down the Option key while drawing forces the selection to draw from the center where you first click down. This can be extremely useful, as you will see later in this book.

Holding down the Shift and Option keys while dragging gives you a perfect circle or perfect square drawn from the center.

Be careful how you click in a file with an active selection. If you click inside the selection, you may inadvertently move the selection slightly. If you click outside the selection, you lose the selection.

If you press and hold down the spacebar after starting a selection, you can move the selection while making it. Release the spacebar to continue changing the selection.

MOVE TOOL

KEYBOARD SHORTCUT: Type the letter V or hold down the Command key.

You use the Move tool to move a selection (not the selection marquee—that you move with the Marquee tool) or the contents of a layer. Click and drag a selection or layer to move it to a new location within your document. You can also use the Move tool to drag and drop a layer from one document to another. If you are using any

Use the Move tool with the Control key to find out what layers exist at a particular location in your file.

other tool, you can hold down the Command key to access the Move tool without deselecting the currently active tool.

AUTO SELECT LAYER allows the Move tool to activate the layer of the object that you click. This can facilitate moving objects around if the boundaries of the object you're selecting are clear. If you're having trouble selecting the appropriate layer, hold down the Control key and choose the layer from the pop-up.

SHOW BOUNDING BOX gives you a rectangle with handles that encompasses the area of that layer which contains pixels. If you move one of the handles, you are immediately in Free Transform mode and the Tool Options bar will reflect that.

Show Bounding Box shows you where the pixel information is on that layer.

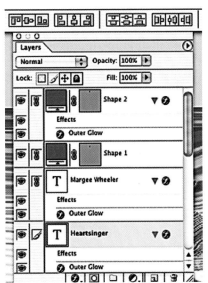

If you have linked layers and you are in the Move tool, you'll see icons for alignment.

ALIGNMENT: Alignment options are available when working with linked layers, a selection and one or more layers, or multiple components of a single path (including multiple shapes on a single shape layer). If you have only two elements selected, you will activate only the first set of alignment icons, which allow you to align edges or entire elements with each other. If you select three or more elements, the second group of alignment icons will also activate, allowing you to distribute the space among the edges or the entire elements as well.

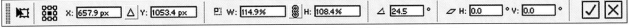

If you move the a handle of the Bounding Box, you are in Free Transform mode and the Tool Options bar looks like this.

LASSO, POLYGON, AND MAGNETIC LASSO TOOLS

KEYBOARD SHORTCUT: Type the letter L. If you type Shift-L, the tool cycles through its three states.

You use the Lasso tool to make freehand selections. Although it's a little clunky to draw with a mouse, you'll find yourself using this tool a lot. You can always get a graphics tablet if you want to draw with a pen. Clicking and dragging gives you a line that follows the track of your mouse. After starting the selection, if you hold down the Option key and click, let go of the mouse button, and then click in a new spot, you can draw with straight lines between mouse clicks. Continue clicking this way to make geometric shapes, or you can hold down the mouse button and draw freehand again. When you let go of the mouse and the Option key, a straight line is drawn connecting the beginning and ending points of your selection, so be careful not to let go of the Option key until you finish your selection. Because the Option key in Photoshop is used for subtracting from a selection, you have to press Option after starting the selection to get the straight line behavior. If you prefer to use the Polygon Lasso tool, you can draw straight lines at every click, without using the Option key. In the Polygon Lasso tool, using the Option key after starting the selection enables you to draw in freehand. The Polygon Lasso tool requires you to click on the selection starting point again to complete a selection, as you also need to do in the Pen tool to complete a path. With the Magnetic Lasso tool, you can set a contrast value for the edge that you're trying to capture, then draw freehand around that edge and let the Lasso decide how to draw the selection. Position your cursor over the edge of the object you want to select and click to set the first fastening point. As you move the mouse, the Lasso lays down more

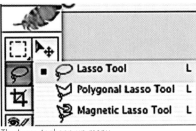

The Lasso tool pop-up menu.

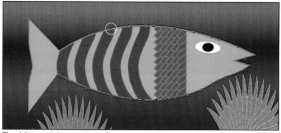

| Feather: 0 px | ☑ Anti-aliased | Width: 10 px | Edge Contrast: 10% | Frequency: 57 | ☑ Pen Pressure |

Magnetic Lasso options.

The Magnetic Lasso at work.

fastening points to define the edge. You can click down at any time to manually place a fastener or hold down the Option key and either drag to access the regular Lasso or click to access the Polygonal Lasso. Draw until you reach the starting point and you get an icon that looks like the one in the Tools palette. If you let go of the mouse, the selection is made. If you double-click or press Enter before you get to your starting point, a line is drawn from the current mouse position to the starting point to complete the selection. Hold down the Option key and double-click to draw a straight line segment between the mouse position and the starting point. Needless to say, this tool works most easily where there is a good amount of contrast between the edges. But, with experimentation, you can get a pretty decent first selection using this tool, and then finesse the selection with some of the more sophisticated selection methods.

WIDTH: Set your Lasso width wide enough to to cover the object edge you plan to trace, but not so wide that you take in many additional areas around the edge. You can use the bracket keys to change the width as you drag if needed, if Pen Pressue is not active.

EDGE CONTRAST: Edge Contrast is the minimum contrast that you want Photoshop to consider when trying to discern the edge. The lower the contrast between the edge you're outlining and the background, the lower you need to set the Edge Contrast.

FREQUENCY: Frequency governs the number of "points" that the Lasso automatically puts down to define the selection.

PEN PRESSURE: Check this box if you want the Lasso width to respond to the pressure you exert on your stylus when using a pressure-sensitive tablet. The harder you press, the smaller your Lasso width.

| Tolerance: 32 | ☑ Anti-aliased | ☑ Contiguous | ☐ Use All Layers |

Magnetic Lasso options.

See Chapter 18: "The Colony Composite," for more information on how to use these Lasso features as well as other selection tools.

MAGIC WAND TOOL

KEYBOARD SHORTCUT: Type the letter W.

Whereas the Marquee and Lasso tools make selections based on physical proximity of pixels, the Magic Wand makes selections based on color values of adjacent pixels.

TOLERANCE SETTINGS: The tolerance that you set determines how close in value pixels must be before they can be selected. The lower the tolerance, the more similar the colors must be, and the higher the tolerance, the greater the range of colors.

CONTIGUOUS: You can choose whether you want Photoshop to select only those pixels within the tolerance value that are beside each other, or to search the entire image and select all pixels that fall within the tolerance. Where you click makes a difference.

Here's the selection that I got using the default tolerance of 32 and clicking in the upper-right area of sky with the Contiguous button checked.

Clicking in the same spot with Contiguous unchecked gives me a selection that would make a pretty good mask.

USE ALL LAYERS: The Use All Layers option makes its selection based on a merged version of all the currently visible layers. Whether you want this option on or off depends on the type of image you are working with and the kind of selection you wish to make. If another layer affects the colors of the object you want to select, you probably want this option on. If all the colors you want to select are on only one layer, leave it off. But remember: Regardless of whether your selection is based on one layer or on merged layers, the edits that you make affect only the currently active layer.

THE GROW AND SIMILAR COMMANDS: The tolerance value that you set on the Magic Wand also affects which pixels you select when you use the Grow and Similar commands from the Select menu. The Grow command selects adjacent pixels that fall within this tolerance, whereas the Similar command selects pixels throughout the entire image that fall within the tolerance range. You can also change the tolerance setting on the Magic Wand between uses of these two commands, to select a larger or smaller range of colors.

THE CROP TOOL

KEYBOARD SHORTCUT: Type the letter C.

Although we often use the Rectangular Marquee tool and the Image/Crop command to crop an image, the Crop tool is more powerful. To use the Crop tool, click and drag a box around the area you want to crop. The area that will be cropped from the image darkens. Click and drag on one of the handles (little boxes in the selection corners and edges) to change the size of the crop area. To cancel the crop, press the Escape key or the Cancel button on the right end of the Options bar. To accept the crop, press Return, Enter, or click the Commit button on the right end of the Options bar.

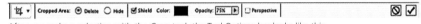

Before you make a selection with the Crop tool, the Tool Options bar looks like this. Here, I've clicked the Front Image button to input the dimensions of the currently active file.

FRONT IMAGE: When you click the Front Image button in the Tool Options bar, the exact dimensions and resolution of the currently active image appear in the input areas.

After you make a selection with the Crop tool, the Tool Options bar looks like this.

You can also enter proportions for the crop manually. Whatever crop you make will be constrained to these proportions, and it will be resampled to exactly these specifications when you accept the crop by pressing Enter. Leave the resolution blank to maintain the specified aspect ratio and let Photoshop resample the file if necessary. For example, if you ask for your crop in inches, and the dimensions are larger than the area you selected, Photoshop lowers the resolution of the file after the crop but does not resample the crop area. However, if you ask for your crop in pixels and the crop is larger than the current file, it maintains the resolution of the image but adds pixels; in effect, it samples up the image. Click Clear to clear all input areas.

DELETE OR HIDE: In general, when you use the Crop tool, you delete the area that you want removed from your image, so Delete is the default here. However, you can choose to simply Hide the other areas of the file, then use the Move tool to relocate the image and decide on the final crop. If you are in a file that only has a Background layer,

Click the Perspective button to allow irregular shaped crops. Using the Shield option colors the area to be deleted with an overlay. I've changed the overlay color to red to get a better idea of the area of the crop.

This is the result of the previous crop using Perspective.

Because I wanted to rotate my crop from the lower right corner, I moved the center point there before beginning the rotation.

The result of the rotated crop.

you'll need to turn the background into a regular layer by double-clicking and naming the layer.

SHIELD CROPPED AREA: After you make a selection with the Crop tool, the Options bar changes and allows you to cover the area that you want to crop out with a colored overlay. You can choose the color and opacity. This helps you check the placement of your crop for more pleasing results.

PERSPECTIVE: Click this button if you want to change the dimensions of your crop disproportionately. This will stretch the image after the crop to fit a rectangle based on the area and shape you chose. This is used primarily to correct perspective distortion that occurs when a photo is taken at an extreme angle.

MOVING AND ROTATING: Click in the middle of the selected area to move the crop boundary without changing its size. Click outside the crop box corners when you see the curved double arrow rotate icon, and drag to rotate the crop boundary. You can move the "center point" around which you will rotate the selected area by dragging it.

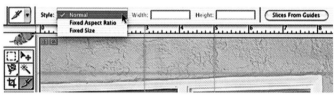

The Slice tool has only a few options, and the style options are the same as for the Rectangular Marquee tool. Slices From Guides will only be active if you have placed guides.

SLICE/SLICE SELECTION TOOL
KEYBOARD SHORTCUT: Type the letter K.

Photoshop is able to create slices directly rather than needing to switch to ImageReady. Slices divide an image into component sections for Web display. Each slice can have its own method of optimization that can increase download speed, and slices are the basic building blocks for animations and rollovers. For complex processing of images for the Web, you'll want to switch to ImageReady, but here's the basics that are available to you in Photoshop.

The Slice tool works with a click and drag, similar to the way you use the Marquee or Crop tools. And like those tools, you can set a Constrained Aspect Ratio or a Fixed Size for the slice you want to create. Whether View/Extras is turned on or off, as soon as you begin to use the tool, the slices will be shown. The preferences for the slice color and numbers are found in Preferences/Guides, Grid and Slices. By the way, User slices have solid lines, Auto slices have dotted lines.

PROMOTE TO USER SLICE: Once you make the slice, Photoshop fills in the other areas of the file with Auto slices. You may have made the slice using the Slice tool or by activating a layer, then choosing Layer/New Layer Based Slice. Auto slices regenerate as you make changes to the size or placement of User slices or Layer slices. Auto slices share the same optimization scheme, so if you want an Auto slice to have a distinctive optimization setting, you'll need to pro-

Click and drag with the Slice tool.

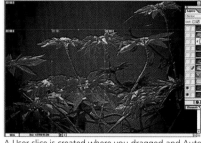

A User slice is created where you dragged and Auto slices are created in the other sections.

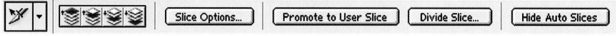

The Slice Selection tool options. In addition to stacking order, Slice Options and the capability of promoting User slices, you can now divide slices by inputting numeric values in a dialog box and you can hide User slices.

mote it to a User slice. If you double-click an Auto slice and set options for it, it automatically becomes a User slice.

SLICE OPTIONS: One of the reasons creating a slice is to be able to set options for it, such as a URL address. Use the Slice Selection tool, click the slice you want, and click the Slice Options button. Or, simply double-click the icon for that slice and the Options dialog box appears. The automatically generated name will appear in the Name input area. For URL, you can enter either a relative or full URL, which must include http://. If you have defined frames in your HTML document, you can enter a target frame in which the URL should open. Message text will display in the status area for that browser, rather than the URL. An Alt tag will display on browsers that cannot use images.

DIMENSIONS: If you are using User slices, you can set both the point of origin and the dimensions of a slice. Click the slice with the Slice Selection tool and use the Slice Options button, or simply double-click the slice with the tool to bring up the Options dialog box.

In addition to the Slice tool, you can create slices using the Layer menu.

In the Slice Options dialog box you input the URL as well as other information.

THE IMAGE EDITING TOOLS

Open the files CeramicFruit, Fish Art, Lighthouse, and Ostrich Egg from the CD to follow the next part of this chapter.

The Pencil and Paintbrush tools are the regular painting tools. The Clone/Pattern Stamp, History/Art History Brush, and Gradient/Paint Bucket tools are more specialized painting tools. The Healing Brush/Patch/Color Replacement tool, Erasers, Blur/Sharpen/Smudge, and Dodge/Burn/Saturate tools edit existing pixels. Note also that the Tool Cursor options you set in your File/Preferences/Display and Cursors preferences control how your tool cursor appears. In general, we use Brush Size for the Painting Cursors and Precise for the Other Cursors. Before we discuss each particular tool, we need to discuss the Brushes palette and some options that are standard to all the tools.

Click the pop-up arrow next to the Brush icon to get the currently loaded brushes.

THE BRUSHES PALETTE

All the image editing tools other than the Gradient/Paint Bucket and Healing Brush/Color Replacement tools get their brush tip information from the Brushes palette. To see this window, you click the Brush palette toggle on the right side of the Options bar just before the Palette Well when a tool that uses brushes is active. You also can use Window/Brushes. The set of brushes (though not all options) is the same for all the tools except the Pencil tool, which has only hard-edged brushes and the Healing Brush, which cannot use custom brush tips. Each tool retains the brush and option set last used for that tool. You can add and save brushes or groups of brushes using the pop-up menu at the top right of the Brushes palette.

Quickly load brushes or change the look of the palette using the pop-up menu on the Brushes palette.

Immediately to the left of the Palette Well on the Options bar is the File Browser icon. To the left of that you'll see the Brushes palette icon whenever you are working with a tool that uses brushes.

This is the running sub head

BRUSH TIPS: *While you are painting, you can change the size of the brush by using the right and left bracket symbols, [and], on the keyboard. Pressing the right bracket makes the brush 10 pixels larger and pressing the left bracket makes the brush 10 pixels smaller. For brushes smaller than 10 pixels, the change is in increments of 1 pixel. If you set General Preference Painting Tools to Brush Size, you can see the brush size as the brush sits over the area you want to paint. You'll see when you've reached the right size. Pressing Shift-] increases the hardness of a brush and Shift-[decreases its hardness in increments of 25%, for brush tips that use a Hardness setting. To cycle through the brushes in the palette, use a period to move to the right (or down) and a comma to move to the left (or up). These last two shortcuts only work if you are using a brush currently defined in the brush presets.*

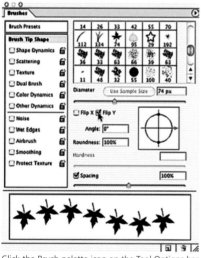

Click the Brush palette icon on the Tool Options bar to get the options for that particular brush. Here, I've increased the spacing on the Maple Leaf brush to 100% and then flipped it vertically by clicking the Flip Y button.

BRUSH PRESETS: When you open the Brushes palette, the first area you enter is the Brush presets. Here you'll see either icons or the names of the currently loaded brushes. This is where you start to build a brush. Choose a preset by clicking it and you can see which options are turned on for that brush by looking for the checks in the boxes on the left of the palette. The only thing that you can change about your brush in this area is the master diameter.

BRUSH TIP OPTIONS: Click the words Brush Tip Shape to enter this area. Here you can change the diameter of the brush (up to 2500 pixels), the hardness of the brush, and the spacing. When you set the hardness to 100%, you get very little or no blending between the color or image you are painting and the background. A hardness of 0 gives maximum blending with the background. Try the same large brush with different hardness settings to see how it can affect the stroke. The spacing controls how closely dabs of the Paintbrush tool are placed together on the screen (the default value for this is 25%, which causes a 75% overlap of each dab, so it looks like a continuous stroke). To learn about spacing, set it to 100%, and then paint using the Paintbrush tool with a big, hard-edged brush. At 100%, the dabs are tangent to each other on the canvas. Now try turning the spacing off (uncheck the Spacing box). With spacing off, the spacing is controlled by how fast you move the brush. Try it!

You can change the angle and roundness of the brush by typing values in the dialog box or by using the handles and arrow on the brush definition area on the lower left of the palette. The Brush icon on the the palette illustrates what that brush will look like. For more on the specifics of Brush options, see Chapter 35: "Painting in Photoshop."

COMMON IMAGE EDITING TOOL OPTIONS

The following options work primarily the same way for all the painting tools.

PAINTING MODES: In Photoshop, you can paint with more than the simple color that's currently the foreground color. By changing the Painting Mode, you can get many different results from your brush. These painting modes are essentially the Blend modes that we cover in Chapter 31: "Blend Modes, Calculations, and Apply Image." If you read that chapter (and experiment with painting) you'll get a feeling for what each of the modes can do.

You can toggle through the different Blend modes as you paint by pressing Shift-+ to move forward or Shift-– to move backward through the various modes. In addition, see the chart for the specific keystrokes for each Blend mode. These keys can also be used to change the Blend modes for layers when you are not in a painting tool.

OPACITY AND FLOW: The default Opacity for brushes is 100%. However, any new brush preset you choose will retain the opacity, flow, and paint mode of the last used brush. This is not true for Tool presets; they maintain the settings that were used when you created the preset. You can change the Opacity of a brush by typing in a number from 0–9 while using one of the brush tools (1 equals 10%, 2 equals 20%...9 equals 90%, and 0 equals 100%). If you type two numbers quickly, like 25, you can set the Opacity to that double-digit percent. Opacity and Flow work hand in hand to determine the amount of paint laid down. I like to think of the opacity as controlling the transparency of the the medium and flow controlling how fully you've loaded your brush. To mimic watercolor, a very transparent medium, I'd keep the opacity low; for thick oil paint, the opacity would be high but I might lower the flow to get more of a blended effect. When Flow is present on the Options bar (and Airbrush is not active) pressing Shift along with a number will set the amount of flow.

MODIFIER KEYS: If you hold down Shift when using any of the painting tools, you draw vertically or horizontally. Also, clicking once with the tool, letting go of the mouse button, and then Shift-clicking somewhere else draws a straight line between these two points with the current brush.

AIRBRUSH: Airbrush is an option on many of the painting tools rather than a tool unto itself. When you turn on the Airbrush option, paint will continue to be laid down when you hold the mouse in one spot until the maximum opacity is reached. When the Airbrush option is checked (either on the Options bar or in the Brushes palette) typing numbers controls the amount of flow rather than the opacity. Hold down the Shift key to type numbers for the opacity in this case. The opacity of one application of pressure using the Airbrush option will never exceed the current opacity setting.

DEFINING A CUSTOM BRUSH: In addition, you can define a custom brush by drawing a rectangle or an elliptical selection around all or part of an image and going to Edit/Define Brush. You can use a color or grayscale selection to define your brush, but the brush appears as grayscale in your palette. Consequently, if your brushes are built in grayscale with a white or transparent background, your results will be more predictable.When you paint with any brush, it uses the density of the gray in the brush to determine the amount of foreground color to lay down. After you have defined your custom brushes, you can use Save Brushes from the Brushes palette menu to give your new set of brushes a distinctive name. You can save the brushes wherever you like, but if you've hit on something you think you're going to use again, save your brushes in the Photoshop/Presets/Brushes folder.

Photoshop includes several custom brush palettes inside this folder already. Someone did a lot of work creating great brushes that give you much better naturalistic results if you are used to painting traditionally or you've been using Painter. You can load these palettes or any palette you create by using Load Brushes from the pop-up options, or if you want to add those brushes to the current palette, choose Append Brushes. Reset Brushes restores the default Brushes palette.

HEALING BRUSH/PATCH/COLOR REPLACEMENT TOOL

KEYBOARD SHORTCUT: Type the letter J. Type Shift-J to toggle between the tools.

If you do much retouching in your work, Photoshop is going to make you very happy. Open The Ostrich Egg.psd file from the *Photoshop Artistry* CD if you want to work with the example shown here. You'll get another chance in Chapter 25: "Restoring Old Photos." For now, here's a bit about how these tools work.

The Healing Brush and Patch tool use pixel information from a source, either a sampled area or a pattern, and then blends those pixels with existing pixels from your image. This is similar to the Clone/Pattern Stamp but these tools do not take the information verbatim; instead, they interpolate it to blend seamlessly with the existing image. This approach covers flaws in your image more quickly and easily than anything that existed before.

Still, there are times when you'll find you need the Clone Stamp to create information, and there's no clear-cut formula to say when you'll need which tool. Both the Healing Brush and Patch tool work best when you are correcting small areas that are not significantly different from what you want the final product to look like. If you have to completely cover an area that differs greatly from the final product, the Clone Stamp may still work best.

To use the Healing Brush, select the brush and options from the Brushes palette and the Options bar. If you want to use a sample from a file, Option-click with the brush to set the sample start point. If you want to use a pattern, click the

TO ACCESS SPECIFIC BLEND/PAINTING MODES

for	Macintosh	Windows
	Option-Shift	Alt-Shift

plus

Normal	N
Dissolve	I
Behind	Q
Clear	R
Darken	K
Multiply	M
Color Burn	B
Linear Burn	**A**
Lighten	G
Screen	S
Color Dodge	D
Linear Dodge	**W**
Pin Light	**Z**
Hard Mix	L
Overlay	O
Soft Light	F
Hard Light	H
Vivid Light	**V**
Linear Light	**J**
Difference	E
Exclusion	X
Hue	U
Saturation	T
Color	C
Luminosity	Y
Airbrush On/Off	**P**

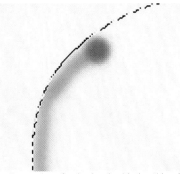

Here, I've used a soft-edge brush with the Airbrush tool. As I got to the top of the stroke, I held the mouse down and you can see that the paint built up in the shape of the brush.

47

Pattern button and choose the pattern from the pop-up. When you use the brush, you lay down a stroke then wait. Photoshop calculates how to blend the information together, then changes the pixel values. For this reason, it's best to work in short strokes and check that the effect is what you want before continuing. You can work with several different blend modes but there is no opacity slider. Therefore, you might want to make a copy of your layer before you retouch it, then change the opacity of the layer if you want more control over the blending of the effect. Photoshop CS can heal onto an empty (transparent) layer as well, giving you another option to maintain the integrity of your original.

The Patch tool works from the same starting point, matching the lighting, texture, and shading from the sample to the source image. Rather than making brush strokes, though, you select an area to work with. The radio buttons on the Options bar now ask you to state whether the selection you make is to be the Source or the Destination for the transformation. If you choose Source, drag the selection you've made to the area that has the information you want to incorporate, or click the Use Pattern button to use the current pattern. If you choose Destination, drag the selection to the area that you want to heal. The selection marquee now moves to that location. You can drag this same selection to new locations to heal other areas. At any point during this process you may click the Use Pattern button to use the current pattern instead of the pixels from the original selection. Clicking the Transparent button for either Source or Destination will give you texture but maintain more of the underlying color and contrast.

You sample an area for the Healing Brush just as you do for the Clone Stamp—by Option-clicking.

As you stroke with the Healing Brush you see a representation of the area from which you are taking information. After a few seconds, the calculations are made and the stroke is blended with the image.

Make your selection with the Patch tool, and then designate it as either a Source or Destination patch.

All the wrinkles worked fine with the Healing Brush, but for the camera strap you need the Clone Stamp.

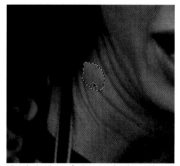

The behavior of the patch depends on whether it is Source or Destination.

The Color Replacement tool is new to this version of Photoshop. It replaces areas of color based on a tolerance value, and what limits you set for the spread of color. You always replace with the Foreground color, so sample it first before you begin to move your mouse or stylus. It seems to work best with areas of flat or similar color, so if you are a cartoonist or animator, you may find it quick and handy. Once you've chosen your color to paint, chose the sampling method for what you will replace. Once will sample the first spot you click and only replace colors within the tolerance value of that one click. Continuous samples all colors, and Background only paints out the color of the current background swatch. The Limits pop-up controls which areas will be colored with Contiguous only painting pixels that fall within the Tolerance value and are next to each other, Discontiguous painting pixels wherever they occur, and Find Edges maintaining the sharpness at the edge of objects. This tool can quickly get rid of "red eye" by choosing the color you want for the eyes, then clicking on the red color and painting.

PAINTBRUSH/PENCIL TOOL

KEYBOARD SHORTCUT: Type the letter B. Type Shift-B to toggle between the tools.

The Paintbrush tool has anti-aliased edges that make the edge of where you paint blend more evenly with what you are painting over. When you use the Pencil tool, the edges of your drawing are jagged because there is no anti-aliasing here. Use the Pencil when you want to be sure to get a solid color even on the edge of the painted area. When you switch from an anti-aliased paint tool, such as the Paintbrush, to the Pencil tool, the brushes in the Brushes palette switch to hard-edge brushes.

When painting with the Pencil or Paintbrush, the Opacity setting from the Brushes palette is not exceeded as long as you hold the mouse button down, even if you paint over the same area again and again.

See Chapter 35, "Painting in Photoshop," to learn all about how to use the Paintbrush and the Brushes palette.

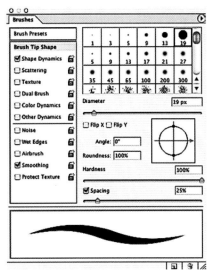

All of Photoshop's brush options are available when you are in the Paintbrush tool. The other image editing tools can only access some of the options. See Chapter 35: "Digital Paint," for information on what each option does.

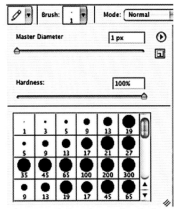

When you switch to the Pencil tool, all currently loaded brushes become aliased.

CLONE STAMP/PATTERN STAMP TOOL

KEYBOARD SHORTCUT: Type the letter S. Type Shift-S to toggle between the tools.

ALIGNED: Both tools allow you to choose Aligned if you want to paint a continuous image or Pattern, even if you let go of the mouse or stylus. With the Clone Stamp, you can clone from an image onto itself, from one layer of an image to another layer, or from one photo to another. With the Pattern Stamp, you can lay down a pattern from the currently loaded patterns using a brush rather than the Fill command.

If you'd like to try some of the options that we show here, open the file Starry Night in the Tools Palette folder on the CD.

Aligned is the option you will use most often with the Clone Stamp. You can use it to remove spots and scratches and also to copy part of an image from one place to another. To use it, pick a brush size from the Brushes palette, then hold down the Option key and click at the location where you want to pick up the image (called the pickup location). Now, without holding down the Option key, click the place where you want to clone the new information (called the putdown location). As long as you hold down the mouse, information copies from the pickup location to the putdown location. Both of these move correspondingly when you move the mouse. When you release the mouse button and then move it and click down again, the relative distance between the pickup location and the putdown location remains the same, but both move the offset distance that you move the mouse. Therefore, you can clone part of the image, stop for lunch, and then come back and finish the job without worrying about misaligning your clone. This makes Aligned very good for removing spots. You also can clone from one image or one layer to another by Option-clicking in the pickup image or layer and then clicking to clone in the putdown image or layer. See Chapter 19: "Overall Color Correction," for more information on removing spots and scratches with the Aligned option. In the Starry Night picture here,

For Clone Stamp (aligned), Option-click at the pickup location...

...then click with no Option key at the location where you want to put down the clone. Notice the + that shows you the current pickup location, and the O that shows the putdown location. We have our Painting Cursors preference set to Brush Size.

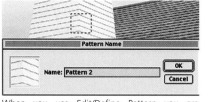

With the Aligned option on, if you let go of the mouse and move to a new location, the Clone Stamp remembers the original location of your Option-click and maintains the relative distance.

With Aligned not on, if you let go of the mouse and move to a new location, the Clone Stamp begins cloning again from the original location.

we've first been asked to clone a group of stars. The Aligned option works well for this.

You would use non-aligned (Aligned unchecked) to copy the same object into various places within the image. When you use this option, the pickup location remains the same when you move the mouse and click down in a new putdown location, which allows you to copy the same part of the image to multiple places within the image. When you want to change the pickup location, you need to Option-click again. Non-aligned would work better if you needed to copy one star over and over.

USE ALL LAYERS: If you have a composite that uses layers, you can clone from the entire image without flattening first by turning on the Use All Layers option. This will clone from whatever is currently visible, so you can turn layers on and off for different effects, even between strokes with the tool.

When you use Edit/Define Pattern you are prompted to name your pattern.

New patterns are added to the current Pattern palette, but you must save that palette to ensure you keep the patterns forever.

PATTERN STAMP: Patterned cloning uses the current Photoshop pattern and copies it wherever you paint with the mouse. If the Align box is checked, painting the pattern is consistent; the patterns line up even if you have released the mouse button and started drawing more than once. This is the tool you want to use if you are painting wallpaper or some pattern that must match. To define a pattern, you select a rectangular area with the Rectangular Marquee, and then choose Edit/Define Pattern. It is then added to the current Patterns palette. If you've added patterns that you really like and want to keep, be sure you save your patterns into a file. See Chapter 33, "Texture and Pattern," for more on creating patterns. In the example here, we used the Lighthouse file and one of the basic Photoshop patterns, then used the Pattern Stamp with Aligned on and our Blend mode set to Normal at 100% to paint the wall. Notice that even if you use discontiguous strokes, the pattern aligns correctly.

Non-aligned means that the patterns do not necessarily match when different painting areas touch up against each other. You would not want to use this option to paint wallpaper, but by changing the Painting modes you might find that you can build up some interesting textures. Here we've used the same pattern but stroked the Pattern Stamp over the same area several times, letting go of the mouse each time. The patterns do not align. While you're here playing, try lowering the opacity or using Multiply, Screen, Dissolve, or Difference as a Blend mode to lay texture over the flat color areas. Groovy.

With the Pattern Stamp, you can paint the pattern wherever you like, including in a channel.

Painting with a non-aligned pattern and using several strokes with different starting points.

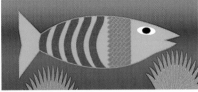

THE HISTORY/ART HISTORY BRUSH

KEYBOARD SHORTCUT: Type the letter Y. Type Shift-Y to toggle between the tools.

This brush works in conjunction with the History palette to give you multiple levels of undo and multiple snapshots from which to paint. You have so many options now you can wander around painting different versions ad infinitum. My head hurts thinking about it. The quick explanation is: The position of the History Brush icon in the History palette determines the state of the file from which you will paint using the History/Art History Brush. One of the primary uses for the History Brush is to recapture effects or states that you used earlier in your work but lost via Undo or further manipulation. Although you can use layers to achieve some effects and, in general, layers give you more flexibility, learning to use the History palette effectively is often very useful. To that end we've devoted an entire chapter to its use, so be sure you read that at some point. One of the main points to remember about History is that it is layer dependent and dependent on the pixel dimensions of the file. That is, you can only paint to a layer information that has existed on that layer. You cannot paint information from a different layer's History state. Also, if you crop the file, you cannot paint from a History state that existed before the crop.

The Art History Brush is another of Adobe's attempts to increase the capabilities of Photoshop to create artwork out of photographs. And although you can achieve some interesting results with this tool, it is unpredictable and takes a lot of playtime to discover methods that are particularly useful. Try out the different tool presets on one of your photos. There are a few nice brushes and quite a few that are merely goofy. My suggestion is: If you want to create naturalistic artwork out of your photos, invest in Painter.

For both the History and Art History brushes, you can use any brush shape currently loaded, and you can use a Blend mode and different opacity. There the similarity ends. The Art History Brush uses styles that control the movement of the strokes laid down, whereas the History Brush is completely dependent on the strokes you make with the mouse or stylus. The Art History Brush can only paint in a few of the Blend modes; the History Brush can use them all, plus Behind. The Art History Brush has additional controls that specify how large a space is covered by the brush

The original Fish art.

The History Brush gives you far more flexibility than the multiple undos of any other program. Here, even though we moved objects and ran filters on them, built new layers and layer masks, and changed Blend modes, we were still able to use the History Brush to paint 45% of the original Green Fan layer back into that layer for a 3-D effect.

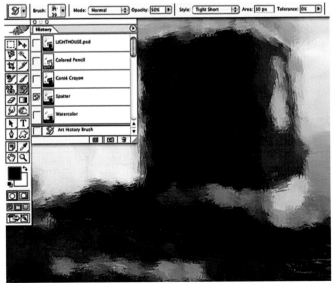

I made a snapshot of a filtered version of the file, then reverted and used the Art History Brush to paint from that version.

These are the types of strokes the Art History Brush can make using the Styles pop-up.

The Art History Brush only paints in these Blend modes.

(Area), and how different the source must be before the brush lays down a stroke (Tolerance).

Eraser/Background/Magic Eraser Tool

KEYBOARD SHORTCUT: Type the letter E. Type Shift-E to toggle between the tools.

The Eraser tool erases to the background color in the Background layer and to transparency in any other layer. The default background color is white but can be any color. Erasing a layer to transparent allows you to see through the erased area to the layers below it. You can choose from three options for the type of eraser nib: Brush, Pencil, and Block. The first two give you eraser nibs that act exactly like their painting tool counterparts in respect to style, so refer to the Paintbrush and Pencil sections of this chapter, respectively. The Block option is most like the Eraser from early versions of the program. It does not have anti-aliased edges, and the size of the area you erase is determined not by brush size, but rather by the magnification of the image you are working with. The higher the magnification, the smaller your erased area, until you reach the point that you are erasing individual pixels.

The Eraser options.

The three different erasers at 100% Opacity.

ERASE TO HISTORY: You usually use the Eraser tool when you want to completely remove something in a small area. If you hold down the Option key when erasing or click the Erase to History option, you get an eraser, which erases to the current position of the History Brush source in the History palette. For more information on using the History palette, see Chapter 8: "History Palette, History Brushes, and Snapshots."

BACKGROUND ERASER: This is a much more refined tool that you will find more useful in helping to separate part of an image from the background. To those who have used Extensis MaskPro, the Background Eraser will be very familiar. The main deficiency of this tool, however, is that, like the Magic Eraser, it deletes image information and replaces it with transparency. If you want to ensure that necessary pixel information is not being thrown away, you need to duplicate the image onto a new layer, as described above, so that the Background Eraser performs its deletion on the copy layer and not the original image (be sure to turn the Eye icon off for the original, so that you can see the effect of the tool). This working method preserves a back-up copy of all your image data in case you need to fill in any areas where the eraser's choices were less than satisfactory. The downside of this is that, in making a duplicate layer of the entire image, you are effectively doubling your file size, which results in more memory and disk space requirements and, on large image files, can cause Photoshop to run slower.

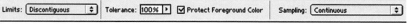

The Background Eraser options.

You may find you need to change the Limits and Sampling options from file to file or even within the same file to use the Background Eraser effectively.

The Options palette for the Background Eraser has three main settings that affect how it performs pixel deletion.

LIMITS: Discontiguous will erase the sampled color wherever it occurs in the layer; Contiguous will erase areas that contain the sampled color and are connected to one another; and Find Edges will erase the sampled color in contiguous areas, but do a better job at preserving the sharpness of object edges.

SAMPLING: From the Sampling options, you can choose Continuous to sample colors continuously as you drag through the image. This option is best for erasing adjoining areas that are different in color. The Once option will erase only areas

containing the color you first click. This is best for deleting a solid-colored area. The Background Swatch option will erase only areas containing the current background color.

TOLERANCE: Finally, you set a Tolerance value similar to the Magic Wand tool. A low tolerance erases areas that are very similar to the sampled color, and a high tolerance erases a broader range of colors.

MAGIC ERASER: This tool functions much like the Paint Bucket tool but clears an area to transparency instead of filling it with color. Another way to achieve the same effect would be to click with the Magic Wand and then delete the resulting selection. Like the Wand and the Bucket tools, it has a tolerance setting to determine the range of pixels that are deleted, as well as Anti-Alias and Contiguous options. The Magic Eraser is useful mainly on images where there is a clear difference between what you want to delete and what you want to keep. And, true to its name, it erases pixel information, leaving you with transparency. Turn on Use All Layers if you have a composite whose background you wish to knock out. Remember that information is deleted with this tool, so keep a copy of your file somewhere if you're not 100% sure that you'll never need those parts again. (No, keep a copy even if you ARE 100% sure.)

One click in the sky with the Magic Eraser and a Tolerance of 12 deleted this area. Although it's possible to delete the entire sky with this tool, you'd have to be very careful not to erase pixels of the light colors on the lighthouse as you erase light colored pixels in the sky.

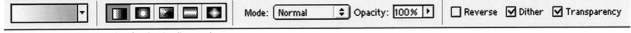

Here's the new Tool Options bar for the Gradient tool.

GRADIENT TOOL/PAINT BUCKET

KEYBOARD SHORTCUT: Type the letter G. Type Shift-G to toggle between the tools.

The basic function of the Gradient tool is to make a gradual blend in the selected area from one color to another color. A blend is accomplished by clicking and dragging a line the length and angle you want the blend to appear. The Gradient tool is often used in a mask channel to blend two images together seamlessly by making a blend from black to white. Black represents one image and white the other. If you'd like to experiment with the tool, open the files TheLeaf and GrColOrPur from the Tools palette folder on the CD. You can use Select/Load Selection to load the Leaf Mask as a selection.

We'll also do a few tricks with layers, so you might want to open the Fish file again. Show the Layers palette (Window/Layers) and click the name of the appropriate layer. Turn on the Preserve Transparency option.

You choose the actual gradient colors that you want to use via the Gradient palette, which appears when you click the pop-up on the Gradient Color swatch on the Tool Options bar. The default setting is Foreground to Background and will compute a gradient for you based on the currently selected foreground and background colors. Using the default palette, the second icon is for Foreground to Transparent. The final icon in this palette is Transparent Stripes, which also uses the current foreground color as the stripe color. Double-click a swatch to view its name or to rename it. Clicking once on the color swatch brings up the Gradient Editor, which is discussed later in this section.

THE DEFAULT SETTINGS: When you set the Blend mode to Normal, the Type to Linear, and the Gradient to Foreground to Background, everything from the edge of the selection to the first click on the line is solid foreground color. Everything from the mouse release to the other end of the selection is solid background color. Along the line, there is a blend from foreground to background color, and at a place 50% along the length of the line, the two colors are blended each at 50%.

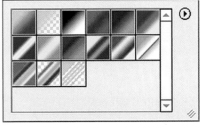

This is the default Gradient palette. The first, second, and last swatches depend on the currently selected foreground color. The first swatch is Foreground to Background and uses both of the current colors on the Tools palette.

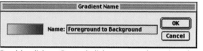

Double-click or Control-click any swatch to view the name or to rename the swatch.

The TheLeaf file. Open this file if you want to play along with the Gradient tool. Now use Select/Load Selection to load the Leaf Mask.

This file, called GrColOrPur, has an orange foreground and purple background. These are the colors we used to illustrate the Gradient tool. To use the same colors as you experiment, use the Eyedropper tool by itself to click the orange square and set your foreground color. Then hold down the Option key with the Eyedropper and click on the purple square to set your background color.

A blend across the selected area with the default setting...

...gives a blend from foreground to background with 50% of each color at the midway point.

A blend that begins or ends before the selection boundaries...

...will be 100% of the foreground color before the beginning of the blend and 100% of the background color after the blend line ends. When using the default settings, the midpoint, where color is 50% foreground and 50% background, will still be at the midway point.

The orange to purple gradient in Color Burn mode at 50% Opacity.

GRADIENT TYPES: Photoshop has five types of Gradient blends: Linear, Radial, Angle, Reflected, and Diamond. These are represented by the group of five icons on the Tool Options bar. Linear is the default and makes a blend based on a straight line that you draw at any angle. Radial creates a radial blend done as a circle. If Gradient is set to Foreground to Background, the first click of the mouse is the circle's center using the foreground color, the line length that you drag is the circle's radius, and the mouse release location is at the outside edge of a blended circle using the background color. The Angle blend gives the effect of sweeping a radius around a circle. The line you draw is the "angle" of the radius in the foreground color (or first color of the blend) that then sweeps around the circle, changing gradually to the background color (or moves through the colors of your selected blend). The Reflected gradient reflects two symmetrical linear gradients outward from your starting point, and the Diamond gradient uses the line you draw as one of the corners of the diamond shape that is created.

BLEND MODES AND OPACITY: You can set the Blend mode and Opacity of the gradient you are about to create using these settings in the Gradient Options palette. We discuss the various Blend modes in Chapter 31: "Blend Modes, Calculations, and Apply Image." However, you might want to try some of the modes, such as Color, Multiply, Difference, and Hard Light, as you explore the Gradient tool.

THE DITHER OPTION: Leaving the Dither option on results in smoother blends with less banding. We recommend that you leave it on unless you want a banded gradient.

THE GRADIENT EDITOR: Click the Gradient Preview swatch on the Options bar to access the Gradient Editor. The currently active Gradient palette is displayed along with the controls to create or edit any gradient. If you want to base your new gradient on an existing one, click the swatch of the existing gradient or use the Load button to load any other palette shipped with Photoshop or created by you.

To modify an existing gradient, just select it and start making changes. When you have something you like, type in a name and click the New button. Your gradient will be added to the palette. If you want to save the gradient forever, you need to use the Save button and give your palette a distinctive name. Otherwise, when you reset the palette, your gradient will no longer be there. To remove a gradient, hold the Option key and click the swatch.

When you click a stop in either the upper or lower row on the color bar, you can change the color or transparency of a gradient.

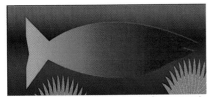
Linear blend from orange to purple, fins to mouth.

Radial blend, center to top of fish.

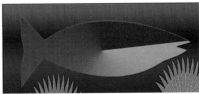
Angle blend, center to nose of fish.

Reflected blend, center to top of fish.

Diamond blend, center to top of fish.

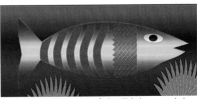
Here we made a copy of the Fish layer and then used the reflected blend shown at the far left on the top copy. We then set the Blend mode of the top layer to Hard Light at 100% Opacity.

Each square below the color bar represents a different color stop. You can add a new stop by clicking below the bar, and you can move this point by dragging from left to right. The Location box tells you the location of this color as a percentage of the length of the line you draw to create the gradient. You can set a point to a particular color by first clicking that stop and then either clicking the color box below and to the left to bring up the Color Picker and pick a new color ,or using the automatic Eyedropper to sample a color from any currently open file. The color point you are currently working on will have its triangle top highlighted in black. The little diamond points under the colored bar represent the halfway point between the color to the left and the color to the right of that diamond point. Click and drag it to have the Location window show you the location relative to the percentage of distance between these two points. The default location of the diamonds is always 50% of this distance, but you can move them left and right.

Click above the color bar to change the transparency of the gradient at points along its length. You can turn off the transparency of any gradient by turning off the Transparency checkbox on the Tool Options bar when you are using the Gradient tool. Try turning off Transparency and then using the Foreground to Transparent option. You get just the solid foreground color. The length of the bar again represents the length of the line you draw when making the gradient. You can place Opacity stops anywhere along the bar by clicking above the bar. When you click a stop, the bottom of it turns black, indicating that it is the stop you are currently editing. The Location window shows you the location of this point relative to the total length of the line, and the Opacity entry area shows you its opacity. The diamonds between stops show you the midpoint between the Opacity stops. Bring the Gradient Editor up and play with it a bit and it will become obvious how it works.

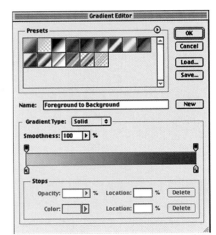
The Gradient Editor set up to adjust the color of the gradient. You access this by typing G to get to the Gradient tool, then clicking once on the color swatch on the Tool Options bar.

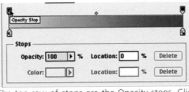
The top row of stops are the Opacity stops. Click one to activate the controls for that stop.

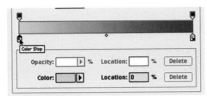
The bottom row of stops are the Color stops. Click one to activate the controls for that stop. In this illustration, the bottom stops use the foreground color on the left and the background color on the right. These stops look a bit different than ones you add yourself.

Here's a more complex gradient. The green color stop on the bottom is the currently active stop. Notice the different icons for the stops on the bottom row.

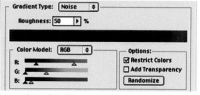

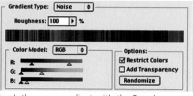

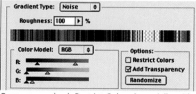

Move the color sliders to assign a range of values for Photoshop to use when computing the colors.

Here's the same gradient with the Roughness setting increased to 100%. With Restrict Colors checked the colors are not allowed to become oversaturated.

Once you uncheck Restrict Colors (especially with a high Roughness setting) the colors become very intense. If you check Add Transparency, certain values are made partially transparent or removed altogether from the gradient.

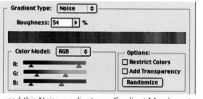

I used this Noise gradient as a Gradient Map layer to produce…

…this effect.

The original image.

NOISE: Photoshop has the capability to build a gradient based on a range of colors. The application computes a gradient composed of colored bands spaced irregularly. The Roughness setting controls how radical the transitions are from color to color, with a lower setting giving you more of a standard gradient and a higher setting giving you something out of a technicolor nightmare. Use Restrict Colors to keep the colors from oversaturating. Transparency removes or partially removes colors from the gradient. Try using a Noise gradient as a Gradient Map layer. Turn on the Preview button and experiment with the sliders, buttons, and Roughness setting. As a gradient map, these gradients offer a quick way to explore color choices that would take much longer to generate as a gradient that you build yourself.

PAINT BUCKET TOOL: The Paint Bucket tool is similar to the Magic Wand in that it fills an area based on the Tolerance value set in the Options bar, and the pixel on which you click. We seldom use the Paint Bucket, preferring to make the selection first with other selection tools and then, once we have the right selection, use the Fill command from the Edit menu. The Fill command (Shift-Delete) also offers more options than does the Paint Bucket. The Bucket is very useful and faster than Fill for colorizing black-and-white line drawings such as cartoon drawings, animations, or solid color areas.

ALL LAYERS: If you are using several layers, you can choose which layers you want the Paint Bucket to search for the color tolerance range. If you click on Use All Layers and have the Eye icon on in more than one layer, Photoshop samples the data in every layer currently visible. The Paint Bucket fills only the currently active layer.

BLUR/SHARPEN/SMUDGE TOOLS

KEYBOARD SHORTCUT: Type the letter R. Type Shift-R to cycle through the three tools.

You use the Blur tool to help blend jagged edges between two images being composited, as well as to remove the jaggies from a diagonal line or just to soften selected parts of an image. You can use the Sharpen tool to locally sharpen an area without making a selection. Both tools work best when you try different levels of pressure (opacity) from the Tool Options bar, and you should start out with a low pressure, as they can work quite quickly.

The Smudge tool causes the image area you brush to behave like wet paint. You can click and drag to smear one color area into another. This blends the colors within the brush area, so the size of the blend depends on the size and softness of the brush you use. The pressure controls the amount of paint that mixes with each stroke and how far into the stroke the paint smears. At 100%, the color that you pick up is laid down the whole length of the stroke. If you hold down the Option key when you start a paint stroke or click the Fingerpaint mode, a dab of the foreground color mixes in with the rest of the colors being smudged. If you find that the Fingerpaint mode doesn't seem to be working, check the Other Dynamics settings of your current brush. You may need to change this setting or turn it off to have the color smudge the way you expect.

USE ALL LAYERS: The Use All Layers option reads all the layers that have the Eye icon turned on to make whatever adjustments are specific to that tool. If you are smudging colors, the Smudge tool looks at all colors in the current composite and smears them together. Ditto for Sharpen and Blur. But be aware that the Smudge, Sharpen, or Blur only occurs on the active layer, so be sure the layer that should show the change is currently active.

DODGE/BURN/SPONGE TOOLS

KEYBOARD SHORTCUT: Type the letter O. Type Shift-O to cycle through the three options.

You use the Dodge tool when you want to make localized areas of your image lighter, and the Burn tool to make localized areas of your image darker. Both tools work best when you try different levels of exposure (opacity) from the Tool Options bar. Start with a low value, about 30%.

When you use the Burn and Dodge tools, you need to specify the part of the image area you are working on. Set Highlights, Midtones, or Shadows depending on the part of the image you are dodging or burning.

Truthfully, we rarely use these tools as there are better ways to burn, dodge, and saturate that are more flexible and accurate. But these tools will suffice for a minor fix.

The Sponge tool allows you to saturate or desaturate the area you brush over. It is useful for desaturating out-of-gamut colors (colors that you can see onscreen but are unprintable) to bring them back into gamut (printable colors). Once again, there are other methods that offer greater flexibility.

VECTOR TOOLS

THE PATH SELECTION/DIRECT SELECTION TOOL

KEYBOARD SHORTCUT: Type the letter A. Type Shift-A to toggle between the tools.

Photoshop becomes more vector savvy with each version of the application. If you are used to working in Illustrator, you'll feel right at home. If you're not used to the vector world, let me assure you that it's worthwhile to learn how to use the Pen tool and all its associated tools.

If you open the Fish Art file and show the Paths palette, you can click on the "fish art" path to activate it. If you use the Path Selection tool and click the path in the image window, you select the entire path and can move the path by dragging it

Blur tool after several applications.

Sharpen tool after several applications.

Smudge tool in action.

Orange foreground color mixed with the image with Fingerpaint mode.

After dodging with the Dodge tool.

After burning with the Burn tool.

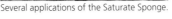
Several applications of the Saturate Sponge.

Several applications of the Desaturate Sponge.

To take a look at a path, click the Fish path in the Paths palette for Fish Art. When you click the path with the arrow, you'll see where the points are located. Notice the "handlebars" for the curved points.

Click the Fish path to activate the path. The icons on the bottom of the palette are for fill, stroke, make a selection, turn the selection into a path, make a new path, and delete a path.

or copy the path by Option-dragging it. If you use the Direct Selection tool, you can choose a particular point to work with. Notice if you click with this tool on a point connected to a curved segment, you get "handles" that allow you to change the shape and length of the curve. If you are using the Pen tool and hold down the Command key, you can also access this tool.

ALIGNMENT: Now open the Temple door file from the *Photoshop CS Aritstry* CD and click on Path 1 in the Paths palette. This is actually four subpaths. Use the Path Selection tool to click on two or more of these paths while holding the Shift key. As soon as two paths are selected the alignment icons will activate. The options for alignment are basically the same as those using the Move tool with linked layers. You must use the Path Component tool (there are no options for the Direct Selection tool) and all the subpaths you select must be in the same path. You cannot Shift-select subpaths from different paths. If you need to combine or align subpaths that are in different path layers, you need to copy and paste them into the same path layer. Select two subpaths to get the alignment options, three or more to get the distribution options as well.

COMBINING SUBPATHS: Just as you can make multiple selections that add to, subtract from, or intersect with each other, you can combine subpaths of a path layer. However, the result depends on the stacking order of the subpaths.

First, the basics. The four Combine icons are Add to, Subtract from, Intersect, and Exclude. You can choose which icon you want before you draw your subpath, or after. If you draw a single shape with the Add to icon active, your selection when you load the path will be the interior of that shape. If you draw a single shape with the Subtract from icon active, your returned selection will be the outside of the shape.

When you create a second subpath, both the stacking order and existing combine state can be important. If your first shape was a "Subtract from" shape and you create an overlapping "Subtract from" shape, you will, in effect, be adding those two shapes together. If, on the other hand, your second shape is an "Add to" shape, you will be subtracting from the first shape. Confusing for me, but those of you who understand math will get it fairly quickly.

This means that you can create two overlapping subpaths and change the selection that will occur when you load the path by clicking different icons each time you load the path. The subpaths remain interactive with the icons unless you click the Combine button. At that point, the subpaths will always return the selection of the icon that was active

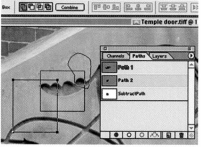

Choosing two subpaths allows you to use the first set of Alignment options to align vertically or horizontally using the edges or centers of the subpaths.

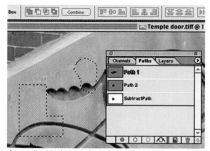

When you select three or more subpaths, you can distribute those subpaths as well as align them.

In this example the subpaths of Path 2 were built from left to right, so the irregular shape subpath is top in the stacking order. The first rectangle is Add to, the second is Subtract from, and the final shape is Add to.

If you drag Path 2 to the Create Selection icon on the bottom of the palette, this is the selection that is returned.

when you clicked Combine, even if you select an additional subpath and use a different method to combine it. Play with the feature a bit; you'll see that it gives you much greater flexibility in making selections from paths.

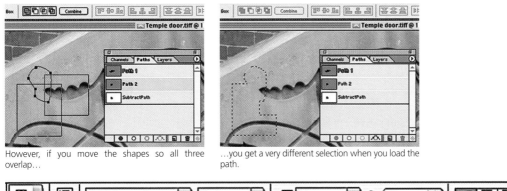

However, if you move the shapes so all three overlap…

…you get a very different selection when you load the path.

Here's the Tool Options bar for the Type tool. The first two icons are for Type tool presets and Change Type Orientation. The first pop-up is for the typeface or font family, then weight, size, and amount of anti-alias. Then comes three icons for alignment, the Color square, the Warp Text button, and the Palettes button for accessing the Character and Paragraph palette.

THE TYPE TOOL

KEYBOARD SHORTCUT: Type the letter T.

This was one of the major advances to Photoshop 6. Vector type that works. We use type in Chapter 34: "Heartsinger CD Cover," so you'll get some practice with it later. When you use the Type tool, you enter text by clicking on the image in the location where you want to insert the text or clicking and dragging to create a bounding box for paragraph type. If you choose either the Horizontal or Vertical Type icon, type is added to your image as a new layer with the type surrounded by transparency. The layer is named using the characters that you just typed in, which makes identifying the layer easy. The two Type Mask tools add a selection of your type boundaries to the currently active layer. This is done by adding a "Quick mask" overlay that remains active until you hit the numeric keypad's Enter key or click the Accept icon on the Options bar. The regular Enter (Return) key just adds a new line for text. If a type layer is the active layer, you'll get a type mask but be unable to do much with it.

You can change the color, kern it, track it, baseline-shift it, and change the attributes character by character. If that's not enough, you can transform the layer or add layer effects and still have vector text.

The text comes in as the current color square on the Options bar. You can highlight portions of the text later and choose a different color in the Options bar, the Swatches palette, or the foreground color square. If letters on a type layer are colored differently, the color square in the Options bar will display a question mark when differently colored text is highlighted or when the entire layer is activated in the Layers palette.

Access type layers through the Layers palette, where you can modify the Opacity and the Paint mode of the layer. This cannot be done on a character-by-character basis.

THE CHARACTER AND PARAGRAPH PALETTES

The Character and Paragraph palettes appear when you click the Palettes button on the Type tool Options bar. Here's a quick rundown of what you'll find on these palettes.

Once you've started typing, the Type tool Options bar will change slightly and show you these two icons on the far right side. These allow you to either Cancel or Commit any edits that you are currently making.

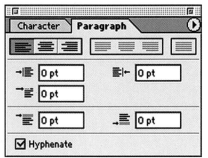

If you click and drag with the Type tool you get a bounding box in which to type Paragraph type.

The Character and Paragraph palettes look almost identical to Illustrator's.

Photoshop has fairly good Paragraph controls. Unfortunately, you cannot set tabs, so Photoshop is not appropriate for all typesetting jobs.

Justification				
	Minimum	Desired	Maximum	OK
Word Spacing:	80%	100%	133%	Cancel
Letter Spacing:	0%	0%	0%	
Glyph Scaling:	100%	100%	100%	☑ Preview
Auto Leading:	120%			

You can set desired word, letter, and glyph spacing using non-justified text; minimum and maximum only apply to justified text.

FONT: The first entry area of the Character palette is for the font or typeface name. Generally, you look for the name of the typeface, such as Times or Garamond (we used ITC Usherwood here), and then select the weight of the face that you wish to use, such as light, book, bold, or italic.

WEIGHT: The second entry area is for the weight of the face, which may be book, bold, light, etc. or may be prefaced by a number that describes the weight.

SIZE: The size at which text appears depends not only on the size you choose in the Type tool Options bar, but also on the resolution and dimensions of the image you set using the Image/Image Size command. Luckily, if you resize your image, Photoshop sizes the type accordingly. To resize the type with a keyboard shortcut, use Command-Shift-> to increase type by two points or pixels, and Command-Shift-< to decrease size by two points or pixels.

KERNING: Photoshop allows you to kern letter pairs; that is, change the amount of space between any two characters. A positive number gives you more space between the letters; a negative number tightens the space. Click between a pair of letters you want to kern, then either type a number in the input area or use the pop-up. Use Option-right arrow or Option-left arrow to kern via the keyboard.

LEADING: Leading is the amount of vertical spacing between the baselines of the lines of text. A positive number gives you more space between the lines, and a negative number, less space. If you set type in all capitals, a negative number usually gives better spacing between the lines. Option-up arrow or Option-down arrow changes the leading by two points or pixels.

TRACKING: Tracking refers to the horizontal letter spacing of the text. Whereas kerning is the space between any two characters, tracking is the space between more than two characters. As in kerning, a positive number gives you more space between the letters, spreading them out, and a negative number draws the letters tighter together. Use the same keyboard shortcuts as kerning when you have whole words or paragraphs highlighted.

SCALING: You can scale some or all of the letters vertically, horizontally, or both by highlighting them and inputting values in the two areas at the top of the third section of the Character palette. Values are written as a percentage of the normal scale of the letters.

BASELINE SHIFT: Some or all of the letters may be shifted up or down from the normal baseline by inputting a value in this area. A positive number shifts the letter up; negative numbers shift the letter down. Use Shift-Option plus the up or down arrows to shift letters via the keyboard.

COLOR: You can click the Color square to change the color of the type at any time. You change the color of all the text when you click the Color square with a type layer active but no text selected. Use the Type tool and select letters to change attributes individually.

CHARACTER STYLING: You can find styles for faux bold, faux italics, all caps, small caps, superscript, subscript, underline, and strikethrough on the bottom of the Character palette. In addition, if you are using Open Type fonts you have other options available to you via the palette pop-up.

ALIGNMENT: The first three icons at the top of the Paragraph palette (they appear on the Type tool Options bar also) are for alignment, either flush left, centered, or flush right.

JUSTIFICATION: The last four icons on the top of the Paragraph palette are for justifying paragraphs. All four justify the paragraph, only the last line is treated differently. You can align the last line left, centered, right, or (the icon that's set apart on the far right) force justification. The specifications for how to justify the paragraph are set using Justify from the Paragraph palette pop-up menu.

INDENTS: The second section of the Paragraph palette controls indents. You can make left, right, and first line indents, which means you can set hanging indents. You also can set hanging punctuation from the Paragraph palette pop-up menu.

SPACE BEFORE/AFTER: The third section of the Paragraph palette allows you to control the amount of space before and after your paragraph.

HYPHENATION: If you want Photoshop to automatically hyphenate a paragraph for you, click the Hyphenate button. Hyphenation is set according to the settings you use in the Hyphenation dialog box accessed via the Paragraph palette pop-up menu.

COMPOSITION: Photoshop is able to use both single-line and multi-line methods of composition. Multi-line is the default and usually gives better line breaks over the paragraph. Use single-line if you want more manual control over the breaks.

WARP TEXT: Photoshop has a fairly robust engine for generating warped type. Click the button on the right of the Options bar to enter this area. We talk more about this in Chapter 34: "Heartsinger CD Cover."

TEXT ON A PATH: Photoshop can now set type on a path. You can draw a path with the Pen tool or use a custom shape to create a path. If the path is open, you are only allowed to put type on the path. If, however, your path is a closed shape, you can put type either on the outside of the path or inside the path. Look at the illustrations here to see the different cursors that appear in each instance.

CHECK SPELLING/FIND AND REPLACE TEXT: Photoshop has the additional capacities to spell check and replace text. Both of these options are found under the Edit menu.

THE PEN/FREEFORM PEN TOOLS

KEYBOARD SHORTCUT: Type the letter P. Type Shift-P to toggle between the pens.

Photoshop 6 added new functionality to the Pen tool. In earlier versions of the application, the Pen tool was used primarily for creating paths that could later be used as selections, or for painting pixels in a layer. It's still great for that. But now, you can also use the Pen tool to create vector shapes more like how you use the tool in Illustrator. Use it in conjunction with the Shapes tool, Shapes palette, and fill layers to create device-independent vector graphics. Before you start to draw with the Pen, check the Options bar icons to determine whether you will be drawing a vector shape that will fill with the current foreground color and be on its own layer, or a path, which is not associated with a particular layer.

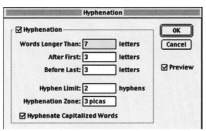

If you want to hyphenate paragraph text, Photoshop gives you control over how to do it, as you would have in a dedicated word processor.

Photoshop uses multi-line composition by default to give paragraph text even color with fewer hyphens. If you want more manual control over the line breaks, select the Adobe Single-line Composer.

If your path is open or you want text on the outside of a shape, this is the cursor you want to see before you click to start typing.

If your path is closed and you want text on the inside of a shape, this is the cursor you want to see before you click to start typing.

Photoshop offers you a fairly sophisticated spell checker.

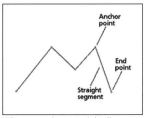

When you draw straight line segments, the anchor points and endpoints have no direction handles.

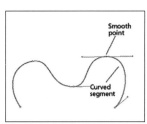

Each curved segment should have two direction points and handles associated with the curve, one at the beginning and one at the end.

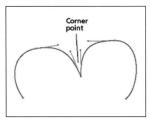

A corner point has two handles that work independently of one another.

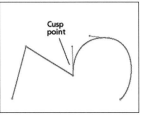

A cusp point that connects a straight line segment to a curve segment has one handle that helps define the curve.

AUTOMATIC FILL: If you have a path active in the Paths palette when you create a solid color fill layer, the color will automatically fill the paths. If you get unexpected results, check the combine status of each subpath of the active path.

When you begin to use the Pen tool to create a new path, be sure you show the Paths palette. This is where you will name your path, fill or stroke your path, turn the path into a selection, or turn a selection into a path. You can also duplicate a path or delete a path. These options are available as icons on the bottom of the palette and from the pop-up menu. In the Layer menu you can designate a path as a vector mask to be included with the file when it is placed in your page layout program (more on this later).

If you've never used the Pen tool, either in Photoshop or a drawing program, you might find it a bit confusing at first. Oh, alright, you might find it absolutely one of the most frustrating experiences of your digital life. But, we promise if you just keep at it, one day you'll have that AHA! experience that lets you know your hand understands something that your brain cannot and somehow you're just able to draw a path. You'll get your feet wet using the Pen tool in Chapter 28: "Rain in Costa Rica," and Chapter 30: "The PowerBook Ad." Till then, let's talk about the basics.

The Pen tool works by placing points and connecting those points with line segments. A segment can be either straight or curved. Each segment has two points associated with it, a beginning point and an end point. (Are you with us so far?) Now, the points that control the segments can have handles. Notice that we say "can." A corner point (that is, a point that connects two straight line segments) has no handles. A smooth point connecting segments in a continuous curve has two handles that are dependent on each other. If you adjust the direction of one of the handles, you affect the other handle in an equal and opposite manner. Simple enough so far. However, a corner point can also join two curve segments that are noncontinuous and abut sharply, as in the two curves forming the top of this lowercase m. In that case, the anchor point would have two handles that work independently of each other. And finally, a straight line segment that joins a curve segment does so by an anchor point that has only one handle, which controls the direction and height of the curve. This type of point is sometimes referred to as a cusp.

To draw straight line segments with the Pen, click where you want to place anchor points. To draw a curved segment, click and drag. To make a corner point with handles that work independently, click and drag out a handle, but after you drag, hold down the Option key to access the Convert tool. Use the tool to drag the handle in a different direction. The handle that controls the previous segment will not change, but when you place a new anchor point, you'll have a corner rather than a smooth curve.

There are actually three types of pens you can use. The Pen tool works like Illustrator's Pen tool and basically the same as it has for many years. In recent versions of Photoshop there's also a Freeform Pen, which allows you to draw freehand style and place points as you go, and the Magnetic Pen (accessed from the Freeform pen), which judges the contrast between two edges to help you draw a path for use as a selection.

AUTO ADD/DELETE: All three pens allow you to automatically add or delete points on a previously drawn path simply by placing the tool over the path. If you are over a segment where no points exist, the Add Anchor Point tool appears. If you are over a point, the Delete Anchor Point

The Pen tool Options bar.

Chapter 4: The Tools Palette

tool appears. This option is on by default, and I find it easier to use when turned on. If you grew up on a previous version of the tool and find it annoying, turn it off.

RUBBER BAND: The Rubber Band option, which you access from the pop-up beside the custom shapes icon on the Options bar, attempts to give you a preview of how the path will look before you place your anchor points. Barry uses it all the time. I think it's bogus. Your choice here.

CURVE FIT: When using the Freeform pen, Curve Fit controls how closely to your drawn path points will be placed. You can input a value between .5 and 10 pixels. The higher the value, the fewer points will be placed, resulting in smoother curves. However, if the number is too high you may find that the resulting path does not reflect the shape you drew. The default is 2 pixels, but you may find that 1 pixel works better if you draw with a very steady hand.

MAGNETIC SETTINGS: The Width is the width of the brush that covers the edge to be defined. It should be large enough to overlap the edge on both sides. The Contrast is how much contrast between values Photoshop should look for when deciding where the edge is. The Frequency is how often anchor points should be placed. If you want the brush to change size based on how hard you press, you can turn on the Stylus Pressure option (if you have a pressure-sensitive tablet). You can use the brush size shortcut keys (left and right brackets) to change the size of the brush also, and I find this easier than using Stylus Pressure.

The beauty of the Pen tool is that once you make a path, it is infinitely editable. You can add points or delete points, change the height or direction of curves, and even turn a curve into a straight line segment or vice versa. It may seem hard to believe if you're a Pen tool novice, but we know many Photoshoppers who rarely use any of the other selection tools. When you do learn to use the Pen, you'll have an "in" to the major drawing programs, and you'll understand why page layout programs are now including tools that draw Bezier curves.

THE SHAPE TOOL

KEYBOARD SHORTCUT: Type the letter U. Type Shift-U to cycle through the tools.

We'll go over the Shape tool in detail in Chapter 32: "Vector Masks, Shape Layers, and Layer Styles." But here's the short version. You can use shapes three different ways. You can make a shape layer, a work path, or a filled region on an existing layer. These three options are the first three icons on the Tool Options bar. The first two shapes will be vector paths that can be edited and are device independent. The third is just like making a selection and filling it; you change the pixels and it cannot be undone later except via the History palette.

The next set of icons are where you choose the tool or shape you want. The first two icons are the Pen tool and Freeform Pen tool, then rectangles, rounded corner rectangles, elipsis, polygons, lines, and custom shapes. Click the shape you want, and then click the pop-up menu to access the settings for that particular shape. There are especially neat settings for the Polygon and the Line shapes. The last icon in the group is the gateway to the Custom Shapes palette. Choose from the default shapes, load a larger Custom Shapes palette from the Presets folder, or create shapes yourself and save them to a new palette. If you have some cool shapes already built in Illustrator, paste them as paths into Photoshop, and then use Edit/Define Custom

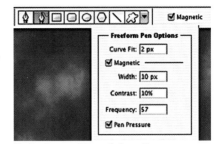
The Freeform and Magnetic Pen settings.

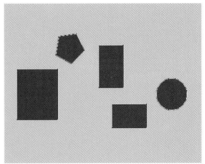
You can have multiple shapes on a single shape layer but all must be the same color.

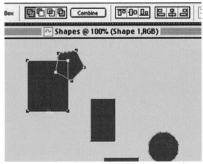
You can combine shapes using the shape area icons and the Combine button.

I've set the Options bar to draw a new shape layer using a five sided polygon in the shape of a star.

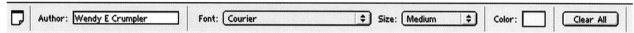

Shape to save them to the Shapes palette. Save the palette with a new name if you want to make sure you keep all your shapes.

As you draw shapes, you need to be aware of the shape interaction icons on the Options bar. These icons are just like the Selection interaction icons. They determine whether the next shape you draw will be a new shape (in this case a new shape layer), added to the existing shapes, subtracted from the shapes, intersected with the shapes, or excluded from the shapes. Once you have several shapes on a layer you can select two or more with the Path Selection arrow to align or combine them.

These are the options for the Notes tool. The Audio Annotation tool has only Author, Color, and Clear as options.

You can move the Note icon away from the actual note.

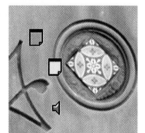

Choose different colors to quickly recognize notes from different authors.

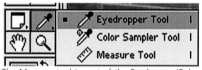

The Measure tool is part of the Eyedropper/Color Sampler tool.

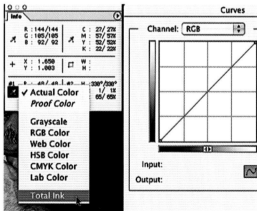

You can set up to four Color Samplers and change the read-out at any time. Here, we've changed Sampler #1 to give us the Total Ink percentage while in the middle of a Curves adjustment.

OTHER USEFUL TOOLS

NOTES/AUDIO ANNOTATION TOOL

KEYBOARD SHORTCUT: Type the letter N. Type Shift-N to toggle between the tools.

You can use either written or audio notes to annotate your files, but you must have either an attached or built-in microphone to record audio notes.

To attach a written note, choose the Note tool and click where you want the note to appear. You can also click and drag to create a notes box in which to input your message. Click in the input window to type your note. While you are there you can highlight the text and change its size and typeface. The color indicator on the Tool Options bar is the color of the note and the author's name. This can be changed from note to note—a quick way to identify the author. You can resize the input window and move the Window and Note icons independently of each other.

When you use the Audio Annotation tool, your options are limited to changing the author or the color. To play the annotation, double-click the icon.

To delete notes of both types, click once on the icon and hit the Delete key, or click Clear All to get rid of all annotations at once.

EYEDROPPER/COLOR SAMPLER/MEASURE TOOL

KEYBOARD SHORTCUT: Type the letter I. Type Shift-I to cycle through the tools.

You use the Eyedropper tool to choose the foreground and background color within an image onscreen. You can click the Eyedropper tool to use it and then click the color that you want to make the foreground color, or Option-click in the image to get the background color. You access the Eyedropper tool by holding down the Option key when using any of the painting tools and then clicking where you want to pick up a new foreground color. You can choose to have the tool sample only one pixel to choose the color, or get an average color of 3x3 or 5x5 pixels.

The Color Sampler tool allows you to place eyedropper-type samplers in up to four locations in your file. During manipulation of your image, you can watch how your changes are affecting the areas where you placed samplers. Samplers can be moved after they've been placed

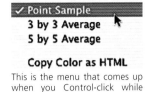

and can be hidden completely by using the Info palette pop-up. You can change the read-out values from RGB to CMYK, Grayscale, HSB, Lab, Actual Color, or Total Ink percentages, even in the middle of making adjustments to the file, by click-ing the specific sampler pop-up triangle. You can delete a sampler from the screen by dragging it off the image. To see how the Color Sampler tool can be used, read Chapter 22: "Color Matching Images."

The Measure tool measurements can now be viewed in the Tool Options bar as well as in the Info palette. If you create a line for measuring, it stays in place even when you switch tools and come back to it. The measurement does not stay after closing a file. When you draw a new measure line, the old one goes away. You can also click the Clear button to get rid of a line.

Copy Color as HTML
This is the menu that comes up when you Control-click while using the Eyedropper tool.

This is the menu that comes up when you Control-click with the Color Sampler tool on a Color Sampler placed in your image.

Here are the Hand tool options. The last three items appear if you Control-click with the Hand tool.

HAND TOOL

KEYBOARD SHORTCUT: Type the letter H.

Use the Hand tool to scroll the image. Scrolling doesn't change your document; instead, it allows you to look at a different part of it. You can access the Hand tool more efficiently by using the spacebar on the keyboard along with a mouse click, which can be done any time. If you double-click the Hand tool in the Tools palette, the image resizes to the largest size that fits completely within the current screen and palette display.

ZOOM TOOL

KEYBOARD SHORTCUT: Type the letter Z.

Use the Zoom tool to magnify the image and, with the Option key, to shrink the image. The location where you click is centered within the bigger or smaller image. Using this tool is like moving a photograph you are holding in your hand either closer to your face or farther away. The actual size of the photograph doesn't change, only how closely you are looking at it. It is best to access the Zoom tool using Command-spacebar-click to zoom in closer, or Option-spacebar-click to zoom out farther. You can use these command keys any time, even when a dialog box, like Levels, is up. If you double-click the Zoom tool within the Tools palette, the image zooms in or out to the 100% size. At 100%, the image may be bigger than the screen, but you see every pixel of the part of the image you are viewing. Use this for detailed work. The Resize Windows to Fit option resizes your normal window to surround your zoomed size, if possible. I leave it off because I don't like my windows automatically resizing.

5 PICKING AND USING COLOR

*A look at RGB, CMYK, HSB, and Lab color spaces,
what they are, when to use each, and how to access them
from Photoshop; the Photoshop Color Picker and the
Picker, Swatches, and Scratch palettes explained in detail.*

There are different color spaces available in Photoshop that you can use for different purposes at different times. Instead of just working in one color space, like RGB or CMYK, it is a good idea to learn the advantages and disadvantages of the different color spaces. Photoshop has various tools for picking and saving colors. We summarize these color space issues in this chapter, mostly for how they relate to picking and choosing color. For more information on setting up and using the RGB, CMYK, and Lab color spaces in Photoshop CS, see Chapter 14: "Color Spaces, Device Characterization, and Color Management."

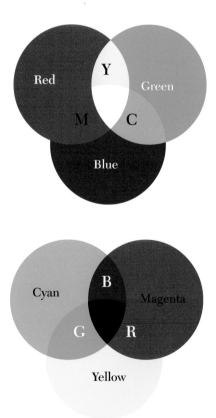

THE RGB COLOR SPACE

For overall color correction and ease of work, using the red, green, blue (RGB) color space offers many advantages. I recommend keeping your final master files in RGB format. Red, green, and blue are the additive colors of light that occur in nature. White light consists of wavelengths from the red, green, and blue spectrums. All scanners, even high-end drum scanners, actually have sensors that originally capture the data in RGB format. You can use RGB for final output to computers, multimedia and TV monitors, color transparency writers, digital video, Web sites, and some digital printers because these all use RGB as their native color space. Plus, RGB files are smaller than CMYK files because they have only three components of color instead of four.

THE CMYK COLOR SPACE

Cyan, magenta, and yellow are the complementary colors to red, green, and blue. Red and cyan are opposites, so if you take away all the red from white light, cyan is what you have left. Cyan is formed by mixing green and blue light. Green and magenta, as well as blue and yellow, work similarly; that is, they are complementary colors. When you print on a printing press, the colors of ink used are cyan, magenta, and yellow. These are called subtractive colors because when you view something that is printed, you actually see the light that is reflected back. When white light, which contains all the colors, hits a surface painted cyan, you see cyan because the cyan paint subtracts the red from the white light, and only green and blue reflect back for you to see. To print red using CMY inks, you use magenta and yellow inks. Magenta subtracts the green light and yellow subtracts the blue light, so what reflects back to your eyes is red light. The cyan, magenta, and yellow dyes that make up printing inks are not pure, so when you print all three of them at the same time, instead of reflecting no light and giving you black, you get a muddy gray color. Because of this problem, the printing trade adds black ink (the K in CMYK) to the four-color process so the dark areas are as dark as possible.

THE AMOUNT OF BLACK

The amount of black ink, and the way it is used in the printing process, depends on the type of paper and press that you use. Newspaper presses typically use a lot of black ink and as little color ink as possible because black ink is cheaper. High-quality advertising color for magazines and other coated stock is printed with much more colored ink and less black. A skilled printer can create the same image in CMYK using a lot of black ink or very little black ink. You can combine the colored and black inks many different ways to get the final result.

CONVERTING RGB TO CMYK

Because of these different choices, converting from RGB to CMYK can be a complicated process. After an image is converted to CMYK, whether by a high-end scanner or by you in Photoshop, managing the relationship between the CMY colors and the black ink can be tricky. That's just one of the reasons you're better off doing your overall color corrections in RGB, so that you are taking a correct RGB file and then converting it to CMYK. You then end up with a CMYK file that has the black in the right place in relationship with the final, or close to final, CMY colors. The main reason to use the CMYK color space is that your final output will be on a printing press or a digital printer that uses CMYK inks or dyes. We discuss color correction in both RGB and CMYK as we present the examples in this book. Because you want to customize the creation of your CMYK file to the type of printing you are doing, and because colors can get lost when you convert to CMYK, you should keep your master file in RGB format, for the highest quality and versatility across all media.

THE HUE, SATURATION, AND LIGHTNESS COLOR SPACE

Another color space used in Photoshop is Hue, Saturation, and Lightness (HSL). You can no longer use the Mode menu to convert an image to HSL mode like you could in some older versions of Photoshop, but the many color tools allow you to think about and massage color using the HSL color space. Instead of dividing a color into components of red, green, and blue, or cyan, magenta, and yellow, HSL divides a color into its hue, its saturation, and its lightness. The hue is the actual color and can include all the colors of the rainbow. A particular red hue differs from a purple, yellow, orange, or even a different red hue. The saturation is the intensity of that particular hue. Highly saturated colors are quite intense and vivid, so much so that they almost look fluorescent. Colors of low saturation are dull and subtle. The lightness of a part of an image determines how light or dark that part is in overall

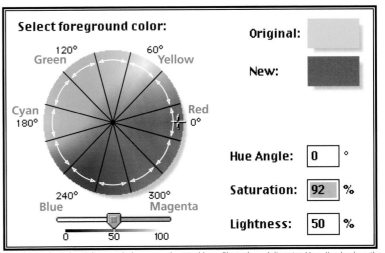

The old Apple Color Picker can help you understand how Photoshop delineates Hue. I've broken the color wheel into 30° segments with black lines, and typed the names (in green) for the six true color segments. Photoshop considers Red hues to be the area from 345° to 15°, with 0° being pure red. Cyan hues (red's compliment) range from 165° to 195°, with 180° being true cyan. The in-between ranges (red/yellow, yellow/green, green/cyan, and so forth) are considered the falloff ranges when you adjust the hue in Photoshop.

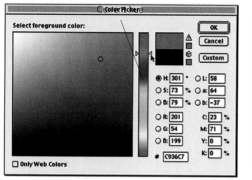

The Color Picker in Hue mode, which is the default. Sliding the color slider (shown with the arrow cursor above) up and down changes the hue in Hue mode. For a particular hue, purple here, click and drag the circle in the color box to the left to pick a particular color. As you move the cursor around in the color box with the mouse button down, left to right movement changes the saturation and up and down movement changes the brightness. You will see the values for saturation and brightness change in the number boxes to the right. You also see the corresponding RGB and CMYK values for each color. Hue is frozen by the color slider position.

Current saturation

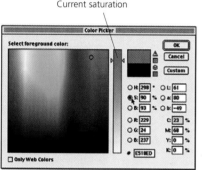

Put the Color Picker in Saturation mode by clicking on the S radio button. Now sliding the color slider up and down changes the saturation. Left to right movement of the cursor circle changes the hue and up and down movement changes the brightness.

Current brightness

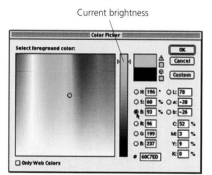

Put the Color Picker in Brightness mode by clicking on the B radio button. Now sliding the color slider up and down changes the brightness. Left to right movement of the cursor circle changes the hue and up and down movement changes the saturation. Brightness here is similar to Lightness, mentioned earlier in this chapter.

Click here to get the Color Picker and change the current foreground color.

density. Lightness is the value in the image that gives it detail. Imagine taking a black-and-white image and then colorizing it. The black-and-white image originally had different tonal values of gray. The details show up based on the lightness or darkness of the black-and-white image. Removing the lightness value would be similar to taking this black-and-white detail part out of a color image. If you increase the lightness, the image starts to flatten and show less depth. If you increase the lightness all the way, the image loses all its detail and becomes white. If you decrease the lightness, the image may appear to have more depth, and if you decrease it all the way, the image becomes black. For working with an image using the HSL, you use Image/Adjust/Hue/Saturation or Image/Adjust/Replace Color. The different Color Pickers also allow you to work in the HSL color model.

THE LAB COLOR SPACE

The Lab color space is a device-independent color space that has as its color gamut the colors that the human eye can see. The Lab color space is used internally by Photoshop to convert between RGB and CMYK and can be used for device-independent output to Level 2 and Level 3 PostScript devices. The Lab color space is quite useful for some production tasks. For example, sharpening only the Lightness channel sharpens the image without "popping" the colors. You can work in Photoshop using Lab color, and we have a Lab color example, Chapter 27: "Bryce Stone Woman," in this version of *Photoshop Artistry*.

USING THE COLOR PICKER

The main tool for picking colors in Photoshop is the Photoshop Color Picker. You access the Color Picker by clicking on the foreground or background color swatch at the bottom of the Tools palette or on the Color palette. You can use this picker in Hue, Saturation, or Brightness mode; Red, Green, or Blue mode; or use Lab color to select using Lightness, the "a" channel, or the "b" channel.

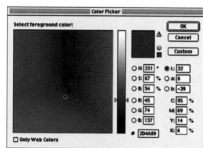

The Color Picker in Lightness mode. The Lightness channel controls the brightness and contrast of the image. Move the cursor circle left to right to change values in the "a" channel, which controls the red to green values. Move the cursor up and down to change values in the "b" channel, or yellow to blue values.

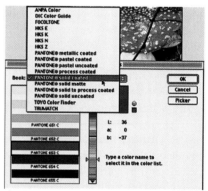

The Custom Colors Picker with the different color systems that it makes available in the pop-up menu. Drag the slider or click on the up/down arrows to locate a color, click on a color to choose it, or type in the number associated with a particular color to choose that one. Choosing OK picks that color, and clicking on Picker returns you to the Color Picker where you can see and pick the RGB and CMYK equivalent to that color.

Chapter 5: Picking and Using Color

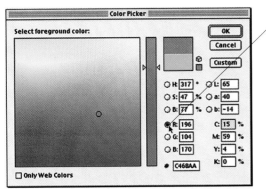

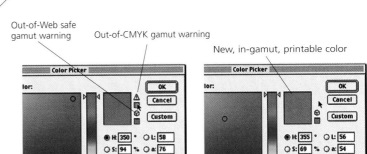

Red mode

Out-of-Web safe
gamut warning

Out-of-CMYK gamut warning

New, in-gamut, printable color

Put the Color Picker in Red mode by clicking on the R radio button. Now sliding the color slider up and down changes the amount of red in your color. For particular blue and green values, click and drag the circle in the color box to the left. Left-to-right movement changes the amount of blue and up-and-down movement changes the amount of green. You will see the values for blue and green change in the number boxes to the right. Red is frozen by the color slider position. The values for cyan, magenta, yellow, and black also change as you move around in the color box. This is a great way to see how the RGB and CMYK components change for different colors. If you are not sure how to adjust a certain color, go into the Color Picker and visually see what will happen to it as you add or subtract different component colors from it.

The exclamation sign shows you that the current color may be out-of-gamut (not printable in CMYK). The small swatch immediately below shows you the closest printable color. Click on the triangle sign or small swatch below it to change the chosen color to the closest in-gamut color (shown at right). See Chapter 20: "Correcting a Problem Image," for a discussion of out-of-gamut colors. The cube icon indicates that the chosen color is not a Web-safe color. Clicking the cube, or the swatch below it, will take you to the nearest color that is Web safe.

See the diagrams here for an explanation of each mode. In addition, you can set a specific color by typing in its Lab, RGB, HSB, or CMYK values.

The Custom button brings up the Custom Colors Picker for choosing PANTONE, Trumatch, and other standard colors. You can use these as separate color channels within Photoshop's Multichannel mode, choose one or more colors for Duotone mode, set spot color channels in CMYK or RGB mode, or the color automatically converts to RGB or CMYK for painting, depending on the active color space.

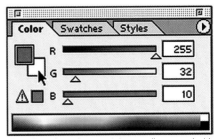

The Color palette shown as it is normally grouped with the Swatches and Styles palettes. The foreground and background colors are shown to the left. You know that the foreground color is currently active because of the double line around it. If you move the sliders, you adjust the foreground color. The arrow cursor is over the background color. If you click on the background color, it becomes the active color, and moving the sliders modifies it. If you click on either color square, you get the Color Picker. This palette also shows you the CMYK Gamut Warning icon.

USING THE COLOR PALETTES

Besides the Color Picker that you access from the Tools palette, you can also access the Color palette and the Swatches palette from the Window menu. Normally these are grouped together on the desktop, but you can separate them by clicking on their name tabs and dragging each of them to some other location on the desktop. Because the big Color Picker is a modal dialog box that you cannot access on-the-fly when using the painting tools, the Color and Swatches palettes come in very handy for getting the colors you need quickly.

THE COLOR PALETTE

In the Color palette, you can move the RGB, CMYK, HSB, or other color sliders to create a color that you like. You pick this color for the foreground or background depending on which of the swatches is chosen in the Color palette. You change the display mode in the Color palette using its pop-up option menu. You can also pick colors from the color bar along the bottom of the palette. This color bar offers different display modes to choose from using the Color palette's options. The Color palette is also useful to have around while you're in Levels, Curves, and the other color-correction tools. It remembers the colors at the last location where you clicked the Eyedropper in an image, and it shows you how the

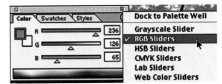

From the pop-out palette menu (click on the triangle in the upper right), you can set the display of the Color palette to Grayscale, RGB, HSB, CMYK, Lab, or Web color. You can also send the palette to the well from here.

The pop-out palette menu also brings up options for how to display the color bar at the bottom of the Color palette. You can choose the foreground color by clicking on a color in the color bar; Option-click for the background color; or choose black or white from the two swatches at the right side of the bar.

69

The pop-out menu of the Swatches palette contains swatch sets for PANTONE, Trumatch, and other standard color systems. Here we see the PANTONE colors loaded into the Swatches palette. When viewed as small swatch thumbnails, if you move the Eyedropper over a particular color, a small label appears, telling you which PANTONE you are about to choose.

The palette pop-out menu also gives you the option to view the swatches in a named list.

You can load and save different sets of swatches to files. If you have certain colors that you use for a particular client, you may want to save these in a file under that client's name. You can append swatches, which adds the swatches stored in a file to the ones you already have in the palette. Reset Swatches just goes back to the default set of swatches.

color adjustments you are making change that location. See Chapter 22: "Color Matching Images," for more details.

THE SWATCHES PALETTE

The Swatches palette is where you store frequently used colors. The palette gives you access to a library of swatch sets, as well as allowing you to save, and then later load, your favorite set of custom swatches. Clicking on a color swatch using the palette's Eyedropper tool will give you a new foreground color. Command-clicking picks a new color for the background. You automatically get the Eyedropper when the cursor moves over the swatches area. If you've chosen a color from your image, or mixed a color with the Color palette, you can save the current foreground color in the Swatches palette; simply position your cursor over the empty gray area at the end of the swatches. Your cursor becomes a paintbucket and, when you click, you are prompted to name your color, and the new swatch is added at the end of the existing swatches. If you want to skip naming the color, you can hold down the Option key as you create the swatch. Pressing the Option key while over an existing swatch gives you scissors which remove the swatch when you click.

Using the pop-up options menu, you can dock the palette in the Palette Well, access the Swatches Preset Manager, change your view of the palette, save a set, or load custom swatch sets, including sets for custom ink colors, such as PANTONE. Remember, however, if you paint with a custom color, it is converted to the current color mode (RGB, CMYK, etc.) and does not separate as a custom color.

If you use the Load Swatches command from the palette pop-up, colors will be added to your palette. You can use Replace Swatches to load only the new set. If you choose an existing color set from the pop-up, you are asked whether you want to append or replace the existing swatch set. When you choose to replace the set, Photoshop asks you if you want to save changes to the current set whenever you've added or deleted swatches from an existing set. Click Save to name your custom set. You can save the set to any folder, but if you'd like to have the set show up in the pop-up list, save it to the Presets/Color Swatch folder inside the Photoshop folder.

Finally, if you are working on files with different color profiles attached, you may see differences in the same Color palette from file to file. Although the color itself does not change, different devices may not be able to render that color. The Swatches palette updates to give you a preview of how certain colors will change depending on how they are used. This helps ensure that the color you choose will render as intended.

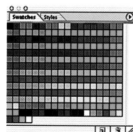

This is the Windows Swatches palette viewed in Adobe RGB, a very large gamut color space.

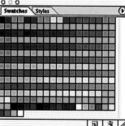

This is the same palette viewed in ColorMatch RGB, a slightly smaller color space. You may notice some colors shifting a bit.

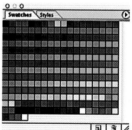

Once again, the Windows Swatches palette, but this time we're looking at a file with a custom profile for the Epson 1270 printer and Matte Heavyweight paper. The same colors look considerably different.

6 SELECTIONS, PATHS, MASKS, AND CHANNELS

Terms and concepts for working with selections, paths, masks, and channels. Knowing the differences between each and also between these and layers.

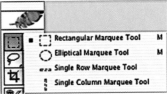

The Rectangular and Elliptical Marquees are the simplest selection tools. Click and drag in the Tools palette on the arrow in the bottom corner of the Rectangular Marquee, or press Shift-M, to change between the Elliptical and Rectangular marquee.

Before you can understand all the possibilities of how selections, paths, masks, and channels are used in Photoshop, you need to know the basic concepts. What exactly is a selection and how do you make a selection using the Photoshop tools? What is a mask channel, how does a selection become a mask channel, and how do you edit a mask channel using different tools to allow you to isolate the necessary parts of an image to achieve a particular effect? This includes understanding what a selection feather or a mask blur is and how these affect the edges of blended selections. We will discuss the concept of opacity, which affects image blending, and show you how to effectively use the Channels palette. We will talk a bit about using paths, which are really just another form of selections. Another basic concept you need to comprehend is that a selection or a mask channel can also instantly become a layer mask for either a regular layer, a fill layer, or an adjustment layer. We will discuss *how* selections become layer masks in the next chapter.

The Magic Wand tool.

MAKING SELECTIONS

Let's start by talking about the concept of a *selection*—an isolated part of an image that needs special attention. You may want to make this part of the image lighter or darker, change its color altogether, sharpen it, or filter it. You might also select something in an image that you wanted to copy and paste into a different image.

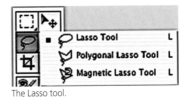

The Lasso tool.

THE SELECTION TOOLS

There are various tools for making selections. The simplest are the Rectangular and Elliptical Marquees, which allow you to draw a box or an ellipse around something by clicking at one side of the area you want to isolate and then dragging to the other side. This will create a box or oval-shaped selection that is denoted by dotted lines around the edge. The next level of selection complexity is the Lasso tool, which allows you to draw a shape around objects to select them. Using the Lasso in Photoshop, you can draw either freehand or straight line segments, or combinations of both. The Magnetic Lasso is a variant of this tool that snaps the selection marquee to an area based on contrast. Selections based on color rather than shape can be made with the Magic Wand, which allows you to click a certain color in an image and automatically select pixels based on that color.

A totally different way to make selections is to use the Pen tool. The Pen tool creates selections, called paths, which are mathematical descriptions of points joined by straight and curved line segments. With the Pen tool, you can create the most

The Magnetic Lasso tool automatically traces around the edge of an object, depending on the way you set up its parameters.

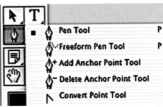

The Freeform Pen tool allows you to make Pen selections in a similar way to using the Lasso tool.

exact paths along subtly curved surfaces. These paths can be converted back to normal selections when you are ready to use them to modify your image or saved as vector masks for specific layers. The Freeform Pen tool is a variant of the Pen that lets you draw a path more naturally and, by clicking a checkbox in the Options bar, you can make the tool magnetic, so the path "sticks" to the edge of an object.

There are ways to increase the size of a selection and also to select all objects of similar color or brightness within the image. In this chapter, we learn about the concept of a selection and how selections fit in with the rest of Photoshop. To learn about actually using the selection tools, go to Chapter 4: "The Tools Palette," and Chapter 18: "The Colony Composite," and for the Pen tool and paths, also look at Chapter 28: "Rain in Costa Rica," and Chapter 30: "The PowerBook Ad."

Here is the Paris Dog where we have used the Lasso to select just the dog.

The selection to the left after choosing Select/Inverse.

WORKING WITH AND INVERSING SELECTIONS

Here you see the Paris Dog image. We have selected the dog using the Lasso tool. If you'd like you can open the Paris Dog image from the folder for this selection's chapter on the *Photoshop CS Artistry* CD. When the dog is selected, anything we do (painting, changing color, and so on) can happen only within the boundaries of the selected area. That is one purpose of a selection, to isolate your work to a particular object or area within the image. If you compare working on an image in Photoshop to painting a mural on a wall, selecting just the dog would be equivalent to putting masking tape everywhere else on the wall, allowing us to paint only on top of the dog. If we choose Select/Inverse, then everything except the dog becomes the selection. Now we have selected the background and not the dog. So, anytime you have a selection of an object, you also have, via Select/Inverse, a selection of everything except the object. Returning to the wall analogy, using Select/Inverse would be like removing the masking tape from the background and putting tape over the area of the dog.

You can use the selection modifier icons at the left of the Options bar to always make a new selection, add, subtract, or intersect with the current Selection.

CHANGING A SELECTION

Changing a selection is a lot easier than moving masking tape. You can add to any selection made using the Marquees, Lasso, or Magic Wand selection tools by using any of these tools with the Shift key pressed down when you create the new selection. You can subtract from a selection by pressing down the Option key when you define the area you want to subtract using these same tools. You can also use the selection modifier icons at the left of the Options bar to always make a new selection, add, subtract, or intersect with the current selection.

Dog selection with no feather filled with green.

Dog selection with a 20-pixel feather filled with green.

SETTING THE FEATHER VALUE

Using most of the selection tools in their default mode is similar to placing masking tape along the edge of the selection, in that there is a defined sharp edge to the selection. Such a selection is said to have a feather value of 0. The selection feather is something that determines how quickly the transition goes from being in the selection to not being in the selection. With 0 feather, the transition is instantaneous. You can change the feather of a selection using the Select/Feather command. If you change the feather of the selection to 20, the transition from being fully selected to being fully unselected would happen over the distance of 40 pixels (actually, at least 20 pixels on either side of the zero feather selection line). If you used this type of feathered masking tape to paint the selection of the dog green, the feather would cause the two colors to fade together slowly over the distance of 40 pixels.

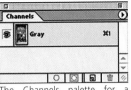

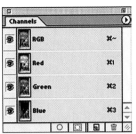

The Channels palette for a grayscale image with the single channel, Gray, which is the image.

The Channels palette for an RGB image. Each of the red, green, and blue channels is a grayscale image. You only see color when you view the RGB channel by choosing Command-~ or clicking the name RGB.

Learn These Shortcut Icons and When to Use Them!

Load selection from channel or path.

Save selection as channel.

New or copied channel, layer, action, or path.

Throw away channel, layer, path, or action.

Double-clicking the name of a mask channel in the Channels palette will allow you to change its name. Double-clicking to the right of the name or on the thumbnail will bring up the Channel options.

PIXELS AND CHANNELS

A pixel is the basic unit of information within a digital image. Continuous tone digital images (scanned photographs of real objects) are a two-dimensional array of pixels. If the image were 2,000 pixels wide by 1,600 pixels high and we were printing it at 200 pixels per inch, then the image would print at 10 inches wide by 8 inches high (2000/200 = 10; 1600/200 = 8).

If we are working with a black-and-white image, each of these pixels contains one byte of information, which allows it to have 256 possible gray values. A black-and-white image has one channel in which each pixel is one byte in size. A channel is just a term referring to a two-dimensional array of bytes. If we are working with an RGB color image, it has three channels (one for each of red, green, and blue). A CMYK image has four channels. You can see these channels by choosing Window/Channels. In an RGB file, Channel #1 is red, Channel #2 is green, and Channel #3 is blue. There is also an imaginary Channel #~, which allows you to see the red, green, and blue channels at the same time. (This is how you see color.) The RGB channel, Channel #~, is an imaginary channel because it is just a composite view of the three color channels and it doesn't take up any additional space beyond that which the red, green, and blue channels take up.

Image with dog selected.

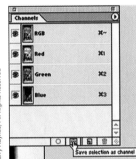

Saving this selection using the Save Selection icon.

SAVING SELECTIONS AS MASK CHANNELS

When you make a selection, you are making what is called a *mask*—the selection masks out the part of the image that you don't select. You can save a selection to a mask channel, which allows you to use it again later or to do further selection editing on the mask with the painting tools. This is especially useful for a complicated selection that you don't want to have to remake later. To do this, choose Select/Save Selection, or just click the Save Selection icon at the bottom of the Channels palette. The new mask channel you would create by doing the Save Selection would be named Alpha 1. When you are working with a grayscale image, Photoshop assumes Channel #1 is the image and Channels #2 and higher are mask channels. In RGB, Photoshop assumes Channels #1, #2, and #3 are red, green, and blue, and that Channels #4 and higher are mask channels.

The mask that gets saved for this selection.

The Channels palette after doing the Save Selection and renaming Alpha 1 to DogMask.

73

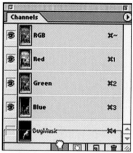

Load Selection the quicker way; dragging the mask channel to the Load Selection icon at the bottom of the Channels palette. The quickest and best way to load a selection is to hold the Command key down and click the mask channel you want to load. You should learn this way because it works in all cases, loading a selection from a mask channel, a layer mask, or even from a regular channel, like Red.

Load Selection from the menu bar.

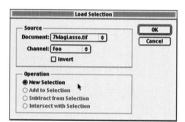

Here are the options you have when you do a Load Selection. The Add, Subtract, and Intersect options only show up if you have an existing selection at the time of the load.

Deleting a mask channel from an RGB image using the Channels palette's pop-up window.

Deleting a channel from an RGB image the quick way by dragging to the Trash icon at the bottom right of the Channels palette.

You can access a channel by clicking on its name in the Channels palette or by using the Command key for that channel (Command-1 for the top channel, Command-2 for the next channel, etc.). You can rename a mask channel by double-clicking the channel, entering the name you want, and then clicking OK or pressing Return. If you Option-click on the Save Selection icon, or choose Select/Save Selection, you can type in the new name right there.

HOW MASK CHANNELS WORK

A *mask channel* is a bit different than the others we've described. When you save a selection to a mask channel, the parts of the image that you selected show up as white in the mask channel, and the nonselected parts (the masked parts) show up as black. When you have a blend between two partial selections, it shows up as gray in the mask channel. Feathered selection areas also show up as gray. A mask channel has 256 possible gray values (32,768 in 16-bit), just like any other grayscale image. A layer mask, which we discuss in the next chapter, is just a mask channel that is being used to mask out (remove) part of a layer. You can also save a selection to a layer mask, using Layer/Add Layer Mask, and that will usually hide the nonselected parts of that layer.

EDITING MASK CHANNELS

You can actually edit a mask channel just like you would edit any grayscale image. Often you may want to make a selection using one of the selection tools, save it to a mask channel or a layer mask, and then edit the selection within the mask channel. When you edit a selection in selection format, with the marching ants around its edge, you use the selection tools. When you edit a selection saved as a mask channel or layer mask, you use pixel-editing tools, like the Pencil, Brush, and Gradient tools. White in a mask means totally selected and black means totally unselected. If you edit a white area to be gray, you make it less selected, or partially selected. You can edit a black area and make part of it white; doing that adds the white part to the selected area. You may save a selection in a mask channel so you can edit it there, or you may just save it so you can use it again later.

We do many things with mask channels in this book. Sometimes we use the terms selection, mask, mask channel, and layer mask interchangeably because they all refer to an isolated part of the image. To do something to the image with a mask that is saved in a mask channel, you must first load it as a selection. Choose Select/Load Selection from the menu bar or click the mask channel you want to load and drag it to the Load Selection icon at the bottom left of the Channels palette. You also can load a selection by Command-clicking on the channel you want to load. When a selection is loaded, you can see the marching ants.

Sometimes people get confused about the need to have both selections and mask channels. Remember, a selection actually masks out the nonselected areas of the currently active channel(s) and layer, so those areas cannot be edited. After you create a selection or do a Load Selection, you can change which channel(s) or layer within a document is active and the selection remains. It always affects what you do to the active channel(s) or layer. A mask channel is just a selection saved for later. Unless the mask channel is currently loaded as a selection, it doesn't affect any other channel(s) or layers or anything that you do to them with the painting tools or filters. You can have up to 53 mask channels in an RGB Photoshop document, plus the Red, Green, and Blue channels, for a total of 56 channels. You can load any of these mask channels as a selection at any time. A layer

74

mask, on the other hand, is a mask channel associated with a particular layer. It is always removing the black areas of the mask from view in that layer. You can access other mask channels using Command-4, Command-5, Command-6, etc. All mask channels are visible all the time within the Channels palette. Only the layer mask for the currently active layer is visible within the Channels palette and you access it using Command-\ .

COMBINING SELECTIONS

When you load a selection, you can combine that new selection with any existing selection present before the load. Command-clicking on a mask channel or layer mask loads it as a new selection and throws out any existing selection. Command-Shift-clicking on a mask channel adds this new selection to any existing selection. Command-Option-clicking a mask channel subtracts this from an existing selection and Command-Option-Shift-clicking on a mask channel intersects the new selection with the existing selection, giving you the parts that the two selections have in common. If you don't want to remember all these command options, they show up in the Load Selection dialog box, which you can access by choosing Select/Load Selection.

DELETING, MOVING, AND COPYING CHANNELS

You can remove a mask channel by clicking that channel and then choosing Delete Channel from the Channels palette's pop-up menu, or by clicking the channel and dragging it to the Trash icon at the bottom right of the Channels palette. If you delete the Red, Green, or Blue channel this way, Photoshop will assume that you want to produce spot color plates of the other two channels and will give you cyan, magenta, or yellow channels, depending on which of the RGB channels you trashed. If you look at Image/Mode, you'll see that you are now in Multichannel mode.

You can copy any channel, including the Red, Green, and Blue channels, by clicking on the channel and dragging it to the New Channel icon at the bottom of the Channels palette. You also can make a copy of a channel by choosing Duplicate Channel from the Channels palette's pop-up menu.

You can move a channel from one location to another by clicking the channel you want to move and dragging it until the line becomes highlighted between the two channels where you want to put this channel. Let go of the mouse at that point and you have moved the channel. You cannot, however, change the location of the original Red, Green, and Blue channels.

USING THE CHANNELS PALETTE EYE ICONS

After you save a selection in a mask channel or a layer mask, you can then work with it in a different way than by just seeing the marching ants lines around the edge of the selection. Notice that the Channels palette has two columns. The left-most column is the thin one that has the Eye icons in it. This column signifies the channels that you are currently seeing—the ones with the Eye icons. The right-most column is the one that has the name of the channel. Clicking in the right-most column for a particular channel highlights that channel, which signifies that you are

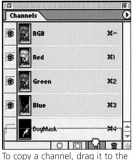

To copy a channel, drag it to the New Channel icon at the bottom of the Channels palette or use Duplicate Channel from the Channels palette menu. Holding the Option key while dragging to the New Channel icon allows you to enter a new name.

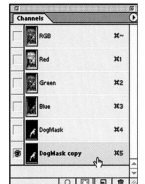

The copied channel appears at the bottom with its name being the same name with "copy" at the end.

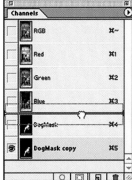

To move a channel, click it and then drag it until the line is highlighted between the channels where you want to put it.

The moved channel appears in its new location.

Normal state for working in RGB, Channel #~, with Red, Green, and Blue Eye icons on and the DogMask off.

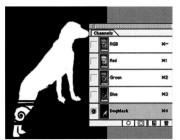

When working on a mask channel or a layer mask directly in black-and-white, you normally have its Eye icon on with its channel grayed. All the other channels have their Eye icons off and they are not grayed.

To change the overlay color, double-click on the mask channel thumbnail to bring up its Channel Options, click here on the color swatch, and change its color.

You can also work on a mask while looking at the RGB image at the same time. To get into this state, first click in the rightmost column of the DogMask channel to activate the mask and then click in the leftmost column of Channel ~ to turn on the RGB Eye icons without activating the RGB channels. Here you will be editing the DogMask channel while looking at the RGB image.

Use Make Work Path from the Paths palette to make a path from a selection.

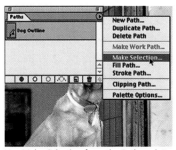

Use Make Selection from the Paths palette to turn a path into a selection.

working on it. That makes it the active channel. Clicking in the right-most column for Channel ~ (the RGB composite channel) highlights the Red, Green, and Blue channels because Channel ~ represents all three of them. If you also have a mask channel defined, like the picture here with the dog mask, then there are different things you can do to work with that mask channel in relation to the other channels.

The Eye icons for the Red, Green, and Blue channels normally are turned on, and those channels are highlighted when you are working with an RGB image. The normal state is displayed in the first dog picture on the previous page.

If you click the rightmost column of the DogMask channel, that channel becomes the active one. It shows up in black-and-white and if you do any editing with the painting tools, you do so in black-and-white in the DogMask channel. The Eye icons for the RGB channels turn off now. The last screen grab on the previous page shows this state.

If you want to edit the mask channel while also seeing the RGB image, do the following. After you make the mask the active channel by clicking in its rightmost column, you can then click the Eye icon column of Channel ~, which turns on the Eye icons for RGB. You will see RGB, but these channels are not active. They are not highlighted, which means that you are seeing them but are still working on the highlighted DogMask channel. The parts of the mask that are black will show up with an overlay color, usually red. If you paint in black with the Paintbrush tool, you add to this black part of the mask, which would represent the non-selected area. The paint shows up in the red overlay color. If you paint with white, which normally represents the selected part of the mask or layer mask, you subtract from the red overlay color. If you want to change the overlay color, double-click the mask channel thumbnail to bring up its Channel Options, click on the color swatch, and change its color in the Color Picker. Be sure to leave its opacity at lower than 100% so you can see the picture through the overlay. You can also rename a channel by double-clicking its name or by using Channel Options, which you can also get from the Channels palette menu.

If you want to, you can also view the DogMask while working on the RGB image. Click the rightmost column of Channel ~, which activates the RGB channels so that when you paint with the Paintbrush, you modify the RGB image. Now if you click the Eye icon column of the DogMask channel, you see this channel as an overlay while you are working in RGB.

CONVERTING BETWEEN PATHS AND SELECTIONS

A path is a special selection created with the Pen tool based on points and lines that are described in an internal model as mathematical objects. A regular selection uses a mask channel, with pixels having 256 possible gray values (32,768 values in 16-bit), as its internal model. Paths are used when you need a selection that maintains a sharp edge, rather than the tiny stair steps associated with a pixel-based selection. Use the Make Work Path and Make Selection commands in the Paths palette to convert between selections and paths or vice versa. To use a path, you will usually convert it into a selection and then maybe into a mask channel or a layer mask. You can use the Layer menu to convert a path directly into a different kind of layer mask called a Vector Mask, which maintains a crisp edge no matter what resolution you print at.

76

7 LAYERS, LAYER MASKS, ADJUSTMENT LAYERS, AND THE LAYER COMPS PALETTE

Terms and concepts for working with layers, adjustment layers, layer masks, layer clipping masks, and the Layer Comps palette for prototyping composites with variations.

Because layers are such an integral part of Photoshop, this chapter is one of the most important for you to understand. Here you will get an overview of what layers are, the different types of layers, and the overall functionality you'll need to know about when working with layers and masks. You'll actually create things with layers, like the image to the right, in the step-by-step chapters.

Think of each layer in an RGB Photoshop document as a separate RGB file. Each layer has its own separate Red, Green, and Blue channels. As you look at the layers in the Layers palette, imagine that the one at the bottom of the palette is a photographic print laying on the bottom of a pile of prints on your desk. Now imagine that each layer above that in the Layers palette is another photographic print laying on top of that bottom one in the order you see them

"Rain In Costa Rica"—an image with many layers. Here we see the final composite. This image is included in the Layers&LayerMasks folder on the CD; open it and follow along while reading this section.

in the palette. You have a pile of photographic prints on your desk. Now imagine that you can look at the top of this pile of photographs and see through them, seeing all of them at the same time, all the way through to the bottom of the pile. It's even better than that because, using Opacity, you can control how much of each photo you see, as a percentage of the whole, and using layer masks or layer clipping masks, you can control what parts of each photo you see. You can run a variety of effects, including layer styles and Blend modes, on each photo in the pile, so the possible combinations of how you can see them all together number in the millions. You can change the order of the photos in the pile and also move them and distort them in relation to each other. When you create a variation that you might want as a final product, you can save a version of the file with the visible layers in position and with their effects in the new Layers Comp palette. All these things and more are what Photoshop layers allow you to do.

LAYERS AND CHANNELS

Layers are similar to channels in the ways you move them around, copy them, and delete them. To work with layers, you use the Layers palette, which you activate from Window/Show Layers or by using F10 with ArtistKeys. If you use layers and

The above four images were used, along with layers and masks, to create the composite at the top of this page.

channels at the same time, which you often will, you will understand their relationship more quickly if you separate these two palettes from their default grouping so you can see them in different places onscreen at the same time. Just click the Layers or Channels name tab at the top of that palette and drag it to a new position onscreen. You can then hide or bring up the Channels palette with Window/Show Channels or by pressing Shift-F10 when using ArtistKeys.

Each layer is like a separate Photoshop file that you can superimpose on top of other Photoshop layers in the same document. Take a look at the "Rain in Costa Rica" image at the beginning of this chapter; we created it using four layers that were originally four photographs on one 35mm roll of film. Each Photoshop layer has its own set of Red, Green, and Blue channels. When working with layers, you can use the Eye icon on each layer to view one layer at a time, several layers at a time, or all the layers at once.

THE *Background* LAYER

If you open any single layer image into Photoshop, such as a TIFF file, and look at the Layers palette, you will notice that the image's layer is called *Background*. It is called *Background* in italics because the *Background* layer differs from a normal layer. The *Background* layer, when it has that name, must be the bottom layer and cannot have any transparent areas. When you choose Layer/Flatten Image, all your layers are compressed into a single layer. This single layer will be a *Background* layer. If you make a selection in the *Background* layer and clear or delete that selection, the selected area fills with the background color (usually white). If you delete a selection in any other layer, that area fills with transparency (the checkerboard pattern). Transparency is a hole where you can look through a layer and see other layers below it. You cannot move other layers below the *Background* layer or move the *Background* layer above other layers. To convert a layer from a *Background* layer into a normal layer, just Double-click it and give it a new name. It then becomes a normal layer and you can move it above other layers, as well as create transparent areas in it. I usually do this when working with my images because I prefer all my layers to have the same full Photoshop capabilities, which a *Background* layer does not. The *Background* layer, or just the first layer in a document, determines the initial canvas size for your layered document. You want to make sure the canvas is large enough to encompass the parts you want to see in all your layers. Therefore, you may want to put your largest picture element, often your main background, down as your first layer. If you add additional layers that are larger in horizontal or vertical pixel dimensions than this bottom layer, you can see only as much of the image as fits on top of the bottom layer onscreen. However, you can still move these other layers by using the Move tool, V, to expose parts left hanging outside the canvas area. In Photoshop, parts that hang off the edge are permanently cropped only when you use the Cropping tool (unless you choose Hide Cropped Areas in the Options bar) or the Image/Crop command. To expose these parts of the image, you can always increase the canvas size using Image/Canvas Size or by choosing Image/Reveal All. You can have a canvas that is bigger than the bottom layer, whether it is a *Background* layer or a normal layer.

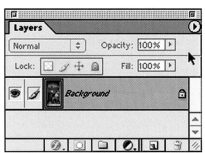

An image with a single *Background* layer. Notice that the Locking icon is on in this layer and the other options are dimmed, indicating that what you can do with it is limited.

The above *Background* layer after double-clicking on it to turn it into a normal layer. Here we named this one Normal Layer by typing in that name after the double-click. Notice now how all the layer's functions have been turned back on.

LAYER MASKS AND ADJUSTMENT LAYERS

To work with the next part of this chapter open the files "Paris Dog" and "Rain in Costa Rica" from the Ch07.Layers folder on your CD. Let's start with the "Paris Dog" image we were using in Chapter 6: "Selections, Paths, Masks, and Channels."

Make sure your Channels and Layers palettes are visible by pressing Shift-F10 and F10 (if you have ArtistKeys loaded), or by choosing Window/Channels and Window/ Layers. You start out with a simple image that has a single layer, called TheParisDog. You can make a copy of this layer by clicking on it in the Layers palette and dragging it to the New Layer icon at the bottom of the Layers palette. Holding down the Option key while doing this opens the Duplicate Layer dialog box, where you can give this new layer a name. We will call it Dog Pointillize, because we're going to run the Pointillize filter on it. Notice that the Layers palette now has a second layer above with the name we gave it. New layers are added above the current active layer, then they become the active layer.

Now choose Filter/Pixelate/Pointillize and run the Pointillize filter on this new layer with a value of 5. Because this layer is on top of the Dog layer, you can no longer see the Dog layer. The Dog Pointillize layer has its own set of RGB channels, so now the document is twice as big as it was when we started.

MAKING A LAYER MASK

Do a Load Selection from the DogMask channel in the Channels palette by Command-clicking that channel. Now we have a selection of the dog. Option-click on the Add Layer Mask icon at the bottom of the Layers palette to add a layer mask to this layer. Notice that the Layer Mask thumbnail now appears to the right of the Dog Pointillize Layer thumbnail and that it is black where the dog is. Also, notice that it shows up in the Channels palette as Dog Pointillize Mask. Now the Dog Pointillize layer is hidden in the area of the Dog where the selection was, and you see the original dog in the layer below. If you press Command-I at this point to invert the Dog Pointillize mask, you can see the original background with the dog now pointillized.

When you first add a layer mask, it comes up in the mode in which you can edit the mask but see RGB. In this mode, the mask's thumbnail has a double border around it in the Layers palette and is highlighted (active) in the Channels palette. **Option-clicking this Layer Mask thumbnail in the Layers palette at this point switches you to the mode in which you can edit and see the mask. The Eye icon is now on for the mask and off for RGB in the Channels palette. Option-clicking again returns you to the original mode where you can edit the mask and see RGB. Try this on the ParisDog sample image.**

To edit the layer itself and also see it, click the Layer thumbnail in the Layers palette. For each regular layer in the Layers palette, the Layer thumbnail is the one to the left and the Layer Mask thumbnail is the one to the right. Just to the right of the Eye icon thumbnail, you see an icon that looks like a mask when you are editing the layer mask and

After adding a layer mask by Option-clicking the Add Layer Mask icon. Clicking the Layer Mask icon hides everything but the selection from this layer by turning it black in the mask. Option-clicking removes the selected area. If there is no selection, clicking on the Layer Mask icon shows the entire layer and Option-clicking hides the entire layer.

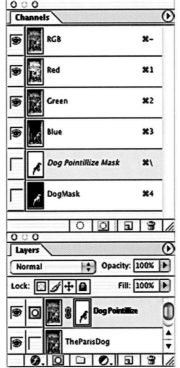

After a layer mask is added, it shows up as a thumbnail to the right of the Layer thumbnail in the Layers palette. It also shows up in the Channels palette below the Blue channel. Because the Eye icons are on for RGB in the Channels palette but only the layer mask is active, we can now edit the mask, but we will see the changes in RGB.

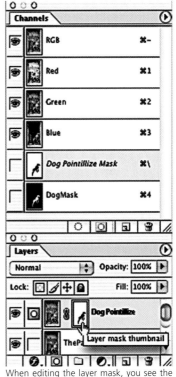

When editing the layer mask, you see the Mask icon just to the right of the Eye icon and the Layer Mask thumbnail has the highlight. In the Channels palette, the Eye icons are on for Red, Green, and Blue, so you can see the results of your mask edits, but the Layer Mask channel is the only one that is actually active.

Layer Masks and Adjustment Layers

When editing the layer, you see the Paintbrush icon just to the right of the Eye icon and the Layer thumbnail has the highlight. The Red, Green, and Blue channels are now the active ones in the Channels palette.

looks like a paintbrush when you are editing the layer itself. The item you are editing, either mask or layer, also has a double border line around it.

You use a layer mask when you want part of a layer to be temporarily removed or made invisible. The black parts of the layer mask are transparent in that layer, which allows you to instantly prototype a layer and its composite with the other layers without seeing the masked-out part. If you later decide you want to restore that part of the image, just turn off the layer mask by Shift-clicking its thumbnail. **Switch to the "Rain in Costa Rica" image now. Try Shift-clicking on the three layer masks within the RainInCostaRicaFinal image, and you'll see what each original photo looked like before the mask was applied.** When you activate a layer that has a layer mask, that mask is also added to the channels in the Channels palette. It only appears in the Channels palette while you have that layer activated. If you want to edit the layer mask while still looking at the layer, just click the layer mask's thumbnail within the Layers palette. When you paint with black in the main document window, you add the black to the layer mask and remove those areas from view in the layer associated with that layer mask.

In Photoshop, you can create a layer mask by choosing Layer/Add Layer Mask/Reveal Selection or by clicking the New Mask icon that is second from the left at the bottom of the Layers palette. If you have a selection at the time of that click, the selected area will become the only thing that is white in the mask and therefore the only visible part of that layer. If you choose Layer/Add Layer Mask/Hide Selection or Option-click the New Mask icon, everything except the selected area will now be visible and the selected area will be made black in the layer mask. If you have a path on your screen, Command-clicking the New Mask icon will create a layer vector mask that, like a layer mask, just shows you the area within the path. When you have a layer vector mask, you can later edit that path, now part of the layer, to change what you actually see. In general you should use a layer mask for any mask that you want to be able to soften or blur the edges of. When you want a very sharp edge that is mathematically accurate no matter what the image size, the layer vector mask is the way to go.

If you Shift-click on the Bus Window layer mask, you'll notice that the original photo this came from was quite different. Driving in Costa Rica is quite exciting; imagine going around a corner and seeing a Bus coming at you! Better to be riding the bus than in a car. Shift-click on the Woman and Red Car layers to see their original images, too.

If you want to edit a layer mask while looking at the mask itself, Option-click the layer mask's thumbnail within the Layers palette. The main document window now displays just the black-and-white mask, and your Layers palette has all the Eye icons dimmed out. The Channels palette now shows this layer mask channel as active with its Eye icon on. When you want to return to editing the layer itself, click the layer's thumbnail within the Layers palette.

ADDING ADJUSTMENT LAYERS

Now that you understand a bit more about layers and their masks, let's go back to the "Paris Dog" image and discover what Adjustment layers are all about. **Click on the Layer thumbnail for the Dog Pointillize layer (that is, the thumbnail on the left, not the Layer Mask thumbnail on the right). You should now see the Paintbrush icon between this Layer thumbnail and the Eye icon. Click on the third icon from the right,**

Chapter 7: Layers, Layer Masks, Adjustment Layers, and the Layer Comps Palette

at the bottom middle of the Layers palette, to bring up the Fill and Adjustment Layer pop-up menu. Choose Curves to create a Curves Adjustment layer. Click in the center of the curve line and drag to pull the curve down and to the right. This darkens the entire composite. (This darkens everything because the new adjustment layer is on top of all the others.) Choose OK, and then double-click on the name Curve in this new adjustment layer in the Layers palette to name this Darken Curve. Although an adjustment layer acts like any other layer, it does not make you pay the price of adding another set of RGB channels for the new layer. The color correction adjustment you make in the adjustment layer applies to all the layers below that adjustment layer. You can turn this correction on and off simply by turning the Eye icon on or off for that particular adjustment layer. The Layer thumbnail, the leftmost one, of an adjustment layer tells you the type of adjustment layer it is. There is a different icon design for each of the 15 different fill and adjustment fill layers. If you double-click the leftmost icon of the adjustment layer, you can actually change the adjustment—in this case, the curve settings—as many times as you want without degrading the color in the file. Just like a regular layer, if you already have a selection when you create an adjustment layer, the adjustment layer's layer mask will be a copy of that selection and so the curve will darken only the selected area. If you have an active path before creating an adjustment layer, that path will be turned into a layer vector mask for that adjustment layer and affect only the part of the image within that path. You can have both a layer mask and a layer vector mask at the same time for any layer. The layer vector mask will always appear on the far right of the Layers palette thumbnails.

Click on the Darken Curve adjustment layer in the Layers palette and drag it down between the Dog Pointillize layer and the Dog layer until you see a double line form between these two layers. Release the mouse button at this point. This moves the adjustment layer down so that now it darkens only the Dog layer and not the Dog Pointillize layer.

You now see *Darken Curve Mask* **in the Channels palette below the Blue channel because now the Darken Curve layer is active. Click back on the Dog Pointillize layer to make it active and notice that the Dog Pointillize mask is now below the Blue channel in the Channels palette. Finally, click back to TheParisDog layer and notice that all the layer masks have been removed from the Channels palette.** Only the layer mask, if there is one, for the active layer shows up in the Channels palette. Use Command-\ to access the layer mask for the currently active layer, no matter what layer it is. The DogMask channel is

Click on this icon to bring up the above pop-up menu and add a fill or adjustment layer from these 15 choices. With ArtistKeys, you can use Command-F2, F3, or F4 to add new Levels, Curves, or Hue-Saturation adjustment layers. Using these function keys, or holding the Option key down while making the above menu choice, allows you to name the layers as you go because each function key brings you into the New Layer dialog box on the way to creating the layer. Choosing Layer/New Adjustment Layer or Layer/New Fill Layer from the menu bar also brings you into the New Layer dialog box. Naming layers is a good idea because it will help you and others to later understand a complex layered document.

Here is the dog image with only the dog itself darkened using the Darken Curve adjustment layer. The leftmost thumbnail in this adjustment layer indicates that its type is a Curve adjustment layer. The white thumbnail to its right is the Layer Mask thumbnail. An adjustment layer will always have a layer mask, although it is often totally white, showing that the adjustment is happening to the entire image area.

Here we see all the different icons for each of the 15 kinds of fill or adjustment layers. The type of each layer is the same as its name and icon.

You can actually click on RGB (or the Red, Green, or Blue channel) in the Channels palette when on an adjustment layer—and you'll even see the Paintbrush icon show up in the Layers palette, but notice that you are not allowed to paint on the RGB channels for this layer because they don't exist.

not associated with any layer, so it stays in the Channels palette all the time. Notice that you use Command-4 to access this channel. If there were an additional channel that was not a layer mask, Command-5 would be used to access it. Adjustment layers and fill layers actually have no RGB data associated with them. Regular layers each have a Red, Green, and Blue channel and take up a lot of space. The purpose of fill and adjustment layers is to be able to make color, fill, and pattern adjustments to all underlying layers at one time; to be able to do so in a way that can be changed as often as possible without damaging the data in any regular layers; and to make these changes in a very space-efficient way. When a Photoshop file is saved, all that must be saved for a fill or adjustment layer is the numerical settings for that particular layer type, the layer mask, and the clipping path. These can all be saved very compactly compared to a regular layer that has real Red, Green, and Blue channels.

SEEING SOME LAYERS IN ACTION

Let's take a look at the Rain in Costa Rica composite image with its five different layers to see how this works. **Go back to the RainInCostaRicaFinal file and use that file to try out the different options that we discuss here.** In the Layers palette for RainInCostaRica, you see that this image has four regular layers and one Curves adjustment layer. Currently, we are looking at all of them because the Eye icons in the left column of the Layers palette

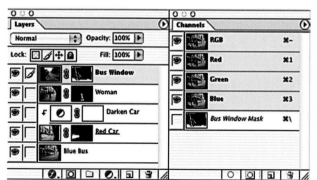

Because all the Eye icons are on in the Layers palette, the Channels palette shows you a view of the Red, Green, and Blue Channel thumbnails of all layers as a composite image. Choose Palette Options from the Layers palette menu to set the size of your thumbnails.

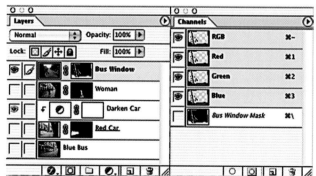
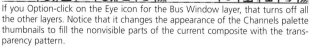

If you Option-click on the Eye icon for the Bus Window layer, that turns off all the other layers. Notice that it changes the appearance of the Channels palette thumbnails to fill the nonvisible parts of the current composite with the transparency pattern.

82

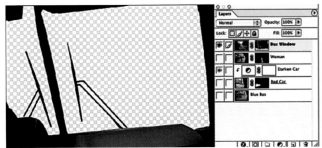

are all on. To see all the details about how this composite was created, check out Chapter 28: "Rain in Costa Rica."

Imagine that all the layers are in a pile with the bottom layer, here called Blue Bus, at the bottom of the pile. As you add layers on top of this, like Red Car, Woman, and Bus Window, they are blended with the layers below them. The active layer that is highlighted, Bus Window, is the layer that is modified by changing the settings for Opacity and Blend mode at the top of the Layers palette. Click on a particular layer's name, in the rightmost column of the Layers palette, to make it active. The active layer will also be changed by anything you do with any other Photoshop tools such as the Paintbrush, Levels, or Curves. If you do something to the active layer while all the other layers' Eye icons are on, you can see the changes to this layer as they are combined with the other layers, but the other layers themselves do not change.

The Channels palette shows you the Channel thumbnails and Eye icon state for the layer you are working on. What you see in the Channels palette thumbnails depends on the layer you have activated and which other layers have their Eye icons on. Notice that if you turn off the Eye icon for the Blue Bus layer, not only does the main part of the image turn into the transparency pattern, but you also see that pattern in the Channel palette's thumbnails. When you add additional layers whose contents are smaller than the *Background* layer, or if you copy a small item and do an Edit/Paste with it, the extra area around these smaller items shows up as transparent (a checkerboard pattern). Areas of an image that are hidden by a layer mask also show up as transparent. When we look at just the Bus Window layer in this image, we see that it is entirely transparent aside from the frame and wipers of the bus window we are supposed to be looking out of. Through these transparent parts, when all the Eye icons are on, we will see the rainy Costa Rican street scene.

If you just want to work on one layer and see only that layer, you can click the Eye icons of the other layers to turn them off. A quicker way to turn them all off is to Option-click the Eye icon in the Layers palette of the layer you want to work on. Doing this also changes the RGB display of the Channel thumbnails in the Channels palette so that you see just the Red, Green, and Blue channel info of the one layer. To turn all the other layers back on again, just Option-click the same layer's Eye icon in the Layers palette. Also, the RGB channel thumbnail display in the Channels palette will once again show a composite of all the visible layers.

Here we see the Bus Window layer as it appears with all the other layers turned off. When you turn them back on, you'll see the other layers through the transparent checkerboard pattern.

To edit the layer mask and see just the mask in the Document window, Option-click the layer mask's thumbnail. You will see the Layer Mask thumbnail to the right of the Layer thumbnail. The Channels palette will display the mask highlighted with the Eye icon on as above. The Eye icons are off for the RGB channels because you don't want to see them. Now Option-clicking the layer mask's thumbnail will toggle between just seeing the layer mask and then seeing the RGB channels, but you will always be editing the mask until you click the Layer thumbnail again or click on RGB in the Channels palette.

To edit the layer mask while still looking at the layer, just click the layer mask's thumbnail. You will see the Layer Mask thumbnail to the right of the Layer thumbnail. The Channels palette will display the mask as above, active, with its Eye icon off. The Eye icons are on for RGB, so you see those channels, yet you edit the mask because it is active.

NAVIGATING LAYERS

You create additional layers in Photoshop by copying something from another image and then choosing Edit/Paste or by clicking the New Layer icon at the bottom

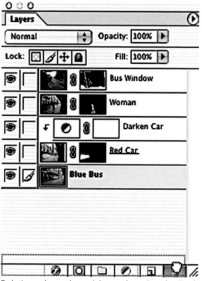

Deleting a layer the quick way by using the Trash icon at the bottom of the Layers palette. If the Layer is active, you can just click the Trash icon. If you don't want the delete warning message to come up, just Option-click. You can also drag any layer to the Trash icon.

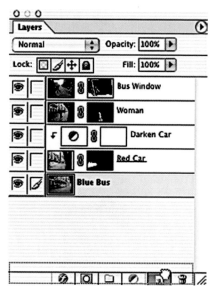

To copy a layer, drag it to the New Layer icon at the bottom of the Layers palette. Holding the Option key down as you do this allows you to rename the copied layer. Just clicking this icon creates a new blank layer with a generic name, or an Option-click allows you to name it while creating it.

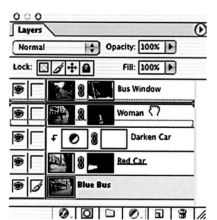

To move a layer, click on it and drag it until you see the double line between the layers where you want to put it.

The moved layer appears in its new location now just below the Bus Window.

of the Layers palette. You can name these layers by double-clicking the names in the Layers palette or by choosing Layer/Layer Properties from the main menu bar or from the Layers palette. Using the Move tool (Command key or V), you can also click a layer in the main document window or the Layers palette in image A, and drag and drop it on top of image B's main document window to create a new layer in image B. In Photoshop, you can also drag and drop a whole group of layers if they're linked together or you are moving a Layer Set. You can move a single layer, or a group of linked layers, from side to side or up and down using the Move tool. Just click to activate the layer you want to move in the Layers palette, then select the Move tool from the Tools palette (V or the Command key). Click on the layer in the main document window and drag it to its new location. If you have all the Eye icons on, you can see its relationship to the other layers change.

You can remove a layer by clicking it, choosing Delete Layer from the Layers palette's pop-up menu or the Layer menu, or by clicking the layer and dragging it to the Trash icon at the bottom right of the Layers palette.

You can make a copy of any layer by clicking the layer and dragging it to the New Layer icon to the left of the Trash icon at the bottom of the Layers palette. You can also make a copy of the active layer by choosing Duplicate Layer from the Layers palette's pop-up menu or from the Layer menu, or by pressing Command-J. The copied layer will have the same name but with "copy" appended to it.

You can move a layer from one location to another in the Layers palette by clicking the layer you want to move and dragging it until the line turns into a double line between the two layers where you want to put this layer. Let go of the mouse at that point, and the layer is moved. When you move a layer, it changes the composite relationship of that layer with the layers around it. Notice how the running woman and red car go away after you move the Blue Bus layer from the bottom upwards to just below the Bus Window layer.

At the top of the Layers palette on the right-hand side are two sliders that affect the opacity of the layer. The first one is obvious—it says "Opacity." The second is called Fill; if you move this slider on a regular layer, it is not immediately apparent why this slider differs from Opacity. Fill is used in conjunction with layer effects to

Chapter 7: Layers, Layer Masks, Adjustment Layers, and the Layer Comps Palette

Changing the Fill Opacity of a layer modifies the opacity of the actual pixels in the layer but doesn't change the opacity of any Layer Styles added to that layer. Changing the Opacity modifies both the pixels in the layer and the Layer Styles added to that layer. To change the Opacity of a particular Layer Style effect, like a Drop Shadow, one needs to use the Opacity slider for that effect within the Layer Style dialog.

allow you to keep the full opacity of any effects you've added to the layer while lowering the opacity of the layer itself. If you used the Opacity slider to lower the opacity of the layer, it affects both the layer and the layer effects. In the illustration here, we have added an outer glow and a stroke to text (text is one area where this technique is used a lot), then lowered the opacity of just the text by moving the Fill slider to 40%. See the "Layer Styles and Blending Options" section of this chapter for a bit more on using layer effects and check out Chapter 34: "Heartsinger CD Cover," to begin using effects yourself.

Here, I've lowered the opacity of the type itself by adjusting the Fill slider to 40%. The opacity of the outer glow and stroke effects remains at 100%.

LINKING AND ALIGNING LAYERS

By clicking in the middle column of a layer in the Layers palette, that layer can be linked with the currently active layer. When you click in this middle column, the Link icon will show up to let you know this layer is linked to the currently active layer. More than one layer can be linked together and when you activate a layer, all the layers that are linked to it will have this Link icon show up in their middle columns. Layers that are linked can all be moved and transformed (scaled, rotated, and so on) together. If you move or scale any of the layers that are linked together, they will all move or scale together proportionately. If you drag and drop any layer that has others linked to it, those other layers will also be copied to the other document. This allows you to link together a group of layers that represent a button, for example, and then drag that button, with all its layers, to any other document. You could use this feature to make up a Photoshop library

Here we have first clicked on Blue Bus to activate it, then we clicked on the Link columns of the three layers above it. Layers that are linked in this way can be moved or transformed as a unit. They can also all be dragged and dropped into another document.

file of the buttons you use most often. When you need a particular button, just drag and drop one of its layers and they all come along for the ride. This is a very powerful feature, especially for Web and multimedia people who use the same elements over and over again.

If you have a bunch of layers linked together and one of them is the active layer, you can use Layer/Align Linked to align the rest of the linked layers with the active layer in six possible ways: Top Edges, Vertical Centers, Bottom Edges, Left Edges, Horizontal Centers, or Right Edges. Remember, the results of the Align Linked command will depend on the layer that is currently active. There is also a Layer/Distribute Linked choice that will distribute the linked layers evenly in the same six ways. The Options bar for the Move tool also displays clickable icons for any of these 12 choices that apply to the currently active layer and any other layers that are linked to it. If you currently have a selection on the screen, you can use Layer/Align to Selection to align the currently active layer and any that are linked to it to the selection in the same six possible ways. For examples of how to use these alignment features, see Chapter 30: "The PowerBook Ad," and Chapter 32: "Layer Vector Masks, Shape Layers, and Layer Styles."

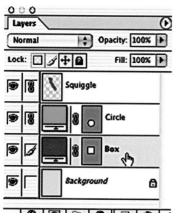

Here are three linked layers. Doing a Layer/Align Linked/Left Edges will align the left edge of the nontransparent parts of the other two layers with the left edge of the Box layer because Box is the active layer.

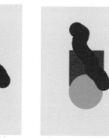

Before Align Left Edges.   After Align Left Edges.

Click on the Blue Bus layer in the Rain-InCostaRica image to make it active and then click in the linking column of the Red Car, Darken Car, and Woman layers above it. Now use the Move tool to drag this entire scene around inside the Bus Window layer, which doesn't move. If you drag it straight up, you can now see the woman's foot on the pavement. Now choose Layer/New/Layer Set From Linked to create a new layer set from all these linked layers. Layer Sets are a great way to simplify your documents by collapsing logical groups of items into a single element. We'll learn more about these later.

CLIPPING GROUPS

A layer can be grouped with the layer or layers below it. The bottom layer in a group determines the transparency for the entire group and is called the clipping mask. The visibility of upper layers will be restricted to the shape of the bottom layer. This also means that if the bottom layer in the group has a layer mask that removes its center portion, that same center area will be removed from all the layers in the group. To group a layer with the one below it,

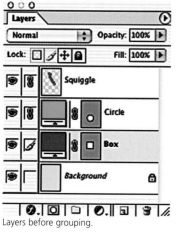

Layers before grouping.

Layers after grouping. Notice the Grouping icon where the cursor is between the Squiggle and Circle layers.

Image before grouping.

Image after grouping.

Chapter 7: Layers, Layer Masks, Adjustment Layers, and the Layer Comps Palette

choose Layer/Create Clipping Mask (Command-G). You can always ungroup a layer later by choosing Layer/Release Clipping Mask (Command-Shift-G). You can also group or ungroup a layer with the one below it by Option-clicking the line between the two layers. It is obvious when layers are in a group because the bottom layer in the group has its name underlined. This bottom underlined layer determines the transparency for the group. The other layers above it in the group are indented to the right with dotted lines between them.

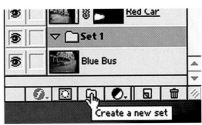

You can create a new layer set in Photoshop by clicking on the Layer Set icon at the bottom of the Layers palette. Doing this creates one, as you see here, with the default name Set 1. Creating a layer set by choosing New Layer Set from the Layers palette menu or using Layer/New/Layer Set or Option-clicking on the above icon allows you to enter your own name as you create the set.

LAYER SETS

A great feature of Photoshop is layer sets. These allow you to group layers into logical sets and then collapse a finished group down into a single element within your Layers palette. This is a great feature for people who have a large number of layers and who want to be able to organize them into functional groups. Once a group of layers is combined into a layer set, the entire set can be turned on and off by just clicking on the Eye icon for the set folder. If you click on the icon for a particular set, you can use the Move tool to move the entire set, even if the layers within the set are not linked. Using the set's icon, you can also drag and drop all the layers in the set into another window. If you want to Scale or Free Transform the entire set, however, all the layers inside the set must be linked, and one of those linked layers must be active. You can add a layer mask or a layer vector mask to a layer set. This applies the mask or path to all the layers within the set as a unit. A layer set also has a possible Opacity and Blend mode.

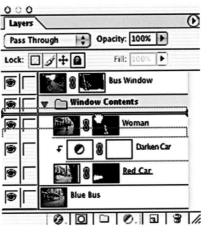

Here we have created a layer set named Window Contents and have already moved the Red Car and Woman layers into that set. We are in the process of dragging and dropping the Blue Bus layer into the Window Contents set. When the Set icon turns black, that is the point to release the mouse and have the layer enter the set.

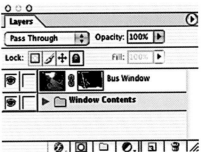

Here we see the Window Contents layer set in its collapsed state. It takes up less room and yet the layers inside the set will continue to act as they did when the set was not there and those layers were just in the Layers palette. Layer sets can be closed so that groups of layers are represented in the palette by a single component. This allows you to simplify complicated documents.

When you first create a layer set, the default Opacity is 100% and the default Blend mode is Pass Through. Pass Through is a Blend mode created for sets that has the effect that all the Blend modes in all the layers within the set will behave as they would if the set didn't exist and those layers were there without the set. You can now nest up to five levels of layer sets.

THE LAYER COMPS PALETTE

Once you've added, moved, scaled, masked, and otherwise edited your layers to create a composite for your ad, poster, newsletter, or fine art, you'll most likely want to save several different versions of the file with slight variations to determine which version is perfect for the project. In the old days, you used to have to do just that— save lots of different files with different version names. Now, however, Adobe's come up with a way for you to do this with only one file via the Layers Comp palette. This palette is capable of saving the Eye icon state, main window position, and effects for each layer. Once you've created a version you like, you click the New Layer Comp icon on the bottom of the palette. You can name your composite, choose which of the three options you need to remain constant, and make notes regarding that comp.

We created the Rainy Street Scene set of layers by first clicking the Blue Bus layer, linking the other three layers to it, and then choosing Layer/New/Layer Set from Linked.

In this comp, called With Hard Light, the Fibers layer Eye icon is turned on, and the Delphinium3 layers is set to Hard Light blend mode.

You can make adjustments to the file and then update a composite by clicking the name of the comp first, and then clicking the Update button (the one that looks like a circle). To view the composite state, you must click the icon to the left of the comp name. Use the forward and backward arrow buttons on the bottom of the palette to quickly cycle through the comps and evaluate them. The Layers Comp palette cannot move layers up and down in the Layers palette hierarchy, though, so it's not a tool to use at the beginning of your artwork process; History and snapshots would be better suited for that. We use the Layers Comp palette in several exercises so look for it in Chapter 30: "The PowerBook Ad."

LOCKING LAYERS AND LAYER SETS

In Photoshop you can lock layers and also entire layer sets. This can stop one from accidentally moving a layer, which can easily happen if you press the Command key, putting you into the Move tool, at the same time as moving the mouse with the button down. If you are working on a complex composite or a color correction where multiple copies of the same image have to line up exactly, I recommend that you lock any layers that you don't want accidentally moved later. Do this by clicking in one of the four lock options at the top of the Layers palette while the layer you want

In this comp, called Without Fibers, the Fibers layer Eye icon is turned off and the Delphinium3 layer is in Normal blend mode. And, I only had to click one checkbox (the icon next to Withouth Fibers in the Layer Comps palette) to make those changes happen.

You'll see the top icon if you try painting on a layer that is locked. The message on the bottom comes up when you try to move a locked layer.

locked is active. You can also lock an entire layer set in a similar way. From left to right the icons are Lock transparent pixels, Lock image pixels, Lock position, and Lock all. If you turn on Lock all, that must be turned off before you can set one of the other locking options. Lock transparent pixels stops you from painting in or changing the transparent parts of the layer, Lock image pixels locks both the transparent and non-transparent areas, and Lock position stops you from moving the layer with the Move tool. Lock transparent pixels does not stop you from painting on the parts of a layer that are made transparent with its layer mask. To stop this as well as to stop painting onto a layer mask and to stop changing a layer clipping path, you need to choose Lock all. None of the lock options stops you from moving the layer up and down the Layers palette in relationship to other layers. Once a layer is locked, you will get the universal Not symbol if you try to paint on it, and you will get a warning message that the layer is locked if you try to move it with the Move tool. Using these features at the right times could save you a lot of grief by removing the possibility for costly accidents!

LAYER STYLES AND BLENDING OPTIONS

If you Option-double-click the layer name in the Layers palette or double-click the thumbnail, the Layer Style dialog box comes up. You can also access it from the Layer/Layer Style menu. As a quick example of what you can do with these features, click on the Bus Window layer to make it the active layer. Click on the leftmost Layer thumbnail to make sure you are working on the layer and not the layer mask. Now choose Window/Styles and click on each of a variety of styles to see the types of things you can do with the Layer Styles palette. Notice as you click on each style that the Layers palette shows you the effects applied to get this style in a list right below the layer name. If you want to explore any particular style, Option-double-click the layer name for the Bus Window layer and the Layer Styles palette will come

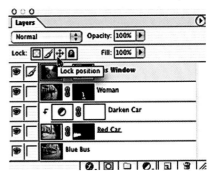

Here you see the four locking options for an individual layer. With a layer set, the only option you can choose for the entire set is Lock all. A gray Lock icon will then appear to the right of all the layers in that set telling you that you must first unlock the set before changing the locking status of an individual layer.

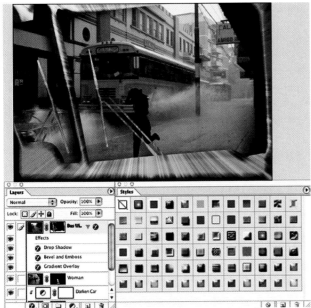

I've appended several style libraries from the Styles palette pop-up and started to play. The Bus Window layer of the RainInCostaRicaFinal image, from this book's CD, was active and I clicked on the Layer thumbnail within that layer. At that point, clicking on the Styles tab, or choosing Window/Styles, will allow you to then click on any style available in the palette and have that style applied to the Bus Window layer. When you see one that is interesting, Option-double-click on the layer name in the Bus Window layer to see how that style is set up using the Layer Style dialog. You can also double-click in the Layers palette on any particular effect listed under the Bus Window layer, and the Layer Style dialog will come up showing you how that particular effect is set up. This layer style is called Angled Spectrum and it's in the Button style library.

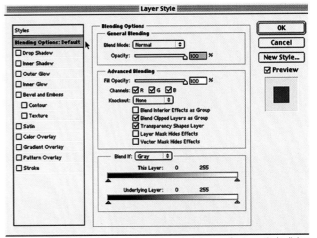

When you first Option-double-click on a layer to bring up the Layer Style dialog box, you may think it's just the Blending Options you see here. Actually, when you click on any of the lines below **Blending Options: Default**, like Drop Shadow, Inner Shadow, etc., each of these has its own special set of options that will then appear to the right. Don't just check the Drop Shadow checkbox but click on the word Drop Shadow; then you'll see all the options available for drop shadows. You can also access this dialog from Layer/Layer Style. From there you can go directly into one of the sub-options areas, like Drop Shadow, for example.

up, allowing you to look at the settings in each of the effects used to create this style. All of the features in the Layer Style dialog box could fill a book in itself, so we will cover them in much more detail in Chapters 31: "Blend Modes, Calculations, and Apply Image," 32: "Layer Clipping Paths, Shape Layers, and Layer Styles," 33: "Texture and Pattern," and 34: "Heartsinger CD Cover."

FLOATING SELECTIONS (PHOTOSHOP HISTORY)

When you have made any type of selection and it is highlighted on the screen with the dotted lines moving around it (those marching ants), you can now Command-Option-click and drag to float that selection. A floating selection is another copy of the pixels of the active layer in that selected area floating on top of the original layer below. A floating selection is sort of like a temporary layer, although it doesn't show up in the Layers palette. To change the Opacity and Blend mode of a floating selection, use the Edit/Fade command. Before Photoshop had layers, it always had floating selections and they were more powerful than they are today. In older versions of Photoshop, all the things we do with layers today had to be done one at a time using a floating selection. You can have only one floating selection at a time, and when you deselect it by clicking outside it, choosing Select/None or by running a filter or any command on it, it becomes embedded in the layer it is floating above. At that point, you can no longer move it. A layer, on the other hand, is like a permanent floating selection; you can have many layers. Layers don't go away like floating selections do. You can no longer turn a floating selection into a full-fledged layer by double-clicking it in the Layers palette. If you really want a layer from a selection, just choose Command-J (Layer/New/Layer Via Copy) to create a new layer with a copy of the current selection. Floating selections had most of their power removed in Photoshop 5. (It might be simpler if Adobe removed them completely.) If you do a Paste on top of an individual channel in the Channels palette, you get a Floating Selection that also doesn't show up in the Layers palette; you must use Edit/Fade to change its mode or Opacity.

USEFUL CONTEXT-SENSITIVE MENUS FOR LAYERS

If you Control-click (right-click in Windows) while working in the Move tool, you will get some very useful context-sensitive menus to speed up your layer work. When using the Move tool, or with Control-Command-click if not in the Move tool (Control-right-click for Windows), you get a context-sensitive menu showing all the layers whose Eye icons are on that have pixels at the location where you clicked. You can then drag through this menu to activate the layer you want to work on. If you are in a selection tool or a painting tool, not the Move tool, you will get a different context-sensitive menu. These context-sensitive menus are great power user tools!

Being in the Move tool, I held down the Control key on my Mac and clicked on top of the red car. This context-sensitive menu came up showing me that the above three layers contained non-transparent pixels at the location where I clicked. Choosing one of these will activate that layer in my Layers palette. If I were doing this on my Windows machine, I'd click with the right mouse button while in Move.

Chapter 7: Layers, Layer Masks, Adjustment Layers, and the Layer Comps Palette

8 HISTORY PALETTE, HISTORY BRUSH, AND SNAPSHOTS

Using the History palette, History Brush, Art History Brush, and Snapshot features to give you added creative power.

The simple explanation for the History palette is that it allows Photoshop to have up to 1,000 levels of Undo. Actually, the History palette allows a lot more flexibility than that. Between the History palette, the History Brush, and the way they work with the Snapshot feature, you may initially wonder if this is yet another flavor of layers. There are some important distinctions between using History with snapshots versus layers and although they can sometimes be used in similar ways, the reasons for using one versus the other are quite distinctly different.

THE SIMPLE CASE OF USING HISTORY

Every time you do a Photoshop command that changes your image, that command gets saved in the History palette as a History state. It may be creating a new layer, painting a brush stroke in your image, or even using the Levels command. In the History palette, you see a list of all the commands you have done in order from the oldest on top to the newest on the bottom. As it has always been, Command-Z toggles between Undo and Redo of the last command you did unless you change this under Edit/Preferences/General. Command-Option-Z moves back up the history chain undoing command after command. Command-Shift-Z goes back and redoes those same commands in the same order they were originally done.

At any time, you can create a snapshot that will remember the state of your image at that particular point. You can have multiple snapshots and they are all saved at the top of the History palette. Photoshop is by default set to automatically take a snapshot of your image when you first open the image. This snapshot is used to implement the Revert to Saved type commands. In the History Options that are accessed from the History palette, you can also choose to have a new snapshot created

Here we see the History palette with five snapshots at the top and then a long list of commands in the lower section. In this photo all the original flowers were red. I used Selective Color, Hue/Saturation, and Replace Color to make versions of this image with all purple, orange, blue, and yellow flowers. As I did this, I made a snapshot of each set of colored flowers. I then kept changing the source of the History Brush, currently set to the Orange Flowers snapshot, as I painted with the History Brush to recolor a flower with any of the five colors. If you wanted to be able to change the colors again after saving the file, you would use adjustment layers to get a similar effect with lasting flexibility. All this history information goes away when you close or quit!

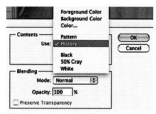

The Photoshop Edit/Fill command has the Use History option. This allows you to Fill a selection, or your entire Layer, from any previous history or snapshot state of that layer.

In the General preferences, you can set the number of History States available in the History palette. The maximum number is 1000.

whenever you save your image. In addition to being able to undo to previous snapshots and history states, you can also use them as the source for the Fill command, the Eraser, the History Brush, and the Art History Brush. I'll talk about the Art History Brush a bit later in this chapter.

The History Brush is a special painting tool that paints from your image as it existed at a particular state within the History palette. Clicking in the leftmost column of the History palette next to any snapshot or history state sets the History Brush to paint on your current image with the image as it looked at that previous point in history. In general, the brush paints from the state of a single layer into that same layer unless you are using a merged snapshot as your source. See the case study with flowers later in this chapter for an example of how this is used. You are not just painting with what that particular step did; you are painting with the cumulative effect of everything you did up to and including that state. This is cool stuff because it makes certain things, like painting with any of the tools that use brushes, much more undoable, repeatable, and totally flexible.

You can bring up this History Options dialog from the History palette menu and use it to turn on Allow Non-Linear History, which will then no longer automatically throw away future history when you go back into the past and change the sequence of events by entering a new command.

MAKING SNAPSHOTS AND DOCUMENT COPIES ALONG THE WAY

When you use the History palette's New Snapshot menu, or the middle icon at the bottom of the History palette, to create a snapshot; this saves not only the current appearance of your image on the screen but also its selection state and the state of the Layers palette and the rest of the file. You can take a snapshot whenever you want to make sure you can get back to this point within your document. If you crop your image after taking a snapshot, you will not be able to paint from this snapshot onto the current state of the document because that state will now have a different canvas size. Just like in the older versions of Photoshop, you could not Clone Stamp from Saved if the saved file had a different crop size. Also, remember that snapshots and history states do not survive after a crash, so you should still save the file often enough to protect from any system failure. If you are in the middle of a project using snapshots and you have to close the file, you can make documents of the snapshots you want to save and then drag the opening snapshots from those documents back into the window of your original document when you reopen it. The snapshots will return to the History palette, and you can continue to paint from those snapshots as long as the image size and Color mode of the snapshots are the same as the current state of the file you're working on. Or, you could make new layers and use Edit/Fill/Use History for each snapshot that you want to save.

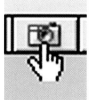

Create a new snapshot from the current history state.

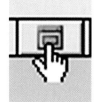

Create a new document reflecting the image at the current history state.

You can click on the leftmost icon at the bottom of the History palette to create a new document showing the image at the current History state. This is like choosing Image/Duplicate, except you don't get the Merged Layers Only choice and the new document will automatically be given the name of the command you just finished doing in the current History palette. This new document will now have its own empty History palette and its own empty set of snapshots and history states, which you will develop as you start to work on it. All the layers are copied into the new document. This allows you to branch off in several directions from a particular state in the history of your image and then explore all the options, each in its own document, until you are happy with the outcome. After working in a new document, you can always go back to the document it came from and all its history will still be intact.

This is somewhat subtle but very powerful, especially for creative people who like to try a lot of options.

PAINTING FROM THE FUTURE

To choose where the History Brush paints from, click in the leftmost column next to a particular history or snapshot state. The History Brush will then paint on your current layer from that particular past state of your file. If you click in the left column of the History palette to set the source for the History Brush on a certain state, then click in the right column of the History palette to return the working image to a state prior to your History Brush source state, your image returns to that previous state. If you start entering more commands, they will be entered *after* the current history state—that is, the previous state where you clicked the right column. All states between the current History state and your History Brush source state will be removed. The state of your History Brush stays there, sort of in the future, as long as that is the location where your History Brush will be painting from. This allows you to, in a way, paint from the future.

Here we see a case where we have the History Brush set on the command called Selective Color, which is in front of the current state we are working on in the History palette. This allows you to paint from the future!

LINEAR VERSUS NON-LINEAR HISTORY

You can turn on the Allow Non-Linear History option by choosing History Options from the History palette. When you do this, the history system does not throw away future history states when you return to a past state. Say you enter 10 commands so you have a History palette with 10 things in it. Normally, if you click the fifth thing to return your image to that previous state, states 6–10 disappear once you do another command. That new command appears at position 6 and states 6–10 are removed. When you turn on Allow Non-Linear History, then states 6–10 stay in the History palette, without actually appearing in your image, and that new command appears at position 11. Your actual image, however, appears as it would if you had done states 1–5 and then state 11. Still, if you click back onto state 8, for example, the effects of states 9–11 go away and you are where you would have been if you never returned to state 5 and then did the new state 11. Non-Linear History makes finding a state in the History palette a bit more confusing, but it always leaves you the option of returning to one of those previously removed states.

HISTORY PALETTE INFORMATION ALL GOES AWAY WHEN YOU CLOSE OR QUIT

If you are doing anything where you want several options created in a way that you can later reopen and change them, you should use layers, layer masks, and adjustment layers to give yourself that capability. By turning layers on and off, modifying layer masks, and switching the settings in adjustment

1. Here we have used five strokes of the Paintbrush to paint a face. Let's say we like the head but don't like the eyes, nose, and mouth. We can click back on the first Paintbrush command, which drew the head, and the other strokes will be turned off.

2. With Linear History, when we make that first paint stroke to draw the new eye, the old paint strokes for the eyes, nose, and mouth go away.

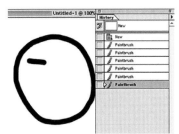

3. With Allow Non-Linear History turned on, the first stroke to draw a new eye skips the old strokes for the eyes, nose, and mouth and starts in a position beyond those. This gives you the option to return to the old face by clicking the stroke just above the currently highlighted one. It also gives you the option to use the History Brush to paint any of those old face parts onto a new face where you might want just one part from the old face.

4. Here, using Non-Linear History, I have painted a second set of eyes and a second nose; then I used the History Brush to paint the old mouth back in from the previous History state. That old mouth state would not have been there if I had not had Allow Non-Linear History turned on.

In the General preferences, choose whether you want to save a History Log, in what format you want it to be saved, and where you want the information to be stored.

Detailed information in the History Log remembers every setting and brush stroke that you made.

layers, you can make almost anything changeable in a variety of ways. You can also now do this in a sometimes simpler way with the History palette. The trouble with the History palette is that it gets cleared every time you close the file and reopen it. Also, if you made a change in the History palette, like a Curves setting, for example, you cannot go back to that history state and double-click it to see what the actual change was, like you could with an adjustment layer; you can only click that state and your image returns to where it was at that state. You can also paint with the History Brush on your current state from the image in that previous state. This History Brush feature adds a lot of power to history, snapshots, and Photoshop.

A More Permanent History Record

Although the actual History states of your files disappear when you close the file, you can now keep a record of what you did to the file. In your General Preferences, at the bottom of the window, you can turn on an option to save a History Log. This file is useful for several reasons. It can keep information on which files have been opened and closed by using the Session Only setting, which could help you track time spent on jobs. Or you could keep a brief record of what you did to a file, listing when it was opened and what adjustments were made to it without detailing the actual steps by using the Concise option. Finally, if you want all the information of where you set every point on a curve or what numbers you used for a Hue/Saturation adjustment, use the Detailed setting. This could be especially helpful if you initially work with a low res version of a file to decide how to alter it, then later need to make the same changes to the larger file. Regardless of which setting you use, you can save the History Log in either the metadata for the file, a separate text file, or both.

A History Case Study with Flowers

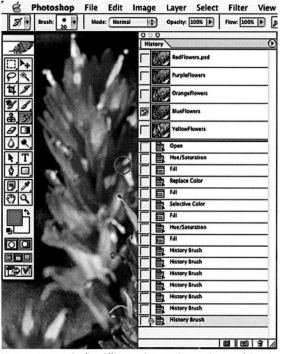

Here you can see the five different color snapshots at the top of the History palette. I'm currently painting with the History Brush from the Blue Flowers snapshot to change this flower from red to blue.

I opened a photograph of some red flowers taken in the High Sierras at Yosemite. I wanted to have this same picture with multiple flower colors. (I wouldn't actually do this to one of my "true nature" photos.) Without making any selections, I used either Replace Color, Selective Color, or Hue/Saturation to change the color of all the flowers to first purple, then orange, then blue, and finally yellow. After each new color, I used the middle icon at the bottom of the History palette to create a snapshot of all the flowers at each of these four new colors. I then clicked in the leftmost column of the Original Red Flowers snapshot to set the History Brush source there and followed that by a Fill from History to return my current state to the original red flowers. I then used one of the color change commands to change this red into yet another color. After I had the five colors I wanted, I then Filled from History to change all the flowers back to red. Next, I set the History Brush onto one of the other colors by clicking in the leftmost column of its snapshot. At that point, I used the History Brush to paint over some of the red flowers with flowers of new colors. I just had to reset the History Brush source on a different color snapshot when I wanted to change colors. With this setup, I could paint over each flower as many times as I wanted and could even go back to the original red flowers at any time. The only problem is that when I close the file or quit Photoshop, my neat snapshot/history

Chapter 8: History Palette, History Brush, and Snapshots

The original photo with the actual red flowers.

The photo after modifying the flowers using the History palette and its snapshots along with the History Brush.

setup goes away. To see how to change the color of objects, check out Chapters 21: "Yellow Flowers," and 22: "Color Matching Images." To see how to set up this type of situation with layers so you can make changes to the flower colors even after saving the file, check out Chapter 26: "Combining Bracketed Photos," Chapter 27: "Bryce Stone Woman," and the other layer color correction examples.

THE ART HISTORY BRUSH

Another interesting feature of the History palette is the Art History Brush. This tool allows you to paint from a history snapshot or history state just like the regular History Brush, but it adds the ability to choose from various brushstroke styles to give your image a painterly look. If you're the type of person who prefers straight photography, then this tool might not be too compelling. But if you like to take an image and explore with Photoshop to see where it takes you, then you can end up having a lot of fun while creating some very interesting effects with the Art History Bush.

Since using the Art History Brush will drastically alter your original image, it's always a good idea to work on a copy layer so you can preserve the original and keep your options open. The method I used here with the image of the man in the blue coat was to create a copy of the background by choosing Duplicate Layer from the Layers palette. I then created a new snapshot by clicking the New Snapshot icon at the bottom of the History palette. This snapshot served as the source state for all of my modifications with the History Brush.

My next step was to fill the duplicate background layer with white, giving me a fresh blank "canvas" to work on. In the History palette, I clicked in the column next to the snapshot I created, which specified that the Art History Brush would use that as its source state. Then I chose a brush from the new Brushes palette. For the Art History Brush, the irregular, rough brushes work well, because they mimic the imperfect characteristics of real-world, natural brushes, but all of the settings of your chosen brush can give you markedly different results. For more on setting brush

This image was originally a black-and-white photo that I colorized using the History palette. After saving a copy of it, I decided to explore a painterly look with the Art History Brush.

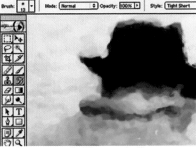

A safe way to use Art History and still preserve your original image: Make a copy layer of your main image, then create a new snapshot. Next, fill the copy layer with white. Select the new snapshot as the source by clicking in the left-hand column next to it, choose the Art History Brush from the Tool palette, choose an appropriate brush size and shape, and start creating your impressionist masterpiece!

The Options bar for the Art History Brush. Style lets you choose from 10 different brush stroke styles; Area determines the size of the area that the brush affects; and Tolerance influences how closely the Art History Brush matches the history state from which you are painting. Remember that brush settings also make a great deal of difference in the look of your "painting."

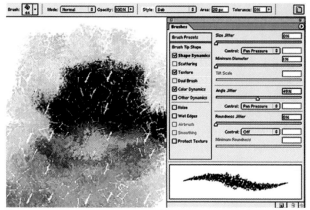

If you are using a pressure-sensitive tablet, you can use stroke pressure to change many variables including shape and angle. I also used 10% Jitter for Hue, Saturation, and Brightness in the Color Dynamics setting and attached texture to my brush. Here, I'm using the Dab style stroke.

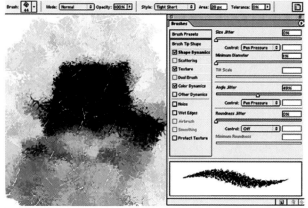

I used the exact settings as above but changed the stroke style to Tight Short.

characteristics see Chapter 35: "Painting in Photoshop." Finally, from the Options bar I chose a brush style (I've found that Tight Short and the Dab styles give you the most painterly look), the size of the Area that I want to paint, and the Tolerance. Lower tolerance values give you more fidelity to the original, but everything depends on the effect you want.

ART HISTORY IN ACTION

Once you have the white-filled layer and snapshot set up, and have chosen your brush and style settings, all you have to do is start painting. As you move your brush back and forth, you'll see that Photoshop is using the source snapshot as a reference for filling in the image in the new Art History style. If you want to have an idea of what part of your image will appear next, try making the white layer partially transparent with the Layer Opacity setting. This technique, as well as setting different Blend modes, can also be useful when you have finished painting with the Art History Brush and want to try combining the altered image with its original counterpart.

Because the result of brushstrokes varies greatly depending on many factors, including brush tip, shape and color dynamics, texture, area setting, tolerance value, and Blend mode, it's best to experiment to get the feel for how different brushes and brush styles affect the image. The illustrations on this page will give you an idea of the tremendous variety of styles that the Art History Brush is capable of if you just dig a bit deeper under its surface.

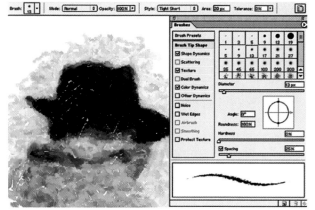

The same settings as version 2 but using a different Brush Tip Shape.

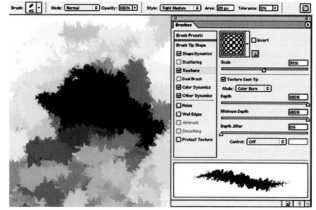

Many different settings for many different looks. Don't forget to set Tool Presets for Art History Brushes that give you looks you like!

9 TRANSFORMATION OF IMAGES, LAYERS, PATHS, AND SELECTIONS

Using the Photoshop transformation features to scale, resize, and distort your images.

One of Photoshop's strengths is its ability to work the way you work—numerically, if you're a by-the-numbers person, or intuitively, if you just like to move things around until they look right. Transforming images, layers, selections, and paths is one area where you'll appreciate this capacity.

In general, you want to initially scan an image at a size that will be big enough to encompass all the needs you will ever have for that image. You then color correct and spot that image to create your master version which you archive. Later, when you want to use that image for a particular purpose, you first resample a copy of it using Image/Image Size, or using the Cropping tool with a fixed target size, set to the dimensions and resolution you will need. This information about scanning and resampling your file is still important when you are going to transform an image, and it is covered in Chapter 16: "Image Resolution, Scanning Film, and Digital Cameras."

This chapter talks about how you can use the Edit/Free Transform command, as well as Edit/Transform/Scale, Rotate, Skew, Distort, and Perspective, to distort a version of a file, layer, or path. In addition, you can use Select/Transform Selection to make the same type of changes to an active selection. We will start with a simple case and then move into more complicated transforms. Let me first mention, however, that whenever you are doing a transform, the Info palette and the Options bar will show you your progress with the current change in angle, position, or dimensions. At any time while in the middle of the transform, you can use the Options bar to show you what you have done to the item so far and allow you to modify those changes numerically. All the Transform

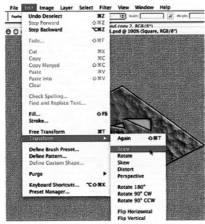

Here we see the Transform menu with all its individual options. You can choose any item from this menu to transform the image in one way at a time. While you are in the middle of a Free Transform, you can still choose any single option from this menu, which allows you to combine single transformation elements, working on them one at a time, before you have to accept any changes. This way, instead of having to type in a Scale value and press Return, type in a Rotate value and press Return, and type in a Skew value and press Return, you are able to begin the Free Transform, choose each option separately, set its value, and press Return only once at the end to make all the changes you entered. This gives you more control than simply dragging handles in a Free Transform.

The Info palette (F9) shows you on-the-fly progress during your transform even when the mouse is down and you are dragging a point. Use this for realtime feedback about your transformations.

At any time during a transformation, you can look at the Options bar to see what changes you have done so far and also to edit those changes on-the-fly while you work. From left to right, the first icon just tells you that you are doing a transform, the second icon allows you to place the center point for rotation in one of nine exact locations, the x and y position values can be shown, using the arrow to the left of the Y, as relative to the position before the transform or relative to the document's zero location. Moving to the right, you then see the percent change in width and height and can click on the Locking icon to make both percentages the same. Next you see the change in rotation angle, then the change in horizontal and vertical skew. All of these values can be edited as you work. A click on the Cancel transform icon (the circle with a line through it), or the Escape key, cancels the transform and a click on the Check icon, or Return, completes and accepts the transform.

Here we see a button that has been made up of three layers. Each of these layers has had layer styles applied to give it shadows, beveled edges, and so on. Because the layers Square, Square 2, and Square 3 are all linked together, with the middle linking column in the Layers palette, any transformation done to any one of them happens to all three of them. Because each layer is an object surrounded by transparency, we do not need to make a selection before transforming the entire object. The transparency itself is assumed to be the selection.

Here we see the Info and Options bar after scaling to 125%, rotating by -14°, and skewing by 9.6°. Being able to both see and change the transform values in the Options bar almost makes the Info palette unneeded for transforms.

The image after scaling to 125%, rotating by -14°, skewing by 9.6°, and then applying perspective.

commands, along with Free Transform, are interrelated, and you can go from one to the other while in the middle of a transform.

Let's take a look at each of these Transform options by themselves and then we'll see how they can be combined using Free Transform and the Edit/Transform menu. Take the case of the Square Button we see to the left. It is a simple shape but you will soon see that we can do a lot to it. Whatever we do to the Square Button, we could do to any image or any piece of an image that is pasted into Photoshop as a layer.

TRANSFORMING A SQUARE BUTTON

To begin, **open the SquareButton file in the Transformation folder of the** *Photoshop CS Artistry* **CD. Type an F to put the image in Full Screen mode, then type Command-Option-0** to zoom to 100%. **Bring up the Info palette (F9) and the Options bar (F12)** so you can see numerically what you are doing as you move the cursor during each transform. **Make sure Square is the active layer in the Layers palette and then choose Edit/Transform/Scale. Click the top-right handle and drag it up and to the right.** Pressing down the Shift key while dragging the corner forces the scale to be proportional. **Scale it to 125% while looking at the Info palette with the Shift key down.** If you can't get 125% exactly, you can actually type this number into the X scale factor of the Options bar, then click the Link icon to make the Y scale factor the same. **Now release the mouse, choose Edit/Transform/Rotate, and use the same top-right handle to rotate the image –14° by dragging up and to the left after clicking the handle. Now choose Edit/Transform/Skew and drag the top-middle handle to the left until the horizontal skew angle is 9.6 degrees. Finally, choose Edit/Transform/Perspective and click the top-right handle again. Drag it down until you see the dimension of the right edge decreasing from both the top and bottom at the same time.** The Options bar shows you the cumulative results of the four transforms you have made so far. The Rotate and Skew angles have changed due to the effects of the Perspective command you did at the end.

Now go ahead and **try Edit/Transform/Distort.** This allows you to click any corner handle and independently drag that corner in any direction while leaving the other corners alone. You can also click one of the handles in-between two corners and this allows you to distort that entire side of the image as a unit. Play around with Distort for a while, and remember that if you don't like the results, you can always exit and cancel the entire transform by choosing the Escape key or the Cancel transform icon at the right side of the Options palette. If you do this though, the image returns to the original rectangular button. While you are entering the individual Transform commands, Photoshop keeps track of all of them while showing you a quick preview. When you press Escape or Cancel transform, they all go away, and when you press Return, Enter, or the Check icon, they are all executed in the final high-resolution image. This final hi-res transform may take a little longer, especially on a large file. **I went ahead and used the Distort transformation to make the button appear as though the bottom of it was closer to me and the top was farther away. To do this in Edit/Transform/Distort, bring the top-right and bottom-left edges toward the center and move the top-left edge a bit until it looks right to you. Now go ahead and choose Return or Enter to finish the transformation and you will notice that it doesn't look as pixelated as the preview did.**

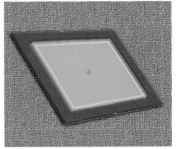

The above image after using Edit/Transform/Distort to make the bottom seem closer and the top farther away.

If you **choose File/Revert to revert your image** to the Square Button again, I'll show you how to do this transformation all in one step. This time **choose Edit/Free Transform (Command-T),** which will allow you to do all the different transformations at the same time. **To Scale to 125%, just click in the top-right handle and drag up and to the right with the Shift key down until you see 125% in the Info palette.** Make sure you release the mouse button before the Shift key to keep things proportional. **Now move the cursor a little above and to the right of the top-right handle and you should see a cursor curving to the left and down.** When you see this cursor, it is telling you that if you click and drag at this point, you can rotate your object. **While seeing the curved cursor, click and drag up and to the left until the angle in the Info palette is -14 degrees. To do the Skew, Command-click in the top-middle handle and drag to the left while keeping the mouse down until the delta H angle is 9.6. Don't move the mouse up or down while dragging to the left or you will also be changing the vertical scaling, and it may be hard to get the angle exactly at 9.6 without the scale changing too. When you get the angle to 9.6, you can release the Command key and you are then just adjusting the vertical scaling.** Since Free Transform does many things at once, it is sometimes hard to keep a particular component of your transform exact and you may have trouble getting back to exactly 125% scaling. The way to fix this is to **now release the mouse, then go into the Options bar to put the exact 125% value back in and adjust any other values.** You are still in Free Transform, so let's do some more transformations before we finish. **To do the Perspective, hold down Command-Option-Shift and then click and drag the top-right handle down and to the right. Finally you Distort by just holding down the Command key while you click and drag in any corner handle and then move it to where you want it. You can now press Return or Enter to finish the Free Transform.**

This is the default location for the rotation point, in the center of the object's area. We have placed the cursor on top of it and you can see the little black circle at the bottom-right of the cursor. This is telling you that you can now click the rotation point and drag it to its new location. Use the Reference Point Location icon at the top left of the Options palette to exactly place this rotation point in the center or on the corners or middle edges.

CHANGING THE CENTER POINT OF A ROTATE

A very useful feature that was added in Photoshop 5 is the capability to change the center of rotation during a transform. Go ahead and **open the original Square-Button file again from the hard disk. Now choose Edit/Free Transform (Command-T) and in the center of the button you will notice a small cross-hair with a circle in the middle of it. Let's call this the rotation point. When you put the cursor on top of it, the cursor gets a small circle at its lower right, as in the middle diagram on**

Here we are rotating the above button around a center point that was moved to the upper-right corner of the button. Now that we have rotated the button, the center point appears just to the left of the top of the button. You can see the curved rotation icon at the bottom below the center of the button.

the previous page. At this point, you can click and drag this rotation point anywhere on the screen. Now when you release the mouse, this moved location becomes the new center of rotation. After releasing the mouse, move the cursor to just outside one of the corner handles of the button until you see the curved rotation icon. Click and drag at that point to rotate the button and you will see that it is rotating around the center point wherever you placed it. You can even place it outside of the button's area. It is very powerful to be able to rotate around any center. You can, of course, move the center point over and over again and then re-rotate around that new center point. If you want to get the rotation point back to the center of the object, just drag it to the vicinity of the original center and it will jump to, and lock on, the center when it gets close enough. You can also use the Reference Point Location icon at the top left of the Options palette to exactly locate the reference point at the center, corners, or middle edges. **Try it!**

TRANSFORMING THE CONTENTS OF A SELECTION VERSUS TRANSFORMING THE SELECTION ITSELF

Choose File/Revert to get back to the original file and click the Square 3 layer in the Layers palette to activate that layer. Now Command-click the thumbnail for that layer to load that layer's transparency as a selection. Actually, the things that are not transparent are loaded as the selection. This layer has the Inner Glow effect on it to create the highlight around the green area in the center of the button. Let's say we want this area to be smaller in the center of the button. **Now choose Edit/Free Transform (Command-T), then Option-Shift-click the top-right handle, and keep the mouse button down while you drag that handle toward the center to make this center square smaller.** Remember that the Shift key forces the Scale to be proportional. The Option key makes the transformation happen symmetrically around the center of the area to be transformed. **Press Return after you have made the square smaller, as shown to the left.** We just did a Free Transform of the contents of a selection. When you have a selection, if you choose Edit/Free Transform and then do a transformation, you transform the contents of the selection within that layer, not the selection itself. To transform the selection and not its contents, you need to use Select/Transform Selection. Your selection should still be there, but if it is not, just Command-click the Square 3 layer again to reload it. **Choose Window/Show Info (F9) to bring up the Info palette. This time, choose Select/Transform Selection**, which puts you in a Free Transform mode where you are working on the Selection itself. **Now hold down Option-Shift while you drag the top-right handle and scale the selection inward until it is at 50% in the Info palette. Move the cursor just outside the top-right handle to get the rotate cursor and then rotate the selection up and to the left until you get –45 degrees in the Info palette.** Notice that the values in the Info palette and Options bar change on-the-fly as you move the mouse with the button down. **If you can't get the exact values you want in the Info palette, get it close using the mouse and then release the mouse button to edit the values inside the appropriate text boxes in the Options bar. Press Return or Enter to finish your transform.** This time you have transformed the selection itself and not the contents of the selection. Again,

Using a simple Elliptical Marquee and Select/Transform Selection can help speed production. I can use this basic selection with a feathered edge to selectively apply corrections such as Unsharp Mask to this young woman's face.

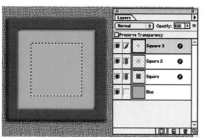
Command-clicking the thumbnail of Square 3 to load its non-transparent area as a selection.

Square 3 after making it smaller with Option-Shift-click and drag using Free Transform of the layer, then Return to finish that Free Transform.

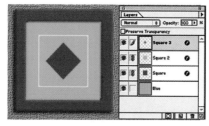
The final button after using Select/Transform Selection to create the center diamond area and then filling it with red.

Chapter 9: Transformation of Images, Layers, Paths, and Selections

the only difference is that to transform the selection itself, you start the process with Select/Transform Selection instead of Edit/Free Transform or Edit/Transform. **Now press I to get to the Eyedropper tool and click on the red color on the outside of the button to load it as the foreground color. Choose Edit/Fill (Shift-Delete) and use the pop-up to fill that selected area using the Foreground Color.** Your image should now look like the last image on the previous page.

TRANSFORM OF A PATH

Click Square 2 in the Layers palette to make it the active layer. Command-click the Square 2 thumbnail to load a selection of the non-transparent area of this layer. Now choose Window/Show Path (Shift-F11) to bring up the Paths palette. Choose Make Work Path from the Paths palette menu to turn this selection into a path and choose OK when asked if you want the Tolerance set to 2.0. You now have a path of the area around the edge of this layer. **Notice that if you go to the Edit menu, the Transform options are now Free Transform Path and Transform Path.** If you have an active path, you'll see these options, even if you have a selection marquee active at the same time. **Now choose Edit/Free Transform Path. Command-click in the top-right point of the path and drag it down and to the left until that point is at the top-right highlight on Square 3. Command-click the bottom-left point and drag it up and to the right until it is at the bottom-left highlight on Square 3. Press Return to complete the path transform, then choose Fill Path from the Paths palette menu to fill this area with the red foreground color. Drag the Work Path to the Trash icon in the Paths palette.** You should now have the Double Diamond image to the right.

LINKED LAYERS TRANSFORM AND MOVE AS A GROUP

The three layers in this example are all linked together, which you can see by noticing that the Link icon, the middle icon in the Layers palette, is on for the other two layers whenever a particular layer is active. Had we not loaded a selection to do the transformations on Square 3, all three layers would have transformed in the same way. Why don't you try this to see for yourself? **Use File/Revert to go back to the original file on the CD, then click on the Square 3 layer and, without loading a selection, choose Edit/Free Transform. You will have to first switch out of the Pen tools (type M for Marquee or H for Hand tool) to be able to access Free Transform again. Now start to scale the image and you will notice that all three layers, the entire button, scale together.** If you use the Move tool to move any of these layers, they will also all move together because they are linked. This is a very useful feature when you create an object that is made up of more than one layer but you want to move it or scale it as a whole. You can also drag and drop this linked object to another document and all the layers will be copied to the other document with the same names as they have in your current document. Combining all the layers that make up this button into a layer set makes this even more convenient. **Press Escape or Command-Period to cancel this transformation, then choose Layer/New/Layer Set from Linked (Shift-F12) to move these linked layers into a set named Button.** Layer sets and linking layers allow you to create component or library documents that contain your stan-

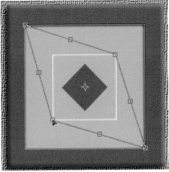

Moving the path points with the Command key down while in Free Transform Path.

The final Double Diamond Button after filling the path with red.

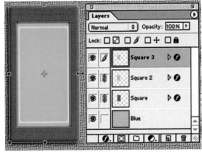

Here we are using Free Transform to scale only Square 3, and yet the other two layers are scaling too because they are linked to Square 3.

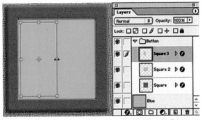

Here we see the same transform as above, after creating the Button layer set. Here only the Square 3 layer is changing because we unlinked it from the other two layers.

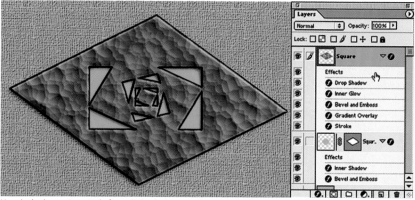

dard objects, like buttons for example. When you need one of these objects, you just open that library document and drag and drop that component into your current working document. To get around this linking so you can move or transform a layer that has other layers linked to it, you need to first click in the Linking column of any other layers where the Link icon shows up. This unlinks those layers from the one you want to change. If there are a lot of other layers linked to this one, it may be faster to just activate one of the other layers and then click the Linking column of the layer you want to modify. This single act unlinks it from all the rest of the group. In either case, you can now transform or move the current layer. If you want to relink the layers after the change, just reclick in the Linking column of the layer(s) you unlinked before and the Link icon should show up again. You can also click and drag through a bunch of layers' Linking columns to do a group linking in one step.

EDIT/TRANSFORM/ROTATE AND FLIP VERSUS IMAGE/ROTATE AND FLIP CANVAS

Edit/Transform/Rotate or Edit/Transform/Flip of a layer rotates or flips the currently active layer and any other layers that are linked to it. This command also affects a layer set full of linked or unlinked layers if the layer set is active in the Layers palette. Image/Rotate Canvas/Rotate or Flip rotates or flips the entire document, including all layers whether they are linked or not.

REAL WORLD USES OF TRANSFORM

You may be wondering just how often you'll have to use Edit/Transform if you work as a photographer. If you do any compositing at all, you'll find being able to use these commands effectively will be an immediate time-saver. And I'm not only talking about fancy, artistic composites; the retouching of the faces in Chapter 29, "The McNamaras," would be very difficult without Free Transform. It's also used in Chap-

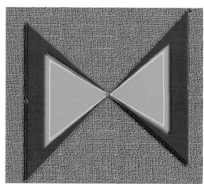

With Free Transform, you can hold the Command key down while dragging the corners across each other to create the bow-tie twist look.

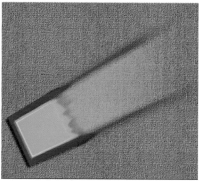

Square Button Reentry Vehicle #1. Free Transform of the button and a stretched ghost image.

Square Button Reentry Vehicle #2. The image above using Color Dodge between the ghost image and the button layers.

Here is the image I created after a little playing, starting with the SquareButton file on the CD. Notice all the effects I added to the Square layer. To create the holes in the middle of this layer, I made rectangular selections, then transformed the selected part of the layer. By rotating and shrinking these selections the holes were created. This file is also on the CD and is called SquareButtonCreation1.

Chapter 9: Transformation of Images, Layers, Paths, and Selections

ter 28: "Rain in Costa Rica," Chapter 30: "The PowerBook Ad," Chapter 32: "Vector Masks, Shape Layers, and Layer Styles," and Chapter 34: "HeartSinger CD Cover."

If you're an architectural photographer you'll find transforms handy when you need to change the perspective of a shot to straighten buildings.

If you're a production person, transformations will be part of the daily routine, whether you're working with images and text for advertising, Web work, television, or film.

And if you're a fine artist, the possibilities are endless as you construct your images.

Photoshop is a powerful tool for compositing and retouching, and the capacity to transform images and selections is part of the reason.

The original 6x7 photograph of this school bus and sky was taken just before sunset from a low camera angle with a wide angle lens. Notice how the bus is wider on the bottom than the top.

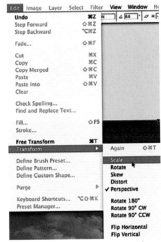

To fix this first we used Edit/Transform/Perspective, which widens both corners equally. Then we switched to Scale, before pressing Return to end the transform operations. Finally we used Distort to stretch out just the top-right side. See the Illustration below-left.

After doing Edit/Transform/Perspective, then Scale, then Distort, here is the way the preview looks on the screen. I sometimes do these in separate increments, versus just using Free Transform, because that gives you more control on each step and avoids an accidental rotate or something like that. Do all the steps, though, before pressing Return to end the transform.

Here is the final image after the transform steps. Notice how much of the original sky is missing at the top of the image and also to the left and right. When you shoot something that will have to be fixed this way, make sure you leave extra image area around the edges as it will get lost like it did here.

10 DIGITAL CAMERAS AND CAMERA RAW

Using the new Photoshop CS Camera Raw Filter to improve digital images shot in Raw format.
My comments on the current state of digital cameras and their use versus the use of film.

My Digital Camera Experiences and What this Chapter Will and Will Not Cover

In this chapter I will do my best to cover the different features of Photoshop's great new Camera Raw filter, which has a lot of improvements over the one that was optionally available as a download for Photoshop 7. If you are using a digital camera and want to get the best quality images, shooting in Raw format is certainly the best way to do this as it gives you many improvement options after actually exposing the original image.

I have spent the last few months using the Adobe Camera Raw filter to make improvements to Raw digital image files captured from cameras including the Nikon D100, Fuji S2, and the Canon EOS Rebel, 10D and 1DS. My experience with this Camera Raw filter is based on working with images from those cameras. Over that last two years, I've also made lots of 22-inch-wide prints from many digital camera files brought in by students who have taken my digital printmaking workshops. This has been my main exposure to digital images from digital cameras so far. I also have colleagues, whose opinions I greatly respect, who work with 120-4x5 film and also digital scanning back cameras for commercial work. We have many discussions about these issues. I've been working with film since I was 14 and have my own Canon 35mm F1 and EOS cameras, a Pentax 6x7 120 camera, and also a Gowland 4x5 camera. I've scanned film using many different film scanners since 1988 when desktop digital imaging had its beginnings. I'm very familiar with what a scanner can get from film and how to get the best data out of film for use within Photoshop. I've owned an Epson 3.2 megapixel point-and-shoot camera for the last several years and have greatly enjoyed the fun, instant feedback and ease of use with digital cameras. I've been waiting for their quality to improve, though, before using one for my landscape photography work where I want to be able to make 20x30 or even larger prints.

Based on these experiences I'm certainly impressed with what digital cameras can now do and I feel that for many people there is no longer a good reason to shoot with film. I'll talk about that film versus digital choice based on the above mentioned experiences. I'm not going to focus on, recommend, or not recommend any particular digital camera, although I will talk about my experiences, and those of my colleagues and students, with some of these cameras. I'm sure that six months from now there will be a whole new set of digital camera products on the market; the important issue for you is why and how you make the decision to buy and use a particular digital camera or continue to use film.

Using Photoshop's Camera Raw Filter

Digital Camera File Types

When you take a photo with a digital camera, there are several steps before that image data gets stored into the camera's memory. The digital camera has a sensor (CCD, CMOS, or some other technology) that takes the place of film to actually capture the scene from the back of your lens. When you save in jpeg and usually tiff format, before saving the file into the camera's memory, this raw data from the sensor usually gets processed and changed by the camera's software based on the camera's exposure and ISO settings, sharpening choice, image compression quality, and other camera preset information. When you save the file in Raw format, then the information from the camera's sensor gets saved directly to the camera's memory card along with the current settings you had on your camera, the white point the camera measured, shutter and f-stop info, etc. Later when you open a digital camera image, if you saved it in normal tiff or jpeg format, the image opens directly into Photoshop. If you saved the file in Raw format, then the file will open into Photoshop's Camera Raw filter, which also sees all the setting, white balance, etc. information from your camera; but now you get to choose what to do with that information as you look at how it alters the color and contrast of the image and its histogram. It is true that you can't change the shutter speed and f-stop that you shot with, which will affect sharpness and depth of field, but there are many other things you can change and improve. This is way better, and you'll see here that shooting in Raw format and using the new Photoshop CS Camera Raw filter allows you to get way more information from your digital camera files.

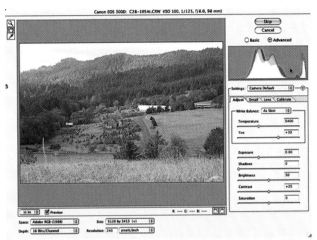

Here we see the entire Photoshop CS Camera Raw dialog. Up in the top-left corner are the Zoom, Hand, and White balance tools. In the bottom-left corner are the zoom percentage menu and Preview button, Space, Depth, Size, and Resolution menus. Just to the right of those are the pixel value readouts and rotate icons. On the top-right side and downward are the Basic or Advanced buttons, the histogram display, the Settings menu, as well as Load and Save pop-up. The four main adjustment windows are below those menus. They are, from left to right, Adjust, Detail, Lens, and Calibrate. We'll talk about each of these parts of this Camera Raw dialog during this chapter.

Philosophy of Using Camera Raw

My workflow for scanning film is to use the scanner hardware and software to get all the information out of the film so I have the most options when I get the file into Photoshop. I generally don't use the scanner's software to do major color correcting work or sharpening on the file since I'm better at doing that with Photoshop. I've taken a similar approach in looking at the Camera Raw filter and its options. I want to know which Camera Raw options will give me a better digital original and also do something that I couldn't do as well or better in Photoshop. For example, if the digital file has already lost its highlight or shadow detail when I first bring it into Photoshop, then there is no easy magic in Photoshop that will bring it back. It would be better if I could change a setting in Camera Raw to bring back that lost Shadow or Highlight detail because it still is actually in the Raw data. Similar things could be said for using Raw to minimize digital sharpening or color noise artifacts or color casts that happen with every file from that camera. I don't want to perfectly color correct and contrast control every image before it comes into Photoshop, especially if this removes important options from what I can do with the file once in Photoshop. Now we'll explain the different features of Camera Raw.

Zoom, Hand, Eyedropper, and Preview Checkbox

To open an image into Camera Raw, first you have to transfer it from your camera to your computer's hard disk and there are a variety of ways to do that. Once on

Here we see the Zoom, Hand, and White Balance Tools. Zoom and Hand work just like in Photoshop.

the hard disk, it's easy to double-click on the raw file from inside the File Browser. In the File Browser you can see thumbnail previews of all your Raw files even when they are still numbered files directly from your camera. While you are in Camera Raw, you can use the Zoom and Hand tools to magnify or de-magnify the preview of the image you are working with on the screen. The standard Photoshop command keys (Command-Spacebar-click to zoom in, Option-Spacebar-click to zoom out and Spacebar to scroll) always work just like they do in Photoshop. I like to click on the Hand tool when I enter Camera Raw—that way I can scroll without using the Spacebar. When I want to Zoom in or out, I just use Command-Spacebar-click or Command-Option-click. There is also a menu in the lower-left corner that shows you the current zoom factor and allows you to pick a new one from 6% up to 400%.

The Eyedropper here is actually called the White Balance tool and will set the white balance at a location that you click on in the image. I prefer to do this inside Photoshop.

SPACE, SIZE, DEPTH, AND RESOLUTION

The Space menu in the lower-left corner allows you to set Adobe RGB, ColorMatch RGB, ProPhoto RGB, or sRGB as the color space your image will open to inside Photoshop.

The Depth menu allows you to open the Raw file in either 8 bit per channel or 16-bit per channel format. We recommend 16-bit per channel as this will keep all the information from your digital camera's sensor and give you the most options once in Photoshop.

You can change the zoom factor by clicking with the Zoom tool, Option-clicking to zoom out, or by using the Zoom menu at the middle left here. To the right side, you see the digital values at the current cursor location and there are icons to rotate left or right. The four menus to the bottom left allow you to set the color Space, bit Depth (8 or 16 bit), file Size, and resolution of the file. Resolution doesn't change the file Size; actually it just sets the default resolution, and therefore size, of a print.

These are the size choices given for a 6 megapixel camera, the Canon 10D or EOS Digital Rebel.

The Size menu allows you to open the file at the size the camera captured it, as shown to the left, or at several smaller or larger sizes. If you are going to res up the file for making larger prints, you'll get better results doing it with Camera Raw than using Image Size in Photoshop to do a one-shot res up. I compared the two and found that the Camera Raw version got fewer sharpening artifacts later in the process. I haven't yet compared a res up in Camera Raw to Genuine Fractals or to doing a res up in 10% increments using Photoshop's Image Size. The 10% increment approach does appear to work a bit better on some digital images. If you do Image Size of 110% seven times, that is very close in size to double the original size. Notice the new ArtistKeys action ResUpby10 (Command-Shift-F1), which does exactly that and gives you a file that is 5987 pixels wide instead of 6144 when starting with a 3072 wide image. I just tried it and I believe it does a bit cleaner res up than doing the res up in Camera Raw. I'll try it on some more images, but I did like what I saw with the test image I've been working with. If you have to res up a file then, compare the res up to 6144 using Camera Raw with opening up the 3072 default file, then running my ResUpby10 Artistkeys action. You may like the action a little better but it does take a bit longer.

The Resolution setting does nothing to the file size or the number of pixels in the file. All it does is set the number of pixels per inch that will be used when the file is printed. You can always change this later using Image/Image Size in Photoshop but if you always print at the same resolution, then you might as well set it here.

ADJUST

When you have Camera Raw set to the Advanced mode, using the buttons in the top-right of the dialog, you get four folder tabs each containing a separate category of adjustments you can make to the raw file before it opens into Photoshop. The ones in the Adjust and Detail section are usually the most important, and the Adjust section is where you will be making most of your image specific changes. It's impor-

Chapter 10: Digital Cameras and Camera Raw

tant to remember that Photoshop remembers the settings you used last time you opened a file with camera raw, and these settings are automatically applied to that file's preview as it appears in the File Browser. You can use Automate/Apply Camera Raw Settings in the File Browser to have the File Browser use the settings for the current file on all the other raw files in the current folder.

I usually start out leaving the White Balance set to As Shot, which sets the color temperature based on what was set and/or measured in the camera. I find that I don't use the preset white balance choices in the White Balance menu. The Temperature setting in the White Balance section actually adjusts your Blue/Yellow balance and the Tint adjustment changes the Green/Magenta balance. You can play with these here to get the basic color balance of the image to look better, but first I'd adjust the Exposure, Shadows, and Contrast below to get the histogram to spread across the full range. Once these are adjusted, if the image seems too yellow or blue, adjust the Temperature; if the image seems too green or magenta, adjust the

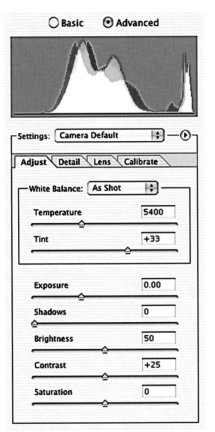

Here we see the Basic settings for the Adjust section and the histogram for this image which has flat shadows and some lost highlights.

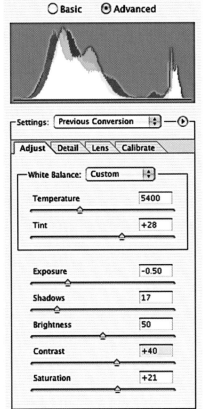

Here we see the Adjust settings for the same image as on the left where we have lowered the Exposure, to bring back highlight detail, increased Shadows and Contrast, to spread the histogram out across a fuller range, and also changed Tint and Saturation.

Tint. I'd do your final color balance adjustments once you get into Levels, as described in Chapter 19: "Overall Color Correction," but Temperature and Tint are good for improving something that is obviously out of adjustment.

The first thing I do when I pull up an image is adjust the Exposure, usually lowering it to bring back any highlight detail that was lost. Holding down the Option key while adjusting the Exposure slider turns the image black and as you continue to increase Exposure, clipped values will show up as non-black. If you needed to get more shadow detail out of an image, you could also increase the Exposure. When the histogram moves away from the far right edge, that brings back your highlight detail. If there is a gap on the left side of the histogram, as seen in the leftmost illustration above, then move the Shadows slider to the right and/or increase the Contrast to spread the histogram further apart; just keep an eye on the right, highlight, end to make sure values don't get all the way to it and off the right side. Holding the Option key down while moving the Shadow slider to the right will show clipped shadow detail as non-white areas. If the image is dark in the midtones, you can increase the Brightness. If colors are dull, you can increase the Saturation, but you could also make those adjustments later in Levels and Hue/Saturation. The most critical adjustments in this section, which you may not be able to make once you get to Levels, are changing Exposure, Shadows, and Contrast so you don't loose any highlight or shadow details.

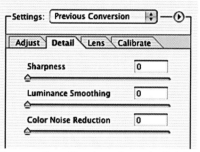

These are the settings I usually use for Detail. I always turn off Sharpness here since I sharpen after my color correction is finished. I often find that having Color Noise Reduction on can really desaturate subtle colors in 3/4 tones and shadows, not to mention the rest of the image, so I usually leave it off, set to 0, unless I see a problem with the colors. I leave Color Noise Reduction on if I'm getting distorted blotchy colors because it helps remove those distortions.

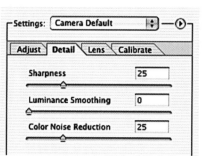

Here we see the Basic settings for the Detail section which includes turning on Sharpening and Color Noise Reduction as you open the file.

DETAIL

The next folder tab over is the Detail section. This section has to do with adjustments that could affect the lightness or image detail values in the image. Sharpness, which has a default value of 25, determines if the digital image is automatically sharpened by the Camera Raw filter. When you save digital camera files in jpeg format, they are often automatically sharpened. The workflow I use for working with images from film is the same that should work best for images from digital cameras. Sharpening uses differences in color and

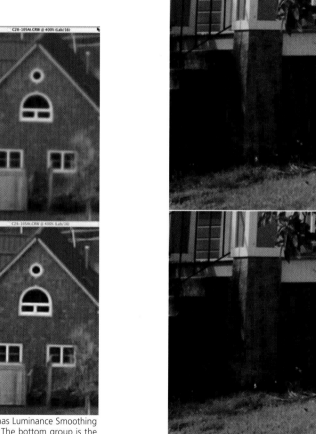

In the top group of two images, the left one has Luminance Smoothing set to 0 and the right one has it set to 100. The bottom group is the same two images we started with on top except that both of them have now been sharpened by the same amount. Notice how much more pixel distortion there is on the sharpened image to the left. We're looking at these images at 400% zoom factor so you can see what Luminance Smoothing does. It does reduce some of these digital-like artifacts, but this also makes the sharpened version appear less sharp when viewed at 100% zoom factor. Thanks to Garth at Cross Roads Camera store in Corvallis for lending me a Canon Digital Rebel and 10D to get these and other shots used in my digital camera evaluations.

The top image has Color Noise Reduction off and the bottom image has it on at 25%. Notice how the top image has more vibrant purple flowers and grass details. The top image also has strange color artifacts in the concrete and in the green color on the house and certainly in the bush leaves. In the bottom image the small purple flowers in the shadows almost disappear and the grass loses detail becoming somewhat blotchy. I'd leave Color Noise Reduction off unless you notice blotchy color artifacts; in that case you'll need to turn it on but when you do, watch out you don't lose important subtle shadow colors and details. Thanks to Pro-Photo in Portland for helping me get these 1DS shots.

contrast to decide what areas or edges to sharpen. When you color correct an image, those edges often become more distinct because you add contrast and saturation to the image. Once the image has its final color and contrast, the sharpening algorithms can do a more accurate job. Therefore I believe it is best to set the Sharpness slider to 0 and sharpen using Photoshop's Unsharp mask filter possibly along with my Sharpen Only Edges BH action script or some other sharpening action or filter technique. If you are going to resample the image using ResUpby10, Genuine Fractals, or some other technique, that is another reason to leave the sharpening to later. A lot of the noise one sees from digital camera images comes from sharpening them too soon using the built-in sharpening software in the camera.

Luminance Smoothing appears to reduce digital artifacts in the lightness values of the image or details of the image. I probably wouldn't turn this on unless your images appear too noisy. When viewed at 400%, as in the illustration on the previous page, these artifacts seem bad, but I believe at many print sizes, or when viewed at 100% on the screen, they can give the image some extra apparent detail.

Color Noise Reduction is also something that I don't turn on unless I have an image with obvious problems. You'll notice that when you turn it on, even at 25%, it reduces the saturation of colors in the image and can almost remove subtle colors in the 3/4 tone and dark shadow areas. If you have really saturated blotches in leaves or other places that don't reflect actual detail in the original image, that is a good time to turn Color Noise Reduction on. You can also open one version of the image with it on and another version of the image with it off, put the two as layers on top of each other, then just paint in the Color Noise Reduction in the areas where you really need it. See Chapter 26: "Combining Bracketed Captures or Scans to Increase Dynamic Range," for the details of how to composite two versions of the same image together and then get the best of each image.

LENS

The Lens section is needed only if your lens has either a Chromatic Aberration or Vignetting problem. I've actually seen these problems on 35mm film I have scanned and suggested to Adobe that they also provide these filters to process any digital image, like one scanned from film.

On certain scans, probably from my zoom lens and not my fixed focus lenses, I've noticed a subtle red or green fringe on distinct edges. When looking at each channel separately, it seemed that those edges were in a slightly different place on the red channel than the green channel. Each channel is in focus but the location is slightly different in each. This problem will get worse as you move away from the center of the image, and you'll have a red fringe on one side of an object and a green fringe on the other side. This problem can actually be caused by a Chromatic Aberration lens defect that focuses reds to a slightly different size than greens. The Chromatic Aberration R/C slider adjusts the size of the Red channel relative to the Green channel. The Chromatic Aberration B/Y slider adjusts the size of the Blue channel relative to the Green channel. If you hold the Option key down while moving the slider, the other Chromatic Aberration problem channel will be turned off so you can view and solve one problem at a time. For example, if you are working with the R/C slider, holding the Option key down will turn off viewing of the B/Y problem making it easier to see when you've fixed the R/C one. These Chromatic Aberration corrections happen to a greater extent as you move away from the center of the image where no correction is needed.

I have a 35mm pocket camera that has a Vignetting problem when I shoot it in 28mm wide angle mode. The corners are darker than the rest of the image and are

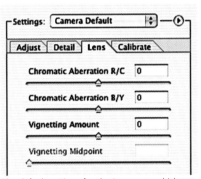

The default settings for the Lens area, which you wouldn't change unless you were having one of these problems with your camera's lens.

Using Photoshop's Camera Raw Filter

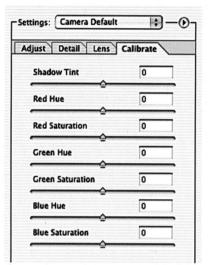

If you are happy with the way Camera Raw brings in images from your camera, leave all these set to 0. You would change these to calibrate Camera Raw's default settings for your type of camera. Doing this with a carefully photographed calibration image would probably be helpful.

If you are unhappy with the Camera Default setting for your camera, you can change it by tweaking any of your settings while looking at a Raw shot of a calibration image while in Camera Raw. Once you get that Calibration image to display correctly in Camera Raw, choose Set Camera Default to set those changes up as the new Camera Default for that Camera. You could have several settings that you switch between depending on the lighting situation you are shooting with. You can go back to Adobe's default profile for that camera by choosing Reset Camera Default.

also a bit out of focus. The Vignetting Amount slider helps to correct this problem and when you move it from the 0 Location, the Vignetting Midpoint slider activates and controls how far out from the center of the image the correction starts to take effect. The larger the number, the closer it is to the corner before the adjustment starts to happen. Positive Vignetting values brighten the corners, which is usually what you want; negative values actually darken the corners. These are great new features when you need them! Wish I could also use them on some of my 35mm scans.

CALIBRATE

If you consistently notice that your digital images have a color cast in them or some other problem that happens on every image or on every image taken in a certain type of lighting condition, you may need to calibrate your camera for that type of shooting situation. The Photoshop Camera Raw filter has built-in profiles for most of the cameras currently on the market and uses those for the Camera Default settings. To calibrate your camera to a certain shooting situation, photograph in Raw format a GretagMacbeth ColorChecker chart, or similar calibrated target, using the lighting that you'd like to calibrate to. You can purchase a ColorChecker chart at most professional camera stores for about $75. Bring the photographed version of the ColorChecker chart up into the Camera Raw filter and choose Camera Default from the Settings menu. That will display the ColorChecker on your calibrated monitor using whatever profile Photoshop has for your camera. Place the physical ColorChecker chart so you can see it lit with the type of light source that is most important for viewing that kind of image, or in a 5000 kelvin light box or under 5000k lights, if you have no particular preference. If the image on the screen does not match the ColorChecker chart, then go to the Calibrate section and Adjust the sliders there to try and make a better match. Shadow Tint only affects color casts in non-neutral shadow areas. If you hold down the Option key while in Shadow Tint, the on screen display will show you if your adjustments are clipping any shadow values, the clipped values will show up in non-white areas. The Red, Green, and Blue Hue and Saturation sliders also affect only non-neutral colors. If you always want your Reds to be more saturated, but not necessarily your Greens for example, changing this with the Red Saturation slider in the Calibrate section is good.

If you want to change your Camera Default to these new Calibrate settings, choose Set Camera Default as shown in the dialog to the left. You can also change other settings, like choosing no Sharpness and no Color Noise Reduction from the Detail section, before choosing Set Camera Default, then those settings will also become part of the new default for this camera. You could also have several default settings, for different lighting situations, that you have each saved by first using Save Settings. When you are shooting under one of those particular conditions, that condition can be temporarily set up as the camera default or just explicitly chosen from the Settings menu. See the section below and the captions on this page and the next page for more information about saving and loading settings.

SETTINGS: LOAD, SAVE, PREFERENCES, AND CAMERA DEFAULT

As mentioned above and explained in the captions on this page and the next page, you can use the Load and Save pop-up menu, from the rightmost arrow button, to Load Settings, Save Settings, Save Settings Subset, or Delete Current Settings, and also to set Preferences. This menu is also used to Set Camera Default to the currently selected settings or to Reset Camera Default to the original profile for this camera from Adobe. If you have a lot of similar images in a series then after changing the adjustments for the first one, you might want to choose Save Settings

Chapter 10: Digital Cameras and Camera Raw

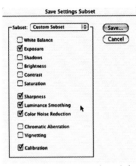

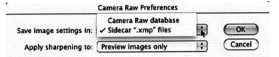

The Camera Raw Preferences are accessed from the Load and Save pop-up menu. If you choose to Save Image Settings in Sidecar .xmp files, then the settings you used to open a particular file will be saved with that file and move with the file from machine to machine. If you choose Apply Sharpening to Preview Images Only, then sharpening will not actually be applied to the files when you open them. These are the settings I use.

If you choose Save Settings Subset, then only the settings that are checked get saved in this settings set. Later when you load settings from that set, only the checked settings will be changed.

on these. When you get to the next image in that series, you can use Load Settings to start with the same settings you used on that first image. Once you have Saved Settings, you can also access those settings from the Settings menu. Use Save Settings Subset to only save certain settings. For example, if you hardly ever have Sharpening or Color Noise Reduction on, then you might want to Set Camera Default with those off and any other settings you always want changed as defaults. You could also do a Save Settings Subset, called Sharp&CNROn, saving just Sharpness and Color Noise Reduction with those on and just those checked. If you do come across an image where you want to have those on, but not change anything else, you can then load that Sharp&CNROn subset and only those two values will change and all your other settings will stay the same. The Preferences choice in the Load and Save pop-up menu allows you to set the two preferences described in the screen grab and caption at the top-center of this page.

The Settings menu shows you settings saved in the default Applications/Adobe Photoshop CS/Presets/Camera Raw folder that is created when you install Photoshop CS. If you save settings in other places, or get some from an outside location, you'd have to access them from the Load Settings item in the Load and Save pop-up menu.

While in the File Browser and having clicked on a certain Camera Raw image, you can choose Automate/Apply Camera Raw Settings from the built-in camera raw menu to apply a particular setting to that image. You can even change those settings while in this menu, but it makes more sense to do that once you are in the Camera Raw dialog since you then get a larger preview and can also see the image's histogram. If you have a group of Raw format images selected in the File Browser, you can apply a particular setting to all of them and their thumbnails will update to that setting when you click the Update button in the Apple Camera Raw Settings dialog.

DIGITAL CAMERAS VERSUS FILM

Without question, using a digital camera is much easier, faster, and cheaper than shooting film when you will be using Photoshop to color correct and print your images. The only good reason to use film these days is when there is an image quality or shooting performance advantage. Digital cameras have improved a lot over the last two years, and you now also get much more for your money. I spent a lot of time over the last few months looking at files from various digital cameras as well as opening and correcting those files within the Photoshop CS Camera Raw filter. For a growing group of people, including many commercial photographers, it no longer makes sense to shoot film. More than 50% of the people who take my digital print-making workshops now have digital cameras, but some of them still use film for their

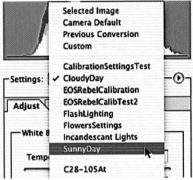

This Load and Save pop-up menu, obtained from the circular pop-up icon to the right, allows you to Load or Save settings defaults and also set Preferences.

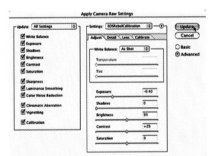

The Settings menu allows you to change your settings from the Camera Default settings, the Previous Raw Conversion for this image, or other settings you have saved before.

You can use the Automate/Apply Camera Raw Settings menu in the File Browser to apply any settings to a particular file and have those settings update the viewing of that file in the File Browser.

highest quality larger format landscape shooting. I'll go through each type of camera and shooting situation and give you my impressions of the issues.

POINT-AND-SHOOT TYPE CAMERAS

For this type of camera and shooting fun and family photos, there is no good reason to continue to use film. We love our little Epson 3.2 megapixel point-and-shoot and have shot thousands of images with it over the last two years. With a digital camera I find that I just shoot away because there is no worry about wasting film. Because of this freedom I've gotten many great shots that I wouldn't have taken with film. I've had a lot of fun with this camera and now Max, our 8 year old, is using and having fun with it. Wendy used it to shoot the annual end-of-the-year slide show (now a digital slide show) at Max's school, and the first-ever digital version of this show was a big success. Why pay to have film and prints processed when you only want 25% of the images anyway. With digital you can just print the ones you want. The inexpensive Epson and HP printers that have slots for your CompactFlash cards allow you to print directly to the printer. For making higher quality prints, bringing the files into Photoshop first is better. For family photos up to 8x10 in size, the 3.2 megapixel models are fine. The 4-5 megapixel cameras should be able to support prints up 11x14 in size when correctly exposed and adjusted in Photoshop. Most of these point and shoot cameras don't support saving files in Camera Raw mode, although the Nikon Coolpix 5700 does and it's a great 5 megapixel camera. A nice thing about these point and shoot digitals is that the built-in zoom lenses are designed for each specific camera so a 28mm lens really is a 28mm lens. With 35mm digitals in the side bar, we explain how your 28mm might really be a 44mm. To get started for cheap you can get a 3.2 megapixel Olympus, Nikon, or Canon camera for $200 to $400 dollars. I'm going to find the smallest of these and just keep it in my pocket all the time to have fun with. We no longer use film for family photos!

35MM TYPE CAMERAS

I've been looking at images from the Nikon D100, the Fuji S2, and the Canon EOS 10D and new Digital Rebel. Many of my workshop students have brought in images from these 6 megapixel type digital cameras, and they usually leave the workshop with several very nice quality 22-inch-wide prints via my Epson 7600 printer. From a 6 megapixel raw file resampled up to 200%, I can make a 17-inch-wide print at 360 dpi or a 25-inch-wide print at 240 dpi. If you shoot with a tripod or image stabilized lens, the quality of these files can be very high, so a res up by 200% followed by a quality sharpening can produce a beautiful print. I've found that many students who had a large investment in Nikon lenses decided to buy the Nikon D100. Some of them, who wanted even larger files, got the Fuji S2, which produces beautiful images. The comments I've heard on the S2 have all been very positive when it comes to image quality. The Nikon D100 seems to rate better for camera feel and features. I used one of my student's S2 and was very impressed with the images I got. The camera seemed fine to me too, but I'm not as picky about camera bodies as some people.

I shot some comparison images of the same scene with my friend Jack Saik's Nikon D100 versus my Canon EOS 10S with Fuji Provia 100. These were close-ups of flowers. I opened the raw files from Jack's camera with Photoshop CS Camera Raw and adjusted the images to have as much highlight detail as possible. For these types of close-up images, I didn't feel that there was much advantage to film. The digital files actually had more shadow details, as they usually do.

One problem with most of the 35mm digital cameras so far is that the digital sensor actually has a smaller surface area than 35mm film that most 35mm lenses were designed for. You can use your existing 35mm film lenses with these cameras but because of the smaller digital sensor, your 28mm film lens, on the Canon EOS Digital Rebel, for example, will really end up being a 28*1.6=45mm lens. Your 50mm lens will end up being a 50*1.6=80mm. This is great if you like to shoot telephoto because your 400mm ends up being a 400*1.6=640mm. If you like to shoot wide angle though, like I do, that 28mm to 45mm transition is a bummer. This has been one reason why I have avoided buying a digital 35mm so far. Recently there have been some new zoom lenses, like the 18-55mm that comes with the Digital Rebel, that help solve this problem. 18*1.6=29mm, I can live with that. One of the things I really like about the Canon 1DS is that its digital sensor is the same size as 35mm film, so the lenses are the same with both film and the 1DS. That's part of the reason it's $8,000!

I also did another comparison between the Canon EOS Digital Rebel and my Canon EOS 10S again shooting Fuji Provia 100. I have similar feelings about close-ups of fall leaves on the grass. The digital close-up images had more shadow detail available via Camera Raw, and the overall quality of the digital files made me think it was time to stop shooting 35mm film. Over the past two months, the cost of buying and processing the 12 rolls of transparencies I shot would have paid for 25% of the digital Rebel. Not to mention the time it took to scan just some of them. I still have lots left in my "to scan one day" pile. There is one test, though, where I felt that the 35mm film images gave me a bit better information than the Digital Rebel. I shot a landscape image from up on a hill looking down over a valley with some homes and a horse stable. These smaller items in the distance, as well as the tree-covered mountains behind them, had more detail in the 35mm film images. Both these scenes were shot with the same exact lens. I took my 28-105 Canon lens off the EOS 10S and used that on the Digital Rebel to also shoot the digital version. Just to compare, I also shot a digital version with the built-in 18-55 zoom that comes with the Rebel. Its quality was about the same as the image shot with my 28-105. I believe I could make a great looking 22-inch-wide print from either the film or the digital camera image. If I wanted to make a 20x30 print, then I believe the file from film would look a little better.

Unless the price of the Canon 1DS comes down dramatically, I'll be buying a Canon EOS Digital Rebel ($899) or a Canon 10D ($1499) soon! I did compare the Digital Rebel with the 10D, including shooting the same images with both, and I believe the image quality will be the same on either. The reason to get the 10D would be the extra durability and/or the extra professional features it has. If you are thinking about buying either one, I'd compare the specifications for both cameras at www.canonusa.com. For $899 that Digital Rebel may be the best deal right now! By the time this book is printed, there will likely be something else newer and maybe even better. That's the digital world.

For most people shooting 35mm, especially people who do a lot of shooting, I believe digital cameras are now the better choice. There is no cost to buy or process film, no cost to buy a scanner, and no more hours spent looking at slides on the light table, cleaning and dusting, then doing scans. How liberating!

My friend Bruce Ashley (www.bruceashleyphotography.com, 831-429-8300), who does great commercial photography, has now converted his entire studio to digital, as have many other commercial photographers. Bruce uses a Canon D60 when he needs to shoot live action or on location for jobs with prints up to 11x17. For still life, extra control, and very large output, he uses a Betterlight 6K-2 4x5 scanning back on his Sinar camera. Bruce is a person who used to have a process camera in his studio (now that's a cool machine) and for many years he did much of the product photography for Apple. Hearing that Bruce has now gone totally digital impressed me greatly because I've always found his work to be of the highest quality.

For those times when I'm shooting landscape photos and I only have one camera on me, like backpacking in the Sierras, I might still be

These are the two comparison images with the film scan on the left and the D100 file on the right. See below for a description to what I did to each of them to end up in a very similar place in the end.

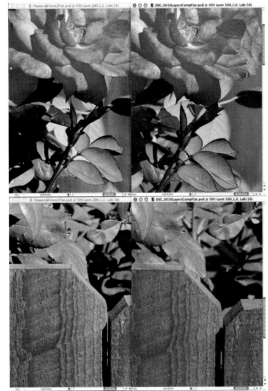

Here we see close-ups of different sections of the Film vs D100 comparison with the film on the left and the D100 Image on the right. Each was color corrected, using the techniques in Chapter 19, so it would look good and also match the other. The Fuji Provia film was scanned at 4000 dpi on a Polaroid Sprintscan 120, the D100 Image was brought in from Photoshop CS Camera Raw at the default D100 Raw size of 3008 by 2000 and color corrected, then a flattened copy was resed up using my ResUpby10 action. Each was then sharpened so they would print well and also match each other in sharpness. To do this with the D100 image, I just sharpened by 500,1,0. The film image was run through my SharpenOnlyEdgesBH action, then the top layer was sharpened by 400,1.5, and 0 and the bottom layer by 200, 1, and 0. The images look and print very similarly and are very close in pixel dimensions. Thanks Jack Saik for your help in getting these images!

shooting film. Actually, though, I'll probably have a digital camera for the fun shots and my Pentax 6x7 for those serious landscape photos!

LARGER 120 FILM CAMERAS VERSUS DIGITAL

I've read several reviews claiming that the Canon 1DS matches the quality of a Pentax 6x7, at least for prints smaller than a certain size. I haven't had the time, or a 1DS, to test them side-by-side. I did take several test shots with the 1DS when it first came out and was quite impressed with what I got, but those shots didn't convince me that it would match my Pentax 6x7. Canon is supposed to be sending me one to test, but it looks like that won't get here in time for this edition of Artistry. My advice is that you do your own test by shooting the same scene with film and your existing film camera and any digital camera you are planning to buy. Test some shots with the type of subject matter that you normally need to shoot. What will work for you will often depend on the type of shooting you do and the texture, detail, and color you like in your prints. A digital camera that works fine for one commercial or landscape photographer may not cut the mustard for someone else. Don't spend $20,000 on a digital back based on a print that you saw at some show, especially if it is not exactly the type of work you shoot. When it comes to the digital world, I've always found it's better to test something yourself than to assume a particular advertising claim or photo proves this is the one you need. There will always be a better digital device 6 months from now, which is great. Once the quality and price gets to the point that the product meets your needs, that is the time to buy. Even better, wait 6 months longer and buy the older one when something new comes along and the price on the old one comes down. How long do you think it will be before the 1DS is $2,000? That is a price I can handle. A commercial shooter could easily save money with it at the $8,000 price, though. There are a variety of digital backs for Hasselblad and other 120 cameras which I have not had the time to evaluate. Many of them are very good and there are a lot of great reasons to stop using film, as I discussed in the 35mm section.

DIGITAL STUDIO CAMERAS VERSUS 4x5 FILM

If you don't have to stop motion and are just doing still life work, having a digital camera may save you time and money. If your work requires that grain look of film, make sure you test that digital back before you buy it instead of that Imacon Scanner. My friend Bruce, who I mentioned before, uses a Betterlight 6K-2 4x5 scanning back on his Sinar camera. He bought his used for $6,000 instead of paying $20,000 for a new one. Imacon Scanners, drum scanners, and digital backs are all expensive specialized pieces of equipment that people buy and sometimes find they can no longer use or never really needed in the first place. If I were going to buy one of these, I'd look for a good deal on a reconditioned used one unless money is no object.

If you really like shooting film, now is a great time to get a used large format film camera. Many people are giving them up and switching to digital. I got a great deal on my Pentax 6x7 ($1,600 with two lenses) early this year when $8,000 for the 1DS seemed a bit much for me. In two years I may be selling the Pentax and getting a 1DS descendant for $2,000. You can get traditional darkroom equipment at fire sale prices but I wouldn't buy that unless you want to own it for life or have it end up at a museum or land fill when you're finished with it.

If you need a digital back for your 4x5 camera, as I mentioned above, I'd test what you plan to buy before you sell your 4x5. A 4x5 piece of film is a beautiful thing; it's the Imacon or drum scanner you need to get all that data into the computer which really costs you the money. That's why I'm using 120 film more these days with my Pentax 6x7. I can get great scans from that with the Polaroid 120 or Nikon 8000. If you do shoot 4x5 film and can't afford an Imacon Scanner, try the $400-$600 Epson 3200 and do 16-bit scans. You have to sharpen the files more and work on them to get deep shadow details, but you can get some beautiful large prints from 4x5 film scanned with the 3200. I have some great 20x30 prints scanned on the Epson 2450; that scanner came out before the 3200.

CONCLUSIONS

This may be a good year for you to buy a serious digital camera. Everyone should have a fun point and shoot digital. I'll be getting either the Canon EOS Digital Rebel or the Canon 10D, unless someone at Canon wants to give me a really good deal on the 1DS! We'll now be using digital for a large portion of our photography but I'll still use my Pentax 6x7 or Gowland 4x5 for my serious landscape photography. For more information on digital imaging and digital cameras check out Rick Sammon's *Complete Guide to Digital Photography* from Norton Press and also Peachpit's *Real World Digital Photography, 2nd edition* by Katrin Eismann, Séan Duggan, and Tim Grey.

I took this image with a FujiS2. It was saved in jpeg format so I didn't open it in Camera Raw. There is plenty of data here for this size or an even larger image. That is a nice digital camera!

11 AUTOMATING PHOTOSHOP

Using Keyboard Shortcuts, the Actions palette, File/Automate, and Scripting to make Photoshop a production workhorse. Sharpen Only Edges, Remove Sky Crud, and other useful ArtistKeys scripts are explained.

If you want to know more keyboard shortcuts than you already do, check out the Help section. There's something for everyone here.

When you want to add or change a keyboard short-cut, use Edit/Keyboard Shortcuts. You can create shortcuts for palette menu items and tools here, too.

Photoshop is a production person's dream application. There are three levels of automation available to you if you work in Photoshop; all are relatively easy to use and all can add speed and ease to the way you work. This is true whether you are a photographer, production person, designer, or video artist.

FIRST STEPS TO AUTOMATION: KEYBOARD SHORTCUTS

Keyboard shortcuts abound in Photoshop and if you've worked in the application for a while, you've probably already been using them for some time. Whenever you type C to access the Crop tool, for instance, that's a keyboard shortcut. The most often used commands and menu items have keyboard shortcuts as well as all the tools. There are special shortcuts for tools in modal dialogs like Liquify and Extract. And now, in Photoshop CS, there are the ones that you assign.

Unlike Actions and Scripts, which can handle many commands with a single stroke, each keyboard shortcut that you set will pertain to one and only one menu item. A keyboard shortcut doesn't remember any settings either. But if you find yourself constantly going up to the menu bar or to a palette pop-up for the same item over and over, a keyboard shortcut is just what you need. It doesn't have to be a task that you'll be doing in the future either; keyboard shortcuts can be set for a short period when you're doing something repetitive, then deleted when the project is completed. When I was doing the chapter on color correction tools, for example, I had to keep invoking the Match Color command. This is not a command I see myself using a lot in my work in general, but it got old fast having to continually go back up to the menu bar for Image/Adjustments/Match Color. As soon as I realized I was going to be using the command a lot, I set up a keyboard shortcut for it.

It's very quick and easy to do. Go to Edit/Keyboard Shortcuts and use the pop-up in the middle section to choose the menu or tool for which you want a new or different shortcut. Click in the Shortcut column for that item, then type the key combination that you want to use. If that combination is already in use for some other command, an alert will appear telling you which command currently has that shortcut. You are then given a chance to disable the current shortcut so you can use the keys you input, or you can simply type a different combination. You must include either the Command key or a Function key in the keyboard combination, except for the Tool shortcuts, where only a single alpha character is acceptable. All 26 characters are currently assigned, however, so if you want to set a new key for one tool, you will have to change the key for some other tool.

Click the Accept button for each shortcut that you set. If you are using the Photoshop Default shortcuts, the set will be renamed, Photoshop Defaults (modified). Clicking the Create New Set icon at the top of the palette at this point will give you an opportunity to save your modified set. This is great for multiple users of the same system. Save the set in the Presets/Keyboard Shortcuts folder and it will be included in the Set pop-up next time you access the dialog. You can also duplicate a set before you start to make changes. If you switch sets, an alert will ask if you want to save changes to the current set before you make the change.

The Summarize button creates an html document that opens in your default browser and allows you to print out all your wonderful new keyboard shortcuts. One nice thing about using more keyboard shortcuts is you can keep your function keys free for more complicated procedures, Actions.

If the shortcut you want to use is already in use, Photoshop will tell you where and give you the option to delete it or change the keys you've tried to input.

ACTIONS SPEAK LOUDER THAN SHORTCUTS

Actions allow you to record and edit single menu items or very complicated sequences of events. You can then run that menu item or series of events over an entire folder full of files. You can execute these events with the press of a function key on the keyboard or a click of a button onscreen. You choose Window/Actions (F11 with ArtistKeys) to bring up the Actions palette. To create new actions or edit them, you need to turn off Button mode from the Actions Palette menu. After you define all your actions, you can turn on Button mode, which shows you the function key associated with an action and also turns the Actions palette into a series of buttons that you can click to play an action.

ARTISTKEYS TO SET UP YOUR ACTIONS

In the Automating Photoshop folder on the *Photoshop CS Artistry* CD, we have given you a predefined set of actions, called ArtistKeys. You should add this set of actions to your copy of Photoshop because we will show you how to use them in this book. Toward the end of Chapter 3: "Setting System and Photoshop Preferences," we show you how to load the ArtistKeys actions into your copy of Photoshop CS. If you haven't already done this, turn to page 29 and 30 and do it now.

What we did with ArtistKeys is go through all the menu items in Photoshop and set up as function keys the ones that you will use most often. For example, F9 through F12 will bring up and close down the palettes you use most often. We tried to do this logically, so F9 is the Info palette and Shift-F9 is the Histogram palette. Both of these palettes deal with measuring color. F10 is the Layers palette and Shift-F10 is the Channels palette. You often use these together. I use F2 through F12 to implement single menu items (and we do mention and use these quite often in the book, so you will find them quick to learn). I consider F1, as well as F13 through F15, optional, so you can use them to reprogram other actions. You can also program most of the Command+ Function key actions as well as all the Shift-Command+Function key ones. Most computer keyboards these days have function keys F1–F12 with some also having F13–F15. Macs seem to be fairly standard in their use of function key. Some of the

The Photoshop CS Actions palette with Button mode turned off. This allows you to edit the actions in many ways. The Actions menu bar shows you all the things you can do with actions. We discuss these in this chapter and explain how they work. Notice the icons at the bottom of the palette that, from left to right, stop recording, start recording, play the current action or command, make a new set of actions, create a new action or command, and allow you to throw an action or command into the trash.

Actions	
Tool Palette	F2
Navigator Palette	⇧F2
LevelsAdjLayer	⌘F2
Save For Web	F3
Color Table	⇧F3
CurveAdjLayer	⌘F3
Unsharp Mask	F4
Gaussian Blur	⇧F4
Hue/Sat AdjLayer	⌘F4
Duplicate	F5
Replace Color	⇧F5
Sharpen Only Edges...	⌘F5
Apply Image	F6
Selective Color	⇧F6
RemoveSkyCrud	⌘F6
Image Size	F7
Threshold	⇧F7
Tool Presets	⌘F7
History Palette	F8
Color Range	⇧F8
Canvas Size	⌘F8
Info Palette	F9
Histogram Palette	⇧F9
Flatten Image	⌘F9
Color Palette	⌘⇧F9
Layers Palette	F10
Channels Palette	⇧F10
Save & Close	⌘F10
Actions Palette	F11
Paths Palette	⇧F11
Horizontal Web	⌘F11
Options Palette	F12

The Actions palette with Button mode turned on. In Button mode, you can click an action to play it, even if it doesn't have a function key alternative as some of the actions lower in the ArtistKeys palette don't.

function keys we've set up for ArtistKeys may have different special functions on various PC systems. On the PC side, with Windows 95, 98, 2000, NT, and XP, as well as all the different companies that make PCs, there are too many possible special features for function keys to cover how to turn these features off. If you are having trouble making certain function keys work with your PC, either learn how to redirect the function keys on your particular model or change the function key assigned to a particular ArtistKeys action so it uses a key that your PC hasn't set up for some special purpose. Later in this chapter, we'll show you how to change the function key assigned to any action.

TO RECORD A SINGLE MENU ITEM ACTION

If you want to set up an action with a function key to perform any menu item, even from the palette menus, here are the steps to take. Make sure the Actions palette is not in Button mode (Button Mode unchecked), by using the Actions Palette menu. While playing with actions here, create a new action set by choosing New Set from the Actions Palette menu. Name this set My Actions. Create a new action by clicking the New Action icon at the bottom of the Actions palette, or by choosing New Action from the Actions Palette menu. Either way, the New Action dialog opens, enabling you to name your action as well as pick the action set, a function key and color for it. Choose My Actions for the set—you do not need to pick a function key or color. When you click the Record button, you can record a single menu item simply by choosing Insert Menu Item from the Actions Palette menu. Doing so opens the Insert Menu Item dialog box shown here. Now choose the menu that you want to automate from the main Menu bar or from a Palette menu, and its name fills the text box. Choose OK and then click the Stop Recording icon at the bottom of the Actions palette or choose Stop Recording from the Actions menu. To play the action you just recorded, press the function key if you chose one. If there is no associated Function key you can click the action in the Actions palette and choose Play from the Actions menu, or click the Play icon at the bottom of the palette. In Button mode, clicking the button for an action plays it. The good thing about actions is that you can record and edit highly complicated sequences of events, and then run them over an entire folder full of files using File/Automate/Batch, Droplets, or the File Browser..

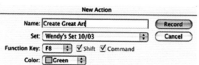

Choosing the New Action command brings up the New Action dialog box, where you can name your action, choose an action set or function key for it, and also a color that shows up in Button mode. If you want to change this information for an existing action you can Option-double-click on the action when not in Button Mode .

Use Insert Menu Item, from the Actions palette menu, to create an action that plays a single menu item. You can pick any menu item from anywhere within Photoshop. Also use this when you don't want the action to insert any values into the command the menu activates.

RECORDING ACTIONS WITH MULTIPLE COMMANDS

To record an action with a sequence of events, you start by choosing the New Action icon or menu item. Name your action, press the Record button, and then go through the sequence of events you want in the action while working on the open file. Each recorded menu item in the sequence is now called a command. Because you want to run this sequence on many other files, you need to be aware of the state of the file when you start recording. All subsequent files will have to be in the same beginning state for the action to work properly. Actions are like computer programs; they have no intelligence to pick the right layer within the file or make sure the file was saved before you start—you'd need a script for that. Take a look at the action within ArtistKeys called Drop Shad (Ob In Actv Lyr). It is meant to add a drop shadow to an object that is in its own layer surrounded by transparency. Open the file called Ball from the Automating Photoshop folder on the *Photoshop CS Artistry* CD. You will notice that the layer called Ball is currently the active layer, and the ball within this layer is surrounded by transparency. Any file that you run this Drop Shadow action on will have to first be in this state for the action to do the right thing. If you have programmed before, this will be obvious, but I know that many of you have not.

To create this action, start with a file in this state (you can use the Ball file; you have it open anyway), then click the Record button and go through a sequence of events to create a drop shadow. In the illustration to the right you can see the steps we took, duplicating the current layer, filling it with black, moving it below the original, offsetting the copy, and blurring it. This drop shadow is created in a more traditional way than some of the layer style techniques you can use to create drop shadows in Photoshop CS. We are just using it as an example to help explain actions. While creating an action, the Actions recording feature records the events as you do the work. If you have the Actions palette open, you can see the events recording as you work. Do absolutely nothing except this sequence of events; otherwise, you record those other things too. After you finish your sequence of events, choose Stop Recording from the Actions Palette menu or click the Stop Recording icon at the bottom of the Actions palette. You have now created the basic action! Now you need to look at the sequence of commands in this action and edit them to make sure it does the right thing when you play it back. Think about it; will you always want all the parameters to each command to be the same, or will some things be slightly different for each use of the action on a different file? One great thing about actions is that you can customize them easily.

EDITING ACTIONS AFTER RECORDING

I wanted people to figure out how to use this Drop Shadow action without any verbal directions, so I added the Stop messages. The unedited Drop Shadow action is shown here at the top of the page with the edited one below it. We added a Stop message by clicking the Drop Shad (Ob In Actv Lyr) line to activate it, and then clicking the arrow to the left of the name, which opens up the action and displays the list of commands in it. Choosing Insert Stop from the Actions menu opens the Record Stop dialog box. That is where you enter the text of the message you want the user to see. The message I entered just explains that to use this action, you need to start with an active layer that has an object surrounded by transparency. Because I was on the name of the action and not a particular step, the Stop command was inserted at the bottom of the action and was dragged to the top, just under the action name, so that the user can click Cancel if the file he is running it on is not in the right state. If the user clicks Continue, the action then goes on to make a copy of the target layer, fill that copy with black using preserve transparency, and then move this new black layer

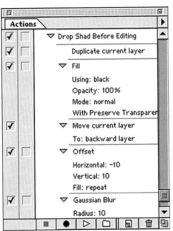

Here we see the Drop Shadow basic action prior to editing. If you play this action, the Offset command always offsets the shadow by −10 horizontal and 10 vertical. The Gaussian Blur of the shadow will always have a Radius of 10. This will not create the correct drop shadow in most cases because the size of the object will be different and the light may be coming from a different direction. You need to edit this to make it user-friendly and object-specific.

Enter the message you want displayed to give the user information about the action that is playing. Turn on Allow Continue so the action will continue when the user clicks OK.

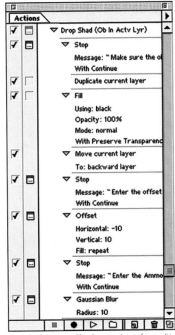

Here is the Drop Shadow action after editing to add the Stop commands as well as the breakpoints in the Offset and Gaussian Blur commands. The Stop commands were added to explain the action to future users. The Break points, which show up as icons in the middle column, allow the user to enter custom values for each invocation of the action.

119

Stop Action Recording or Playback.   **Begin Recording.**

Play Current Action or Command.   **Create a New Action Set.**

Create a New Action or Duplicate Current Action or Command.   **Throw Away Action or Command.**

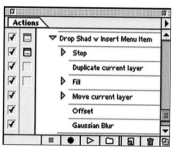

Here we have a Drop Shadow action where the Offset and Gaussian Blur were created using Insert Menu Item. These will automatically stop and allow the user to specify the parameters each time. There are no default values if you create a step using Insert Menu Item.

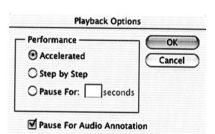

Choose Playback Options from the Actions palette menu to bring up this dialog for your Playback options. If you have a newer, faster computer, you may have to put a Pause For several seconds between each action to have time to see them as individual steps on the screen.

below the original target layer. To turn this new black layer into a shadow, we need to now offset it from the original and then blur it to make its edges soft. I added another Stop message by clicking the Move current layer step and using Insert Stop again. This added a stop before the Offset command, explaining that the user needs to adjust the offset numbers to fit the object in question. The direction and amount of the offset will depend on the lighting on the original. To allow the user to change these values, I put a break point on the Offset command by clicking in the middle column to the left of this command in the Actions palette. Adobe calls these break points, modal controls, and it means that at these points there must be user input. The action stops until the user presses either Return or Enter. Finally, I added another Stop to explain that the Gaussian Blur amount also requires editing to make sure the shadow looks right for this situation. So the user can actually edit the Gaussian Blur amount, I then added a break point on the Gaussian Blur, again by clicking in the column to its left.

FURTHER EDITING REFINEMENTS

The preceding example illustrates the types of editing you can do to actions. After you understand how this Drop Shadow action works, you could turn off the Stop commands by clicking their check marks to turn off each check in the leftmost column next to each Stop command. You could also throw away the Stop commands, as you can any command or action, by dragging it to the Trash icon at the bottom of the Actions palette. If you were using File/Automate/Batch to run this Drop Shadow action on a bunch of items that all have the same offset and blur values, you could turn off the breakpoints on the offset and blur steps by clicking in the middle column next to each of them. You could change the actual value of the default offset or blur by clicking that command line and then choosing Record Again from the Actions Palette menu. It will play that command line and allow you to change its default value within the action. If you want the user to always enter the values for a particular command when he uses the command, you need to use the Insert Menu Item option from the Actions menu when recording that command, and choose that command as the menu item to insert. Recording a command this way doesn't actually execute the command until the action is played, so the user has to enter the values at that time instead of having default values.

ADDING TO ACTIONS

After you record an action, you can add to it by selecting a particular command within the action and choosing the Start Recording menu from the Actions menu bar, or by clicking the Start Recording icon at the bottom of the Actions palette. New commands are recorded right after the command you select. You can click an existing command and drag it to the New Action/Command icon, at the bottom of the Actions palette, to make a copy of that command. You can then drag that copy, or any command, to another location in the current action or in another action. If you want to start playing an action in the middle, just click the command at the point at which you want to begin and choose Play from the Actions menu to play the action from that point forward. You can also play an action or command by clicking the Play icon at the bottom of the Actions palette.

THINGS THAT ACTIONS DON'T SUPPORT

Some menu items in Photoshop don't do anything during the recording of an action. If, while recording, you choose a menu item or click a tool, or do anything, and a new command doesn't show up in the Actions palette, then that thing is not recordable. If you want to include any of them as part of an action anyway, you can choose Insert Menu Item, which will play that menu item when the action plays. You can't put default values into these commands, but at least you can get the user to respond to them.

OTHER ACTIONS FEATURES

Actions can be organized into different sets. To create a new set, choose New Set from the Actions Palette menu or click the third icon from the right (looks like an empty folder with a tab) at the bottom of the Actions palette. You can then drag actions into the set. Use Sets to organize your actions into different functional groups. The function keys are global across all the sets, so you can't use the same function key twice for two different actions, even if they are grouped in different sets.

BATCH FILES AND DROPLETS

The File/Automate/Batch menu enables you to specify an action along with a source and destination folder for that action. If you specify a source folder and a destination folder, Photoshop opens each file in the source folder and runs the action on the file and then saves that modified file in the destination folder. If the source folder has subfolders, you can choose to have Photoshop also process the files in the subfolders. You do not have to put Open or Close commands in your action; the Batch command automatically adds these at the beginning and the end. If your action has any Open commands in it, the Override Action Open Commands checkbox in the Batch dialog box allows you to tell it to ignore those commands. Another checkbox lets you tell the Batch command to ignore any Save commands. You select the action you want to perform by using the Action pop-up menu in the Batch dialog box and choosing the Source and Destination folders by clicking their respective Choose buttons. If you choose None for Destination, Photoshop leaves the modified files open. If you choose Save and Close, they are saved back in the folder in which they started, under the same name. You can also create a Multi-Batch action that records more than one Batch command. You can then play this Multi-Batch action, which allows you to batch one action after another on the same set of files, or to batch the same action over and over again on different files in more than one folder.

Photoshop also has the capability to log errors to a file, whose name and location you choose. After the error is logged, the action continues. When running actions on a large group of files within a folder, this allows the action to process the other files even if there is an error with several of them. When an error comes up, you can also choose to have Photoshop stop the action and put an error message on the screen.

Droplets take this process one step further by allowing you to create a small applet that can reside on your desktop or

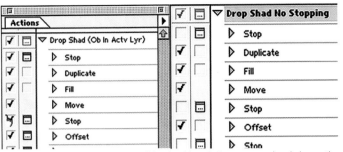
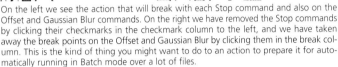

On the left we see the action that will break with each Stop command and also on the Offset and Gaussian Blur commands. On the right we have removed the Stop commands by clicking their checkmarks in the checkmark column to the left, and we have taken away the break points on the Offset and Gaussian Blur by clicking them in the break column. This is the kind of thing you might want to do to an action to prepare it for automatically running in Batch mode over a lot of files.

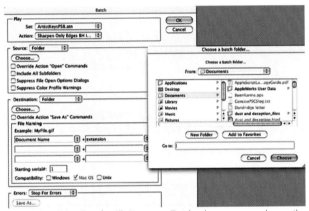

Here is the dialog box for File/Automate/Batch where you can choose the Action Set and Action, Source, and Destination for your Batch. Notice the features that let you Override Action Open Commands, Include All Subfolders, and Suppress Color Profile Warnings during the playing of an action. You are also allowed to Log Errors To a File. When you use one of the Choose buttons, for Source or Destination, this brings up the dialog box at the right. Click the Choose button in that dialog when the folder you want is highlighted. The dialog here is set to choose the folder called Documents.

The Create Droplet dialog box is very similar to the Batch command dialog. You do not need to choose a source folder because you will drag your folder onto the Droplet to initiate the action. You simply choose where you want to save your droplet. Other than that, your options are the same.

Here's what Photoshop CS droplets look like on the Mac desktop. I created the droplet from an actions in the ArtistKeys and created a destination file to hold the results.

Editing Actions After Recording

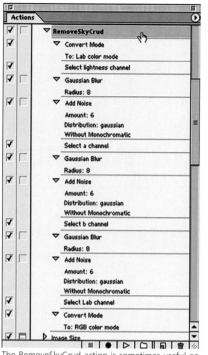

The RemoveSkyCrud action is sometimes useful on images that have large clumpy grain in the sky. To use this action, first make a flattened copy of your Master Image and then run this RemoveSkyCrud on this flattened copy. This turns the copy into Lab color mode, then blurs each channel separately and also uses Add Noise after the blur to return some sort of grain pattern to the channel. When finished, this action converts this copy of your image back to RGB color using your RGB working space. You would then use the Move tool with the Shift key down to drag and drop this copy of your image back on top of your Master Image layers. You then want to add an all-black layer mask to this Crud Removed layer and use a soft Airbrush with a low Opacity, like 07%, to paint white in the mask only in the areas where you need to remove the clumpy grain in the sky. Depending on the amount of grain in your Master Image sky, you may want to change the Radius values, within this action, for Gaussian Blur and Add Noise.

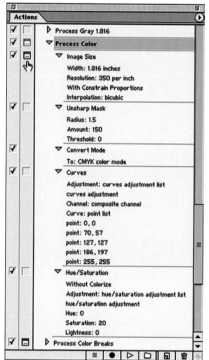

Here we see the Process Color action, which is in the ArtistKeys set but doesn't have a function key assigned to it. This is a generic version of the basic action I used to process all the screen grabs within *Photoshop CS Artistry*. The Image Size command within this action has a break point attached to it, which allows me to set the width I want for this particular screen grab. The other commands here will always just run and do the same thing. After resampling the screen grab to the width of its box in Quark at 350 dpi, the file is then sharpened, converted to CMYK, has a Curve run on it to compensate for contrast loss due to CMYK conversion, and has Hue/Saturation run on it to saturate the colors again after the CMYK conversion. Notice that there is another similar action called Process Color Breaks that has break points on the Unsharp Mask step and the Hue/Saturation step. I use this action when I want to double-check the amount of sharpening or the amount of color saturation.

in a folder on your hard drive. You don't need to even have Photoshop up and running to drag a folder of images on top of the droplet. Photoshop will open and run the appropriate action on all the files and subfolders dependent on how you have saved the settings in the File/Automate/Create Droplet command.

Let's get some action into our lives!

VERY USEFUL ACTIONS IN THE PHOTOSHOP CS ARTISTKEYS SET

The Sharpen Only Edges BH, RemoveSkyCrud, and Process Color actions are useful actions included with ArtistKeys, but they need some explanation. On this page are screen grabs of RemoveSkyCrud and Process Color, along with detailed captions that explain how to use them. The third, and very important script, Sharpen Only Edges BH, is explained and used in Chapter 26: "Combining Bracketed Photos," at the end of the chapter. A recent script that may be useful to you if you shoot digitally is ResUpby10. This script is explained in Chapter 10: "Digital Cameras and Camera Raw." Please let me know, at barry@barryhaynes.com, how useful you find these actions and if you discover any new and better variations of them.

THE BIG GUNS: SCRIPTS

When you need something more than actions, you'll want to learn some basic scripting (and not so basic for you true production geeks). When Wendy was writing and producing her book, *Photoshop, Painter, and Illustrator Side by Side*, we found that trying to organize the hundreds of screen shots into appropriate size folders and batch process them as we had done for this book was tiresome, faulty, and didn't give us much flexibility to change the layout during the editing process. So, she got PhotoScripter™ from Main Event Software to make Photoshop 6 AppleScriptable. She had been using AppleScript to make her Filemaker database automatically export pictures with appropriate section numbers and captions into a Quark layout, and it worked really well. The missing link was getting Photoshop to talk to the other applications. Through much trial and error she finally got her system to go to the Quark layout for a chapter and then ask Photoshop to open each picture in the chapter, read its width from Quark, resize in Photoshop to that width, and then run the Process Color action that is included in ArtistKeys.

Processing files, which had taken hours (sometimes days) before could be done in a matter of a few minutes. This is the power of scripting. Photoshop Actions cannot speak to other applications, nor can they be set to run differently depending on file variables. Scripts can do all of this and more. We've been using AppleScript ever since our first experience with it and Photoshop CS makes implementation of scripts easier than ever.

Which Language?

Photoshop CS can be scripted using a variety of languages. The scripting language you use depends on which platform will be doing your production, and to some extent, your previous scripting experience. The most often used languages are VisualBasic and JavaScript on the PC side, and AppleScript and JavaScript on the Mac side. Tom Burbage of Adobe's Scripting Support team tells me that, "In actuality, your choices for scripting are more varied than this as Scripting Support essentially turns Photoshop into a standard COM Automation Server. What this means is that any programming or scripting environment that can act as a COM Automation controller/client can be used to automate tasks.

This might be accomplished using Windows' built-in scripting capability (VBScript), perl, JavaScript, VisualBasic, using VBA from Word, Excel, or Access. For larger scale production support applications, Visual C++ or Borland's C++Builder or Delphi could even be used. Of course, there are others."

If you're a designer who's already had to learn some JavaScript to accomplish your Web work, you'll be able to extend that knowledge now to help you with simple production tasks directly in Photoshop. If, on the other hand, you've worked in AppleScript with Quark or Filemaker or VisualBasic in Microsoft Word or Excel, you might want to stick with one of those languages.

Another important consideration is whether you need only Photoshop to do the work, or is there another application or part of your operating system that will need to interact with Photoshop. If Photoshop will stand alone, JavaScript gives you the flexibility of being completely cross platform. If you need application interaction, other languages may be more appropriate.

Installed Scripts and Where to Find Out More

Photoshop CS automatically installs several very useful JavaScript scripts that you can find under the File/Scripts menu. These scripts can export layers of a multi-layered Photoshop document to separate files for building effects and animations, or create separate documents and Web Photo Galleries out of the comps you've created in the Layer Comps palette. These are the scripts that show up in the menu, but there are many more sample scripts for you to view and begin to work with.

The first place to go when you want to start learning about scripting is the Photoshop CS Scripting Guide in the Scripting Guide folder of Photoshop CS. I say start with this guide rather than the guide to the specific language because it covers very important concepts specific to how Photoshop is set up for scripting. Understanding these concepts will make it easier to comprehend what's being described by a particular script.

Also in the Scripting Guide folder are PDF guides to the three major scripting languages as well as sample scripts for each one. Most of these scripts are mere snippets but they employ some core functions and can serve as the basis for more complicated scripts.

This script will output four files, one for each of the layer comps in this palette. You can choose where to save the files and the file format you want from within the script.

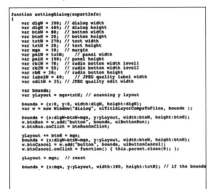

This is part of the JavaScript code that accomplishes the above script.

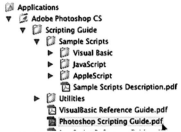

Start with the Photoshop Scripting Guide to familiarize yourself with what Photoshop can and cannot do with scripts. Then move on to the specific guide and sample scripts for the language you want to use.

123

COLOR CORRECTION AND CALIBRATION TO CREATE A MASTER DIGITAL IMAGE

CALIBRATION, COLOR SPACES, AND COLOR MANAGEMENT

OVERALL COLOR CORRECTION AND CREATING A MASTER IMAGE

THE ZONE SYSTEM FOR DIGITAL IMAGES

IMAGE SIZE, RESOLUTION, AND FILE PIXELS PER INCH VERSUS PRINT DPI

8- AND 16-BIT SCANNING, DIGITAL CAPTURE, AND HISTOGRAMS

Paris Cafe was shot around 1985 through a window on a rainy night with my Canon F1. This image has not been manipulated other than to correct the color. It has always been one of my favorite images and is one of my most requested prints.

12 COLOR CORRECTION TOOLS

Overview of Photoshop's many color correction and gamma adjustment tools, which ones are most useful for what and why, and which ones are fairly useless for the professional.

The color correction tools are in the Image/Adjustment menu. When you use them from here, they permanently modify the pixels they are adjusting in the currently active layer. Changing the pixels over and over again can damage the integrity of the image.

Doing an adjustment using an adjustment layer creates a special layer above the currently active layer, which allows you to change this adjustment as many times as you like without modifying or damaging the original pixels or the integrity of the image. It also keeps a record for you of the changes you have made.

Photoshop offers many tools for adjusting color and modifying image gamma or contrast. This chapter gives you a quick overview of what the different tools do and when to use each tool. The color correction tools are in the Image/Adjustments menu, and most are also available as adjustment layers. Levels, Curves, Hue/Saturation, Replace Color, Selective Color, Color Balance, and Channel Mixer are the color correction tools we use most. Auto Levels, Auto Contrast, Auto Color, Brightness/Contrast, Desaturate, Gradient Map, and Variations are the ones we don't use as much. New adjustments added in Photoshop CS are Match Color, Photo Filter, and Shadow/Highlight. Though we haven't used these a lot, they show great promise. You will notice that *Photoshop CS Artistry* color corrects mostly with adjustment layers because those corrections can be changed as many times as you like without destroying the integrity of the file. In later hands-on chapters, we actually go through the details of each tool's features and how they're used in real-world examples. Invert, Equalize, Threshold, and Posterize are used more for effects and masking, which are covered in other parts of this book.

USING THE INFO/COLOR SAMPLER AND COLOR PALETTES

When you use any of the color correction tools, it is very helpful to have the Info palette, and sometimes the Color palette, visible onscreen. Use Window/Show Info (F9 with ArtistKeys) and Window/Show Color (Shift-F9) to bring up these palettes. While working in any color correction tool, Photoshop automatically gives you the Eyedropper tool for measuring colors in the image. The Info palette shows you the digital RGB, Lab, and/or CMYK values of the pixel or group of pixels you currently have the Eyedropper tool above. It shows you these values both before (left of slash) and after (right of slash) any changes you have made during the current iteration of the color correction tool you are now using. The Color palette has a subtle but important difference from the Info palette in that it displays the values of the last place where you clicked with the Eyedropper versus wherever the Eyedropper might currently be located that the Info Palette displays. This allows you to click on a picture tone or color area and see how the pixel values of that particular area change as you make adjustments with the Color tool you are currently working with. The Color palette also has colored sliders that give you hints as to how a certain color change, like adding red, will affect the color of the location where you last clicked. The Color Sampler tool, an option of the Eyedropper in the Tools palette, allows you to click (Shift-click while in a color tool or the regular Eyedropper) up to four locations where you want to monitor the color of your image while working. These four color values show up in the bottom of the Info palette. This is a great feature because you can see how the color values at these four locations change throughout your color correction process. You don't have to measure them again; their values will constantly update as you work. Each open image can have up to four Color Samplers attached to it.

When adjusting a digital image, you usually want to make as few separate file modifications as are necessary to achieve

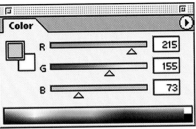

The Color palette remembers the values at the last location you clicked with the Eyedropper. If you made that click after entering a color adjustment tool, this palette will then show you how the values at the point you clicked change as you make adjustments using that color adjustment tool.

the desired result. A file modification is when you click the OK button for any of the color correction tools and you are not in an adjustment layer. Each file modification changes the original data, and too many changes can eventually degrade the quality of the data. Therefore, you don't want to constantly go from one color correction tool to the other frantically trying to get the effect you need. You want to use these tools intelligently, knowing what each one is good for and keeping the total number of uses to the minimum required to do the final adjustments on a particular image. If you do your changes using adjustment layers, the actual image pixels do not change until the image is flattened. Adjustment layers allow you to go back and change the color over and over again without suffering from this cumulative degrading effect on the digital values.

COMMON COLOR CORRECTION TECHNIQUES

All the color correction tools share a few things in common. When using a color correction tool, you need to turn the Preview button on to see the changes happen to the image. With the Preview button off, you are seeing the image as it appeared prior to the changes made by the current invocation of the tool you are using. You can see before and after by quickly turning the Preview button off and on. When you turn the Preview button on, Photoshop has to change the data in the file, based on the changes you have made in the color correction tool, before you can see the changes on the screen. With today's computers this happens very quickly, but it still involves a lot of calculations.

In all Mac versions of Photoshop before version 6, having the Preview button off in some of the color correction tools, like Levels and Curves, would use Video LUT Animation to give you an instant preview with constant feedback as you made changes. Clicking on the title bar with the Preview off would show you an instant before version of the image. These were implemented using a feature supported on all Macintosh video cards called Video LUT Animation. Most Windows cards didn't support Video LUT Animation, and now support for it has been removed from Photoshop on both platforms. It did provide some useful features in some circumstances, and I wonder if support for it would have been removed if it worked on Windows platforms as well? Having it work the same way now on both platforms certainly makes it easier to explain, but it does seem that the world has lost some functionality here because Microsoft didn't support it.

When working with a selected subarea, comparing one window to another, or adjusting an area in one layer to blend with nonadjusted items in other layers within Levels, Curves, Color Balance, or Brightness/Contrast, you usually work with the

The Info palette with the before values to the left and the after values to the right of the slash. In this Info palette we have created two Color Samplers, #1 for the highlight position and #2 for the shadow position.

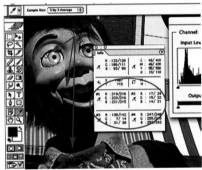

By Shift-clicking on the screen while in a color correction tool, you can place up to four Color Sampler points whose values will show up at the bottom of the Info window and will continue to update as you make color changes. These locations continue to update throughout your editing session, even as you switch tools and measure other locations with the regular Eyedropper.

Preview button on so you can compare the changes you make to the selected area to the rest of the image.

In any of the color correction tools, you can Option-Cancel (Reset) to stay in the tool but cancel any changes you have made in that tool so far. Many of these tools also let you load and save a collection of settings. This is useful when you have many very similar images in a production situation. You could carefully make your Levels setting for the first image and then use the Save button to save those settings in a file. If you have subsequent images in the group, you can use the Load button to automatically run the same settings or load them into an adjustment layer.

LEVELS AND CURVES

The Levels and Curves tools have the broadest range of capabilities of any of the color correction tools. When you color correct an image from its original scan, you want to do so in a particular order. (We discuss that order in great detail in Chapter 17: "Steps to Create a Master Image," and you should read that chapter for a better understanding of this overview.) The first step after you do a scan is to do overall color correction; that is, correct the complete image without any selections. Levels is the best tool to use because it gives you a histogram of the data in the image as well as a quick way to pinpoint the lightest and darkest spots of your image. You can use the histogram to judge the quality of the scan and to fix many scanning problems. You can also use Levels to precisely adjust the highlight and shadow values, the overall brightness and contrast, and the color balance, while viewing the results onscreen and in the histogram. You make all these changes in one step and must choose OK only once after making all these improvements. When using an adjustment layer, you can go back in and tweak your Levels settings as many times as you like. Levels is the color correction tool we most often use first.

You can also use the Curves command to do your initial overall color adjustments of the entire image. Curves enables you to do all the same adjustments that Levels does plus more specific adjustments in particular image data ranges. The Curves command has a different user interface than Levels, however. Instead of furnishing a histogram, it provides the curve diagram shown here. The horizontal axis of the diagram represents the original image values with black and shadows on the left and white and highlights on the right. The vertical axis represents the modified image values with the shadows at the bottom and the highlights on the top. When the curve is a straight diagonal, as shown here, the image has not been changed. Moving the curve down in the middle darkens the image, and moving it upward lightens the image. The endpoints of the curve are used to change the highlight and shadow values. Using Curves, you can measure individual colors, see the range of values they represent on the curve, and then change only that color range. Curves' advantage is that it allows you to independently modify specific portions of the image's tonal range in different ways with more flexibility than Levels. Now, with the addition of the Histogram palette, you can have histogram data available to you while you are in Curves or a Curves adjustment layer. We'll let you know if this changes the way we work.

Levels and Curves are the most powerful color correction tools. See Chapter 19: "Overall Color Correction," for a detailed introduction to Levels and Curves, and also Chapters 20: "Correcting a Problem Image," and 24: "Desert Al," for good discussions of using Levels and Curves in the ways for which they are best suited. Also read Chapter 13: "Digital Imaging and the Zone System," to understand how Levels histograms and Curves relate to the original photograph.

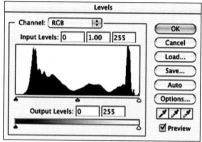

The Levels tool with its histogram is best for doing the overall color correction right after bringing in a scan or a digital camera image.

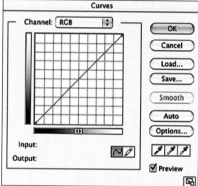

The Curves tool with a curve showing no adjustments to the image. The horizontal axis shows the original image values and the vertical axis shows these values as modified by the curve. Option-clicking on the graph toggles it between the 4x4 default divisions and the 10x10 divisions you see here.

THE HUE/SATURATION COMMAND

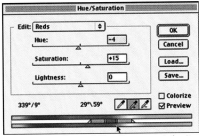

I often use Hue/Saturation to increase the saturation of all the colors by 10% to 20% after doing the overall color correction using Levels and Curves. This change is done with the Master button on. Using the Reds, Yellows, Greens, Cyans, Blues, or Magentas, you can change the hue, saturation, or lightness of objects in the image that have one of these standard colors as their primary color without actually making a detailed selection. You can then fine-tune these color selections further using the Hue/Saturation Eyedroppers. You should use Hue/Saturation when you want to change the color, saturation, or lightness of a particular object or color range without changing its gamma or other characteristics. The first part of the process is to select the object(s) you want to change and use the Hue/Saturation Eyedropper with plus and minus to get a model of the representative color. This model shows up in the Color Strip at the bottom of the Hue/Saturation window. This Color Strip shows changes to your representative color as you make them.

The Hue slider looks at hues in a circular fashion, sort of like the Apple Color Picker or a rotary color wheel type color picker. The initial Hue value, 0, is the degree value where you find your initial color. To change just the color, slide the Hue slider to the right (like rotating counter-clockwise on the Apple Color Picker). If your initial color was red, then red would be your 0. A Hue change of 90 degrees would make the color green. A Hue change of –90 degrees would make your color purple. A Hue change of 180 or –180 would yield the opposite of red, which is cyan. Sliding the Saturation slider to the right makes the selected items more saturated and sliding to the left makes them less saturated. This is like moving further from the center or closer to the center on the Apple Color Picker.

Moving the Lightness slider to the right takes away gray values and moving it to the left adds gray values (similar to the sliding bar on the right side of the Apple Color Picker). See Chapter 19: "Overall Color Correction," and Chapter 22: "Color Matching Images," for more information on the Hue/Saturation tool.

The Hue/Saturation tool. Usually you want the Preview button on when using Hue/Saturation. Notice the color bars and sliders at the bottom of the dialog box. These, along with the Eyedroppers, allow Photoshop to do a much better job of picking a color range to modify with Hue/Saturation. The color bars are always available. When you make an adjustment, the bottom color bar will change to show you how the colors are being shifted. If you are adjusting one of the component colors from the Edit pop-up, you also get the sliders between the two color bars. This shows you the range of colors that Photoshop is considering when making an adjustment. Using the Eyedroppers can expand or contract that range to make your change more exacting. You can move the sliders manually as well.

THE REPLACE COLOR COMMAND

The Replace Color command allows you to make a selection based on color and then actually change the color of the selected objects using sliders built into the command's dialog box. The selections are similar to selections made with the Magic Wand, but this tool gives you more control over them. The Magic Wand requires you to make a selection by using a certain tolerance setting and clicking a color, and then selects adjacent areas based on whether their colors fall within the tolerance value you set for it. If the selection is incorrect with the Magic Wand, you need to change the tolerance and then select again. This process can take a lot of time and iteration. The Replace Color command allows you to change the tolerance on-the-fly while viewing the actual objects or colors you are selecting.

The tolerance here is called Fuzziness. Increasing the Fuzziness, by moving the slider in the dialog box to the right, enlarges your selection, and decreasing it shrinks the selection. You see a preview of what is happening with the selection in a little mask window in the dialog box.

After you perfect the color selection, you then use the Hue, Saturation, and Lightness sliders in the Replace Color dialog box to change the color of the selected objects. You can see this color change in the image by clicking the Preview button, and the Preview button also allows you to make further tweaks on the selection while actually seeing how they're affecting the color change. Replace Color changes the

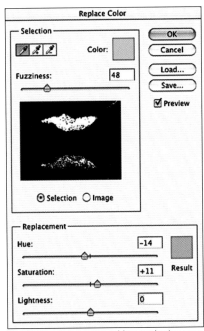

The Replace Color command has a selection capability based on object color and has some of the controls from Hue/Saturation built into it. Use it for quickly selecting and changing the color of objects. Use the sample swatch as a quick reference to see how your color will change; then use the Preview button to see the change happen within the file.

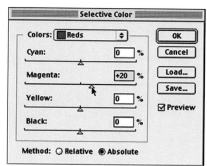

The Selective Color command is used for adding or subtracting the percentage of cyan, magenta, yellow, or black inks within the red, green, blue, cyan, magenta, yellow, black, neutral, or white colors in the selected area of a CMYK image. These percentages of change can be relative to the amount of an ink color that is already there or they can be absolute percentages.

The Channel Mixer allows you to take a percentage of the color from one channel and use it to create part of another channel. Here, we are taking 25% of the Red channel and 75% of the Green channel and using it to create a new Green channel.

color of the objects it picks from the parts of the entire image selected with the selection tools before you entered Replace Color. To learn more about using Replace Color, see Chapter 21: "Yellow Flowers."

THE SELECTIVE COLOR TOOL AND CMYK

The Selective Color tool works great when you are working with CMYK images. It is a good tool for making final tweaks to CMYK colors after converting from RGB to CMYK. With this tool, you adjust the amount of cyan, magenta, yellow, or black ink within the red, green, blue, cyan, magenta, yellow, black, neutral, or white colors in the selected area. It's also a great tool for fine control over fixing color areas that fade a bit when converted to CMYK. For more information about using this tool, see Chapter 21: "Yellow Flowers," and Chapter 22: "Color Matching Images."

THE CHANNEL MIXER

The Channel Mixer allows you to take a percentage of the color from one channel and use it to create part of another channel. This technique can be used to improve CMYK separations and also for the process of creating a black-and-white image from a color image. It is also very useful in repairing images where one of the emulsion layers of the film may not have been exposed properly or may have been damaged over time. I've found this happens often with digital cameras where the blue channel is sometimes poorly exposed. You mixed channels in the past using Image/Calculations or by just pasting one channel on top of another and changing the opacity; the Channel Mixer just makes this process easier and allows you to see a preview of the results as you are working. Also, because you can use the Channel Mixer as an adjustment layer, you have the advantage of being able to create several versions and select areas that work via layer masks. See Chapter 24: "Desert Al," where we repair a damaged color photograph, for an example of using the Channel Mixer.

If you simply go to Mode/Grayscale with the Manhattan Sunrise picture, this is the result.

Chapter 12: Color Correction Tools

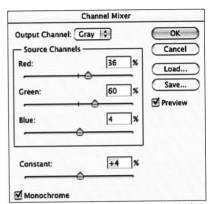

Here are the settings I used to convert the Manhattan skyline photo from RGB to Grayscale. I used the Channel Mixer as an adjustment layer in case I wanted to make changes later. For even more control over the tones in the image, I would use curves adjustment layers with layer masks.

Using the Channel Mixer and taking some of all three channels gives me better contrast in the buildings and more detail in the trees of Central Park.

COLOR BALANCE, BRIGHTNESS/CONTRAST, AND VARIATIONS

You will notice that we don't use Color Balance, Brightness/Contrast, and Variations tools much in this book. We consider them less precise than the other six color correction tools previously mentioned. We explain the advantages and disadvantages of using these three tools in this section. In general, they are more for color beginners and don't offer as much control as the Levels, Curves, Hue/Saturation, Replace Color, Selective Color, and Channel Mixer commands.

THE COLOR BALANCE TOOL

The Color Balance tool shows the the relationship between the additive colors (red, green, and blue) on the right and the subtractive colors (cyan, magenta, and yellow) on the left. You move three sliders, the Cyan/Red slider, the Magenta/Green slider, and the Yellow/Blue slider, either to the left to get the CMY colors or to the right to get their complementary RGB colors. If you don't understand the relationship between RGB and CMY, this tool makes it a little easier to see. When you use Color Balance, you need to adjust your shadows, midtones, and highlights separately, which can take longer than using Levels or Curves. The best feature of Color Balance is that you can make adjustments with the Preserve Luminosity button on, which allows you to radically alter the color balance of a selected object toward red, for example, without the object becoming super bright like it would if you made such a radical adjustment in Levels or Curves. There are times when this is very useful. The Preserve Luminosity option can be useful when you need to remove a color cast from the image without changing the brightness and contrast of the image.

In general, the Color Balance tool is much less powerful than Levels or Curves because you can't set exact highlight or shadow values, and you don't have much control over brightness and contrast. Moreover, if you have a setting that you use all the time in Levels, Hue/Saturation, or Curves, you can save it in a file and load it later to use on a similar image. This can be very useful when you want to save time and make a group of images have similar color adjustments—once again, the Color

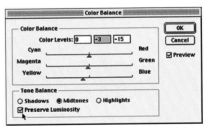

The Color Balance tool. Color levels of 0 means that no adjustment has been made. Negative values mean adjustments in the CMY direction, and positive values are adjustments in the RGB direction. Preserve Luminosity is the main feature this tool has that allows it to do something that you can't do using Levels or Curves.

131

Balance tool doesn't have this option. However, as we've said, there are times when this tool will be useful, especially as an adjustment layer that can be tweaked at will. Generall, I would say that the Color Balance tool is more of a beginning color correcting tool and not the main tool I would recommend for imaging professionals.

THE BRIGHTNESS/CONTRAST TOOL

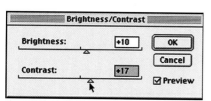

The Brightness/Contrast tool. Moving the sliders to the right increases the brightness or contrast, generating positive numbers in the respective boxes. Moving the sliders to the left decreases brightness or contrast and results in negative numbers.

The Brightness/Contrast tool allows you to adjust the brightness and/or contrast of your image using Brightness and Contrast sliders. Usually we adjust the brightness and contrast using Levels or Curves because those tools allow you to also adjust the color balance and highlight/shadow values at the same time as well as allowing you to Save and Load adjustment values. Like the Color Balance tool, I would say that Brightness/Contrast is more of an entry-level tool. Most professionals use Levels and Curves. The only time you might use Brightness/Contrast is when you don't need to make any color adjustment and need only a subtle brightness or contrast adjustment.

THE VARIATIONS TOOL

The Variations tool is a neat idea, but it has several serious flaws. Variations is useful for the person who is new to color correction and may not know the difference between adding a little cyan and adding a little green to an image. When you use it, you see the current image surrounded by different color correction choices. The main problem with Variations is that you cannot zoom in on the current image or any of its new choices to see the details of what will happen when you make possible changes.

Variations works better on a 19" or 21" monitor, simply because the small images used to illustrate the changes are bigger on a larger monitor. Still, when you make the changes and say OK to Variations, you are often surprised by how the changes that looked cool in small size inside the Variations dialog box have adversely affected certain color areas. Like the Color Balance tool, you can't set precisely where the highlight and/or shadow values begin. You have to adjust highlight and shadow values separately using the radio buttons at the top right of the Variations dialog box. You can't set the highlights or shadows to known values like you can in Levels and Curves.

In Variations, you can also adjust the saturation by selecting the Saturation radio button. The saturation, highlight, and shadow settings show you out-of-gamut colors if you have the Show Clipping box checked. When shadows are going to print as pure black or highlights as pure white, these clipped areas show up as a bright complementary warning color. In Saturation mode, colors that are too saturated for the CMYK gamut show up the same way.

If you are not used to doing color corrections, Variations is a good way to prototype the corrections you want to make. Maybe you'll decide to add some yellow, darken the image, and increase the saturation a bit. After you make these decisions with the aid of Variations, you probably want to go back to Levels,

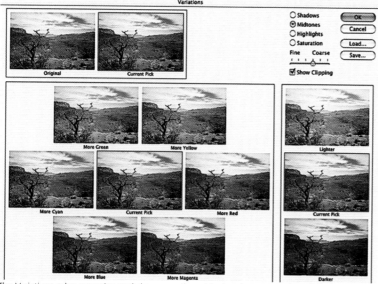

The Variations color correction tool shows you the original and current version of the image up in the top-left corner. As you change the current image, you can easily compare it here to the original. The big box in the bottom-left corner shows the current image in the middle surrounded by versions with more green, yellow, red, magenta, blue, or cyan added to it. You click one of these surrounding versions of the image if you like it better. It replaces the current image in the middle of this circle (also at the top), and then another round of new color iterations surround this new current image. On the right side, the current image is in the middle with a lighter one above and a darker one below. Again you can click one of these to make it the current image.

Curves or Hue/Saturation and make the corresponding changes there. Then you can also set the highlights and shadows more exactly and see the details of the changes you are making as you make them. We do not use Variations in this book. For more details on Variations, see the Photoshop manual or built-in Help menu.

MATCH COLOR

Adobe lists two uses for this adjustment. The first is correcting the color in a single image where the image is both the source and the target. The second is matching color between images, layers, or selections.

The first instance is one of those adjustments I feel is for people who have neither the time nor the inclination to actually learn the application. It's fast, it does an okay job on some images, but it's extremely limited. There's a button to neutralize color casts, but how in the world does it judge what the color is supposed to be? And yes, you can brighten the picture and increase or decrease its saturation, but there are better tools.

However, there are times when you need to match the color of the light between two photos. This might happen when you have portraits of several people taken by different photographers or at different times that need to have a unified look, say for a spread about the Board of Directors. Or, it might be that you've color corrected a landscape that has lush greens and vivid blues and you'd like to bring another photo in line with those same colors. If time is short, this might be the tool for you.

I've illustrated both of those types of situations here, but I don't want you to think that this tool is a magic bullet for anything. I had to search to find photos that worked well and as I'm sure you'll notice in the case of the portraits, the background is exactly the same, only the time of day differed. One reason I don't forsee using this tool a lot is that you can do virtually the same thing with adjustment layers and have a lot more flexibility. In the portraits here, and the aspen pictures on the next page, I could have made a layer set of the adjustment layers used to color correct one photo and simply dragged the entire set over for the initial adjustment to the other image.

If you do decide to use the tool, make sure that the layer you plan to change is active when you enter the dialog. If you intend to modify a layer that has important information, make a copy of the layer first. Also, make sure the layer you use as the source has all the color information you intend to use. If it is being affected by adjustment layers, you'll need to flatten the image first, or select the Merged option in the Layers pop-up in the Source section of the dialog box.

In some instances you will want to use only selected colors to modify your target image. In this case, make a selection in the source image first, then switch to the target image, selection, or layer and invoke the Match Color Command. You can also make a selection in the Target image if you want to modify only that area (such as a face), but unlike an adjustment layer where you can modify the layer mask if your selection is not perfect, you need to have a really good selection. If you're going to

Mary's photo has been color corrected.

LuAnn was shot after the Oregon clouds rolled in, and no correction has been done.

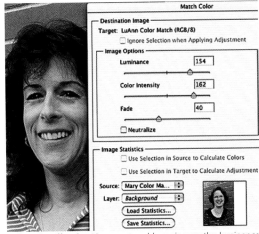
Fading the effect by 40 percent and bumping up the luminance and saturation gave a pretty good and very quick match.

This is the result of the above correction. No other adjustments have been made to the image.

This is an uncorrected scan of aspen and wildflowers that we want to quickly correct.

This image has excactlly the colors we need in the flowers and trees, but we don't need the sky, so I've made a selection of the areas that are useful.

go to all that trouble, it's just as easy to use adjustment layers and masks. Easier, really.

In the third example, where I'm simply "borrowing" the mood of a photo, for example warming up the Manhattan sunrise, don't be afraid to move the sliders. Just like filters, the default result might not be something you'd actually use, but modifying the result may give you a wonderful effect. If you do find a particular photo that gives you the tones you want and you think you might want to use those settings again, you can save the settings and then load them later. Your source will then be listed as Statistics File rather than the name of the image. This is particularly helpful because you don't have to have the image open to use its statistics.

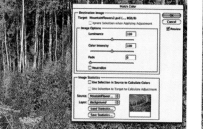

If I ignore the selection in the source image, my colors are skewed toward the blue of the sky.

Using only the colors in the selected area gives me the result I was expecting.

This is the Ceiling Lights file.

This is the original uncorrected digital camera file of the Manhattan sunrise.

This is the Side of the House file.

Here I matched the color to the Ceiling Lights file using settings of 100, 100, 50. No other corrections were made.

Here I matched the color to the Side of the House file using settings of 135, 135, 35. No other corrections were made.

SHADOW/HIGHLIGHT

Adobe continues to add "automatic" adjustments to Photoshop, some of which are more sucessful than others. With the Shadow/Highlight adjustment, we have a semi-automatic adjustment that's very good at what it does within certain limits. Shadow/Highlight is set by default to correct for shadows obscuring a backlit subject. If you simply open the adjusment (available only from the Image/Adjustment menu), you'll probably be disappointed with the result, no matter how you slide the sliders. However, click the Show More Options checkbox and this becomes a handy tool for quick corrections. In a rather complicated bit of programming, Photoshop looks at a range of pixels to determine which areas of the photo are in deep

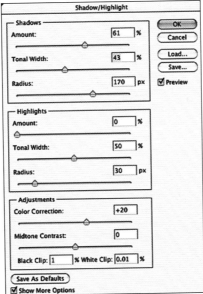

The default values in the Shadow/Highlight adjustment are for a backlit subject like this man's face.

Here are the settings I used to lighten the man's face in the second picture.

shadows as opposed to simply dark areas that are correctly exposed. You set the range yourself via the Radius slider. In experimenting with Shadow/Highlight, I've had the best results by setting this slider first with the default 50% for both Amount and Tonal Width. Get the best look you can and then adjust the Tonal Width slider to select the range of values within your radius setting that are to be adjusted. Finally, tweak the Amount slider. You may find that you need to move between the Tonal Width and Amount sliders, adjusting back and forth. Also, one other setting that I found really makes a difference is the Black Clip setting. For the illustration here, I set the clip to 1%, but I've used other photos where I set the amount as high as 5%. The Highlight sliders work exactly the same, only on the highlight values. In the bottom of the dialog box, the Color Adjustment slider increases the saturation of any area that has been adjusted, and Midtone Contrast is just exactly what it says. I've had better luck using an additional curve after the Shadow/Highlight adjustment to increase contrast rather than the Midtone slider.

This is the result using only the Shadow/Highlight adjustment settings shown here.

With a few adjustment layers to open and color correct the face a bit more, you have this.

PHOTO FILTERS

If you've sometimes wished that you had shot a certain scene with a color filter, here's your chance to apply the filter after the fact. Photoshop CS has a list of standard filters that can be accessed as either an adjustment or adjustment layer. This is similar to setting a solid color layer above your image in color blend mode at about a low opacity, but look closer and you'll see that it's not the same.

What Adobe has attempted to do here is correct for exposure issues, just

In this Riotgrrl photo, note the blown out highlights as well as the overall coolness of the scene.

The #85 Warming Filter warms up the skin tones and the neutrals adding density to the image.

as you might judge a situation when you're shooting by metering the highlights and shadows of the scene and choosing a filter to compensate for problems that you expect. It is recommended that you turn off the Preserve Luminosity checkbox to more closely mimic exposure compensation. Photo Filters give you some filters that you'll immediately recognize and the option to set your own colors. Also, because you can use the Photo Filters as adjustment layers, you can mask out all or some of the effect wherever you need to.

THE AUTO LEVELS, AUTO CONTRAST, AUTO COLOR, DESATURATE, AND GRADIENT MAP COMMANDS

The Auto Levels command does an automatic Levels color correction of your image; Auto Contrast does an automatic contrast adjustment. Auto Color does an automatic color correction of your image. I would not recommend using these for quality color control, but it's okay for a quick fix to an FPO proof or for low-end reproduction. If you are in a production environment where speed is of the essence and you decide to use these tools, make sure you set up options that will work for the majority of photos that come in. To do that go to Level or Curves (you can do this in an adjustment layer as well) and click on the Options button. This allows you to set target values for the highlights, shadows, and midtones, as well as clipping percentages for black and white pixels. Save the values you set as defaults.

The Gradient Map command added to Photoshop 6 and 7 is pretty cool for adding effects to an image. It converts the image using the gradient you select from the Gradients palette. There is a Dither option, which will tend to give you smoother gradients and a Reverse option, which will reverse the direction of the gradient. The gradient we chose here turns this color image of the Santa Cruz boardwalk into a Duotone type effect. If you add a Gradient Map as an adjustment layer, the original image pixels are not modified and you can always go in and change the gradient at a later time by double-clicking on the Adjustment Layer icon. That's the best way to use this tool.

The Desaturate command completely desaturates your image, taking all the hue or color values out of it, leaving you with a black-and-white image in RGB or CMYK mode. Desaturate does not do exactly the same thing as Image/Mode/Grayscale; with Desaturate, the image appears flatter. To convert from color to grayscale, I would correct the color image first and then choose Image/Mode/Grayscale. If you need an RGB image to send to your printer, for example, then convert this grayscale back to RGB. You get better contrast that way.

The Gradient Map command is a useful effect. It is great for getting a Duotone type look by converting the 0-255 values in your image to the corresponding values in the gradient chosen. This doesn't have the level of control that the Duotone feature has, but you could use it to quickly get standard appearances with an image that will still end up being in the RGB format when you are finished. If you like this type of effect, you might also try using the Gradient Overlay effect within the Layer

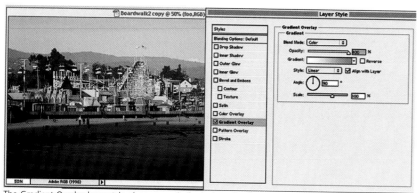

The Gradient Overlay layer style gives you a similar look to Gradient Map but has a few more options that you can play with. Here we have set the Blend mode to Color.

Style dialog box. You get to this by double-clicking on a Layer thumbnail of a regular layer or by choosing Layer/Layer Style/Gradient Overlay. Layer styles won't work for a *Background* layer unless you convert it into a normal layer by double-clicking on its thumbnail and then renaming it.

WHERE TO LEARN MORE

To learn more about the color correction tools mentioned in this overview, read Chapters 13: "Digital Imaging and the Zone System," 17: "Steps to Create a Master Image," and do the step-by-step examples in Chapters 19: "Overall Color Correction," 20: "Correcting a Problem Image," Chapters 21: "Yellow Flowers," 22: "Color Matching Images," and 24: "Desert Al." Chapters 26: "Combining Bracketed Captures or Scans to Increase Dynamic Range," and 27: "Bryce Stone Woman," also have valuable color correction techniques.

RGB to CMY Relationship

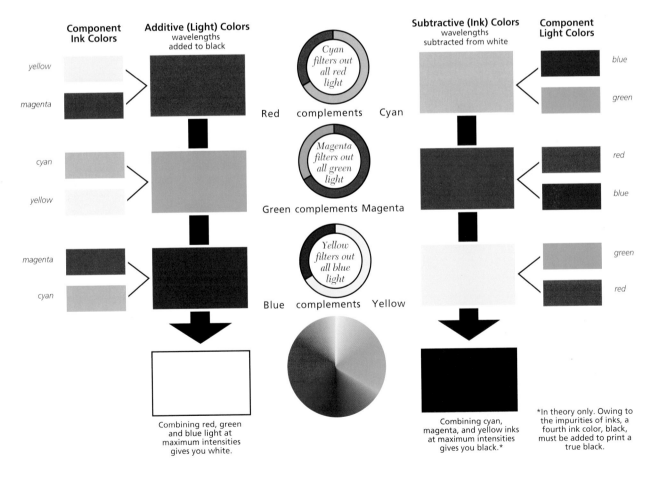

13 DIGITAL IMAGING AND THE ZONE SYSTEM

*Digital imaging as it relates to traditional
photography and the Zone System, and
how to create a high-quality original photograph.*

Images in nature that you see with your eyes have the greatest beauty because they usually are illuminated by wonderful light and have depth and texture that we can only simulate on a print or computer screen. The range of light, from the darkest black shadow to the brightest sparkling highlight, reflected from reality to our eyes is far greater than we can reproduce in any printed or screen image. Our eyes can adjust as we gaze into a shadow or squint to see a bright detail. When you look at a scene in nature, it has the best quality and the most detail. The T.V. set, which we watch so much, has the least amount of detail and sharpness. Go out and see the real world!

TRANSITIONS TO THE DIGITAL WORLD

There are many reasons to copy a scene from nature, a pretty face, or a product, and reproduce the image so it can be carried around and seen again. How to do this, and get the best quality, is an important subject of this book. I give thanks to Ansel Adams, perhaps the most well-known nature photographer, and his great series of books, *The Camera, The Negative,* and *The Print,* for my introduction to an understanding of artistic photography. These titles by New York Graphic Society Books are must-reads for anyone who wants to understand how to take the best quality photographs. *Ansel Adams: An Autobiography* is also a wonderful book. Many of Adams' discussions are about black-and-white photography, but the concepts still apply to color and even digital imaging. The depth and joy of his philosophies are something all people who deal with images should have a feeling for.

Although he died in 1984, before digital imaging became easily available and popular, Ansel Adams was ahead of his time and says in his book *The Negative:*

"I eagerly await new concepts and processes. I believe that the electronic image will be the next major advance. Such systems will have their own inherent and inescapable structural characteristics, and the artist and functional practitioner will again strive to comprehend and control them."

This chapter should help you to understand the nature of an original image and how to control and improve it in the digital world.

ACHIEVING YOUR VISUALIZATION

The Zone System, developed by Ansel Adams in 1940, gives photographers a way to measure an image in nature and then capture it on film so it can be reproduced with the photographer's intentions in mind. Adams uses the term "visualization" to explain a technique where photographers imagine what they want a photo to look like as a print before taking the photo. Once this image, the visualization, is in the photographer's mind, the photographer uses the Zone System to get the correct data on the film so that visualization can be achieved in the darkroom. Getting the right data on the film or into a digital camera is very important in the process of creating a digital image too. We use the Zone System to explain what the right data is, and then we discuss how to get that data onto film or into a digital camera. If you get the right data into a digital camera, you can transfer it directly into your computer. When you capture the image on film, you need to scan it correctly to make sure all the information gets into your computer.

Capturing the Dynamic Range

When you look at an image in nature or in a photography studio, you can use a photographic light meter to measure the range of brightness in the image. On a very sunny day, out in the bright sun, you may have a very large range of brightness between the brightest and darkest parts of your image area. We will call this range the *dynamic range* of that image. Each photographic film, and each digital camera, has its own dynamic range of values from brightest to darkest that the particular film or camera can capture, called its *exposure latitude*. Many photographic films and digital cameras cannot capture the full dynamic range of brightness present in the original scene, especially on a bright, contrasty day. I'm sure you have all taken photographs where the prints don't show any details in the shadows or where a bright spot on a person's forehead is totally washed out. The objective of the Zone System is to measure, using a light meter, the brightness range in the original scene and then adjust your camera so the parts of that brightness range that you want to capture actually get onto the film or into the digital camera.

Dividing an Image into Zones

The Zone System divides an image into 11 zones from the brightest to the darkest. Ansel Adams uses Roman numerals to denote the zones from 0 to X. These zones in the printed image reference how light or dark each area will be. In a photograph, a Zone 0 area would be solid black, with no detail showing whatsoever; in a halftone you would see no white dots in the solid black ink. Zone I is still a very dark black, but it is not pure black and has no real measurable detail. If you look at a Zone I halftone with the naked eye, it still looks black without detail, but if you were to use a loupe or other magnifier, you would see very small white dots in a sea of black ink.

On the other end of the scale, Zone X is solid white. In a print this would be the color of the paper; in a halftone there would be no dots in a Zone X area. You would use Zone X to represent a specular highlight like the reflection of the sun on a chrome bumper. Zone IX is a very bright white without detail, but again you can see some very small halftone dots if you use a loupe. The range of image brightness areas that will have obvious detail in the printed image include Zone II through Zone VIII. Zone VIII will be very bright detail and Zone II will be very dark detail. In the middle of this area of print detail is Zone V. In a black-and-white print, Zone V would print as middle gray, halfway between pure black and pure white. In a color print, a Zone V area would print as normal color and brightness for that area if you were looking at it in normal lighting conditions with your eyes adjusted to it. When you set the exposure setting on your camera, areas in the image that have a brightness equal to that exposure setting are getting a Zone V exposure. We will explain this further in this chapter.

GETTING A GOOD EXPOSURE

Let's talk for a moment about how you take a picture with a camera. We will use black-and-white negative and color positive transparency as examples in this discussion. Normally, when you take a transparency picture with a camera, you measure the range of brightness in the original scene and set the exposure on your camera so as to reproduce the range of brightness on the film to look the same as it appeared in the original scene. The automatic cameras of today have computerized light meters that do all this for you, although you sometimes still need to do it manually to get exactly what you want. When you use a manual camera with a hand-held light meter, you need to do it manually. Even though many of you probably have automatic cameras as I do, let's describe the manual camera process so we all understand what needs to happen to take a good picture. This discussion also applies to getting a good exposure with a digital camera.

MEASURING THE BRIGHTNESS

To get a good exposure, you need to measure the brightness range of different subjects within the photograph. Let's say you were taking a photograph of a Spanish home in Costa Rica. You want to set the exposure somewhere in the middle of the brightness range that occurs naturally in the setting. That middle position, wherever you set it, then becomes Zone V. A hand-held spot light meter allows you to point at any very small area in a scene and measure the amount of light reflected from that area. The light meter measures the brightness of light, the *luminance*, reflected from the metered part of the image. Unless you plan to use filters or different film to modify the light's color, this is all you really need to measure regardless of whether you are taking a black-and-white or color photo.

In the Spanish home picture, the brightest areas are the little bit of sky at the top and the reflection of the sun in the right side of the window frame at the bottom. The darkest areas are the shadows in the bottom-right corner. Measuring these with a light meter that allows spot readings might produce readings like exposure value 17 for the bright section of sky at the top and exposure value 7 for the dark shadow at the bottom. Each change in the exposure value settings on a professional light meter is equal to a difference of two in the amount of light measured.

In the building picture to the left, if we have exposure value readings from 7 in the darkest area to 17 in the brightest area, there is a difference of 1,024 times the brightness from the darkest amount of light to the brightest amount of light. This is because each jump in the exposure value represents twice as much light. Here's how we get 1,024 times as much light: exposure value 7 = 1 (the lowest amount of light), EV 8 = 2 (twice as much light), EV9 = 4, EV10 = 8, EV11 = 16, EV12 = 32, EV 13 = 64, EV14 = 128, EV15 =

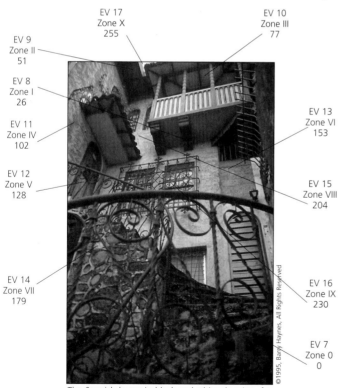

EV 17
Zone X
255

EV 9
Zone II
51

EV 8
Zone I
26

EV 11
Zone IV
102

EV 12
Zone V
128

EV 14
Zone VII
179

EV 10
Zone III
77

EV 13
Zone VI
153

EV 15
Zone VIII
204

EV 16
Zone IX
230

EV 7
Zone 0
0

The Spanish home in black-and-white showing, for each zone, the exposure value (EV) read by an exposure meter, the corresponding zones, and lastly the 0 to 255 digital value based on placing Zone V at exposure value 12 on the door.

140

256, EV16 = 512, EV17 (the brightest reading) = 1024. This is 1,024 times as much light from the darkest area to the brightest.

PLACING THE ZONE V EXPOSURE

After measuring the range of exposure values within a scene that you want to photograph, you usually set the camera's exposure to a value in the middle of that range. The value that you set your exposure to causes the areas that have that exposure value within the scene to show up as a middle gray value on the film and print in black-and-white or as a normal middle detail exposure in color. Where you set your exposure on the camera is called "placing your Zone V exposure." Here we are placing our Zone V exposure at exposure value 12, the reading we got from the door. Usually you set your exposure to the area within the image that you want to look best or most normal. If a person were standing on the steps in this photo, you might set the exposure to a reading that you would take off the person's face.

When you decide where to set the exposure, you affect what happens to each of the zones within the image area, not just Zone V. If the Spanish home image were a transparency, it would reflect an exposure where you set Zone V based on the reading taken from the middle of the door. If the film is then processed correctly, the middle of the door in the transparency would look correct, as though you were looking straight at it with your eyes adjusted to it. When you set the exposure to the middle of the door, the areas that are lighter or darker around it, the zones above and below Zone V, become correspondingly lighter or darker on the film. The bright window, at exposure value 16, will then be placed at Zone IX and will show up as very bright and with almost no detail on the film. This is because it is four zones above, or 16 times brighter than, where we set our exposure (at exposure value 12).

If you were to set the exposure on the camera to exposure value 16, the exposure value for the bright window, you would do to the camera and film what happens to your eye when you move up very close to the bright part of a contrasty scene. The iris of your eye closes and you start to see a lot of detail in that bright area. It is no longer a white area with no detail, because the focus of your field of vision moves up and your eyes adjust to encompass just that area. If you set the exposure on your camera to exposure value 16, that bright window area in the picture would show up as a middle gray for black-and-white or a normal color in a transparency. By changing this exposure, you would then be placing Zone V at exposure value 16. Now the door would be at Zone I, 16 times darker, and everything darker than the door would be in Zone 0, totally black. This would give you details in the highlights, but you would lose the details in the darker parts of the scene. By measuring the scene and noticing that the bottom of the stairs has exposure

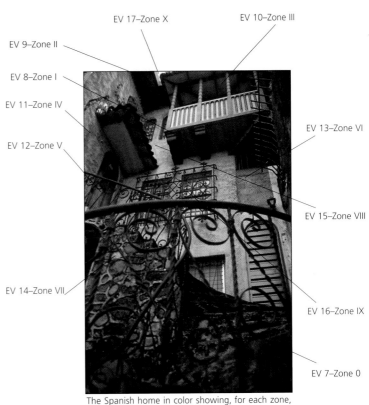

The Spanish home in color showing, for each zone, the exposure value read by an exposure meter and the corresponding zone based on placing Zone V at exposure value 12 on the door. For the color image, the RGB digital values vary for each color channel depending on the color of the area.

141

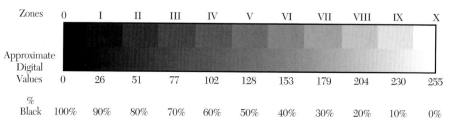

Zones	0	I	II	III	IV	V	VI	VII	VIII	IX	X
Approximate Digital Values	0	26	51	77	102	128	153	179	204	230	255
% Black	100%	90%	80%	70%	60%	50%	40%	30%	20%	10%	0%

A stepwedge file of the 11 zones in the Zone System with the approximate corresponding digital values and percentages of black ink. The digital values shown here fall somewhere in the center of each zone. Where the actual zone values and digital values appear for each image depends on the type of output you choose. You have more latitude where the Zone I detail begins and Zone IX details end when you print at a higher resolution and line screen. If you are printing to newsprint, all of Zone I may print as 100% black and all of Zone IX as 100% white.

If you want to know more about the Zone System and how to take the best photographs, you should read Ansel Adams' book The Negative. It contains very useful information. It also shows you some very good techniques for extending or shortening the exposure latitude of your film by under- or over-developing. Another great book on the Zone System is The New Zone System Manual by White, Zakia, and Lorenz from Morgan Press, Inc.

value 7 and the sky has exposure value 17, then setting the exposure on your camera in the middle at exposure value 12, you place Zone V at exposure value 12, thereby obtaining the full range of these values on the film.

UTILIZING YOUR EXPOSURE LATITUDE

Different films and different digital cameras have different exposure latitudes. The *exposure latitude* of a film is the number of different exposure values it can record at once. The Zone System covers a range of 11 exposure values, a brightness going from 1 to 1,024 times as bright. Most films cannot capture detail in so broad a range of lighting situations. This range of light would be found in a contrasty scene on a sunny day with the sun shining directly on it. Some films can capture detail over a range of seven exposure values and some over a larger range. In Adams' description of his zones, detail is captured only from Zone II through Zone VIII, or over a seven-zone range. Things in Zones 0, I, IX, and X are pretty much void of detail and either black or white. Many digital cameras, like the Dicomed digital backs, have a larger dynamic range than most film. If you know the exposure latitude of your film or digital camera when taking a picture, you can determine which parts of the picture will have detail and which will be black or white by measuring the range of your image area and setting your exposure, your Zone V area, so that the other zones or brightness ranges you need fall where the camera will catch them.

We could have gotten more details in the highlights in this picture by placing Zone V, our exposure setting, at exposure value 13 or 14 instead of 12, but then the shadow areas at exposure values 8 or 9, the areas underneath the roof and balcony overhangs, would have shown up as totally black. Some pictures will not be very contrasty, and you will know by taking light measurements that the exposure latitude of your film or digital camera can handle the total number of zones in the image. All you need to make sure of then is that you set the exposure in the middle of that range so all the areas of different exposure values fall within the latitude of the film or digital camera and you thus capture their detail.

The measurements and diagrams in this chapter don't accurately measure any particular film or camera. They simply illustrate how the process works.

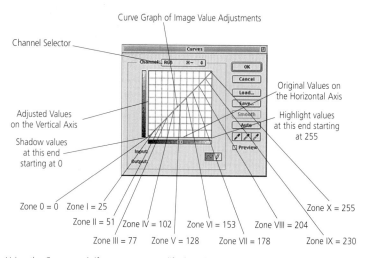

Curve Graph of Image Value Adjustments
Channel Selector
Original Values on the Horizontal Axis
Adjusted Values on the Vertical Axis
Highlight values at this end starting at 255
Shadow values at this end starting at 0
Zone 0 = 0 Zone I = 25
Zone II = 51 Zone IV = 102
Zone III = 77 Zone V = 128
Zone VI = 153
Zone VII = 178
Zone VIII = 204
Zone IX = 230
Zone X = 255

Using the Curves tool, if you want to modify the colors or brightness of the items in a certain zone or zone range of the image, this diagram points out the part of the curve you would modify to change those zones. Using the Eyedropper tool with Curves, you can measure any part of the image and the location of its values will show up on the curve as a small circle. This makes it very easy to adjust any range of values or colors using Curves.

Chapter 13: Digital Imaging and the Zone System

THE ADVANTAGES OF A DIGITAL IMAGE

Once you have captured all the information you need on the film, you want to move it into your computer by making the best possible scan. If you have a digital camera, you don't need to scan; you can digitally transfer the image from the camera to the computer. Your objective is to make sure that your image retains all the zone detail you captured for you to play with. Photoshop is able to work with Camera Raw files, which allows you to have more control over the information captured by your high-end digital camera. For more on scanning and bringing images into the computer, see both Chapter 10: "Digital Cameras and Camera Raw Format," and Chapter 16: "Image Resolution, Scanning Film, and Digital Capture."

When you look at the histogram of a digital image using the Levels or Curves commands or the Histogram palette in Photoshop, you see all those values, all those zones. You can move them around and adjust them with much more precision on the computer than you would have in the darkroom. In addition, some digital cameras let you see the histogram on the camera back. One quick look tells you if you've captured the values you need for a great print.

If you are not familiar with Levels and Curves, read Chapters 19: "Overall Color Correction," 20: "Correcting a Problem Image," and 17: "Steps to Create a Master Image," later in this book.

Looking at a scan of the Spanish home image in Levels, we can actually see how many values in the image fall within each zone. Notice that in this image many values fall in Zones I, II, and III. That's because this image has a lot of dark areas. There are not many values in Zones IX and X because this image does not have many very bright areas. To move the values that are in Zone V toward Zone IV, making the image brighter, or toward Zone VI, making the image darker, you can use the Brightness/Contrast slider in Levels. To move the values in Zones I and II over to Zone 0, making the shadows darker, you can use the Input Shadow slider. In later chapters, we show you how to use these techniques with the Levels command to give you more control over the different brightness and color zones in your images. We will also show you how to use Curves to do pretty much anything you want with your image data.

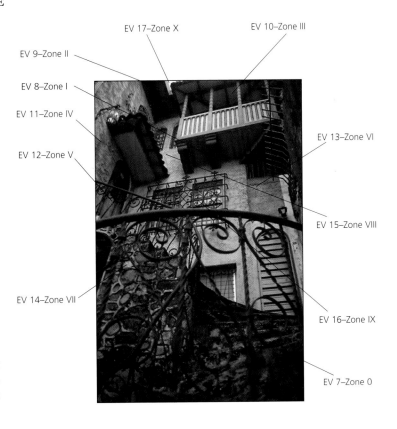

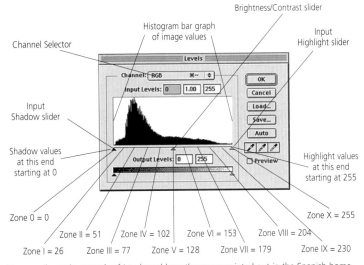

Here are the main controls of Levels and how the zones pointed out in the Spanish home image above show up in the histogram of that image. The approximate digital value, in the 0 to 255 range, is also shown for each zone. If you work on 48-bit images in Photoshop, then each pixel in each of the Red, Green, and Blue channels has 65,536 possible tonal values. If your scanner or digital camera software allows you to save more than 8 bits of data per channel, save the file this way and you will capture more of the tonal variations and details from the film or digital camera.

COLOR SPACES, DEVICE CHARACTERIZATION, AND COLOR MANAGEMENT

An overview of how we see color; measure color; calibrate color scanners, monitors, and printers; and what color working spaces and file bit-depths to use in Photoshop.

WHAT IS COLOR AND HOW WE SEE IT

It's night and we can barely see; then the sun slowly comes up, and things begin to become recognizable. The light from the sun is allowing us to see more and more things. In that early morning light, things seem very warm and yellow. Then as the sun gets higher in the sky, that warm yellow goes away and we get a whiter light. That white, midday light is made up of many wavelengths of light. Light is actually waves of excited electronic particles, and those waves come in different wavelengths. When those light waves hit a surface, each different type of surface absorbs some of the wavelengths of light, and other wavelengths are reflected back toward us if we are looking at that surface. Now instead of the white light that comes from the sun, we only see part of that light reflected back from a surface. The part, or wavelengths, that are reflected back to us determines the color of that surface.

Our eyes have sensors called rods and cones. The rods sense brightness or light intensity, but it is the cones that actually detect color. There are three different types of cones, each sensitive to a different wavelength of light. One type of cone is more sensitive to red light, one is more sensitive to green, and the third is more sensitive to blue.

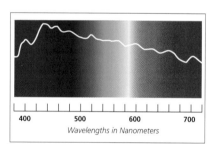

The wavelengths of light and how you see them. The white line is an approximation of daylight wavelengths.

AN IMAGE ON PAPER

When we look at an image printed on paper, the color we see depends on the color of the incoming light that is illuminating the paper; that incoming light supplies all or most of the wavelengths of light that we could possibly see, although there might be several different types of light illuminating the paper that increases the possibilities. The color and surface texture of the paper itself will subtract some of the wavelengths from that incoming light source and give the paper a certain color. The inks or other types of color that are painted on that paper will subtract further wavelengths from that original light and reflect back different colors that are the remaining nonsubtracted wavelengths. The angle that you view the paper might also influence how much light is reflected back. When you are considering how a particular image might look on a certain printer, the digital values in the original image, the type of inks that you use, the type of paper that you print on, and the way the printer puts the ink on the paper all work together to create a specific range of colors you can see in that one situation.

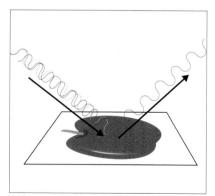

Seeing color by light reflecting back off a surface while the other colors are absorbed.

AN IMAGE ON A COMPUTER MONITOR

Color on a computer monitor comes from particle energizers, a type of light source, behind the monitor's glass that hits the coating on the inside of the monitor glass and produces different colors and light intensities depending on the numerical values that are driving the different colored light particle energizers. There is also light hitting the monitor from the outside due to other light sources within the room, and this light will have some effect on the color and brightness that you see from the internal monitor particle energizer. The way you see color on a computer monitor is quite different from the way you see color on a printed piece of paper. It is difficult to exactly match the brightness, color, and contrast characteristics of these two media. We will show you how to get as close as possible to a match using calibration.

SLIDE ON A LIGHT TABLE

When you see color by looking at a slide on a light table, the color you see there depends on the color of the light source behind the slide, the colors in the emulsion of the slide material, and on the amount and intensity of the other light sources in the room.

COLOR GAMUTS

There is a very large range of colors, wavelengths of light, that the human eye can see. There are also wavelengths of light that our eyes can't see. A particular range of colors is called a color gamut. The color gamut of the human eye is described in a color space called Lab color. A color space is a description of a range of colors to be used for a particular purpose. In the 1930s, an organization called the CIE (Commission Internationale de l'Eclairage) did a bunch of scientific measurements with human observers to develop a description of the colors the human eye could see. Without filling in all the details here, this description has evolved into two very useful tools we will use in this book for measuring and quantifying color. (Note: to learn a lot more about the CIE and color history and theory, I'd recommend *The Reproduction of Color* by Dr. R.W.G. Hunt, Fifth Edition, 1995 by Fountain Press.) One of these tools that Photoshop supports is the Lab color space, which consists of a color gamut of the range of colors that the human eye can see. The second tool is the CIE xy chromaticity diagram that shows these colors on an xy graph, again representing the colors the human eye can see. This CIE xy chromaticity diagram is useful for plotting other color gamuts and comparing one against the other. When you are working on a project using the Lab color space, you won't be throwing out colors that the eye can see and you won't be working with any colors that the eye cannot see. Using the Lab color space, you can potentially be working with all the colors the eye can see; however, the eye can actually see more colors than most of the cameras and printers we work with can reproduce. Some of the step-by-step examples in this book use the Lab color space.

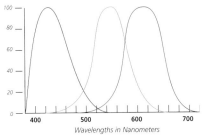

Wavelengths of light the eye can see.

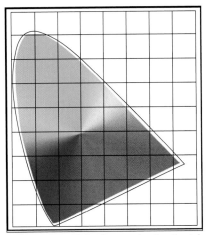

A CIE xy chromaticity diagram showing the Lab color space.

MEASURING COLOR

To measure color, we need to be able to measure wavelengths of light. A device called a spectrophotometer does this best, and we will be talking about how a spectrophotometer, along with various color calibration software, work together to improve our use and accuracy of digital color. We want to be able to measure the colors that a particular film or digital camera can record, a particular scanner can scan, a particular monitor can display, and a particular printer can print. To do this, people have developed test target systems, such as the IT8 color target from the CIE, to

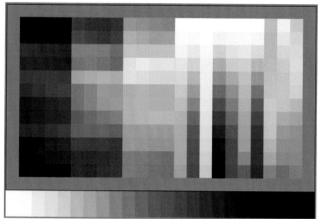

An IT8 color measuring target.

measure color. In its purest form, this IT8 target consists of a group of many color swatches, light wavelength descriptions, covering a large range of colors that the human eye can see, as well as various films could capture, scanners could scan, monitors could display, and printers could print. I use the word could here because you need to know that each color device—each film, digital camera, scanner, monitor, or printer—has its own color gamut. The color gamut of a device is the range of colors that particular device can detect, reproduce, or display. With a spectrophotometer, one can use the IT8 target or one of many other similar targets to measure the color gamut of any particular device.

Measuring the Gamut of a Film

To measure the gamut of a film, you photograph a scientifically printed version of the IT8 target when that target is illuminated by a known type and color temperature light source. You then process that film exactly and use the spectrophotometer to measure each swatch in the target as it is reproduced on that film. Different film manufacturers will sell you film swatches with IT8 targets already correctly exposed on them for you to scan and measure. The film needs to be illuminated by a known light source while taking the measurements. Those measurements are then entered into a profile-making software program, which generates an ICC color profile of that film. The software program knows the empirical values each swatch is supposed to have and did have on the scientifically produced original that was photographed. Based on the differences between the original values of each swatch and the values actually recorded on the film, an ICC profile is generated that characterizes that particular film. A characterization is a description of the differences from the original empirical values, which ends up also telling you the color gamut or range of colors that film can represent. ICC stands for International Color Consortium, which is basically a group of companies and international organizations that have agreed on a standard for specifying color. The ICC profile standard is that standard, and an ICC profile is a description of color that is in a standard format that can be recognized by many different color software applications, including Adobe Photoshop, Apple ColorSync, QuarkXPress, Adobe Illustrator, and Adobe InDesign.

Characterizing a Scanner

To measure the color gamut, or characterize a scanner, you need a scientifically produced IT8 target on film, which you can get from the film manufacturer, or on a printed medium that can be scanned with the scanner. The resulting digital values that the scanner gets are entered into the profile-making software that will make an ICC profile that describes that particular scanner. In Chapter 15: "Photoshop Color Preferences, Monitor, Scanner, and Printer Calibration," we'll talk about several packages you can use to make custom scanner profiles.

Characterizing a Monitor

To characterize a monitor, a scientifically created digital file of the IT8 target or some other target is measured with a colorimeter or spectrophotometer while being displayed on the screen in a room lit with controlled lighting conditions. Then those measurements are entered into the profile-making software to generate the

Chapter 14: Color Spaces, Device Characterization, and Color Management

ICC profile of that monitor. In Chapter 15, we'll show you several hardware/software packages you can use to calibrate your monitor.

CHARACTERIZING A DIGITAL PRINTER

To characterize a particular digital printer or printing press, the scientifically produced digital version of the IT8 target, or some other target, is printed on that printer or press using the standard process for outputting to that device. Then the results are measured with the spectrophotometer, and the profile-generating software creates an ICC profile from those results.

Now we know what ICC profiles are and how they are made. By the way, there are various targets that the industry uses to create ICC profiles; the Kodak IT8 is just an example, and there are various companies that create ICC profile-making software. These companies and their products include Monaco EZ Color, Proof and Profiler, ColorVision OptiCal, Profiler RGB and Profiler Pro, GretagMacbeth Eye One Photo and Profilemaker, and many others. Calibration products have become much more popular since Photoshop 5 first began to support ICC profiles. When you are using this process to characterize, or describe, the color gamut, or range of colors, that a particular device can record, scan, display, or print, the accuracy of this characterization is based on the accuracy of the way the test was performed and measured. When you make a profile or have a profile made, make sure it is done properly, or the profile you get might actually do you a disservice. In the next chapter, Chapter 15, we will go through the process of making profiles using some of the more popular products now on the market.

CHOOSING YOUR COLOR WORKING SPACE

When you are working in Photoshop CS, you have the option of choosing different color spaces as your working color space. Color spaces available with Photoshop CS use either the RGB, Lab, or CMYK color model. Each color space also encompasses a particular color gamut. So when working in Photoshop CS, you need to decide which color model, RGB, CMYK, or Lab, makes the most sense for your type of work, and then, within that model, what color gamut you need for the work you are doing.

Let's first discuss the color gamut issue. For any particular body of work that involves human viewing, you will probably not need to work with colors outside the gamut of Lab because this is the set of colors the human eye can see. If you are outputting your work on color film, digital printers, computer monitors, or printing presses, you also need to consider the color gamut of those devices. It turns out that the color gamut of a CMYK printing press is much smaller than the color gamut of the human eye, the Lab color space. If you are only outputting to CMYK presses but you are working within the Lab color space, you may be constantly disappointed because many of the colors you would see on the screen could not actually be reproduced on a printing press. The color gamut of computer monitors, color film recorders, and some of the new digital color printers is much larger than that of a CMYK press. So if you are also outputting to devices other than a press, you would not want to limit your gamut to colors only available on a press, especially if your goal is to produce art prints for gallery use or exciting colorful images for the Web and multimedia. The ideal circumstance would be to work in a color space that encompasses the entire color gamut of all the input scanners or digital cameras, display monitors, output color film recorders, photographic and ink-based printers, digital printers, and CMYK or 6-color presses that you would be outputting to now and in

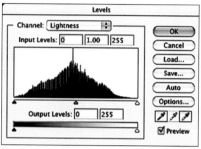

The Lightness channel in a Lab color image looks similar to an RGB histogram, but check out the a and b channels below where very small adjustments can make major changes.

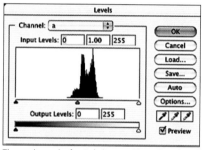

The a channel of a Lab image. There is a lot of unused space on either end of the histogram that could be used for a more detailed spec of this color if this were a reduced gamut Lab space like Lab LH.

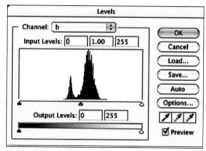

The b channel of this same Lab image.

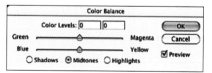

The Color Balance tool gives you different controls when working in Lab color, and you may find that you use it more in this color mode.

the reasonable future. I got the term "reasonable future" from my friend Bill Atkinson, and it seems like a good term because foreseeable future could include a time when we all wear special glasses, like Geordi La Forge on *Star Trek*, that increase the gamut of what the human eye can see. That would complicate things too much. We could measure the gamut of each of those devices and plot those gamuts on a CIE chromaticity diagram. If we then created a color space that encompassed the gamut of all those devices, then we would be set!

Now let's discuss the color model issue. What we have available in Photoshop is Lab, RGB, and CMYK. In the Image/Mode menu, there are also Index color, Duotone, and Grayscale, but I would put them in the category of special case models that we only work with under certain circumstances.

THE LAB WORKING SPACE

The Lab model has the advantage that its color gamut encompasses all the colors that the human eye can see. This is a very wide gamut and would certainly encompass the devices we would be working with in the reasonable future. Bill Atkinson and Charlie Cramer, two photographer friends of mine whose work I really admire, have actually worked a lot in the Lab color space using Photoshop. Bill does his scans on a Tango drum scanner using LinoColor software. He uses this software on the scanner to do his overall color correction on a Lab file, which he then uses in Photoshop to do final masking and tweaking with layers. Bill's images can be seen at www.billatkinson.com and Charlie's at www.charlescramer.com, and both their prints can be seen at the Ansel Adams gallery in Yosemite and in Carmel. Charlie has also been working with Lab color but is now switching to RGB, experimenting with several advanced wide gamut RGB color spaces. There are certain features of Photoshop that are not available when working in Lab color. To see what these are, use Image/Mode/Lab Color to convert one of your RGB images into Lab, then browse through the Photoshop menus and notice the ones that are now disabled, light gray.

I have used the Lab color space for my art prints but the potential problem with the Lab space is that it encompasses a larger gamut than most of the output devices I will be using. These are LightJet 5000, Epson 1280, 2200, and 7600 digital prints, prints on other digital printers, output to color film via a film recorder, and display on color monitors. Another potential problem with Lab is that the tools for working in Lab within Photoshop are sometimes not as easy to work with than when working in RGB. In the Lab space, there are three channels: Lightness, a, and b. The Lightness channel allows you to adjust the brightness and contrast of the image as well as sharpen the image without modifying the color of the image. Using Levels to look at a histogram of the Lightness channel of a Lab image is similar to looking at a histogram of RGB—all three channels at the same time. The color values in Lab are stored in the a and b channels. The a channel controls the red/green range of color, and the b channel controls the yellow/blue range. Most of us are used to working with color using red, green, and blue along with their complements of cyan, magenta, and yellow. Using a and b takes a little getting used to, and it works pretty well in Photoshop if you start out with a scan that is very close to what you want. When you have to make major color shifts with the a and b channels in Photoshop, this can be more difficult.

Bill and Charlie have used LinoColor, which has color controls that are more flexible in Lab, to get their colors close while scanning, then used it in Photoshop for all the final color tweaks, masking, spotting, sharpening, and final image production. The other thing about the a and b channels in Lab images is that if you look at their histograms, you will see that the values are usually all within the center part of the

Chapter 14: Color Spaces, Device Characterization, and Color Management

histogram. The blank parts at the left and right side of the a and b histograms represent colors that are in the very wide gamut Lab space but were not captured by the film or scanner, and therefore don't get represented in most Lab images. To represent a digital image in 24 bits of digital space in Lab, we have 256 possible lightness values, 256 possible a values, and 256 possible b values. The concern about Lab is that for most images, the a and b channels are using much fewer than the 256 possible range of values. The possible color range for the a and b channels is so wide that the actual range used is often covering a span of only 140 to 160 values or fewer within the center of the histograms. This brings up the concern of posterization of color values within Lab images. In a well-adjusted Lab image, one usually has a Lightness channel that has a range of values that stretches completely across the 256 possible values. According to Bill Atkinson, the Lightness channel is the one that is most important to avoid posterization. If the a and b channels contain fewer than 256 tonal values, even as few as 64 tonal values, the human eye will probably not be able to detect many more than that anyhow. Bill, Charlie, and I have not noticed any problem with color posterization when working with images in the Lab space. To address this potential problem, though, LinoColor has actually defined a smaller Lab space called Lab LH that encompasses a smaller a and b gamut that is more in line with actual digital output devices, but I don't believe Photoshop CS supports that space. Another way to better deal with the large Lab color space, which Photoshop CS now allows even when using Adjustment layers, would be to work with Lab images that have 16 bits per channel of color information. You'll notice, though, that some Photoshop functions, some filters mostly, still don't work with 16-bit Lab color. When you are working within an RGB space, both lightness and color values are represented in each of the Red, Green, and Blue channels, so it is harder to adjust one without the other changing as well.

THE RGB WORKING SPACE

Working in RGB is probably the most common way people work with digital images. The sensors on scanners actually scan in RGB, digital cameras capture images in RGB, most digital imaging software uses RGB as the default space, RGB is the format for images on the Web, RGB is the format used to print on the Light-Jet 5000 and Fujix digital printers, it is the preferred format for Epson and HP printers, and the format used to print to color film recorders. There are lots of reasons to work in RGB, and it is the color model that is most fully supported by Photoshop. Photoshop allows you to also look at and work with color using other color models, such as Lab, Hue/Saturation/Lightness, and CMYK, and you need to learn when and why it makes sense to work with color in a model other than RGB. RGB is the color model most people will use use most often. Working in RGB is a way to look at and interpret color data, but within the RGB world there are also different interpretations of RGB data.

If you scanned the same transparency with several different scanners, you would get different numerical results and the colors and contrast would also probably look somewhat different. Before Photoshop 5, there was not really a way to quantify those differences, all those files were just RGB files and you brought them into Photoshop and adjusted them to get what you wanted. Since Photoshop 5 and Photoshop's support of ColorSync and color management, you can actually make profiles for each of those scanners, and then when you bring those files into Photoshop, you can convert them from their respective scanner profiles to a standard RGB color space that you want to work with in Photoshop. If done properly this should make these different scans look more similar and also look more like the original transparency as you view

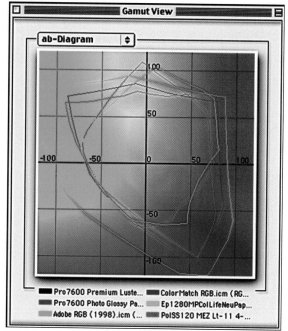

You can use the RGB pop-up in Photoshop/Color Settings to set your default RGB workspace; here it is set to Adobe RGB.

them on the screen within your standard Photoshop working space. Photoshop CS allows you to view each of these files on the screen in either a standard RGB working space or in the working space of the scanner itself by working on them in the color space of the scanner's profile.

When using the RGB color model in Photoshop, you usually want to pick an RGB working space for each file that you work with. Older versions of Photoshop, before Photoshop 5, assumed the gamut of your RGB space was the gamut of your monitor as described by the old Monitor Setup dialog. This caused colors outside of that space to be clipped (thrown out) even though those colors might have been printable on higher gamut output devices like color film recorders or the Epson 2200 digital printer. With Photoshop CS, you use the Photoshop/Color Settings dialog in the Working Spaces RGB area to specify the gamut and other characteristics of your RGB space. You can choose an RGB color space that has a wider gamut than your monitor and Photoshop will adjust the display of your space to preview as accurately as it can on your monitor, but Photoshop CS will not clip the colors that are outside of the monitor's gamut from your RGB file. That way you will still see those colors when you print the image.

With Photoshop 6 - CS it is easier to work with different RGB color spaces for different purposes than it was with Photoshop 5 & 5.5. The Photoshop 5 versions always displayed RGB files on the screen within one standard RGB workspace, so if you opened a file that was created in a different RGB workspace than your preferences were set to, you needed to change your preferences or that file needed to be converted to your standard space for the file to be displayed correctly. In Photoshop 6 - CS, you can work on many files at the same time, each with a different RGB workspace, and yet each file will be displayed correctly on the screen. Photoshop 6 - CS will simultaneously display files in Lab color and various CMYK color spaces correctly on the screen as well. The RGB Working Space that you set in Photoshop/Color Settings is the RGB space that will be assigned to and used to view new RGB files and is also the space in which untagged files, those with no assigned profile, will be viewed in on the screen.

Using the RGB pop-up menu, you can choose from the default RGB spaces Adobe has provided. If you choose the top Custom RGB choice, you can also enter your own Gamma, White Point, and Primary values using CIE xy values. To be sure he can work with all the colors his film captures, Joe Holmes, a well-known photographer, has created his own Ektachrome RGB space, which is bigger than Adobe RGB. Unless you have the tools available to measure the gamut of your input and output devices and create your own RGB workspace, you should probably pick one of the spaces provided by Adobe or something that seems to be moving toward becoming some sort of an industry standard. Of the spaces provided by Adobe, only three of them have much interest to people dealing with professional images. I will describe those here, and you can look in the Photoshop CS documentation for information about the other spaces if you want it. The three most commonly used spaces are Adobe RGB, ColorMatchRGB, and sRGB.

In the ab-diagram above, the Lab color space includes all the colors in the diagram. The Adobe RGB space is all the colors inside the green line, ColorMatch RGB includes the colors inside the blue line, the black line and the red line right on top of it are the profiles for the Epson 7600 Premium Luster and Premium Photo Glossy papers, the cyan line is a Monaco Proof profile I made for my Epson 1280 printer, and the purple line is the Polaroid Sprintscan 120 film scanner. Notice that the Adobe RGB color space encompasses all or most of the colors defined by any of the spaces shown here. In Photoshop CS you can preview an image within a CMYK or RGB printing space using the View/Proof Setup dialog. It is a good idea to do this before printing to be sure those non-printable colors don't spoil the effect of your image.

Chapter 14: Color Spaces, Device Characterization, and Color Management

Adobe RGB (1998)

The widest gamut of these spaces, Adobe RGB, was originally a proposed standard for HDTV production. Some people call this Adobe RGB (1998), but I just call it Adobe RGB. The gamut of Adobe RGB essentially includes the entire CMYK gamut and more because it also better encompasses the gamut of things like color RGB film recorders, the LightJet 5000 digital printer, various Epson and HP printers, and other more advanced color output devices. If you set your RGB working space to Adobe RGB, you will least likely be throwing out values that you'll be able to see in most of today's digital output devices, and yet the gamut is not so large that you'll be wasting a lot of your color space and risking posterization problems. I usually use Adobe RGB when I'm working with art prints in the RGB color space. With Adobe RGB, though, you will be able to see more colors on a good monitor than you'll be able to print in CMYK on a press. The technical description for Adobe RGB is: white point = 6500, gamma = 2.2, red x = .6400 y = .3300, green x = .2100 y = .7100, and blue x = .1500 y = .0600.

ColorMatch RGB

The ColorMatch RGB space has a smaller gamut than Adobe RGB but bigger than sRGB and AppleRGB. This space is based on the Radius PressView monitor that was an earlier industry standard for quality color work. There are several advantages to the ColorMatch RGB space, especially for people who are doing print work. One is that people who have been working with a PressView monitor can open their old untagged files into this space without any conversions. The other advantage is that it has a fairly large gamut, at least for CMYK print work, and it is a well-known space within the color industry. If you had been working in Photoshop 4 or earlier versions with a quality monitor, like the Radius PressView calibrated to gamma 1.8 and 5000° Kelvin color temperature, then ColorMatch RGB will give you a very similar working situation for your files within Photoshop CS. I have worked within the ColorMatch RGB space for the screen grabs and most of the work on previous editions of Artistry where the main intention for the files is printing on a CMYK press. The technical description for ColorMatch RGB is: white point = 5000, gamma = 1.8, red x = .6300 y = .3400, green x = .2950 y = .6050, and blue x = .1550 y = .0750.

sRGB

The sRGB color space is the current default for Photoshop CS. This space is good for people who are primarily working on Web images and want to see what they are going to look like on a typical PC monitor. The problem with sRGB is that it is the smallest gamut space of the three RGB spaces, and working in this space will mean that you are potentially throwing out certain colors, even for CMYK print work, and you are certainly throwing out colors if you are planning to output to a color film recorder or LightJet 5000 type digital printer. Photographers working on art prints should certainly change their RGB working space to something other than sRGB. If you are working in a larger gamut space, like Adobe RGB or Lab, and you want to create an image for the Web, you could use Image/Mode/Convert to Profile to convert a copy of your file from the larger space into sRGB for Web use. This would allow you to do your main work in Adobe RGB or Lab space and keep more colors; then use sRGB to preview the work as it will look on the average PC Web user's monitor. You can resave the file under a different name, or in JPEG format for your Web consumers, in the sRGB space that is optimized for that market. If you are a service bureau, you will probably find that you get a lot of files from the sRGB space just because it is the Photoshop 5 - CS default and many people who don't take

In the initial Photoshop 5.0 release, the Adobe RGB color space was called SMPTE-240M. Adobe renamed it to Adobe RGB, actually Adobe RGB (1998), in version 5.02 of Photoshop. If you see the name or color space SMPTE-240M, just know that it is exactly the same color space as Adobe RGB, and vice versa.

the time to learn about color won't bother to change this. Many digital cameras also default to sRGB. If you are opening an sRGB file from a digital camera and you are planning to color correct the file, you should use Image/Mode/Convert to Profile to convert it to Adobe RGB. This can also be done automatically in the Open dialog. If you are not going to color correct the digital camera file, and thus increase the color saturation, you can just leave it in sRGB and it will be displayed or printed correctly. The technical description for sRGB is: white point = 6500, gamma = 2.2, red x = .6400 y = .3300, green x = .3000 y = .6000, and blue x = .1500 y = .0600.

AppleRGB

The AppleRGB space is based on the old standard Apple 13" Trinitron color monitor. There are probably a lot of files out there in this space because older Illustrator and Photoshop versions have been using it as their default RGB space for a long time. Its gamut is not that much better than sRGB, so we really are not suggesting you use this as a current RGB working space. You will probably find it useful to use this as a Source Profile when opening old, pre-Photoshop 5 files that were not from Radius PressView monitors, especially files from people who never changed their Photoshop Monitor Setup from the default settings. You'd be surprised how many people never change this. The technical description for AppleRGB is: white point = 6500, gamma = 1.8, red x = .6250 y = .3400, green x = .2800 y = .5950, and blue x = .1550 y = .0700.

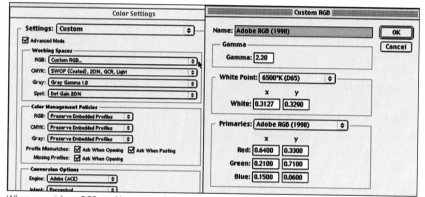

When you pick an RGB working space, that also sets up the default Gamma, White Point, and CIE xy primaries that describe that workspace. With Advanced Mode checked, you can go in and modify any of these by hand by choosing Custom RGB from the top of the RGB pop-up menu. Modifying any of the values of the standard RGB spaces will change them from that space to another of your own making, so be sure to change the name of the space too so you don't overwrite the standard. An example where you might want to define your own space this way would be if you measured a particular new film or digital camera that you are using and determined from its ICC profile that the Adobe RGB primaries did not contain a small portion of the film's color range. You could then change the Red, Green, or Blue xy values of Adobe RGB to extend the range of the Adobe RGB space. You'd want to call it something like Adobe RGB Plus!

Other RGB Working Spaces

Some photographers and imaging professionals may choose to develop their own custom RGB working space. This can be done by creating an ICC profile of a certain film that you like to work with. It can also be done by modifying an existing RGB working space to add a wider range of color in a particular area, like reds or greens for example. If you go to the top of the pop-up menu for your RGB Working Space, you can choose Custom and then edit the Gamma, White Point, and XY Primaries to create your own custom color space.

CMYK Master Workspace

The CMYK print gamut is smaller overall than the gamut of any of the RGB color spaces we just discussed, but there are a few colors CMYK can print that sRGB and Apple RGB don't include. These days, it is not that common for people to have images that are only used in CMYK print. Even if you are using an image for just CMYK print, it is likely that you may have to print that image several times, at several sizes, and on different types of paper. For these situations, it is better if you have your master image in RGB or Lab; then when you resize the file, you can get more exact sharpening and you can also more accurately generate new CMYK separations for different papers and presses. Most of us will be using the same image in print, on the Web, and for output to several digital printers. Because the RGB and Lab spaces are both bigger in color gamut than CMYK, it makes more sense these days to leave our master image in RGB or Lab format. If you do still decide to create your master images in CMYK, remember that some of the Photoshop filters don't work in CMYK either. In any case, while viewing your CMYK images on the screen, even if the separations were done elsewhere, Photoshop compensates for the appearance of the image on the screen based on the CMYK profile the image is tagged with. If the image isn't tagged with a profile, Photoshop will display it using the CMYK settings you set for your CMYK working space using Photoshop/Color Settings. If you open an image that was separated to be used in a 20% dot gain situation and display it in Photoshop with a CMYK working space set up for 30% gain, the image will appear too dark on the screen. When you reset the Photoshop settings to 20%, the same image appears correct again. You need to be careful when opening untagged CMYK images that your preferences are set up correctly for their display.

WORKING WITH 16-BIT PER CHANNEL SCANS AND FILES

A very useful technique, especially when working on the highest-quality art prints, is to do 16-bit scans, or digital capture, then work in 16-bit per color channel mode instead of 8-bit color. This gives you up to 16 bits per RGB, Lab, or CMYK channel of information instead of the usual 8 bits. Photoshop CS now has full Layer and Adjustment Layer support for 16-bit files and it also supports many other things in full 16-bit mode. The filters that photographers use for regular photography are supported in 16-bit mode, but many of the effects filters only work in 8-bit mode. To convert an image to 16-bit color, just choose Image/Mode/16 Bits/Channel, but to actually get the extra info that 16 bit is great for, you need to scan or digital capture in 16-bit mode to start with.

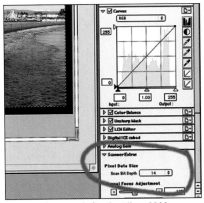

Here are the controls for the Nikon 8000 scanner set up to do 16-bit per channel scans. This scanner actually scans 14 bits of information per channel, but in Photoshop CS the two choices are either 8 bits per channel or 16 bits per channel, so when you actually do 12 or 14 bits in your scanner and save this as a TIFF file, it will show up as 16 bits within the Photoshop user interface.

If you get a scan from most of today's scanners, they will actually be scanning the files getting more than 8 bits per channel of RGB information. When you adjust the curves and other controls in the scanner software, what you are really doing is deciding how to convert from the more than 8 bits of information that the scanner gets down to the 8 bits of information per channel that is in a standard RGB file. When you do that conversion to 8 bit, you are throwing away information that you got from the scanner, and often you end up throwing away the wrong information or you want some of it back later. At this point, you may need to rescan your original to get that information. Most scanners these days, including the Nikon 4000 & 8000, the Polaroid Sprintscan 120, and the Epson 2450 and 3200, allow you to save all 16 bits per channel of information exactly as it comes from the sensors on the scanner— a raw scan. This way, assuming you have a great scan from a great scanner, you might never need to scan the original again because you can always reprocess that 16-bit per channel raw scan data down to 8 bits in a different way to pull out a different area of detail. Now with Photoshop CS, you can permanently leave your file and layers in 16-bit per channel color!

You should do your overall color correction on 16-bit per channel files using Photoshop CS to improve the histogram, colors, and contrast of that original raw scan without throwing away any information. This allows you to do one raw scan and then save that and actually be able to make most of your scanner decisions later without actually rescanning. In Chapters 19 and 26 of our step-by-step examples, *Photoshop CS Artistry* will show you how to change your workflow to do your overall color correction or all your color correction using 16 bits per channel and get much more from your scans. Check out Chapter 16: "Image Resolution, Scanning Film, and Digital Cameras," to get a lot of good ideas of things to consider when making 8-bit or 16-bit per channel scans.

15 PHOTOSHOP COLOR PREFERENCES, MONITOR, SCANNER, AND PRINTER CALIBRATION

Here you learn how to set up your Photoshop color preferences and to calibrate your monitor, printers, and output devices using ICC profiles and color management.

To fully understand this chapter, you should also read Chapter 3: "Setting System and Photoshop Preferences," Chapter 14: "Color Spaces, Device Characterization, and Color Management," and Chapter 17: "Steps to Create a Master Image." In the first part of this chapter, we will go through the Photoshop CS Color Settings and describe each setting and our recommended choice for it and what that choice means. The second part of the chapter will explain the choices for calibrating your monitor, scanner, and printer, which can dramatically affect the quality and predictability of your results.

SETTING YOUR PHOTOSHOP CS COLOR PREFERENCES

In Photoshop, bring up the dialog to the left and choose Photoshop/Color Settings (Command-Shift-K). We will be working with this dialog for some time because I'm going to try and explain each of the settings, why you make a particular choice, and what that choice will mean and do to your files. Get your coffee or your Coke (mine is right beside me) and if you are tired or bored, just choose the settings on the left and then come back and read this chapter later. The color settings and calibration are not the most fun part of Photoshop, especially for me, but they will dramatically affect the quality and accuracy of your results. If you are not happy with the results you are getting, this chapter must

Go to Photoshop/Color Settings (Command-Shift-K) in Photoshop CS to bring up this dialog. Make sure the Advanced Mode checkbox, at the top left, is checked so you see this entire dialog box. Once you have all your color settings the way you want them for a particular type of project, click the Save button to save these settings in a file that can later be reloaded in one step using the Load button.

be understood before you continue, as the problem may be your lack of understanding of what is herein.

WORKING SPACES

The top section of the Color Settings dialog is called Working Spaces. Choose Adobe RGB (1998) in the first RGB pop-up menu. After making this choice, notice that if you put the cursor on top of that same menu, the description area at the bottom of the dialog will tell you something about the setting you have chosen. As you are learning to understand all these settings, Photoshop will give you some information about each setting in this description area whenever you put the cursor on top of that setting. Please do that and read the description information for each of these settings as we go through them. We have now set the RGB working space to Adobe RGB. The RGB working space is the space that will be assigned to new files that you create using File/New, and it is the space that you will view untagged files in on the screen even if you don't tag them with Adobe RGB when you open them. Files that are already tagged with some other color space, like some of the files on the *Photoshop CS Artistry* CD that are tagged with ColorMatch, will usually be opened and viewed within that other color space, unless you choose to do otherwise in the next "Color Management Policies" section. To learn more about the Adobe RGB color space and the other default RGB spaces, see Chapter 14: "Color Spaces, Device Characterization, and Color Management." If you are a photographer and don't have another default custom RGB space you want to work in, like the color space of your film, then Adobe RGB is a good space for you to choose. If you are doing exclusively Web work, then you might want to choose the sRGB space. If you are doing exclusively work for CMYK print, then you might want to choose ColorMatch RGB. Setting your RGB working space causes certain things to happen in Photoshop in conjunction with how you set the Color Management Policies for RGB in the next section of this dialog. We'll talk about those issues there.

For the second CMYK pop-up menu, I recommend that you choose the U.S. Sheetfed Coated v2 settings, which have worked very well for me when I'm doing CMYK work. Most of my day-to-day printing is of my landscape art prints on the Epson 1280, 2200, and 7600. All these printers require RGB files, and in most cases I'm converting my RGB or Lab master files to a custom profile for those prints. My CMYK experience involves doing all the color separations for *Photoshop 6 Artistry, Photoshop 7 Artistry, Photoshop CS Artistry,* and Wendy's book, *Photoshop, Painter, and Illustrator Side-by-Side.* I also occasionally do an effect for a magazine cover or advertisement and usually separate these, too. *Photoshop 6 Artistry* was printed at Graphic Arts Center (Indianapolis) from Quark files containing my separated CMYK TIFF files direct-to-plate on sheetfed presses. *Photoshop 7 Artistry* and Wendy's *Side by Side* books are also printed at GAC, but using a direct-to-plate web press. I always go to the press check for the

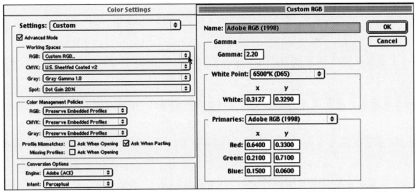

When you pick an RGB working space, that also sets up the default Gamma, White Point, and CIE xy primaries describing that workspace. You can then go in and modify any of these by choosing Custom RGB from the top of the RGB pop-up menu. Modifying any of the values of the standard RGB spaces will change them from that space to another of your own making, so be sure to change the name of the space too so you don't overwrite the standard. An example where you might want to define your own space this way would be if you measured a particular new film or digital camera that you are using and determined from its ICC profile that the Adobe RGB primaries did not contain a small portion of the film's color range. You could then change the Red, Green, or Blue xy values of Adobe RGB to extend the range of the space adding those colors. You'd want to call that Adobe RGB Plus or something like that!

155

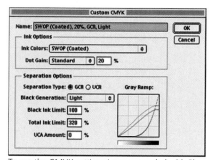

To use the CMYK settings I recommended with Photoshop 5 & 5.5, choose Custom CMYK from the CMYK pop-up, change Black Generation to Light and Total Ink Limit to 320%, and then choose OK. More advanced users who want to set custom Ink Colors can get the below dialog by choosing Custom from the Ink Colors dialog here. You can also set custom dot gain curves by choosing Curves from the above Dot Gain pop-up. Using the above settings, I've had very good results in printing *Photoshop 5 & 5.5 Artistry* on a sheet-fed press, *Photoshop, Painter, and Illustrator Side-by-Side* on a web press, as well as separating various brochures and magazine covers. We used the U.S. Sheetfed Coated v2 settings, shown to the right, for the more color critical pages in *Photoshop 6 Artistry* through *Photoshop CS Artistry*. For newspaper presses, non-glossy papers and other printing situations, you may need to use other settings. To be sure, you should run tests with the proofing mechanism at your print shop.

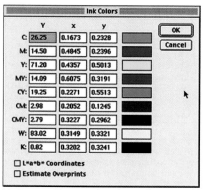

Most users will not need to change these. I would not recommend changing them unless you really know what you are doing or have real good recommendations. You may find more info about editing the Ink Colors in *Professional Photoshop 7* or *Real World Photoshop 7*.

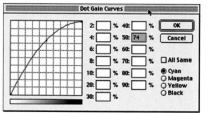

Photoshop CS allows you to create your own custom dot gain curves. If you work in a print shop and know a lot about color separations, you may want to do this, but most users won't. I would not recommend changing these unless you know what you are doing or have really good recommendations.

first printing of *Artistry*; then they do a great job on reprints using the press sheets from that first printing. When the web projects came up, I did some tests with the printer's Kodak Approval proofs comparing these same settings of mine with the settings normally recommended by the printer. Because this was a web press, I expected the printer's settings to work better, but my settings actually looked a bit more open on the Approval proofs. Approvals are digital proofs that actually show the dot patterns that will appear on the direct-to-plate printing plates. For more info on Photoshop CS CMYK settings and options, see pages 161 through 165 of this chapter and the information in the screen grabs and captions on those pages.

For the Gray pop-up menu, I'm using the Gray Gamma 1.8 option, which matches the gamma that I've set my Mac monitor to, which I've used with grayscale images in the past. Photoshops 6 through CS tag grayscale images with a profile showing the gamma that they have been created or adjusted with. The most important thing with grayscale images is that you stay consistent with the gamma that you use, either 1.8 or 2.2, because the appearance of the image will change dramatically if you view a gamma 1.8 image within a gamma 2.2 environment, or vice-versa. There are other choices available for your Gray working space, including pre-set dot gains of 10% up to 30%. You can also choose Custom Gamma to set the grayscale gamma to any custom value and Custom Dot Gain to set your own dot gain curve. You would use these options when printing grayscale images on presses and papers with different dot gain values or when you needed a gamma value other than 1.8 or 2.2.

Photoshop CS provides these CMYK default settings. We used the U.S. Sheetfed Coated v2 settings for the more color critical pages in this book. The older screen grabs were printed with the settings shown at the top-left of this page. If the settings I recommend on this page are not working for you, you may want to try the appropriate setting for your type of press and paper shown in this screen grab. See pages 161–165 of this chapter for more CMYK information. If you want even more CMYK information, I recommend that you check with the *Adobe Photoshop CS User Guide* or the books *Professional Photoshop 7* and *Real World Photoshop 7*.

For your Spot working space, which controls the dot gain on spot color channels, you should choose a dot gain that is comparable to the dot gain you are using with your CMYK working space. If you are adding a spot color plate to a certain print job, the dot gain for that plate should be similar to the dot gain you are getting at that printer in CMYK. I've set mine to the Dot Gain 20% setting, corresponding to my CMYK settings, but you might want to check with the print shop that is running a spot color job for you and see what they suggest. You can also choose Custom Dot Gain from the top of the Spot working space pop-up menu. This allows you to enter a custom dot gain curve, which you should only do if you know what you are doing and have specific dot gain measurements from the print shop.

COLOR MANAGEMENT POLICIES

The "Color Management Policies" section helps you deal with files that are different from what you normally expect. Photoshop CS assumes that you will normally be working with files that are tagged with profiles from your RGB, CMYK, or Grayscale working spaces. When you open or paste from a file that is tagged with a profile that is different from your working spaces or that isn't tagged with any profile, Photoshop lets you choose what to do. The settings I recommend, shown on the next page, will always warn you when you open or paste from an untagged file or a file that is tagged with a profile other than your working spaces. When I'm working on photographic images, I usually have my RGB working space set to Adobe RGB, but when I'm working on a book or printing project, I'll sometimes set it to Color-

In the Color Management Policies section, you have the same three choices in each of the RGB, CMYK, and Gray pop-ups. For each one, I recommend that you choose the middle choice, Preserve Embedded Profiles. I also recommend that you turn on Ask When Opening for Profile Mismatches and Missing Profiles that happen when you open a file, and turn on Ask When Pasting for Profile Mismatches that happen during a paste.

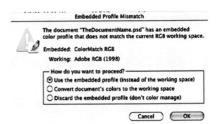

If you often work with files from different color spaces, it might be a good idea to set the info area at the bottom of your window to show the Document Profile. You will then see the profile that Photoshop has assigned to that particular document. In the case of an untagged document, that document will normally be displayed using the default RGB or CMYK working space.

Match RGB. Leaving the Color Management Policies as shown here will always give you a heads up when you are opening a file that is different from your current settings. If you always leave your working spaces set to the same values and you are always working with files in those same spaces, you should never get bothered by these settings.

If you often work with files from other color spaces, the above settings will cause Profile Mismatch dialogs to come up when you open a file or paste from a file in a different color space. The dialogs also alert you that a certain file is from a different color space or maybe doesn't have a profile at all. Because Photoshop CS allows you to work with several files from different color spaces on the screen at the same time, there is no need, as there was in Photoshop 5 and 5.5, to convert a file into your working space or to change your working space so a file from a different space will be displayed correctly. When you open a file from a different color space, and you get the Embedded Profile Mismatch dialog (top right), you will usually want to use the embedded profile. If you will be combining or pasting from that file into a master file that is in your working space, it might be faster to convert this file into the working space now. Otherwise, every time you copy from or drag and drop from that file into your master file within the working space, or within any different space for that matter, you will get the Paste Profile Mismatch dialog (bottom right) and will have to consider doing the conversion then. Opening an image that has no profile attached will bring up the Missing Profile dialog (middle right). This dialog allows you to leave the file as is (without a profile) or to assign the working space profile, or to assign some other profile you can choose from a pop-up menu. If you make this last choice, you can also turn on a checkbox to convert the file from that profile you assign into the working space.

If you turn off the Ask When Opening options for Profile Mismatch and Missing Profile, or Ask When Pasting option for Profile Mismatch, you won't get the dialogs, you'll just get the behavior from the appropriate pop-up menu in this Color Management Policies section. I do not recommend turning off these warning dialogs unless you are really sure you understand what you are doing and you are bothered by the dialogs. With the warning dialogs turned off, if you choose Preserve Embedded Profiles for RGB, then when you open a file that has a different profile from the RGB working space, that file will automatically open and be displayed correctly using the RGB profile that was attached to that file. If Convert to Working RGB was your menu choice, the file would automatically be

Actually, even when Ask When Opening is turned off, Photoshop will put up this dialog to let you know that the embedded profile will be used instead of the working space. Notice, however, that you can click the Don't show again checkbox here and this warning message will not show again unless you click on the Reset all Warning Dialogs button in Photoshop/Preferences/General.

When you open a file that has an embedded profile different from your working space, you will get a dialog like the one above. If you choose Use the embedded profile, the image will be correctly displayed on the screen, taking that profile into consideration, and it will continue to use that profile. If you choose Convert document's colors, the colors in the document will be converted so the document looks correct when displayed in the working space, and the document will be tagged and displayed with the working space. If you choose Discard the embedded profile, the profile will be tossed but the document will be displayed using the working space. To no longer get this dialog, turn off the Ask When Opening checkbox for Profile Mismatches; you will then automatically get the behavior chosen in the Color Management Policy pop-up for that RGB, CMYK, or Gray file type.

When you open a document that doesn't have a profile, you will get the Missing Profile dialog. I believe that the standard default here is to Assign the working space, but this dialog is sticky. That means that if you make a particular choice, Photoshop will remember that choice and offer it next time. When working with my book, I usually assign the Adobe RGB profile to my screen grabs, so Photoshop has remembered that and now offers it to me as the default. Notice that you can also assign a profile and then convert the file to your working RGB space. This option is useful, for example, when opening files from a scanner that doesn't save a profile with its files but that you have made a profile for and want to always convert from the scanner profile to your working space. To no longer get this dialog, turn off Ask When Opening for Missing Profiles.

When you paste from a document having profile A onto a document having profile B, you get this dialog, and usually you will want to choose Convert to have the colors of the pasted image look correct within the document you pasted it into. If you don't convert the colors, the pasted image may look wrong!

157

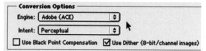

This Conversion Options section controls some of what happens when an image is converted from one color space to another using Image/Mode/RGB, Lab, or Grayscale or Image/Mode/Convert to Profile. The Use Dither option should usually be on because it will make it less likely that you will get banding when converting from one color space to another. Banding appears as a choppy gradation of subtle color changes and is not usually desirable. I usually leave the Use Black Point Compensation option off when converting from one RGB space to another, like from Adobe RGB, or even from Lab, to an ICC profile for my Epson 2200 printer or the LightJet 5000. If you have this off and then you don't like the way your blacks and dark shadows look, try the conversion again with Use Black Point Compensation on. With my files, turning it on seems to make the blacks more muddy and gives me less snap in the shadows. What you get will depend on your image as well as how the source and destination profiles were actually created.

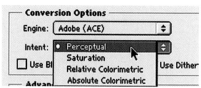

The Engine pop-up controls which software actually does the conversion. Adobe (ACE) is the built-in Photoshop software that you should normally use. An example where you might want to use Apple ColorSync, Apple CMM, or Heidelberg CMM would be if there were a new version of one of those packages that contained a feature that ACE didn't support or where that feature was more accurate using ColorSync or some other engine.

The Perceptual Intent is usually what photographers want for photographs because it preserves the overall look and feel of the image. For my RGB and Lab conversions for Epson 1280, 2200, and 7600 output, I use Perceptual with Black Point Compensation off. Relative Colorimetric, with Black Point Compensation on, is the Photoshop CS default. This may work well for you also. I actually like the onscreen proofs better on Relative Colorimetric with Black Point Compensation off. You may want to try that combination if the Perceptual choice is desaturating your images too much. The Saturation option is useful when you want really intense colors, like for business graphics. Absolute Colorimetric is not the choice most photographers will want because the white points of the source and destination are not compensated for. You may find it useful if trying to match the look of one media, like a Match Print for example, on another media, like an Epson printer proof.

converted to the RGB working space but you would receive no notice of this conversion. If you had chosen off for your RGB Color Management Policy, then that file would be opened without a profile attached at all. If you look at the Document Profile name in the lower-left corner of the window, it will be named Untagged RGB. The pixels in the file will still be viewed on the screen using the RGB working space.

Here we summarize the three Color Management Policies, which include: Off, Preserve Embedded Profile, and Convert to Working RGB, CMYK, or Gray. New documents are tagged with the current working space profile unless Color Management is set to Off, in which case they are left untagged. When opening an existing untagged document, all three options will use the existing working space for viewing and editing the document but they will leave it untagged. When you open an existing tagged document, that document will be tagged with the current working space. All three options view and edit this in the current working space and also leave it tagged with that space. When opening an existing tagged document tagged with a profile other than the current working space, the Off option untags the document and views it in the current working space. The Preserve Embedded option preserves the embedded profile and views it correctly in that profile's space. The Convert to Working option converts the document from the other profile space into the current working space and then retags the document with the current working space. When pasting or importing data onto an existing document, the Off option just pastes the color numbers without doing any conversions. The Preserve Embedded option converts if the data has a source profile, but if not, or in the case of CMYK data, the numbers are pasted without any conversions. The Convert to Working option converts the data to RGB or CMYK unless it comes from a source without a profile.

CONVERSION OPTIONS

At the top left we see the Conversion Options section of the Photoshop CS Color Settings. These influence what happens when an image is converted from one color space to another using Image/Mode/RGB, Lab, Grayscale or Image/Mode/ Convert to Profile. The Use Dither option should usually be on. This option makes it less likely that you will get undesirable banding when converting from one color space to another. I usually leave the Use Black Point Compensation option off when converting from one RGB space to another. If you have this option off and don't like the way the blacks and dark shadows look in your prints, redo the conversion with Use Black Point Compensation on. Having it on has not helped my images when working with color prints and profiles generated by Monaco or other more current sources. For me, turning this on seems to make my blacks more muddy and gives me less snappy shadows. What you get will depend on the images you are working with as well as what software and settings were used to generate their source and destination profiles. If your printed blacks are coming out too dark, plugged up, or muddy, try reprinting with Use Black Point Compensation on.

See the screen grabs and captions to the left for information about the Engine and Intent pop-up choices. It is important to set these correctly and, in general, you will want to set the Engine to Adobe (ACE), the built-in Photoshop conversion software, and the Intent to Perceptual. Perceptual, with Black Point Compensation off and Use Dither on, is a common setting for photographers when converting an RGB or Lab master image, with a large gamut, to a CMYK or RGB print image within a smaller gamut printer space. If you find that the Perceptual setting is desaturating your colors too much, you might want to try the Relative Colorimetric setting with Black Point Compensation on or off. A good way to compare these settings is to use the wonderful Photoshop CS onscreen proofing while comparing several versions of the same image on the screen. See the illustration to the right for an explanation of one way to do this. For the ultimate test, you can also print several versions of the same image, converted with different Conversion Options, and compare the printed results.

ADVANCED CONTROLS

Most people will want to leave the Advanced Controls off unless they are using a very wide gamut RGB space, one that is much wider than Adobe RGB. If you are using such a space, see the screen grab and caption about Advanced Controls at the bottom of this page.

OTHER PREFERENCES RELATING TO COLOR

EYEDROPPER TOOL SETUP

Usually when you measure digital image values in Photoshop, you want the Eyedropper set to measure a 3 x 3 square of pixels. That gives you a more accurate measurement in a continuous tone image because most colors are made up of groups of different pixels. If

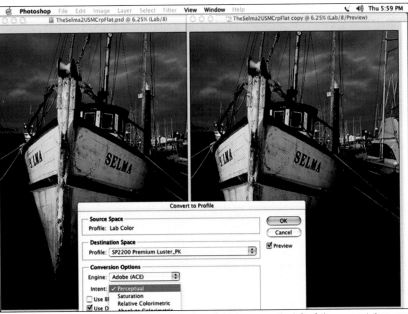

To set this up, I started with my Lab master version of this image on the left of the screen. I then used Image/Duplicate to create the copy to the right and arranged the two windows so I could see both at once. While working on the version to the right, I chose Image/Mode/Convert to Profile and picked the profile for Epson Premium Luster paper with my Epson 2200 printer. With the Preview button on, I can then choose either the Perceptual or Relative Colorimetric Intent options, and turn Use Black Point Compensation on and off while looking at a preview of the printed results in the image to the right. For this particular image, the Perceptual choice with Black Point Compensation off seemed to match my original Lab version the best. Another thing you could do is use Image/Duplicate to make several copies of the image and convert each one in a different way with different settings. You could also compare these on the screen. The final step in the test would be to make and compare test prints after converting the image with one setting versus the other. The onscreen preview should simulate the results you get in your test prints if your monitor is correctly calibrated and you are viewing your test prints with the correct viewing light color temperature. Remember that there are many variables in the process to get this right: the printer settings, the scanner or spectrophotometer used, the ink cartridges and paper, where you bought them, the temperature and humidity, etc. I sometimes have to edit a profile or add a curve to get the printed images to more closely match my monitor. We show you how to do that later in this chapter on page 153. Another sometimes more efficient way to use screen previews to compare printer profiles is to use Window/Arrange/New Window then View/Proof Setup/Custom. This is described on page 156, you should check it out!

The Advanced Controls should be left off unless you are using a very wide gamut color space. Photoshop 5 had a built-in RGB space called Wide Gamut RGB. This was a very wide gamut space and was probably removed from the Photoshop 6 default list because it was really too wide to be useful in 24-bit color. If one were using such a wide gamut space, it would only be really useful in 48-bit color mode, but it is unlikely the colors in that space could be accurately represented on a normal computer monitor. If you were using a large gamut space, you could turn on Desaturate Monitor Colors By to try to somehow estimate your colors on the screen. If you did this, the screen display would probably not be able to match your printed output.

Blend RGB Colors Using Gamma controls the blending of RGB colors, probably from one layer into the next. When it is turned on, RGB colors are blended using the chosen gamma. A gamma of 1 is considered colorimetricly correct and is supposed to create the fewest edge artifacts. When this option is disabled, RGB colors are blended within the document's RGB color space, which matches what most other applications do.

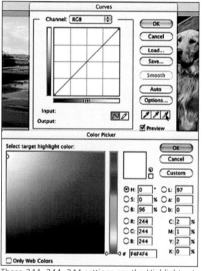

Usually you want the Eyedropper set to measure a 3 by 3 average when measuring continuous tone color. Setting either the Eyedropper Options or the Color Sampler Options to 3 by 3 Average will set both of them to 3 by 3 Average.

you were to measure a Point Sample, the default, you might accidentally measure the single pixel that was much different in color from those around it. Click on the Eyedropper tool and set its Sample Size in the Options palette to 3 by 3 Average. You can also do this by Control-clicking (right mouse button on the PC) in an image when the Eyedropper is the active tool, which will bring up a context-sensitive menu allowing you to change the dropper options. Setting the Eyedropper to 3 by 3 Average also sets up the Photoshop CS Color Samplers to read a 3 by 3 average, which is what you want.

HIGHLIGHT AND SHADOW PREFERENCES

The last preferences items that you need to set up for color separations are the Highlight and Shadow settings, which you can reach by choosing either Image/Adjust/Levels or Image/Adjust/Curves. While in Levels or Curves, double-click the Highlight Eyedropper (the rightmost one). The Color Picker opens. Set the R, G, and B values to 244, 244, and 244. Depending on your preference settings for your CMYK workspace, you may get different CMYK alternatives for these RGB values, but that is OK as long as your RGB values are neutral. Even if you are using different settings than ours, if your final output space will be RGB, you should make sure your RGB values are equal so you get a neutral highlight color when setting the highlight with the Eyedropper in RGB. Click OK in the Color Picker to return to Levels, then double-click the Shadow Eyedropper (the left-most one). Set the RGB values in the Color Picker to 8, 8, 8 and you'll notice that the CMYK values that correspond to these RGB values will be different depending on what you set your CMYK working space to in the Color Settings preferences we talked about at the beginning of the chapter. I have actually used Shadow settings between 2, 2, 2 and 8, 8, 8 depending on how dark I want my blacks to be and where I am setting my black. A value of 8, 8, 8 may need to be set in an area of the image that represents the darkest place where you want any detail; a value of 2, 2, 2 or even 0, 0, 0 should be set where you want absolute black. You can certainly adjust the black setting depending on the type of output you are doing and how dark you like your

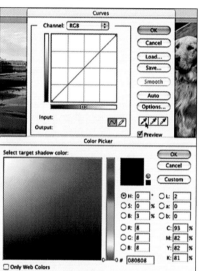

These 244, 244, 244 settings are the Highlight settings we recommend for RGB. The corresponding values you get in CMYK will depend on your chosen RGB and CMYK workspace settings. For RGB output to the Web, film recorders, and digital printers, and general RGB overall color correction of a file, you should make sure the RGB values shown here are neutral and around 244, 244, 244. Double-click the Highlight Eyedropper in Levels or Curves to change these settings for different output devices or situations.

These 8, 8, 8 values are the Shadow settings we recommend as starting values for RGB output to film recorders, digital printers, and general overall color correction of a file. Double-click the Shadow Eyedropper in Levels or Curves to change these settings. I actually use Shadow settings between 2, 2, 2 and 8, 8, 8 depending on how dark I want my blacks to be and where I am setting my black. A value of 8, 8, 8 may need to be set in an area of the image that represents the darkest place where you want any detail, a value of 2, 2, 2 or even 0, 0, 0 should be set where you want absolute black.

shadows. Click OK in the Color Picker and then click OK in Levels. In Photoshop CS, when you click on OK in Levels, you may get an additional dialog asking you if you want to "Save the New Target Colors as Defaults." If you get this dialog, click on the Yes button, which is not the default button, otherwise the defaults will go back to what they were before. To learn more about these Highlight and Shadow settings and how you use them, turn to Chapter 19: "Overall Color Correction," which takes you through all the basics of color correction and shows you when and how to use the Eyedroppers.

Chapter 15: Photoshop Color Preferences, Monitor, Scanner, and Printer Calibration

SETTINGS FOR OS X COLORSYNC ON THE MAC

If you are working on a Macintosh computer, you want to have ColorSync installed. ColorSync comes with the Mac OS and you can also get free updates for ColorSync from the Apple Web site. ColorSync allows various color applications on the Mac to all get their color information from the same place, but the ColorSync Workflow setting in the Photoshop Color Settings dialog doesn't do everything that you might want.

To set up ColorSync with Mac OS X, choose System Preferences from the Apple menu, then click on ColorSync in the Hardware area. You can then use the Default Profiles section to enter the standard profiles you want all your color applications to use. See the diagrams to the right for the details on how to do this.

To import those profiles from ColorSync into Photoshop, you could then use the ColorSync Workflow setting from the Settings menu in Photoshop's Color Settings dialog. This ColorSync Workflow setting gets Photoshop's RGB, CMYK, and Grayscale Working Space settings from ColorSync, but there are potential pitfalls in doing it this way as we will explain. It is safer to explicitly set these things in the Color Settings dialog as I mentioned at the beginning of this chapter. If you do use the ColorSync Workflow setting, then you need to make sure you undo the changes this does to the Conversion Options within the Color Settings dialog. **The problem with the ColorSync Workflow setting is that it also automatically sets the Engine to Apple ColorSync, the Intent to Relative Colorimetric, and it turns on Use Black Point Compensation. You then need to remember to go down to the Conversion Options section of the Color Settings dialog and set these back to the settings you prefer.** See the screen captures and captions here for my recommendations about resetting these Conversion Options.

SAVING AND STANDARDIZING YOUR PREFERENCES

After you make major changes to your standard Photoshop CS preferences, you should quit from Photoshop immediately. When you leave Photoshop in OS X, it saves its current state (preferences, tool option choices, palette locations, and so on) to several files within the Users/[Your User Name]/Library/Preferences/Adobe Photoshop CS Settings folder. In Windows XP, these files are at: C:/Documents and Settings/[Your User Name]/Application Data/Adobe/Photoshop/CS/Adobe Photoshop CS Settings. Quitting after changing preferences ensures that Photoshop saves your preferences changes to these files. If you were to crash before quitting Photoshop, you would lose these latest preferences changes, and Photoshop would revert to the preferences it had when you last quit from Photoshop.

It may be a good idea for everyone in your company to standardize on a set of separation and workspace preferences, especially for the same publication, and vitally important to standardize separation and workspace preferences if you are doing color corrections and separations. You can copy a standard version of these files to the Photoshop Settings folders on everyone else's machines, or print up a standards document and have your systems administrator make sure that everyone is using those settings.

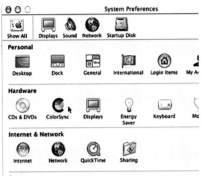

To find ColorSync in OS X, you double-click on the ColorSync icon shown above by the cursor in the Hardware section of System Preferences.

You can use the Default Profiles section of Colorsync to enter the standard profiles you want all color applications to use. To get Gray Gamma 1.8 here, I had to use Save Gray to save the Gray Gamma 1.8 setting from Photoshop's Color Settings. Then I used the yellow helper, shown above, to learn what folder this ICC profile needed to be in to show up in ColorSync.

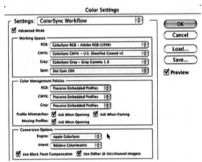

Once you have the ColorSync Default Profiles set, as explained in the caption above, you can then choose ColorSync Workflow from the Settings menu in Photoshop's Color Settings dialog to import those profiles into Photoshop. The problem with doing this, as pointed out in the area shown by the black cursor above, is that this changes the Conversion Options to settings you don't really want. You should change the Engine back to Adobe Ace, the Intent back to Perceptual, and uncheck Use Black Point Compensation.

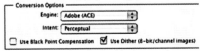

As we mentioned earlier in this chapter, these are the conversion options you will probably want most of the time. Make sure you put Conversion Options back to these from the different ones that ColorSync Workflow chooses.

161

HARDWARE MONITOR GAMMA VERSUS WORKING SPACE GAMMA

Another thing you need to consider when working in Photoshop is the hardware gamma your monitor is calibrated to and whether you work in an RGB workspace that is 1.8 or 2.2 gamma. If you are using your monitor to work with images that are for CMYK print output, you may be better off if your monitor hardware gamma is set to 1.8, which is the standard gamma of Mac systems. If you are doing primarily output to the Web, you may want to set your monitor hardware gamma to 2.2, which is the typical gamma of PC systems. Now the gamma of your RGB workspace is a different story. Regardless of what you have your monitor gamma calibrated to, provided your monitor is calibrated accurately, Photoshop should compensate for a different gamma in your RGB Working Space if necessary to give you a correct display of your images on the monitor.

An RGB Working Space that has a gamma of 2.2 does a more even job of displaying the values in a histogram and allows you to see more separation in the shadows. Your shadow detail will less likely be posterized. Many people in the print world are used to working with the ColorMatch RGB workspace with their gamma set at 1.8. In general, people who work in print have been working with a workspace that has a gamma of 1.8, and people who use the Web or work on the Web are more likely to use a workspace with a gamma of 2.2. If you open a file that has been color adjusted in a gamma 1.8 space into a gamma 2.2 space without converting, the file will seem darker and more contrasty. Similarly, if you initially corrected the file in a gamma 2.2 space and then opened it into a 1.8 space without converting, the file will seem too flat and light. Whatever space you adjust your files in, you will get used to it and make the appropriate color adjustment choices. When you open or print that file into a different gamma environment without compensation, you will notice a problem.

Open an image that was corrected and tagged with a gamma 1.8 workspace, like ColorMatch RGB, and then choose Image/Mode/Assign Profile and assign a gamma 2.2 profile, like Adobe RGB, to this file without conversion. See how this changes the appearance of the file? Although I'm a Mac user, these days I calibrate my monitors to 6500 and 2.2 and I usually color correct in Adobe RGB, which is a gamma 2.2 color space. These settings seem to do the best overall job in Photoshop of matching my various monitors to the canned Epson paper profiles and Bill Atkinson profiles that I use on my Epson 2200 and 7600 printers.

Lately I've been calibrating my monitors to 6500 and 2.2. OptiCAL provides many choices for what gamma and color temperature you use. The custom choice allows you to type in any white point or gamma. This can be a useful option if one of the standard choices (6500 and 2.2, 5000 and 1.8, etc.) don't exactly match your monitor to your prints.

Current monitor calibration solutions, including Monaco Optix, Color Vision Optical 3.7.5, and GretagMacbeth EyeOne Display and EyeOne Photo now all support calibration of either CRT or LCD monitors.

CALIBRATION OF MONITORS, DIGITAL PRINTERS, AND SCANNERS

One of the most common questions I get from the readers of my *Photoshop Artistry* books and students in my digital printmaking workshops has to do with how they can better calibrate their monitors, printers, and scanners. Calibration can allow you to get from your printer the same color and contrast that you see on your monitor, to get very similar color and contrast when printing the same image on a number of different papers and/or printers, and also to improve the results you get from your scanner. Apple ColorSync and Photoshop CS provide an effective framework for people to accurately calibrate the production of digital images using Photoshop on the Macintosh and to also get very accurate soft proofs of printed images on the screen. This can also work well in a Windows XP environment. Doing this calibration accurately, however, requires color measurement instruments and calibration software. When ColorSync and Photoshop 5 first came out, the only calibration and measurement products available were both expensive and difficult to use. Recently

Chapter 15: Photoshop Color Preferences, Monitor, Scanner, and Printer Calibration

this has changed, and there is now a variety of software and hardware products that help you to calibrate. Here, I'll categorize and discuss some of those products and their effectiveness for different types of users. I'll help you understand the type of user you may be and try to match you to the calibration solution that will work best for you. These solutions include: 1. doing and buying nothing, 2. buying several of these calibration products, depending on your needs, and using them to calibrate yourself and, 3. hiring a calibration expert to do the work for you using the most expensive and accurate calibration products and also the expert's knowledge.

WHAT ARE CALIBRATION, COLORSYNC, AND ICC PROFILES?

Calibration is the process where you measure the color gamut of a particular monitor, printer, or scanner and produce a detailed description of this color gamut in the format of an ICC profile. The color gamut of a device is the range of colors that a device can reproduce. The ICC is an international standards organization that has developed the ICC Profile format, which has become an industry standard for describing and dealing with the color gamuts of different color devices. ColorSync is a system software component that is built into the Macintosh that provides a framework for other applications, like Photoshop, Illustrator, Quark, etc., to make use of ICC profiles to accurately deal with the differences in color input and output on different devices. ColorSync and its use by other applications allows the user to get matching, or close to matching, color on each device. For calibration to work correctly, one needs to accurately make an ICC profile of each device and then correctly use these ICC profiles within a world of ColorSync-savvy applications.

DO YOU NEED TO CALIBRATE?

If the color on your monitor matches the color on your digital prints and if you and your clients are happy with the results of your digital image creations, you may not need to calibrate any further. Seriously! A few years ago I had been using my Epson Stylus Photo 1200 to create low-cost proofs for later final output to the Light-Jet 5000. The LightJet 5000 is a $200,000 digital printer that prints onto 60–year, color-permanent Fuji Crystal Archive photographic paper up to 50" wide. Until the Epson 7600 and 9600 came along, the LightJet was the standard for archival digital photographic output. With the Epson 1200 using the methods and settings described in the Latest Tips area of www.barryhaynes.com, I had been able to get images on my monitor and from this printer that were often quite close to having the same image printed on the LightJet. This is more likely to be the case if your Epson, HP or other printer is the only output you are interested in and if you are lucky enough to have a monitor that matches the printer's output.

If images on your monitor don't match your printer, then you should certainly pay close attention to the rest of this chapter. I'm interested in, as exactly as possible, matching my Epson 1280, 2200, 4000, and 7600 prints to my LightJet 5000 prints and also in matching Epson 1280, 2200, 4000, and 7600 prints on several different papers. To do this I used to create my own ICC profiles for each printer and ink combination. The canned profiles that come with the Epson 2200 and 7600 for Epson papers, as well as Bill Atkinson's profiles for the 7600 and 9600, are very good and much better than the canned profiles that came with older Epson printer models, like the 1270 and 2000P. Since getting the 2200 and 7600, I use those canned or Bill Atkinson profiles with the Epson papers. If I were using a 3rd-party paper or ink, then I'd be more likely to need to make my own printer profiles. These days, many 3rd-party paper companies, like Red River Paper, also provide good canned profiles on their Web sites. I'm very picky about color so I may require more accuracy than you need. The amount of color accuracy you require will depend on the type of color user you are and also on the amount of time and money you can spend.

WHAT CATEGORY OF COLOR USER ARE YOU AND HOW MUCH TIME AND MONEY DO YOU HAVE TO SPEND?

There are a lot of color calibration products now on the market, and they are obviously designed for different categories of color users. I'll try to come up with some user categories to help describe who might want to go with each type of calibration solution. The four categories I'll describe here are hobbyist, serious hobbyist, professional color user, and finally color management expert.

A "hobbyist" user is someone who uses Photoshop and other desktop applications to make prints to send to friends and relatives, to make their own Xmas cards, and just for fun. If you are this type of user on a Mac, you may be happy using System Preferences/Displays/Color/Calibrate to calibrate your monitor. The hobbyist user doesn't have a lot of time and money to spend on calibration products and probably won't spend more than $250 on calibration. Even if you are a hobbyist, I'd recommend using Monaco Optics, the Color Vision Spyder, or the GretagMacbeth EyeOne Display to calibrate your monitor. Any of these can usually be purchased for under $200 and they will do a more accurate and consistent job than calibrating by eye.

A "serious hobbyist" user is someone who creates digital images and really cares about more exact color control of those images. This type of user will be willing to spend some time and money on calibration products but probably won't want to spend much more than $500 to $1,500. If you want to calibrate your monitor as well as making printer and scanner profiles, you could get Monaco EZ Color for about $500, or for more accurate measurement spend about $1,500 on the GretagMacbeth EyeOne Photo system. Another product to check out is the new Color Vision Print Fix system for making printer profiles.

I'll call the next category the "professional color user." This type of user needs to have exact repeatable color on more than one output device for commercial and/or art sales of their images. The professional color user will pay considerably more than $1,500 to get control over their color and will also invest the time required to get repeatable consistent results. For making printer and/or scanner profiles, this type of user may want to purchase Monaco Proof with the X-Rite DTP-41 spectrophotometer or the GretagMacbeth EyeOne Photo or EyeOne Match system.

The highest category of color user is the "color management expert." This is a person who is in business to make color profiles and calibrate other customers' color environments. The color management expert will spend up to $10,000 and maybe more for the software and hardware needed to do the job. He or she will also spend weeks and months learning how to use these calibration products in a variety of situations.

SHOULD YOU CALIBRATE YOURSELF OR GET A PROFESSIONAL TO HELP YOU?

Most people should buy their own monitor calibrator and calibrate their own monitors. These systems work quite well if you have a decent monitor. If you are using an Epson 2200, 4000, 7600, or 9600 and Epson papers, you probably won't need to make printer profiles because the profiles that come with these printers are quite good. If the canned profiles are not working for you, I'd make sure your print dialogs are set up correctly (see page 170) before you decide to make your own profiles. Using the wrong print dialog settings is the most common cause of poor print color with the people who take my workshops.

If you are using 3rd-party papers or don't like the canned profiles, then you may want to make your own printer profiles. If you are a hobbyist and need to make a lot of profiles, then I'd say you should calibrate yourself using some of the less expensive solutions I'll describe below. Most color management experts who actually know what they are doing will charge you more than what you will be willing to pay for their services.

The exception to this statement is that you might want to hire a color management expert to make a custom profile for you or try a profile from a place like ProfileCity.com or Chromix.com, which will make a profile for you remotely for about $100. As with ProfileCity.com, some color management experts will send you a calibration file, which you print out on your printer via their instructions; then you mail it back to them and they measure it and mail you a profile. This can work if done correctly and can be as cheap as $100. I've talked and emailed with quite a few serious color users who are happy with the profiles ProfileCity has made for them. Because ProfileCity is in the business of making profiles, they get a lot of experience with particular printers, inks, and papers, which will help them make the correct choices for the profiles they make. They also use higher quality hardware and software than you may be willing to purchase. Because the test targets are printed on your printer by you and then sent through the mail, ProfileCity, or a similar organization, is not in complete control of the process. This is a process that can easily be thrown off by using the wrong print dialog setting, having a test swatch file accidentally converted to a different space by Photoshop, or some other mistake the inexperienced user could easily make when printing their swatches. Several people have mentioned to me that their ProfileCity or other profiles didn't help them much; this may have been due to those people's setup problems.

If you are a serious hobbyist, you might want to try some of the low to moderately priced calibration solutions and calibrate your own system. The deciding issue here might be whether you will need to calibrate more things in the future. If the canned profiles don't work, you'll want to make an ICC profile for each printer and paper combination that you use regularly. If you are using the Epson 1280, for example, and only the Epson Semigloss ColorLife Photo Paper and maybe the Epson Matte Paper Heavyweight, that will require a profile for each of these papers and calibration of your monitor and maybe a scanner. If you will be happy with those profiles for some time to come, then getting a color management expert, or a place like ProfileCity.com, to do it for you may save you time and money and get you more accurate profiles. See the small list or profile making services later in this chapter. If, on the other hand, you want to try Lysonic and MIS third-party inks with your Epson 1280 or 3000, and you are using a variety of papers and are using several scanners or printers, then you will probably save money by purchasing your own calibration products. For my Epson 7600, I've not had to make any profiles when using the Epson papers.

If you are a professional color user, the same issues come up for you, too. I'm assuming you will have more money to spend on a solution than the serious hobbyist and that time may also be a factor for you. If you are, for example, a busy commercial photographer or design agency, you may not have the time to learn how to correctly use the calibration hardware and software products you will need to do a good job. It took me several weeks to decide which products to evaluate for my earlier *Communication Arts* calibration article and then several more weeks to learn how to use the products well. To use them really efficiently in a variety of circumstances takes longer, and it is a constantly changing process because the products are changing and improving all the time. Your time might be better spent hiring a color management expert, who will also bring the best software and hardware to the task. On the other hand, if your organization is large and you have a lot of different color scanners, monitors, printers, inks, and papers to calibrate, you might save money, make it more convenient for yourself, and have more control if you purchase your own calibration products and learn how to use them.

The color management expert is going to want to have the highest quality calibration software and hardware available and will likely have to spend at least $10,000 to get what they need. A calibration expert may also want to have several solutions available, so they can charge different amounts depending on the accuracy required by the customer and also the amount of money a customer can spend.

Whether you decide to use canned profiles, make your own profiles, or get someone else to make your profiles, you may find that it will take some effort to get exactly what you want. Some of the profiles I make look right and match my monitor right away. Quite often though I have to edit a profile or create a Photoshop compensation curve to adjust the profile to produce what I want. Sometimes one will have a profile that looks good everywhere but in the shadows or in the highlights or in an image with a subtle sky color change. In many cases, this is not yet an exact science because the general public has not been making custom profiles for that long. The scanners, monitors, and printers are changing all the time and so is the profile-making software.

Here is a quote via an email I received from Howard Cubell, an *Artistry* reader with an Epson 10,000 who obviously has a lot of color expertise. It describes the type of experience you may have as you go through this calibration process: "So, what I decided to do was buy a custom profile, to have a custom profile shootout by hiring three well-regarded companies to make a custom profile for me for the same ink/paper combination. First, I hired ProfileCity and their profile was a major improvement over the standard Epson profile for the Premium Luster paper in terms of color gamut and depth of the blacks. However, the shadows in my test prints were somewhat blocked up with this profile. I believe that ProfileCity used a Spectrolino and its own profiling software to make the profile. I then tried a guy who is a prolific contributor to the Colorsync List and the Epson/Leben List. His profile was not quite as good as ProfileCity's, and it had a serious problem with deep blues, turning such hues toward magenta. It turns out that this person uses ColorVision's Profiler Pro to make his profiles, and that software has a known defect in dealing with blues. Finally, I hired Steve Upton at www.chromix.com to make a profile. His was the best. All of the advantages of the ProfileCity profile—great color gamut and blacks—but no problem with the shadows blocking up. I think he uses a Spectrolino with Gretag's ProfileMaker software. Chromix has been great to work with. They charge $99 for a profile, and they give you a money back guarantee."

I heard similar stories from other readers who are very happy with their ProfileCity profiles. For about $100 each, you could also try the ProfileCity (www.profilecity.com) and Chromix (www.chromix.com) shootout. If you try it, let me know what printer and paper you were working with and how your profiles worked out.

Monitor Calibration for Free?

Photoshop 6 came with a tool called Adobe Gamma, which allowed you to visually calibrate your monitor. On the Mac in System Preferences/Displays/Color/Calibrate there is a built-in visual calibrator. This system works similarly to the old Adobe Gamma. I calibrate my monitor to a color temperature of 6500 kelvin and a gamma of 2.2, which works well for printed photographs. I've found it hard to correctly and consistently calibrate many monitors to these settings using visual calibration techniques like this. Even if you calibrate one monitor correctly, it is harder to match the results on other monitors and get the same results each time. Most modern monitors also have buttons on the front of the monitor that allow you to set the color temperature and gamma; these are sometimes quite accurate, but often not that accurate. If you have a good eye for monitor color and some patience, it may be possible to get reasonable calibration on some monitors using one of these techniques. If this doesn't work or your prints are not matching your monitor, then you should try one of the third-party hardware monitor calibration techniques discussed later in this chapter. In general the hardware calibrators from ColorVision, Monaco, and GretabMacbeth work very well these days and will usually calibrate your monitor more accurately and consistently than you can do visually.

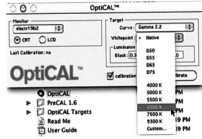

Lately I've been calibrating my monitors to 6500 and 2.2. OptiCAL provides many choices for what gamma and color temperature you use. The custom choice allows you to type in any white point or gamma. This can be a useful option if one of standard choices (6500 and 2.2, 5000 and 1.8, etc.) don't exactly match your monitor to your prints.

INEXPENSIVE CALIBRATION SYSTEMS

GOOD SOLUTIONS FOR MONITOR CALIBRATION ONLY

The products described here all include software and a USB hardware device to measure and calibrate your monitor's contrast, white point, and color. All these products also now work with both CRT and LCD monitors. I believe all three of these products are priced at under $200 for the software and hardware. Prices change from month to month so I'm not going to quote the exact price on each system.

The ColorVision Spyder with OptiCAL is a good product that I have been using for several years. The nice thing about OptiCAL is that it allows you to choose any color temperature or gamma instead of just the standard 5000, 6500, 1.8, and 2.2. That gives you more monitor tweaking options when your monitor image doesn't exactly match your prints.

The new Monaco Optix product is also great for just calibrating your monitor. I like the way the new Optix device easily attaches and detaches from a monitor without accidentally falling off and yet not sticking at the end when you are trying to remove it. Optix also allowed me to correctly calibrate external monitors attached to several iMacs with built-in monitors that were no longer calibratible. In that situation OptiCAL recognized that OptiCAL was attached to an IMac so OptiCAL didn't allow me to use the more advanced features I wanted for the external monitor. In all other cases, both OptiCAL and Optix worked fine and similarly.

The GretagMacbeth EyeOne Display product, just for calibrating monitors, is also a great entry level system that does a good job on monitors. This new Gretag product uses a similar sensor to the Monaco Optix device. Both have many small suction cups that are easy to attach and remove from the monitor. The EyeOne Display uses a measuring device that only calibrates monitors. The more expensive EyeOne Photo or Match products have the EyeOne Pro measuring device, which can calibrate monitors, printers, scanners, etc.

Current monitor calibration solutions, including Monaco Optix, Color Vision OptiCAL 3.7.5, and GretagMacbeth EyeOne Display and EyeOne Photo now all support calibration of either CRT or LCD monitors.

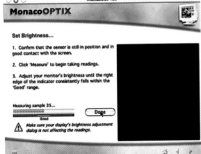

All three of the monitor calibration products can measure the brightness and color temperature of your monitor, then allow you to adjust it before measuring color patches and creating the final profile. The amount of adjustment possible depends on the type of monitor you have and its possible internal adjustments.

TO CALIBRATE SCANNERS, MONITORS, AND PRINTERS

You only need to calibrate your printer if the canned profiles are not working for you and/or you need to make profiles for 3rd-party papers. If the canned profiles make good prints, then all you may need is one of the monitor calibrators described above. You only need to make a scanner profile if it is important to you to have your original scan match the original as closely as possible. Because my prints always are corrected to look better than the original and I also like to work with raw scans, I don't worry too much about having a scanner profile. If you do need to make scanner and/or printer profiles, here are some solutions that may help you.

Monaco EZ Color 2.5 can make monitor profiles (if you get the Optix sensor), printer profiles, scanner profiles, and it also has a profile editor.

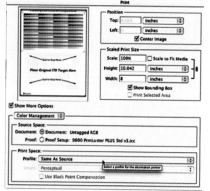

When printing swatches to make a printer profile, make sure Source Space is set to Untagged RGB and Print Space is set to Same as Source. Also make sure that the Color Management dialog is set to No Color Adjustment.

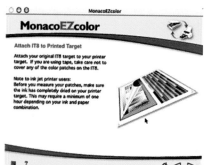

The IT8 target gets attached to your printer swatches. Monaco uses the target to make a profile for your flatbed scanner, then with that scanner profile in hand, it can make a profile for your printer by reading the swatches.

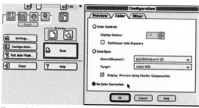

Turn this No Color Correction feature on in the Epson Twain software to make sure the scanner does no color management when scanning swatches to make a profile.

For the lowest price and easiest-to-use solution for calibrating your flatbed or film scanner, monitor and inkjet printer, I recommend Monaco EZ Color 2.5, for $299 without their monitor Optix sensor and $548 with the sensor. Monaco EZ Color developed a very smart system that uses your flatbed scanner to create a profile for both your scanner and printer. Monaco EZ Color steps you through the simple process and explains it very well. It first prompts you to print a profile from your printer. Instead of printing directly from Monaco, I recommend that you have Monaco write the profile to a file and then open that file and print that profile directly from Photoshop. This way you will be sure to use the same print options that you use when printing your profiled images. Use the print options I show here for printing the profile from Photoshop with the Epson 2200 printer; use similar options for other Epson printers. With any printer, you will want to print in a way that turns off all the color management done by the printer software.

An important thing I discovered is that the Epson dye-based inks, and some other inkjet inks, change in color as the ink dries for several days. I found that my profiles were more accurate if I let the test swatches dry for 48 hours or longer before reading them with the scanner or spectrophotometer and making the profile. The dye-based inks can actually take up to five days before all initial color changes stop, so you might want to wait that long before reading your swatches when using Epson dye-based inks. I'd wait just 24 hours with the pigment-based inks like the Ultrachrome inks on the 2200, 7600, 4000, or 9600. After printing the swatches with Monaco EZ Color and letting them sit in a place where they won't get dusty for the colors to stabilize, you then tape an IT8 target to the indicated place on the printed swatch page. The IT8 target comes with EZ Color and is a standard set of color swatches that are produced using exact specifications. See the third page of Chapter 14: "Color Spaces, Device Characterization, and Color Management," for a picture of an IT8 target. You then place this letter-sized swatch printout, with the IT8 target attached, on your flatbed scanner and scan the entire thing, making sure that all color management on your scanner is turned off.

Due to poor software or documentation, making sure all the color management on your scanner is turned off is often hard to do but is very important, because leaving the scanner's color management on can undermine the results of making a profile this way. I've found that Epson 1600, 1680, 2450, and 3200 scanners work well for making these profiles, and the Epson Twain software that comes with them has a setting in the Configuration section for No Color Correction. You want to turn this on to make sure the scanner does no color correction. If you are not sure how your scanner will work, or how to turn off all the scanner's color management, check with Monaco tech support or the scanner manufacturer. You then save the scanned RGB file in tiff format. Monaco EZ Color then reads in the information from this scan and compares the results from the scan to the empirical results of the original swatch colors. It then uses the results of scanning the IT8 target to create a profile for your scanner. You can save this scanner profile and use it when you are scanning prints with this scanner. With the scanner profile in hand, Monaco can then analyze the scan of your printer's swatches to create the profile for your printer. I've made a number of profiles using Monaco EZ Color with different papers and Epson printers. I've found that the same image printed with the

168

correct Monaco EZ Color profile on these different printers and papers looks very similar. This is a good solution for the price and well worth a try for the hobbyist or the serious hobbyist.

Monaco will also sell you IT8 targets on film so you can use EZ Color to calibrate a film scanner. These cost $40 for 35mm and $100 for 4x5 film and you can also order them bundled with EZ color for a similar price increase. To make a film scanner profile, you scan the 35mm or 4x5 film IT8 target, following Monaco's directions, and then read this scanned file into Monaco where it will analyze the scanned version and create a profile for your film scanner. I have tried this with the Nikon 4000 and the Polaroid Sprintscan 120 and it works well, with the goal being to start out with a scanned image that comes closer to matching your original transparency. After you have made a profile for your scanner, you would then do your scans in the same way as you scanned the IT8 target. If your scanner software will not allow you to assign a custom profile directly, which would be the easiest thing to do, just save your scans with no profile attached. When you open a scan into Photoshop, use Image/Mode/Assign Profile to assign your scanner profile to this scan. If you then want to work in Adobe RGB, you can use Image/Mode/Convert to Profile to convert the image from the scanner profile you just assigned to the Adobe RGB working space. Whether you leave the image with the assigned scanner profile or convert it to Adobe RGB, it should now look very close on your calibrated monitor to your original transparency before you even start color correcting in Photoshop.

I was not that impressed with the Monaco EZ Color system for visually calibrating a monitor. With the hardware Optix sensor it works much better, so if you are getting Monaco EZ Color and you haven't already purchased ColorVision OptiCAL or another product to calibrate your Monitor, I'd get the $548 bundle that comes with Optix. If you already have ColorVision PhotoCal or OptiCAL, you can continue to use that to calibrate your monitor and use Monaco EZ Color to make scanner and printer profiles.

MAKING EPSON PRINTS WITH CANNED OR CUSTOM PROFILES

Remember that when you print an image using an Epson canned or custom profile, you can convert to the printer profile within the Print with Preview dialog (Command-Option-P) or you can first use Image/Mode/Convert to Profile to convert your flattened sharpened master image from your Lab or RGB Color Space into the space for your printer created by this profile. Then in your Print with Preview dialog, you want to set your print options as described on page 170. By Epson canned profile I'm just referring to the profiles that get installed on your system when you install the software that comes with your printer. The Bill Atkinson profiles for the 7600 or 9600 or a profile you made yourself are examples of a custom profile.

The three screen grabs and captions across the top of page 170 show three important variations of using the Photoshop CS Print with Preview dialog, which is now the default that you get with Command-Option-P. The Page Setup in the middle and the two screen grabs and captions down the right side of page 170 show the rest of the printer dialog settings, which should be essentially the same no matter which of the top variations you are working with. Read through each of the captions on page 170 to see how to set your prints up correctly. The variation at the top right of page 170 shows you the settings to use when you are printing the Monaco EZ Color RGB Print Patches file that you have to print to make a printer profile. In that case the Source Space should be set to Untagged RGB and the Print Space to Same as Source.

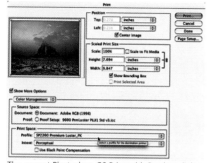

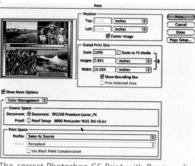

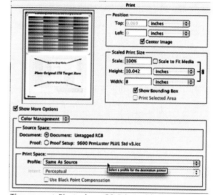

The correct Photoshop CS Print with Preview dialog when printing a file that you want Photoshop to convert on-the-fly while printing from your default color space to a canned or custom profile for your printer. In this case the Source Space will be the name of your default color space (like Adobe RGB or Lab) and the Print Space will be the name of the custom profile for your printer. Photoshop will convert the image on-the-fly, just for this print, to your custom printer profile. The other print dialogs would look the same as the Page Setup and other two lower dialogs to the right.

The correct Photoshop CS Print with Preview dialog when printing a file that you have converted using Image/Mode/Convert to Profile from your default color space (like Adobe RGB or Lab) to a canned or custom profile for your printer. In this case the Source Space will be the name of that custom profile and the Print Space will be Same as Source. The other print dialogs would look the same as the Page Setup and other two lower dialogs to the right.

The correct Photoshop CS Print with Preview dialog (Command-Option-P) when printing the Monaco EZ Color RGB Print Patches file. Source Space should be Untagged RGB and Print Space should be Same as Source.

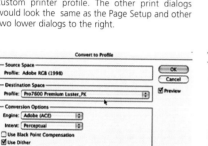

When printing an image using a canned or custom profile, I sometimes first use Image/Mode/Convert to Profile from Photoshop to convert my flattened, sharpened master image from its default color space, Adobe RGB in this case, into the space defined by the custom profile. I then print the image using the middle Print with Preview settings above. Depending on the image I'm working with, I may set the Intent to either Perceptual or Relative Colorimetric and I may occasionally turn on Black Point Compensation. With the Preview checkbox on as shown here, you should get an accurate on-screen preview to help you in making those Conversion Option decisions. My most common choice for Epson printers is Perceptual with Black Point Compensation off. I often use the PSCSArtistryCal-ibrationImage, found in the Ch15.Color Pref and Calibration folder on the *Photoshop CS Artistry* CD, as a test for the profiles I make or use. After making or getting a new profile, you can print this image and use it to compare profiles made on other papers or with other printers and inks. It is a good image to evaluate a profile because it contains neutral swatches as well as images that have various properties that can be difficult to profile. If you are doing Image/Mode/Convert to Profile with my calibration image, your Source space will be ColorMatch and your Destination space will be the profile you want to test. Don't convert the calibration image to Adobe RGB or any other space before converting it to your printer space to test the profile or this will invalidate the test.

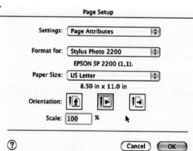

When you click on Page Setup from the Photoshop CS Print with Preview dialog seen in all three above, you get this. Choose the printer you want to use from Format For and the paper size from Paper Size. If you need to define a new paper size, choose Custom Paper Size from the Settings menu. See more info on the next page about creating custom paper sizes.

Once you have set your Print Settings and Color Management choices, as shown to the right, you can choose Save As from the Presets menu to create a new preset with these settings. The next time you make a print, all you have to do is choose this Preset instead of going into the Print Settings and Color Management area again.

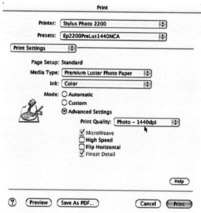

Clicking the Print button in the Print with Preview dialog brings up this dialog. First choose your printer from the Printer section, then go into Print Settings shown here. Now you want to choose your Media Type. Here is the recommended setting for Epson Premium Luster Photo Paper on the 2200. Click on Advanced Settings, then set Print Quality to 1440 and turn off High Speed if you want the best print quality. On the PC these settings will look slightly different, but they should all be there.

After choosing Print Settings, shown above, choose Color Management and set it to No Color Adjustment. The profile you chose in the Print with Preview dialog is doing your color management for you and you don't want to color manage twice!

170

Chapter 15: Photoshop Color Preferences, Monitor, Scanner, and Printer Calibration

The middle variation at the top of page 170 shows you the settings to use when you have previously used Image/Mode/Convert to Profile to convert your image to the colorspace of a custom printer profile for a specific printer, paper, and/or ink combination. In this case Source Space should be the name of your custom printer profile and Print Space should be set to Same as Source. If you use the top-middle dialog then you have already converted the image into the printer space, using Image/Mode/Convert to Profile, before entering the print dialog. If you have the same image that you print with the same printer, inks, and paper over and over again, this setting may be more efficient because you could just save this converted image.

The top-left variation on page 170 shows you the correct settings if you want Photoshop and its print dialog to convert your image on-the-fly from your working color space into the space of a custom printer profile. If you are using these top-left settings, you don't use Image/Mode/Convert to Profile first because this conversion is done while you are making the print. In this case Source Space should be set to your working RGB, Adobe RGB for example, or Lab working space. Print Space should be set to the canned or custom profile for your particular printer, ink, and paper combination. The top-left choice requires the Print dialog to do the printer mode conversion every time a print is made that may take more time.

If you use the same conversion options, the top-left and top-middle choices should give you the same results. The top-middle option, by first using Image/Mode/Convert to Profile, allows you to see a few more conversion options, like changing the Conversion Engine and turning Dither on or off, and it also allows you to see on-screen previews of these different options while in the Convert to Profile dialog. That is an advantage to the top-middle approach. You should develop a workflow and try to make your prints the same way each time. That way you are less likely to make mistakes due to inconsistencies in the way you make prints. I use the top-middle approach, which uses Image/Mode/Convert to profile first if I want to add an adjustment layer after doing the conversion but before outputing to the printer. This adjustment layer would be a tweak for this paper and printer only. This gives you a way to edit a profile without having to use expensive profile-editing software. For more info on this process see the "Editing Profiles with Profile Editors and/or Photoshop Adjustment Layers" section later in this chapter. The top-left approach is a bit faster, especially if you are only making one print of each image.

The screen grabs on this page and page 150 were made in Mac OS X using Photoshop CS and the Epson 2200 and 7600 printers. With Windows systems, the dialogs will look somewhat different, but you'll find the same functionality and you should have the same workflow options. If you are using an Epson 1280, 2200, 4000, 7600, 9600, 10,000, or some other Epson pinter, you'll be able to use a similar workflow and you'll also find similar dialogs, but you'll notice that an option here or there will be different. If there are differences you really can't figure out, after actually studying this book and the Epson manual, send me an e-mail along with an attached small compressed jpeg version of the screen grab in question. Small means 150k or less. I don't appreciate getting e-mails that have files much bigger than that attached because we don't have access to a fast internet connection where we live.

If you have an Epson 7600, 9600 or other Epson printer that uses roll paper, you will often need to define a custom paper size. In OS X you do this by choosing Custom Paper Size from the Settings menu in the Page Setup menu. This gets you into the dialog below where you need to first choose the New button then name your new paper size. After that, set the Width, Height and Margin sizes using the text boxes towards the bottom of this dialog. Finally click on the Save button to save your new paper size. When you leave this dialog, by choosing Page Attributes from the Settings menu, then you have to choose this new paper size from the Paper Size menu.

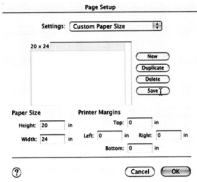

GETTING ACCURATE ONSCREEN SOFT PROOFS OF YOUR OUTPUT TO RGB PRINTERS, CMYK PRINTERS, AND PRESSES

One of the best features Photoshop CS gives you is the capability to accurately preview your printed images using the monitor. To do this for an RGB device, like a LightJet 5000 or Epson 1280, 2200, or 7600, you will need an accurate ICC profile of your RGB printer when printing using a particular ink and paper combination. This could be a canned profile that comes with the printer or the profile could be made using one of the techniques discussed in this chapter. You can compare the way the image will look when printed using this profile to the way it looks within your Lab or RGB working space. Start by choosing Window/Arrange/New Window to give you an alternate window on your image. This is not another copy of the image, like you would get with Image/Duplicate; it is just another way to look at the same file you

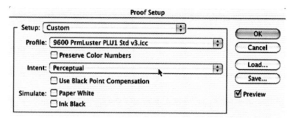

Here we see the View/Proof Setup/Custom dialog. You use the Profile pop-up menu to select the printer profile for your printer and the Intent menu to select your rendering intent, which is usually Perceptual when working with photographs.

have open. Now arrange the original window of the image and the New Window of it so their windows are next to each other and you can see them side by side. After doing that, choose View/Proof Setup/Custom, which will bring up the Proof Setup dialog, allowing you to choose the Profile you will use when printing to your printer and also the rendering intent you want for this image.

With the Preview box checked, you can actually try out several profiles and rendering intents to see which settings come closest to matching the original image, in the other Window, in your Lab or RGB working space. You can then use Window/Arrange/New Window again to create a third view and set that one up to do a soft proof to a different printer. This allows you to compare how the image will look on a LightJet 5000 versus your Epson 7600 versus the original in Adobe RGB or Lab. With a well-calibrated system, as mine is, the images on the screen are a very accurate simulation of what the print will look like. This is a great way to compare one profile to another, one rendering intent to another, or even to decide if you want Black Point Compensation on or off! To use it accurately with RGB printers, you will need an ICC profile for your printer, an accurate calibration of your monitor, and the correct viewing lights for comparing your prints to your monitor.

USING PROOF COLORS AND GAMUT WARNING

To get soft proofs for your RGB files or to see how they will look on CMYK printers or CMYK presses, you can just choose View/Proof Colors (Command-Y) and Photoshop will show you how the file will look and print on your RGB printer or in CMYK depending

Here I used Image/Duplicate to make a couple of copies of my calibration image. The one on the left is the original still in ColorMatch RGB. Notice the different Document Profile display in middle one, which I converted using Image/Mode/Convert to Profile to the canned Epson 2200 Premium Luster profile. This automatically gives you a soft proof using that profile. With the copy on the right I used View/Proof Setup/Custom to get a soft proof using Bill Atkinsons Epson 7600 Premium Luster profile. I used the Epson 2200 with the canned premium luster profile to make first proofs for images I will later print larger on my Epson 7600 with Bill Atkinson's profile. As you can see, all three images look very similar, but there are subtle differences!

on your View/Proof Setup/Custom choices. If you have already converted the file to CMYK, then you are already seeing it as it should print on your CMYK device, provided you are calibrated correctly. It is very important that your CMYK settings in the CMYK working space area of Photoshop/Color Settings are set correctly when using Command-Y to preview RGB files in the way they will look within CMYK. If you open an existing CMYK file, it should be displayed correctly on the screen provided that the file has an embedded ICC profile and your screen and output devices are correctly calibrated.

When you initially choose View/Proof Setup, it is set up so using Command-Y to see Proof Colors will show you how your RGB file looks when separated into CMYK using the current CMYK settings within the CMYK Working Space inside the Color Settings dialog. If you choose View/Proof Setup/Custom, as we mentioned, you can change that default for the current file to show the preview using an ICC profile for your printer or other output device. When you choose View/Proof Setup/Custom while working on an open file, this sets the preview on a file-by-file basis or actually on a window-by-window basis, as shown in the illustration on the previous page. If you open Photoshop and then immediately go into View/Poof Setup/Custom, while no files are open, this sets the default proofing environment for Photoshop, which is normally set to Working CMYK when you install Photoshop. You can change this setting to that of an ICC profile for your RGB printer, or some other profile, by setting it when no files are open and then quitting from Photoshop

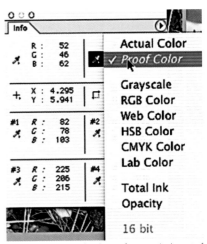

When you turn Proof Color on for a particular set of Info palette display values, you'll see the numbers that you'd get at that location if you did Image/Mode/Convert to Profile using the Profile currently set up in View/Proof Setup. You're seeing Proof Color values when the *R:*, *G:*, and *B:* letters are displayed in italics, as they are in the screen grab above except for the top left set of values which show the R:, G: and B: as they normally appear.

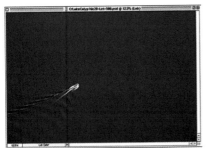

Here is my Crater Lake image as shown on my screen in Lab color. This image has very deep saturated blue colors, as does Crater Lake, one of the clearest lakes in the world.

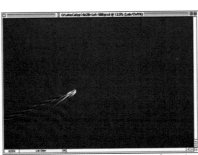

Here is the same Crater Lake image after using Command-Y to get a CMYK preview. Notice that the title bar at the top of the window has changed its name from Lab to Lab/CMYK.

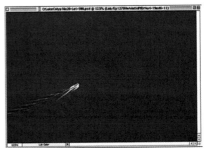

Here it is previewed using the profile for my Epson 1270 printer on Matte Paper Heavyweight. This deep blue is way out of the gamut for the CMYK gamut and also partially outside of the gamut for my Epson 1270. The prints of this image on the LightJet 5000 do show this deep blue because it is within the gamut of that printer with Fuji Crystal Archive paper.

Using Command-Shift-Y to get a Gamut Warning for a CMYK version of Crater Lake, you see that the entire blue image is out of gamut.

A Gamut Warning with the ICC profile for the Epson 1270 using Matte Paper Heavyweight shows that many blues are out of gamut, but not as many as with CMYK. This is one of only a few of my images that has a gamut problem with this printer and paper combination.

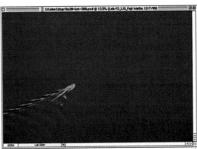

Even on the LightJet 5000 using Fuji Crystal Archive paper, there are a few colors out of gamut in the water highlights around the boat. I often print images with small gamut warnings anyhow and they usually look fine. Using Command-Y to get the onscreen preview often tells you the most about whether you will like the image using a particular printer, ink, and paper.

173

right after making that setting. When you later restart Photoshop, you will notice that Command-Y now shows you how your RGB file will look when printed on your printer using that profile.

Notice that if you choose View/Gamut Warning (Command-Shift-Y), Photoshop will show you the colors in your RGB file that are outside the gamut of the profile that is currently set in View/Proof Setup to be your proofing profile. If you want that to show the out of gamut colors for your current CMYK settings, then View/Proof Setup should be set to Working CMYK. If you want it to show you the out of gamut colors based on the ICC profile for your RGB printer, then you need to use View/Proof Setup/Custom to set Profile to the ICC profile for your printer.

EDITING PROFILES WITH PROFILE EDITORS AND/OR PHOTOSHOP ADJUSTMENT LAYERS

Once you make a profile, have one made for you, or even with canned profiles, it is possible to edit the profile to change it and fix small areas you are not happy with. According to my friend Bruce Bayne, a color management expert, it is very common to have to make small edits to many of the profiles that are created. You will want to have this capability even if someone else makes a profile for you. Many of the profiles I have made were essentially good except for some minor flaw, like having a magenta cast in the 20% and 10% highlight areas.

I use a GretagMacbeth ColorChecker chart, available at good camera stores, to compare the neutrals in a test print with standard neutrals in the ColorChecker. If the calibration image prints correctly using a particular profile, with totally neutral gray values as well as good contrast and saturation, you may not want to tweak that profile but instead change the calibration of your monitor so the onscreen version of the image matches the print. It is usually easier to change the monitor calibration than to get a really great profile. If the print itself is not neutral or if it has inadequate contrast or saturation, then you might do better editing the profile. If the profile is really far off and bad, you should just get or make a new profile.

Monaco EZ Color 2.5, Monaco Proof, and many other profiling packages now contain profile editors. These allow you to edit and improve a profile after making it. Another technique I've found to be very useful, and sometimes easier to use, is to create a Photoshop Curves or Hue/Saturation Adjustment layer to edit a profile. Let's say you create a profile, or have one made for you, and then test that profile with your images, or with the calibration image in the Chapter 15 folder on the *Artistry* CD. Say you find that the entire image has a green or magenta cast, it might be a bit too flat or contrasty, or when looking at the gray swatches you may see a magenta cast in just the 10% and 20% swatches. For all these types of problems, you can often create an adjustment layer, which will fix this problem. The steps to take are as follows:

1. Make sure your monitor is correctly calibrated. Bring up the PSCSArtistryCalibrationImage.psd file from Chapter 15 on the *Artistry* CD and leave it in the ColorMatch RGB color space.
2. Choose Image/Mode/Convert to Profile to convert this test image from ColorMatch RGB into the color profile you made for your printer.
3. Print this image using the top-middle Print with Preview dialog shown on page 150 of this chapter. Follow the directions on that page to set up the rest of your Print dialogs correctly for your printer and paper combination using a custom profile with No Color Correction in the Color Management dialog.
4. Make a print and let it dry overnight, for Ultrachrome or pigment-based prints (Epson 2200, 4000, 7600, and 9600), and for at least 48 hours for dye-based inks

Monaco Proof is a higher-end calibration package that uses a spectrophotometer, like the X-Rite DTP-41 UV, to get more accurate readings from color swatches to make better profiles for your color printers. Here we see the profile editor in Monaco Proof, which allows you to use Curves to edit profiles. This gives you more control than with the profile editor in Monaco EZ Color, which doesn't have a Curves tool to edit specific color ranges but instead allows you to edit Overall, Highlight, Midtone, or Shadow areas. It is great that both these Monaco products do include profile editors. With the really high-end systems, you have to pay a lot more to edit profiles. Another solution to profile editing is the Photoshop solution I show you to the right.

Chapter 15: Photoshop Color Preferences, Monitor, Scanner, and Printer Calibration

(Epson 1270, 1280, etc). This will allow the colors to stabilize.

5. Bring up the original PSCSArtistryCalibrationImage on the screen, then use Image/Duplicate to make a copy of it. Choose Image/Mode/Convert to Profile to convert this copy from ColorMatch RGB into the color profile you printed your test print with. Arrange your windows so the original calibration image is on the left and the copy is on the right and you can see the same parts of each. If your monitor is correctly calibrated, the image on the right should give you an accurate on-screen proof of your print.

6. The problem is that sometimes your print does not match this screen correctly. If that is the case, then create Levels, Curves, Hue/Saturation, or other adjustment layers to modify the rightmost image on screen until it looks like your print. Make sure you are viewing your print with a standard lighting situation that you will use all the time.

7. Once the rightmost image on screen looks like your print, you can then create yet another adjustment layer, or two, to modify the rightmost image on screen to make it look the way you really wanted your print to look, i.e. like the original image on the left. Once you get the rightmost image to match the leftmost image, use the Save button in each adjustment layer's color correction tool to save just the adjustment layer settings you added in step 7.

8. Now make yet another test print starting with the original calibration image again but after step 2 (after Image/Mode/Convert to Profile) create adjustment layers of the types and in the order used in step 7, then use the Load button in each of those adjustment layers to load your saved settings from step 7 into each. After your test print dries for the correct amount of time, see if your adjustments improve the results. When you get the printed calibration image to look like the original calibration image onscreen, then you can use those same saved adjustment layer settings to adjust all your images for this printer, ink, and paper combination. I usually have to go through steps 7 and 8 several times until I get adjustment layers that do exactly what I want with the profile. When using this technique, I create an action to do the Image/Mode/Convert to Profile, then add each adjustment layer and Load the settings for each. I run this action as a final step when I want to make a print using this calibration technique.

Here you see the setup for tweaking a profile with the original calibration image on the left, still in ColorMatch RGB space, and the copy of it on the right which has been converted to the profile we are trying to tweak. The bottom adjustment layer in the layers palette was used to get the rightmost image to match the test print. That was created in Step 6. Then in Step 7 we created the topmost two adjustment layers which make the rightmost image match the original on the left. These topmost two are the ones who's settings you save then later load when making future prints to that printer with that profile.

These saved settings are actually being used to edit the profiled image on-the-fly before making your print. I do this all the time to "edit my profiles," and you can try it without having to buy an expensive profile editor. I find that it works great, and for small adjustments I can often avoid step 6 and just make a guess at what my step 7 adjustments will be. I try them out and tweak them once or twice and then I end up with a Curve, or some other adjustment, that I can use over and over again just to tweak the changes made by my profile so things look just right on the printer. You may need to make a set of these saved tweaks for each profile, but you can keep them in an appropriately named folder and just load them into adjustment layers with a print action when you need them.

Editing Profiles with Profile Editors and/or Photoshop Adjustment Layers

COLOR MANAGEMENT EXPERTS:

Bruce Bayne of Alder Technology
(They make profiles for $200 each)
13500 SW 72nd Ave, Suite 200
Tigard, OR 97223
503-603-0998 or 1-888-318-8230
www.aldertech.com
bruceb@aldertech.com

Jim Rich
Rich and Associates
4601 North Park Ave, Apt. 301
Chevy Chase, MD 20815
301-652-7266

ONLINE PROFILE-MAKING SITES:
www.profilecity.com
www.chromix.com

COMPANIES MENTIONED
IN THIS CHAPTER:

X-Rite
3100 44th Street S.W.
Grandville, MI 49418
www.x-rite.com
888-826-3059

Monaco Systems
100 Burtt Road, Suite 115
Andover, MA 01810
www.monacosys.com
978-749-9944

Color Vision
1430 Vantage Court, Suite 101
Vista, CA 92083
800-554-8688
www.colorvision.com

Gretag Macbeth
617 Little Britain Road
New Windsor, NY 12553
www.gretagmacbeth.com
914-565-7660

MID-PRICED CALIBRATION SYSTEMS

The mid-priced calibration systems that seem to be most popular today are the GretagMacbeth EyeOne system and Monaco Proof. Monaco Proof is a higher-end system similar to Monaco EZ color except that Monaco Proof can use a variety of color measurement devices (see the list at the bottom of the next page) to measure color swatches instead of the flatbed scanner that Monaco EZ color uses. This and the higher-end software allow it to make more accurate profiles. You also get more options for how you make those profiles than with Monaco EZ Color. You can buy Monaco Proof without a sensor or with the X-Rite DTP-41 bundled in. See the captions on the next page for price information as of November 2003. Prices may change by the time this book is in print.

The GretagMacbeth Eye-One system, which includes profile-making software and the Eye One Pro measurement device, comes in several configurations. The EyeOne Display system just includes the software and hardware to calibrate monitors and it costs about $259. EyeOne Photo at $1299 would be the system most photographers would want. It comes with the EyeOne Pro measurement device. This device can be used to calibrate monitors as well as make printer and scanner profiles. You need to pay an additional $359 to enable the EyeOne Photo to make scanner profiles.

Both the X-Rite DTP-41, which you use with Monaco Proof, and the GretagMacbeth EyeOne Pro are exact devices which come with certificates of conformity that they have been inspected and work to a known calibration standard. They both have a mechanism for reading an entire strip of color swatches at a time. That is faster than earlier devices which required you to click on each swatch to read its color value. These products give you more assurance of getting a higher quality result than when using a variety of scanners with a system like Monaco EZ color. My experience has been that some scanners work well with EZ color and some don't work quite as well.

For my *Making the Digital Print* project, I plan to work with the X-Rite DTP-41 UV strip-reading spectrophotometer and Monaco Proof and compare that to the Eye One system as I delve more deeply into making profiles. Because the canned profiles that come with the 2200, 7600, and 9600, as well as Bill Atkinson's profiles, have been so great, I've found myself concentrating on making more prints and working with my art instead of making a lot of profiles. Still, I'd like to compare Monaco Proof and EyeOne profiles to these canned profiles to see if there is a good reason to make my own profiles. Right now it seems to me that the main reason I'd want to make profiles would be if I were using 3rd-party papers where I couldn't get quality profiles. With Epson papers the canned and Bill's profiles have made me quite happy. The new Epson 4000, which I plan to get ASAP, will allow me to more easily switch between matte black and photo black ink and therefore experiment more with heavy papers. Those will probably require making some profiles.

Because *Photoshop CS Artistry* is already quite a thick book, whose main focus is to teach photographers and artists how to work with Photoshop, our plan is to eventually create *Making the Digital Print* as a second book or training CD/DVD. This new book and/or DVD will assume that you already have *Photoshop CS Artistry* as an external resource, so *Making the Digital Print* can focus entirely on digital printmaking issues, like calibration, and other more advanced tricks you can use in color correcting to make better scans and digital prints. Check www.barryhaynes.com for more information about this book and/or DVD, its contents, and when it will be available. For those of you who have been patiently waiting, it will come along even-

Chapter 15: Photoshop Color Preferences, Monitor, Scanner, and Printer Calibration

tually. Every time a new version of Photoshop comes along, updating Photoshop Artistry takes Wendy, Sean and I about 6 months! Hope you like this latest version.

EXPENSIVE, "PROFESSIONAL," CALIBRATION SYSTEMS

The professional color user and the color management expert would probably want an X-Rite DTP-41 or the even more expensive Gretag Macbeth Spectrolino spectrophotometer with the SpectroScan X-Y table. The Spectrolino is a spectrophotometer that can take readings from your monitor, a swatch printed on paper, and also through film. The SpectroScan X-Y table allows you to place a page of swatches on the table, hook up the Spectrolino to its holder on the table, and then automatically read all the swatches on the page without any further user intervention. If you are in the business of making profiles and you have to make a lot of them, this is the professional tool of choice. If you are a professional color user and you need to make a number of printer profiles, only then may the DTP-41 or the Eye-One Pro be a more cost-effective solution for you that still allows for some automation. X-Rite also makes more advanced versions of the DTP-41 that allow you to take readings from both film and paper.

The professional level software packages include Gretag Macbeth's Profilemaker and Monaco Profiler. These are the products that the color calibration expert will want to check out. I have not evaluated these products myself so far because most of the people I work with would not want to spend that much money on calibration.

COLOR MANAGEMENT SYSTEMS AND HOW THEY FIT INTO THE PHOTOSHOP CS ENVIRONMENT

Color management systems, like ColorSync, take an image that you have corrected on your computer screen and remap that image based on the color gamut of the particular output device it is being printed on. The color gamut of an output device is the set of colors and brightness ranges that the output device can print. Each different output device, such as a digital printer, CMYK proofing system, transparency writer, and so on, has its own specific gamut. If you take the same digital file and print it, unmodified, on a number of different output devices, each print will look different from each other, and also probably different from the image on your screen. The purpose of a color management system is to adjust for these differences so the same image will look as close as possible on different computer monitors and will print as closely as possible on different types of output devices.

A color management system measures the difference between different types of output devices and creates a device profile for each device. Photoshop and ColorSync use ICC profiles to characterize devices. When you send an image to a particular device, the color management system changes the image, using that image's device profile, to try to make it print in a standard way on that device. If you print the same picture on many devices, the color management system does its best to make all those pictures look as close as possible to each other. I say "does its best" because you cannot always get the same colors on one device that you can on another. Each device has its own color gamut, the range of colors that device can scan, display, or print.

Apple's ColorSync color management system is a generic one that allows many other third-party companies to contribute device profiles for their specific products. I have, for example, an Epson Stylus Photo 1280 inkjet printer. I love the photographic quality prints it gives me, but if I took the digital file that produced a print

EyeOne Photo (~$1299 for software and EyeOne Pro calibration device) or Match are mid-priced calibration systems. With EyeOne Photo you can make RGB printer profiles and calibrate monitors. EyeOne Match also allows you to make scanner profiles and CMYK printer profiles. If you get EyeOne Photo, a good place for photographers to start, you can later add the ability to make scanner profiles by paying a fee (~$350) to update your software.

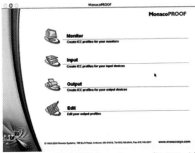

Monaco Proof (~$1399 for software, ~$2,845 with DTP-41) is a mid-priced calibration package that uses a spectrophotometer, like the X-Rite DTP-41 UV, to get more accurate readings from color swatches to make better profiles for your color printers. We may evaluate using this system versus the EyeOne in our future *Making the Digital Print* book or training CDs. If you want to find out more about these products, you can access their Web sites from the Useful Links area of www.barry-haynes.com or check out the URLs on the previous page.

Monaco Proof can use all the color measurement devices listed here from X-Rite and GretagMacbeth. This makes it a very versatile system.

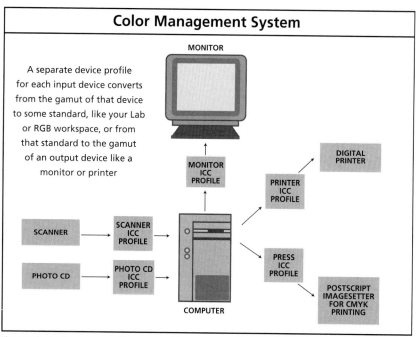

Color Management System

A separate device profile for each input device converts from the gamut of that device to some standard, like your Lab or RGB workspace, or from that standard to the gamut of an output device like a monitor or printer

MONITOR

MONITOR ICC PROFILE

SCANNER

SCANNER ICC PROFILE

PHOTO CD

PHOTO CD ICC PROFILE

COMPUTER

PRINTER ICC PROFILE

PRESS ICC PROFILE

DIGITAL PRINTER

POSTSCRIPT IMAGESETTER FOR CMYK PRINTING

The standard color space your files are stored in, on your computer and in Photoshop, should be either Lab or your default RGB working space. The ICC profiles will then translate files into that standard space, from a scan or digital camera, and out of that space to display on a monitor or print on a printer of some kind.

on my Epson printer and printed the same file, unmodified, on someone else's different model of Epson printer, you would see differences between the two prints. The other printer might have a different batch number on its inks, it might be slightly out of alignment, the temperature and humidity at the other printer's location might be different, and for whatever reason, there may be other subtle differences.

To solve this type of problem, a color management system needs to be able to measure the output from your particular device and create a custom ICC device profile for it at any particular time. That is what we have been talking about doing in the previous sections of this chapter. Color management systems can characterize different types of scanners and film input types, different types of monitors, and other factors that affect color production along the way to final output. Given the great many variations in what can happen to the colors, it's no wonder color calibration and correction often prove so difficult.

Color management systems can help you deal with the differences in the gamut and characteristics of different types of input and output devices, and they are improving all the time. Some color management system marketing implies that these systems can automatically scan, correct, and output images so that they print like originals. It's usually not that easy and it needs to be done carefully and correctly. Although color management systems can be adjusted to give you a high degree of calibration and control between devices, doing this correctly still requires a lot of measurement and control of every part of your color production system.

CALIBRATING YOUR OUTPUT DEVICE

Many issues arise in attempting to get quality output to a digital printer, film recorder, or imagesetter. First among them are calibration issues. You must calibrate the output device and keep it calibrated. When your output device is not calibrated and consistent, any calibration and correction you do on your computer is less useful. The job of a digital printer, for example, is to print exactly the same way every time. If you change the batch of ink or the type of ink or paper, that may change the results of the printer and require you to recalibrate. The supplier of your inks and papers must have strict controls to keep them consistent or else you will have to recalibrate every time you get new inks or papers even if you are using the same type of ink or paper. Some printers, like the Fuji Pictrography printers, have a built-in system to calibrate the printer itself whenever the paper and chemicals are changed. This ensures that the output of the printer is consistent; then all you have to do is make a profile for that printer. When calibrated correctly you should be able to send some known, good test output to your output device and compare that output print to previous versions of that image on that printer with that ink and paper and the result should be the same.

When you scan or capture an image or have it scanned, you need to be sure to get the best scan or capture, and it would be very helpful to have an ICC profile of your scanner or digital camera. The Photoshop CS Camera Raw filter has built-in profiles for a variety of digital cameras. Using Camera Raw is covered in Chapter 10: "Digital Cameras and Camera Raw." If you are not doing the scanning yourself, you need to know how to check the scans that others have done to make sure that the maximum amount of information is available. And, you need to understand how to make the most of the information that you have. We cover the scanning part of the process in Chapter 16: "Image Resolution and Scanning."

Trying to calibrate your monitor or perfect your process of making color corrections doesn't do any good unless the output device you are sending to (imagesetter, color printer, film recorder, or whatever) is consistent and is calibrated. A good way to test this calibration is to send a group of neutral colors to your output device. I have created a file, called the StepWedgeFile, for use as a test file for calibrating your output device. The StepWedgeFile consists of wedges of neutral gray that have a known value. Two issues are involved in calibrating your output device. The first issue is whether the device will print the correct density. If you send a 50% density value to the device, it should measure and look like 50% when it prints. All densities should print as they are expected. The second issue is getting colors to print correctly. Using all its colors, if you get the output device to print these neutral gray values correctly, it's a good sign that it will also print colors correctly. You want the densities on the gray wedges to be correct, and you also want each wedge to continue to look gray because when you see a cast in your printed grays, that cast usually gets added to all color correct images. The original StepWedgeFile was created using an older version of Photoshop and it wasn't tagged with an ICC profile. In that version of Photoshop, I was working in a Gamma 1.8 RGB Working Space similar to ColorMatch RGB, but that was before Photoshop used ICC profiles. With Photoshop 5-CS, I've noticed that, depending on the color space I am working in, the density readings from the Info palette could change when reading neutral values from the untagged StepWedgeFile. To make them simpler to use with Photoshop CS, I've now included three versions of the StepWedgeFile within the Calibration folder on the CD. The StepWedgeFileUntagged is the same StepWedgeFile I've included with older versions of *Photoshop Artistry*, which contains correct neutral grayscale values but is not tagged with any particular profile. The StepWedgeFileGamma1.8 and StepWedgeFileGamma2.2 are explained in the caption to the right, which you need to read and understand before using these files!

Checking RGB Printer Output or Photoshop CMYK Separations on Your RGB or CMYK Printer or a CMYK Press

I have created a Photoshop printer test file from some of my prints and the StepWedgeFile. It is called PSCSArtistryCalibrationImage.psd and is included in the Ch15.Color Pref and Calibration folder on the *Photoshop CS Artistry* CD and also printed on the next page. This RGB file in ColorMatch RGB space can be used to test output to your RGB printer or other RGB output device. Before doing any tests, be sure to set up your Color Settings preferences as shown at the start of this chapter. If you are doing CMYK output to a CMYK printer or printing press to see if your Photoshop color separation settings are working well, we will show you how to use this image to create a Photoshop separation test.

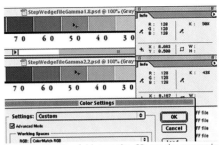

In the Calibration folder on the CD are the grayscale StepWedge files. You can use them to test your printer and see if it is printing neutral grays as neutral. I usually open one of these, and then copy or drag and drop it onto the white canvas edge of a print. Then I print the image and see if the grays come out neutral in all density areas. If they don't then you know the part of your printer or profile that needs further calibration. There is a file called StepWedgeFileGamma1.8, which you should use with RGB or grayscale images that are in a grayscale or color space like ColorMatch RGB that has a gamma of 1.8. The file called StepWedgeFileGamma2.2 should be used with images that are in a grayscale or color space like Adobe RGB that has a gamma of 2.2. When you use the matching gamma stepwedge file, the RGB values will read correctly in the Info palette after that file has been pasted on top of another grayscale or RGB file.

The Info palette readings that you get from these grayscale files, and from RGB files that they are pasted on top of, will depend on the RGB working space preference that is currently in place. In the illustration above, two Info palette readings are shown from the 50% gray swatch when the RGB Working Space is set to Color Match RGB. In this case the RGB values for the Gamma 1.8 and 2.2 files will both be 128, 128, 128; the Lab values will both be 61, 0, 0, and the black (k) values will be 50% for the Gamma 1.8 file but only 43% for the Gamma 2.2 file. If we change the RGB Working Space to Adobe RGB, that makes the RGB values in both files 145, 145, 145 and both the Lab values are still 61, 0, 0 and black(k) values are still 50% for the Gamma 1.8 file and 43% for the gamma 2.2 file.

Since a Gamma 2.2 environment is more contrasty, 43% black there will look the same as 50% black in the Gamma 1.8 environment. The data in the Gamma 2.2 file was converted from Gamma 1.8 to Gamma 2.2 so the files will match on the screen, when used within their correct gamma environment, and should match when you output them after correctly using profile conversions to your printer's color space.

When you convert either of these two grayscale files to ColorMatch RGB, the resulting RGB value of the 50% swatch will be 128, 128, 128, the Lab value 61, 0, 0 and the K value 50%. When you convert either file to Adobe RGB, the RGB values will be 145, 145, 145, the Lab values 61, 0, 0 and the K values 50%. Again, in a Gamma 2.2 space, an RGB value of 145 will look the same as an RGB value of 128 would look in a Gamma 1.8 space.

Play around with these two files as you change the Info palette readouts between RGB, Grayscale (K), and Lab and also as you change the RGB Working Space, and make sure you are aware of the differences that can occur in the Info palette readings. Photoshop CS has the very useful Proof Color option in the Info palette, which shows you the numerical values you will get if you convert the image to the Proof Colors profile.

Calibration Image from Photoshop 6 Artistry. All images © 2001, Barry Haynes, All Rights Reserved

100 98 95 90 80 75 70 60 50 40 30 25 20 10 5 2 0

You are given permission to print this to calibrate your output devices only. Large Archival prints of these and other images by Barry Haynes are available for sale at www.barryhaynes.com.

To make your own test image, create an 8.5x11 canvas in RGB mode, fill it with a neutral gray background, and save it as MyPrinterTest or something like that. Now use Image/Mode/RGB to convert the grayscale StepWedgeFile, in the Ch15.Color Pref and Calibration folder on the CD, to your RGB Working Space, and then paste it into your test file. Next, find some color corrected RGB images that are typical of your normal work. Copy these images and paste them into your test file. Save the final RGB version of your RGB test file.

Use your test image, or ours, to output to your RGB printer or device in the way that you would normally use that device. If you have a profile for the printer, then use Image/Mode/Convert to Profile to convert a copy of the test image to that color space. Then print the image using printer settings that do no further color management or changes, because the profile should have done that for you. If you are not using a color profile, then use whatever settings you would normally use with your printer. The PSCSArtistryCalibrationImage prints well on most Epson printers on an 8.5x11 sheet of Epson paper. If you have

This is the *Photoshop CS Artistry* printer calibration image. It can be used as an RGB test image to check your screen calibration and your printer output to an Epson RGB printer, LightJet 5000, or Fuji Pictrography printer and a variety of RGB devices. The Photoshop file is in ColorMatch RGB format and can be converted to a printer profile for print tests using Image/Mode/Convert to Profile as described earlier in this chapter when talking about making printer profiles and printing using those profiles. If your monitor is calibrated correctly and you have a controlled lighting monitor and print-viewing space, then this image should match your prints when viewed on the screen using View/Proof Setup/Custom correctly set to your printer's profile, which was used to make your prints.

To use this file to test CMYK output, make sure your Photoshop CS CMYK preferences are set up for the type of CMYK press and paper you will be using, and then choose Image/Mode/CMYK to convert this file to CMYK. If you are calibrated, then this image onscreen, after it is converted to CMYK, should look like your best press proof from your printer.

an Epson 1270, 1280, 2200, 4000, 7600, 9600, or similar Epson printer, use the print dialog recommendations on page 170 of this chapter. If you have an older Epson printer, check out my recommended printer dialog settings for printing with no profile at www.barryhaynes.com in the LATEST TIPS section. If you have another Epson printer of similar vintage to one of these, you should be able to get the same settings in your print dialog; they might just be in different places.

When comparing your test print to the image on your monitor, make sure you view the test print in the lighting you have calibrated for and the image on the screen should be previewed using View/Proof Setup using the profile you made for your printer. If you are not using a profile, then just view the image on screen using your normal Lab or RGB Working Space. I view my art prints under halogen floods with a color temperature of around 2700K because that is the light source used in most galleries. When working on a book that will be printed on press, I view proofs from the book's print shop using my Soft View D5000 Transparency/Print Viewer, which lights them at 5000K, the standard for most press rooms in the USA. The light you view your print under will make a big difference in the way it looks!

If converting the test file to CMYK for a CMYK printer or a press, make sure your CMYK Color Settings preferences are set correctly for the type of printer or paper and press you are using. If you normally use Image/Mode/CMYK to convert from RGB to CMYK, do just that with your separation test. If you use someone else's separation tables, do it that way. If you normally save your files as Photoshop EPS or

DCS and then put the files into Quark, do the same thing in your test. Save your final CMYK version of the file under a different name than the RGB version. Whenever I'm going to print a new version of *Photoshop Artistry*, I always have the printer make a set of proofs using their current best color proofing system. Lately, the printer has been using Kodak Approval proofs, which are digital proofs that can be printed on the actual paper the book is being printed on. The paper of your proof can also make a difference in the color.

When evaluating your test image, the densities should look correct in the gray stepwedge and they should also look gray. If the stepwedge densities are not right, or if they have a cyan, magenta, or some combination of color casts, it's a sign that either the RGB or CMYK output device, imagesetter, platemaker, or proofer isn't calibrated or something's not right about the way you created this output. You should not have altered or color corrected the stepwedge file using your monitor, so it should be gray. If it doesn't look gray or the densities are not correct, you will have to calibrate your printer, edit your printer profile, or for CMYK adjust your separations to solve this problem. See the section titled "Editing Profiles with Profile Editors and/or Photoshop Adjustment Layers," earlier in this chapter, for another idea about how to make your monitor color closer to your printer output. If the stepwedge looks good and this test prints with the correct densities and no color casts, you know your output device is calibrated.

CREATING CUSTOM SEPARATION SETTINGS

If you want to calibrate Photoshop separation settings for a newspaper, a particular type of web press, or other custom CMYK output, you can do this using Photoshop CS. First, you need to find out the correct CMYK values for the full range of neutral colors in a stepwedge file, like the one included in the Calibration folder on the *Photoshop CS Artistry* CD. The press expert at your print shop should know this information. Next, you adjust Custom CMYK at the top of the CMYK Working Spaces menu in Color Settings, as well as the way you set highlights and shadows, using the techniques described in the illustration on page 164 of this chapter, until you get the CMYK values closest to the CMYK values from your press expert for neutral colors in the stepwedge file. Using those settings in Photoshop usually gets you very close to the separations that you want.

Neutral RGB 0...255 values				Sample Target GCR type CMYK values to print these as neutrals			
	Red	Green	Blue	Cyan	Magenta	Yellow	Black
highlight	243	243	243	5%	3%	3%	0%
1/4 tone	192	192	192	25%	16%	16%	0%
midtone	128	128	128	50%	39%	38%	4%
3/4 tone	64	64	64	69%	58%	58%	30%
shadow	13	13	13	76%	66%	65%	85%

Actual CMYK values (plus or minus 1) when separating the unmodified StepWedgeFile using sample Photoshop separation settings

	Cyan	Magenta	Yellow	Black
05% highlight	5%	3%	3%	0%
25% 1/4 tone	24%	16%	16%	0%
50% midtone	49%	37%	36%	3%
75% 3/4 tone	67%	57%	56%	29%
95% shadow	75%	65%	64%	84%

The preference settings we chose don't exactly match the values in the target CMYK table, but they give the closest overall settings to these values, which also are the most useful starting point settings.

NEWSPAPERS AND OTHER CUSTOM SETTINGS

Our default highlight and shadow values usually are good for most RGB output purposes, including output to film recorders and also for CMYK separations to coated stock. If they are not working for you, use this process to change them. Newspaper presses tend to vary much more than web or sheetfed presses for coated stock. If you are doing output for newspapers or some other special process, first get a set of correct values for printing neutral colors from your press person. It should look like the preceding table but with different numbers. For newspapers, start out with Custom CMYK set to SWOP (Newsprint) with a Standard Dot Gain of 30%. Set the Separation Type to GCR, Black Generation to Medium, Black Ink Limit to around 85%, and Total Ink Limit to around 260%; again, get these values from your press person. Set the Highlight and Shadow preference values in Levels initially as your press person recommends for the brightest and darkest place that can still carry a dot or not be solid black on your press.

Bring up the StepWedgeFile, which starts out as grayscale, and convert it to your RGB working space using Image/Mode/RGB. Bring up the Info palette and use Color Samplers to measure the RGB and CMYK values you get at different density areas along your stepwedge. Compare the CMYK numbers with the ones you got from your press person. Adjust the Dot Gain (remember, you can now use the Curves setting to adjust each curve separately and exactly if needed), Black Ink Limit, and Total Ink limit settings in Custom CMYK until you get values that are as close as possible to those your press person gave you. You can also change the Black Generation curve between Light, Medium, and Heavy as well as create a custom Black generation curve by choosing Custom. Photoshop doesn't give you direct control over the Cyan, Magenta, or Yellow generation curves, but you can affect them via changes you make to the Black curve. You can also separately adjust each of the dot gain curves by choosing Curves from the Dot Gain pop-up.

You will have to play with all these settings until you get a feeling for the relationship they have with each other. The settings we have recommended for coated stock have worked quite well in producing this book and for many other projects that I have done. We don't recommend particular settings for newspapers because they tend to vary from paper to paper. For more information on output to black-and-white halftones, you should get *Photoshop in Black-and-White: An Illustrated Guide to Producing Black-and-White Images with Adobe Photoshop* by Jim Rich.

You can also load a custom ICC profile to run your separations. This custom profile would decide for you how to convert from RGB to CMYK. There are companies that sell custom separation tables and ICC profiles for Photoshop. If you have another color separation system that you would like to import into Photoshop, like from Scitex or some other high-end system, you can do that also by converting that to an ICC profile.

MORE ABOUT THE CMYK WORKING SPACES

Photoshop CS has a lot more options for controlling CMYK separations. There are two main types of choices for how to specify your CMYK Model in Photoshop CS. You can choose an ICC profile directly from the CMYK Working Spaces pop-up menu, and Photoshop CS has provided the canned CMYK ICC profiles shown at the top right of this page. The Euroscale Coated v2 and Euroscale Uncoated v2 are the settings to use with European inks and presses for either coated (i.e. glossy) or uncoated stock. Japan Standard v2 is the setting to use when printing with standard inks in Japan and there are the new 2001 Japanese options to try with CS. The U.S. Sheetfed Coated v2, which we used for this book, and U.S. Sheetfed Uncoated v2 are Adobe separation settings to use with sheetfed presses when using either coated or uncoated paper. The U.S. Web Coated (SWOP) v2 and U.S. Web Uncoated v2 are Adobe settings to use with web presses, with the Coated (SWOP) one being for the SWOP web press printing standard.

When you choose Custom CMYK, you get a set of controls that are identical to the previous built-in CMYK options for Photoshop 5 & 5.5. These should give you the same good results you could achieve with Photoshop 5 & 5.5, provided you make the correct choices. These settings also allow you to tweak your own CMYK curves.

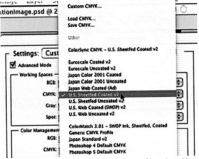

These are the canned CMYK ICC profiles that Photoshop CS provides. Choosing one of these, or adjusting your Photoshop CS CMYK settings yourself using Custom CMYK, should all give you good results, provided you choose the right setting for your print job, paper, and press. To print this book, we used the U.S. Sheetfed Coated v2 settings because these seemed to give slightly cleaner separations with more saturated color than the settings described below on this page.

INK OPTIONS

INK COLORS: This setting tells Photoshop the types of inks you will be printing with on a press. Because printing inks are fairly standardized, you will probably find it unnecessary to change this setting after you pick the right ink. For printing this book on a sheetfed press, I previously used the SWOP coated setting. You would want to choose the SWOP Newsprint for newspapers or the SWOP Uncoated for uncoated paper. If you are printing with Toyo inks, which I was impressed with the time I used them, you would pick one of those settings. You can also choose Custom and enter the xyY values or Lab values in the case of special custom inks. When you convert from RGB to CMYK, the actual CMYK values you get for a given RGB value depend on a combination of the Color Settings in RGB Working Space, CMYK Working Space, and also where and how you set your Highlight and Shadow values in Levels or Curves.

DOT GAIN: The Dot Gain setting adjusts how dark Photoshop displays an untagged CMYK image on the screen as well as how dense Photoshop makes each of the CMYK separation channels when you convert from RGB to CMYK. The Dot Gain value represents how much the printing inks will spread when printed on certain papers. If you set the Dot Gain to 30%, Photoshop will separate each CMYK color with less density and display the colors of untagged CMYK files on the screen darker than if the Dot Gain were set to 20%. As a general setting, you should start with a Dot Gain setting of 20% or less for coated stock. You should talk to the press expert at the printshop you will be using to find the exact Dot Gain settings for the press and paper combination you will be using. Most print shops are familiar with Photoshop settings these days. Photoshop CS allows you to use this dialog to specify each of the Cyan, Magenta, Yellow, and Black dot gain curves separately instead of just picking one Dot Gain value to use for all four. Again, you should discuss the expected dot gain with your printer and set the Photoshop Standard single value or the new dot gain curves accordingly.

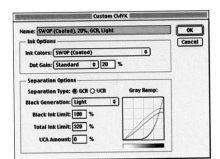

For the recommended CMYK settings I used in Photoshop 5 & 5.5, choose Custom CMYK from the CMYK pop-up and then change Black Generation to Light and Total Ink Limit to 320% then choose OK. More advanced users who want to set custom Ink Colors can get the Custom dialog by choosing Custom from the Ink Colors dialog here. You can also set custom dot gain curves by choosing Curves from the above Dot Gain pop-up. Using the above settings, I've had very good results in printing *Photoshop 5 and 5.5 Artistry* on a sheet fed press, *Photoshop, Painter, and Illustrator Side-by-Side* on a web press, as well as separating various brochures and magazine covers. We used the **U.S. Sheetfed Coated v2** setting, for the CMYK Workspace pop-up in Color Settings, to print *Photoshop 6 Artistry* and *Photoshop 7 Artistry*. For newspaper presses, non-glossy papers, and other printing situations, you may need to use other settings. To be sure, you should run tests with the proofing mechanism at your print shop.

SEPARATION OPTIONS

The Separation Options further control RGB to CMYK conversion values. The Gray Ramp is a curve diagram showing how cyan, magenta, yellow, and black are generated for neutral colors as the image goes from highlights on the left to shadows on the right. There is more ink used in the shadows, and black ink gets used only in the darker half of the color ranges. If you adjust the settings for Black Generation from Light to Medium or Dark, you can see how the black setting affects the Cyan, Magenta, and Yellow curves. You can also choose Custom for the Black Generation

183

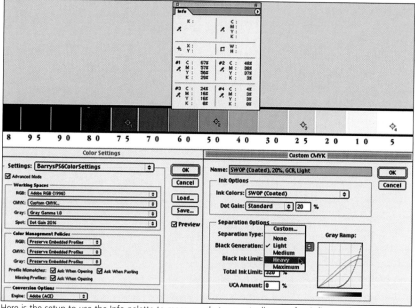

Here is the setup to use the Info palette to measure what you actually get, after influence from Ink Colors, Dot Gain settings, and Separation Options, when making a separation. Change some of the settings, and you can measure the differences using the Eyedropper, Color Sampler tools, and Info palette. You need to make sure the Preview button is on in the Color Settings dialog to be able to see the changes in the Info palette. Here we have four Color Sampler settings to measure the values at 5%, 25%, 50%, and 75% within a stepwedge file that comes in the Calibration folder on the *Photoshop CS Artistry* CD. When we change any parameter seen here, including the Dot Gain curves, Black Ink Limit, Total Ink Limit, UCA Amount, and so on, we see what separation values those changes will actually give us in the five measured areas. You should be able to use this technique to tweak the built-in separator to get very close to what your press person wants for a particular press. First, though, I'd try the built-in Photoshop seps we talk about earlier, and you might find that even if the numbers are different than what you normally get, the results are much better than they were in Photoshop 5.5 or in older versions. You can also use this type of measuring technique to compare the CMYK values you would get using different ICC profiles, including the new built-in Adobe separations for U.S. Sheet Fed, U.S. Web, etc.

curve, and this will bring up a Curve dialog that allows you to manually modify the black curve. You cannot manually modify the Cyan, Magenta, or Yellow curves here, although you can now modify their dot gain curves. Changing the Black Ink Limit, Total Ink Limit, and UCA (Under Color Addition) also affects all the curves shown in the Gray Ramp. The Separation Type lets you choose between GCR (Gray Component Replacement) or UCR (Under Color Removal) separations. Our recommended settings for Separation Type are GCR (Gray Component Replacement) turned on; for Black Generation, Light; for Black Ink Limit, 100%; and for Total Ink Limit, 320%. If your were printing on a web press, your total ink settings would probably be somewhat lower, around 280, and for a newspaper press, they would be lower still. Each newspaper press is a little different. We are leaving the UCA (Under Color Addition) amount set to 0, but you can increase the UCA value if you find that the GCR separations are removing too much colored ink in the non-neutral areas. Again, if you are not happy with the results you are getting, the best thing to do here is talk to your print shop and run some tests with different settings until you get the results you like. If the Custom CMYK controls don't allow you to get what you want, you can also use profile-making software to create a custom profile for a particular press, paper, and ink combination; then choose that ICC profile as your CMYK Working Space.

Using an ICC Profile for Separations

When you set your CMYK Working Space to an ICC profile, you will set the Profile to a special ICC profile for your press and paper conditions. There are standard profiles available for particular presses and inks, and you might want to ask your printer or service bureau if they have any of these to recommend. In theory, though, the best thing to do is to make a custom profile for your particular press, paper, and ink condition. To do this, as described earlier in this chapter, you have to first choose the profile-making software and hardware you are going to work with or a color management expert in the business of creating color profiles for you.

The process would be to print a standard test target, made up of many swatches of color and neutral values, on your press using standard ink densities and printing conditions. This test target would then be measured with a spectrophotometer to see how these standard color swatches printed on this press with this paper and ink. Those measurements would be entered into a software package, like Monaco Proof, which would then create the ICC profile for that press, ink, and paper combination. That profile would then be used as your CMYK Working Space. When you printed

Chapter 15: Photoshop Color Preferences, Monitor, Scanner, and Printer Calibration

those separations, you should get the best results when printing with the same standard ink densities and printing conditions that were used to make the profile.

When you use a profile for your separations, your results will be based on three things: These are the accuracy of the printing test proof that was used to take the measurements from, the accuracy of the person and equipment making the measurements from that proof, and finally, the quality of the software making the ICC profile from those test results. If the persons running the test printing and making the profile do a good job, you might get the best possible results from this approach; however, if it doesn't work that well, you may have less control over any changes you need to make unless you actually own all the software, equipment, and knowledge to make further tests and correct the situation.

USING SEPARATION TABLES FROM OLDER VERSIONS OF PHOTOSHOP

If you are happy with the color separations you were getting from an older version of Photoshop and want to continue to use them with Photoshop CS, here is how you can do that:

1. Go to your old version of Photoshop, in this case Photoshop 5.5 or older, and make sure your Monitor Setup, Printing Inks Setup, and Separation Setup settings are correct for the tables you want to move over to Photoshop CS as an ICC profile.

2. Go to File/Color Settings/Separation Tables, and click the Save button to save your old tables.

3. Quit from your old Photoshop and start up Photoshop CS. Now go to Photoshop/Color Settings and then choose Load CMYK from the CMYK Working Space pop-up.

4. After you have these old tables loaded, choose the Save CMYK menu item from the CMYK Working Space pop-up and resave them into the ColorSync folder on the Mac. On the PC, save this ICC profile into the folder where your particular Windows version saves ICC Profiles. You will now be able to choose this as an ICC profile setting from the CMYK Working Space pop-up menu within Color Settings. When you add ICC profiles to the ColorSync Profiles folder, depending on the operating system you are using, you may need to quit from Photoshop CS and then restart Photoshop CS for those profiles to show up within Photoshop CS.

5. In general, you should find the Photoshop CS separations better than those from older versions of Photoshop, so I would not recommend just using your old tables. However, if you were happy with your old tables and you just got Photoshop CS and need to do some work before having time to test the new Photoshop CS separations, you can load your old tables and use them until you set up the new Photoshop CS stuff the way you want. I do really encourage you to use the new Photoshop CS separation engine, however, because it is much better when you get it set up correctly for your needs.

16 IMAGE RESOLUTION, SCANNING, DIGITAL CAPTURE, AND HISTOGRAMS

Here you learn how to make 16- or 8-bit scans or set digital captures at the appropriate resolution and file size, how to use histograms to evaluate and improve scans and digital captures, and how to compare film scans on popular multiformat scanners.

Silver Reeds.

Sunset at Swamp. Taken hand held after my friend no longer had enough light to shoot with his film camera on a tripod. This image and the one above were all taken by Barry with the Epson PhotoPC 3000Z, a 3.3 megapixel digital camera, using the 2048 x 1536 image size.

WHAT ARE BYTES, BITS, AND DPI?

When working with digital images, you need to understand resolution and the issues involved in determining what size to make the scan or digital capture. Because we're going to be talking about size in bytes, let's take a minute to talk about bytes, bits, and dpi. A *byte* (8 bits) is the most common unit of measurement of computer memory. All computer functionality is based on switches that can be turned on and off. A single switch is called a *bit*. When a bit is off, it has a value of 0. When a bit is on, it has a value of 1. With a single bit, you can count from 0 to 1. With two bits lined up next to each other, you can count from 0 to 3 because now there are four possibilities (00=0, 01=1, 10=2, and 11=3). Add a third bit, and you can count from 0 to 7 (000=0, 001=1, 010=2, 011=3, 100=4, 101=5, 110=6, and 111=7). When there are 8 bits, or a byte, you can count from 0 to 255, which is 256 possible values. When there are 12 bits, you have 4,096 possible values, and when there are 16 bits you have 65,536 possible values.

A grayscale 8-bit digital image has one byte of information for each value scanned from the film. A value of 0 is the darkest possible value, black, and a value of 255 is the brightest possible value, white. Values in between are different levels of gray, the lower numbers being darker and the higher numbers being lighter. You can think of these values like you would think of individual pieces of grain within a piece of film: the more values you have per inch, the smaller the grain in the digital file. Also, the more of these values that you have per inch, pixels/inch, the higher the resolution (also referred to as ppi [pixels per inch] or samples per inch) in your file. An 8-bit RGB color digital image has three bytes of information (24 bits, one byte for each channel of red, green, or blue) for each value scanned from the film. And CMYK files have four bytes per pixel. A 16-bit per channel grayscale file has two bytes and 32,769 (0-32,768 is 32769 values) possible tonal values per pixel or sample. A 16-bit per channel RGB file, 48 bits in all, contains 32,769 possible tonal values per color channel. With today's scanners, scanning 16-bit per channel images is something well worth considering. This 0-32,768 value range is what the Info palette of Photoshop CS shows when you turn on the Show 16 bit values option in its Palette Options menu. This number actually represents the 15-bit range, but it is plenty.

If you have an enlarger in the traditional darkroom, you can make a 20x24 print from a 35mm original. Its quality will not be as good as a 20x24 print on the same paper from a 4x5 original of the same type of film, because the 4x5 has more film area with which to define the image. If you were printing on different types of paper, the paper's grain would affect the look of the final print. It's the amount of grain in the original film that makes the difference when you project that film on the same paper to make a traditional darkroom print.

When you make a print on a digital printer, the dpi (dots per inch) of the printer is analogous to the grain in the photographic paper. The dpi of a digital printer is the number of individual sensors, or ink jets, or laser spots, that the particular printer can put down per inch. Each digital printer has its own maximum possible dpi, based on its own specific physical limitations. The relationship between the pixels per inch of a digital file and the dpi of a digital printer is analogous to the relationship between the grain size of film in the enlarger and the grain size of the paper you are printing on in a traditional darkroom. A digital file at 100 ppi will print on a digital printer that can output at 720 dpi, but it won't look as good as a 300 ppi file of the same image for the same printer. A digital capture with 2000 pixels across the image area won't usually print with as much detail as a digital capture with 6000 pixels across the same image area. Similarly, a print on photographic paper from ASA 1600 (large grain) film will look grainier than a print from ASA 25 (small grain) film.

The ppi that you scan a file at is based on the size of the original piece of film you are scanning from. When you print that file, you will often lower the ppi used in making the print so you can print at a larger size.

When you make a print on a printing press, the line screen of the halftone is somewhat analogous to the grain in the photographic paper.

HOW BIG SHOULD I MAKE A SCAN OR A DIGITAL CAPTURE?

When you are having an image scanned, you should know the intended purpose of the scan well ahead of time. When you have more than one purpose and image size, scan the image at the maximum size you would use or at the maximum optical dpi of your scanner. Scanning at higher than the optical dpi of your scanner just means that the scanner software is upsampling your file. Photoshop can usually do as good a job or better upsampling as your scanner software can, so there is usually no need to scan at higher than the scanner's optical resolution. With digital cameras, I usually shoot raw files at the maximum resolution for the sensor on the camera. For more info on this, see Chapter 10: "Digital Cameras and Camera Raw."

The formula for calculating the required byte size for a scan of a 6x7 image, for example, to be printed using 300 ppi is (6x300 ppi) x (7x300 ppi) x 3. This file would be 11,340,000 bytes in size. (The final factor represents the number of bytes for each pixel in the image; 3 is the number for an RGB color image.) If you were saving the

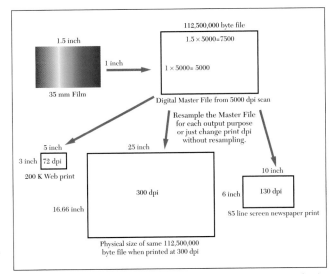

If you will use the scan for more than one purpose, make the original scan for the size of the biggest file you will need. Do your overall color correction, image enhancement, and spotting on this biggest master file. You can then resample that corrected file down to whatever resolution and file size you need. Above you see some sample uses. When scanning most files on a high-end scanner, you will find that you will not get any more detail information from the film by scanning it at more than 5000 dpi. If you scan at a higher dpi than this, you probably will not get any better data than just resampling up the 5000 dpi file. A file of this dpi can certainly be resampled down with Image Size or the Cropping tool to 72 dpi for the Web, 300 dpi for a digital art print, 170 dpi for a newspaper print, or anything else you need.

If the image is to be published as a halftone on a printing press and you want the best quality, you need to scan it at a ppi (pixels per inch or scan samples per inch) of at least twice the line screen of the publication. For example, if you are printing a six-inch by seven-inch photograph in a 150-line screen publication, you should scan it at 300 dpi for the number of inches you're printing it.

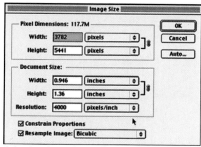

Going into Image/Image Size on a file that was just scanned using a Polaroid SprintScan 120 at 4000 pixels/inch. The Width and Height in the Document Size area are still set to the size of the crop on the actual 35mm film. Notice the Pixel Dimensions.

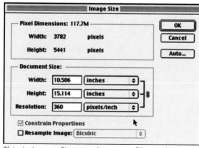

This is Image Size on the same file as the initial Image Size at the top of this page. Here we turned Resample Image off then changed the Resolution to 360 pixels/inch. Now we see in the Width and Height values in Document Size how big of a print we'd get from this file when sending 360 ppi to the printer. Notice that the Pixel Dimensions values have not changed since Resample Image is off.

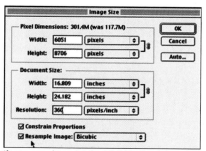

If we wanted to print the 16x24 to the right at 360 ppi, we'd turn on Resample Image, then type in 360. Notice that Pixels Dimensions have changed because doing this adds pixels to this file. Study the Image Size command and make sure you understand all its possible variations. Study the Image Size command and make sure you UNDERSTAND all its possible variations. Yes, I said this twice because this is the most misunderstood thing within Photoshop, but it is also the most important to understand! For best results when upsampling a digital capture file, do it in the Camera Raw filter; see Chapter 10.

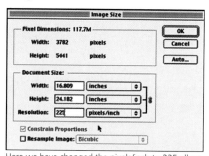

Here we have changed the pixels/inch to 225 allowing us to make a 16x24 print from this same file. Notice that Pixel Dimensions still have not changed.

complete file after scanning at either 12- or 16-bits per channel, or anything more than 8-bits per channel, you would end up with a 16-bit per channel file in Photoshop, which would double the above file size making this final factor 6. For an 8-bit CMYK scan, the factor is 4 instead of 3 because there are 4 bytes for each pixel in a CMYK image. If you do a black-and-white scan, you can remove this factor because they require only 1 byte per pixel, 2 bytes for a 16-bit grayscale scan. Here's the general formula for the required byte size of final publication scans:

Scan Size = ((height of image) x (2 x line screen dpi)) x ((width of image) x (2 x line screen dpi)) x 3 (for 8-bit RGB) or x 6 (for 16-bit RGB).

If you scan a file for output to a digital printer, such as the Epson Stylist Photo 1280, 2200, 4000 & 7600, or the LightJet 5000, you don't need to do the scan at the same ppi as the resolution of the printer you plan to use. After scanning the file, the resolution can be set to different values depending on the printer you are using for that print. For output to the LightJet 5000, which has a print resolution of 120 pixels per centimeter (304.8 dpi), the formula and byte size would be (6x304.8 dpi) x (7x304.8 dpi) x 3 = 11,705,783 bytes. The Epson Stylist Photo 1280, 2200, 4000, 7600, and 9600 have printed dpis of from 720 up to 2880. The way the Epson printers use dots, however, is different from digital printers like the dye subs and the LightJet 5000. I have found that for these types of Epson printers, you get good results if you use a file of about 360 ppi or higher. For 1440 dpi Epson prints, I'll use 360 or 480 ppi files for optimal prints, but most people won't see the difference so long as the ppi is over 240 and some digital camera files look great at 180.

Another thing I often do, instead of resampling my larger scans when doing letter size test prints, is turn off Resample Image in the Image Size dialog, then set the Resolution to a high enough ppi so I can get a letter size print. Looking at the screen grabs for Image Size dialogs to the left, with Resample Image off, we could set the Height to the maximum letter size of 10.3 inches, which would change the pixels/inch to 528.252. I don't like the fractional values so I would then change the pixels/inch to 530, which would give me a letter size print 10.266 inches high and 7.136 inches wide. This allows me to make a letter size test print of my image without resampling it and maybe having to resharpen it, which one sometimes has to do after resampling. With some ink and paper combinations, you might find that printing using digital files that have a different ppi can affect the colors in the print, in which case you would always want to resample your images so the ppi of the file you sent to the printer was a standard 360 or 480 or whatever works for you. I haven't found color shifts with different ppis to be a problem with my images.

I recommend scanning your film at the highest optical ppi of your scanner, up to around 5000 ppi (4000 ppi with the Nikon 4000 and 8000 and also the Polaroid Sprintscan 120, 5760 ppi or higher with the Imacon scanners and 35mm film), then color correcting this large master file. You can always downsample the master file for smaller uses. If you have the option of scanning or capturing at 12, 14, or 16 bits per channel and saving all that information in your file, you will be able to do more with that information color correcting in Photoshop CS.

Chapter 16: Image Resolution, Scanning, Digital Capture, and Histograms

If you scan a file for output to a film recorder, such as the Kodak LVT (Light Valve Technology) or Cymbolic Sciences' LightJet 2000, remember that they require a very high ppi. If you want the output to have the same quality as original film, the ppi can be around 2000 or more. Outputting a 4x5 RGB transparency at 2,000 ppi requires a file size of (4x2000) x (5x2000) x 3, or 240,000,000 bytes. For film recorders, the ppi of the file needs to match the maximum dpi of the film recorder for optimal quality. If you don't have a file that large, you may still be happy with the film recorder output—you should ask your service bureau for their recommendations.

If you have trouble remembering formulas and don't want to bother with a calculator, there is an easy way to calculate the file size you will need: by using the New command in Photoshop. Choose File/New, and then enter the width and height dimensions in inches for the largest size you expect to print the image you are scanning. Based on the current discussion, set the Resolution in pixels/inch to match what you will need for your line screen or printer resolution. Now set the mode to Grayscale, RGB, or CMYK, according to the type of scan. The Image Size that shows up at the right of the dialog box is the size in megabytes that you should make your scan. Now you can cancel from this dialog box; Photoshop has done the calculation for you. If the scan you are making will be 16 bits per channel, then change the bit depth pop-up to 16 bits as shown in the illustration on this page.

If you scan small files, usually measured in pixel dimensions, for Web sites or multimedia applications, you often can get better results if you scan a simple factor larger in each dimension. I did some Web images where the final spec for the GIF file size was 180x144 pixels. I scanned the files at 720x576 and did all my color corrections and masking at that larger, more detailed size. One of the final steps before creating the GIF files was to scale the corrected and sharpened files to 25% of the larger size. This 25% scale factor is a simple ratio that allows for very accurate scaling.

If you need some digital files to prototype a project, you don't need to start with the large scans we describe here. I find that RGB scans of about four megabytes usually provide plenty of screen detail for prototyping. When you decide on the final dimensions for the images in your project or printed piece, you can do a final scan for the intended output device at those final dimensions. When you get a big final scan, archive the original digital file as it was scanned and use copies of it to do color corrections, color separations, and crops, so that you can go back to the original if you make a mistake. Happy scanning!

EVALUATING HISTOGRAMS TO MAKE BETTER SCANS AND FINAL IMAGES

Now that you know how big to make a scan or capture, you need to know how to make a better scan or capture using Histograms. The key to

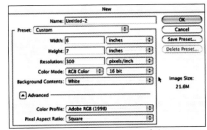

Use File/New to calculate the size of the scan you will need. Notice that Photoshop CS now has a Preset sizes pop-up in the New dialog as well as an Advanced area allowing you to set the profile and Pixel Aspect Ratio, usually Square, of the new file. Just to the right of Color Mode is the Bit Depth pop-up, which is set to 16 bit here.

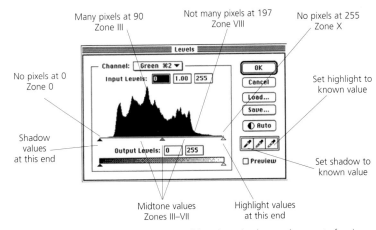

A histogram, like the one in this older Layers dialog above, is a bar graph you get of an image when you look at it in Photoshop's Levels dialog or the new Histogram palette or in various scanner software interfaces. For more information on Levels and histograms, turn to Chapter 19: "Overall Color Correction," where we furnish a detailed introduction to Levels. Also refer to Chapter 13: "Digital Imaging and the Zone System," to see how histograms relate to traditional photography and light.

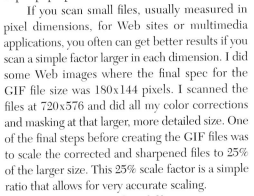

The new Histogram palette with an image that has lots of dark values. Click and drag across an area (blue) to see info on that range of values.

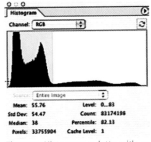

A histogram that has a full range of values. The shape of histograms in the midtone area, not the extreme highlights or shadows, is different for each image depending on ranges of its tonal values.

189

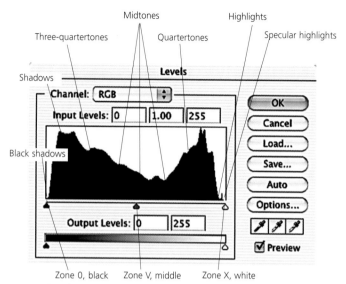

Here is a diagram showing what the different parts of a histogram refer to.

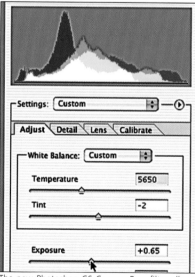

The new Photoshop CS Camera Raw filter allows you to adjust the histogram of a raw digital camera file to optimize it before converting the file into a normal RGB format. See Chapter 10: "Digital Cameras and Camera Raw," for more info on this.

these techniques is learning how to use the histogram displays in scanner software, built into a digital camera, or in Levels, and the Histogram palette to evaluate initial scans and captures as well as your image as you improve it during the color correction process.

A *histogram* is a bar graph of the samples of each possible setting in the 0 to 255 range in the entire image. This range may actually be a 0 to 32,768 range when working with 16-bit images. The diagrams here show you some of the useful information that a histogram can provide. When you have normal subject material, the best possible circumstance is to have an original image, transparency, or negative that has a good exposure of the subject matter and shows a full range of values from very dark to very bright and some detail in all areas. Chapter 13: "Digital Imaging and the Zone System," tells you how to create a high-quality exposure with a camera. If you have a high-quality image that contains values in all zones and has been scanned or captured correctly, you often see a histogram like the one shown to the left.

When you photograph a normal full brightness range scene, you should aim to get a scan or digital capture that has a full range of the values present in the original. For a typical image, you want a histogram that has similar traits to the one above.

SCANNING OR CAPTURING SHADOWS AND HIGHLIGHTS

When you photograph or capture an image and then later scan it, there are several areas in which you need to be careful what values you obtain. There can be places within the image that are totally black. These should occur only if the original has areas that are totally black (*black shadows*, Zone 0). Then there are the regular shadows, which are the darkest places in the image that still show texture or detail when printed (Zones I and II). On the other end of the spectrum are specular highlights, which are areas in the original that are totally white, such as the reflection of the sun in the chrome bumper of a car (Zone X). Next, there are regular highlights, the brightest areas of the image where you still want to see some texture or detail (Zones VIII and IX). When you photograph the image, you need to be aware of the dynamic range of your film or digital camera, which is the amount of brightness variance it can capture. If your film or digital camera does not have enough dynamic range to capture all the highlights and shadows in a scene, it can sometimes help to bracket exposures. One exposure would get all the shadow information and a second exposure would get all the highlight information. When the camera is on a tripod, it is possible to combine these two images with Photoshop to get a full range of values.

To some extent, we can call everything between the regular highlight and shadow areas *midtones*. At the dark end of the midtones, are the *three-quartertones* (shadow areas where you can see a fair amount of detail) and at the bright end of the midtones, the *quartertones* (highlight areas where you should also be able to see a fair amount of detail).

ADJUSTING THE SCANNER TO GET THE RIGHT VALUES

When you do a scan or correct a digital capture, the values that you want to obtain for the shadows and the highlights may depend on the type of output device you are directing the final image toward. If you are not sure of the output device or

Chapter 16: Image Resolution, Scanning, Digital Capture, and Histograms

if you might be using different output devices, the highlights (Zone IX) should have a value in the range of 245–250 and the shadows (Zone I) should have a value in the range of 5–10. With an original image that has a full range of colors in each of the Red, Green, and Blue channels, you need to adjust the scanner or Camera Raw filter to get these types of

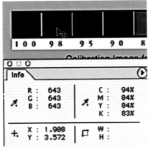
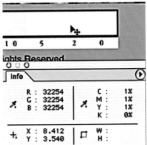
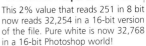
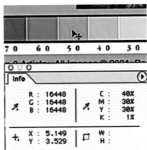

After converting my calibration image to 16 bit, this value that did read 5 in 8 bit now reads 643. Pure black is still 0!

This 50% value that reads 128 in 8 bit now reads 16,448 in a 16-bit version of the file.

This 2% value that reads 251 in 8 bit now reads 32,254 in a 16-bit version of the file. Pure white is now 32,768 in a 16-bit Photoshop world!

8-bit highlight and shadow values. With 16-bit files, you can choose Show 16-bit values in the palette options for the Info palette and you'll get quite different numbers. The 5 to 10 range above would be 643-1,300 or so. See the illustration above for a comparison of 8-bit versus 16-bit values. If you get the highlight and shadow values correct, the values of the quartertones, midtones, and three-quartertones usually fall between these endpoint shadow and highlight values. With this complete scan, you can always adjust the image in Photoshop to get different highlight, midtone, and shadow values, as well as different brightness and contrast, and you will know that you started with all the information from the scanner or digital camera. This is why many digital cameras and most scanner software include a histogram display of the file. I usually start out doing my scans or Camera Raw adjustments with the normal default settings. Some scanners allow you to add a curve or histogram display that adjusts the image as you scan it. If the scanner preview is too light or dark or the contrast is way off, I might use a curve or histogram in the scanner software to fix this. My objective with most scanners, though, is to get all the information out of the film without throwing any of it away. When the file you are saving is an 8-bit per channel file, the scanner software will then have to decide how to convert the 12 to 16 bits of information the scanner is actually getting down to 8 bits per channel in the file that will be saved. When you are doing 8-bit scans, it is very important to use the settings in the scanner software to optimize how the scanner converts from the higher bit depth down to 8 bits. With 16-bit scans, you can make most of these decisions later in Photoshop, which gives you more control.

Scanning up to 16 Bits Per Color Per Pixel

Most scanners these days scan a lot more than 8 bits of information per color per pixel. The scanner gets this information out of the film and then, often by default, the scanner software uses a curve or other scanner settings to reduce this down to 8 bits per pixel when it gives it to you in Photoshop. If you later decide you are not happy with the 8 bits of information you got, you will have to rescan the image to get a different set of values. For example, the scanner may actually pull more shadow range information from the film but, due to the fact that 8-bit files are limited to a total of 256 tones per color, the scanner software throws out a lot of this shadow info when it reduces the file to 8 bits. Because Photoshop CS now has full support for working with files that have more than 8 bits per color, it is much better to open into Photoshop all the information the scanner gets from the film before the scanner software reduces it down to 8 bits. That way you can save this extra info on disk and modify it many different ways without having to rescan the image. Photoshop CS now allows you to work with up to 16 bits of information per channel using almost all of its tools, including Layers and Adjustment layers. Most scanners these

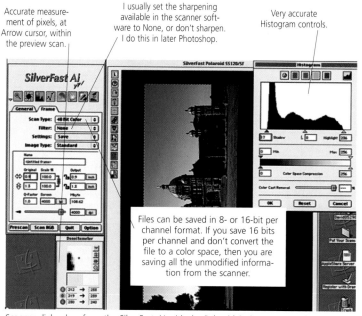

Accurate measurement of pixels, at Arrow cursor, within the preview scan.

I usually set the sharpening available in the scanner software to None, or don't sharpen. I do this in later Photoshop.

Very accurate Histogram controls.

Files can be saved in 8- or 16-bit per channel format. If you save 16 bits per channel and don't convert the file to a color space, then you are saving all the unmodified information from the scanner.

Scanner dialog box from the SilverFast AI with the Polaroid Sprintscan 120. This is a good scanner interface because you can create the cropping box in the prescan window in the center, and set its dimensions and its dpi independent of each other. You can also see accurate histograms, like those shown here, and measure pixel values. SilverFast is quality scanner software that is available for a variety of scanners; allowing you to switch to a different scanner without relearning the scanner software.

days allow for the saving of files with more than 8-bits per color channel. This is an important feature to check for when buying a scanner to use for high-end color work. I wouldn't purchase a scanner that didn't allow me to save the full information from the the scanner's sensors.

My preference is to save the full bit depth from the scanner into a file and then use the Photoshop Levels, Curves, and Hue/Saturation Adjustment layers, which usually give me more control than the scanner software, to do the adjustments on the 16-bit per channel file. Remember that in Photoshop any image of more than 8-bits per channel will open as 16-bits per channel. The hardware sensors on many scanners actually do whatever they do without much adjustment possible; the software controls in most scanners adjust how the data from the scanner's hardware sensors is converted from 12 up to 16 bits down to 8 bits when the file is saved. Saving the data directly from the scanner's hardware sensors into a 16-bit per channel file allows you to use the more accurate Photoshop tools to readjust that scan as many times as you would like without ever having to rescan the file. This is the strategy that makes the most sense for fine artists and people who want to tweak their images to the max. With many scanners, doing raw scans that don't have scanner software adjustments is actually a lot faster. If your raw scans are really dark or have other serious flaws, you may want to use the scanner software to do some adjustments before saving the scans and then working on them in Photoshop. If you are a service bureau or doing production scans for a magazine or newspaper, then you may want the scanner software to do as much of the work as possible and just give you an 8-bit file you can place and print, maybe even a CMYK file.

SCANNING STEP BY STEP

Whenever I scan in Photoshop, using any scanner, I always use the same simple technique. First I set up the default brightness, contrast, and color balance controls on the scanner. I remove any pre-set curves that would change the contrast of the scan from the scanner setting. I make sure that I set the scanner for the correct type of film. I then do a prescan, which shows me the image in the scanner's preview window. Using the scanner software, I set the crop of the image to scan the area I want to scan, usually the full image. For evaluating the histogram of this scan, it is best if this crop does not include any black or white borders around the edges of the film. In the Silverfast scanner dialog box at the top of this page, the prescan and crop are shown with the image preview in

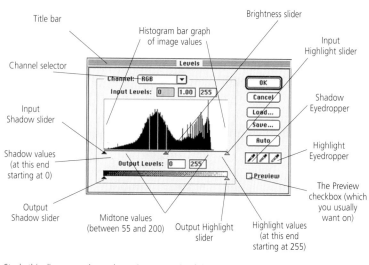

Title bar

Histogram bar graph of image values

Brightness slider

Input Highlight slider

Channel selector

Input Shadow slider

Shadow values (at this end starting at 0)

Shadow Eyedropper

Highlight Eyedropper

Output Shadow slider

Midtone values (between 55 and 200)

Output Highlight slider

Highlight values (at this end starting at 255)

The Preview checkbox (which you usually want on)

Study this diagram to learn the various controls of the Levels tool.

the center. If the scanner software doesn't have an accurate histogram display, I set the scanner to do about a 4MB test scan. I usually don't tell scanners to sharpen the image, because sharpening works best when customized to each final image size, and I can usually get better sharpening with the Photoshop Unsharp Mask filter and the Sharpen Only Edges BH Action. If I get a good focused raw scan from the scanner, I know Photoshop sharpening can do a great job. The next step is to evaluate the histogram based on the scanner software preview or do a 4MB scan at the default settings and look at the histogram in Photoshop. If you have to preview the histogram in Photoshop, it helps to have a scanner that has a Photoshop plug-in allowing it to scan directly into Photoshop.

Next, I evaluate the histogram using the scanner software itself or using the 4Mb scan with Levels or the new Histogram palette in Photoshop. Later in this chapter, I show you sample histograms and explain their problems and how to correct them by adjusting the scanner.

Keep on doing scanner previews or small 4MB scans and adjusting scanner settings each time until you get the best histogram you can for this particular image. Once you get the histogram to look correct in the scanner software or on the small 4MB scan, use the same scanner settings for exposure and color balance, and increase the size of the scan to give you the final number of megabytes that you will need. I suggest doing the final scans at more than 8 bits of information per color channel and saving all that information to your file. The Imacon and Polaroid Sprintscan 120 does scans at 16-bits per channel; the Nikon 4000 and 8000 does them at 14 bits. Both allow you to save all this scan info into your file. Especially when doing 8-bit scans, it is best to get a good-looking histogram from the scanner before you make corrections to the histogram in Photoshop. On the other hand, if your scanner software doesn't have a histogram display, a 16-bit raw scan with no adjustments in the scanner software, other than for film type, is often all you need. That 16-bit file can be corrected quite nicely in Photoshop. If you aren't personally doing the scan, you at least now know how to evaluate the scans you get. When you cannot improve the scan using the scanner itself, the next step is to correct the histogram after the scan using Photoshop's color correction utilities and the Overall Color Correction process.

GETTING THE RIGHT HISTOGRAM

Time and again I am asked in classes, "What is a good histogram?" Let me ask a question in response. If you have three different photographers take a picture of a basket of apples, which would be the "good" photograph: the one that is dark, moody, and mysterious; the one that is light, delicate, and ethereal; or the one that is an accurate representation of a basket of apples in the sunshine? In actuality, any or all of the three may be excellent photographs. Judging a histogram is similar, in that many different histograms could be the "right" histogram for a given photograph, depending on the artist's interpretation of the subject.

COMPARING THE HISTOGRAM TO THE ORIGINAL

The histogram cannot be evaluated separately from the original slide or photo. A good histogram of the original is one that accurately reflects the amount of information in the original. A good histogram of the final output accurately represents the artist's visualization. Never does the adage "garbage in, garbage out" apply more fully than in digital imaging. If you have an original piece of film with no highlight detail, there is absolutely zero possibility that even a high-end scanner can give you something to work

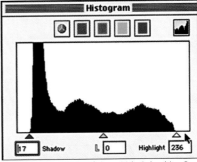

Here is the histogram of the British Columbian Parliament buildings as set up in the Silverfast on the Polaroid Sprintscan 120 with a RAW scan. As scanned, this image is dark and has dark shadows as shown below.

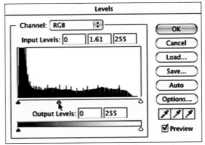

After running the above Levels adjustment layer on the above image, which opens the shadows and the entire image, we have converted the histogram moving the skinny shadow area above to a wider, more spread out shadow shown below. Look on the next page to see the final histogram and image.

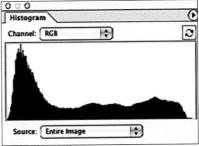

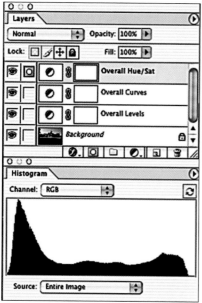

After adding a small s-curve to adjust the contrast and a Hue/Saturation adjustment, we see a final histogram showing what the Overall Color Correction process has done to it. The image below shows what those adjustments, along with sharpening, have done to improve this image.

When opening Photo CD files, you want to navigate to the numbered files within the IMAGES folder within a folder called PHOTO_CD inside your Photo CD icon on your desktop. With Photoshop CS, you have the added advantage of seeing the Photo CD image previews from the File Browser.

with. A good scan of a good original gives you a full range of information that can be manipulated digitally, just as you would manipulate information in the darkroom.

If you start with a very low contrast original, your histogram will have a shortened value scale; that is, the representation of the pixel values will not stretch across all the values from 0 to 255. In general, as you color correct this scan, you force the values of the pixels in the scan to spread out along the luminosity axis all the way from deep shadows (between about 3 and 10) to bright highlights (around 245-250)—notice that we say "in general." If the effect that you wish to achieve is a very low contrast image— say, a photo that appears ghosted back— you may need to do very little adjustment to the histogram. Just as you use the Zone System to set where the values of the actual subject matter will fall on the film, in digital imaging you choose (by manipulating the histogram) where the values of the scan or digital capture will fall in the final output. Therefore, you must view the histogram in the context of the original input and the desired output. You must ask yourself, "What is actually there?" and "What do I want the audience to see?"

MODIFYING WITH LEVELS AND CURVES

Once you get a good scan with a good histogram, you can modify it with Levels and Curves to get your visualization of that image for your final print. If you move the Levels Input Highlight slider to the left, you move your Zone VIII and IX values toward Zone X, brightening the highlights. If you move the Output Highlight slider to the left, you move your Zone X, IX, and VIII values toward Zone IX, VIII, and VII, respectively, dulling the highlights. Similarly, you can use the Shadow sliders to move the zone values around in the shadow parts of the histogram. If you move the Input Brightness slider to the right, you move Zone V values toward Zone IV or III, making the midtones darker and more contrasty. If you move the slider to the left, you move Zone V values toward Zone VI or VII, making the image lighter and brighter.

The Curves tool allows you to make even finer adjustments to values in specific zones. Read Chapter 19: "Overall Color Correction," Chapter 20: "Correcting a Problem Image," and Chapter 24: "Desert Al," to try out these techniques and see how digital imaging gives you more power to realize your vision. As Ansel Adams says in his book *The Negative,* "Much of the creativity in photography lies in the infinite range of choices open to the photographer between attempting a nearly literal representation of the subject and freely interpreting it in highly subjective 'departures from reality.'" Many people think of Adams's prints as straight photos from nature. Actually, Adams did a lot of adjusting with his view camera and in the darkroom to create the visualization of the image that would bring forth his feelings and impressions from the original scene. I believe he would enjoy digital imaging and all the extra control it would give him.

WORKING WITH PHOTO CD IMAGES

Photoshop CS has pretty good built-in support for Kodak Photo CD. First let's talk a little about Photo CD. When you get an image scanned onto Photo CD, there are two possible formats: Regular and Pro Photo CD. Regular Photo CDs have five scans of different sizes of each image. The five pixel dimensions are 192x128, 384x256, 768x512, 1536x1024, and 3072x2048 pixels. For about $1 to $2 a photograph, you get all five sizes of scans of each photograph. The largest of these is an 18MB file, which is useful for a 10"x6.8" print at 300 dpi.

Kodak also offers Pro Photo CD scans. These scans have the same five resolutions as above, plus a sixth resolution that is 4096x6144, or up to 72MB in size—big enough for 11x17 by 300 dpi without resampling up the scans. I have made high quality 16x20 LightJet 5000 prints from 4x5 Pro Photo CD scans. The Pro scans cost about $15 to $20 each, and they seem to be very good as long as you give them a proper original exposure. The Photo CD scan puts your image onto a CD. A regular CD, be it an audio CD, multimedia CD, or whatever, can hold up to 650MB of digital information. The Photo CD scans are compressed so that even if a file is 18MB when you open it, it takes up only 4MB to 6MB of storage on the disk. That means you can get about 100 to 120 regular Photo CD scans on a single CD. The Pro format takes much more disk space; you can only get about 30 of them on a single CD.

When getting Photo CD scans, it is important to find a service bureau that you can trust with your film and also does good work. These days, it is becoming harder to find a service bureau that still supports Photo CD scans. If you had this type of scan made in the past, however, it is still important to know how to open them.

If you have a difficult negative—one that is improperly exposed, too dark, or too light—and you want to get the absolute most out of the scan, you may do better with a high-end drum scan or a scan from an Imacon, Nikon 4000 or 8000, or a Polaroid Sprintscan 120. On the other hand, if the original is a good exposure with a full range of data, and you make sure that you tell the people doing the Photo CD scans the type of film you are sending them, it is possible to get very usable scans.

Bringing Photo CD into Photoshop

Photoshop CS has very good built-in Photo CD support available from the Open dialog that allows me to open Photo CD images in an ICC profile compatible way. To Open a Photo CD file from the File/Open dialog, choose File/Open, then use the Open dialog to navigate to the numbered files within the PHOTO_CD/IMAGES folder on the Photo CD disk. In Photoshop CS, if you use the File Browser to navigate to this folder, you'll see the image previews for all the numbered files in that folder. This makes it much easier to choose the image you want to open. Double-clicking one of the numbered images brings up the Kodak PCD Format dialog to the right. Use the Source Image Profile pop-up to set the ICC profile that describes the "Film Term" used to scan your type of original. There is usually one for E-6 scans and one for Kodachrome scans. Set the Destination profile to RGB or LAB 8- or 16-bit files. Choose which of the five (or six with Pro) Pixel Sizes you want, and then click OK to bring up the image.

Some Scanners I Recommend

I've been comparing scanners a lot over the years, especially in the last three years. There are now several scanners that I can recommend and feel that you will be quite happy with. Most of the readers of this book are interested in scanning film. If you are just scanning 35mm film, I'd recommend the Nikon Super Coolscan 4000, at about $1100, which does great 8- and 16-bit scans of 35mm film at up to 4000 optical dpi. If you need to scan 35mm and 4.5x6, 6x6, 6x7, 6x8, or 6x9, then I'd get the Nikon Super Coolscan 8000, at about $2,400, or the Polaroid Sprintscan 120, at about $1500 (if you can find this good discontinued scanner), which both scan up to 4000 dpi optical with either format. The Imacon Flextight Photo, at about $5000, is also a great scanner for 35mm and 6x sizes. If you want to scan 35mm, 6x6 or 6x7

Here are the controls for the built-in Photo CD Opening software that you access from File/Open or the File Browser. This dialog allows you to specify an ICC profile for the Source Image and the Destination Image. The Source Image specification is an ICC profile that you should get from your Photo CD provider. The name they seem to use for it is a film term, which will describe what the Photo CD scanner will do with a particular type of film. There is usually one film term for Kodachrome and another for E-6. The Destination Image Color Space should be set to your RGB working space or Lab. If you choose RGB 8 bits/channel or RGB 16 bits/channel, then this dialog will convert your file into your RGB working space. With the LAB choices, it seems to open the file without doing a conversion at the end. I have had very good results opening my own and various students' Photo CD files into LAB color. When you have an accurate Source and Destination profile, Photoshop CS appears to give you pretty good results with Photo CD scans.

Here are all the possible sizes for a Pro Photo CD scan. Regular Photo CD scans have all the same sizes except for this biggest 4096x6144 choice.

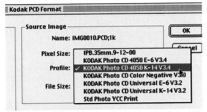

Here we see some typical choices for the Photo CD Source Image Profile. KODAK Photo CD 4050 E-6 V3.4 is the film term I have been using for film processed in E-6, and KODAK Photo CD 4050 K-14 V3.4 is the film term I have been using for Kodachrome. These seem to work especially well when the Image Info Product Type, at the bottom left of the dialog, is set to Film Scanner 405. The Color Negative film term here also seems to work well, but I haven't used it a lot since I shoot mostly transparencies. The version 3.2 E-6 and K-14 film terms seem to be older versions that I have not used lately. These may work better with the older Photo CD scans.

Corrected Photographs and Their Good Histograms
(The shape of each histogram is quite different depending on the image)

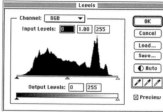

Lots of ¾ tones on the dark parts of the beach. The large number of ¼ tones are probably in the sky and the waves.

Santa Cruz sunset from the boardwalk.

Young Lakes.

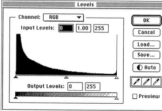

Lots of very dark areas show to the left of the histogram and a few very bright areas in the spike to the right. Even totally black and white are OK in this photo.

The Paris Cafe.

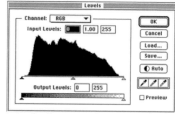

Lots of values everywhere across the full brightness range.

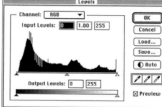

This histogram has lots of dark shadows in the trees and the fence. The spike at the far right is the white buildings.

The Burnley church.

Shells in Costa Rica.

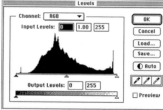

Notice the small spike for the dark shadow areas that are small but so important in the photograph.

Man on the beach at sunset.

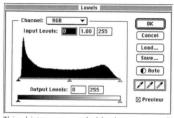

This histogram probably is so smooth because all the objects have a similar range of colors and subtle tones.

or 6x9, and also 4x5 or larger film, a less expensive solution would be to get a Nikon Super Coolscan 4000 for the 35mm and then use the Epson Perfection 3200 flatbed scanner, or another similar flatbed scanner, at about $399, for 6x6 cm and 4x5 inch scans at up to 3200 optical dpi. You could also get the Nikon 8000 and just use the Epson to scan 4x5s. All flatbed scanners I've tested don't focus as sharply on film as dedicated film scanners, but you may find the quality of scans fine for the larger 6x and 4x5 film formats. I use the Polaroid Sprintscan 120 for 35mm and 120 film, then scan 4x5s with my Epson Perfection 2450 (the predecessor to the 3200), which produces beautiful 20x30 prints when sharpened properly! The best desktop scanners I've tested that do all three formats of film are the Imacon Precision II, III, and the newest 848. I have used many Imacon scanners and am very impressed with them. Now that the 848s are out, used Precision IIs and IIIs are considerably cheaper than the $15,000 they were when they first came out. For great 4x5 scans, I borrow my friend's Imacon!

Scanner prices tend to drop quickly when something new and better comes out, so these prices here may be higher than the current ones by the time you read this. For my scanner comparisons I've always scanned, among others, two particular images—both transparencies. The first one is a 35mm Kodachrome 25 photograph of the Santa Cruz beach and boardwalk that was shot from the Santa Cruz pier with a great Canon 50mm lens using my trusty, old Canon F1 mounted on a tripod. This is a very sharp and low-grain photograph that I can print sharply at 25 inches wide on the LightJet5000 when scanning with a Tango drum scanner at 5000 dpi. The second image I used for comparison is a 4x5 inch original of the harbor in Bandon Oregon shot on Kodak Ektachrome with a 4x5 camera using a 210mm Nikor lens. Both of these images are very sharp originals that have a broad range of values going from bright white down to dark black and lots of sharp details.

When looking at scanners, I don't go into great lengths about the details and features of their software. I've found over the years that scanner vendors try to sell their scanners by wowing people with all the features of the scanner's software or the bundle of toys that come with the scanner. Many of these features duplicate things that Photoshop CS can do just as well and often better. If you just get a reasonable raw scan from any scanner and are able to save this as a 16-bit per channel file, then you can use Photoshop's Levels, Curves, and Hue Saturation tools, among others, in a standard way to get great results from many different scanners. If you are saving 8-bit per channel files from the scanner, then you need to rely on the scanner's software not to damage the data, and also to optimize it as it transforms that data from 12-, 14-, or 16-bits per channel that the scanner hardware gets (down to 8 when saving the file). My main philosophy in scanning these days is to get 16-bits per channel of info from the scanner, then do most of my corrections in Photoshop. It certainly helps if you start with a scan that matches the original film fairly closely. Making a custom profile for your scanner using Monaco EZ Color 2.5, the Gretag MacBeth Eye One system, or other software, can often help simplify that step. People who are doing hundreds of batch scans daily may want to use their scanner's software or a custom scanner profile to automate this process.

IMACON FLEXTIGHT SCANNERS

The Imacon FlexTight Precision II, III, and 848 scanners are at the high end of the non-drum scanners. The Precision II can scan a 35mm at 5760 dpi, a 6x6cm at 3200 dpi, and a 4x5 inch at 1800 dpi maximum optical resolution. The newer models do even better. They use a unique mounting system where the film is placed and lined up on one of four thin metal backing holders, one for each film size. After you

The Santa Cruz California beach boardwalk image which is a 35mm original.

The Bandon Oregon harbor image shot with 4x5 inch film.

Here we have the Imacon's general setup controls set for the 1800 dpi maximum optical resolution on 4x5 film. We are set for a 16-bit per channel RGB scan of a transparency. Imacon recommends leaving the Enhanced shadow detail setting on.

An Imacon tip that is not in the manual is that you can tweak the focus calibration on the Imacon using the Descreen function that you see in the middle of this dialog. A setting of zero gives you the focus setting that was saved the last time you calibrated the focus. A setting in the positive or negative direction will either make that focus slightly more blurry or possibly slightly sharper, only if the calibrated focus was off. I found that calibrating the focus with the calibration target that came with the Imacon actually made it worse at times; but I was able to dial directly in on the grain by tweaking this descreen setting until the grain was as in focus as possible.

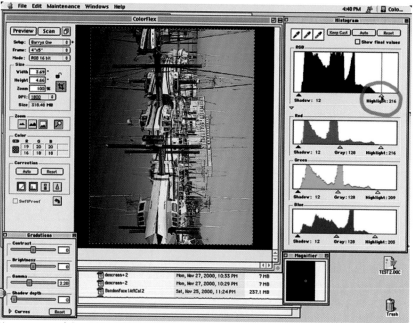

Here are some of the more important controls on the Imacon Precision II scanner using its ColorFlex software. In this 320 meg 48-bit scan of the Bandon 4x5, notice the very exact histograms within Imacon's Histogram dialog to the right. You can keep this dialog up all the time, and the histograms get updated every time you make a new Preview or new crop. As you can see me doing with the cursor in the topmost RGB histogram, you can exactly adjust the highlight and shadow points for RGB, which adjusts all the settings, and you can also adjust each color separately. When doing a 16-bit per channel scan, you can afford to be conservative and adjust the histograms so no values get lost from the highlights or shadows. When I do my scans in this way with a great scanner like the Imacon, Nikon 8000, or Polaroid Sprintscan 120, I probably will never need to scan that piece of film again. That scan got all the useful data out of the film, and I can reinterpret the original 48-bit scan data as many times as I like. You can bring the 48-bit scan into Photoshop and fine tune those highlight and shadow points while zoomed in to look at the highlight and shadow details you care the most about. You can adjust one layer to keep the extreme highlight details and another for the midtones and shadows. These can be combined in Photoshop with layers and masks and, now with Photoshop CS, the entire project can stay in 16 bit! Most images don't require this much work, however.

Using these Imacon ColorSync settings allows you to save the raw unmodified information from the scanner. The file is not tagged with any profile and it is not converted before saving. Once you are in Photoshop, this allows you to use Image/Mode/Assign Profile to retag the original unmodified scan with any profile, like a newer and better custom scanner profile you made even long after the scans were made. Once you tag the file, you can still use Image/Mode/Convert to Profile to convert it to your working space, and you can do the conversion using the Photoshop conversion choices that work best for this image. For the artist who wants to have the most flexibility to tweak their images later, saving without a profile, or tagging with a custom scanner profile and not converting, leaves you with all the options on the original unmodified scan.

line up the film, a hinged magnetic flap is dropped down over the film to hold it in place. A hole is cut in the metal backing holder and also in the magnetic flap, allowing you, and the scanner, to see the film through this holder. After the film is mounted, one frame at a time, the holder is then placed on a light table attached to the front of the scanner. The holder snaps in place and is held in place by magnets. After setting the correct preferences for the type of film you are using and the type of scan you want, pressing the Preview button in the scanner's ColorFlex software creates a preview of the scan, which you then crop as you would like. To actually do the scan, the FlexTight film carrying mechanism bends the holder, and the film within it, so they are wrapped around a drum as they are drawn into the scanner. The drum in this scanner is actually two metal bands that contact the holder on each side and bend the holder and the film into a position so it doesn't buckle and is a consistent distance from the scanner's CCD sensor. It's like bending the film around a real drum scanner drum but with no actual drum surface, just air, where the film passes over the sensor. It is much easier to do than real drum scanning, and yet you get some of the same benefits in the way the film is bent into a known plane of focus. With a real wet-mounted drum scan, there are some benefits to having the film surrounded by liquid since the liquid will fill many scratches and imperfections that might be on the film's surface. The disadvantage to wet mounting, though, is that your film must be cleaned before and after the process. It is best to have clean and dusted film for any scans, but wet-mounted drum scans put your film through more torture, and are more work for the scanner operator, than most other scanning processes.

EPSON PERFECTION 2450 AND 3200

These Epson flatbed scanners allow you to scan printed matter and film formats up to 4x5 in size. The Epson Perfection 3200 has a color bit depth of 48 bits. It allows you to scan at an optical resolution of up to 3200x6400 dpi, although I've found that these unbalanced optical resolutions usually do their best job at the lower balanced number, which would be 3200x3200 dpi. The reason for the imbalance in many flatbed scanners is that the scanner's CCD actually gives you only the lower resolution in one direction, but the stepper motor moving the CCD over the image steps at the higher value. We are getting 3200 dpi from the CCD and 6400 from the stepper motor.

One nice thing about the film holders that come with both Epson scanners was that they didn't cut much from the edges of the image area. I was able to scan the full frame of the 35mm shot and very close to the full frame of the 4x5. I actually

Chapter 16: Image Resolution, Scanning, Digital Capture, and Histograms

have the 2450, but it looks and works very much like the 3200, which came out soon after the 2450. For the money, $399, both these scanners are a great deal. Now you just want to get the 3200. I wouldn't use them for high-end scans of 35mm, but they would be great for web scans or smaller prints for the 13" wide or smaller Epson printers. One the other hand, I have made beautiful 22-by-28 prints from 4x5 film originals scanned at 2400 dpi with the 2450. These images require more color correction work and sharpening than if they were scanned with an Imacon, but the final prints are quite impressive. If you shoot 4x5 and can't afford an Imacon, $399 for a 3200 would be money well spent.

If you don't already have Monaco EZ color 2.5, the $599 professional bundle comes with Monaco, Silverfast scanning software, and a Monaco 4x5 film target for making scanner profiles. These 2450 and 3200 scanners are also good if you need a flatbed to make Monaco EZ color printer profiles. I talk about making profiles in Chapter 15. The Twain software that you see here did not include any histogram options, but the SilverFast software, which also comes in the $599 bundle, does include histogram support. Making a Monaco EZ Color scanner profile will make it easier to have your scan files initially match the colors on your original film.

The problem I've always had when trying to scan film from a flatbed scanner is getting sharp scans. I have not found a flatbed scanner yet that gives scans as sharp as a film scanner with a good focus mechanism. These Epson 2450 and 3200 scanners also fall into that category with the film scans not being as sharp compared to the ones on the Imacon, Nikon scanners, or the Polaroid Sprintscan 120. If you scan a 4x5 piece of film, though, or maybe even a 6x6cm image, you can get prints that will appear quite sharp and acceptable to most people; just use the Sharpen only Edges BH action script described in Chapters 11 and 26. Another difference between most flatbed scanners and the dedicated film scanners we discuss here is the scanning density range. If you have images that have really deep shadow detail that you need to capture in a scan, you'll find that the dedicated film scanners we discuss here generally do a better job.

Another way to use a flatbed scanner when working with 4x5 black-and-white negatives is as follows. Some of my friends in the Corvallis Photo Arts guild are making beautiful black-and-white prints by first making a good 8x10 print in the darkroom from their 4x5 negative, then scanning that print on a flatbed scanner, like the two mentioned above. That scan of a print, which these scanners do a great job of, can then be further improved in Photoshop. Let's say, for example, you shoot a 4x5 original on film and then make an 8x10 very sharp and high quality black-and-white print from that film in the darkroom. Now you could scan that 8x10 print at 2400 dpi on on the above scanners and get a great scan. After improving the digital file in Photoshop, you could then make a great Epson 9600 print with it, without resampling, and at 360 dpi this print would be 53x66 inches in size! If you wanted to output the image at 600 dpi to an imagesetter, this would give you a black-and-white digital negative at 32x40 inches in size, which you could then very easily contact print back onto darkroom paper. My friend, Dave McIntire, has been making wonderful black-and-white prints this way.

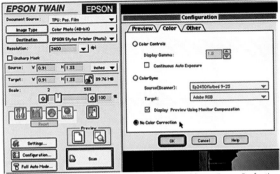

These are the control settings I use to scan film with my Epson Perfection 2450. With the Epson 3200 the controls are similar but you would set the resolution to 3200. Notice that I'm using the Color Photo (48-bit) setting and scanning at 100%. I've clicked on the Configuration button to the left to bring up the dialog on the right. In that dialog I turn on No Color Correction, which gives me a RAW scan. These RAW scans are often dark but you can open up the shadows using Levels and Curves in the Overall Color Correction process, as shown in Chapter 19. This No Color Correction setting is also what you want to use when scanning swatch patterns for making Monaco EZ Color 2.5 printer profiles.

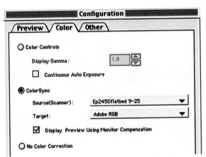

With the Epson Twain software, and with other scanner software, if you want your scans to look like your originals when you first bring them into Photoshop, you should make a profile for your scanner, then assign that profile to your scans. The above ColorSync settings in the Configuration of Epson Twain allow you to assign the Source profile to a scan, then convert it to Adobe RGB upon saving it. Using the above settings, the scanner preview can also be displayed using Monitor Compensation. These scanners actually do a reasonable job of auto color correcting a file, and for people who do a lot of production scans, this may be the way you want to scan. Doing the scans and adjustments as I do manually in Photoshop, as shown in the dialog at the top of the page, gives you ultimate control over highlight and shadow values as well as other decisions, but may make color correction more work.

The Nikon Super Coolscan 4000 and 8000

The Nikon 8000 scans both 35mm and 120 film formats at up to 4000 dpi optical resolution. With a scanning density range of 4.2, the 8000 may be considered a more economical Imacon. The 35mm scans are very sharp, similar to the Imacon's, but maybe just a tad less sharp. They are certainly so close to the Imacon and Photo CD Pro scans that just a small sharpen on the Nikon 8000 35mm scan will make it equal in sharpness to the Imacon or Photo CD Pro. The Imacon Precision II actually scans at 5760 dpi, a little bigger, and the Photo CD Pro scans are at 4000 dpi, like the Nikon 8000 or 4000. The 120 holder on the 8000 has the wonderful feature of clamping the film along both long edges so it can be stretched tight! This is a great film holder and should help solve the problem of 120 film buckling or sagging in the center. The software for 120 size supports 6x4.5, 6x6, 6x7, 6x8, and 6x9 but since it is a long undivided holder, you can actually scan 6x17s by doing two scans and piecing them together later in Photoshop. The NikonScan software that comes with the 8000 and 4000 is certainly the most versatile that I have tested and appears to be on par with that of Imacon. Both these scanners actually allow the intensity of the lamps to be increased in the hope of getting more detail out of very dense film. This software shows updated histograms after all adjustments, has similar adjustments to the other better packages I tested, and also has an additional LCH curve adjustment for doing Luminance, Chroma, and Hue adjustments. Very Cool! NikonScan allows scanning in either 8 bit or 14 bit on either scanner, and you can also make more than one scan pass and average the results together for a more accurate scan. I used the four pass setting for my scans. The 8000 comes with a 35mm slide holder that holds up to five mounted slides at a time, a 35mm strip film holder that can hold two 6-frame strips side by side, and a 120 holder that holds the 120 formats I mentioned.

When scanning images that had very dark shadows, I discovered that if I did raw 16-bit scans, then later opened up the shadows on the 16-bit file using Photoshop Levels, that there were streaks in the dark shadow area within pixels in the range of 0 to 30 or so. My initial impression was that this scanner, with its large dynamic range, was just picking up shadow detail that other shadows didn't get and therefore I could just turn this to black and that would fix it. I played with this idea some but found that when comparing this Nikon 8000 scan to a Photo CD Pro scan of the same image, the Nikon 8000 scan didn't handle these dark shadows as well and left streaks in the shadow area where I actually got useful, very dark detail from the Photo CD Pro scan. The scans from the Polaroid Sprintscan 120 also looked better in these very dark shadow areas. You probably wouldn't notice this unless you scanned an image with large areas that were black or very near black. I discussed this problem with Nikon and they mentioned that if this problem occurs it can be solved by setting the scanner to scan with just one of the three sensors normally used when scanning. Look in the Nikon manual for a description of how do this to cure the problem of streaks in your shadows. I've had emails from several trusted sources and I've tried this myself confirming that using just one sensor does solve this problem.

Using Monaco EZ color 2.5, Gretag EyeOne, or another profiling package to make a custom profile for the scanner will help you to get scans that initially match your original slide. I've tested this with Monaco EZ Color and a Nikon 4000 using the optional 35mm IT8 film target, and it works quite well. Once you make a profile for your film scanner, you want to assign this profile to your scans. If the scanner software won't allow you to attach the profile directly, save the file without a profile. When you open the file into Photoshop CS, use Image/Mode/Assign Profile to assign the profile you made to the files you scan. If you then want to work in a specific color space, like Adobe RGB, choose Image/Mode/Convert to Profile and convert from

Chapter 16: Image Resolution, Scanning, Digital Capture, and Histograms

the scanner profile you just assigned to Adobe RGB. The image on your screen should now look very similar to your original scan when that scan is viewed using a 5000 kelvin viewing box.

THE POLAROID SPRINTSCAN 120

The Polaroid Sprintscan 120 is a great scanner with similar functionality to the Nikon 8000. The Sprintscan 120 will scan 35mm and 120 film at up to 4000 with either 8-bit or 16-bit per channel scans. The Sprintscan 120 comes with a 35mm mounted slide holder that holds up to four slides. It also has a 35mm strip film holder that holds up to a 6-frame strip. The 120 holder and software supports 6x4.5, 6x6, 6x7, and 6x9 formats but doesn't have the mechanism to stretch the film tight across the width as the Nikon 8000 holder has. The scans I have made with the Sprintscan 120 are very similar in sharpness to those of the Nikon 8000 with the Nikon being just a tad sharper. The difference between the two is minimal and could probably be made up with a small Unsharp Mask factor. I use the Sprintscan 120 with the Silverfast scanning software, which is a fully featured package offering similar features

A close-up of a section of the 35mm Santa Cruz boardwalk image scanned at 5760 dpi with the Imacon and zoomed to 100% within Photoshop.

to the Nikon 8000 and Imacon software. The Sprintscan 120 is a very good scanner and compares better to the Nikon scanner in sharpness than the previous Polaroids have compared to their Nikon counterparts. If you get the Sprintscan 120 and want scanning software with a lot of features, make sure you get it with the Silverfast software. I believe Polaroid is no longer making this scanner; it's too bad because I'm very happy with the one I've been using. I heard that B&H photo bought the remaining stock, but I'm not sure if any are still available.

Between the Polaroid Sprintscan 120 and the Nikon 8000, I believe I like the software that comes on the Nikon a bit better, and I also like the Nikon's 120 film holder. Both scanners are a great improvement over what was available at this price in the past, and I'd certainly recommend either scanner. If you get a Polaroid Sprintscan 120 at this point, I'd make sure someone will continue to provide support and service. If you are just doing 35mm scans, then I'd get the Nikon 4000; and if you have to scan a lot of 35mm images, their batch scanning attachment allows you to scan up to 50 slides automatically. A friend of mine who shoots stock and has to do a lot of scans is very happy with his Nikon 4000.

The same area scanned at 4000 dpi with the Nikon 8000 and zoomed to 100% in Photoshop. All images on this page have been color corrected.

Scanned at 5000 dpi with the Lino Tango Drum scanner zoomed to 100% within Photoshop and color corrected within Photoshop.

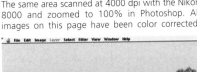

A Photo CD Pro scan done at Palmer's at 4000 dpi zoomed into 100% in Photoshop and color corrected in Photoshop.

The same area scanned at 4000 dpi with the Polaroid Sprintscan 120 and zoomed to 100% in Photoshop, color corrected by me in Photoshop.

Each of the images above was scanned with the respective scanner at the stated dpi without any sharpening turned on in the scanner. The amount of sharpness that you see here is a factor of the focus and scanner optics without software Unsharp Masking. Each of these images can be further sharpened using either the scanner's sharpening software, the Sharpen Only Edges BH action, or Unsharp Mask in Photoshop.

17 YOUR WORKFLOW, STEPS TO CREATE A MASTER IMAGE

Choosing your color working space, the color correction process, archiving the master, and then targeting resampled versions for different uses, sharpening, soft-proofing, device-specific tweaking, and saving final output files.

CHOOSING YOUR MASTER COLOR SPACE

Versions of Photoshop before version 5 assumed the gamut of your RGB working space was the same as the gamut of your monitor. Photoshop 5 allowed you to choose an RGB or Lab workspace that is not limited by the gamut of a particular monitor or device. You need to decide which RGB working space, or the Lab space, you are going to use as your default color working space. To help you in making this decision, you should read Chapter 14: "Color Spaces, Device Characterization, and Color Management." This very important chapter is an overview of the workflow you will use to create master images within your default color working space, usually Adobe RGB, and then color correct those images, archive the final color correct master and, finally, output copies of it to several different device-specific color spaces, like CMYK, the LightJet 5000 color laser printer, the Epson 2200 inkjet printer, a film recorder, and also to the Web.

Here we see the Image/Mode/Convert to Profile dialog showing a conversion from a Polaroid Sprintscan 120 scan, using a custom scanner profile, into the Adobe RGB color space. For images one would usually use the Perceptual Intent, but if you are not happy with that, you could also try Relative Colorimetric and you could try turning on Use Black Point Compensation if you are not happy with the way the shadow areas of the image are converted. If your scanner scans into the Adobe RGB space, or if your scans look good with that space assigned, you may not have to create a custom scanner profile.

GETTING AND CONVERTING YOUR SCAN OR DIGITAL FILE

I create my master digital photographs from scans that are big enough to make the largest print that I might want. In scanning 35mm color transparency film, experimentation has shown that a scan from a good drum scanner of around 5,000 dpi will get all the information from the film. Good scans from an Imacon scanner, the Nikon 4000 & 8000, and the Polaroid Sprintscan 120 also do a pretty good job. For larger film formats, like 4x5 for example, a smaller dpi will often give you as big a file as you will need. Most scanners these days allow you to obtain a file with more than 8 bits of information per channel. If you want to get the most information from the scanner, start with a file of up to 16 bits per channel. If getting your work done as quickly as possible is your goal, then letting the scanner software convert the file down to 8 bits per channel may save you time. When working with a digital camera, one would use either the largest resolution the camera could get or the resolution needed for the job at hand. See Chapter 16: "Image Resolution, Scanning Film, and Histograms," for more information about scanning, resolution, file sizes, and so on. It would then usually be best to use the scanner software or Image/Mode/Convert to Profile to convert the scanner output file from a source ICC profile that describes the color gamut of the scanner into the destination color gamut of your preferred RGB or Lab working space. I usually use the Adobe RGB color space to do my color corrections and create my master images. When I'm working with an image that is exclusively for CMYK presses, I may choose ColorMatch RGB as my RGB working space. I use the word master image because once this image has been color corrected, I should not normally need to color correct it again to be able to print it with the same, or very similar, color on a number of different devices.

COLOR CORRECTING YOUR SCAN OR DIGITAL CAMERA IMAGE

Even after getting a great scan or digital camera image, you usually need to do some further color correction work. The first step in color correction is to work some more on the histograms until you get them as close to perfect as you can given the data available. Before you start the color correction process, make sure that your Photoshop preferences are set up correctly for all the color spaces you will be working in for this project; that is, if your RGB working space is Adobe RGB, but you will print a version of this image in CMYK on a sheet fed press, you need to be sure your prefs are set up correctly for your RGB working space and your CMYK working space for that press and paper. The parts of the preferences that affect color correction and the appearance of images onscreen are all described in Chapter 15: "Photoshop Color Preferences, Monitor, Scanner, and Printer Calibration." You should usually do your color correction in a specific order following the recipe we discuss in this chapter. The next few pages offer an overview of the order and steps you should use in making color corrections and in creating a master image, and your device-specific images. Chapter 19: "Overall Color Correction," goes into much greater detail, as it follows this process step-by-step while working on a photograph.

GETTING SET UP TO COLOR CORRECT

The first step in color correcting is to bring up the Info palette by choosing Window/ Info (F9). The Info palette shows you the RGB and CMYK values of the current location of the Eyedropper tool while in Curves, Levels, Hue/Saturation, or any color correction tool. It also shows you how your color correction is modifying these values by displaying before values on the left of the slash and after values on the right. When you move the cursor into the Levels or Curves dialog boxes, the values in the regular Info palette go away, but you can use a Color Sampler to keep track of values at specific locations you choose or you can use the Color palette to keep track of values at the last location you clicked with the Eyedropper. The Color Sampler tool is grouped with the Eyedropper Tool pop-up menu in the Tools palette. To add a color sampler value to the Info palette, just click on the image using the Color Sampler tool or Shift-click when in the regular Eyedropper tool. The Color Sampler values, up to four per image, show up at the bottom of the Info palette. It is useful to always have the Info palette and, sometimes, the Color palette showing when you are making color corrections. When you click in a particular location with the Eyedropper, the values in that location show up in the Color palette. These values change only when you click in a new location or use Levels, Curves, or Hue/Saturation to make a color adjustment that affects the location where you last clicked. When you use all color correction tools, the color values at all the color sampler locations are updated to reflect any changes in color.

Before you start any color correcting, make a copy of the original scan and color correct the copy, so that you can return to that original if you make any mistakes. You

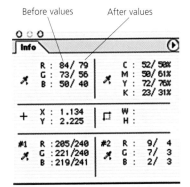

Here we see an Info palette with the standard RGB and CMYK readouts as well as two of the possible four Color Sampler readouts. The Info palette shows you the original values, that you had when entering a tool, on the left of the slash. On the right, after the slash, it displays the values resulting from the adjustments you made with the tool after you entered it this time.

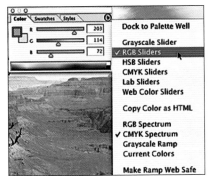

The Color palette shows values at the last place you clicked. You can see how the values at that location change when you make an adjustment using one of the color correction tools. The color bars in the Color palette give you hints as to how adding or subtracting one of the color components will change the color of the last place you clicked. The Color palette can display color bars in grayscale, RGB, HSB, CMYK, Lab, and Web colors. You can use the spectrum at the bottom of this palette to pick a new color by clicking on it. That spectrum can be in the RGB, CMYK, Grayscale ramp, or Current Colors space. Current Colors gives you a ramp from the current foreground color to the current background color.

also want to make sure your original scan is scanned for the biggest possible usage for that image. For example, I make 16x22 prints of my 35mm transparencies. For this type of print, I scan at 16-bit per channel at 4,000 dpi with the Polaroid Sprintscan 120, which gives me about a 112MB file. I do my color corrections on this file, which becomes my master image after it is corrected. I can then resample the file down for smaller prints, this book, and for my Web site. The basic order for a color correction workflow when starting with an RGB scan or capture is as follows:

OVERALL COLOR CORRECTION
(16-Bit Image or 8-Bit Image, Use Adjustment Layers Either Way)

Step 1. Crop any unneeded black or white borders off your image, then go into Levels (Best to use a Levels Adjustment layer. Have Info and Histogram palettes up and positioned out of the way.)

    a. Set the Highlight (using eyedroppers or manually).

    b. Set the Shadow (using eyedroppers or manually).
Note: Highlight and Shadow Color Sampler locations can alternatively be chosen before the Levels step using Threshold. You still need to click on them to force them to the default values using the Levels eyedroppers.

    c. Adjust overall brightness of the image with the middle RGB slider.

    d. Go into the Red, Green, and/or Blue Levels channels and remove color casts, being especially careful that neutral colors stay neutral and don't have a cast.

    e. Turn Levels Preview checkbox on and off as a final check. Save your Levels or Curves settings in a Levels or Curves adjustment layer, so you can change them later without image degradation.

Step 2. If needed, use the RGB channel of Curves to adjust the overall contrast of the image and the Red, Green, or Blue channels to adjust color casts in particular color ranges within the entire image.

Step 3. Use Hue/Saturation to increase or decrease overall saturation. Make adjustments to the hue, saturation, and lightness of specific color areas. (If you don't want to use and save 16-bit adjustment layers, use the Save button in each of Levels, Curves, and Hue/Saturation to remember the settings for that tool. Then use Layer/Flatten Image followed by Image/Mode/8-Bits/Channel to convert 16-bit images to 8–bit.)

COLOR CORRECTION OF SPECIFIC AREAS USING MASKS, SPOTTING

Step 4. Make color changes to specific image areas using Levels, Curves, Hue/Saturation, and other adjustment layers, each with a mask to isolate its target correction area. There can be many of these but try not to change the same image area too often as that could degrade it.

Step 5. Remove spots and scratches from your Master Image background layer, or a background copy, and do any required retouching.

Step 6. Save and archive your Master Image on disk and then to a CD. Make a copy of important CDs and put them at an off-site location.

RESAMPLE A COPY, SHARPEN, CONVERT, FINAL TWEAKS

At this point, you have a color-corrected master RGB or Lab image with all its adjustment layers. You will archive this Master Image and then use a flattened copy of it to make prints. If you need to resample the flattened copy up or down, do this now. After the flattened copy is at the final size, you then do a final sharpening and spotting. You can print sharpened copies of this image directly to RGB printers, or output to an RGB film recorder to make transparencies. If you have a profile for the printer, you would first do Image/Mode/Convert to Profile to convert the copy from your RGB working space into the space for that printer. Sometimes that conversion can be done on the fly within the print dialog. You can use a specific RGB copy for Web and multimedia projects and as the final file if you are using a non-Photoshop method to convert your images to CMYK. You can also use Image/Mode/CMYK to convert an image to CMYK if using Photoshop to get CMYK press output.

Step 7. Resample each copy of the image to a final size, if necessary, then do final sharpening, and after the sharpen, a final spotting.

Step 8. If you are going to output files to a LightJet 5000, Epson 1280, 2200, 7600, or other RGB printer that you have an accurate ICC profile for, use Image/Mode/Convert to Profile, or the Print with Preview dialog, to convert to that printer's RGB color space. When using Image/Mode/Convert to Profile or View/Proof Colors, Photoshop will give you a soft proof of what your converted image will look like in the printer's color space. If you need CMYK, convert to CMYK using Image/Mode/CMYK. This will automatically soft proof the converted file using the simulated CMYK colors on your screen, so make sure your CMYK working space is correct for the press you will be using.

Step 9. After a mode conversion or when using View/Proof Colors, you can make minor color adjustments to specific color areas, while viewing the soft proof, using Hue/Saturation, Curves, Selective Color, and other Adjustment layers with or without a mask.

You should review the previous 9 steps or even post them on your wall until you get this workflow remembered. People who have taken my workshops often forget this and ask me to write it down for them. Here it is written down for you.

OVERALL COLOR CORRECTION DETAILS

USE 8 BITS/CHANNEL OR 16 BITS/CHANNEL FILES

When color correcting your image, it is helpful to do as many of the color correction steps as possible using adjustment layers. Each new step is added as a new adjustment layer on the top of the Layers palette with the bottom layer being your original scan, which remains unmodified as long as you do all your work with adjustment layers. Now with Photoshop CS, you can use Adjustment layers in both 8-bit and 16-bit per channel images. This is a big improvement if you want to be able to save all the information about your images. Whether your scanner or digital camera saves 10 bits, 12 bits, 14 bits, or 16 bits per channel of information, as long as it is over 8 bits per channel, it will show up in Photoshop at Image/Mode/16 Bits/Channel. Even though you can now use almost all of Photoshop's features in 16-bit files, you will find that 16-bit files with adjustment layers take up more than just twice as much memory and disk space as their 8-bit counterparts.

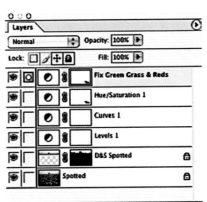

Here is the Layers palette for my file Chumley'sWalk, which we talk about as an example of the sizes for 8-bit files versus 16-bit files.

For example, the 16-bit 4000 dpi original scan of the Chumley'sWalk 35mm image is 111 megs. After adding 4 adjustment layers and a sky only spotting layer, this 16-bit file is now 302 megs. The 8-bit version started out being 55.5 megs, then after adding all the same layers, the final layered file is 130 megs. To add 4 Adjustment layers and a sky spotting layer to the 8-bit file took 74.5 more megs than the original file size, so the final file was 234% larger than the original. To add the same layers to the 16-bit file took 191 more megs than the original file size so the final 16-bit file was 272% larger than the original. If speed and storage are really important then you may find that working with 8-bit files, after doing your initial adjustments in 16-bit, is still the best for you. If keeping all the detail from your 16-bit images is the highest priority, with CS you can now do it all in 16-bit per channel mode!

When working with a 16-bit per channel file, you will usually do your overall color correction steps, steps one through three two pages ago, using 16-bit adjustment layers for Levels, then Curves, then Hue/Saturation in that order. This way you can go back and forth between these steps until you get your histogram optimized. You can keep track of the histogram by using the new Histogram palette, which will show you the cumulative histogram as you add adjustment layers to your image. If you are going to convert your file into 8-bit to save space, then once you are happy with your histogram, double-click on the layer thumbnail for each of Levels, Curves, and Hue/Saturation, then click on the Save button in each to save these settings. This will allow you to save the settings you used for each adjustment layer so you can redo them and change them later if you are not happy with the results. To change them though, you would have to go back to your original, unmodified scan and start over versus just double-clicking and changing an adjustment layer if you leave the file in 16-bit. If you were going to convert to 8-bit, then after saving your settings you'd use Layer/Flatten Image followed by Image/Mode/8 Bits/Channel.

The advantage of doing your first three overall color correction steps on a 16-bit file is that a 16-bit file has up to 65,536 tonal values per color channel, whereas an 8-bit file only has 256 tonal values per channel. You can make many color adjustments and mode conversions, even radical ones, to a 16-bit file and yet, when you convert it down to 8 bits of information, you still get a very accurate 8-bit file with a great histogram. If you make many color changes or mode conversions on 8-bit files, especially when these adjustments are major, the 8-bit file starts to loose details and its histogram starts to have many gaps in it. You need to flatten the image before converting to 8 bits so those adjustment layer changes are done using the full 16 bits of information to allow for more accuracy.

After doing the first three overall color correction steps and getting your histogram correct on a 16-bit per channel file, you can then use Image/Mode/8 Bits/Channel to convert that file to 8 bits per channel for the final, more subtle specific color adjustments. If space is not an issue, you can now also leave the image in 16-bit mode. If you plan to convert the file from Lab to Adobe RGB or from your scanner's RGB space to Adobe RGB or ColorMatch RGB, you might want to do that conversion while still in 16 Bits/Channel space, and then convert down to 8 bits per channel once you are in your final 16-bit working space. That will make it less likely that your 8-bit file will have lost information due to the mode conversion. In Photoshop CS, steps 4 through 8 can now be done in either 16- or 8-bits per channel color, and in either case you should do them using adjustment layers and masks.

STEP 1-A, SETTING THE HIGHLIGHT

Creating a Levels Adjustment layer can be done using Layer/New Adjustment Layer/Levels from the pop-down icon at the bottom of the Layers palette, or by using Command-F2 with ArtistKeys. Within the Levels dialog, you work in Channel RGB, the composite channel, to set the highlight and shadow. The *highlight* is the brightest point in the image where you still want to have texture. Everything brighter than the highlight prints totally white, with no dots. Once the highlight is set, the RGB values here should read somewhere in the range of 240 to 250,

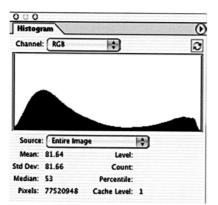

New to Photoshop CS is the Histogram palette (Shift-F9) which allows you to see, while they are being made, how adjustments in the various color correction tools are affecting the histogram of an image. This is a great new tool.

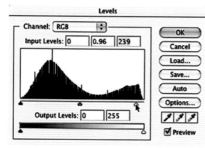

It is often hard to distinguish what point is the brightest on the computer screen. You can find the highlight by holding down the Option key while moving the RGB Highlight slider to the left. The first area to turn white on the screen is usually where you want to look for the highlight. Make sure you move the slider back to 255 when you see where the highlight is. For this to work with Photoshop CS, you need to do it with the Preview checkbox checked.

Chapter 17: Steps to Create a Master Image

depending on your output device. Remember that after you set the highlight, everything brighter than the highlight location will usually print totally white. Setting the highlight also removes color casts from the whole highlight part of your image. You need to set the highlight at a place you want to be white in the end, a place that was white in the original scene as well as at a location you want to print as a neutral value. You want to pick a spot where the detail or texture is just fading but is not completely gone. This usually falls at the brighter end of Zone IX in the Zone System. First Shift-click at the spot where you want to set your highlight; this will place a Color Sampler there and allow you to follow the color values of this spot throughout the entire color correction process...a very useful thing to do. Now, after clicking on the rightmost highlight Eyedropper in the Levels dialog, click at the location where you want to set the highlight (where you just set your Color Sampler), and at the same time, watch how the Info palette shows the values (before and after in RGB and CMYK, or Lab). When you click, the after values to the right of the slash should change to the default preference white point values or very close to those values. Because not all images have a good white point, you can also set the highlight by going into each of the Red, Green, and Blue color channels and moving their Highlight sliders separately. The Highlight slider is the rightmost slider in the top set of three sliders. We'll show you exactly how to find and set these highlights in the step-by-step examples starting with Chapter 19: "Overall Color Correction."

STEP 1-B, SETTING THE SHADOW

Now pick the point where you want to set the shadow. The RGB values here should read between 0 and 8 when you are finished. It should be at a location you want to print with a neutral shadow value. This location would be at the darker end of Zone I in the Zone System. Everything darker than this point usually prints as totally black after you set the shadow. If you want a lot of totally black places in your image, set the shadow at a location that isn't very dark, say 15, 15, 15. Everything darker than that location goes black. If you want a lot of shadow detail in your image, set the shadow at a location that is as close as possible to 0, 0, 0 in RGB. If you Shift-click at the spot where you want to set your shadow, this will place a Color Sampler there and allow you to follow the color values of this spot throughout the entire color correction process. Using the leftmost shadow Eyedropper, click at the location where you want to set the shadow (where you just set your Color Sampler), and at the same time, watch how the Info palette shows the values (before and after in RGB and CMYK, or Lab). When you click, the after values should change to the default preference black point values or very close to those values. Because not all images have a good shadow point, you can also set the shadow by going into each of the Red, Green, and Blue color channels and moving their Shadow sliders separately. The Shadow slider is the leftmost slider in the top set of sliders. We'll show you how to set these in the step-by-step examples starting with Chapter 19: "Overall Color Correction."

These initial RGB highlight and shadow values vary somewhat from image to image. The purpose of setting the white and black is to normalize these values to neutral grays and also to set the endpoints of detail in the reproduction. Some images do not have a good point at which to set the highlight and shadow with the Eyedroppers. See Chapter 20: "Correcting a Problem Image," and Chapter 27: "Bryce Stone Woman," for examples of how to deal with that situation.

STEP 1-C, ADJUSTING THE OVERALL BRIGHTNESS

Use the RGB channel of Levels again for this step. Move the middle slider, in the top set of three sliders, to the right to make the image darker. Move it to the left

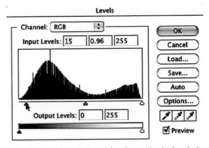

It is often hard to distinguish what point is the darkest on the computer screen. You can find the shadow by holding down the Option key while moving the RGB Shadow slider to the right. The first area to turn black on the screen is where you want to look for the shadow. Make sure you move the slider back to 0 when you see where the shadow is. You need to do this with the Preview checkbox checked.

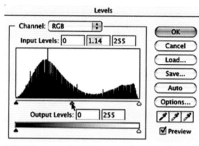

Adjust the overall brightness and contrast by moving the middle slider using Channel RGB.

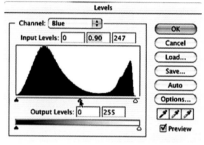

Now deal with color casts by adjusting the middle slider in the color channel that affects the color cast.

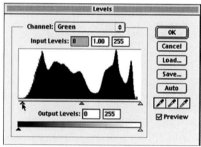

Here we can see the unbalanced values in Color Sampler #2. The green value is greater.

Make the change using the Shadow slider from the Green channel while looking at the values in the Color Sampler in the Info palette.

Now the Color Sampler shows the correction implemented to neutralize the shadow value in green.

to make the image brighter. Move it around until the image has the level of brightness that you want. If the image is too flat or too contrasty, you will adjust that in your next tool by adding a contrast adjustment curve. With an image in Lab color, you'll do all the work we've covered so far using the Lightness channel.

STEP 1-D, ADJUSTING THE OVERALL COLOR CAST

If the overall image seems too green, use the Channel pop-up to go to the Green channel in Levels and move the top-middle slider to the right. This will add magenta to the midpoint values in the image and remove the green cast. Moving it to the left would add green. If the image is too blue, go to the Blue channel and move the middle slider to the right to add yellow to the image. You just need to remember that the Red channel controls red and its complement, cyan; the Green channel, green and magenta; and the Blue channel, blue and yellow. When adjusting an image for color casts, try to remove the worst color cast first and then move on to the lesser ones. You do it in this order because removing one cast will change the appearance of the others. The middle sliders of each channel are going to mostly affect the midtones as well as the quartertones and three-quartertones.

The rightmost Highlight and leftmost Shadow sliders should have already been adjusted correctly when you set the highlight and shadow earlier, but you can always tweak them after setting the middle slider if you need to. If your highlight and shadow Color Sampler positions are no longer neutral (the same value in Red, Green, and Blue), that is a sign that you may want to tweak them. Sometimes you can get a color cast in the highlight or the shadow if the point at which you set the highlight was not a neutral location. Some images do not have neutral locations. Use the Highlight or Shadow sliders for the color channel(s) that are out of adjustment to correct the numbers in the Color palette or Color Sampler. Afterward, you may have to go back to readjust the midtone sliders to slightly adjust the midtone color cast.

You should modify all these corrections in the Levels dialog box as one step. You don't want to click on OK until you complete all these steps. If you choose OK too many times in the Color Adjustment dialog boxes and you are not using adjustment layers, you can degrade the image. You don't want to go into Levels or Curves repeatedly. Do it all in one step if possible, and then go back and tweak it later if you did it with adjustment layers. After you finish all the above color correction steps in Levels, and only then, choose OK in the Levels dialog box. To have the ability to modify your changes over and over again, do this step with an adjustment layer. For hands-on examples using these techniques, see Chapter 19: "Overall Color Correction," Chapter 20: "Correcting a Problem Image," and Chapter 24: "Desert Al." If you find that doing a color shift by moving the middle slider of a color channel in Levels affects the brightness and contrast too much, you can use the Color Balance tool with Preserve Luminosity turned on. This will change the color without changing the brightness or contrast. If you were working in Lab color, you would make these cast changes using the A and B channels and they would not affect brightness or contrast.

STEP-2, ADJUSTING THE OVERALL CONTRAST AND SPECIFIC COLOR RANGES

Use the RGB Channel of Curves for this step with Layer/New Adjustment Layer/Curves. If your image is too flat or too contrasty, Option-click inside the curve graph until you get the graph with four sections each, horizontally and vertically. Place a point at each of the three intersections along the diagonal line going from the bottom left to the top right. To make the image more contrasty, move the top-right point up and to the left and move the bottom-left point down and to the right. This

Chapter 17: Steps to Create a Master Image

creates a curve that looks like an S. To make the image less contrasty, move the top-right point down and to the right and move the bottom-left point up and to the left. This creates a reverse S-Curve. If you need to enhance a specific range of color within the entire image, Option-click within the curve graph until you get the graph with 10 sections each, horizontally and vertically. Go to the color channel that will most affect the color you want to change. This would be the Red channel for red and cyan, the Green channel for green and magenta, and the Blue channel for blue and yellow. Click on the intersection of every graph point along the line going from bottom-left to top-right. This will lock down the curve in each place. Now put the Eye-dropper cursor over the color area in the image you want to modify and, with the mouse button held down, move the cursor over the range of color you want to change. A larger circle will appear on the curve diagram showing you the range of values in that color channel that affect that part of the image you want to change. Remove the lock down points from the graph within that range by clicking on each point and dragging it entirely outside the Curve dialog box. Now click a new point along the diagonal line in the center of that range and drag it up and to the left to add red, green, or blue, or down and to the right to add cyan, magenta, or yellow. Radical curve adjustments over posterize the colors. Choose OK if you are in an adjustment layer, or Save to save your Curve settings, and then OK if you are not in an adjustment layer.

STEP 3, MAKING OVERALL AND SELECTED CHANGES TO HUE, SATURATION, AND LIGHTNESS

You often want to increase the overall saturation of colors using the Hue/Saturation tool, especially if you had to brighten the image in Curves or Levels. Choose Layer/New Adjustment Layer/Hue/Saturation. To increase the overall saturation, move the Saturation slider to the right with Master selected in the Edit pop-up menu. You can also selectively correct color if a certain color range in the image is off. For example, if the reds in the image were too orange, you could make them redder by first selecting Reds from the Edit pop-up and then moving the Hue slider toward the left. This operation would add magenta to only the red areas of the image. This method differs from adding magenta using Levels or Curves because the latter method usually adds magenta to all colors in the image.

When the Red Edit menu item is selected, only the parts of the image that are red have their color changed. If these parts were unsaturated, you could add saturation to just the red items by moving the Saturation slider with Red selected. Similarly, you could add or subtract lightness in the reds. If your image contains different tones of red, and you only want to adjust some of them, you can use the Eyedroppers in the Hue/Saturation dialog to fine-tune the range of reds you want to adjust by adding to the default red tones using the +Eyedropper tool, and subtracting from the default red tones using the –Eyedropper tool. Choose OK if you are in an adjustment layer. If you are not in an adjustment layer, then click Save to save your Hue/Saturation settings, and then choose OK. The Color Range, Replace Color, and Selective Color tools are also good choices which you could for tweaking colors.

After making the Levels, Curves, and Hue/Saturation Adjustment Layers, you can double-click on the Layer thumbnail of any step and go back and tweak that adjustment. As you are making these adjustments, you should keep track of the Histogram palette to make sure your histogram is not being degraded by loosing shadow or highlight information. A vertical bar at either end of the histogram is a sign that highlight or shadow info has been lost. We'll show you more about how to check and correct the histogram in Chapters 19 and 20.

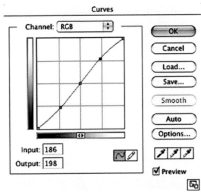

Here we see an S-Curve that would increase the contrast in the file it was applied to.

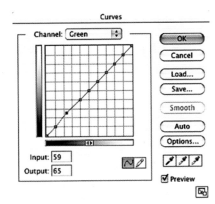

Here we see a lock down curve to pop the greens in the three-quartertones.

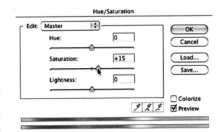

Using Hue/Saturation with Edit set to Master to saturate all the colors by +15.

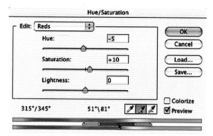

Using Hue/Saturation with Edit set to Red to saturate just the Reds by an additional +10. We have also moved the Hue slider to the left, which adds magenta to the Reds. Additionally, we have used the Eyedropper plus tool and dragged over some reddish-orange colors in the image. This has increased Photoshop's definition of what is red, as you can see where the black cursor icon is, so now some of the reddish-orange colors will also be more saturated and get some magenta added to them. Using the Eyedropper plus and Eyedropper minus tools within Hue/Saturation can be a very powerful color correction technique.

If you are working on a 16-bit per channel image at this point, you can continue to do the entire project in 16-bit to keep all the information. Now would be a good time to use File/Save or Save As to save what you have done so far. If you want to convert to 8-bit to save space, now is a good time to do that. To convert to 8-bit, first choose Layer/Flatten Image to create a single 16-bit layer with all your adjustments integrated. Then choose Image/Mode/8 Bits/Channel to convert the file to 8-bit. If you want to keep your initial 16-bit adjustments, then save the 8-bit version using a different name, otherwise save on top of the 16-bit version to save space.

COLOR CORRECTING SPECIFIC AREA DETAILS

STEP 4, MAKING COLOR CHANGES TO ISOLATED AREAS USING SELECTIONS, LAYER MASKS, AND ADJUSTMENT LAYERS ALONG WITH LEVELS, CURVES, AND HUE/SATURATION

The color corrections I have discussed so far have been overall color corrections to an entire image. If a particular area is the wrong color, too light or too dark, too flat or too contrasty, you now should make a selection of that area using Photoshop's selection and masking tools. Then you may want to adjust the colors in that area using Levels, Curves, Hue/Saturation, Color Balance, etc., but in all cases doing this with an adjustment layer gives you the ability to change the correction or the mask, which determines exactly what gets corrected.

When you have a selection on the screen, creating an adjustment layer at that point automatically sets up that selection as the layer mask for that adjustment layer, so only the selected part is adjusted. The selection's marching ants go away and are replaced by white in that adjustment layer's layer mask. After making the adjustment, you can later go back and tweak the mask, and thus exactly what is being adjusted, by using the painting tools. Painting with white adds to the adjusted area and painting with black takes away from it. You have much more fine control when painting in a mask using the painting tools than you do when editing a selection using the selection tools. You often want to use the selection tools to create an initial rough selection, then edit the corresponding mask with the painting tools to make your selection perfect. Each new adjustment layer will tweak a particular part of the image and is usually added to the top of all the other adjustment layers you have created so far.

Go through Chapter 20: "Correcting a Problem Image," Chapter 27: "Bryce Stone Woman," and Chapter 24: "Desert Al," for a complete description and some hands-on practice in using these techniques to change isolated areas.

STEP 5, SPOTTING THE IMAGE

You will want to clean up your Master Image by removing spots, scratches, and other blemishes with either the Rubber Stamp tool, the Healing brush, or the Dust and Scratches filter. You will usually do this to the bottom layer in your Layers palette, which will be your original scan. If you have to do some complicated retouching, you can do that on a copy of your original scan layer or a section of your original scan layer. That way, if you make a mistake, you won't have damaged your original scan layer. You can also merge all your layers into a new "Merged" layer at the top of all your existing layers and then spot that. If you spot the original scan at the bottom of the Layers palette, you won't need to respot if you later change any of your adjustment layers. You save time by spotting the Master Image because you only do that once; then the spots that have to be removed after you sharpen each resampled version later will be a lot fewer and often none. Many of the step-by-step examples show you how to spot using different techniques.

You can use Image/Duplicate Image to make onscreen copies of your Master Image, one for each usage. Choose Duplicate Merged Layers Only to compress all the layers in the master into just one layer in the duplicate.

Chapter 17: Steps to Create a Master Image

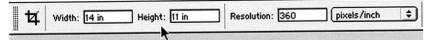

The Image Size dialog in the illustration to the right does not allow you to crop and resample your image at the same time. To do that, you want to use the Cropping tool with Fixed Target Sizes, as shown here.

STEP 6, SAVING YOUR MASTER IMAGE

After spotting, your Master Image is ready to be saved and archived. You can now use this image for any future projects or prints to RGB printers, film recorders, CMYK print jobs, Web, or for multimedia use. For any of these uses, you will make a flattened copy of the master, rename it, resample it (possibly) to the size needed, and convert it to the format needed for this particular purpose.

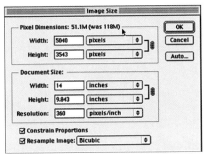

Make sure the image Width, Height, and Resolution are set correctly for your layout dimensions and line screen when printing on a press. You don't want Quark or InDesign to resample your image. For best results, place it into other apps at 100%. For Web images, change the inches pop-up to pixels before typing in your pixel dimensions.

RESAMPLE COPY, SHARPEN, CONVERT, TWEAK DETAILS

STEP 7-A, MAKING RESAMPLED COPIES FOR EACH USAGE

With your Master Image open, you can choose Image/Duplicate and turn on Duplicate Merged Layers Only to make a nonlayered copy of the master that is already open and on your screen. After you have a flattened copy on the screen, you can choose Image/Image Size, or use the Crop tool with a fixed Height, Width, and Resolution to resample the image to the size and resolution you need for this particular project. See Chapter 16: "Image Resolution, Scanning Film, and Digital Cameras," or Chapter 19: "Overall Color Correction," to learn the details of this resampling process. Just remember that you will get better results when you take a big image and sample it down, than if you take a small image and sample it up. If you had already scanned your original at 4,000 to 5,000 dpi from film, or if your original is the highest resolution from your digital camera, then sampling up is certainly a viable choice. When you scan film with a good scanner at more than 5,000 dpi of optical resolution, it is unlikely you will get any more real information. For my photography art prints on Epson printers, I rarely resample my original 4,000 dpi scans. In Image Size I turn off Resample Image, then I just change the Width, Height, and Resolution to get the print size I want. This way I only have to sharpen once since I'm not changing the number of pixels in the image.

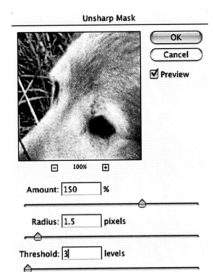

Here we see the Unsharp Mask filter dialog with its three parameters of Amount, Radius, and Threshold.

STEP 7-B, SHARPENING THE IMAGE

As a final step, on each resampled version of your image, you will want to use Filter/Sharpen/Unsharp Mask (F4) to sharpen the image. You will have to run some tests to determine the type and amount of sharpening that works best for your different categories of images and output devices.

Let me explain the three parameters of Unsharp Mask.

AMOUNT: Controls the overall amount of sharpening. When you compare sharpening effects, use Command-Option-0 to zoom the image to 100% so you can see all the detail. Compare different copies of the same image area using different settings for Amount and you will notice that the larger the number, the sharper the image becomes, but at some point the grain gets enhanced also.

RADIUS: Photoshop sharpens an image by looking for edges in the photograph and enhancing those edges by darkening one side of the edge and lightening the other side. *Edges* are sharp color or contrast changes in an image. The Radius setting in the Unsharp Mask filter controls the width of pixels along an edge that are modified when you sharpen the image. Again, try running the filter with different settings, as well as comparing two copies of the same image side by side.

THRESHOLD: When you set the Threshold to 0, everything in the image becomes a candidate edge for getting sharpened. At a setting of 0, an image can easily be made to look too grainy by sharpening because even the changes caused by the grain will get sharpened and increased, which is especially noticeable in skies and clouds. If you set the Threshold to 10, Photoshop finds and sharpens an edge only if there is a difference of at least 10 points (in the range from 0 to 255) in the pixel values along that edge. Areas like clouds will not be sharpened and the grain there will not be increased. The larger the value you give to the Threshold setting, the more contrasty an edge must be before it is sharpened, and the more you are just sharpening the edges. I usually set my Threshold values between 3 and 5 depending on the image. When you find the correct Unsharp Mask values, use them to sharpen the entire file. See Chapter 20: "Correcting a Problem Image," for a detailed, hands-on example of using Unsharp Mask. For more control over your sharpening, you can also use the Sharpen Only Edges BH action from the ArtistKeys actions that come on the *Photoshop CS Artistry* CD. This action builds an edge mask so only the parts of the image that really need sharpening are affected by the Sharpen filter. This allows you to sharpen those areas even more and yet not get unwanted grain effects in skies, clouds, and other areas that don't improve when sharpened. Using this filter is described in Chapter 26: "Combining Bracketed Photos."

STEP 8, CONVERTING FROM YOUR RGB OR LAB WORKING SPACE TO THE FINAL OUTPUT COLOR SPACE

If you are working on an image for output to an RGB printer, like the LightJet 5000 or the Epson Stylist Photo 1280, 2200, or 7600, you can leave the resampled and sharpened image in your RGB or Lab workspace and still get a soft proof on the screen of how the image will look when printed to that output device. To do this, you choose View/Proof Setup/Custom and pick the ICC profile for your printer from the Profile pop-up menu. The Rendering Intent will usually be Perceptual or Relative Colorimetric, you can try each one while looking at the soft proof of the image on your screen. After choosing OK from this dialog, Command-Y will toggle between showing you a soft proof of the image as it will look on this printer, and as it looks in your working space. See the "Getting Accurate Onscreen Soft Proofs of Your Output to RGB Printers, CMYK Printers, and Presses" section of Chapter 15: "Photoshop Color Preferences, Monitor, Scanner, and Printer Calibration," for more information on the best ways to set this up. This is a very useful feature, check it out!

If this will be a CMYK-specific version of your image, make sure that your CMYK preferences are set up correctly for the type of press and paper you will be using; then choose Image/Mode/CMYK Color to convert the image from RGB or Lab to CMYK. If you don't correct the RGB or Lab file before converting to CMYK, Photoshop could create the Black channel on your CMYK file incorrectly. Unless your scans are done directly into CMYK, you should do overall color correction on your master RGB or Lab file before converting to CMYK. Scans made by high-end scanners in CMYK should already have had overall color correction done for you by the trained scanner operator.

STEP 9, MAKING FINAL SUBTLE COLOR ADJUSTMENTS

When you are comparing the image on your screen to a print from a particular RGB printer, you want to compare the Lab or RGB version of the image onscreen with Proof Setup set to the ICC profile for your printer. There are colors that will show up on an RGB monitor, and in your RGB or Lab workspace, that may not be printable with your RGB printer. Proof Setup should display these out of gamut col-

Here we are using Image/Mode/Convert to Profile to convert a file from Adobe RGB to the ICC profile for an Epson 9600 printer. Depending on the image, set the Intent to either Perceptual or Relative Colorimetric. I usually leave Use Dither on and Use Black Point Compensation off. If you don't like the way your blacks look, try turning Use Black Point Compensation on.

Chapter 17: Steps to Create a Master Image

ors more like they will print on your printer. When comparing a CMYK print proof with the image onscreen, you want to be looking at the CMYK version of the image; in which case, Photoshop automatically soft-proofs the CMYK colors on the screen, based on the ICC profile stored within the CMYK file. If you are working with CMYK files that don't have embedded ICC profiles, files that may have been separated elsewhere, you need to be sure that your CMYK working space preference values are compatible with the type of CMYK separation you have or the file may not be displayed correctly on the screen.

Because the CMYK or RGB soft proof image onscreen more closely matches the image on a press or your printer than your Master RGB Image, you may need to do final subtle color corrections in CMYK or RGB soft proof mode. For some images, the CMYK or RGB soft proof version will look the same on the screen as the Master RGB version, depending on the colors in the image and the gamut of your output device. Certain colors, for example bright, saturated red or deep blue, may get duller or change when you convert to CMYK. Also, the shadow or highlight areas may require a slight modification to ensure the correct balance is achieved in the neutral areas. To add contrast to CMYK images, you may want to run an S-Curve or increase the black midtone values. You can make these final color adjustments using Curves, Levels, Hue/Saturation, Replace Color, or Selective Color. See Chapter 11: "Automating with Actions and Scripts," for a discussion of the actions we use when processing all the CMYK files for our books.

If this version of the image is destined for the Web, you might want to use Image/Mode/Convert to Profile to convert the image from your regular RGB or Lab working space to the sRGB space. Now you should see an accurate example of how this image will display on the average PC monitor. If you save this copy of the file at this point, it will now be tagged with sRGB, which may be best for a Web image for general industry consumption.

SAVING THE DEVICE-SPECIFIC IMAGE

For output to a press or imagesetter, especially if printing directly from Photoshop, you might need to go into File/Print with Preview to adjust some of the settings. You should talk to the print shop or service bureau doing the output and ask them if you need to set Negative or Emulsion Down. Also, ask the service bureau how to set the Halftone Screens. Often, they will want you to not set either value in Photoshop because they will set them using Quark, the imagesetter, or platemaker. Also ask the service bureau whether they want you to save the images as Photoshop EPS, use one of the Photoshop DCS options, use CMYK TIFF, or use some other format because this varies according to the type of output device that particular bureau uses. For our books, which we lay out in Quark, we usually use the CMYK TIFF format, which works well and is simple and compact to save in.

If you save an image in Photoshop EPS format for input into Quark, you should check the Include Halftone Screen box only if you set up the screen angles and frequencies using the Screens dialog box (which you access from the File/Print with Preview dialog box). If the screens are going to be set in Quark, leave the Include Halftone Screen checkbox unchecked. Good luck with your color. If you have any questions or comments about these techniques, please email us at www.maxart.com or reach us via our contact information at the end of the book.

If you are outputting to an RGB printer, like an Epson printer, check the print dialog information on page 170 to make sure your print dialogs are set up correctly. This can make a big difference in the quality of your prints.

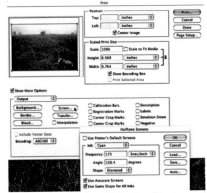

The Photoshop CS Print with Preview dialog box and its Halftone Screens dialog box, which you can access when Show More Options is set to Output. When separating files for use on a press, check with your service bureau for how to set the screens and other settings here. They usually want you to leave these unset in Photoshop as they are often planning to set them in Quark or some other layout application at the print shop.

If you set this pop-up menu, located at the bottom left of your Photoshop windows, to Document Profile, then the profile that is assigned to your document will be displayed to the left of the pop-up menu. The profile displayed above is of a CMYK document.

213

OVERALL COLOR CORRECTION, SELECTION AND LAYER TECHNIQUES

MAKE DETAILED COLOR SELECTIONS AND MASKS

COLOR MATCH IMAGES

OVERALL COLOR CORRECTION

REPLACE COLOR, COLOR RANGE, AND SELECTIVE COLOR

USING 16-BIT LAYERS, SHARPENING, AND SPOTTING

HISTOGRAM PALETTE, CORRECTING A PROBLEM IMAGE

Garibaldi Harbor is just north of Tillamook on the Oregon coast. It's one of my favorite photographic stops which we usually visit during our Oregon Coast advanced workshops. This image was shot with my 90mm and Gowland 4x5 using Fuji Velvia film.

18 HANDS-ON SESSION: The Colony Composite

A simple composite offers opportunities to work with different selection tools and techniques, the Channels palette, and several layers.

STEP 1: The original Colony Colors file that will serve as the background for this composite.

STEP 1: The initial portion of the selection was made by drawing freehand with the Lasso, but now I'm using the Option key as well to draw straight lines.

Making selections is one of the most basic Photoshop tasks, but also one of the most important. Often the difference between work that looks polished and work that looks hack is dependent upon how well you make your selections. In this simple composite we use several selection methods to isolate parts of images that we want to use. We'll show you a couple of different ways to achieve the same result. With practice, you'll find which tools you're most comfortable with and which give you the type of accuracy and flexibility you need. If you haven't already done so, you might want to read Chapter 6: "Selections, Masks, and Channels," before starting this exercise.

PREPARE THE BACKGROUND

STEP 1: You need to make some minor color adjustments to the file you'll be using as the background for your composite. **Open the ColonyColors.psd file from the Colony Composite folder.** The window in the upper right of the image has a reflection that's a bright yellow bordering on yellow-green. You're going to make a quick selection and use Hue/Saturation to warm that area a bit. In most of the exercises in this book we suggest methods of working that allow you to easily make changes down the line. However, this is your first real hands-on lesson and we're going to do parts of it more simply than we normally would. The Lasso tool is one of the primary selection tools for working with non-geometric shapes. It lets you draw a freehand selection around an area. You can also use the Lasso tool to draw straight line segments of a selection by holding down the Option key and clicking rather than dragging. Let's try it on this reflection.

Type L to select the Lasso tool and in the Options bar set its feather to 2. The feather will give a gradual transition when you make the color adjustment. You don't need the small strip on the left side of the window pane, just the major area on the right, so start your selection at the upper left of the large yellow area and move down the left side. Draw freehand style until you come to the bottom of the reflection. Now, without letting go of the mouse button, hold down the Option key. Once the Option key is down, let go of the mouse button and move the mouse. Notice the straight line that follows the mouse but is not creating the selection yet. Move the mouse to the lower point of the reflection and click the mouse button. This attaches or anchors a point for your selection. Still holding the Option button but letting go of the mouse button, move the mouse again. Another straight line segment

216

is waiting to be placed. Instead of using another straight line at this point, though, you want to draw freehand again to get this bottom curve. Start where you placed the anchor point. No need to let go of the Option key, you're going to need it again in just a moment. All you have to do is hold down the mouse button and draw. The option key is ignored—it's like drawing without it. Draw freehand only until you trace the next small curve, then let go of the mouse button and use straight line segments to finish the rest of your selection. You may find it more accurate to use small segments rather than large lines. Continue until you're back at the starting point, then let go of the mouse button, then the **Option key.** When you draw in straight line segments you are accessing the Polygonal Lasso tool. This tool is also available from the Toolbox and you can draw with it if your selection will be mostly straight lines. If you start out in the Polygonal Lasso, adding the Option key gives you the regular Lasso. But I generally find it easier to stick to the Lasso itself and switch to the Polygonal Lasso by adding the Option key as you did here. **If your selection is not what you want, type Command-D to deselect the area and start your selection over.** In a moment, I'll show you how to add to and subtract from your selection and even save the selection to edit later, but for now, practice with this tool. If you do much work in Photoshop, you're going to use it a lot.

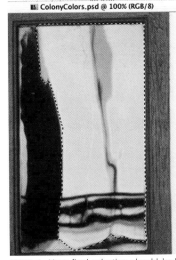

STEP 1: Your final selection should look something like this. It doesn't have to be perfect, but if there are large areas you don't have selected or you've included too much, try again.

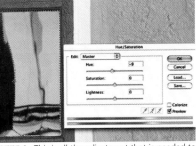

STEP 2: This is all the adjustment that is needed to bring the color in line with the rest of the image.

STEP 2: **Once you have a selection that you like, use Image/Adjustments/Hue/Saturation or type Command-U to bring up Hue/Saturation. You may want to type Command-H at this point to hide the edges of your selection; you can do this while in the Hue/Saturation command. Move the Hue slider to the left to about -9, which warms up the yellow and makes it more orange. Use File/Save As to save your file and name it ColonyComp.** Now you're ready to start selecting other pieces for this image.

SELECTING THE DELPHINIUM

STEP 3: **Open the file Dephinium.psd from the Colony Composite folder on the CD.** This time you are going to use the Magic Wand to start your selection, the Lasso tool to finesse your selection, and the Channels palette to save your selection. **Click the Magic Wand tool in the Tools palette or type W to access it. In the Options bar, use the default setting of 32 as the Tolerance value, and make sure Contiguous is unchecked. Also, click the second of the selection interaction icons just to the right of the tool preset icon.** This will assure that each click of the wand will add to the selection rather than making a brand new selection each time. With the Magic Wand you're only going to try and get the major areas of color on the flowers, so **make your first click in the more purple flowers to the left. Check the illustration here to see where I made my first click.**

STEP 3: Here's where I made my first click with the Magic Wand.

STEP 3: When you hold down Shift with the Magic Wand, the second selection interaction icon will be highlighted because you are adding to a selection. If you use Option, the third icon shows that you will be subtracting from the selection. And, if you use Shift-Option you will take the intersection of the selections and the final icon is highlighted.

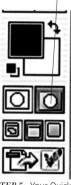

Quick Mask mode selector (Quick Mask icon)

STEP 4: I made my second click in these blue flowers.

STEP 5: Your Quick Mask icon should look like this. This causes an overlay to cover areas outside of the selection you've made. It masks out everything except your selection. Hence the term Quick Mask.

STEP 5: Clicking the Quick Mask icon at this point gives you an overlay that looks something like this one.

STEP 5: If your image looks like this after you click the Quick Mask icon, Option-click the icon to have the mask overlay cover the green background rather than the flowers.

Step 6: After the Grow commands your selection looks like this.

STEP 4: **Use the Magic Wand again to click on the medium blue flowers on the right side of the picture to include these colors in your selection. Again, check the illustration to see where I clicked.**

STEP 5: At this point it may be difficult for you to tell what is selected and what is not. **To help you see which colors are selected, click the Quick Mask icon at the bottom of the Tools palette. This will put a red overlay on top of everything that is not selected. Your screen should look something like the illustration here. If your mask does not look like mine, your Quick Mask may be set to show you the selection instead of the mask. Make sure your Quick Mask icon looks like the one pictured here. If not, Option-click the Quick Mask icon.** What we want to see using Quick Mask is all of the delphinium flowers but none of the green background—that should all be covered in the red overlay. But this quickly shows me that there are still large areas of color I haven't selected. I especially **note the big area on the flower about halfway down on the right. Click the Standard Selection icon on the left of the Tools palette to get you back to regular selection mode and use the Magic Wand again to click the area of that flower. You can click again with the wand if you feel you can get more areas of the flowers without taking the background, or move on to the next step. If you get much of the green background area in your selection, undo your last step and click in a different location.**

STEP 6: You may have noticed that I haven't asked you to click on any of the darker purples in this image. If you do, you will most likely get areas of the background that are similar enough in color to be included. Instead of continuing to click, we're going to use the Grow command, which will add colors in the tolerance range, but only colors that are adjacent to those already selected. **Use Select/Grow to add colors to your selection now. Continue to use the command two or three more times until you have most of the flowers selected. The white centers will remain unselected, but you are going to use the Lasso tool to add those in the next step.** Click back on Quick Mask mode if you'd like to check your selection.

STEP 7: Now you're going to use the Lasso tool to clean up your selection. This time you're going to be adding and deleting from your selection and it's going to be a hand-eye coordination test. **Type L to get the Lasso or click its icon in the Tools palette. Enter a one pixel feather value in the Options bar. Click the first selection interaction icon, which normally would give you a new selection each time you click and drag. You'll be using the Lasso in conjunction with keyboard shortcuts to modify the selection.**

First you are going to add some areas of the flowers to the selection. This includes some of the dark areas as well as the white centers of the flowers. **Hold down the Shift key before you start to draw, and make sure it is down to keep from accidentally moving the selection instead of adding to it.** When you hold down the Shift key, the second selection interaction icon activates and the cursor appears as either a crosshair or the Lasso, depending on how your preferences are set up. You will see a little plus to the bottom-right of the cursor telling you that you are adding. When the Shift key is not down, the cursor looks like a white pointing arrow with a selection box. Clicking and dragging inside the existing selection at this point will move the selection. If you do this by accident, immediately choose Edit/Undo (Command-Z), or if you notice that you moved the selection a few steps ago, use the History palette to back up to a state where the selection had not been moved. **Use Shift with the Lasso tool to circle all the areas not selected. When adding to the selection, first put the cursor on top of an area already selected, and hold the Shift key down. Next, press and hold down the mouse button while circling the areas you want to add. If you accidentally select something along a border that you don't want to select, move the cursor into an area nearby that isn't selected, hold the Option key down, press the mouse button down, and use the Lasso to circle the part of that border area you want to deselect.** When you hold down the Option key, you see a minus to the right of the cursor signifying a subtract from the selection. The selection interaction icon on the Options bar also changes. When doing selections along a border with the Lasso tool, you have to trace the edge pixel by pixel. The Lasso tool has no intelligence to detect where color or brightness changes, so this is a hand-eye coordination exercise. If you find it easier to click the appropriate selection interaction icon on the Options bar, that's okay too.

STEP 7: You can lasso large areas while holding down the Shift key to add them to your selection. In this illustration the Display and Cursors preference is set to Standard for non-painting cursors. If you are using the Precise setting, your Lasso will be a crosshair with a plus sign at the bottom.

After you have started a Lasso selection, addition or subtraction, the mouse button is down and you are drawing with the button down. At this point, if you hold the Option key down, you can release the mouse button and draw straight line segments between mouse clicks with the Polygonal Lasso as we did in the first part of this exercise. If you want to draw in freehand again, hold the mouse button down again while drawing. In any case, either the Option key or the mouse button needs to remain down until you are done with this selection change, because when you release the Option key and the mouse button at the same time, the two end points of the selection will join. The hand-eye-mouse coordination in this maneuver can be tricky! Let's go through the most difficult case, when you are subtracting from the existing selection. Make sure you are using the first selection interaction icon, then press the Option key and hold until you click down on the mouse button. Starting with the Option key down tells Photoshop you want to subtract. Next, you click the mouse button and hold it down while drawing in freehand. Now you can release the Option key as long as you keep the mouse button down. If you want to draw straight line segments, press the Option key again after its initial release. Now each time you mouse click, you are defining a corner point and straight lines will be drawn between clicks. To draw in freehand again, press and hold down the mouse button while drawing. When you have looped around what you wanted to subtract, release the Option key and the mouse button, and the end points of this selection will be joined. Remember, this works for both adding to (Shift key starts) and subtracting from (Option key starts) a selection.

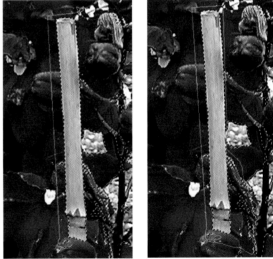

STEP 7: Hold down Shift to add to the selection, start to draw, then hold down Option to access the Polygonal Lasso and draw with straight line segments. This is a good way to add the stake to your selection.

STEP 7: At any time you can switch back to the regular Lasso by holding down the mouse and drawing freehand rather than clicking to anchor line segments.

Selecting the Delphinium

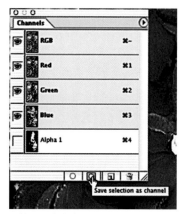

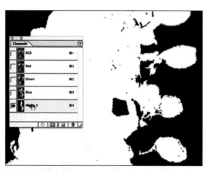

STEP 8: Click the Save Selection icon at the bottom of the palette to save your selection as a new channel.

STEP 8: Click the name or thumbnail of the channel to show only that channel and not the color information for the file. The selection that you made is still active as well here, so you can see the selection marquee.

SAVING A SELECTION

STEP 8: During this selection process you've probably wondered what to do if you inadvertently lose your selection. It would be very annoying to have to repeat all the work you've done so far. So, you need to save your selection. **Make sure the Quick Mask icon is set to its default state with gray on the outside and a white circle in the middle. If not, Option-click the QuickMask icon. Next, use Window/Channels or type Shift-F10 if you are using ArtistKeys to to open the Channels palette.** You'll notice that there are three channels for this document—a Red, a Green, and a Blue channel—as well as a composite image that is labeled RGB. The RGB is not an actual channel, it merely lets you see how the three color channels will look when you combine them. **Now click the Save Selection icon at the bottom of this palette; it's the second one from the left. This creates a new channel in the palette named Alpha 1. Look at the thumbnail for this channel and you can see that all of the areas of color you selected are white and the background areas are black. To take a closer look at exactly what you selected, click on the name Alpha 1 in the Channels palette. This turns off the RGB layers and shows you only the mask channel that you just created. Type Command-D to deselect the marching ants so you can see clearly where you need to add to or delete from the selection. Retrieve your selection from the mask channel by choosing Select/Load Selection of a New Selection and set the Channel pop-up to Alpha 1. A shortcut for doing Load Selection is to hold the Command key down and click Alpha 1 in the Channels palette. That selects the white parts in the channel.**

STEP 9: **Click back on the thumbnail for the RGB information. Your selection is still active and you can continue to add or delete areas with the Lasso. After you've added or deleted several areas, go to Selection/Save Selection and choose Alpha 1 from the pop-up menu and Replace Channel from the options. This will overwrite the channel you just created and edit the mask.**

AN EASIER WAY TO EDIT A SELECTION

STEP 10: Switching back and forth between making selections and resaving the selection will become tiring fairly quickly, so now I'm going to show you the easy way to edit the selection mask. **Click the thumbnail for the Alpha 1 channel so it becomes the active channel. Now click the first column of the Channels palette beside RGB to turn on the view for that information. Because the Alpha 1 channel is highlighted in the palette, it will be the channel that you edit when you use a painting tool.** Once you turn on the RGB for the file, you may notice that your file looks a lot like it did in Quick Mask mode. There is a colored overlay over part of the image. This is the portion of the file that is "masked out."

Type B to use the Brush tool and click the Brush pop-up on the Options bar to choose a 13-pixel brush with a soft edge. If you've loaded Barry'sPhotoBrushes, use the 13-pixel brush in the third row. If not, just make sure the Hardness of the brush is set to zero. As you paint, use the left and right bracket keys to make your brush larger or smaller. Type D to get the default colors. Note that when you are working on a mask channel while viewing the mask channel, the default foreground color is white and the background is black. This is opposite from the default colors when you are working on an RGB layer, or working on a mask while viewing the RGB layer. When you paint with white you will be adding to the selection, black will remove areas from the selection. Use the Paintbrush tool, in Normal mode, with 100%

Opacity. If you are not sure how to pick brush sizes and options, see Chapter 4: "The Tools Palette."

Paint with white any areas of the flowers that are covered in the red overlay. If you accidentally paint beyond the edge of the flowers, you can erase mistakes by typing an X, which exchanges the foreground and background colors and allows you to paint with black. Depending on how well you made your initial Magic Wand selections and your Lasso additions, you may have a lot or a little painting to do. This is a very intricate mask, so don't get frustrated.

STEP 11: There are areas of color on the flowers that are slightly red, and you may wonder if they are actually red or merely covered in the red overlay. Here are two quick ways to check your mask. First, change the color of the mask. **Double-click the thumbnail for the Alpha 1 channel. This brings up the Channel Options palette.** You'll notice that you can switch the overlay from covering the masked areas to covering the selected areas and doing this can often help you perfect a mask. The third option, Spot Color, lets you build a channel mask that can be included in a file to furnish traditional print shops with plate information for special inks. **What we're interested in right now is the color square on the bottom left. Click once on this color and the Adobe Color Picker appears. Now you can choose a new color that might work better for this file's overlay. I chose turquoise, which worked nicely on most areas. Once you've changed the color (you can change the Opacity setting as well), go back to your mask and do some more touch-up.**

STEP 12: **When you feel you've made most of the corrections, click the Eye icon to the left of the RGB composite thumbnail to turn off all three RGB channels and view only the mask. You may notice little dots of black or white that need to be painted over, or areas of gray that should be cleaned up.** Sometimes it's easier to see it in black and white and make the changes that way.

As you work on the mask, you'll have to make some choices about which stems to include and where the edges of some of the petals really are. What you're working for here is to get a nice mask, it doesn't have to be absolutely perfect. It's more important right now that you become comfortable with the techniques. If you'd like, you can click the Eye icon for Alpha 1 to turn off the mask you're working on and turn on the icon for Delphinium Mask, the one I built for this example. I decided to leave out the separate petals on the left and the one single petal at the bottom. I included quite a few stems and even one leaf. **After you make all your edits, click back on the thumbnail for RGB to activate the color information for the file.**

MOVING THE FLOWERS TO THE COLONYCOMP FILE

STEP 13: Now that you have a beautiful mask channel to work with, it's time to load the channel as a selection and move your flowers to the ColonyComp file that you worked on earlier in this example. **First, switch back to the ColonyComp file by choosing it from the bottom of the Window menu. Type F to put this file into Full Screen mode. Move the Channels palette to the upper right of your screen and use Window/Layers to show the Layers palette if it is not already onscreen. Now bring the Delphinium file forward by choosing it from the Window menu. Move it to the left side of your screen. Command-click the thumbnail for the Alpha 1 channel to load your selection from this channel. Type V to switch to the Move tool, then click and drag the selected flowers over the top of the ColonyComp file. When you release the mouse, the ColonyComp file will activate and the delphinium will drop**

STEP 11: Double-click the thumbnail of the channel to bring up these options, then click the color square to use the Color Picker to change the overlay color.

STEP 11: I chose a turquoise color for the overlay. This avoided some of the confusion in the red areas of the flowers and also showed some edges that I had missed as well.

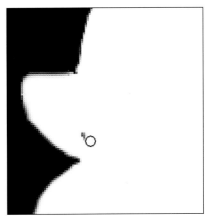

STEP 12: When only the Alpha 1 channel Eye icon is on, you are viewing only the mask. Because this is a grayscale image you can quickly see areas within the main selection that need to be tidied up.

STEP 13: As you begin to drag the delphinium to the ColonyComp file your screen will look like this. Don't panic! You are not actually cutting the flowers out of your file. When you move a selection outside of its image window, Photoshop knows that you are copying the information.

onto this file as a new layer called Layer 1. Move the flowers to the right side of the image over the orange wall.

SELECTING THE DESPACHO

STEP 14: We are going to use the Lasso tool again, but this time we'll use the Magnetic Lasso option. This tool creates selections based on color and contrast differences between the element you are selecting and the background. **Open the file Despacho.psd from the *Photoshop CS Artistry* CD. Type Shift-L until you see the icon for the Magnetic Lasso; then go to the Options bar and set your Feather value at 1 and turn Anti-aliased on. Start with 5 as the Width setting. If you are using a pressure-sensitive table, this is one place where I suggest leaving Pen Pressure off, so uncheck that box in the Options bar. The Frequency is how often the Lasso will put down anchor points to anchor the selection marquee. We're going to use 20. For Edge Contrast, type in 10%.**

   Before we actually begin the selection, it's important to note that the Magnetic Lasso is sometimes not as ideal a selection tool as it might seem. The accuracy of its selections depend not only on the settings that we discussed in the paragraph above, but also on the particular image and specific edge that you're working on. For high-contrast edges you can use higher Width and Edge Contrast settings and draw a looser selection. Low-contrast images require lower settings, more care in tracing the edge, and more manually placed anchor points. For this image, which was taken with a digital camera and has strong shadows, the Magnetic Lasso works fairly well. However, it does seem to have difficulty with sharp points, so I found that it's best to let the Magnetic Lasso trace the edges that curve, but click down to manually place anchor points at the tips of the leaves or anywhere else the transitions are sharp.

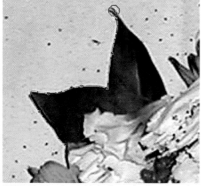

STEP 15: The tip of this leaf was the first place that I needed to click the mouse to place an anchor point. You may have needed to place one before this where the two leaves meet.

STEP 15: **Begin at the upper-left set of leaves at about the ten o'clock position. Set your zoom magnification to 200% by using the Navigator palette, or type Command-+ enough times to bring you to 200%. Click once on the edge of the leaf to set the first anchor point and start the Magnetic Lasso selection; then begin to guide the mouse around the edge of the despacho. You do not need to have the mouse button pressed down after the initial mouse click.** If you have your cursor preference set to Brush Size, keep the middle of the circle over the leaf's edge. If you see that the selection is being drawn around a piece of confetti or it's not taking something that you want, you can move the mouse back over the previous selection, retracing your steps until you get back to the last anchor point that was laid down. If you've placed the last anchor point in a poor position, you can delete that anchor point by pressing the Delete key. Continue to retrace your path, pressing the Delete key until you get back to a place where you like the path you've drawn. Continue forward again, clicking once to add an anchor point where you feel one is needed. If at any time you become hopelessly entangled in Lasso lines, you can press the Esc key to quit drawing and start again. **When you need to scroll the image to continue drawing your selection, simply hold down the Spacebar to access the Hand tool and move the image in its window. After scrolling this way, you may need to return the cursor to the point where you interrupted your selection or the Magnetic Lasso may try to connect to where your cursor is after the scroll.** If you think you might find it useful to switch to the Polygonal Lasso tool, you can access the tool while in the Magnetic Lasso by holding down the Option key and clicking from point to point, releasing the mouse button between points. (The Lasso will draw the line but not place anchor points.) To switch back to the Freehand Magnetic Lasso, click the mouse and release the Option key to continue drawing. Once you are sure the tool has resumed its magnetic behavior, you can release the mouse button and continue to guide it along the edge.

Finish the selection by drawing all the way back to your starting point. You'll see the Magnetic Lasso icon again, with a little circle at the bottom-right, which means that when you click, the selection will be closed. The selection will also close if you double-click at any time or press the Enter key.

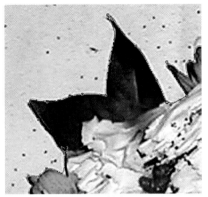

STEP 16: When you complete the selection, click the Save Selection icon on the Channels palette to save this selection as a new channel. Alternately, you can go to the Selection menu and use Save Selection, choosing New Channel as the destination. Type Command-D to deselect the marquee and then click the thumbnail for your new channel called Alpha 1 in the Channels palette. Note that in this mask there are no errant pixels of black that need to be removed from the central white area, nor white pixels in the black background area. This will save a lot of painting on the mask to perfect it. Click the Eye icon next to RGB in the Channels palette to turn on the color information and once again you'll see the red overlay over the background. It should be fairly simple to see where the edges of the selection are imperfect. Type B for the Brush tool and use the same brush as last time to begin painting. You will probably need to make your brush smaller for much of this edge. If you have edges that need painting and are straight, you can click on one end to begin a stroke, then Shift-click at the other end to paint a straight line. This one small technique can save you quite a lot of time on some images. You should have very little touch-up to do on this mask, as the Magnetic Lasso has probably made a good selection of the despacho. A despacho, by the way, is a traditional Andean spiritual offering.

STEP 16: When you see this icon, you have completed the selection and you are back over the point of origin. Click now to close the selection and get a selection marquee.

PUTTING IT ALL TOGETHER

STEP 17: Now that the despacho mask is complete, click back on the thumbnail for the RGB information, then Command-click the Alpha 1 thumbnail to load the mask as a selection. Just as you did previously with the delphinium selection, type V to access the Move tool and move the despacho over to the ColonyComp file. The ColonyComp file will activate and you can continue to use the Move tool to place the despacho in the upper-left corner of this image. At this point, you have three layers. Double-click on the name Layer 1 and rename this layer Delphinium. Double-click on Layer 2 and rename that layer Despacho. Type Command-S to save your file.

STEP 17: After you copy the despacho to the ColonyComp file, your image and Layers palette will look something like this.

STEP 18: To complete the composite, drag the Despacho layer to the New Layer icon on the Layers palette to make a copy of it, then use the Move tool to drag that copy to the center-left side of the image. Now drag this layer to the New Layer icon and position this second copy at the bottom of the image. Make two copies of the Delphinium layer the same way and arrange the three flowers on the right side of the image in a way that pleases you. You are now finished with this composite, but you will be working on more complex composites in Section 5 of this book.

STEP 18: Here's my final version of the composite. You can open this from the Extra Info folder in the Colony Comp folder on the Photoshop CS Artistry CD.

223

19 HANDS-ON SESSION: Overall Color Correction

Introduction to Histograms, Levels, Curves, and Hue/Saturation for overall color correction and the fundamental steps in creating a master image.

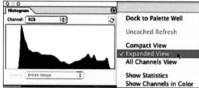

Here we see the new Histogram palette along with its menu options. The Expanded View, shown here, gives you a larger, more exact display than the Compact View. The All Channels View shows the RGB channel plus each of the Red, Green, and Blue channels. You can use the Histogram palette to see in real time how adjustments you are making in Levels, Curves, and Hue/Saturation are effecting the histogram of your image. This is a very useful and powerful tool!

In Chapter 3: "Setting System and Photoshop Preferences," we showed you how to set your Photoshop preferences for doing high-quality color correction. This overall color correction chapter is done using those Color Settings and, specifically, with the RGB working space set to Adobe RGB and the CMYK working space set as in Chapter 3. If you didn't already do so, go through Chapter 3 before doing this exercise or any of the other color correction exercises. Before you proceed, also read Chapter 14: "Color Spaces, Device Characterization, and Color Management," Chapter 15: "Photoshop Color Preferences, Monitor, Scanner, and Printer Calibration," Chapter 16: "Image Resolution, Scanning Film, and Digital Cameras," and Chapter 17: "Steps to Create a Master Image." These chapters give you an overview of the entire reproduction process, show you how to calibrate your monitor, and give you a further understanding of the Levels, Curves, and Hue/Saturation tools you will be using here. Chapter 17 pages 204 to 205 have the color correction workflow you will be using, which you need to practice and remember. You should make sure your monitor is calibrated before proceeding with this chapter.

INTRODUCTION TO LEVELS AND THE HISTOGRAM PALETTE

Before you start actually color correcting the Banff Lake image, let's take a tour of the Levels tool and explain its different parts and functions. Levels contains two sets of controls, Input Levels and Output Levels, which can make the image lighter or darker as well as change its contrast. The Input controls on top include the histogram, the Input Levels numbers, and three sliders. The Input Shadow slider, on the left, darkens shadows as you move it to the right. The Input Highlight slider, on the right, lightens highlights as you move it to the left. The Brightness slider, in the middle, adjusts the brightness of the image. The Output controls on the bottom of the Levels dialog contain the Output Levels numbers and two sliders. The Output Shadow slider, on the left, makes shadows lighter as you move it to the right. The Output Highlight slider, on the right, makes highlights darker or duller as you move it to the left. The names "Input" and "Output"

The initial uncorrected Banff Lake image. Notice the overall flatness of the image.

are chosen by comparing what happens with the Levels Highlight and Shadow sliders to what happens in Curves when you move the end points of a straight curve either along the horizontal (Input) axis or along the vertical (Output) axis. This might seem a bit obscure at this point, but I believe it will make more sense to you after you read the entire chapter.

STEP 1: **From the Overall Color Correction folder on the CD, open the BanffLake16.tif file in Photoshop**. If your RGB working space is not set to Adobe RGB, you will get the Embedded Profile Mismatch dialog. In that case, you should make the Use Embedded Profile choice to leave this file in the Adobe RGB space and work on it in that space. That way the Info palette numbers and Levels histograms will look the same as in the book. **Type F to get Full Screen mode, and then press the Tab key to get all your palettes off the screen. Type Command-0 to fill the screen, then type C to get the Crop tool. After choosing the Crop tool, hit the Enter key to bring up the Options bar and double-check that you are not cropping to any specific size. Click and drag to draw a crop box around the entire outside of the image, then click two of the diagonal corner handles and drag them inward to remove the black borders from around the end of the original transparency. You'll notice that as you try to move the corner handle close to the corner, it may snap to the edge of the image. While holding the mouse button down on the corner handle, press the Control key and hold it. This will turn off the snapping to the picture edge and allow you to exactly place the corner handle to remove the black crud around the edge of the image without removing any extra info. When you have the corner handle where you want it, release the mouse button and the Control key. You can now zoom in to any of the handles to check their exact location before cropping. To do the crop, press Return. Uncheck View/Snap To/Document Bounds to turn off the default edge snapping of the cropping tool. I usually turn this feature off. Use File/Save As BanffLakeLayers.psd in Photoshop format on your hard disk; it is always good to save things in Photoshop format while you are working on them because it saves all your channels and layers.**

STEP 2: **Bring up the Info and Histogram palettes from the Window menu. If you have loaded ArtistKeys, the predefined set of function keys explained in Chapter 3, press F9 to bring up the Info palette and Shift-F9 for the Histogram palette. Be sure to set up the Info palette's Options to show you both RGB and CMYK values or RGB and Lab values. Set the Histogram palette to Expanded View. Move both these palettes to the screen edge so they won't be over the lightest or darkest places on the image.**

STEP 3: **Choose Layer/New Adjustment Layer/Levels and then click and drag the Levels title bar, at the top of its dialog box, to move the Levels dialog box out of the way as much as possible. You want to see as much of the image as you can while color correcting it. Switch the Source pop-up menu in the Histogram palette to Adjustment Composite which allows you to see both before and after histograms. Otherwise the Histogram palette just shows the adjusted histogram. Use the Levels Overview diagram at the top of this page as you review or learn the basic functions covered in steps 4 through 9. Make sure the Preview button is turned on.**

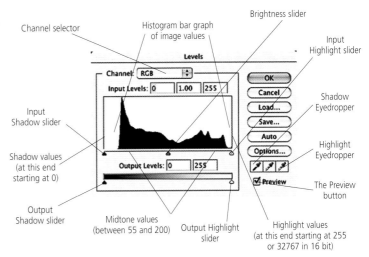

Study this Levels Overview diagram to learn the various controls of the Levels tool.

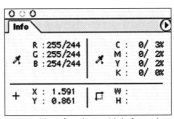

STEP 2: The Info palette with before values on the left of the slash and after values on the right. The before-after slash shows up when you are in a color correction tool and you have made changes with that tool. Here we see 8 bit values.

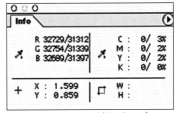

STEP 2: Here we see 16 bit values after setting the highlight in the Levels tool. You can get 16 bit values by choosing Show 16 Bit Values from the Info Palette Options menu.

STEP 3: Here's how I have my screen set up to work with this image. Notice the Options bar at the top and the Navigator at the top-right edge.

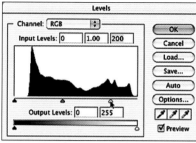

STEP 4: Move the Input Highlight slider to the left so the right Input Level reads about 200.

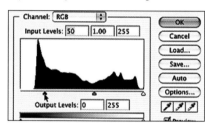

STEP 4: The black histogram shows what the above Levels move did to the original gray histogram. Click on the yellow triangle or the circle arrows to get a more accurate display. To see both the black and gray histograms, the Source menu has to be changed to Adjustment Composite. You have to change this after entering your first Adjustment Layer, i.e. after entering Levels here.

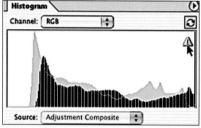

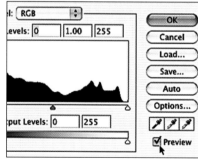

STEP 6: Leave the Preview checkbox checked in Levels and other color correction tools to see your changes as you make them. To see the image as it looked before this round of changes, uncheck the Preview button. When you are working in an adjustment layer and you are entering the Levels dialog for this layer for a second or third time, having Preview checked shows you the changes since the last time you entered Levels, and unchecking shows you how the image looked with your previous set of Levels adjustments. To see the image without this Levels adjustment layer altogether, turn off the Eye icon for this layer in the Layers palette.

STEP 4: **Move the Input Highlight slider to the left and observe that the highlight areas in the clouds get brighter and the Input Levels number on the right decreases from 255. Move the slider until the number reads about 200. Let go of the slider and move the cursor over an area of the image where the clouds have turned completely white.** When you use any of the color correction tools, you automatically get the Eyedropper tool when you move the cursor over an area of the image. The Info palette shows you two sets of values for this white area. The values to the left of the slash are the original values at the Eyedropper location when you first entered Levels, and the values to the right of the slash show you what your levels changes have done to the digital values at the Eyedropper location. You can now see that moving the Input Highlight slider to the left makes the highlights brighter, but it also causes you to lose detail in the highlights if you move it too far. The original RGB values that were in the range of 220 to 240 have now all changed to 255, which is pure white and prints with no color or detail—and you don't want that. Notice how the black histogram in the Histogram palette has shifted to the right showing you what this change did to the histogram. The gray histogram in this palette is your original histogram. See the caption to the left about a possible bug. **Move the Input Highlight slider back to 255.**

STEP 5: **Move the Input Shadow slider to the right until the Input Levels number on the left goes from 0 to about 50 and the shadow areas of the image darken. Move the Eyedropper over a dark area and measure the changes in the Info palette.** The RGB values originally in the range of 0 to 50 have all moved to 0 and have become totally black. **See how this change effected the Histogram display. The Histogram palette shows you how changes effect the histogram. Click on the triangle or the circle arrows at the top right of the Histogram palette to get a more accurate display.**

STEP 6: You always should have the Preview checkbox checked to see the changes in the image as they happen in Levels or any color correction tool. To see the image the way it looked before any changes were made in the current invocation of Levels, or any tool, uncheck the Preview checkbox.

    Now, hold down the Option key and click the Cancel/Reset button. The Cancel button changes to Reset, and clicking it restores the levels to their starting values when you entered Levels this time. All your changes are removed, but you don't leave Levels. Calculating the Levels histogram can take a long time when you're working on large files, and this Reset feature saves time when you want to start over.

    Notice that the values in the Info palette change when you move the cursor around on the screen. Move the cursor out over the image, while holding the Shift key down, and click the image area. Notice that a new set of numbers appear at the bottom of the Info palette. This is called a Color Sampler, and the Info palette will always show the values at this location no matter where the cursor is located, even if the cursor is inside the Levels dialog. When you want to precisely set the digital values at a certain location, Shift-click there to create a Color Sampler; then go back into the Levels dialog and move the controls until you get the values you wanted at that location. Using the Color Samplers lets you remember the values at a particular location and see how a change in Levels modifies those values.

STEP 7: **Choose Window/Color (Command-Shift-F9) to bring up the Color palette. If your Color palette is docked in the Palette Well, drag it out onto the area surrounding your image. Use the Eyedropper tool to click a midtone value in the Banff Lake image; clicking the lake itself will work great. When you press down on the mouse button, the values in the Color palette change. Now Shift-click the lake. This creates**

Chapter 19: Overall Color Correction

another Color Sampler at the bottom of the Info palette that will always show you the values at that location. Now move the cursor back into Levels; notice that these values in the Color palette and Color Sampler don't go away, even when you're in the dialog box. Press down on the Input Brightness slider, the middle one, and move it to the left; the image gets brighter and the numbers in the Color palette and Color Sampler get larger. Move the slider to the right, and the image gets darker, while the numbers in the Color palette and Color Sampler get smaller. Also, observe that the middle number (the gamma) in the Input Levels numbers boxes is changing. When you move the Brightness slider to the left, the gamma goes above 1.0, and when you move it to the right, the gamma goes below 1.0. If the Input Levels numbers read 0, 1.0, 255, you know you haven't changed the Input Levels. When you click another area of the image, the Color palette's values will change to show you the reading at that new location. The Color Sampler you created before will not move or change, however. If you Shift-click in a new location, a new Color Sampler (up to four per image) will be created at that location. To move an existing Color Sampler, you need to Shift-click on top of the old sampler location and drag it to a new location. **Hold the Option key down and click the Reset button, formerly the Cancel button, to move the Input values back to 0, 1.0, and 255.**

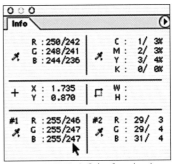

STEPS 6 AND 7: A Color Sampler shows up at the bottom of the Info palette. A Color Sampler will always show you the before and after values at the location where you placed that color sampler even when the cursor is inside the Levels dialog.

STEP 8: **Move the Output Highlight slider to the left until the Output Levels number on the right reaches 200. Then measure the brightest cloud values; notice that values originally in the 200 to 220 range have all dropped below 200.** You changed the Output Levels number from 255 to 200, and the difference of 55, or close to it, has been subtracted from all these highlight values, darkening and dulling your highlights.

STEP 9: **Move the Output Shadow slider to the right. Notice how doing that makes the shadows lighter and duller.** If you measure the changes with the Eyedropper and Info palette, you will notice that moving this slider increases the shadow's numerical values (which makes the shadows lighter).

SETTING THE HIGHLIGHT AND SHADOW VALUES

STEP 10: Steps 4 through 9 show you the basic functions of the different parts of the Levels tool. It is important to use those functions in the right order and to take careful measurements of your progress using the Info palette, Color Samplers, and Color palette. We will start out working with the Highlight and Shadow Eyedroppers to set the highlights and shadows on this image—a very important step in this process. All reproduction or printing processes, including sheet-fed presses, web presses, newspaper presses, digital printers, and film recorders, have certain end points to their reproduction process defined by the highlights and shadows. Many newspaper presses can't show detail for shadow values that are more than 85% to 90% black, and some newspapers are even worse. Sheet-fed presses, on the other hand, can sometimes show detail in areas with more than 95% black. In an 8-bit digital file, these percentages are represented by numerical values ranging from 0 (100% black) to 255 (white, or 0% black). 0 to 255 is actually 256 possible values.

In a 16-bit file, you can look at the 16-bit values in Photoshop 8 by turning on "Show 16-bit values" using the Pallete Options choice of the Info palette's menu. When working with 16-bit values, 0 is still 100% black but 100% white is actually 32,768. There is a big difference between 32,768 possible tonal values and a mere 256, which is why working with 16-bit files keeps all the information in your digital

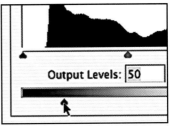

STEP 9: Moving the Output Highlight and Shadow sliders and looking at the Output Levels numbers.

227

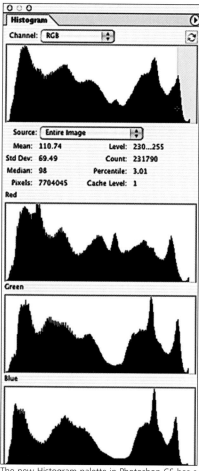

The new Histogram palette in Photoshop CS has a palette menu option called All Channels View, which expands the palette to show you the histograms of all your channels at once. This really allows you to see in detail what happens when you change something in the color correction tools. If you also turn on the Show Statistics option, then you get numbers shown here below the RGB histogram display. Notice that the Level number there is reading 230..255. This is because I have clicked and dragged from 255 down to 230 in the RGB histogram display and the statistics are showing me, with Count, the number of pixels in that 230-255 range and, with Percentile, what percentage of the total pixels that Count represents. This makes it easy to see how many pixels, possibly 0, are in a certain range of values. If there are no pixels in a range of the highlight or shadow values, then you might want to clip that range of values by moving the Input Highlight or Shadow slider up to the right or left edge of that range. This allows the values in the middle of the histogram to spread out and give your image a larger dynamic range. This new palette is very cool!

image and gives you more options. The difficulty when working with 16-bit files is that many of Photoshop's tools, like the Levels histogram for example, still only show 256 possible values. It is also true that today's computer monitors can't show you the subtle changes that 32,768 values would allow. Also, it is true that you won't be able to see a difference in many printing situations. For subtle gradient transitions from one color to another or from light to dark, however, I do believe 16-bit images will have an advantage. If you work with 16-bit images now, then you will be able to display and print those images on future devices and get even better results as printing and monitor technology improves over time. I work with 16-bit per channel images whenever I can.

When you color correct an image, you don't want that image to contain bright and dark areas that the output medium you are using can't reproduce. Setting the highlight and shadow values correctly for your output device ensures that this won't happen. You also want the white parts of your image to print as white (not with a color cast of yellow, cyan, or magenta) and the black parts of your image to print as black (not dark gray with a green cast). You can ensure this by setting your highlights and shadows correctly. When you set the highlight, the idea is that you are setting the brightest point in the image that is a neutral color, white, and that still has a dot pattern or some ink (doesn't print as pure white paper). The highlight would be the brightest part of Zone IX in the Zone System. Most points brighter than the highlight will print as totally empty paper with no dots or ink. When you set the shadow, you are setting the darkest point in the image that is a neutral color, black, and that still has a dot pattern. The shadow would be the darkest part of Zone I in the Zone System. Most points darker than the shadow will print as totally black ink with no white dots to give detail.

STEP 11: **To start the actual color correction of this image, Option-Shift-click any Color Sampler points you previously set to remove them from the image and the Info palette. Press the Cancel button to leave the Levels tool. Close the Color palette and choose Window/Navigator to bring up the Navigator palette. Move it mostly off the screen on the right side, but leave enough of it so you can see your zoom factor number in the bottom left of this palette. All you need on the screen is this small piece of the Navigator and the Info and Histogram palettes in screen locations that won't be on top of where you need to set the shadow or highlight. If you have two monitors, put your palettes on one and leave the other just to look at your image.** The image we are working on here was scanned at 16-bits per color channel, using an Imacon Flextight scanner. The original scan was over 200 megs in size and scanned at over 5700 dpi. I have resampled down the file so it would fit on the CD and be a good size for this book. **If you are starting out with either a 16-bits per channel scan or an 8-bit scan, using Photoshop CS, you should now choose a Levels adjustment layer with Layer/New Adjustment Layer/Levels. Name this Overall Levels, then choose OK in the New Layer dialog.**

Photoshop allows you to decide where you want it to set the highlight. The highlight should be the brightest neutral point that still has detail. **Double-click the Highlight Eyedropper button, the rightmost Eyedropper inside the Levels dialog, and make sure that the RGB values in the Color Picker are 244, 244, 244.** These are the neutral values you would want your highlight to have for a sheet-fed press on coated paper, and they also work for most other purposes, including the LightJet 5000 and most Epson printers like the 1280, 2200, 4000, and 7600. Due to the impurities in printing press inks, you often get a neutral color in CMYK by having more cyan than magenta or yellow. The CMYK equivalent of 244, 244, 244 may be 5, 3, 3, 0 or maybe 3, 2, 2, 0. Because this is a highlight, there is no black in the CMYK values. Click the OK button in the Color Picker if you need to change any of the RGB values, otherwise just click Cancel.

STEP 12: **Now double-click the Shadow Eyedropper and make sure the shadow values are 8, 8, 8 in RGB.** If you have different values than these, compare your settings to those in Chapters 3 and 15. As discussed in Chapters 3 and 15, the shadow preference values should be somewhere between 2, 2, 2 and 8, 8, 8 depending on how dark you want your shadows to be. Click the OK button if you need to change any of the values, otherwise just click Cancel.

SETTING THE HIGHLIGHT

STEP 13: Next, you use the Highlight Eyedropper to click a highlight, which should be the brightest white area in this image. You want the highlight to be a neutral white area—the last possible place where you can see a little texture. The RGB values in the Info palette should be in the 240 to 255 range and the CMYK values in the 0 to 10 range. If you have specular highlights (the sun reflected off a chrome bumper, for example), these will not have detail and should have values of 255. You're looking for something just a hair less intense than that. **Click on the Highlight Eyedropper to select it. Move the Levels dialog box out of the way so you can see the entire clouds and snow area. To find the correct place for setting the highlight, with the Levels Preview checkbox checked, hold down the Option key and move the Input Highlight slider to the left. The whole image area first turns black and then, as you move the slider to the left, brighter and eventually white areas appear. The first white area that appears in the snow on top of the mountains at the left is the area you should set as the highlight. Remember where that location is in the window. Now move the Input Highlight slider back to 255 because you were only using it to locate the brightest point.**

Zoom in to the area of the snow on top of the mountain until you are zoomed in about 400%. Click the Highlight Eyedropper in the Levels dialog box. Now move this Eyedropper up to that bright place in the snow, and move it around in the area while looking at the RGB values in the Info palette for the highest set of numbers. When you find those numbers (I chose 255, 255, 255), Shift-click once to set a Color Sampler at the spot where you want to set your highlight. Now move the cursor back on top of the circle where you set the Color Sampler and, when the cursor disappears, click without the Shift key to set your highlight value at that point. When the cursor disappears, you have the Color Sampler and the location for setting your highlight lined up exactly. The numbers to the right of the slash in the Info palette at your #1 Color Sampler location should now display 244, 244, 244 for RGB at that exact spot where you clicked. By setting the highlight here you have actually lowered the brightness of this snow to a value that will still have a dot when printing on a press and will actually get some ink dots when printing with a digital printer. If you wanted this snow to be a specular highlight, you could adjust this value to 255. As we go through this example, you can watch this Color Sampler location and you may notice the values get a bit higher than 244, 244, 244. You will be able to decide if this snow prints as pure white paper at 255, 255, 255 or still has a bit of detail by printing a smidgen darker.

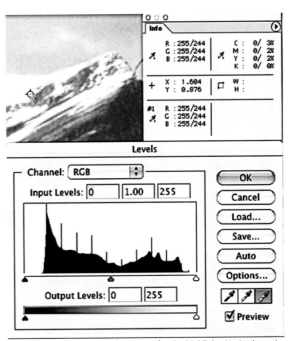

STEP 13: The before and after values for the highlight. Notice how the totally white snow was replaced by the 244, 244, 244 values by clicking using the Highlight Eyedropper. You can increase the brightness of these 244, 244, 244 values, and thus the snow, by going into each of the Red, Green, and Blue channels and moving the Output Highlight sliders back to the right. After moving the Output Highlight sliders back to the right all the way, moving the Input Highlight sliders to the left will make the image even brighter.

229

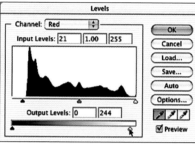

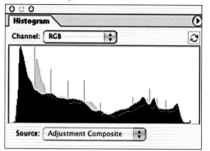

STEP 14: Notice that after setting the highlight and shadow with the eyedroppers, if you go into the Red, Green, and Blue channels, you will see that the Output Highlight sliders have been moved to the left, making the highlights duller, and the Input Shadow sliders have been moved to the right, making the shadows darker. See below how the Histogram palette has changed.

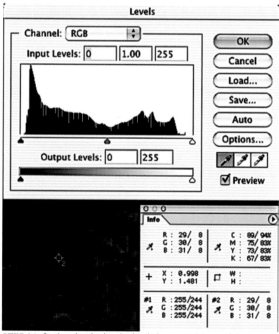

STEP 14: Setting the shadow in the dark area at the top of the tree. As you can see with the #2 Color Sampler, the initial values at this point were 29, 30, 31, but after we set the shadow that changed them to 8, 8, 8. Right after clicking your Color Sampler point with the Shadow Eyedropper, use Command-Z to toggle back and forth between having the new shadow value set and right before that. As you do that, notice how the shadow part of the RGB histogram on the left moves back and forth as each of the Red, Green, and Blue shadow values are changed when you click with the Eyedropper.

Now go to the Preview checkbox and turn off Preview. When Preview is off, you see the original image. When Preview is on, you see the image after the highlight change. Notice that this process of setting the highlight has darkened the image somewhat. As we go through the color correction process, click the Preview on and off from time to time to see what has happened to the image. **Turn Preview on again for now.**

Setting the highlight actually moves the highlight sliders in each of the Red, Green, and Blue channels, which in turn moves the highlight part of the histogram in the Levels Channel RGB display to the left or to the right. **Press Command-Z once to undo and then Command-Z again to redo this change while watching the RGB histogram and the white color or the sky. See the differences? Use the Channel pop-up menu at the top of Levels to look at each of the Red, Green, and Blue channel histograms. The Output Highlight slider in each of them should have changed to 244 or thereabouts. Clicking the snow with the Highlight Eyedropper caused each of these Red, Green, and Blue sliders to move. To change your Color Sampler highlight value to something other than 244, 244, 244, you could just manually move any of these Red, Green, or Blue Output Highlight Eyedroppers. Move the Channel pop-up back to RGB, which you can also do by using Command-~.**

SETTING THE SHADOW

STEP 14: Now we are going to use the Shadow Eyedropper to click a shadow. The shadow should be the darkest neutral area where you still want a little detail or you may want your shadows totally black. This depends on the image you are working on, where you click with the Shadow Eyedropper and the actual numerical values you use for your shadow. When looking for a location to set your shadows, the RGB values in the Info palette should normally be in the 1 to 10 range, but they may be higher than this for a particular scan like they are with this image. **Move the Levels dialog box to the top of the screen and zoom out so you can see the entire bottom half of the image. To find the correct area for setting the shadow, hold the Option key down while moving the Input Shadow slider to the right. The whole image area first turns white, and then as you move the slider to the right, black areas appear. The first black area to appear, in the upper tree to the lower left, is the place where you should set the shadow. Now move the Input Shadow slider back to 0 because you were only using it to locate the darkest point. Click the Shadow Eyedropper, the leftmost Eyedropper, in the Levels dialog box to select it. Now move this Eyedropper up to that darkest place, and then move it around in the area while watching the RGB values in the Info palette. You might want to zoom in to that particular area to around 400% before you pick the darkest spot. When you find the right spot, Shift-click there first to place a Color Sampler, then click once again without the Shift key in exactly the same location. You know that you are exactly on top of the Color Sampler when the cursor disappears.** The numbers for the #2 Color Sampler in the Info palette should now display 8, 8, 8 (or very close to it) for that exact spot where you clicked. The location you click will get a value of 8, 8, 8, or whatever preference value you have set for Shadow Eyedropper. If the point you click for the shadow is the darkest point in the image, then you won't lose any shadow detail that wasn't already in your scan, even if

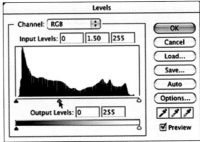

you set this to 0, 0, 0. On the other hand, if you click at a place that wasn't the darkest place in your image, you may end up removing some of the shadow detail from the scan. Be careful where you click to set your highlight and shadow values. **Now you can turn the Preview checkbox on and off to see the changes made to this image so far. Leave it on when you are done.**

SETTING THE OVERALL BRIGHTNESS OF THE IMAGE

STEP 15: As you look at this image, notice that it's pretty dark at this point. **Move the Input Brightness slider to the left until the middle Input Levels number reads about 1.50.** This opens up the image and makes it even a bit flat looking. If you think back to our discussion of the Zone System, you can equate the initial location of the Brightness slider with Zone V, the middle gray values. Moving the slider to the left moves Zone V down toward Zone III or IV, depending on how far you move it. What was a Zone IV value now becomes a Zone V value; lighter, and possibly a bit flatter. This effect is similar to the one you would get by setting the original camera exposure at Zone IV or lower, except moving the Brightness slider by a zone or two wouldn't change Zones I and IX as much. Notice that the RGB values for your #2 Color Sampler have changed to around a value of 22 instead of 8. If you leave them here, this will make your shadows look washed out. Since the shadows in this image don't have much detail anyhow, it is better to make sure they are black than have them end up a muddy gray. **Go into each of the Red, Green, and Blue channels and move the Input Shadow slider to the right until that channel has a value of around 6 to 8 at the #2 Color Sampler in the Info palette. Try to match the value, within 1 point anyhow, to get a neutral shadow. Once you click in the Input Shadow slider and move it a bit, the leftmost Input number is highlighted. At this point you can use the up and down arrows in the lower right of your keyboard to nudge the number up or down by a single digit.** This nudging works with most number entries in Photoshop and is often more accurate and less tedious than using the slider with the mouse button down.

CORRECTING FOR COLOR CASTS

STEP 16: **Many adjustments so far have been done with the Levels Channel selector set to RGB (Command-~). You can now use the Channel selector in Red (Command-1), Green (Command-2), and Blue (Command-3) modes to control the color balance of the image and to correct for color casts. You can switch between channels by clicking the pop-up menu and dragging up or down, or by using the key combinations Command-~ through Command-3.** The Red channel controls red and its complement, cyan; the Green channel controls green and its complement, magenta; and the Blue channel controls blue and its complement, yellow. Try to commit this set of complementary colors to memory. To learn more about the complementary colors, refer to the RGB/CMYK table at the end of Chapter 12: "Color Correction Tools." This image has a slightly blue color balance, which makes it seem a little cold. **Use the Channel selector or Command-3 to move to the Blue channel. Move the Input Brightness slider far to the right until the middle Input Levels number reads about 0.5 and notice how yellow the image is. Now move the same slider far to the left to about 1.5. Notice how blue the image is.** You can use this middle slider to control the color balance of the midtones. Remember that when the Brightness value reads 1.0 for any channel, that is the position where you haven't made any changes. **Move this slider back to the right until it reads about 0.86 and notice the differences in the**

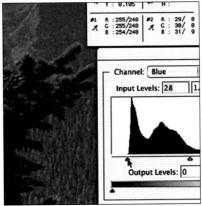

STEP 15: Move the Input Brightness slider to the left to about 1.50 to open up this image.

STEP 15: Here we are moving the Red, Green, and Blue Input Shadow sliders to the right to darken and re-neutralize the shadows.

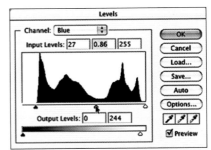

STEP 16: Here we are adjusting the color cast by moving the Blue Brightness slider to 0.86, which adds yellow to the midtones of the entire image.

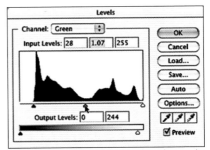

STEP 17: Here we are adjusting the color cast by moving the Green Brightness slider to 1.07, which adds green to the midtones of the entire image.

231

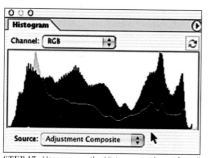

STEP 17: Here we see the Histogram palette after all the Levels adjustments are finished. Notice the white line showing the original histogram, which didn't have such a wide range left to right from black to white and also didn't have as many color values vertically in each area. This is now a better histogram!

color. You have added yellow to remove the blue cast in this image.

STEP 17: **Press Command-2 to switch to the Green channel. As you move the middle slider to the left, you add green, and as you move it to the right, you add magenta. Move this middle brightness channel to about 1.07 to add a little green to the entire image and improve the look of the trees.** Now when you turn the Preview checkbox on and off, you are seeing the difference all the Levels changes have made in this image.

If you press Command-1, you can use the middle slider to move between red and cyan. I changed this to 1.06 to add just a little red. You may make these adjustments differently depending on your preferences for color and your monitor. So long as you have calibrated your monitor and your output devices, you should be able to obtain results that you like. Whenever you make major cast changes to any particular channel, go back to RGB (Command-~) and then double-check your overall Brightness adjustments. **Take a look at your Histogram palette and notice how the histogram has changed since you started your Levels adjustments. Now click the OK button to complete all the changes you have made in this 16-bit Levels Adjustment layer.** With earlier versions of Photoshop, we were not able to create Adjustment layers in 16-bit but Photoshop CS allows this, which is much better. If you start with a 16-bit scan, I recommend you always do your initial Levels, Curves, and Hue/Saturation adjustments as 16-bit Adjustment layers. **At this point, choose File/Save As and save this as BanffLake16Layers.psd in case you want to revert to this version of the image later.**

INTRODUCTION TO CURVES

This section shows you how to adjust specific contrast and color ranges using Curves. Before you start making further adjustments to the Banff Lake image, take a moment to examine the Curves tool and its different parts and functions.

Curves is a graph of input and output values with the input values at the bottom of the graph on the horizontal axis and the output values to the left side of the graph on the vertical axis. When you use Curves, the input values are the original unadjusted values before you invoked Curves. The output values are the adjusted values and depend on the shape of the curve graph.

In Levels, the histogram is a picture of the actual data that makes up the particular image. In Curves, you see a graph of how this curve would modify any image, but you don't actually see the

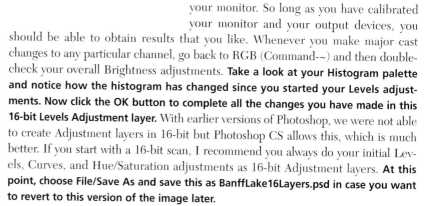

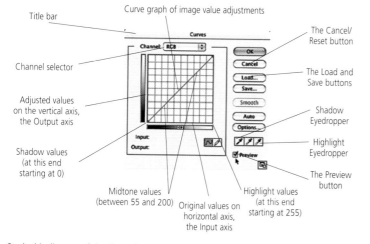

Study this diagram of the Photoshop Curves dialog to learn the controls of the Curves tool.

Chapter 19: Overall Color Correction

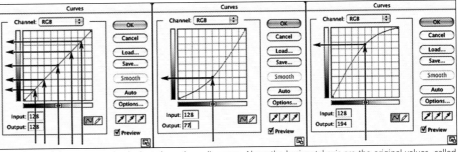

data that is part of the image. That is why I recommend using Levels first, after you do a scan, because you can see how the scan worked by looking at the histogram and then use Levels to create the best possible histogram from the scan you started with. Many of the controls in Curves are the same as those in Levels, but with Curves you don't see a picture of the data in this particular image. The power to see what a Curve is doing has greatly increased with Photoshop CS,

To understand the curve graphs, look at these three diagrams. Along the horizontal axis are the original values, called Input, with 0 (black) on the left side and 255 (white) on the right side. On the vertical axis of the curve, to the left side, are the modified values, called Output, with 0 (black) on the bottom and 255 (white) at the top. Imagine that the original values are light rays that travel straight up from the bottom of the diagram. When they hit the curve graph, they make an immediate left and exit the diagram on the left side. When the curve is the straight default curve, the values go out the same as they come in, as you can see by the leftmost curve above. When the curve is dragged downward, like the middle curve, a value that comes in at 128 hits the curve sooner so it will go out at 77. Because lower values represent darker numbers, pulling the curve down makes the image darker. When the curve is dragged upward, as in the right curve, the input value of 128 doesn't hit the curve until it gets to 194, and that is the brighter output value.

however, because the new Histogram palette allows you to see what a curve is doing to your image's histogram while you are doing it within Curves. Both Levels and Curves provide an OK button, which you press when you want the changes to become permanent, and a Cancel button, which you press when you want to leave the tool without any changes taking effect. If you hold the Option key down and then press Reset, you stay in the tool, all changes are undone, and the curve goes back to the default straight curve. Both Levels and Curves also have Load and Save buttons that you can use to load or save settings to the disk.

If you particularly like a curve that corrected one image, you can click Save to save it, go into Curves while working on another image, and click Load to run those saved settings on the other image. Curves, also like Levels, has Highlight and Shadow Eyedropper tools to set the highlight and shadow the same way you do in Levels. In fact, Curves uses the same preference values for the highlight and shadow numbers as you set in Levels. These preferences are systemwide. The curve graph is just a picture of what happens to all the values from 0 to 255. To move the curve, you click it and drag it to a new position. When you let go, Photoshop leaves a point along the curve graph, a point that causes the entire curve to move. To get rid of a point, click and drag it outside of the Curves window. When you do this, the curve bounces back to where it would be without that point. Let's experiment a bit now with Curves before you make final adjustments to the Banff Lake image.

STEP 18: Make sure your Histogram palette (Shift-F9) is visible for these steps and watch what happens to your histogram as you adjust the curves. Using the same image you saved at the end of Step 17, choose Image/New Adjustment Layer/Curves (Command-F3) and look at the Curves dialog box. You'll need to first choose OK from the New Layer dialog. If the Curves graph area is divided into only four sections horizontally and vertically, it is possible to get a more precise grid. Move the cursor to the middle area of the Curves graph, and Option-click in this center area. Now the Curves graph will have 10 sections in each direction. Option-clicking again will get you back to 4 sections in each direction. To get a bigger Curve window, where you can enter points with greater precision, click the grow box at the bottom-right of the curve diagram. Clicking in this area again will go back to the smaller curve diagram. Make sure that the Preview button is on so you can see your changes as you work with Curves.

STEP 18: In Photoshop CS, the grow box in the bottom right toggles the Curves window size.

By default in Curves, the horizontal axis shows the shadows on the left. The grayscale on this axis is a hint at this, which is easy to remember because Levels does the same thing. Some curve diagrams show the shadows on the right. If you click the arrow in the middle of the grayscale, you can flip this curve to put shadows on the right. Doing this turns everything else in the curve adjustment into a mirror image of what it was. Therefore, we recommend leaving shadows on the left. When you set the shadows on the right, the Input and Output values read as percentages between 0% and 100%. If you are more comfortable reading percentage values than the 0..255 values, you can make your Curves tool work this way.

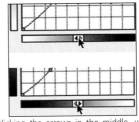

By clicking the arrows in the middle, you can make the horizontal axis have shadows on the left or the right. Leave the shadows on the left, like on the bottom here, for working with this book.

Introduction to Curves

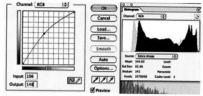

STEP 19: This curve makes the image lighter and brighter. To do this in Levels, move the Input Brightness slider to the left. The light gray in the Histogram palette shows the before histogram and the black is the after histogram.

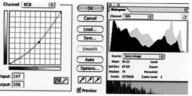

STEP 19: This curve makes the image darker. To do this in Levels, move the Input Brightness slider to the right. Notice how the black after histogram has more values to the left, which is the shadow side.

STEP 19: This S-curve makes the midtones more contrasty and the shadows and highlights less contrasty. You can't do exactly the same thing in Levels. Notice how this black after histogram actually has more values at either end.

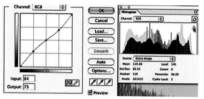

STEP 19: This reverse S-Curve makes the midtones flatter and increases contrast in the highlights and shadows. You can't do this exactly in Levels. To get the more accurate histogram displays shown in the three diagrams above, click on the yellow triangle when you see it. This indicates that your histogram is in a less accurate display mode. Clicking on the triangle causes the histogram to be recalculated using all the image data so it sometimes takes some time.

STEP 19: Now click the middle of the curve and move the mouse up and down, left and right, and notice how the curve shape changes. Also notice the corresponding changes to the image. Try all the curves in the diagrams above and on the next page. Option-Cancel between each one to reset the curve to the original, straight diagonal. Make sure you understand why each curve changes the image the way it does. Remember that each input value has to turn instantly to the left and become an output value as soon as it meets the curve. Trace some values for each of these examples, and I think you will understand how the curve graphs work. You need to understand these curve graphs because they come up all over the place in Photoshop (in Curves, Duotones, Custom CMYK, and Transfer functions), as well as in many books and other applications dealing with color. Cancel the Curves dialog when you are finished.

CHANGING CONTRAST WITH CURVES

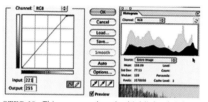

STEP 19: This curve makes the highlights brighter. This is similar to when you move the Input Highlight slider in Levels to the left. Notice how this looses highlight details that have all changed to 255 in the black after histogram.

STEP 20: **Use Window/Layers (F10) to bring up your Layers palette. Choose Layer/New Adjustment Layer/Curves (Command-F3) to add a Curves adjustment layer to your image. The New Curves dialog will come up and you should name this layer Overall Curves and press OK to bring up the Curves dialog. For this curve, you will want the curve diagram with 4 section dividers. If you currently have a graph that is divided into 10 sections, Option-click in the middle of the curve graph until you get only 4. Click once on each of the 3 intersections along the diagonal line, across the curve, which will place a point on each of those points. Move the bottom point down and to the right, the top point up and to the left, and leave the middle point where it was.** This will create an S-shape curve that

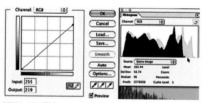

STEP 19: This curve makes the highlights duller. This is similar to when you move the Output Highlight slider in Levels to the left. See, where the arrow cursor is, how the after histogram has now moved to the left producing duller highlights.

The Adjustment Composite histogram displays seen on this page alway happens if you do Image/Adjustments/Curves but if you want to see this double histogram display while in an Adjustment layer you need to choose Adjustment Composite from the Source menu in the Histogram palette after creating your first Adjustment Layer. You'll only see this double histogram display while inside a color adjustment tool that has changed the image.

will make the image more contrasty. Play with the different points on this curve to see how moving them effects the image. The final values we used for the bottom point were Input of 70 and Output of 56, for the middle point we used Input of 130 and Output of 125, and for the top point we used Input of 183 and Output of 195. After clicking any point, you can either drag to move the point, type in a new value for Input or Output, or you can use the up and down arrows on your keyboard to move any point up or down in value. **If you don't like the way the image looks with these values, move the points around until you get what you like.** The bottom point has more control

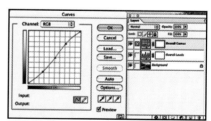

STEP 20: Here you see the Overall Contrast curve that we have added as an adjustment layer on top of the Overall Levels adjustment layer on top of the *Background* layer in the Layers palette. After choosing OK and closing this Curves dialog, you can go back to it and even change it as many times as you want to by double-clicking the little curve graph, which is the leftmost layer thumbnail for this Curves adjustment layer. When you change an adjustment layer, you are not permanently modifying the values in the background layer as you would if you chose Image/Adjustments/... then made changes. Adjustment layers also keep track of your changes for you.

over the shadow areas, the top point, the highlights, and the middle point controls the midtones. If you move the middle point up and to the left, the midtones will become lighter. Moving it down and to the right darkens the midtones. To see where any location in the image actually appears on the curve, click that point in the image and hold the mouse button down; you will see a circle on the curve showing the values relating to that point. You could now move that part of the curve and the contrast of that point, and similar ones, will change. With Curves you have a lot of control! **Press Return (OK) when you are happy with the contrast of the image.** Since you did this curve as an adjustment layer, notice that the Layers palette now contains the Overall Contrast Curve adjustment layer on top of the Overall Levels adjustment layer on top of the *Background* layer.

ENHANCING COLOR WITH HUE/SATURATION

STEP 21: Now you are going to create another adjustment layer of type Hue/Saturation. **Choose Layer/New Adjustment Layer/Hue/Saturation (Command-F4) to create a new Hue/Saturation adjustment layer.** Using the Master selection in the Edit pop-up menu at the top, the Hue/Saturation tool allows you to adjust the hue balance and color saturation of the entire image. Using this tool, you can add contrast and drama to an image without losing shadow detail. **In Master, move the Saturation slider to +12 to increase the saturation of all colors. Move the Hue slider from left to right and notice how this changes the color balance of the entire image. Put it back to 0 when you are finished playing with it.** When you saturate all the colors, mainly the midtones change; the highlights and shadows remain the same. You can verify this by looking at the values in your highlight and shadow Color Samplers in the Info palette.

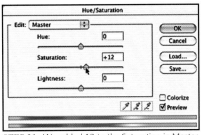

STEP 21: We added 12 to the Saturation in Master, which will saturate all the colors. Notice that if you move the Hue to the right, that makes the colors a bit warmer and more magenta, if you move it to the left, the image looks more green.

Now change the Edit pop-up to Reds and move the Hue slider left and right while noticing how this changes the color of the dirt in the foreground. Change the Reds settings so the Hue slider is set to +8 and the Saturation slider to +12. When Reds is selected, only parts of the image that contain red will change in color. This change removes the red cast the dirt had in the foreground. **Note: If you just wanted to see the effect of the additional red changes, first make the suggested changes to Master and then choose OK. Now double-click the leftmost Layer thumbnail for this Hue/Saturation layer to bring up the Hue/Saturation dialog again. Now move the Edit pop-up to Reds and go ahead and make your red changes. Since you made the changes to Master within the initial invocation of this dialog, turning the Preview checkbox off will now show you the image with just the Master changes applied. Turning the Preview checkbox on will show you the image with the Master changes and the Red changes.** The Preview checkbox, for this second invocation of the tool, now just shows you the changes you added for the Reds. To see your changes as you work, make sure the Preview checkbox is checked while working in this tool and all color correction tools.

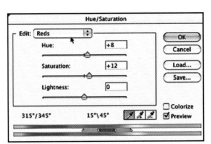

STEP 21: Here we see the suggested changes with Edit set to Reds.

Now change Edit to Yellows and set the Hue to -4 and Saturation to +16. This further changes the color of the dirt in the foreground and also makes subtle changes to the mountains further back. You may need to zoom to 100% (Command-Option-0) and turn the Preview button on and off to notice these subtle changes. **Now change the Edit pop-up to Greens and make the Hue +10 and Saturate the greens by +20. Click on the Eyedropper plus tool, to the bottom right of this dialog, and drag this**

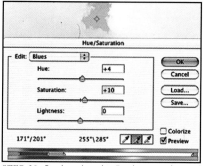

STEP 21: *STEP 21: By dragging the Eyedropper plus tool across the patch of blue sky, we change the left-most range of blues to 171/201 degrees.*

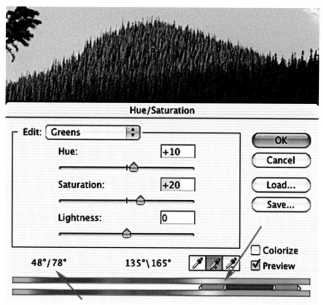

STEP 21: The goal here is to enhance the Saturation and Hue of the green trees. First set Edit to Greens, then move the Hue to +10 to add cyan to the greens, then set the Saturation to +20, which makes them more intense. The colored sliders at the bottom of the Hue/Saturation diagram show you, above the dark gray area, the range of colors Photoshop considers to be green. The colors above the lighter gray areas on either side are greens but are affected to a lesser extent. As shown in the image area above, move the Eyedropper tool, the cursor, over the top of the brighter green trees below the lake, then click and drag the Eyedropper over this green tree area. Notice how the width of the darker gray area increases to include the more yellow greens shown here with the rightmost red arrow. The leftmost red arrow points out the exact numerical Hue settings I chose with my Eyedropper. These numbers can be edited by hand by clicking on the two leftmost gray bars under the rightmost red arrow above. Adjusting the definition of Greens, or any of the Edit colors, this way is a very powerful feature of the Hue/Saturation tool that I use often.

tool across the green tree area shown in the illustration to the left. This has now corrected the range of greens we are affecting to be the specific tree greens within this image. See the illustration to the left for more info on this adjustment. With Greens selected, only parts of the image that contain these greens will change in color. Removing some greens from the colors to be modified can be done with the Eye-dropper minus tool by clicking and dragging over the colors you want to remove. **Finally switch Edit to Blues and set the Hue to +4 and the Saturation to +10. Now click on the Eye-dropper plus tool, then drag it across the center of the patch of blue in the top center of the sky. See the illustration above on this page.** Notice that this changes the range of blues to be affected by the Blue Hue/Saturation adjustment by extending them more into the cyan colors. This changes the sky blues as well as the blues in the shadows of the mountains at the back center of this image.

The color of the lake in this image may seem a bit strange, but this lake in the Canadian Rockies is filled with water from a melted glacier and it actually does have this unusual color. **Choose OK when you are happy with the Hue and Saturation, then choose File/Save to save your changes so far.**

ADJUSTING SELECTED COLOR AREAS USING MASKS

STEP 22: During the Overall Color Correction steps, which we just completed, the goal is to correct the overall image without using selections or masks to fine-tune the color, or contrast adjustment, of any particular areas. We are looking at the entire image and trying to make the largest areas of it look correct. Now that we have completed those steps, we should have a histogram for this image that we are happy with, having correct and neutral highlight and shadow values, an overall brightness and contrast that we like, and also a good overall color saturation. Now we want to find the isolated parts of the image that will require a selection or mask to be improved even more.

You should notice the dark shadows to the top of the tree at the left and also in the trees behind the person to the front of the image. One of the greatest things about 16-bit scans from many of today's scanners (Imacon, Polaroid Sprintscan 120, Nikon

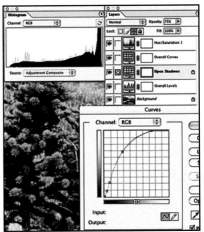

4000&8000, Epson 3200, etc.) is that you can pull a lot of highlight and shadow detail from these scans if you know how to do it. When you make the scans this detail needs to not be thrown away. See Chapter 16: "Image Resolution and Scanning," for details of how to correctly make the scans. What we want to do now is insert a curve, to bring out shadow detail, between the Overall Levels and Overall Curves layer. **Click on the leftmost Layer thumbnail of the Overall Levels layer in the Layers palette to make this layer active. Now choose Layer/New Adjustment Layer/Curves, name this layer Open Shadows, then choose OK to bring up the Curves dialog again. Click the point at the top-most right of the curve line and drag it straight to the left quite a way.** This increases the slope of the shadow areas in the lower left and you should notice the shadows in the trees getting lighter. **Add several points down in the bottom left of the curve moving this part of the curve even further to the left. Add a point in the middle left, you can see these points in the diagram to the right for step 22. Now that you have the three points to hold the middle and bottom of the curve in place, drag the top point, the one you started this curve with, back over to the top-right side. Choose OK when your curve looks like the one in step 22 to the right here.** Notice that most of the image is now very light and flat, but the dark shadows have much more detail. **Now choose Image/Adjustments/Invert which will make the mask for this Adjustment layer all black.** The black mask removes this adjustment from everywhere. The mask for an Adjustment layer is all white by default, as in your other three Adjustment layers, which means everything is being adjusted. **Now type a B to choose the Paintbrush from the Tools palette. Use Window/Options (F12) to bring up the Options bar, then choose Airbrush 7% from the Tool Presets pop-up at the very left of the Options bar.** Note: This preset will only be available and work correctly if you loaded BarrysPhotoBrushes and ArtistryCSToolPresets in your Tool Presets as described in bold print on page 30 in Chapter 3. **Type a D, for Default Colors, which will make the foreground color white when you are working in a mask. You are now going to paint with white, on top of the darker areas in the tree, using the soft brush set up with the Airbrush 7% setting. You are actually painting in the mask but seeing its effect on the dark trees. The longer you hold down the brush, the more white is applied to your mask and you should see details begin to appear in these darker areas. If too much shadow detail appears, use Command-Z to undo your last brush stroke or use the History palette (F8) to undo several strokes. You can also type an X, for exchange colors, to change the foreground color to black. Painting with black in the mask will remove some of the shadow detail you added. Use the left bracket key to get a smaller brush and the right bracket key to get a larger brush. Paint white in other tree shadow areas to bring out more detail.** To toggle between seeing the image and the layer mask, Option-click on the rightmost Layer Mask thumbnail for this Open Shadows layer. You can open the BanffLake16Layers.tif file from the Overall Color Correction folder on the *Photoshop CS Artistry* CD and compare your mask for this layer to the one I made. **When you are happy with the shadow detail added, click on the Hue/Saturation Layer at the top of the Layers palette so the next layer will be added above it.**

STEP 23: **Make sure that the active layer in the Layers palette is the topmost Hue/Saturation Adjustment layer. The active layer is the one that is highlighted; you can click the name of a layer to highlight it. We are going to create a new Curves adjustment layer, which will appear on top of the Hue/Saturation layer and that means this new layer's corrections will happen after the Hue/Saturation corrections have already occurred. Choose Layer/New Adjustment Layer/Curves or just press Command-F3, if you have ArtistKeys installed, to make yet another adjustment layer,**

STEP 22: Here you see the Open Shadows curve that we have inserted between the Overall Levels and Overall Curves. The idea of this curve is to increase the slope, or angle, down in the lower-left corner, where most of the dark shadow values are. Increasing the slope on these values adds contrast to this area and also makes the values much lighter. Notice, in the Histogram palette, how the shadow values to the left side of the histogram are spread out which opens them up a bit.

STEP 22: Choosing Airbrush 7% from the Options bar. To do this you must be using the Paintbrush tool (B), then click and drag in the Presets icon (see the black arrow above) at the top left of the Options bar.

Adjusting Selected Color Areas Using Masks

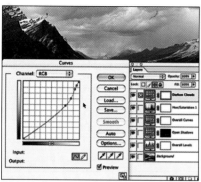

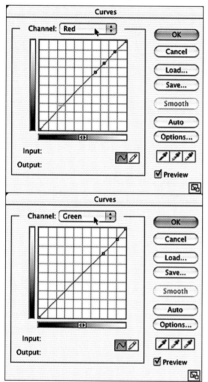

STEP 23: Here we see the RGB part of the Darken Clouds adjustment layer while its mask is still all white. Notice how dark the image is.

STEP 23: Here are the changes I made to the Green and Red channels of the Darken Clouds curve. These changes removed the undesirable color casts.

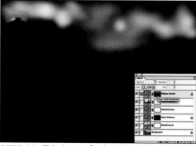

STEP 23: This is my final Darken Clouds mask, which I observed by Option-clicking on the Layer mask thumbnail. Option-clicking a second time on this thumbnail allows me to see my image again.

which you should name Darken Clouds. Click a point in the top-center of the diagonal line and drag it down and to the right until the clouds have more drama and you like the way they look. I added several points to make the top part of the curve more vertical. See the illustration to the left. Don't worry about the rest of the image looking too dark, just get the clouds to look the way you want them, actually a little darker and more contrasty than you want in the end, then choose OK.

Notice that this Darken Clouds adjustment layer in the Layers palette has two thumbnails associated with it. The leftmost one is the Layer thumbnail and it contains the little icon that looks like a curve diagram, which shows you that this is a Curve type adjustment layer. The rightmost thumbnail is the Layer Mask thumbnail and it is completely white, which means that right now this adjustment is happening to the entire image. **Choose Image/Adjustments/Invert (Command-I) to invert this Layer Mask thumbnail, and the layer mask, to completely black. Now this curve change doesn't apply to any of the image. Type a B to switch to the Paintbrush tool, then choose the Airbrush 7% preset as you did before from the top left of the Options bar. Type a D for Default Colors, which will make your foreground color white and your background color black, then use the right bracket key to increase your brush size a bit. Now paint over the parts of the clouds where you want the clouds to be darker and more contrasty.** As you paint white in the mask, you are selectively applying this Darken Clouds adjustment layer to the areas where you paint. The more you paint, the more of the adjustment you apply until that part of the mask is totally white. If you want more darkness or contrast at that point, you'd have to go back and edit the curve. **Continue to paint until all the cloud areas that need to be darker or more contrasty are changed. Don't bring the brush too close to the tops of the mountains, as you don't want them darkened by this Curves adjustment. If you accidentally paint too close to the mountains and they get darkened, you can use Command-Z to undo the last brush stroke or use the History palette (F8) to remove several brush strokes. You can also just type an X, for Exchange, to switch the foreground color to black. Painting over the mountains with black will again remove the curve adjustment from the black painted areas. Type X a second time to switch back to white.**

You may notice that this curve has added a green or magenta color cast to different parts of the clouds. If you are having this problem, zoom into those parts of the curve until your Navigator shows 100%. Now double-click on the leftmost Layer thumbnail for the Darken Clouds layer, which will bring up the Curves dialog again. Switch to the Green channel, then click and drag the mouse over the area of the clouds where you are seeing the cast and move the cursor around while the mouse is down. A circle will appear on your curve graph showing you where those values are in the curve. If the clouds are too green, click in that area of the curve and drag it ever so slightly down and to the right to add a little magenta. If the clouds are too magenta, drag up and to the left to add green. You may find that the adjustment needs to be made in the Red channel where down and to the right will add cyan and up and to the left will add red. See the curves to the left here so you can check out the adjustments I made to tweak the color.

FIXING CLOUDS AND REMOVING SPOTS

STEP 24: Now we are going to fix the top left and top right of the image where the lens shield of the camera caused a vignetting effect with this 28mm wide-angle lens. **Click the word Background in the *Background* layer to activate that layer. Type an M to switch to the Rectangular Marquee tool. Shift-M will toggle between the Rectangular and Oval marquee, by the way. Use the Rectangular Marquee to select all of**

the cloud area of the image as shown in the illustration here. Now choose Layer/New/Layer via Copy to turn this selection into a new layer right above the

STEP 24: Select this area with the Marquee to start the process of fixing the clouds.

Background **layer.** You will work on this copy of the clouds so if you make a mistake, the original undamaged clouds will still be in the *Background* layer below. **Click the Lock Position icon at the top of the Layers palette to lock the position of this layer so you don't accidentally move it with the Move tool. Type an S to switch to the Rubber Stamp tool, called the Clone Stamp tool in Photoshop 7 and CS, and choose the 100-pixel soft brush from the Brush pop-up in the Options palette at the top of your screen. Make sure Opacity and Flow are set to 100%. Move the cursor over some good-looking clouds, a bit below and to the left of the dark top-right corner area.**

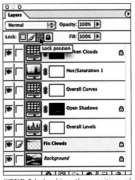

STEP 24: Locking the position of the Fix Clouds layer so it can't be accidentally moved.

STEP 24: This is what it should look like in the Rubber Stamp tool with the mouse button down as you replace the black area with good clouds. The + shows you where clouds are being copied from and the circle shows you where the clouds are being copied to. Make sure the Use All Layers option is off (that is, unchecked).

Option-click at the spot where you want to copy the clouds from. Now release the mouse button and move the cursor over to the top-right corner where you need to replace the black area with good clouds. Click and hold the mouse button as you drag across the black area and see it replaced by good clouds. While the mouse button is down, you'll see a + where Photoshop is copying new cloud data from and a circle where the data is being copied to. Do this slowly and over and over again until you understand what is happening and get some good-looking clouds in the top-right corner. You can always choose Command-Z to Undo one step, then try it again. If you really mess up the area, bring up the History palette and click back before you started using the Rubber Stamp tool. **When you have fixed your clouds, double-click on the default Layer 1 name for this layer and rename it to Fix Clouds. Turn the Eye icon off for the *Background* layer for now, so you are just seeing image data from this Fix Clouds layer.**

Now zoom to 100% by choosing View/Actual Pixels (Command-Option-0), then zoom in one more time, using Command-Spacebar-click, to get the image to 200%. Press the Home key on your keyboard to scroll the image to the top-left corner, then choose the third brush from the top left in the Brushes pop-up. You should still be using the Clone Stamp tool. You can now press the Tab key to remove all your palettes from the screen. If you are still in Full Screen mode, you will just see a close-up of the top-left corner of the screen. You now want to scroll through your image one full screen at a time and remove any dust or spots until you have a totally clean image. When you see a dust spot, or a larger piece of dirt, move the cursor next to the spot on top of an area that matches the color and contrast where the spot is. Hold the Option key down and click once where you want to copy image data from to fix

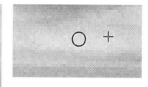

STEP 24: A spot to the left with the Option key down and cursor on the right. Option-click next to the spot to show Photoshop where to pick up color and detail.

STEP 24: Click the spot without the Option key down. The cursor should look like this before you click, and the spot should be removed when you click using the pixels from where you Option-clicked before.

STEP 24: The circle and the crosshair that you see while cloning with the mouse button down. Photoshop picks up detail from the crosshair and places it down at the cursor circle.

the spot. Release the mouse button. Now move the cursor on top of the spot and click without the Option key down. The data will be copied from where you Option-clicked to where you clicked without the Option key. If you hold the mouse button down and drag, you'll see a + where Photoshop is copying from and a circle where it is copying to.

Once you initially Option-click and then click without the Option key, this sets up the spatial relationship between where Photoshop copies from and where it copies to. If Aligned is on in the Rubber Stamp's options, this spatial relationship will stay the same until you Option-click again, so you don't have to use the Option key each time. You can just click and data will always be copied from the left, right, bottom, or top of where you click, depending on your initial set of Option-click and then click. **To remove a big spot or piece of dust, you'll have to click multiple times, or hold the mouse button down and drag, until the spot is gone. You only need to Option-click again if the color of where you are copying from no longer matches where you are copying to.** If you are having trouble getting the Rubber Stamp tool to work correctly, look at page 49 of Chapter 4: "The Tools Palette," for more details about how it works.

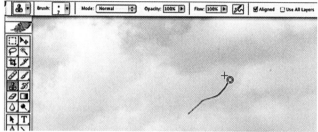

STEP 24: This long piece of dust with three straight sections can actually be removed in about three short steps. Option-click to the top left of the dust to pick up clean sky from there, then click at the top of the dust as shown here, which will remove the top end of the dust. Release the mouse button and move the cursor down the straight piece of dust and Shift-click just before the dust piece curves to the left. Shift-clicking will clone from where you first clicked in a straight line to where you Shift-click. You can repeat this process for the three straight sections of this strip of dust to remove it more quickly.

When you have removed all the spots from this section of the screen, you can use Command-Page Down to scroll one screen full to the right. Now you remove the spots from this section and continue to scroll to the right until you reach the right side of the screen. At that point you can press the Page Down key on your keyboard to scroll one full screen down. Now you are fixing a full screen, then choosing Command-Page Up to scroll a full screen to the left. Move through the entire Fix Clouds layer until you have removed all the spots in this layer. Now use Tab to bring up your palettes again and click the word Background to activate the *Background* layer. Press Tab again to remove your palettes and then continue stepping through screens of the *Background* layer until you have removed all the spots there, too.

SCRATCH REMOVAL A: First, Option-click below the left end of a scratch using a brush slightly bigger than the scratch.

SCRATCH REMOVAL B: Second, click the left end of the scratch, centered on the scratch, directly above where you Option-clicked before.

SCRATCH REMOVAL C: Third, Shift-click the right end of the scratch, centered on the scratch. The scratch should disappear! You can use this technique to remove scratches made in film by the film processor. After the initial removal, you may need to do some further Rubber Stamp cleanup on some parts of the scratch.

SAVING AND ARCHIVING YOUR MASTER IMAGE

STEP 25: **Now that you have spotted your master image, you need to save this file and go ahead and make a test print to be sure you are happy with the color. We will show you how to prepare the test print in Step 26 and beyond. After making the test print, you may need to come back to one or more of your adjustment layers and tweak the color before you achieve a final print. To tweak an adjustment layer, just double-click on its Layer thumbnail, which will bring up that layer's Levels, Curves, or Hue/Saturation dialog and show you the adjustments you already made. You can then make subtle changes to what you have already done based on what you want to change in the print. When bringing up an adjustment layer a second time, turning the Preview checkbox off shows you the image based on the first set of adjustments; turning on the Preview checkbox shows you the image with the changes you have added after bringing it up the second time. To see the image without this**

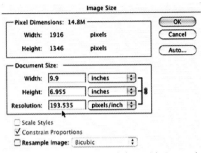

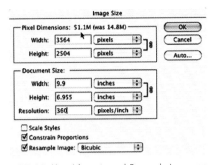

STEP 26: The Image Size dialog with Resample Image off and the Width set to 9.9 inches, my normal letter size test print width. Having resample off shows me that when I take the 1916 pixels in the width of this image and divide that by 9.9 inches, I'll be printing using 193.535 pixels of digital file per inch on the printer. For a test print, I would usually just change this resolution to a close whole number, 195 for this image, and not resample.

STEP 26: Here I have turned Resample Image on and changed the Resolution to 360. This changes this file from 14.8 megabytes up to 51.1 megs. The added pixels won't be quite as accurate as the original ones, but 360 and 480 pixels/inch are optimal resolutions for Epson printers. I've found that most people won't notice the difference between 300, 320, or 360 dpi in a print so I don't always resample to 360 or 480 as I used to. My 35mm Originals are scanned at 4000 to 5000 dpi. Just using that data, without resampling, I usually make 9.9-inch wide test prints at 500-600 dpi and 20-inch wide final prints at 240-360 dpi. My 6x7cm and 4x5 inch originals create much larger files where my large final prints are often set at 480 dpi. I rarely resample my original scan, which allows me to do just one very careful sharpening of that original data after the color correction process.

adjustment layer at all, you need to turn off this layer's Eye icon in the Layers palette. When you are finally happy with all your adjustments to this image, save and archive this as your master layered image to a CD or some other permanent backup storage.

Resampling and Retargeting Copies of a Master Image for Different Size Prints and Other Uses

Making an RGB or CMYK Print Version

STEP 26: After saving your master layered file, choose Image/Duplicate (F5) to make an onscreen copy of your master image. Turn on the Duplicate Merged Layers Only option in the Duplicate dialog and enter a name for this image of LakeTest 300 dpi 4x6. Choosing Merged Layers Only in Photoshop CS will blend all the layers in this copy into one Photoshop background layer. Press F for Full Screen mode and then Command-0 to fill the screen with this copy. Go into Image/Image Size (F7) and turn off the Resample Image option at the bottom of the dialog. This allows you to play around with numbers to see what you will get without resampling your image. If you don't need to resample, that is better, and when you do resample, you want to resample down and make a larger image smaller, rather than resample up. Set the width to 9.9 inches, which is the width you'd want for a centered test print on letter size paper on most Epson printers. At 9.9 inches, the resolution is 193.535. What I'd usually do at this point is just bump the resolution up to 195, or a larger even number in the case of the bigger original scan, and then make my test print. If you wanted to resample the image, which I usually don't for my art prints, you could now turn on Resample Image and then add or take away pixels. Choose OK as you have now set your print size. Note: This is a downsampled file because I had to have room for it on the *Photoshop CS Artistry* CD. The real original scan started at 5760 dpi, which is the maximum 35mm optical resolution for the scanner I used.

STEP 27: Now we need to sharpen the image because it is at its final size and we have not sharpened it before, even while scanning. You will get better sharpening results if you don't sharpen the image till it reaches its final resampled size. Choose View/Actual Pixels (Command-Option-0) to zoom the image to 100% and then do Filter/Sharpen/Unsharp Mask (F4). The details of the Unsharp Mask filter are explained in the next chapter, but what you need to know

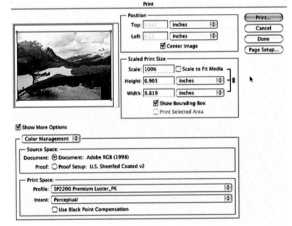

Step 27: When you are printing directly using a profile for your printer-paper-ink combination, you can convert to that profile while printing using the Color Management options at the bottom of the Print with Preview dialog. Source Space will be set to your RGB working space, usually Adobe RGB, and Print Space will be set to the correct profile for your printer-paper-ink combination. The Intent is usually set to Perceptual for photographs with Use Black Point Compensation off. See pages 169-175 in chapter 15 for details on how to tweak canned profiles, make your own profiles, and calibrate your monitor to your printer. Other printer settings and alternatives are also discussed there.

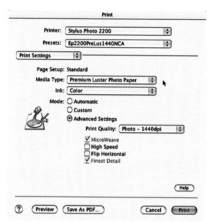

STEP 27: When you press the Print button at the top right of the Print with Preview dialog, you get this main Print dialog in Mac OS X. Choosing Print Settings allows you to choose your Media Type and other Advanced Settings. With Epson printers, it is very important to set all these print settings correctly, especially choosing the right Media Type as that determines how much ink is used. The Advanced Settings I've chosen above are what I recommend for high-quality prints on the Epson 2200, 7600, and other Epson printers. Setting the Print Quality at 2880, versus 1440, will not be noticeably different for most images but the prints will take longer. Setting it to 720 also produces quite good results, prints more quickly, and uses less ink. I use 1440 for my art prints but 720 for cards and mass printing jobs.

STEP 27: The Color Management part of the Print dialogs is also important. When you are converting to a profile for your printer, you want Color Management set to No Color Adjustment. In the Workshops I teach, the most common reason people's Epson prints don't look right is that they set the Print dialogs incorrectly and/or inconsistently.

If the 3 and 2 in the Options bar get the letters px after them, your rulers are set to Pixels instead of inches and you are about to resample your image to 3x2 pixels! If you see px instead of in after the dimensions, press the Escape key at the top left of your keyboard to exit the Crop tool, then use Edit/Preferences/Units and Rulers to change your Ruler Units to inches.

here is that you will use different settings in this filter, depending on the size of the image and also on the particular image. Also, you are usually best judging the results of a sharpen or a blur while looking at the image at 100%. **For this image, I have decided to use the 100, 1.0, and 3 setting. Start with these values and then you can play with the settings and see what they do to the image, as long as the Preview button is on in the Unsharp Mask dialog.** Again, we will go into the details of what each setting does in the next chapter. You may want to check and respot your image after the final sharpening; there should be little additional work! **Do Command-S to save your image in RGB format. If you were going to make a test print on an Epson or other RGB printer, this would be the image you'd test. See the illustrations here to see how to print this on the Epson 2200 or similar digital printer.**

STEP 28: **If you were going to print this as a CMYK press proof of some sort, make sure your CMYK working space in the Color Settings preferences was correct for this print job, then you'd choose Image/Mode/CMYK to convert this image to CMYK. Depending on your monitor calibration and your other preferences setup, you might notice a certain color and/or contrast shift after converting to CMYK. You can use Command-Z to toggle back and forth between RGB and CMYK to help you decide if you need to make adjustments after converting to CMYK. When View/Proof Setup is set to the default of Working CMYK, you can actually do this and make the adjustments in RGB mode by turning on View/Proof Colors to see what your RGB file will look like when converted to CMYK.** Because I don't usually adjust my RGB master files based on how they will look in CMYK, my normal workflow is to go ahead and do the conversion to CMYK and then fix any problems in that particular CMYK version at that time. This is my preference because the main focus of my images is my larger art prints that are destined for RGB output devices, like the Epson 4000 or 7600 or 9600.

MAKING A WEB VERSION

STEP 29: **Use the Window menu to go back to your BanffLakeLayers master image; then choose Image/Duplicate again with Duplicate Merged Layers Only on naming this file BanffLakeWeb300x200. Press the Tab key to remove all your palettes, then choose F for Full Screen mode and View/Fit On Screen (Command-0) to fill the screen with this image. Type C to switch to the Crop tool, and press Return to bring up its options in the Options bar. Set the Width to 3 and the Height to 2; then draw the crop box across the full width of the image. Release the mouse and then click inside the crop box and drag down to center the crop area, so an even amount is cut from the top and bottom of this image. Press Return to actually do the crop. The Crop tool will have now forced the image to the aspect ratio you have chosen. Now choose Image/Image Size (F7) to bring up the Image Size dialog again and set the dpi (Resolution in Pixels/Inch) to 72, then set the top Width, in the Pixel Dimensions area, to 300 pixels. Press OK to resample your image for the Web. Now choose Command-Option-0 for 100% and then press F4 for Unsharp Mask and use the 200, .5, and 0 settings.** Larger amounts and smaller Radius values seem to work better for the small Web images. **Now choose File/Save As and save this file in JPEG format with the Quality set at High (8) and Baseline Optimized On.** These JPEG settings are explained in great detail in the last section of the book: "Images for the Web and Multimedia."

In versions of this book before *Photoshop 6 Artistry*, we had used an image called the Grand Canyon for this initial Overall Color Correction exercise. For *Photoshop 6 Artistry*, I decided to move on to a new image with a slightly different

Chapter 19: Overall Color Correction

approach. The Grand Canyon image, however, is a great image to illustrate that setting the highlights and shadows to neutral values can do a lot towards the color correction of many images. **To gain extra understanding of what we are doing here and why, you might also want to go through the Overall Color Correction process described in this chapter using the Grand Canyon image, which is still on the CD, called GrandCanPCDRaw.jpg, in the folder for this chapter. My color corrected version of this image, called GrandCanyonLayers.psd, is in the Extra Info Files folder for this chapter.**

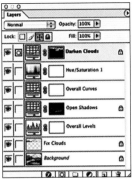

The final Layers palette for this master image. Notice that each layer with image data or a non-white layer mask has been locked against accidental movement.

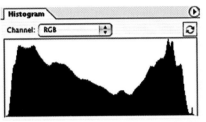

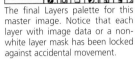

STEP 29: Here is the JPEG version of this image but printed at 300 dpi.

Here is the final greatly improved histogram for this image. Compare this to the original one on the first page. Values now go all the way from white to black and there are many more saturated values.

STEP 29: The final version of the Banff Lake image after sharpening and resampling to 6 inches wide. For my final art print of this image, I also removed the people and the post in the front right of this image. Doing that is a bit advanced for the first exercise in this book. Later in this book, you'll learn to do that type of thing and more.

243

Resampling and Retargeting Copies of a Master Image for Different Size Prints and Other Uses

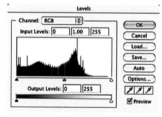

20 HANDS-ON SESSION: Correcting a Problem Image

Overall color correction using adjustment layers on a problem scan without good white or black points. Using advanced selections and adjustment layers with Curves, Hue/Saturation, and Unsharp Mask to finish color correcting a problem scan; soft proofing and fixing out-of-gamut colors.

The initial Kansas Photo CD scan.

STEP 2: Original RGB histogram with lack of highlight values.

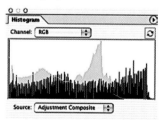

STEP 2: Histogram palette display of above histogram after highlights are set. The original histogram is now gray.

In this example, you will do overall color correction but use some different techniques than in the Banff Lake session because the histogram of this scan looks different. For the purposes of this example, we assume that you have done the Banff Lake, Chapter 19: "Overall Color Correction," example.

SETTING HIGHLIGHTS WITH CHANNELS

STEP 1: **Open the file KansasRawPhotoCD from the Chapter 20 folder on the *Photoshop CS Artistry* CD. When you get the Embedded Profile Mismatch dialog, leave this file in ColorMatch RGB space to have your color correction adjustments to match the books. The other choice would be to convert the file to Adobe RGB, which is what you would do when opening a scan with a scanner profile attached.** This is a 4MB 8-bit Photo CD scan of a Kodachrome shot I took while driving through Kansas during a summer vacation when I was in college in 1977. Old Kodachromes tend to fade! **In the Crop tool (C), delete the Option bar values in Width and Height if they are still there from the last exercise. Use the Crop tool to crop the copyright notice from the bottom. Choose File/Save As and save this file as KansasLayers. Put the image in Full Screen mode (F) by clicking the middle icon at the bottom of the Tools palette. Bring up the Info palette (F9 with ArtistKeys) and the Histogram palette (Shift-F9), and then choose Image/New Adjustment Layer/Levels (Command-F2) to enter Levels giving this adjustment layer the name Overall Levels.**

STEP 2: Look at the original RGB histogram pictured here and notice that the values don't go all the way to the right (highlight) side, which is why the picture looks dull. **Press Command-1, then Command-2, and then Command-3 to look at the Red, Green, and Blue channels, respectively.** I always do this when I first look at a scan to see if it has any potential problems. In this image, all the channels have dull highlights, but each of them has highlight detail that ends at a different point on the histogram. **Press Command-~ to go back to RGB and then hold down the Option key while dragging the Input Highlight slider to the left.** Remember, the Option key technique only works if you have the Preview checkbox on. You would normally set the highlight at the first area to turn white. In this photo, there is no good, neutral place to set a highlight, which should be pure white after that setting. The "white" buildings aren't really that white, and the brightest area is actually somewhere in the blue clouds. That's a sign that the Eyedropper may not be the best way to set the highlights in this image. **Type Command-1 again and move the Red Input Highlight slider to the left until it reaches the first real histogram data, at about 213. Do the same thing for the Green (189) and Blue (171) channels, and then press Command-~ to return to RGB.** Notice how much brighter the image looks now and how much more complete the RGB histogram looks. We have set our highlight for this image.

STEP 3: Notice that the shadow values in the Blue channel suddenly drop off a cliff on the left side, unlike those in the Red and Green channels, which taper off like they should. This is a sign that the scanner did not get all the shadow detail in the Blue channel or that there was no more detail in the film. Because this is a Photo CD scan, we have to live with it or buy our own scanner. When this happens to you, look at the original transparency and see if there was actually detail in this area. If there was, you might be able to get better results by rescanning with a high-end drum scanner, a better scanner, or just better scanner settings. **However, in the real world, we often have to correct problem images and scans. Back in the RGB channel, hold down the Option key and move the Input Shadow slider, the top-left slider, to the right to test for a shadow point. There are some good shadow locations on the right side of the wheat, at the bottom, and also within the big green tree by the house. Move the Input Shadow slider back to 0. Measure these shadows with the Eyedropper until you find the darkest neutral spot (I found a few in the wheat that had initial values of 5, 5, 5) and then Shift-click on that spot to create Color Sampler #1 in the Info palette. Go into each of the Red, Green, and Blue channels and move the Input Shadow slider to the right until the Color Sampler for your shadow point reads around 2, 2, 2 and your black shadows look neutral. If they don't, click a new darkest neutral spot until your shadows look and measure neutral. Now you have set your shadow. Turn the Preview checkbox off and on to see what you have done to the image so far.**

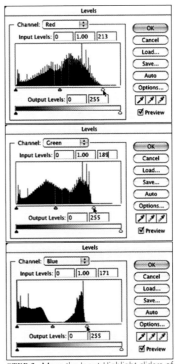

STEP 2: Move the Input Highlight sliders of the Red, Green, and Blue histograms to the left until they touch the beginning of the data. This moves all the data to the left of that point all the way to the right, spreading out the values in each histogram. If you hold down the Option key as you move each color channel highlight slider to the left, you can see, in that color, any highlight values that will be clipped. Don't clip any values that would remove important highlight details from your image.

BRIGHTNESS AND COLOR CAST

STEP 4: **Move the Input Brightness slider in the RGB channel until the overall brightness of the image looks correct. I moved it to the left to 1.15 to bring out a little more shadow detail in the foreground wheat and in the dark trees around the house. You can't bring out more detail in an area that is totally black, so don't go too far on this shadow detail thing.**

STEP 5: Now we need to go into each channel and correct for color casts, which is easiest to do if you try to fix the most annoying cast first, and then fine-tune the other colors and casts that appear along the way. The wheat in the foreground seems to have a greenish cast. I often have a hard time with these greenish casts because they're sometimes both green and cyan. This one looks greener, so go to the Green channel (Command-2) and move the middle slider to the right to add magenta; that should improve the situation and make the wheat look more golden. Move the slider until the wheat looks too magenta, move it back until you start to see the green again, and then add just a little magenta. If the image still has a greenish tinge, it might be that there is a cyan problem too, so move to the Red channel (Command-1) and add a little red by moving the middle slider to the left. Finally, add a little yellow by moving

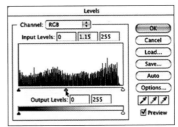

STEP 4: After setting highlight and shadow, set overall brightness. Move the middle slider to the left in RGB.

245

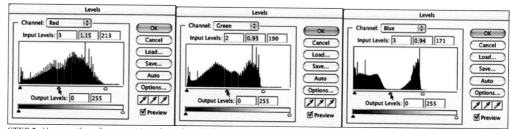

STEP 5: Here are the adjustments I made to the middle sliders of the Red, Green, and Blue channels to adjust for color casts in this image. Because the wheat is the major component here, getting that to look good was the main goal. Other parts of the image can be fine-tuned later.

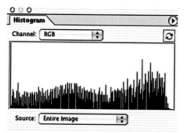

STEP 5: Kansas, after all the Levels adjustments.

the middle slider in the Blue channel a little to the right. The color choices you make may be different than mine depending on your taste. That is certainly fine! When your color appears correct, look at the RGB values of your Color Sampler for the shadow in the Info palette. If they are no longer neutral, you can go back into each color channel and move them back where you want them using the Input Shadow slider for that channel. When you're happy with the color, you should click OK to complete your Levels changes. Because you have your Levels changes in a Levels adjustment layer, you can turn these changes on and off using the Eye icon for that layer, which is above the *Background* layer in the Layers palette. Choose File/Save to save your changes. Now you have done the initial Levels adjustment on this difficult image.

SATURATING COLORS AND ADDING CONTRAST

STEP 6: After the Levels adjustments, you could add a Curve adjustment layer to change the contrast of this image with an S-Curve. We are first going to saturate the colors using Hue/Saturation and see if that gives us enough contrast. We could always insert a Curve layer between the Levels and Hue/Saturation layer afterward. **Choose Layers/New Adjustment Layer/Hue/Saturation (Command-F4), calling this layer Overall Hue/Saturation, then press OK. Make sure that the Preview checkbox is on when you reach the Hue/Saturation dialog.** For flexibility later, you should create a Hue/Saturation adjustment layer instead of just doing Image/Adjust/Hue/Saturation. When you first enter Hue/Saturation, the Edit Master menu is selected. Any master changes you make apply to all the colors at the same time. **Move the Saturation slider to the right to about 15, making all colors more vivid.**

STEP 7: Because the wheat is mostly composed of yellow, this is an important color to tweak. **Choose the Yellow Edit menu to restrict the changes you make to apply only to the yellow parts of the image. Move the Saturation slider to the right by 15 and**

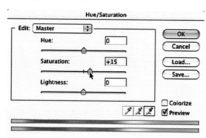

STEP 5: Here we see the Histogram after the Levels adjustments. Choose All Channels View from the Histogram pop-up menu. Notice the white gaps in the R,G, & B channels.

STEP 6: In Edit Master, saturate all the colors by 15.

Chapter 20: Correcting a Problem Image

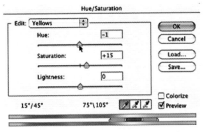

move the Hue slider a little to the left toward red; –1 makes the yellows a little warmer and more intense. The changes you make might be a little different depending on your personal taste and exactly how you have adjusted your version of this image so far.

STEP 7: In Yellow saturate the yellow colors by 15, and move yellows slightly toward red.

STEP 8: **Choose the Red Edit menu and move the red Hue toward the left by –3,** add magenta, and saturate the reds also by 5. Choose the Cyan Edit menu and move the cyan Hue toward the right (blue) by 5, and saturate them by 10. The cyan changes mostly affect the sky. When you choose OK in this Hue/Saturation dialog, your changes are archived in a Hue/Saturation adjustment layer that you can tweak as many times as you like, without damaging the original image, even after saving the file. Choose All Channel View from your Histogram palette, then choose Uncached Refresh to get the most accurate histogram display. Notice that the gaps that were there in the Red, Green, and Blue channels after the Levels adjustment are now mostly removed by saturating the colors.

STEP 8: Red Hue/Saturation changes.

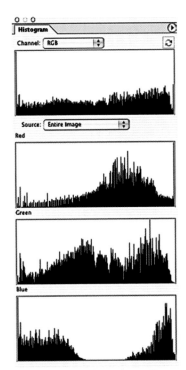

STEP 9: **Click back on the Overall Levels Adjustment layer to activate it, then choose Layer/New Adjustment Layer/Curves (Command-F3) to add a Curves adjustment layer between Levels and Hue/Saturation. New layers are added above the currently active layer. Create an S-Curve similar to the one on the right. Play around with the shape of the curve and notice how this affects the contrast of the image and also the histogram. Choose OK when you are happy with the image. If you are not sure how much contrast to use, make it a bit more contrasty than you need, then reduce that contrast using the Opacity slider for this Curves layer at the top of the Layers palette. Click back on the Hue/Saturation adjustment layer to activate it so the next layer you add will be on top of it. Use Command-S to save the image at this point.**

STEP 8: After completing the Hue/Saturation adjustments, choose All Channels View from the Histogram pop-up menu. Notice that the white gaps in the Red, Green, & Blue channels have now been removed.

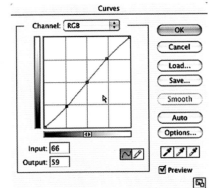

STEP 9: The curve we added has the threequarter-tone point set at 66/59 and the quartertone point set at 187/194 with the midtone point left at 128/128.

STEP 9: Kansas after Levels, Curves, and Hue/Saturation adjustments using adjustment layers.

Saturating Colors and Adding Contrast

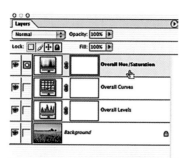

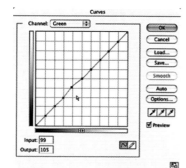

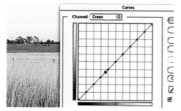

STEP 9: The Layers palette after step 9.

STEP 10: **Type a W to switch to the Magic Wand tool and look in the Options bar at the top of your screen to make sure that the Tolerance is set to 32 and that Anti-aliased and Contiguous are on; these are the defaults.** You are going to select parts of this image and improve their color balance and/or density. **Start out selecting the green strip of grass that separates the field from the sky; you will have to Shift-click on it several times to get the entire green field. The center part of this area seems a bit too magenta to me. Click the grass and then Shift-click to add to the selection until you have selected all the grass. If you accidentally select something that you shouldn't, choose Edit/Undo (Command-Z) and try again. You can also use the Lasso**

STEP 11: Create the selection of the green field with the Magic Wand and Lasso tools. If you find the tolerance value of 32 on the Wand too high, undo the selection and then press Return, 16, Return to change that tolerance without having to move the mouse. Remake your selection with this lower tolerance, which usually works better.

STEP 11: My final adjusted Green curve.

STEP 11: Measuring where the greens occur in the green grass. Command-Shift-click to add a point to the Red, Green, and Blue curves at the same time or just Command-click to add a point at the corresponding location in the curve you are currently looking at, as we did with the Green curve.

tool (L) with the Shift key to add to the selection, or with the Option key to subtract from the selection. After you select the entire area, choose Select/Feather and enter 1 to create a 1-pixel feather. This feather will blend the color changes you will make along the edge of the selection.

STEP 11: **Choose Layer/New Adjustment Layer/Curves and name this new adjustment layer Green Field, and then press OK in the New Layer dialog. Use the pop-up at the top of** the dialog to go to the Green channel, and then press the Load button in the Curves dialog to load the LockdownGreen curve from the Lockdown Curves folder within the Ch03.Preferences folder on the *Photoshop CS Artistry* CD. This places points all along the curve so you can make changes to a selected part of the curve. You could have placed these points manually, but the Lockdown Curves save you time. **Click on the image with the Eyedropper and hold the mouse button down in the area where the green grass seems a bit too magenta. Look at the circle that appears on the curve. Move the cursor around a bit in the green area, while holding down the mouse, until you can see where an average magenta/green area is. At that point, Command-click on the image and Photoshop will place a point on the curve representing the place you clicked. Move that point in the curve diagram up and to the left to add green to that part of the curve. If you click in the grow box at the bottom right of the Curves dialog, you will get a bigger dialog that makes it easier to place more detailed points. When you are happy with your color changes, choose OK.**

STEP 11: If you Option-click on the Green Field layer mask thumbnail, the rightmost thumbnail, you will see the mask created from your Wand selection. That is the only thing adjusted by this adjustment layer. Option-clicking a second time will return you to the display of the composite image.

Chapter 20: Correcting a Problem Image

STEP 12: Here we see the tree selected as we did using the Magic Wand tool. Now we choose Select/Similar after setting the Magic Wand's Tolerance setting to 12.

STEP 12: After using Select/Similar to select the other dark green parts of the image, you then use the Lasso tool with the Option key held down to circle the area seen in red above here. When you release the mouse button, this part of the selection will go away and only the trees and bushes will remain.

STEP 12: **Use Command-Spacebar-click to zoom in on the trees; then select the darker parts of the big tree with the Magic Wand (W), as shown in the illustration to the right. Now go to Select/Grow and notice how this increases the size of that selection with that local area. Use Command-Z to undo the grow; then do Select/Similar and notice how this selects similar areas throughout the entire image, but with the Wand Tolerance at 32, this selects too much. Use Command-Z again, then press Return, then 12, then Return again and notice that the Wand's Tolerance is now set to 12. Now try Select/Similar again and you should see a selection that is like the one at the top of this page. You want to have the trees and bushes selected, but not the shadow areas in the fore-**

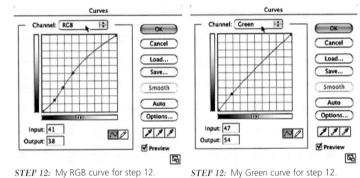

STEP 12: My RGB curve for step 12. STEP 12: My Green curve for step 12.

ground. Type an L to switch to the Lasso tool and use Option-Spacebar-click to zoom out so there is gray area surrounding the image. While holding the Option key down, circle the area shown in red in the illustration below and the Lasso tool will remove those foreground shadows from the selection. Now choose Command-F3 to create a new Curves adjustment layer and use the Curves dialog to brighten up the shadow areas and also the green color of the trees and bushes. Don't over do it here, you want small subtle adjustments like those shown to the right; otherwise, your trees will look posterized. When you are finished, you should have a Layers palette that looks like the one you see here. **Now choose File/Save (Command-S) to save your work on this example so far.**

STEP 13: Now we'll show you a useful tip you can use when selecting areas of isolated color. **Type an L to switch to the Lasso tool and press the Return key to select the Lasso's feather value. Type in a 2, then press Return again to accept the feather change. Using the Lasso tool, make a very loose selection around the red barn, like you see in the illustration on the next page. Use Command-F4 to get a new adjustment layer of type Hue/Saturation and call it Paint the Barn. Now move the Edit menu to Reds and then move the Hue slider to –10, which will make things that are already red look like they just got a new coat of paint.** Because there is no red

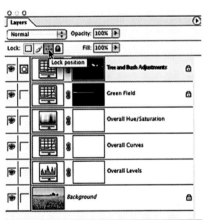

STEP 12: How your Layers palette should look after step 12. Notice that I have locked the top two layers so they can't accidentally be moved using the Move tool. To do this, just click on the Lock position icon for the active layer at the top of the Layers palette.

249

STEP 13: Close-up of the Barn selection. Don't let the selection go down into the yellow field because that does contain some red and the change won't work as transparently.

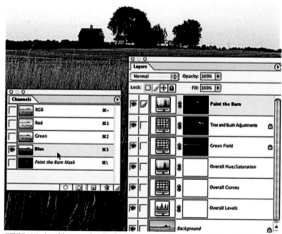

STEP 13: In Edit Reds, move the Hue slider to -10 and you'll notice that the barn gets a new paint job.

component to the sky or green grass, this works well and saves you from making a detailed selection of the barn. Setting the Lasso feather to 2 before you started makes the edge of this selection soft, which helps it blend with the parts of the image that have not been changed. **Choose Command-S to save your file.**

STEP 14: Notice that each time you create a new adjustment layer, your Layers palette grows toward the top. Also notice that these last three adjustment layers have mostly black Layer Mask thumbnails in the Layers palette. **If you Option-click one of these Layer Mask thumbnails, you will notice that you see a mask and that mask is black everywhere except the area that was selected before you created the adjustment layer.** When you create an adjustment layer when having a selection, Photoshop assumes the selection is the part you want to adjust and creates a mask that is white only in that area. Only the white parts of the masks are actually changed in color or contrast by the adjustment layer. The first three adjustment layers in the Overall Color Correction area have totally white Layer Mask thumbnails because those layers adjust the entire image. **If you type a B for brush, then a D for default colors, and then pick the third brush from the top left in the Brushes palette, you can now paint 100% white over the top of the red roof on the small building at the left of the green field. This will add white into the layer mask for the Paint the Barn adjustment layer, and will make that red roof a more saturated red just as it did for the barn.**

STEP 15: **Use Command-0 to zoom out until you can see the entire image. Now bring up the Channels palette (Shift-F10) and click on each of the Red, Green, and Blue channels, one at a time, until you find the one with the most contrast between the sky and the rest of the image. Click on the word Blue in the Blue channel and make sure the Eye icons are off for RGB, Red, and Green.** The Blue channel has the most contrast in this image, so we are going to use it to create a mask separating the sky from the rest of the image. This is a useful technique that I use all the time, but it is quite often a different channel than Blue that has the most contrast. **To make a copy of the Blue channel, drag the Blue channel down to the New Channel icon next to the Trash icon at the bottom of the Channels palette. You should now just be working on this grayscale channel called Blue copy, so choose Image/Adjustments/Levels and move the Input Highlight and Input Shadow sliders toward the center to increase the contrast between the sky and everything else. As you move the Input Highlight slider left, you will notice the sky being etched away. Moving the Shadow slider right makes the buildings and foreground turn towards black.** An ideal mask would be a pure white sky, with everything in the foreground being pure black, then a subtle gray along the horizon, which will blend any change in the sky seamlessly into the rest of the image.

Move the Input Brightness slider, the middle one, to the left to make the transition area lighter, and to the right to darken it. Zoom into the horizon area, especially in the area of the buildings and trees, and turn the Preview button on and off to see how accurately the horizon is captured by the mask. Notice how changing the three Input sliders changes the makeup of the horizon. When you have the mask as close as possible in Levels, choose OK. Type B to get the Paintbrush, then use a large, solid brush to paint black anything that is still gray in the foreground, and paint white anything, like large dust, that is not white in the sky. The horizon line should have some gray transition values.

STEP 15: Looking at the Red, Green, and Blue channels to decide which one to copy to make a mask.

Chapter 20: Correcting a Problem Image

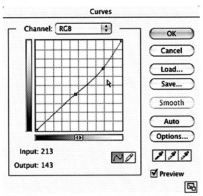

Command-click on the thumbnail for the Blue copy channel that you have been working on in the Channels palette. This will load the white areas of this channel as a selection. Using Command-click is the universal way to load a selection and you will find it is the easiest and most useful, so make it a point to learn. Now click on the word RGB at the top of the Channels palette and the color image should come back into display. Make sure the Paint the Barn layer is the active layer and choose Layer/New Adjustment Layer/Curves (Command-F3) to create a Curves adjustment layer you should call Darken Sky. Move the Eyedropper around in the sky while the mouse button is down and notice where the sky values are located on the curve. Click a point in the center of that sky area on the RGB curve and drag the curve down and to the right to darken the sky. Choose OK when you are happy with your darker sky. Check out the below right caption about blurring the mask! At this point, this mask of the sky is saved in the layer mask of the Darken Sky adjustment layer, so you can now drag the Blue copy channel, in the Channels palette, to the trash if you would like. Press Command-S to save your file.

STEP 15: Here is the setup for creating the mask for the Darken Sky layer. You are using Image/Adjustments/Levels on a copy of the Blue channel in the Channels palette. Notice the positions of the Input Shadow and Input Highlight sliders. When you think you have the mask right, turn the Preview button off and on to make sure the mask matches the horizon and you don't lose small details like the power poles you see at the top right above.

STEP 16: **To further modify any of your adjustment layers, double-click the Layer thumbnail of that adjustment layer and your old modifications will come up, allowing you to change them again and again without slowly destroying the integrity of the original image. One thing you should do to the *Background* layer, however, is use the Clone Stamp tool to remove all the spots and scratches. Click the *Background* layer to activate it and then use the Clone Stamp techniques you learned in the last chapter to spot this image, especially the sky.** Another easier way to spot skies is to use the Dust and Scratches filter. You only want to use this filter on soft skies, and you need to use it correctly so you don't lose the grain pattern in your sky, but only the spots. **Command-click on the Layer Mask thumbnail of the Darken Sky adjustment layer to reload this mask as a selection. Choose Select/Modify/Contract and use a Contraction value of 10 pixels. This moves the selection away from the horizon so the filter doesn't blur any details along the horizon. Use Command-Option-0 to zoom in to 100%, then Command-Spacebar-click to get you up to 200% while looking at the sky in the area behind the buildings. This allows you to see the details while you are working on your *Background* layer. Type L to get the Lasso tool and use this with the Option key down to circle and remove any selection over the power poles to the right of the buildings. We don't want this filter to run on the poles as it will think they are dust and blur them. Choose Filter/Noise/Dust & Scratches and set the Radius to 2 and the Threshold to 0.** Notice that all the scratches and clumpiness in the sky is removed, but so is the natural grain pattern. The Radius is the number of pixels around a spot or scratch that Photoshop will change to get rid of the spot. **Leave the Radius at 2, but increase the Threshold to around 4 or 5. Your grain pattern returns, but the large clumps, spots, and scratches are now removed. Choose Command-H to hide the selection edge and see how this sky blends with the horizon at the bottom. Turn the Preview button in the filter off and on to see the sky as it was before and after the filter. This is a good way to save time when spotting skies! You may still have to do a few large dust spots with the Rubber Stamp tool. First, do a Command-D to deselect the selection so you can work anywhere in the file. Do another Command-S to save the latest changes.** This would actually be your

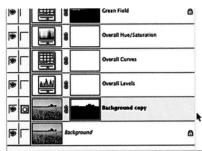

STEP 15: Here is the curve I used to darken my sky. After choosing OK to this Curves dialog, choose Filter/Blur/Gaussian Blur (Shift-F4) to bring up the Gaussian Blur filter. Doing a Gaussian Blur of 1 on this type of mask will usually make the transition between sky and the rest of the image a bit smoother. Zoom into 100% or 200% and notice how the telephone poles show up better after blurring the mask. Try it!

STEP 16: A safer way to run the Dust and Scratches filter is to run it on a copy of the *Background* layer with a layer mask to reveal the parts you want to see. That way you can always undo the effects of this filter.

251

STEP 16: The Kansas image after specific color corrections using selections and adjustment layers and before sharpening.

master layers version of this image, so this is the one you would archive for future uses and different sizes. Note: My editor keeps reminding me that the Rubber Stamp tool is now called the Clone Stamp tool. I'm sure in this book you'll see it referred to as the Rubber Stamp tool a lot because I've been thinking of it with that name for over 14 years.

THE UNSHARP MASK FILTER

STEP 17: If you are going to resample your image by either adding pixels to make it bigger or removing pixels to make it smaller, you should do that first before sharpening your file. In the Image/Image Size dialog, if you are just changing the Pixels/Inch with the Resample Image option turned off, this should not affect the sharpening of an already sharpened file as you are not adding or removing pixels.

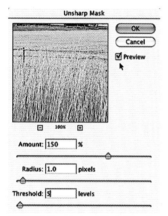

STEP 17: The Unsharp Mask filter dialog box with the settings I used to sharpen my KansasVersion1 file.

Another technique for sharpening very saturated files is using Image/Mode/Lab Color to convert the file to Lab Color mode and then sharpening the L channel. This method prevents your saturated colors from popping too much during the sharpening. You can actually print to an Epson printer directly from Lab color so you don't need to convert back to RGB. Another sharpening option is to just sharpen one of the RGB channels.

Choose Image/Duplicate (F5) to make a copy of this master layers file called KansasVersion1, turning on the Duplicate Merged Layers Only option and then choosing OK in the Duplicate dialog. Type an F to put this single layer copy in Full Screen mode. Now you will use Filter/Sharpen/Unsharp Mask to sharpen your image for final output. The Unsharp Mask filter has three different settings (Amount, Radius, and Threshold) that affect different parts of the sharpening process. You will have to run some tests to determine what value to use in each of these settings. It is often useful to compare tests on a small section of the image. Photoshop does have a Preview button in the Unsharp Mask filter that allows you to see the effect on a selected area of the image, but it doesn't allow you to compare one group of settings to another. Once you get familiar with the amount of sharpening you like on your various types of prints, you can turn the Preview button in the Unsharp Mask dialog off and on while trying different settings to decide the amount of sharpening you want. Turning the Preview button off and on will change the part of the image that is visible on your computer screen from not sharpened to sharpened. The small window inside the Unsharp Mask filter will always show part of the image as sharpened, but if you click down and hold inside that little window, that part of the image will toggle to unsharpened. Click anywhere in your image to reset what actually shows within this window inside the Unsharp Mask filter.

A good way to compare different sharpening settings is to use the Marquee (M) to select a section of the image that can represent the entire image, and whose sharpness is most important, and make a copy of it using Edit/Copy. (See the images on the next page to see what I selected from this photograph.) Now choose File/New (Command-N) to create a new file. Because you just made a copy, the new file will be the size of the copied section. Click OK in the New dialog box and then do Edit/Paste (Command-V). Repeat this action several times, until you have five or six small files that you can place next to each other on the screen for comparison. Now run different tests on each file to see what each of the three parameters of Unsharp Mask do. Speaking of those three parameters, here is what they do:

AMOUNT: This setting controls the overall amount of sharpening. When you compare sharpening effects, you want to zoom in on the image (to 100% and occasionally to 200%) to see all the detail. Compare different copies of the same image

STEP 17: Image with no sharpening. We need some!

STEP 17: Unsharp Mask 150, 1.5, 0. Too much grain!

area using different settings for Amount. You sharpen an image by looking for edges in the photograph and enhancing those edges by making one side of them darker and the other side of them lighter. Edges are sharp color or contrast changes in an image.

RADIUS: This setting controls the number of pixels along an edge that you modify when you sharpen the image. Again, try running the filter with different settings and compare several copies of the same image side by side.

THRESHOLD: When you set Threshold to 0, everything in the image becomes a candidate for being an edge and getting sharpened. If you set the Threshold to, say 10, then an edge will only be found and sharpened if there is a difference of at least 10 points (in the range from 0 to 255) in the pixel values along that edge. The larger value you give to the Threshold setting, the more contrasty an edge needs to be before it is sharpened.

STEP 17: If you name the layer in your document with the sharpening value you used, that information will help later if you decide the sharpening amount wasn't correct.

When you find the Unsharp Mask values that look best, use those to sharpen the entire file. If the original image is very grainy, I might increase Threshold, which lessens the sharpening of the grain. If the image is very fine grained, I might decrease Threshold, which allows me to sharpen the file a bit more, without getting more than the normal grain appearance in the final image. You have to be careful not to over-sharpen. If your final output is a halftone, you can get away with more sharpening than you can for a transparency film recorder, or even a digital print output, because the screen angles and dots in a halftone tend to lessen some sharpening artifacts. All artifacts show up if you output to a color transparency film recorder, however. We usually use the Unsharp Mask filter instead of the other Photoshop sharpening filters because Unsharp Mask provides much finer control over the many different types of images.

Another way to sharpen your image and avoid sky grain, which I usually use, is the Sharpen Only Edges BH action script. This is explained in Chapter 11: "Automating with Actions," and also at the end of Chapter 26. You should check it out, as it produces very sharp files without the grain!

STEP 17: Unsharp Mask 450, 1.5, 0. Too much sharpening and grain!

STEP 17: Unsharp Mask 150, 4.5, 0. Too large a Radius for a real look.

Respotting with the Clone Stamp

STEP 18: **After you sharpen any image, you should zoom in to at least 100% and then go through each section of the file, checking for spots that appeared after sharpening.** Sharpening tends to enhance spots that may not have been obvious before, which is why you should double-check the spotting of your master file after any final sharpening. The procedure is the same as the spotting work demonstrated in Chapter 19: "Overall Color Correction." **Do another File/Save (Command-S) to save your final spotted file.**

STEP 17: Unsharp Mask 150, 1.5, 8. I used to use this a lot but now I experiment more on each image.

STEP 17: Unsharp Mask 300, .5, 4. Compare this to the ones on either side.

STEP 17: Unsharp Mask 500, .5, 8. Let's see how this prints.

OUT-OF-GAMUT COLORS

Step 19: You can see many vivid colors on the computer screen in RGB or Lab that won't print in CMYK on a press. If you are working in RGB to send your final output to a film recorder and color transparency film, you can get more colors on film than you can on a press. If your final output is some Web or multimedia presentation, you can also get the colors there. You need to realize that each different type of computer monitor or digital color printer, or even press and paper combination, usually has a different color gamut. The gamut of your output device is the range of colors it can actually print. For more information about these issues, see Chapter 14: "Color Spaces, Device Characterization, and Color Management." If you are going to print this file on a press in CMYK, or if you are using View/Proof Colors to soft proof RGB output devices, you might want to check your out-of-gamut colors and see if you need to correct them. This might be a good time to review the discussion of View/Proof Colors and View/Proof Setup in Chapter 15: "Photoshop Color Preferences, Monitor, Scanner, and Printer Calibration." **Choose View/Proof Setup/Working CMYK for now as we go through this discussion. Now choose Select/Color Range, and then choose Out of Gamut from the Select pop-up at the top of the dialog box. Click OK to see a selection of all the colors that you can see in RGB, but which won't print exactly the same in CMYK or on your RGB device when Proof Setup is set to soft proof for an RGB output device. Choose View/Extras (Command-H) to hide the edges of this selection.**

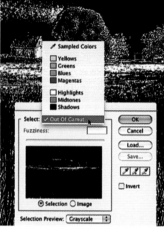

STEP 19: In Color Range, selecting out-of-gamut colors. Notice that we have set the Selection Preview to Grayscale so we see a large preview of the out-of-gamut colors in the image area behind the dialog. Play around with the other Selection Preview choices as you might find them useful.

STEP 20: Some out-of-gamut colors, like red, often look quite different, and usually muted, when printed in CMYK. In many other colors, you might not notice the difference. **Turn View/Proof Colors on (Command-Y) for an estimate of what the image will look like when printed in CMYK while you are still working in RGB or Lab. If you made the red barn really bright, you will notice it fades a bit.** View/Proof Colors is on when there is a checkmark to the left of it in the menu bar. How many other changes did you see in the image? The sky might look a bit duller. **Now choose View/Gamut Warning (Command-Shift-Y), and all these out-of-gamut colors will change to gray or whatever color you have set in Preferences as the gamut warning indicator. Remember that you have a selection, which you made using Color Range, of all the colors that are actually out-of-gamut. With Gamut Warning on, you can use this selection in conjunction with the Hue/Saturation command to fix much of the gamut problem.** Colors often are out-of-gamut because they're too saturated. **Choose Command-U for Hue/Saturation and move the Saturation slider to the left. Notice that the Gamut Warning areas get smaller the more you desaturate the selected out-of-gamut area.** You might want to desaturate your out-of-gamut colors in several stages, or use the Sponge tool from the Tools palette, so you don't further desaturate colors that have already come back into gamut. To desaturate in stages, move the Saturation slider to the left, to –10. Choose OK and then choose Select/None. Now go back to Color Range (see step 19), and choose the new smaller set of out-of-gamut colors. Reduce the saturation on these, also, by –10. Continue this iterative process until you have no more out-of-gamut colors, or until the out-of-gamut areas are so small they won't show.

STEP 21: Gamut Warning is a very useful tool for seeing colors that are going to be difficult to reproduce in CMYK, or on your RGB output device when soft proofing to an RGB device. However, if you always desaturate all your colors so that no Gamut Warning areas show up, you may end up with duller colors on press or your device than you would have gotten if you were a little less strict about desaturating all your RGB colors. I compared two conversions to CMYK of this image. The first had been pre-adjusted, via steps 19 and 20, to remove out-of-gamut colors, and the second was of the same image without the out-of-gamut adjustments. The pre-adjusted image didn't change much at all when converted to CMYK, which is good. The image that I hadn't pre-adjusted for out-of-gamut colors did change and got a little duller, as with the red barn, but overall was a bit brighter and more vivid in CMYK than the pre-adjusted image was. **So if you work in RGB and use bright colors, even out-of-gamut ones, you might get brighter color results by going ahead and converting these to CMYK. You know that some bright colors may get a bit duller, but you can deal with those dull or changed colors when you are in CMYK mode, instead of dulling them ahead of time by desaturating based on Gamut Warning and possibly desaturating them too much. Do some tests to see what works best for you!** When printing on an RGB device, like the LightJet 5000, you might find you lose a few less details in your extreme saturated areas if you bring things into gamut with the device a bit, before sending a file to the printer. Again, you should experiment and see.

CONVERTING TO CMYK

STEP 22: Now you have your final color corrected version of the RGB image for this particular job. If your final output device is an RGB device, such as a film recorder or a video screen, your work is done. If you use a color management system or printer software that automatically converts your file from RGB to CMYK as you output it, you also are done. If your final output device is CMYK and you are going to do the conversion from RGB to CMYK in Photoshop, you need to make sure all the preferences are set up correctly for CMYK conversion and for this particular printing project. **Choose Image/Mode/CMYK to convert the image to CMYK.** When in CMYK, Photoshop automatically adjusts the image display on the monitor to try to simulate your actual CMYK printed output. Consequently, some of the brighter colors may get duller or change slightly. **You might want to do additional small color tweaks now that you are in CMYK, using the same tools you used in RGB. You can also use the Selective Color tool and other tools to tweak CMYK colors, as explained at the end of Chapters 21: "Yellow Flowers," and 22: "Color Matching Images." When you are happy with your CMYK image, save it as Kansas-FinalCMYK.**

STEP 21: The final RGB version of Kansas after all color corrections and using the Unsharp Mask filter.

21 HANDS-ON SESSION: Yellow Flowers

Using Color Range and Replace Color
to change the colors of flowers and to
enhance those colors; using Selective Color
to improve the CMYK version.

Original version of the flowers picture. We will select the flowers and change their color.

The Color Range tool lets you make selections based on these different color choices. When you use the Sampled Colors choice, you click on the colors you want to select within the image.

In this session, you use the Color Range and Replace Color tools to select the flowers and change their color from yellow to orange. You then use the Selective Color command to enhance the color of the orange flowers. This image is tagged with ColorMatchRGB and was created in a ColorMatchRGB workspace. Using a different workspace to do this example might yield slightly different measured values.

ABOUT COLOR RANGE AND REPLACE COLOR

The first thing you do in this example is select all the flowers. There are two similar tools for making selections based on color in Photoshop. Select/Color Range allows you to specify a color using the Eyedropper tool and then shows you a mask of all the areas in the current selection that contain that color. You can add to or subtract from that mask using + or − Eyedroppers, so that when you leave Color Range, you have a selection that contains the final colors you specified. Another command that is similar to Color Range is Image/Adjustments/Replace Color. It lets you make selections similarly and also change the colors of the selections at the same time, using controls that are like those in the Hue/Saturation command but not quite as powerful. You can load and save color selection sets between these two tools, so you need to understand the subtle but important differences between them.

The Color Range tool always returns a selection, which you can then use as you would any other selection to modify the selected areas using an adjustment layer or other Photoshop tool. Because Color Range lets you make selections, it furnishes some very useful features for seeing exactly what you have selected. When you choose the Sampled Colors option from the Select pop-up menu in Color Range, you select colors by clicking on them with the Eyedropper (you do the same in Replace Color). You can add to the colors that you select by using the regular Eyedropper and Shift-clicking, and you can subtract from the selected colors by Option-clicking. Also, the + and – Eyedroppers always add to or always subtract from, respectively, the selected areas. You see what colors are selected by looking at a black-and-white mask window in the dialog box. Here, white shows you the selected areas. To see the selected items in the most detail, choose the Quick Mask option in the Selection Preview pop-up of Color Range, and you will get a Quick Mask overlay on top of the unselected areas in the Actual Image window. If you choose the correct color for your Quick Mask (notice the purple in the diagram here), you can see when your selection is complete. You choose the color for your Quick Mask by double-clicking on the Quick Mask icon at the bottom of the Tools palette. (You need to do this before you enter Color Range.) See Chapter 18: "The Car Ad," for a discussion of Quick Mask mode. You can also choose no preview in the image area, or a Grayscale, Black Matte, or White Matte preview. These can also be very useful in different types of situations. Try them all and see what works best for you. By the way, the other options in the Select pop-up allow you to select all the reds, yellows, greens, cyans, blues, magentas, highlights, midtones, shadows, or out-of-gamut colors in the part of the image that you selected before you entered Color Range. The out-of-gamut colors option can be very useful (see Chapter 20: "Correcting a Problem Image"). Although Replace Color doesn't give you these other Select options, you can get them by using the Save button in Color Range to save selections made with these options, and you can use the Load button in Replace Color to load these selections.

The Replace Color tool also allows you to select colors with the Eyedropper in the same way as Color Range, but it has no Quick Mask Preview mode and no Select options. Replace Color doesn't provide as many options for selecting the colors or for seeing the selection as Color Range does, but after you make a selection in either one, you can click on the Save button to save the description of the selected colors. This feature allows you to select similar colors in other images or make the same color selection in the current image from Color Range or from Replace Color by going into either tool and using the Load button to load that color selection description. When you have the selection you want, the Replace Color tool allows you to change the color of the selected items by using the Hue, Saturation, and Lightness sliders at its bottom. The Preview box here shows you the color changes happening in the image on the screen. For changing color, Replace Color is even better than a selection preview because you see whether the selection is correct as you actually change the colors you want. So, when you use Color Range, you are selecting a range of colors in an image and ending up with a selection. When you use Replace Color, you select a range of colors and replace those colors simultaneously. Now, let's try this out!

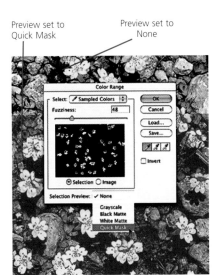

Preview set to Quick Mask

Preview set to None

In the top part of this illustration, the Selection Preview is None and you see the image. At the bottom of the illustration you see the purple Quick Mask preview, which is very useful.

The Quick Mask icon

Click here to change the Quick Mask color.

Double-click on the Quick Mask icon to get the Quick Mask Options dialog box, and then click on the color square and select a new color with the Color Picker.

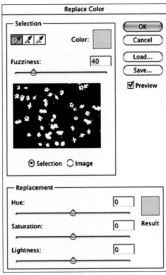

The Replace Color dialog box with a mask showing the flowers selected.

USING COLOR RANGE TO SELECT THE FLOWERS

STEP 1: **Open the FlowersYellow image in the YellowFlowers Example folder. Put Photoshop into Full Screen mode by pressing F or by clicking on the middle icon at the bottom of the Tools palette. Double-click on the Quick Mask icon, click on the colored square, and then set the color to medium blue or purple. Find a color that has no yellow in it so that any flower parts not selected show up easily. Make sure the Opacity is set to 50% and that Masked Areas is clicked. Click OK to these dialog boxes and click back on the regular Selection icon to the left of the Quick Mask icon. Now press the Tab key to remove all the tool windows from the screen. Choose Select/Color**

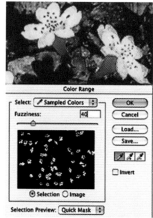

STEP 2: Part of the flower on the right is covered by purple. Shift-click on it to add it to the selection.

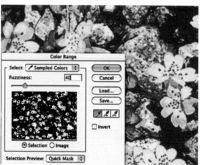

STEP 2: Here we have selected too much. You can see the mask coming off things that are not flowers, like the green leaves to the left of the flowers. Use Command-Z or the − Eyedropper to fix this.

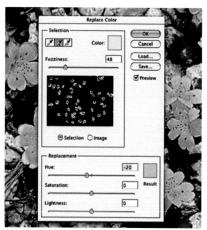

STEP 4: The Replace Color dialog box previewing yellow to orange. The Color swatch at the top shows you the color you want to change. This swatch initially shows current foreground color, but you can click in the image to change it if need be.

Range. **Set the Fuzziness to 40.** The Fuzziness, which works the same in Replace Color and Color Range, is like the Tolerance on the Magic Wand; the higher the Fuzziness, the more similar colors are selected. Unlike using the Magic Wand, you can move the Fuzziness after you make a selection to change the range of selected colors. **Set Select to Sampled Colors and set Selection Preview to None, for now. Use the Eyedropper to click on the yellow flowers in the image window and you will notice that wherever you see a flower, you should get some white showing up in the mask window. Hold the Shift key down and click on different areas of the flowers, adding more to the mask. If white areas or spots show up in the mask window where there are not any flowers, press Command-Z to undo that last Eyedropper click. When you think you have selected all the flowers—and no areas that are not flowers—set the Selection Preview to Quick Mask.**

STEP 2: **In Quick Mask, you will notice a see-through purple layer covering everything not selected by the mask. That's the Quick Mask preview. If you notice that parts of the flowers are covered by purple, Shift-click on them to add them to the selected areas. If you select a really bright part of the flower or a really dark part of the flower, you may also notice the purple overlay coming off other areas of the image that are not flowers. If so, you have selected too much, and should press Command-Z.**

STEP 3: **When the purple mask doesn't cover any flowers but still covers everything not a flower, you have done what you can do with Color Range to select the flowers. You might want to try the Grayscale, Black Matte, or White Matte Selection Preview modes to see if there are any errors that show up there. If so, just use the + or − Eyedroppers to fix them. It's also helpful to click the Invert button to switch the mask to the non-selected areas, but don't forget to switch back. Click on the Save button and save this set of colors as ColorRangeToRC. Click on OK now and you end up with a selection of the flowers.** If you wanted to work on these selected items with one of the other color correction tools, such as Hue/Saturation or a filter, you could have used this procedure to get a selection of the flowers. We had you do the first part of this exercise in Color Range so that you could see the differences between it and Replace Color. You could have done the whole session in either Color Range or Replace Color. Just so you know, you can click inside the preview window itself with the Eyedropper tools to add and subtract in Color Range. This may not be accurate enough for this difficult selection, but it can be faster in simpler selections.

USING REPLACE COLOR TO SELECT AND CHANGE THE COLOR

STEP 4: **You are now going to use Replace Color for the rest of the exercise. Choose Select/None (Command-D) because you're actually going to improve on this selection using Replace Color. Press Tab to bring your palettes back into view, and then click the Eyedropper tool and set the Sample Size to Point Sample. Choose Image/Adjustments/Replace Color, and click on the Load button. Select the ColorRangeToRC file you just saved from Color Range.** This will give you the same selection you just had, but this time you only see the black-and-white mask in the dialog box. As an alternative to loading the selection you created in Color Range, you can also choose the colors to change directly in Replace Color. **If you want to start over using Replace Color, just initially click down on an average yellow color within one of the flowers. If you are doing the selection over again, then you want to switch to the + Eyedropper tool and click with it in various places within the flowers until you have**

clicked on bright, medium, and shadow yellow flowers. When you believe you have created a selection
of all the yellow flowers, either by loading one from
what you did in Color Range or by starting over
using Replace Color, then choose the middle + Eyedropper tool and click on a yellow flower at a place
that is a middle yellow color. This color should be a
shade of yellow that best represents the flowers as a
whole. Notice that the sample box at the top of the
Replace Color dialog now has the yellow color you
clicked on in it. Getting the color into the sample box
is why you clicked here with + Eyedropper. This tool
adds a color to the color selection range instead of
starting a new selection range. **Now go down to the
Hue slider and move it to the left to –20. The yellow
sample is now orange. With the Preview button on,
all the selected yellow flowers will turn orange.** This
is the one type of selection preview that you can't do

The flowers, after changing them to orange.

in Color Range, and it is very useful. **If most of the flowers look orange but have a
little bright yellow around their tips, you have 'em right about where you want 'em.
If all the flowers are orange without a trace of yellow, you should look around the
rest of the image and make sure you didn't change the color of anything else that
had some yellow in it but wasn't totally yellow, such as the green leaves on the
ground.**

STEP 5: **Now you need to change the yellow in the tips of the flowers to orange.
Because the Eyedropper is set to Point Sample, this will allow you to select minute
color differences that are only one pixel in size. Zoom in (Command-Spacebar-click)
on any flowers that still have too much yellow around the tips of their petals. Zoom
in close enough so you can see individual pixels at about 400%. Carefully click on
those yellow tip colors and add them to the color set. As you do this with Preview
on, the tips of other flowers also turn orange. You can also increase the Fuzziness;
you will notice that more little dots show up as selected in the mask. This may also
improve the blending of any remaining yellow in the flower tips. Some of the
brighter tips may actually just be highlights, so you don't need to change every last
one. They just need to look natural as orange flowers. Some of the flower petals
tips, which look almost white, were originally burned and dried on the yellow flowers, so don't try to get them to turn orange also. If you do, you will make the color
set too large and change colors where you shouldn't.**

*NOTE: Control-clicking in the
document window while Replace
Color is open gives you the contextual menu so you can change
the Eyedropper tool sample size
on-the-fly if needed.*

**Click the Save button in Replace Color and save the final color set as Yel-
lowFlowerSet.** Later in Step 9, you will use YellowFlowerSet to learn about a more
advanced way to do this that gives you more control over your flower color details.
**For now though, click on the OK button in Replace Color when you are happy with
your flowers. It may be faster to change the dried tips using the Clone Stamp tool,
cloning color from another flower or another part of the same flower. You still will
want to do this with Aligned turned on in the Clone Stamp options using either the
Normal or Color Blend mode.**

STEP 6: **Use File/Save As to save the file as FlowersOrange, and then open the original Flowers file and compare the two images. The flower colors and tones should
look as natural in orange as they did in yellow. Bring back the Tools palette by press-**

259

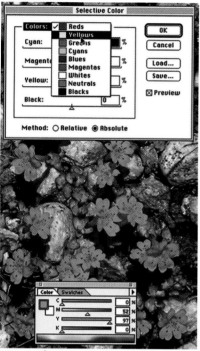

STEP 7: After measuring the orange flowers, we notice in the Color palette that this orange color is made up of 97% yellow and 52% magenta. You may get slightly different values. We then choose yellow as the color to change in the Colors pop-up.

ing Tab, and then use the Options bar pop-up to set the Eyedropper tool Sample Size back to 3 by 3 Average.

USING SELECTIVE COLOR

STEP 7: **When you are happy with the RGB version of this image and have saved it (in Step 6), you should convert it to CMYK using Image/Mode/CMYK. You may notice a slight dulling of the flowers when the image converts to CMYK, although this particular orange color converts to CMYK quite well. When in CMYK, it is often helpful to use the Selective Color command to make further subtle tweaks on colors. This command changes a particular color based on the respective amounts of cyan, magenta, yellow, and black that comprise it. Bring up the Color palette using the Window menu (Shift-F9 with ArtistKeys). If you had this palette in the Palette Well at the top right of the Options palette, drag it onto the screen using its Color tab. Use its Palette Options pop-up menu to change it to CMYK Display mode. Now choose Image/Adjustments/Selective Color to bring up the Selective Color tool.** With this tool, you have to select the main color that you would like to change using the Colors pop-up menu at the top. The choices are Red, Yellow, Green, Cyan, Blue, Magenta, White, Neutral, and Black. If you want to change the orange flowers, you'll probably notice that orange is not one of these colors. **Use the Eyedropper and click on an orange flower in a shade of orange typical of the orange color of all the flowers. Notice in the Color palette that this bright orange consists mainly of yellow and magenta. Because yellow is the main component of this orange color (it's around 97% yellow, in fact), you should now choose Yellow from the Colors pop-up. Next, you change the percentages of the other colors that make up your yellows.**

STEP 8: The orange flowers after adding 20% magenta. Notice that the Magenta value actually changes from 52% to 61%.

STEP 8: The orange flowers after removing 25% magenta with Selective Color. If you click on a sample color after entering Selective Color, the Color palette shows you the actual new CMYK percentages as you make adjustments in Selective Color.

STEP 8: **Notice that the orange color already is very close to completely saturated in yellow but that the magenta component is only around 52% saturated. On the top-left side of the Color palette, you see a swatch of the color where you last clicked. The Magenta bar in the Color palette shows that if you add magenta to this color, the flowers will look a deeper orange, and eventually reddish, in color. If you take away magenta, the flowers will become more yellowish. Move the Magenta slider in Selective Color (not in the Color palette) to the right, to +20%. In our example, the Method radio button at the bottom of the dialog box is set to Absolute, which should mean that you're adding 20% magenta ink to the 52% magenta already in the yellows, resulting in 72%.** If you were to set Method to Relative, you would add 20% of the 52% of magenta already there, which should bring it up to about 62%. In reality, Absolute mode brings the 52% magenta up to 61%, and Relative mode brings it up to 57%. **If you are trying to add a specific percentage, you should measure the results you actually get using the Color palette rather than assume the percentages in the Selective Color dialog box will be exact. Now subtract 25% magenta from these orange flowers to get the lighter, more yellowish orange you see in our third Selective Color illustration.** When you do this exercise, the color values you get will probably be a little different than mine.

These operations are examples of how you use the Selective Color tool to make subtle tweaks in specific color ranges. When you set Colors to Neutral, Selective Color is also very good at removing color casts in the neutral areas. Photoshop is good at identifying which colors should be composed of equal quantities of cyan, magenta and yellow. There are a couple of other things to note about Selective Color. It is available as an adjustment layer (like Hue/Saturation in the next step), and it works in RGB as wel as CMYK. We most often use it after converting to CMYK where it is particularly useful.

The flowers with the burned petals have to be fixed with the Rubber Stamp tool.

STEP 8: The orange flowers after the color correction choices have been made with Selective Color.

A MORE FLEXIBLE WAY TO SET THIS UP

STEP 9: For a more advanced way to set this up, try this. **Re-open the original FlowersYellow image from the** *Photoshop CS Artistry* **CD. Choose Select/Color Range, use the Load button to load the YellowFlowerSet that you saved in Step 5, and click on OK. You now have a selection of the parts of this image that you want to change. Now choose Layer/New Adjustment Layer/Hue/Saturation, name this new layer Orange Flowers, and then click on OK. This adds a Hue/Saturation adjustment layer above the existing yellow *Background* layer. Now you are in the Hue/Saturation dialog box, so set the Hue to –20.** Your flowers will now change to orange, and only the flowers will change because your selection will have been automatically put into the layer mask of this Hue/Saturation adjustment layer. When an adjustment layer is active, you are automatically working on this layer mask. **With the adjustment layer active, you can now use Gaussian Blur and the painting tools to fine-tune the adjustment layer's built-in layer mask, and you can double-click on the adjustment layer thumbnail at any time to change the color of the flowers. I found that a Gaussian Blur of 1 on this adjustment layer's mask improved the color change blend. Choose Filter/Blur/Gaussian Blur (Shift-F4) and set the Amount to 1. Try Command-Z several times to Undo and Redo this Gaussian Blur and notice how the darker reddishorange spots on the flowers look more natural and less pixelated after the Gaussian Blur is added to the mask. You can also turn the Eye icon on and off on the Orange Flowers layer to see that the tonality of the orange flowers with the blurred mask matches the tonality of the original yellow flowers more closely.** This solution allows for an infinite number of changes to the color and also to the mask without degrading the image. See the Yellow/Orange Layers file in the Extra Info Files folder for this chapter and try this out for yourself!

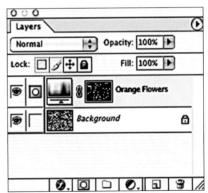

A MORE FLEXIBLE WAY: The Layers palette for this more flexible way to change the color of the flowers and leave your options much more open.

261

22 HANDS-ON SESSION: Color Matching Images

Measure and adjust the color of objects so differently colored items can be changed to match, and do subtle color tweaks after CMYK conversion to deal with faded CMYK hues.

The long shot is a red car, and you need to end up with two matching red CMYK images.

The close-up shot is a green car; you need to change its color to match the red car to the left.

Imagine that you want to create an advertisement using two photos of the Acura Integra. One of the photos is of a red Integra and the other is a green one. You need to convert the green car photo so that its color matches that of the red one. You also need to convert both cars to CMYK and do some final color matching there. **The files in this example were saved using the ColorMatchRGB settings and the example was done with ColorMatchRGB as the RGB working space. Your numbers should come out very similar if you leave your files in the ColorMatch space for this example, but you might get somewhat different numerical values if you choose to convert these original images to another RGB workspace.**

CHOOSING THE COLOR MATCH SPOTS

STEP 1: Here is the color match spot in the red car.

STEP 1: Here is the color match spot in the green car.

STEP 1: **Open the RedAcuraCM and GreenDetail files from the Color Matching Cars folder. Find a spot on the red car where the color appears to be an average, intermediate color that could represent the color you want for the whole car. Both of these photos have highlight and shadow areas that you are going to want to match also. I've found that if you can locate a good midtone area in both images and get those midtone areas to match, the rest of the image will also match pretty well. I used the area on the front of the car to the right of the chrome Acura emblem, just above the word Integra embossed in the red bumper. Because this spot exists—and the lighting on it is similar—in both photos, you can use this** location on both cars to get the colors to match. We call this location the color match spot. Bring up the Info palette (F9) and set the top-left viewing area to HSB mode. Type an I to choose the Eyedropper tool; then Shift-I to switch to the Color Sampler Eyedropper. This tool was added in Photoshop 5 and it allows you to place a measurement location within an image and then see how the values at that location change when you make color adjustments. You can place up to four Color Sampler locations in each image that you have open. **Press Return to bring up the Options bar for the Color Sampler if it is not currently visible and make sure the Sample Size is set to 3 by 3 average. Put the Eyedropper over the color match spot and click to take a measurement. Hold the mouse button down and measure around a bit to make sure the spot you are using as this first measurement is an average measurement for this area. I used the area just above the E in Integra. When you release the mouse, the Color Sampler added to the bottom of the Info palette will remember values for that location. Change the current display of those values for that Color Sampler to HSB and write down the HSB values within the Red image. I got 358 for the Hue, 89 for the Saturation, and 81 for the Lightness, but slightly different values will work also. We will now match these in the green image.**

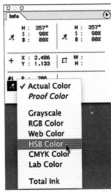

STEP 1: Choosing the Color Sampler tool and setting the Sample Size to 3 by 3 Average.

STEP 1: Setting your Color Sampler readings to HSB.

STEP 2: **Switch to the green car and find the same location right above the embossed E. Click here to create a Color Sampler reading in this image, too. Change the Color Sampler display of this spot in the Info palette to HSB.** If you ever have trouble seeing the Color Sampler part of the Info palette, which is at the bottom, you can always choose Hide Color Samplers followed by Show Color Samplers from the Info palette's options and this will bring all your Color Sampler values back into view. **Choose Image/Adjust/Hue/Saturation (Command-U) to bring up the Hue/Saturation color adjustment tool. Move the Hue slider so that the Hue value in the Info palette for your color match spot for the green image matches the one you wrote down for the red image. You need to have the windows open on the screen so you can see both cars at the same time, and you might want to zoom in so that you see this part of both cars at the same time. Now move the Saturation and Lightness sliders back and forth until you get saturation and lightness values in the Color Sampler that match the numbers you wrote down for the color match spot on the red car. The Color Sampler continues to show you how the color match spot, where you set it in the green car, has changed based on the Hue/Saturation slider movements. Try to get all three numbers to match exactly, but don't worry if one of them is off by one point in either direction. The Saturation and Lightness settings influence each other as you move them. As you change one, the other also changes, so you must tweak both of them for a while until you get as close as possible to what you had in the red car. You can use the Tab key to move quickly between the input areas, and when a number is highlighted, you can use the up and down arrow keys to increase or decrease the values by one. When you are happy with the adjustments, click the OK button in Hue/Saturation.** You could have also made a Hue/Saturation adjustment layer if you wanted to easily go back and modify these settings again later.

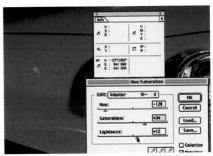

STEP 2: Adjusting Hue, Saturation, and Lightness to get the green color match spot to match the values in the red car.

STEP 3: **Now click and drag the little Eyedropper pop-up menus in the Info palette to convert the Color Sampler displays for both images to RGB mode. Write down the Red, Green, and Blue values from the color match spot in the original red car. My values were 207 for Red, 23 for Green, and 29 for Blue. Switch to the green car, now**

Choosing the Color Match Spots

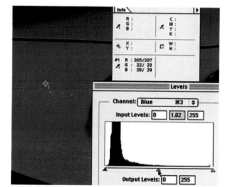

STEP 3: Using the Red, Green, and Blue channels in Levels to match the green car's RGB values to the red car's values.

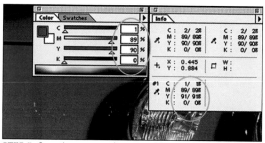

STEP 5: When you put the Eyedropper tool exactly over the color match spot, the circle and crosshair will disappear and you will just see the number 1 that denotes Color Sampler number 1's position. At this point, you can click and get all the values to match exactly between the different palettes.

STEP 5: Sometimes, even when everything appears to line up correctly, the values will not match exactly between the different palettes or even between two readouts from the same palette. Just get things as close as possible.

converted to red, and choose Image/Adjust/Levels (Command-L). Go into the Red channel (Command-1) and move the Input Brightness slider, the middle slider, until the Red value in the Color Sampler matches the Red value you wrote down for the original red car. Switch to the Green channel and do the same thing until the Green value matches on both. Finally, do the same thing for the Blue channel. Now the two cars should match fairly well. Click OK.

CONVERTING TO CMYK MODE

STEP 4: **Now bring up the Color palette (Command-Shift-F9), which is useful here because it shows you, with its colored sliders, how to adjust colors to get more of what you want.** In older versions of Photoshop, I always used the Color palette for all my matching color situations. Since Photoshop 5, the Color Sampler gives you the advantage of remembering the location of the sample point and also having up to four sample points for each image. It is good to know the trade offs between using the Color Sampler and the Color palette, and here we'll learn them. **Using its Palette Options menu, switch the Color palette to CMYK display. Also convert all your Color Sampler readouts to CMYK. Type Shift-I twice to switch the Tools palette back to the regular Eyedropper tool. This is the tool you will use for getting measurements into the Color palette. Drag the Color palette out of the Palette Well if it is there.**

STEP 5: **Make sure your File/Color Settings/CMYK Setup settings are set correctly, as described in Chapter 3: "Setting System and Photoshop Preferences," and then use Image/Mode/CMYK Color to convert both cars to CMYK mode.** Based on your CMYK preference settings, the colors onscreen should now be as close as possible to your printed colors. You might notice the intense red of these cars fades somewhat as you convert to CMYK. Now we'll use the Selective Color tool to do subtle, final tweaks of your red colors in CMYK mode. Selective Color is a great tool for doing subtle adjustments to particular color areas in CMYK. **Switch to the original red car, the long shot, and make sure you can see both the Info palette and the Color palette. Now go into Image/Adjustments/Selective Color (Shift-F6). Make sure that Colors is set to Reds because you're going to be adjusting the red colors in the car. Set the Method to Absolute, so that you can make the color adjustments more quickly. Move the cursor until it is exactly on top of the color match spot; at that point the circle and crosshair will disappear (make sure you're using Precise Cursors). At this exact point, click to take another measurement at the color match spot on the car and notice that when you click, the values come up in the Color palette.** Values only change in the Color palette when you click or take a reading with the mouse button down. The values in the top-left area of the Info palette change whenever you move the mouse, and the values in your color match spot in the Info palette will only change when you change the color of that color match spot. **These values in the Color palette should now match the values in the color match spot within the Info palette—although, as we show you in the illustration, the match might not be completely exact.**

Chapter 22: Color Matching Images

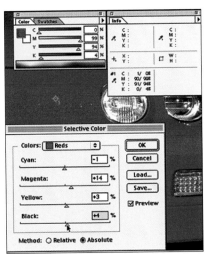

STEP 6: **Notice that the color consists mostly of magenta and yellow.** The colors of the sliders on the Color palette show you how the color at the color match spot will change if you add or subtract more cyan, magenta, yellow, or black ink. **If the Cyan value is greater than 0, subtract cyan using the Selective Color slider, until the Cyan value reads 0 in the Color palette; 1 may be as low as it will go. You should also now see the 0 value in your Info palette Color Sampler reading. This maneuver adds red to the car color. Add magenta with Selective Color until the Magenta value in the Color palette is about 99 to make the car a deeper, richer color. Adjust the yellow until the Yellow value in the Color palette reads about 94. To get a slightly darker, richer color, add some black until the Black value in the Color palette reads about 4. The colors in the Color palette's sliders will give you hints on what to do to improve the CMYK color of the spot you are reading in your image. You don't have to use the exact same numbers that we have; just adjust the cyan, magenta, yellow, and black percentages on the color match spot until you like the car's shade of red. Write down these adjusted CMYK values from the Color palette. Click OK.**

STEP 7: **Switch to the image that was originally green and again enter the Selective Color tool (Shift-F6). Press down on the mouse button while taking a measurement of the color match spot in this image. The values in the Color palette should now match those in the color match spot for this image in the Info palette. Now adjust the cyan, magenta, yellow, and black inks, using the sliders in Selective Color, until the percentages in the Color palette (or Info palette) match the final adjusted percentages you just wrote down from the other image.** We used Cyan = 0, Magenta = 99, Yellow = 94, and Black = 4, but your values can be different. You just want the two red colors to match and both to look the way you like them. This method is a good way to match the colors of objects that start out differently, but have to end up the same.

STEP 6: Here are the final Selective Color adjustments we made to get the 0, 99, 94, 4 values for the car that was originally red.

The final green car after converting to red and CMYK adjustments.

The final long shot of the original red car after conversion and adjustment in CMYK.

265

ADVANCED COLOR CORRECTION AND RESTORATION TECHNIQUES

USING DUOTONES FOR HIGHER TONAL RANGE

RESTORING OLD PHOTOGRAPHS

WORKING IN LAB VERSUS RGB

USING MASKS FOR VARIED COLOR CORRECTION

COMBINING BRACKETED PHOTOGRAPHS TO INCREASE DYNAMIC RANGE

RESTORE DAMAGED FILM AND RETOUCH FACES

I shot this image in 2003 with a Canon 3.2 megapixel digital point-and-shoot at Fotofusion. Fotofusion is my favorite Photography conference, which I attend every year at Palm Beach Photographic center. Come down and have some fun in January 2004; see www.fotofusion.org for info. I usually teach a week long Digital Printmaking workshop there after the conference.

23 HANDS-ON SESSION: Burnley Graveyard

How to work with duotones, how and why to adjust duotone curves, and how to save and calibrate your duotone output.

STEP 1: The BurnleyGraveyard image printed as black and white using only black ink.

Duotones are used when printing black-and-white photos on a press to get more tonal range. Black-and-white (B&W) digital images can have up to 256 tones in digital format, but you can't get those 256 tones on a printing press with just the single black ink. If you use two or more inks to print B&W images, part of the tonal range can be printed by the first ink and part of it by the second ink. Many of Ansel Adams' well-known B&W posters are actually duotones. Besides giving you a larger tonal range, duotones allow you to add rich and subtle color to your B&W images.

Typically, you use black ink for the dark shadows and a second color, a brown or gray, for the midtones. You can add a third and even a fourth color to enhance the highlights or some other part of the tonal range. Many books are printed with two colors, black for the text and a second color, such as red or blue, for text section titles, underline, and other special colored areas. If this type of book has photographs, you can often make them more interesting by using duotones instead of just B&W.

CREATING A DUOTONE

STEP 1: This photo was originally a color transparency, but I felt a B&W or duotone printing of it would better convey the feelings I have about this stark graveyard where my grandfather and uncle are actually buried. Before using Image/Mode/Grayscale to convert the image to B&W, I did the overall color correction with Levels to get the best version of the RGB image I had scanned. It is usually best to do overall color correction before converting an image from RGB to either B&W or CMYK. After converting to B&W, I edited the contrast of the sky and the foreground separately to bring out the drama of the scene. I also fixed a section of the sky which was blown out due to the high dynamic range of the original photo. I plan to add the full step-by-step process for this image, including the color work and conversion and then masking in black and white, to my upcoming book: *Making the Digital Print.* **Open and crop the BurnleyGraveyard image from the Ch23.Burnley Graveyard folder on the CD. Choose Image/Mode/Duotone to start working with the Duotone options. Start with the Type set to Monotone and the curve for Ink 1 straight. If the**

STEP 1: Change Type to Monotone mode and start with a straight curve.

curve is not already straight, click on the Curve box (the leftmost one) for Ink 1 and bring up the curve. Click and drag any extra points in the middle of the curve to outside the dialog box to remove them, or hold down Option and click the Reset button to remove all the points. The horizontal axis of the curve diagrams in Duotone Options has the highlights on the left and the shadows on the right—the opposite of the default for Levels and Curves. The numbers in the boxes represent a percentage of black. Box 0, for the brightest highlight, should read 0, and box 100, for the darkest shadow, should read 100. All the other boxes should be blank when you have a straight curve. **Click on OK in the Duotone Curve dialog box. The Ink box for Ink 1 should be black and Black should be its name. Change the Type to Duotone to activate Ink 2 with a straight curve. To pick the color of Ink 2, click in the Color box (the rightmost one) for Ink 2 to bring up the Custom Colors picker, and then select a PANTONE, Focoltone, Toyo, Trumatch, or other color from one of the Custom Color Systems.** Look in Chapter 5: "Picking and Using Color," if you need help using the Custom Colors Picker. If you were going to print your duotone on a two-color book job or a job with a spot color, you would probably use one of these color systems. **We selected PANTONE Warm Gray 10 C for Ink 2. You now have a black ink and a medium gray ink, both with straight curves. Make sure the Preview button is on in the Duotone Options dialog box to give you a preview of what it should look like with the current inks and curves.** Printing two inks, both with straight curves, is like printing the image in black and then printing the exact same image again with the second ink color. When printing with halftone screens, the second ink will be printed with a different screen angle to add some additional tonality over using one ink. Printing the two inks using the same curve will cause the image to have too much density and seem very dark. This is not taking advantage of the real possibilities for duotone improvements.

STEP 1: The BurnleyGraveyard image created in Duotone mode as a duotone with black and PANTONE Warm Gray10 C inks, both having straight curves, and later converted to CMYK for this final output.

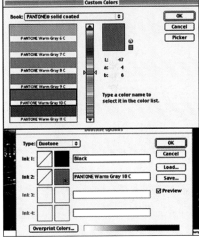

STEP 1: Picking the second color by clicking on the rightmost color square for Ink 2.

ADJUSTING YOUR DUOTONE CURVES

STEP 2: **Click on the Curve box (the leftmost box) for Ink 1. You want to adjust the black ink to make it prevalent in the shadows, but less prevalent in the midtones and highlights. To do this, click on a point in the middle of the curve and drag that point downward to remove black from the midtones and highlights. Now click on the shadow end of the curve (to the middle right) and drag it up to add a little more black to this area of the image. See the illustration of the black curve here. Click on the OK button for black and then click on the Curve button for Ink 2 (warm gray) so you can work on its curve. Because we want the dark areas of the image to be represented mostly by black, we need to remove the gray from the shadows. Click at the top-right of the curve and drag it down to about 55. Now you need to put the gray back into the highlights and midtones, so click a couple of points in the middle of the curve to pull it up so it looks like the curve here. When the Preview checkbox in Duotone Options is on, you should be able to see these changes as you make them. You have now made the basic adjustments for your duotone curves. Now change each curve just a little bit, one curve at a time. Tweak these curves until you are happy with your duotone; then choose OK to Duotone Options and use File/Save As to save the image as BurnleyGraveyardDuo.**

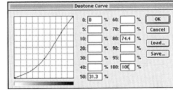

STEP 2: The black curve emphasizing the shadows.

STEP 2: The midtone curve for Ink 2, lowering this color in the shadow areas.

269

STEP 2: The BurnleyGraveyard image created in Duotone mode as a duotone with black for the shadows and PANTONE Warm Gray 10 C for the midtones and high-lights, after adjusting the curves for those two colors, and then converting to CMYK.

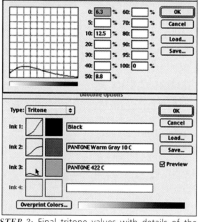

STEP 3: Final tritone values with details of the highlight curve. Notice how this curve actually starts above 0 on the Y axis. This adds density in the very brightest areas.

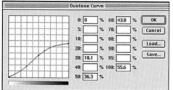

STEP 4: The Info palette measuring a high-light in Tritone mode.

STEP 4: Set the Info palette to Actual Color for duotones.

STEP 5: The midtone curve for the tritone with a small dip in the highlight area and a bigger dip in the shadows.

CREATING A TRITONE

STEP 3: To further enhance this image, you can add a third ink for the highlight areas to alter them in subtle ways. Before doing so, however, take time to make a copy of the two-ink version of the image so you can compare them onscreen. **Choose Image/Duplicate (F5) and name this copy BurnleyGraveyardTri. Choose Image/Mode/Duotone, and select Tritone from the Type menu in Duotone Options so that a choice for Ink 3 will be added. Click on the Ink Color box and choose a lighter gray for the highlights. (For Ink 3 we chose PANTONE 422 C.) Adjust the curve for this highlight color so that it has ink only in the brightest part of the image. The Step 3 illustration shows the curve we chose for the third ink. Notice how we moved the 0 posi-tion of the curve up to 6.3 instead of leaving it at 0.** This strategy actually adds some density to the brightest parts of the image—that is, in the clouds and where the sun reflects off the gravestones, two areas that previously were pure white. Here, we are using a third ink to subtly fine-tune the main image created by the first two main inks.

STEP 4: **You may want to measure some values on the screen using the Eyedropper. When working with duotones, you want to set the top-left area in the Info palette to Actual Color, so that it will give you measurements of the ink density percentage of each color. If you measure one of the highlight areas in the clouds, you can see that there is no density there from Inks 1 and 2, but that Ink 3 has 6% density in that area. If you measure a shadow area, the maximum density there will be from Ink 1, black. There will be some density from Ink 2 and there will be no density from Ink 3 because its curve specifies no ink in the shadow areas.**

STEP 5: **You have added a third color specifically for the highlights; therefore, you may want to go back to Ink 2 and remove some of the midtone ink from the high-light areas. Click on the Curve box for Ink 2 and lower its curve in the highlight areas by clicking a point there and dragging it downward. Here is the final curve we used for Ink 2 in the tritone. Our final tritone image appears on the next page.**

STEP 6: **Go back and try some different colors and different curves for this duotone or tritone. Try some blues, greens, purples, magentas, yellows—lots of wild things. Experiment with some radical inverted curves to discover the great range of effects you can achieve with the Duotone options.**

CALIBRATING AND OUTPUTTING YOUR DUOTONES

If you are not having any particular calibration problems, especially if you are converting duotones to CMYK for final output, we recommend that you leave your calibration and preferences set up the same as those for your CMYK workspace as described in Chapter 3: "Setting System and Photoshop Preferences."

When you output your duotones, you have several choices to make. If you actu-ally print with PANTONE or some other custom spot color, you need to save the file as a duotone in Photoshop EPS format. You can set your screen angles for the duotone in Photoshop using File/Print With Preview with the Show More Options checkbox on. Use the pop-up to select Output, then click the Screen button. You can also set your screen angles in QuarkXPress or InDesign if you are placing your duotone into one of those page layout applications. Talk to your service bureau about how and where to set your screens and what screen angles and frequencies to use. One important issue is to make sure the name of each color is exactly the same (including upper- and lowercase letters) in your page layout application; otherwise, your duotone may be output as CMYK. To save from Photoshop as a duotone, leave the Mode menu set to Duotone, choose File/Save As, and then set the Format to Photoshop EPS. In the EPS dialog box, set the Preview to Macintosh (8 bits/pixel) and the Encoding to Binary, and then click on the Include Halftone Screen checkbox only if you have set your screens and frequencies using Print With Preview in Photoshop. On Windows, you may want to set the Encoding to ASCII, depending on the page layout application you're placing the duotone into. Check with that Application's manual.

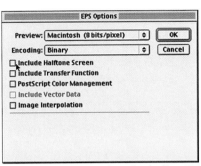

The dialog box and settings for saving the file as EPS Duotone.

If you want to convert the duotone to CMYK to output it with process colors, use the Image/Mode menu to convert the image to CMYK color. For more information on the options for saving CMYK files, see Chapter 17: "Steps to Create a Master Image." You can also convert your duotones to RGB format if you want to composite them with other images for Web or multimedia use, or for output to a film recorder or some other RGB device, like an Epson printer. To do the conversion to RGB, just select Image/Mode/RGB.

When you work on a duotone or tritone, the Channels palette displays a single channel—your original black-and-white image. When you print the tritone, this same black-and-white channel prints three times, and each time the separate curve for the particular tritone color is used to modify it before it goes to the printer. If you want to see each of these three-color tritone channels as they will look after the curves are applied, switch the Image/Mode menu to Multichannel. The Channels palette will now show you three channels: Channel 1 for black, Channel 2 for PANTONE 10, and Channel 3 for PANTONE 422. You can then click on each channel in the Channels palette to see how that channel will look on film. If you wanted to edit each of these channels separately, you could do so now, but after doing that, you could not convert them back to Duotone mode. These three channels would now have to be output as three separate black-and-white files. If you were just looking at the three channels and not editing them, you would choose Edit/Undo Multichannel to undo the mode change and put things back into Duotone mode.

Converting a file from Duotone to CMYK format for output to process colors.

The final BurnleyGraveyard image created in Duotone mode as a tritone with black shadows, PANTONE Warm Gray 10 C midtones, and PANTONE 422 C highlights, then converted to CMYK for final output.

24 HANDS-ON SESSION: Desert Al

Retouching this problem scan using adjustment layers, the Channel Mixer, intralayer blending, and the Healing Brush to produce a print with natural, consistent, and pleasing tones overall.

The original uncorrected image.

One of my favorite pictures has always been this photo of my best buddy Al, taken on a desert trip we made together back around 1980. I always wanted to make a print of it, so when I got my Epson Stylist Photo printer, I had it and many other favorite pictures put onto Photo CD. When I brought in the photo from the CD, it was obviously oversaturated in the shadow areas of the face. Because this is not a major area of the image, the first step to correct it is to do overall color correction to get the rest of the image to look right. This file was saved using ColorMatch RGB, so if you want your values and histograms to look the same as in the book, leave this file in the ColorMatch RGB space.

OVERALL COLOR CORRECTION

STEP 1: **Open the OrigAl.psd file from the Desert Al folder on the CD. Crop any areas from around the edge of the image that are not going to be in the print.** In this case, my copyright notice is the only thing you need to crop. **Double-click on the *Background* layer and name it Original Al; then click on the Lock Position icon, second from right at the top of the Layers palette, to lock the position of this layer. Use F9 to bring up the Info palette. Now use Command-F2 to create a Levels adjustment layer and use the steps outlined in Chapter 19: "Overall Color Correction," to set the Highlight, Shadow, overall Brightness, and finally the color cast. Here are the Levels settings I ended up with for Al. To set the highlight, I used the Highlight Eyedropper in Levels and set it to the white area on the tip of Al's right shoulder (on the left side of the image). For the shadow, I used the Shadow Eyedropper and set it to the shadow on the black tuft of hair below Al's ear and behind his neck. I then adjusted the overall brightness, as well as the color balance. When you are done with your basic color corrections, choose OK to save your Levels adjustment layer.** If you want to compare your settings to mine, double-click on the Levels thumbnail in your new adjustment layer and then click on the Load button and load the file named Step1LevelsSettings.alv from the Extra Info Files folder on this chapter. Turning the Preview button off will show you your settings and turning it on again will show you mine. If you Cancel Levels, you'll go back to your settings, and if you choose OK, you'll convert to mine. Just make sure that the color on Al's face looks good!

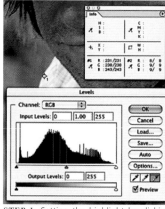

STEP 1: Setting the highlight by clicking with the Highlight Eyedropper on the whitest area of Al's shirt.

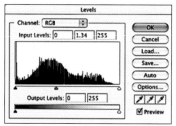

STEP 1: The overall corrected RGB histogram.

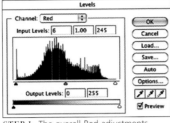

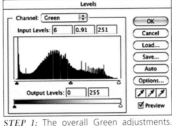

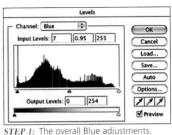

STEP 1: The overall Red adjustments.   STEP 1: The overall Green adjustments.   STEP 1: The overall Blue adjustments.

STEP 2: **Use Command-F4 to add a Hue/Saturation adjustment layer above the Levels adjustment layer.** Here to the right are the settings I made in Hue/Saturation. The goal was to saturate all the colors, as I normally would do, but then to not add more saturation to the reds in the face. **To get the set of reds that I wanted to desaturate in the face, I first used the Hue/Saturation Eyedropper and dragged it over the really saturated areas of his face because these are the ones that need desaturation. I then used the –Eyedropper to subtract away the normal red flesh tones by dragging over them, and then the +Eyedropper to add any oversaturated colors back in.** As you are doing this, notice that the range of reds that are selected changes based on the width of the gray slider bars between the two rainbow color bars in the Hue/Saturation dialog. Try my settings and feel free to modify them and make your own to improve the image. **Don't try to fix the red shadow areas around the eyes here, just desaturate them a little bit. They should still look a bit too saturated when you finish with Hue/Saturation.**

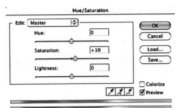

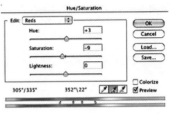

STEP 2: The Master Hue/Saturation setting.   STEP 2: The Red channel Hue/Saturation setting.

FIXING THE OVERSATURATED AREAS WITH CHANNEL MIXER

STEP 3: **Use Shift-F10 to bring up the Channels palette. Click first on the word RGB, and then the word Red to look at the Red channel. Make sure the Eye icons are off for the RGB, Green, and Blue channels. Now look at just the Green and just the Blue channels in the same way. This will tell you if one of the channels has a noticeable pattern within the oversaturated area on Al's face.** The Levels and Hue/Saturation layers actually have no Red, Green, and Blue channels themselves because they are adjustment layers, but this is showing you what each of these channels will look like when the layers you've created so far are merged. **You can see that the Green channel is very dark (which will print as magenta) in all the saturated areas. Make sure the Hue/Saturation layer is active and then choose**

STEP 3: Al's RGB before using the Red channel to fix the saturated areas.

STEP 3: The Red channel we will use to fix the Green and Blue channels.

STEP 3: The unfixed Green channel is dark in all the saturated areas.

STEP 3: Al's RGB after fixing the Green and Blue channels using the Channel Mixer.

273

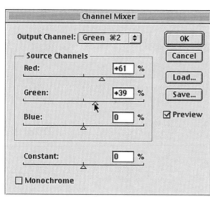

STEP 3: Here we see the Channel Mixer settings for the Green channel.

Layer/New Adjustment Layer/Channel Mixer. Channel Mixer is a feature in recent versions of Photoshop that makes this kind of operation much easier and more flexible than it used to be. We are going to use the Red channel to fix the oversaturation problems in the Green and Blue channels. **Make sure the Preview button is on in the Channel Mixer dialog; then set the Output Channel to Red and leave the Source Channels set to 100% Red. Now set the Output Channel to Green; then change the Source Channels to about 61% Red and 39% Green.** This will change the Green channel to actually be made up of 61% of the Red channel and you will notice more detail returning to the saturated areas of Al's face. **Now set the Output Channel to Blue; then set the Source Channels to about 47% Red and 53% Blue.** You can change these percentages as many times as you like, and as you do, you will notice small changes in color balance and the amount of detail in the saturated areas of Al's face. You can use the Load button to load the file Step3ChannelMixer.cha, which is my Channel Mixer settings. To fix the Green and Blue channels, you want to use the least amount of the Red channel that both repairs the dark areas and keeps a compatible color balance that will be flatter than the previous image, because much of the detail is coming from the Red channel after using the Channel Mixer. While in the Channel Mixer dialog, if you turn the Preview checkbox off, you'll see the original image as it was before fixing. With the Preview button on you'll see the fixed image. It is OK if the fixed image is flatter than the original because we are only going to use the fixed image in the areas where we need it. The main goal here is to get the color close to the original and realize that it will be flatter for a moment here. **Choose OK to complete your Channel Mixer step.**

Using the Channel Mixer Only Where We Need It

STEP 4: **Choose Image/Adjustments/Invert to invert the layer mask of the Channel Mixer adjustment layer and make it black.** Now your image should look like it did before you added the Channel Mixer adjustment layer. We are now going to airbrush in this Channel Mixer adjustment only where we need it. **Type a B to switch to the Brush, pick a 30 pixel brush, and click the Airbrush icon to the on position (highlighted) in the Options bar. Use a soft brush, one that has a Brush Tip Shape Hardness set to 0. Set the Opacity to 100% and the Flow to 7%. Make sure you only use the left and right bracket keys to change your brush size—that way the Airbrush option will stay active. Type a D for default color and paint white in the Channel Mixer layer mask. Doing so lets you slowly remove dark and oversaturated parts of the image to apply the lighter fixed version of the Channel Mixer where you need it. Use Command-Option-0 to zoom into 100% or maybe even 200% so you can see details. Do this slowly with a light touch and start out with less-complicated areas like the redness around the ears and where the sideburn hair meets the face. When you get the idea there, move on to more complex areas. Don't worry if the color balance of Channel Mixer version isn't exactly right; just work on getting the saturation down in the damaged areas. You want to airbrush with white very little to get a gray value in the layer mask so just barely enough of the Channel Mixer layer is revealed. Painting too much in the mask is the most common problem students have in getting this example to work for them. If your mask in the fixed areas is totally white, then you overdid it. You can always type an X to switch and paint with black, and then paint black on the mask in areas where you over did it painting with white. Typing X again switches back to white.** If you are having trouble making this work, see the AlAllFinalLayers.psd

STEP 4: Al before retouch and sharpening.

Chapter 24: Desert Al

file in the Extra Info Files folder of this chapter to check out my layer mask for the Channel Mixer layer. **When you are happy with the basic detail that you have added using the Channel Mixer layer mask, use Command-F2 to add a new grouped Levels adjustment layer called Fix Channel Mix above the Channel Mixer layer. To have this adjustment layer grouped, you need to turn on the Use Previous Layer to Create Clipping Mask checkbox in the New Layer dialog. Now you can use Levels to change the color balance and brightness of the Channel Mixer layer while watching how these changes affect its composite with the other layers underneath. You should find that you can get Al's face to look much better when you match the color and brightness of the two. Choose OK when you are happy with your changes. You can also use the Load button to load my settings from the file Step4ChannelMixerAdjust.alv from the Extra Info Files folder on the CD. My settings may not help your image, however, because your mask is different from mine. Click on the Channel Mixer layer again and then use white or black with the Airbrush to make further changes to the mask and fine-tune the face composite. You can also double-click on the Layer thumbnail of the Fix Channel Mix layer if you want to tweak the color of the fixed areas some more.**

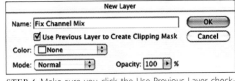

STEP 4: Make sure you click the Use Previous Layer checkbox so the Levels adjustments you make in this step only affect the Channel Mixer layer.

STEP 5: **When this is looking as good as you can get it, click on the Fix Channel Mix layer to activate it. Now Option-click on the New Layer icon, to the left of the trash can at the bottom of the Layers palette, to add a new layer above the Fix Channel Mix layer, named Retouch Clone. Now, with the Option key held down, choose Merge Visible from the Layers palette menu to merge the five lower layers all into this new layer. Make sure you release the mouse button first and leave the Option key down until the computer stops thinking about the merge. Otherwise the underlying layers will disappear, which you don't want to happen.** Using a new Merged layer for retouching allows you to just retouch a single layer and to also have the option of throwing this layer out and starting over again if you make an uncorrectable mistake.

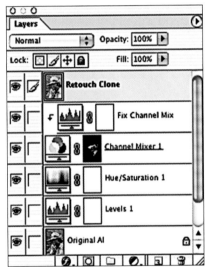

STEP 5: The Layers palette as it should look after step 5. Check out my version named AlAllFinalLayers.psd in the Extra Info Files folder on the *Photoshop CS Artistry* CD.

CLEANING UP SOME BLEMISHES WITH CLONING AND HEALING

When we teach this example as well as some others, there's a great deal of confusion about when you need to use the Clone Stamp and when you're better off working with the Healing Brush. I'm afraid there's no hard-and-fast rule to guide you. Each photograph is different, so you'll probably have to experiment with both tools until you feel comfortable with their capabilities. It's important to remember that you have more control over exactly what gets copied with the Clone Stamp, but the Healing Brush may give you a more natural look with less effort. In this exercise, we'll use both so we can compare how the tools work.

STEP 6: **Type an L to choose the Lasso tool, then type Return and then 1 and then Return again, to put a one-pixel feather on Lasso selections. Now use the Lasso tool with this feathered edge to select the white part of Al's left eye. Use Command-H to hide the selection edges and then go into Hue/Saturation (Command-U) and try to brighten the white of Al's eye and make it more white. I added +10 to the Lightness in Master mode, and then I moved the Hue to +8 in Reds mode, all of which made the eye stand out a little better and removed some of its red tint. Choose OK to finish Hue/Saturation and then Command-D to deselect the eye.** This is another place you could use an adjustment layer with a layer mask, but it's a small area and a minor adjustment, so we've chosen not to add a layer here.

STEP 7: **Now use the Clone Stamp tool (S) with different size soft brushes and opacities to remove any blemishes and to tone out areas that are too magenta.** If you set the Opacity to 30–50% and then clone from an area next to the one you want to fix, it's easy to even out color areas that aren't quite right without losing the original detail in that area. You can also clone with the Blend mode set to Color to change the color of something without losing its original detail. Type Shift-Option-C to use Color mode, Shift-Option-N to return to Normal mode. Remember that you can change the Opacity of the Clone Stamp tool by typing a number on the numeric keypad between 0 and 9. Zero is for 100%, 9 for 90%, 8 for 80%,…1 for 10%, or even 25 for 25%. You can also use the bracket keys, [and], to move to the next smaller or the next larger brush. **For this type of cloning, I usually use the top row, 100% hardness, or second row, 80% hardness, of brushes in the BarrysPhotoBrushes set that you loaded while setting your Photoshop preferences in Chapter 3. It is also a good idea to have your History States set to a large number when retouching like this.** Photoshop allows you to save up to 1,000 History States, although you normally wouldn't want to save that many as it takes up lots of hard disk space. Make sure that you use Edit/Preferences/Display & Cursors to set the preferences for Painting Cursors to Brush Size so that if the cursor is over your image, you can see the brush size relative to your image and zoom factor as you change the brush size with the bracket keys. **Be careful not to blur the facial detail with too much cloning.** To see what is possible with Clone Stamping, open the AlAllFinalLayers file from the CD, turn off the top three layers, then turn the Eye icon off and then on again in the Retouch Clone layer.

STEP 8: Al, after retouching with Clone Stamp and sharpening.

STEP 8: **Option-drag the Retouch Clone layer of your file to the New Layer icon and name the copy Retouch Clone USM. Go into Filter/Sharpen/Unsharp Mask (F4) and use the techniques demonstrated in Chapter 20: "Correcting a Problem Image," to find the right sharpening settings for Al. I used 150%, 1.5, and 3. You may want to rename this USM layer with the sharpen settings you used. This will help if you need to change them later. After doing the sharpen, you may want to do another quick sweep at 100% to check for spots that the sharpen might have added. I did my sharpen in a layer that is a copy of Retouch Clone to give me the option of later trying a different sharpen amount!**

Photoshop CS now allows you to heal to a transparent layer. This means you can Option-click to sample a layer, and then use the Healing Brush on an empty layer above the main image layers. Working this way gives you the opportunity to experiment with the transparency and blend mode of a healed area.

STEP 9: Now we are going to experiment with the Healing Brush. **Turn off the Eye icons for the Retouch Clone layer and your USM layer that you made in steps 5 through 8. Click on the Fix Channel Mix layer to activate it again and then go through step 5 again, but this time call your new merged layer Healing Brush. Go ahead and redo step 6 on this Healing Brush layer. Type a J to choose the Healing Brush and set its options in the Options bar to a 21-pixel brush, Blend mode of Normal, and Source set to Sampled. With the Healing Brush in this type of situation, I'd leave the Aligned option off, which is the default for the Healing Brush.**

When using the Healing Brush, look for an area of the face that is discolored or has the wrong texture. That is the area you want to heal. Now Option-click on an area of similar texture to the area you want to heal. You will be healing using the area that you Option-clicked on as an example to heal by. Now without the Option key down, click on the area you want to heal. If the area you want to heal is a bit lighter or darker than the area you sampled with Option-click, the Healing Brush appears to normally figure this out and do the right thing. I found that multiple clicks in the area I wanted to heal often worked better than a click and drag because the click and drag may start to use a part of the sampled area that doesn't have the right color and texture. You can use the left and right bracket keys to change the brush size, but you'll notice that the normal Brushes palette brushes are not available to the Healing Brush. To change the Brush attributes with this tool, click on the brush at the top left of the Options bar.

Using the Healing Brush is different than using the Clone Stamp (Rubber Stamp) tool and to some extent you have to play with it to get the feel for it. With less work and more quickly, using the Healing Brush, I was able to do a better job removing the blemishes on Al's face. I even gave him a partial shave! As with the Clone Stamp tool, though, it is easy to get carried away and click too many times. That is why you'll want your History States (Command-K for General Preferences) set to at least 100 when you are doing this. That allows you to use the History palette to back up enough steps if things start to look too pixelated or if a pattern starts to form.

STEP 10: Al, retouched with the Healing Brush and then sharpened.

STEP 10: **Make a copy of the Healing Brush layer and sharpen this by the same 150,1.5, 3 amount that you used on the Retouch Clone layer. This allows you to compare the two by turning off and on the Eye icon of the top Healing Brush USM 150,1.5,3 layer as you see the sharpened Retouch Clone USM layer below that. If you turn both of these off, you can then turn off and on the Eye icon of the Healing Brush layer to compare it with the Retouch Clone layer below that. Notice that I locked the position of all layers that contain pixel data, or a mask. That is a good habit to get into so the Move tool can't harm you. If I were printing this image on my Epson 1280 or 2200, I probably would have only sharpened it using the 100, 1, and 0 setting, but the 150, 1.5, 3 setting looks good when printed on a press!** Save the file as your final RGB version of Al, and call it AlFinalRGB or something like that. You want to save the flattened version under a different name to preserve the layered RGB version for later use.

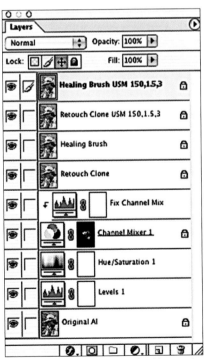

STEP 10: The final Layers palette for this example. Check out my version named AlAllFinalLayers.psd in the Extra Info Files folder on the *Photoshop CS Artistry* CD.

277

25 HANDS-ON SESSION: Restoring Old Photos

Techniques for restoring and colorizing old photographs are explored as we restore a black-and-white photo of the Cochrane train station taken in the '30s by Arthur F. Lynch, Jr. and provided for use in this book by the Adams Collection.

Since I have been teaching the Printmaking for Photographers workshop in my studio, various students have brought in old photographs they wanted to restore. I am very impressed with what we have been able to do to restore these old black-and-white as well as color photographs so I decided to add a restoration example to *Photoshop 6 Artistry*. I had been looking for the right photograph to restore and mentioned this during one of my courses. A student at the course, John Adams, happens to collect old photographs so he sent me this as a possible candidate. It is a great shot, taken in the 1930s by Arthur F. Lynch, Jr., and is just what I was looking for. Thanks to the Adams Collection for providing this photograph for use in this book. You can gain access to the Adams Collection via their Web site at www.adamscollection.com.

The original faded and scratched photograph was not that different from this size.

SCANNING THE ORIGINAL

STEP 1: Scanning an old photograph can be done quite well using a flatbed scanner. This one was scanned on the Epson Expression 1640 XL at 1600 dpi. This scanner does a great job scanning prints and has a large bed, allowing you to scan prints up to 12.2 x 17.2 in size. The file you will be working with here is 25% of that 1600 dpi scan. The important thing to do in making a scan of an old photo is to try to capture all the detail in the photo. Try not to lose any highlight or shadow detail that is in the original print. It is important to have the focus right on, which is usually not a problem when scanning prints using a flatbed scanner. I scanned this at 16 bits per channel. **Your first step will be to use File/Open to open the file CochraneOrigScanAt25%.psd from the Ch25.Restoring Old Photos folder on the *Photoshop CS Artistry* CD. This is a 16-bit per channel grayscale image so use Image/Adjust/Levels to do the initial adjustment. The settings I used are shown to the left. Choose OK in the Levels dialog and then choose Image/Mode/8 Bits/Channel to convert this to an 8-bit grayscale image.**

STEP 1: The Levels settings I used on the 16-bit per channel grayscale file.

ADDING CONTRAST

STEP 2: **Create a Curves adjustment layer using Layer/New Adjustment Layer/Curves (Command-F3). Use Option-click in the Curves graph area until you have a graph with just four divisions in each direction. Now make an S-Curve like the one to the right to increase the contrast of the scene. Make sure the shadow detail in the train and on the station platform doesn't get too dark.** You may notice that the shadow detail in the train wheels and also on the station platform is sort of plugged up. What we need to do to solve this problem is create a curve that increases contrast in these areas but then only apply that curve to these areas. **Use Command-F3 to create a second Curve adjustment layer called Add Contrast to Shadows. While looking only into the shadow areas, adjust the curve until you add contrast to these areas. We are going to isolate this adjustment to these areas so it doesn't matter a whole lot what this curve does to the rest of the image. Choose OK in the Curves dialog, and then choose Image/Adjust/Invert (Command-I) to invert the layer mask on this adjustment layer and make it totally black. Now this adjustment is doing nothing...for the moment. Type B to switch to the Paintbrush tool and set the Flow, in the Options bar, to about 7%. Click on the Airbrush Icon to the right of Flow in the Options bar, which, when gray, turns on Airbrush mode. Pick a soft brush of about 30 to 50 pixels in size, and then type D to get the default colors of a white foreground and a black background. Paint on your layer mask in the shadow areas of the train wheels and the station platform to reveal the extra contrast and detail only in those areas. The longer you hold the Airbrush down, the more paint is applied and the more contrast you'll see in these areas.**

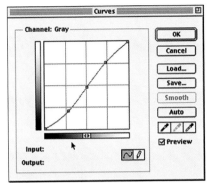

STEP 2: The initial S-Curve to increase contrast. Notice that these curves have their shadows to the left. You can use the double arrows in the middle to display your curves with shadows on either side.

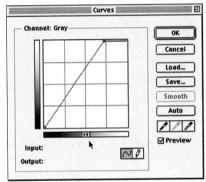

STEP 2: The Shadow curve that is applied to specific areas using the mask below and to the left. This increases the slope of the shadow areas, making them more contrasty, but it also pulls the curve up, making those areas brighter.

STEP 2: The Shadow curve mask that applies the Shadow curve only in the areas where the mask is white.

DARKENING THE BRIGHT, WASHED-OUT AREAS

STEP 3: We want to do a similar, but opposite thing to darken the bright and washed-out areas and also add some contrast to them. **Use Command-F3 again to make another Curves adjustment layer and name it Fix Highlights. Adjust this curve to make the flat, dull highlight areas on the station roof and in the tracks area darker and more contrasty. The curve pictured to the right worked well for me. While making this curve, only look at those areas of the image. After you choose OK in the Curves dialog, choose Command-I to invert the mask and make it totally black. You now want to paint white with the Airbrush in the areas you want to enhance.** This will take a while but it is worth the effort. The images on the next page show you the

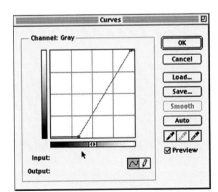

STEP 3: The curve used to darken the bright and washed-out areas. Because the slope of the curve in the highlights is increased, that adds contrast to these flat areas. Pulling the curve downward also makes those areas darker.

279

STEP 3: The Cochrane station before we darken the roof and foreground with the mask to the right.

STEP 3: The Cochrane station after we darken the roof and foreground with the mask to the right.

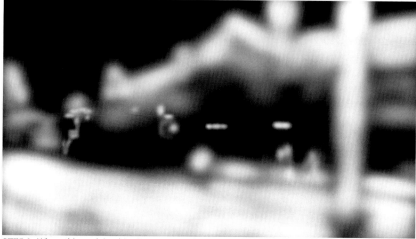

STEP 3: Where this mask is white, its accompanying curve makes the bright areas of this image darker and more contrasty.

![Curves dialog]

STEP 4: A final, more subtle S-Curve was added to the entire image to add just a little more overall contrast.

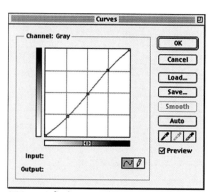

STEP 5: The Layers palette after making the RetouchCopy layer. Notice that I have locked four of the layers against accidental movement.

before and after versions of this photo. These curves adjustments can have a dramatic effect on an image. Use File/Save As to save your file as CochraneLayers.

A FINAL CONTRAST TWEAK

STEP 4: **The image still looks a bit flat overall, so use Command-F3 one more time to add another adjustment layer with a more subtle S-Curve to the entire image. This curve is pictured to the left. Depending on the curves you created so far, you may or may not need this step.** My final CochraneLayers file as well as each curve definition is in the Extra Info Files folder for this chapter on the CD. Compare my masks and curves to the ones you have used so far. If you want to try them, you can load my curves using the Load button in the Curves command.

SPOTTING AND RETOUCHING

STEP 5: This image obviously has a lot of spots, scratches, and other blemishes. We want to fix them but also be able to make sure we don't destroy the original integrity of the image while doing so. Doing these fixes on a copy of the original image allows us to keep the original as a backup and also to look at it from time to time to double check that we are really making positive progress. **Double-click on the *Background* layer to turn it into a regular layer and name it Orig Scan. Drag this Orig Scan layer to the New Layer icon, to the left of the trash, and make a copy called RetouchCopy. This RetouchCopy layer should now be right above the Orig Scan layer. See the illustration to the left to make sure you have it set up correctly. Lock the Orig Scan, RetouchCopy, Add Contrast to Shadows, and Fix Highlights layers so they can't be accidentally moved with the Move tool. Make sure the RetouchCopy layer is active, and then type an S to switch to the Clone Stamp tool. Check in the Options palette to be sure the Opacity and Flow are set to 100%, that Aligned is turned on, and that Use All Layers is turned off. Pick the third brush from the top-left in the Brushes palette as a starting point. Make sure you are in Full Screen mode, press the Tab key to get rid of all your palettes, use Command-Option-0 to zoom in to 100%, and then press the Home key to scroll to the top-left corner of your document. You may want to use Command-Spacebar-click to zoom in to 200%. Now you need to spot, remove scratches, and retouch each section of this image.**

Chapter 25: Restoring Old Photos

The big spots in the sky and elsewhere are fairly easy to remove. It's the fingerprints and tiny scratches in the station and station platform area that you can spend a lot of time on. Be patient and don't get carried away with the Clone Stamp tool. Fix one section at a time and you may find that you don't need to fix every last blemish to make the photo look a lot better. Because the Orig Scan layer is underneath the RetouchCopy layer, you can turn the Eye icon for the RetouchCopy layer off and on again from time to time to see how much you have improved things.

STEP 5: Before retouching, you can see the scratches in the top right of this part of the building and there is also a fingerprint slightly above and to the left of the Cochrane sign.

STEP 5: After retouching with the Clone Stamp tool. It took me about an hour to retouch this entire image. It's still not perfect but looks a lot better.

You can use the Healing Brush along with the Clone Stamp tool to get even better results. I found that the Clone Stamp tool works best when you want to remove some pixels and you know exactly what you want to replace them with. Since you are just copying pixels from one place to another you get exactly what you expect with the Clone Stamp tool. It is great for removing spots in the sky or copying something, like along the edge of a roof or a pattern where you need to copy the exact pattern from one place to another and control precisely where it will be copied to. **Using the Healing Brush tool (J) on this image seemed to work best where I could use Option-click to copy from a texture that didn't have any scratches in it to an area with a similar texture, and there were so many scratches that it would have been very time consuming or impossible with the Clone Stamp tool. The area that you are fixing by copying to it does not always need to have the same lightness or darkness as the area you are copying from because the Healing Brush usually keeps the destination brightness as it was.** Often the Healing Brush will work quite well but sometimes it doesn't give you exactly what you expected and you'll need to go back several steps in the History palette. **When doing this type of retouching work, I use Command-K to set my History states to 99. That allows me to go back quite a few steps when needed. In Photoshop you can set up to 1,000 History states!**

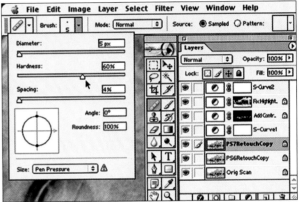

STEP 5: Use the Healing Brush (J) to improve on the damaged areas of the image. First Option-click on a similar undamaged area that has a good texture. Now click and paint on the damaged area in a similar way that you would with the Clone Stamp tool. The Healing Brush won't totally replace the damaged area but tries to use the texture from the good area to fix irregular areas in the damaged area. Try It! Remember that the Healing Brush does not use the regular Brushes palette so you need to click in the Brush area, at the top-left of the Options palette, to change the parameters of your brush. The one that I used for this project had the settings shown here. You can still use the left and right bracket keys to change the brush diameter. For more info on this brush, see Chapter 4: "The Tools Palette."

SHARPENING

STEP 6: **When you have finished spotting and retouching the RetouchCopy layer, choose File/Save (Command-S) to save your final layered file. Now choose Image/Duplicate (F5) to make a copy of your master layered file and make sure Duplicate Merged Layers Only is checked in the Duplicate dialog. With this flattened copy of your file, choose Filter/Sharpen/Unsharp Mask (F4) to sharpen it. I did an overall sharpen of 150, 1, and 0. This improved the image somewhat and also added a normal grain pattern. Now go to the Channels palette and make a copy of the single grayscale channel by dragging it to the New Channel icon next to the trash can**

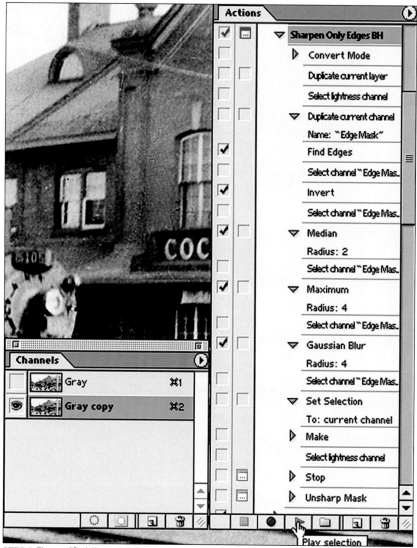

STEP 6: The modified Sharpen Only Edges BH action and the setup in the Channels palette so it will work on a channel by itself. After sharpening the channel, turn the other steps back on. You could also start out by just dragging this entire action to the New Action icon at the bottom of the Actions palette. This will make a copy of the entire action. Rename the copy to Sharpen Only Edges BH Grayscale. Now you could just remove the steps you don't need by dragging them to the trash. This will leave you with a Sharpen Only Edges action that you can use on any channel. To sharpen any RGB image, this new action could be used on one of the Red, Green, or Blue channels of that RGB image instead of converting that image to Lab color as the Sharpen Only Edges BH action does.

To learn more about Photoshop Actions, make sure you read Chapter 11: "Automating Photoshop."

STEP 6: We sharpened the bottom layer with the Unsharp Mask filter at 150,1,0. We then copied this sharpened version in the Channels palette and used that to make the mask with the modified Sharpen Only Edges BH action. We also copied the sharpened version as a layer and sharpened it again at 150,1,0 but applied it through the edges mask as shown here.

at the bottom of the Channels palette. Press F11 to bring up your Actions palette and turn Button Mode off using the pop-up Options menu in the Actions palette. Open up the Sharpen Only Edges BH action and turn off the steps shown to the left (the steps without checkmarks). This modifies the action so it will only run on this new channel you just made in the Channels palette. Play the action on this extra channel and when the action is finished, turn those steps back on again so the action will work normally the next time you use it for a color image. To load it as a selection, Command-click on the Mask channel you just created with the Sharpen Only Edges BH action. Click back on the top channel in the Channels palette to activate it again. Now switch to the Layers palette and drag a copy of your single layer to the New Layer icon to make a copy of this layer. You should still have the selection loaded from the sharpen mask so now choose Layer/Add Layer Mask/Reveal Selection to turn this into a layer mask on this top layer. Click on the leftmost Layer thumbnail for this top layer so you will be sharpening the layer and not the mask. Now use F4 again to go back into Unsharp Mask and sharpen this top layer. I used the same value of 150, 1, and 0 but this time only the areas that are white in the mask are going to be adding sharpness. The final setup for the sharpening is shown to the lower left. Use File/Save As to save this as Cochrane USMLayers. Use Image/ Duplicate (F5) again to make a flattened copy of this and name that copy CochraneColorLayers. Choose Image/Mode/RGB to convert that image from black and white to color. You will now have a Red, Green, and Blue channel in your Channels palette instead of just a single grayscale channel.

COLORIZING

STEP 7: The process for colorizing the image involves creating various Hue/

STEP 7: For each of the adjustment layers in the Layers palette on the next page, we have done a similar adjustment with the Colorize checkbox on in Hue/Saturation. The difference between each one is where we moved the Hue and Saturation sliders. That will determine the color created as we colorize this black-and-white image. These are the settings for the first HueSatBrown layer. You can open my final color version of this image, including all the layers, by looking in the Extra Info Files folder on the CD.

STEP 7: Here is the mask for the Hue/Sat Gray layer. We wanted the train engine to be a darker blue-gray than the other areas so we painted using 100% white. The Opacity of the Paintbrush was changed in the other areas to get the shade of blue-gray we wanted. The straight tracks were done by clicking at one end and then Shift-clicking at the other end, which draws a straight line between the two ends.

Saturation adjustment layers and turning on the Colorize option in each one. The final Layers palette for my colorized Cochrane image is on the next page. **First use Command-F4 to create the HueSatBrown adjustment layer. Using the settings shown above-left, this gives the entire image a brown sepia tone effect. Using the Paintbrush (B), paint black in the mask for this adjustment layer at either 100% or a lower Opacity to remove this effect from the windows of the station. Now use Command-F4 again to create a Hue/Saturation adjustment layer, using the Colorize checkbox again, with a blue-gray color (I set Hue at 218, Saturation at 18, Lightness at -6). Next, type Command-I to invert the mask on this Hue/Sat Gray layer so it won't affect anything. Use the Brush tool to paint in the adjustment layer's mask with white at either 100% or a lower Opacity to add this color to the train engine and other parts of the image. Remember that, while painting, you can type a number to change the Opacity of the brush. Create a Green (92, 15, 0) and then a Red (0, 38, 0) Hue/Saturation layer in a similar way, inverting each of their masks, and then painting white in each mask where you want that color in the image. The final Hue/Saturation colorizing layer you need to create is the one for the Roof (Hue = 9, Saturation = 8, Lightness = 0), which is used to give the roof of the station a more gray color. The only problem left now is a sky with no color or detail in it. To create a sky, use Layer/New Layer to make a new normal layer named Sky at the top of all the other layers in the Layers palette. Click on the Foreground color, at the bottom of the Tools palette, to get into the Color Picker and pick a sky blue color. Be sure white is the background color, and then use Filter/Render/Clouds, which creates a sort of cheesy cloud effect. Setting the Opacity of this layer to 15% or 20% makes this effect somewhat believable. Use Command-0 to zoom out and see the entire image. For a moment, turn off the Eye icon for this top layer, and then click on the Hue/Saturation Roof layer to make it active. Now click on each of the Red, Green, and Blue channels in the Channels palette, while turning off the Eye Icons for the other channels, so you can look at each channel and find the one having the most contrast between the sky and clouds. Make a copy of the**

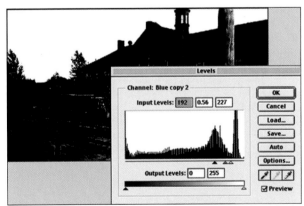

STEP 7: Here we are using Levels on a copy of the Blue channel to make the mask for the new sky. Notice that I have moved the leftmost Input Shadow slider to the right to a value of 192. The rightmost Input Highlight slider is moved to the left to a value of 227. This makes the sky pure white and the foreground mostly black and gives you a contrast separation between the sky and the foreground images. Now adjust the middle Brightness slider to darken the midtone values in the foreground and get an edge that is accurate between the sky and the buildings and trees. I set my Brightness slider to 0.56. You may also want to readjust the Highlight slider and the Brightness slider while turning the Preview checkbox on and off to make sure the horizon in the mask accurately divides the sky from the building and trees.

STEP 7: The Layers palette after adding all the Hue/Saturation Colorize adjustment layers to create the image at the right.

The final color version of the Cochrane train station after making the initial improvements to the black-and-white version, sharpening and then finally colorizing as previously explained.

Blue channel, and then use Image/Adjustments/Levels on that copy to increase the contrast between the sky and everything else. You want the sky white and all else black, so do your best when moving the top left and right Levels sliders toward the middle and adjusting the middle Brightness slider to fine-tune the mask. Choose OK in Levels and then use the Paintbrush (B) to fine-tune the mask so it is white only in the sky and black everywhere else. Command-click on this mask to load it as a selection and then click back on the word RGB in the Channels palette. Bring back your Layers palette (F10) and click on the Sky layer to reactivate it. Now choose Layer/Add Layer Mask/Reveal Selection to add this sky mask as a layer mask to the Sky layer. For more details on how to make this type of sky mask, see Chapter 20: "Correcting a Problem Image." Now you should have a completed color image of the train station. You can always fine-tune things by clicking on any adjustment layer and then editing its mask with the Paintbrush. To change the color of a particular layer, double-click on its Layer thumbnail and change the Hue, Saturation, or Lightness values. Have fun with this and if you have any questions, be sure to check my final version, in the Extra Info Files folder for Chapter 25 on your CD.

HANDS-ON SESSION: Combining Bracketed Captures or Scans to Increase Dynamic Range

Taking three bracketed photos and/or three 16-bit scans to get the full range of detail in a high-contrast image; then using layers, adjustment layers, and layer masks to color correct the image by combining the all versions into one final print.

GENERAL INFO ABOUT THIS EXAMPLE

The dynamic range of film, and also of digital cameras, is often less than the range of light values in a contrasty outdoor scene. To get all the information in the scene, one can shoot three exposures of the same scene, called bracketing your exposures. Shoot one at the suggested exposure on your camera's light meter, then an exposure at one stop under and another at one stop over the suggested exposure. Shooting these with the camera on a tripod makes combining them later in Photoshop much easier, especially if you are shooting with a digital camera since the images will then line up exactly. If you don't have a tripod available, go ahead and shoot the 3 exposures hand held, and we'll show you here how to line them up. When shooting with film, even on a tripod, you'll have to line up the images in Photoshop because it is hard to scan each image at exactly the same location when using almost all scanners.

Having the three images within Photoshop allows you to get most of your final scene from your main exposure, then get some highlight details from the under-exposed version and shadow details from the over-exposed version. If you want to be sure of the full dynamic range when shooting the scene, measure the brightest and darkest places in the scene with a spot meter, then adjust the amount of your exposure bracketing to compensate for the full dynamic range of the scene. See Chapter 13: "Digital Imaging and the Zone System," for more information on how to get all the information within a scene onto your film or digital file. In this example we'll use several techniques to make initial masks to combine 3 images and get a more complete final version. We'll color correct that final version, fine tune the initial masks, tweak each image's color, do final burning and dodging, then use sharpening techniques to get a final image. We'll also discuss the technique differences in combining digital files verses scans from film.

OPENING AND LINING UP THE IMAGES

STEP 1: **Open the EPSN0004.JPG, EPSN0005.JPG, and EPSN0006.JPG files from the Ch26.CombiningBracketedPhotos folder on the *Photoshop CS Artistry* CD. When you get the Embedded Profile Mismatch dialog upon opening, go ahead and convert these files from the sRGB space into Adobe RGB.** These were taken with my small Epson 3.2 megapixel digital camera, which does not support the RAW format. If your digital camera shoots in RAW format, I recommend shooting that way and you

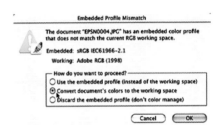

STEP 1: The Epson digital camera saves its files in the sRGB color space. Since you will enhance the colors as you correct these images, you should convert the files to Adobe RGB as you open them. This will make Adobe RGB's larger color gamut available to you as you color correct this image.

STEP 1: Here is the original normal exposure of the valley and horse stables we will be correcting in this example. Notice that the colors here are quite muted and the highlight details in the barn roof are gone.

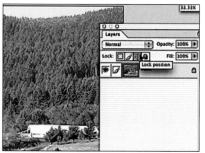

STEP 1: Here we have renamed the Background layer as Main and we've clicked on Lock Position to lock this layer from accidental movement.

STEP 1: Here we see the Layers palette as it should look after getting all three images into the Horse-FarmLayers file and locking all three layers.

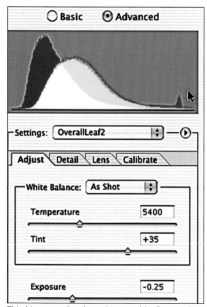

This histogram has been improved in Camera Raw from the one at the right by lowering the Exposure to get back highlight details and lowering the Contrast to return the shadow details.

should see the upcoming comments about RAW. **After opening all your images, make the EPSN0004.JPG image active, then choose File/Save As and save this in Photoshop format as HorseFarmLayers.psd. Type F to put HorseFarmLayers into full screen mode. Double-click on the** *Background* **layer and name this layer Main, then click on the Lock Movement Icon at the top of the Layers palette to lock this layer from accidental movement. Now use the Window menu to activate EPSN0005.JPG, which is the underexposed version and has more detail in the barn roof. You should now see the EPSN0005 window on top but still be able to see some part of the HorseFarmLayers image underneath. Type V to get the Move tool, and with the Shift key held down put your Move cursor on the EPSN0005 image, then drag and drop this until the Move cursor is on top of some part of the HorseFarmLayers image, then release the mouse button before letting up on the Shift key.** If done properly, this will "drag and drop" the EPSN0005 image as a layer on top of the Main layer in the HorseFarmLayers image. Holding the Shift key down while you drag and drop forces the new layer to be centered within the HorseFarmLayers image. Because both these images are exactly the same size and they were shot on a tripod, they will now line up exactly! **Double-click on the new layer name, now called Layer 1, and rename it to Highlights, then click on the Lock Position icon to also lock this layer. You should now use the Window menu to reactivate, then close EPSN0005. Now activate EPSN0006 and drag and drop it on top of HorseFarmLayers naming this new top layer as Shadows and also clicking on Lock Position to also lock this layer from accidental movement. Now use Window to activate and close EPSN0006. You should now have only the HorseFarmLayers image open with your layers palette looking like the one to the left here. Choose File/Save, Command-S to save this image.**

What if you Were Opening these Files with Camera Raw or Just Had a Single Shot and Wanted to Improve It with Camera Raw?

When the images you shoot with your digital camera are exposed in Camera Raw mode, you have the option of improving their histograms before bringing the files into Photoshop. If you just had one shot of an image that had a histogram like the one shown to the right, you could lower the Camera Raw Exposure slider to bring back the highlight detail, lowering the Contrast slider will also sometimes bring back shadow detail. If you shot just one exposure in RAW mode, another option would be to open several versions of that same exposure using different Camera Raw settings for each version. The main version could have settings similar to those on the left. You could always open a 2nd version that had a higher exposure setting, for exam-

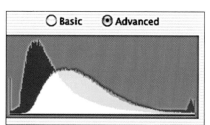

If you open an image in Camera Raw and its histogram looks like this, you can use settings like those to the left to improve the histogram and return shadow and highlight details. If you see a spike at the far left of a histogram, like in this one, that's a sign that shadow detail has probably been lost. When the rightmost highlight end of the histogram has a spike, or just drops straight off, as this one does, that shows lost highlight detail.

ple, that would bring out more shadow detail than the first version. Make sure you open your Camera Raw images in 16 Bits/Channel mode to give Photoshop the most detailed information. For more information on Camera Raw and shooting digital images, see Chapter 10: "Digital Cameras and Camera Raw."

Chapter 26: Combining Bracketed Captures or Scans to Increase Dynamic Range

Lining Up the Images when They are Scanned from Film

If you were working with these same three images but they were scanned from film in a flatbed or dedicated film scanner, you'd have to also line up the layers to get to the same place the HorseRanchLayers file is now at the end of Step 1. To do this, you'd open all the files and combine them in the same way we did with the digital camera files, but then you'd probably find they were a bit out of alignment. Note: if Shift-drag and drop of a 16-bit layer does not center that layer, as it does with an 8-bit one, this may be a temporary bug in Photoshop CS. Once you had all the layers combined in one file, you'd turn off the Eye icon for the Shadow layer, then click on the Highlight layer to make it active. Then you'd set the Opacity of the Highlight layer to 50% and use Image/Adjustments/Invert to invert that layer.

Note: If you take any image layer, make a copy of that image layer on top of the original, invert it, and set its Opacity to 50%, you'll notice that all you see is plain gray. If you then use the Move tool along with the Arrow keys to move that layer a pixel or two in any direction, you'll see an embossed pattern similar to the one you see in the image at the top of this page. Try this it's fun and useful too!

When two scans that are different exposures of the same scene, like we have here, you can use this "invert 50% emboss" technique to line up the two images by Moving the top image until the embossed pattern is as subtle as possible. Since the two bracketed scans are not the exact same exposure, you won't get just plain gray, but when they are lined up, the embossed pattern will be very minimal. See the illustrations and captions at the top of this page and to the right for the details of how to use this technique to line up scanned bracketed exposures. Once you line up the Highlights layer, you invert it back to normal and set its Opacity back to 100%. You can then activate the Shadow layer and use the same technique to line it up with the other two. When they are all lined up, make sure you turn on the Lock Position option on all three layers.

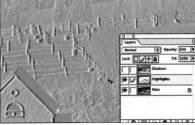

To set up scanned images for lining them up, the layer containing the highlights should be on top of the main layer with its Opacity set to 50%. Use Image/Adjustments/Invert to invert the Highlight layer and it will look like this after using the Move tool to line it up as close as possible. Use Free Transform, in the below illustration, for final alignment.

After lining up a layer as closely as possible with the Move tool, bring up the Options palette (F12), then use Edit/Free Transform to rotate the layer and also move it at the same time. While in Free Transform you can use the arrow keys to move the layer one pixel at a time, or you can type new x and y values into the x and y text boxes at the top left of the Options palette. To rotate the layer, you need to use the curved arrow on one of the corners. Remember that in Photoshop CS you can use the Hand tool (Spacebar) to scroll the image to one corner even in the middle of a Free Transform while in Full Screen mode! To rotate by small increments, type a new number into the angle text box, which reads -0.2 degrees here. If you change the value of a text box, press Return (only once) to get the cursor out of the text box. If you press Return a 2nd time, before entering another text box number, that will end the Free Transform. The layer will be lined up best when the embossed effect is as small as possible. At that point, press Return to end the Free Transform, then Command-I to invert the layer back, then set Opacity to 100%, and click the Lock Position icon for this layer.

Making Rough Masks for Each Image

Using a Channel to Make a Highlight Mask

STEP 2: Regardless of whether your originals came from a digital camera or from scans, at this point all three original exposures are lined up as layers in one document with a layer palette as pictured on the left side of the previous page. **Click on the Highlights layer to make it active, then turn off the Eye icon on the Shadows layer.** From this Highlights layer we want to get the details from the Barn roof, details in the white horse stall posts, and other highlights around the image like maybe the sky and the long dry grass in the foreground. **Use Shift F-10 to bring up the Channels palette. Click on the word Red in the Red channel, then turn off the Eye icons for Green, Blue, and RGB if necessary.** Now you should only be looking at the Red channel of the Highlights layer. See how much contrast there is in these highlight parts of this channel compared to the rest of the channel. To make your mask, you want to

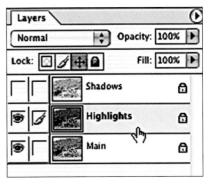

STEP 2: Here we see the Layers palette as it should look before we start making the highlight mask.

STEP 2: Here we see the Channels palette as it should appear as we are looking at just the Blue channel and are actually making a copy of the Blue channel by dragging it to the New Channel icon.

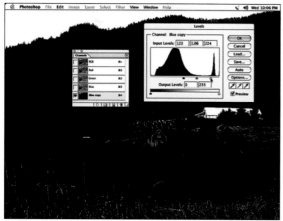

STEP 2: Here we see the entire screen as it looks while we are making the highlight mask from the copy of the Blue channel.

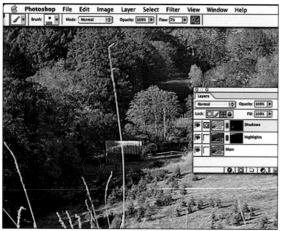

STEP 3: Adding shadow detail by painting white into the Shadows layer mask using the Airbrush 7% setting from Tool Presets.

choose a copy of the channel with the most contrast in these highlight areas compared to the rest of that channel. Now look at just the Green channel and finally just the Blue channel. The Blue channel is lighter in the sky and also has a lot of contrast between the Barn as well as other white areas and everything else. **Click on the word Blue in the Blue channel, then drag this down to the Create New Channel icon just to the left of the Trash icon at the bottom of the Channels palette.** This makes a copy of the Blue channel, and we will use that copy to make our mask. **Zoom your image to about 50%, which will just fill the screen if it is set to 1024x768. Press Tab to remove all the palettes.**

Choose **Image/Adjustments/Levels, not a Levels Adjustment layer, as we are going to tweak the copy of the Blue channel into the mask we need. Move the Levels Input Shadow slider, the top left one, to 122. Move the top middle brightness slider to 1.06 and move the top right slider to 224.** These settings should work as a good starting point for this mask as the treeline and sky are a very exact blend here with some gray values along the edge to blend things. The barn and white fences also look good. **Choose OK in Levels, then click back on RGB in the Channels palette. Now Shift-click the Blue copy channel to load the white parts of it as a selection. Choose Layer/Add Layer Mask/Reveal Selection to make a mask showing only these parts of the Highlights layer.** Don't worry if the edge blending of this mask is not perfect right now; it is better to fine tune that later after Color Correction is more or less complete. **Choose Command-S to save this file.**

Using an Airbrush to Bring Out Shadow Detail

STEP 3: **Click on the word Shadows in the Layers palette to turn on and activate the Shadows layer.** Since this layer is one stop overexposed and it is on top of the Layers palette, we are now only seeing just this layer. Notice that the shadow areas in this layer have more detail in them, but they are also a bit flat for dark shadows. **Choose Layer/Add Layer Mask/Hide All to add a black layer mask to the Shadows layer, which now hides this entire layer. Press the Tab key to remove all the palettes, then Type a B to bring up the Brush tool. Press F12 to bring up the Options bar and use the Tool Preset Picker at the top left of the Options bar to choose the Airbrush 7% preset.** You should have loaded this preset when you set up your Tool and Brush preferences in Chapter 3. **Now type a D to get the default colors of white as the foreground color and black as the background color. Paint on the image in the shadow areas, and you will see more shadow detail coming up as you hold the mouse down longer.** You are actually painting white onto the all-black layer mask that you just created for the Shadows layer. You will only see this layer, partially, where the white is painted. The more you paint, the more of the layer you will see. **Only paint this layer in where you need more shadow detail and don't worry right now if that shadow detail is a bit flat.** Don't forget that you can use the left and right bracket keys to change the size of your soft brush. **Paint in shadow details in** other parts of the image also, but don't overdo it at this point because you'll be able to tweak this mask later after color correction. When you are finished painting, choose H to switch back to the Hand tool so a random click doesn't put a spot where you don't want it. Choose File/Save, Command-S, to save your file again.

OVERALL COLOR CORRECTION OF THE COMBINED LAYERS

USING THRESHOLD TO MARK THE HIGHLIGHT AND SHADOW

STEP 4: The image we are seeing at this point is actually a composite of all three exposures of this scene. We now want to do the Overall Color Correction for this scene but the Highlights are coming from one layer and the shadows from another. We are going to create a temporary layer that integrates everything we have done so far into one layer, then use that just to find the highlight and shadow points. **Choose Layer/New Layer to create a new layer on top of the Layers palette called Temp. While holding the Option key down, choose Layer/Merge Visible and hold the Option key down until all the calculations have finished. If all your layers go away except for this new layer, then choose Undo because you didn't hold the Option key down long enough. If you did this correctly, everything from the three lower layers will be merged up into this Temp layer on the top. Use Tab to remove the palettes from the screen. Use F9 to bring up the Info palette and place it in the lower-right corner as that part of this image will not be the location of the brightest or darkest point. Now choose Image/Adjustments/Threshold and move the slider toward the right to isolate the highlights. As you do this, you'll notice that the brightest areas are to the left side of the barn. Use Command-Spacebar-Click to zoom into that part of the image. I zoomed into 600%, then moved the slider farther to the right to isolate the brightest places. This isolates them much better than Levels does, and with Photoshop CS you can now also use Threshold with 16-bit images. Measure around in these brightest areas and when you find the brightest one (highest Info palette numbers), then Shift-click at that point to add the Highlight Color Sampler to the Info palette. We'll actually set this highlight in Levels. Now use Command-0 to zoom back out, then move the Threshold slider to the left to isolate the shadow areas. In this image, I marked a shadow in the lower-left part of the image. Using this technique, if you zoom way in, you really can locate the darkest pixel. Just make sure the location you pick has a similar numerical color trend than that of other dark areas so you don't pick some location that is the one pixel that is way different from the rest of the shadows. When you find the shadow spot, Shift-click again to add Color Sampler #2. Once that is done you want to Cancel from Threshold, and you can actually drag the temp layer to the trash icon at the bottom of the Layers palette.**

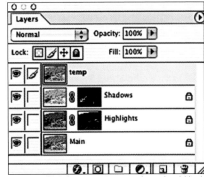

STEP 4: This is how your Layers palette should look after doing the Merge Visible on the temp layer.

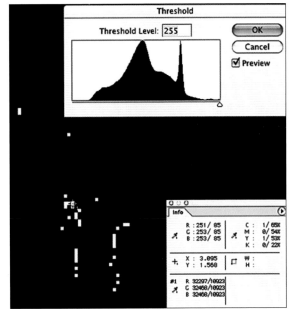

STEP 4: Zoomed in to 600%, we just Shift-clicked to add the #1 Highlight Color Sampler to the Info palette. Notice that we have our palette to read 16-bit values, at least for the Color Samplers, here.

ADDING OVERALL LEVELS, CURVES, AND HUE/SATURATION ADJUSTMENT LAYERS ABOVE ALL THREE IMAGE LAYERS

STEP 5: By using the Main layer plus parts of the Highlights and Shadows layers, we have now created a composite version of this image that we will use for Overall Color

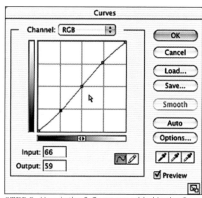

STEP 5: Here is the S-Curve we added in the Overall Color Correction step to add some contrast to the image. We also moved the middle of the Green curve with a point from 128 to 129 adding a little green, and we added a point in the Blue curve from119 to 115 adding some yellow to the overall cast.

STEP 5: You can manually change the range of one of the Edit colors by dragging the 4 control points on the gray slider at the bottom of this dialog. This gives you extra color selecting power!

Correction. We will not do Overall Color Correction on a single merged layer, however, because we want to keep our options open to tweak the masks for the Highlights and Shadows layers later after color correction. Adding Levels, Curves, and Hue/Saturation Adjustment layers on top of the three existing layers will actually color correct the cumulative effect of those three existing layers. **Bring up your Options (F9) and Histogram (Shift-F9) palettes and place them in locations that won't cover your highlight or shadow Color Sampler locations or any other important color areas.** For this image, I put my History palette in the top-left corner, Info at bottom middle-left and also had my Navigator (Shift-F2) hanging off the top-right edge so I could just see the zoom factor, which I had at 50% so I could sharply see the entire image. **Now choose Layer/New Adjustment Layer/Levels (Command-F2) for your overall Levels adjustments. Zoom into the Color Sampler you created with Threshold for your highlight setting, then choose the Levels rightmost Highlight eyedropper and click with it exactly on top of this Highlight Color Sampler point. I zoom into about 800% then make sure the eyedropper is lined up exactly on the Color Sampler point before I click. This will set the highlights to 244, 244, 244 and correct for any color casts. Use Command-0 to zoom back out, then zoom in to the shadow Color Sampler point and click on that with the leftmost Levels Shadow eyedropper to set your shadow value starting at 8, 8, 8. Zoom back out again, then set your Brightness using the middle RGB Levels slider. Finally correct for color casts using the middle sliders of the Red, Green, or Blue channels. All I did there was set the middle Blue slider to .96, which adds a little yellow. Choose OK in Levels.**

Now choose Layer/New Adjustment Layer/Curves (Command-F3) to add a Curve adjustment layer. This image seems a bit flat to me so I added an S-Curve, shown at the top left of this page, which increases contrast. Using the numbers described in the S-Curve's caption, I also added some Green and some Yellow by slightly changing the Green and Blue channel's curves.

Now we want to add a Hue/Saturation adjustment layer (Command-F4) to saturate our colors, which also adds some more contrast. Because this image seems quite flat, I set the Master saturation at +25, which is more than I usually use. With Edit set to Yellows, I set the saturation to +12 and the Hue to -7, which adds some warmth and saturation to the default range of yellows. For the Cyans I set the saturation to +10 and the Hue to -2 and also dragged the Eyedropper plus tool across a section of the sky, which extended the Cyan range into the blues using numbers of 212/242. These numbers that specify the color range of this Cyan are at the bottom right of the Hue/Saturation dialog above the colored strips, and they can be manually changed by dragging the gray sliders that are between the two colored strips. You can also change them by dragging the Eyedropper plus or minus tools across a color area in the image. Using these make the Hue/Saturation tool much more powerful for selecting an exact range of colors. The changes we made to Cyan here affect the color of the sky and also the darker green trees toward the top part of this image. **Use Command-S to save your image so far.**

SPECIFIC COLOR OR CONTRAST CORRECTION FOR A PARTICULAR LAYER

STEP 6: To improve the shadow areas of this image, open them up a bit and yet not have them be so flat, we can use a curve and we want that curve to affect just the shadow parts of the image. **Click on the Shadows layer to make it the active layer.** Whenever you add a new Layer or Adjustment Layer, it will be added on top of the currently active layer. **Choose Command-F3 to add a new Curves adjustment layer**

Chapter 26: Combining Bracketed Captures or Scans to Increase Dynamic Range

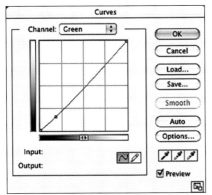

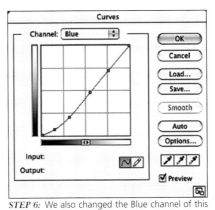

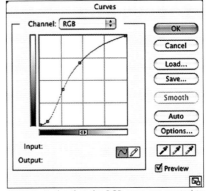

STEP 6: We made a subtle change to the Green channel of the Shadows curve to take a greenish cast out of the shadow areas.

STEP 6: We also changed the Blue channel of this curve to take the blue cast out of the shadow areas.

STEP 6: Notice that the RGB curve we created to Improve Shadow Contrast increases the slope (steepness) of the curve from the darker shadows, to the left, up to the midtones at the middle vertical line. The extreme dark shadows are actually made darker by adding that point at the bottom-left corner. The part of the curve to the top left, where the slope has been reduced, is not influencing the parts of this image that have been selected by the Shadows layer mask.

and turn on the Use Previous Layer to Create Clipping Mask option in the New Layer dialog. Name this new layer Improve Shadow Contrast, then choose OK to the new Layer dialog. Since you turned on the Clipping Mask option, this curve will take on the layer mask of the Shadows layer as its own mask, so what you do here will only affect the shadow areas you have already selected with the Shadows layer mask. To improve the shadow contrast, you need to increase the slope of the shadow parts of the curve. **While holding the mouse button down, move the cursor over the shadow areas to the lower-left side of this image and notice the small circle that shows up on the curve diagram showing you where these shadow areas appear on this curve. Those are the parts of the curve where you want to increase the slope. Because the mask is affecting only the shadow areas though, you can actually move most of the curve without changing the parts of the image where the mask is black. See the curve diagrams and captions above where we explain how we changed each part of the curve. Once you create your curve and choose OK in curves, you can click back on the Shadows layer to re-edit the shadows layer mask. Type a B to go back to the Brush then, using the Airbrush 7% Preset option, paint with white to have more shadow areas effected by this curve or paint with black to reduce the effect in certain shadow areas. You can also lower the Opacity of the Improve Shadow Contrast curve layer to reduce its effect on the Shadows layer, or lower the Opacity of the Shadows layer itself to reduce its overall effect on the final composite. Another thing you can do is double-click on the Improve Shadow Contrast layer thumbnail to go back and re-edit this curve after you have modified the mask a bit. There are many things you can tweak until you get the shadow parts of your image looking just right!**

FINALIZING THE MASKS SEPARATING THE LAYERS

STEP 7: Now that we've done most of the color correction, we can go back and improve the mask on the Highlights layer. We already did some work on the Shadows layer mask in the last step. Whenever I create a mask using a channel, in the way we did for the Highlights layer mask, I always go back and Gaussian Blur that mask after doing the required color corrections. The reason you want to wait until after doing the color corrections is that the color corrections often increase the contrast and saturation of your image, which tends to make errors in the mask show up more. Waiting till now to fix the mask saves you from having to do this twice. **Click on the Layer Mask thumbnail, the rightmost one, for the Highlights adjustment layer. Zoom**

STEP 7: Above we see the Barn before the mask blur, below we see it after the blur.

STEP 7: Above we see the mask before the blur of 2; below we see it after the blur. Having soft edges on this type of mask helps blend things.

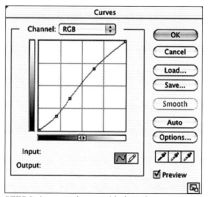

STEP 8: I was not happy with the colors or contrast of the trees in the top parts of the image. The above RGB curve fixes the problem with the contrast. We also added a bit of red, a lot of green, and some yellow by moving the center parts of the Red, Green, and Blue channels toward red, green, and away from blue respectively. Below is the mask used to apply this curve with a soft brush only in the areas needed.

into the horse barn at 100% or 200% and notice that the edges of the barn are a bit pixelated. This will become more apparent if you turn the Eye icon for this Highlights layer off then on again. The jagged edges are caused by the sharp edges on the mask for this layer. While looking at the barn edges, choose Filter/Blur/Gaussian Blur (Shift-F4) and set the amount to 2. While in the Gaussian Blur filter with the Preview button on, you can change the blur amount to see how it affects this edge blur. You can turn the Preview button off and on to see before and after differences. Use the Spacebar to scroll up to the top of the trees and see how blurring the mask affects how the tree tops blend with the sky. I found that a blur of 2 made these highlights blend in the most pleasant way, but you may like a different setting better. The important thing is that you do blur these masks; it always seems to help. **Choose OK in Gaussian Blur when you are happy with the amount of your blur.**

Another thing I did to improve my Highlights mask is use the Blur Tool (R) with a 200 pixel soft brush and the Strength setting of this tool, found in the Options bar, set to 15%. While looking at the lower part of this image at both 50% and 100% zoom, I painted (Blurred) on the Highlights layer mask until I was happy with how the grass highlights blended in with the rest of the image. Blurring this area just a bit more removed a subtle pixelized look in some of the grass area highlights. Remember that this tool works like an airbrush, the longer you paint over the same area, the more blurring you get.

OVERALL COLOR FINE TUNING, BURN & DODGE LAYER

STEP 8: Don't forget that in the Extra Info Files folder for this chapter, 26, on the *Photoshop CS Artistry CD* is my final layered file of this image. You can open this file and compare my colors to yours, my masks to yours, etc. If something in this example is not working for you, it would be a good idea to compare what you have done to my final version in case there is some difference between the two that can explain your problem or question.

Before adding your fine-tuning layers, click on to activate the topmost Hue/Saturation layer so the new layers will be added at the top of the layer stack and thus work on the cumulative effect of everything we have done so far. The first fine-tuning Adjustment layer I added was a curves Adjustment layer called Add Tree Contrast, Remove Blue. **Use Command-F3 to add a curves layer of that name and make an S-Curve similar to the one at the left. While you are doing this, just look at the trees in the top parts of this image and do what will make them look better without worrying what it does to the rest of the image. Now go into the Red, Green and Blue curves channels and make slight adjustments to the center parts of each while looking at what these adjustments do to the trees. See the caption to the left, and also my final layered version of this image, for a description of the adjustments I made. Once you have the adjustments made and have clicked on OK in Curves, choose Image/Adjust/Invert (Command-I) to invert the mask for this layer. Now type B to get the brush, D for default colors, giving you white, and choose Airbrush 7% from the Presets pop-down to the left end of the Options palette (F12). Paint white over the parts of the trees where you want to apply this curve; the more you paint the more you get; if you overdo it, type X then paint with black to lessen the effect.**

Chapter 26: Combining Bracketed Captures or Scans to Increase Dynamic Range

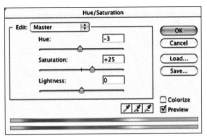

The next adjustment layer I added was to improve the look of the grass in the foreground. **While looking at this grassy area, I added the Hue/Saturation Adjustment layer, settings shown to the right, then pressed OK in Hue/Saturation. I then used Command-I to invert the mask and typed B followed by D to paint in white. My AirBrush 7% setting was already in force so I just painted over the parts of the grassy area until I had added the amount of saturation I needed.** When making these adjustment layers whose mask you are going to paint in, it is best to overdo the adjustment a bit. That way you can just paint in the amount you need and you know you will have enough. If you are too subtle with the adjustment then even when you paint 100% white, you'll have to go back and change the adjustment, to get what you need.

The final tweak to the layers of this image, and many of my images, is to add what I call a Burn&Dodge layer. **Choose Layer/New/Layer and name it Burn&Dodge, then set the blend Mode to Soft Light from within the New Layer dialog, then turn on the "Fill With Soft-Light Neutral Color (50% Gray)" checkbox which will automatically fill this layer with 50% gray. Now you can choose OK in the New Layer dialog.**

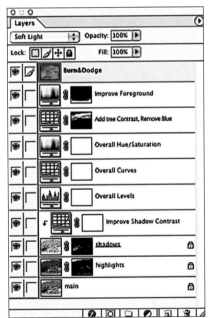

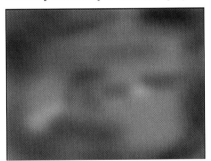

Type D, for default colors, and you'll find that the foreground color is actually black this time. D gives you white when working on a mask but since this is a real layer, D gives you black. You can always type X to exchange those two black and white colors. **Painting with white, using Airbrush 7%, on this layer will lighten the underlying image and painting with black will darken it.** The keyword for this type of layer is "subtle," be subtle. **You may want to set the Flow of your brush from 7% to 3% so the changes you make will happen very slowly.** Look at my final image for this chapter, called HorseFarmComposite, in the Extra Info

STEP 8: Here is my Burn&Dodge layer for this image, used with a layer Softlight Blend Mode. The general idea is to make the image a little bit darker around the edges to focus the eye's attention to the middle of the image. Certain things in that middle may have been lightened or darkened depending on need.

Files folder. Turn the Eye icon off then on again for my version of this layer to see what can be done with a Burn&Dodge layer. It is great! **Use Command-S to save the final Master Image with all your layers for this image.**

USING SHARPEN ONLY EDGES BH AND/OR UNSHARP MASK TO SHARPEN A FLATTENED VERSION OF THE IMAGE

STEP 9: **After saving the master image with all its layers, use Image/Duplicate (F5), with the Duplicate Merged Layers Only checkbox on, to create a flattened version of this image.** I use Image Size (F7) to set the size and resolution for my printer and resample if necessary. I usually don't resample because I start out with the maximum size image from Camera Raw or from my Scanner. For smaller, especially test, prints just print those using the same file at a higher dpi. **Make sure you are in Full Screen Mode, use TAB to remove your palettes and Command-Option-0 to zoom to 100%. Run the Sharpen Only Edges BH action script (Command-F5 or Command-Shift-F5 for the one with Breaks), which is described in detail in the large caption on the next page.** When this action script is completed, your image will be in Lab Color mode with two layers separated by a layer mask that the action created. The bottom layer is your original flattened image and you will be sharpening the top layer. Only the

STEP 8: The final Layers palette for the master image of this composite. You can open my version of this file from the Extra Info Files folder inside the CD folder for this chapter.

293

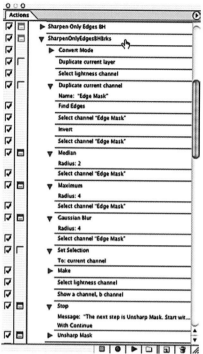

The Sharpen Only Edges BH action is an embellishment of one that I originally got from Bill Atkinson. This script uses the Lightness channel of a Lab version of your master image to create a mask that applies sharpening to only the parts of the image that really need to be sharpened. The BH version adds a step at the front that converts your image to Lab color, which does nothing if your image is already in Lab color. The BH version also sets up the created mask as a layer mask on a copy of the original layer. The mask that both of these sharpening actions create is made by using the Find Edges filter, followed by Invert, Median, Maximum, and then Gaussian Blur to massage these edges into a mask that will sharpen only what you need. Sharpen Only Edges BH works well on images that are 50 to 150 Mb in size to be printed at 300 or higher dpi. If you are working on larger or smaller images, you may want to adjust the Radius settings on the Median, Maximum, and Gaussian Blur filters to see if you can get better results. If you plan to adjust these, use the new Sharpen Only Edges BH Brks action, which has breakpoints on these steps so you can tweak the settings. When making sharper prints, you might want to increase the radius and for smaller prints decrease it. The CS versions of these actions now automatically correctly set up the Channels palette to sharpen just the Lightness channel. The last step of Sharpen Only Edges BH is to run Unsharp Mask to sharpen the Lightness channel. This allows you to change the amount of sharpening, while watching the effect of the sharpening with the Preview checkbox on within the Unsharp Mask filter. You are actually sharpening the entire Lightness channel of the copy of your master image. The layer mask shows only the portions of the sharpened copy that are really needed. After finishing the Unsharp Mask, you can then paint white or black to further edit the mask to add more or less sharpness to specific areas. After running Unsharp Mask, you can also lessen the amount of sharpening by lowering the Opacity of the top layer.

parts of the top layer that need to be sharpened will be seen because the mask will hide the sharpened areas that usually won't improve your image. **The final step of this action will end up in Unsharp Mask (F4), where you can tweak the settings.** This will be sharpening only the Lightness channel, but you will be seeing the results in color since the Eye icons are turned on for the other channels too. **With the Preview button on in the Unsharp Mask filter, you can adjust the amount of sharpening until you think it is optimal for this image.** When using one of these edge masks, you can actually sharpen more than you would normally without grain appearing in flat areas, like skies. **For the top layer of this image, I used an Amount of 125, a Radius of 1, and a Threshold of 0.** For 4000 dpi scans from film, I usually use values close to the defaults of 350,1,0. For larger prints use a larger Radius and sometimes Amount. For smaller prints or Web images, use smaller Radius values and sometimes smaller Amounts.

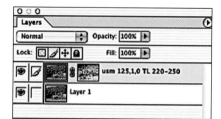

STEP 9: These are the Unsharp Mask layers used to produce the bottom final image. To do this sharpening, you start with a flattened copy of your master layer image and you run the Sharpen Only Edges BH action script on that. That converts the image into Lab color mode, copies the background layer to a 2nd layer on top, which has a layer mask added to it containing the most crucial areas to be sharpened. For this image, I sharpened the Lightness channel of the top layer by 125,1,0. The mask on the top layer combines the two to give you the final sharpening effect. To add even more sharpness in selective areas, use the Airbrush to paint white into the mask. To lessen the sharpness, paint black where you feel it is too sharp. You can lessen the overall sharpness by lowering the opacity of the top of the two layers. You can remove popping highlights caused by sharpening by Option-double-clicking on the top layer, then moving the rightmost sliders in the This Layer part of Layer Styles. For this image, I set those sliders to 220 and 250. That means the values from 250-255 are completely removed and the values from 220-250 are slowly blended out. Notice my notation on the top layer which reminds me of the settings I used on this image. That way I can change them later while knowing what I used this time.

Remember that you can turn the Preview checkbox off and on in the Unsharp Mask filter to see before and after this amount of sharpening. After choosing OK to the Unsharp Mask filter, if you Shift-click on the layer mask for the top layer, that will turn the mask off and you can actually see the large amount that this layer was sharpened. Shift-click again to turn the mask back on.

Sometimes just sharpening the top layer's Lightness channel is enough, especially when your original scan is tack sharp to the grain of the film. If you are not totally happy after sharpening the Lightness channel of the top layer, you can also sharpen the original layer on the bottom a bit too. Most digital files from scans have a grain pattern you can see when you look at them at 100% on the screen. You don't want that grain pattern to be very heavy; but if it is not there at all, that may indicate that the scan focus was a bit soft. **To also sharpen the Lightness channel of the bottom image in the sharpening layers stack, click on the Layer thumbnail for the bottom layer and activate only its Lightness channel in the Channels palette with just the Eye icons for the other channels on in the Channels palette. You also want the Eye icon to be on for the top layer in the Layers palette. Now go back into Unsharp Mask (F4) and sharpen this bottom Lightness channel, but be careful not to sharpen it anywhere near as much as the Lightness channel in the top layer. While doing this, you want to keep a careful eye on your sky and other areas of flat detail to make sure they don't get too grainy.** I didn't sharpen the bottom layer of this image since it started as a digital camera jpeg, so it was probably already sharpened a bit by the camera's software. A digital file coming from Photoshop's Camera Raw will likely not already be sharpened since I recommend turning off the sharpening in Camera Raw and leaving that sharpening till now.

Chapter 26: Combining Bracketed Captures or Scans to Increase Dynamic Range

If you are going to print this Unsharp Mask layered image on the LightJet 5000 or an Epson printer, you should just leave it, or the flattened versions of it, in Lab color. You don't want to do yet another mode conversion back to, for example, Adobe RGB before printing. If you have an ICC profile for your printer, then you can use the Print dialog to convert from Lab color to that specific ICC profile for this paper and printer. See the Print dialog information on page 170 of Chapter 15, which will show you exactly how to correctly print your images on Epson printers.

If you are working with Grayscale images or don't want to convert your images to Lab color as part of your sharpening actions, try my new "Sharpen Only Edges BH Grayscale" or "Sharpen Only Edges BH in RGB" actions that are a bit lower down in the Photoshop CS ArtistKeys actions that come with this book. These allow your final image to avoid the mode conversion to Lab. I don't actually believe the mode conversion to Lab loses a significant amount of information because Lab is a larger space than Adobe RGB. Converting from Lab back to Adobe RGB could lose information, and there is no reason to do this anyhow because you can print the Lab image directly.

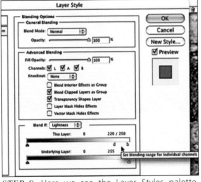

STEP 9: Here we see the Layer Styles palette, which comes up when you Option-double-click on the top sharpening layer. You can remove white highlight spikes from this sharpening layer by moving the rightmost "This Layer" slider to the left. Option-drag the left part of this slider to split them. Here values above 250 are completely removed while the values from 220 to 250 are slowly blended out. This is a hot tweak!

The final version of the combined Horse Ranch image after flattening and sharpening.

Using Sharpen Only Edges BH and/or Unsharp Mask to Sharpen a Flattened Version of the Image

27 HANDS-ON SESSION: Bryce Stone Woman

*Color correcting an image in Lab color, versus RGB, using
most of the techniques in this book.*

The final Bryce Stone Woman image after correcting it in Lab color. You can see the "before" version of this image on the last page of this chapter.

This is one of my favorite photos of Bryce Canyon. The light rock formation in the front center, if you use your imagination a bit, could be a naked woman with long bushy hair sitting on the rock and admiring the view. Because the rocks are predominately red, it is hard to make the rocks look their best without making the green trees and shrubs look too dark and magenta. The solution is to use a layer mask to combine several versions of the image, one that optimizes the red parts and another that optimizes the green parts. You should read Chapter 14: "Color Spaces, Device Characterization, and Color Management," to learn more about Lab color before doing this example. Also, this will not be a normal step-by-step example; because this is an example in Lab color, I decided to share the experience of creating the image with you instead of worrying about writing down every step. Therefore, to better understand this example, you should first do the examples in Chapters 21: "Yellow Flowers," 24: "Desert Al," 26: "Combining Bracketed Photos or Two Scans to Increase Dynamic

Range," and 28: "Rain in Costa Rica." These chapters use similar techniques but include all the details.

When I first got the scan for this image from Bill Atkinson and his Tango drum scanner, I converted it to RGB from the Lab format in which he had given it to me and made a very nice LightJet 5000 print of it. When I started working on this example, I took my master RGB image from that print and thought I would start over with the original Lab scan to see if I could duplicate what I had done in RGB, using Lab this time. The following is the process I went through to arrive at the Layers palette, shown here, for the final Lab image printed on the previous page. **You should open my final Lab image, called BryceLab.psd, from the Ch27.Bryce Stone Woman folder on the CD. You can then look at the layers setup on your screen and turn each layer on one at a time as we go through the purpose of each layer.**

TRYING TO DUPLICATE WHAT I DID IN RGB

STEP 1: When I reopened the Lab scan, I realized that it was still uncropped and I had already cropped the RGB version I was trying to duplicate. I had not resampled the RGB image though, just done a crop, but I would need to line the two up. **To do this, I went into Image Size on the RGB version and noted the actual number of pixels in each dimension. This would be the crop size I would use on the Lab version, too, so I set the Fixed Size Style on the Marquee to that width and height. When using the Marquee or Cropping tool, if you want a fixed size in pixels, you need to use Photoshop/Preferences/Units and Rulers to set the Ruler Units to pixels, or make sure you type px after you input values to specify pixels. Then the sizes in the Marquee and Cropping tool will show up in pixels instead of inches.**

Next, I copied the flattened version of my RGB image and pasted it on top of my Lab version, and of course, it was a bit smaller. I inverted this temporary RGB layer and set its Opacity to 50% because a positive and negative image on top of each other at 50% Opacity gives you 50% gray if they are perfectly lined up. If they are not lined up, you get an embossed effect. I then used the arrow keys while in the Move tool to nudge the inverted layer until the embossed effect went away and it lined up with the Lab image I had to crop underneath. At that point, I turned the Eye icon off for the layer underneath and then clicked with the Marquee, which was already set for the correct size, and lined the Marquee up with the edges of the already cropped RGB image on top. Now my Marquee selection lines were lined up exactly, so I chose Image/Crop to do the crop and then threw away the temporary layer on top.

STEP 2: You might be wondering why I wanted to crop this Lab image so it lined up exactly with the RGB image I had made before. The reason is that there were some

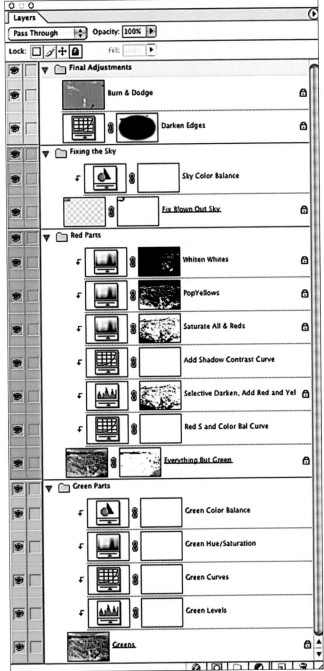

Here is the final Layers palette for this example. We are going to go through the steps I went through in creating this image and all its layers. We have added the layer sets to help delineate the four parts of this composition.

297

Trying to Duplicate What I Did in RGB

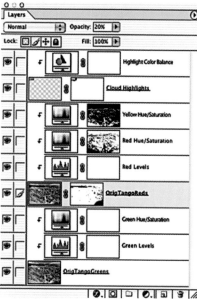

STEP 2: The Layers palette from my earlier RGB rendition of Bryce. Because I made sure the crop was exactly the same on my newer Lab version, I was able to reuse the layer mask separating the Red and Green elements, as well as the Yellow Hue/Saturation mask and the Red Hue/Saturation mask, although the way I used them was sometimes different in Lab color.

STEP 2: The layer mask that separates the Green and non-Green layers in my RGB and Lab images. The white areas of the mask are where you will see the non-green areas from the upper of the two layers, and the black and gray parts of the mask are where you will see all or some of the image from the Green layer.

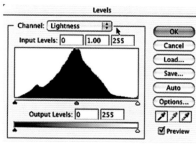

STEP 2: The Lightness channel for the Everything-ButGreen layer. This histogram looks very similar to a corrected RGB histogram. The Lightness channel contains the brightness and contrast information for a Lab image.

complex masks I had created for the RGB version of this image, and I was hoping to reuse them in doing the Lab version. Here is the Layers palette for my previous RGB version of this image, and I did reuse the masks as you will see.

My traditional Overall Color Correction steps for an RGB image are to first use Levels to correct the histogram; then use Curves to adjust the contrast and then follow that with Hue/Saturation to saturate the colors. What I did in the RGB version, as you can see to the left here, is create one real layer, OrigTangoGreens, for the Green elements in the photograph and a second real layer, OrigTangoReds, on top of that, for the Red elements. The layer mask to the right of the OrigTangoReds layer controls which parts of the image come from each of these two main layers. You'll notice several Grouped Adjustment layers above the OrigTangoGreens layer that set its Levels and Hue/Saturation settings. Then above the OrigTangoReds layer is the grouped Adjustment layer for the Red Levels, and then two different Hue/Saturation Adjustment layers above that. For this image I used one Hue/Saturation layer to adjust the reddish tones and a separate one for the yellows, each with its own layer mask. Trying to do it all with one Adjustment layer caused too much crossover between the Red and Yellow areas, especially where they mixed a lot. The layer mask that separates which part of the image comes from OrigTangoReds and which part from OrigTangoGreens was created using Image/Adjust/Threshold in a similar way that we created the Darken Sky mask with Levels in Chapter 20: "Correcting a Problem Image." To create the Red and Yellow Hue/Saturation masks, which are close to inverses of each other, I went into Select Color Range to create a selection of either the Red or Yellow areas and then used Select/Save Selection to save that selection in the Channels palette where I edited it, and then later used Load Selection to load it before creating my Red Hue/Saturation layer. For more details on this mask creation technique, see Chapter 21: "Yellow Flowers."

When I started working on the Lab version, I went ahead and created one layer for the Greens and a second layer for the Reds. You can see in the Lab Layers palette that these two layers, called Greens and Everything But Green, and the layer mask separating them remained. In the Lab version, I've put the layers that control the green appearance into a layer set called Green Parts and then put the layers that control the red appearance into a layer set called Red Parts. I tried to use Levels to do the initial overall color correction on the Red and Green layers. You can see these two layers, called Selective Darken Add Red and Yellow, and the other, Green Levels. I discovered that in Lab mode, the Lightness channel is great to work with for setting the highlight and shadow values because there are not color balance problems mixed in with setting the brightness and contrast. The difficulty for me came when I went to the A and B channels within Levels and tried to adjust the color balance. Try this out for yourself using the BryceLab you have opened. Turn off all the Eye icons above the Everything But Green layer and click on that layer to activate it. Shift-click on the layer mask to turn it off and now turn the Eye icon on for the Red Parts layer set. Now create a new Levels adjustment layer above it. You'll notice when you go into Levels that you are in the Lightness channel. This is a pretty normal histogram, and you do the obvious thing of moving the endpoints in to where the data starts. Then use the middle slider to adjust the brightness. It is great to be able to adjust this separately from the color balance. Also, if you just sharpen the Lightness channel of a Lab image, you avoid the color shifts you can get when sharpening all the channels of an RGB image. There is no need to sharpen the A and B channels within a Lab image because they only contain color information and no brightness and contrast information as all the channels have in an RGB or CMYK image. That is why the Sharpen Only Edges BH script converts the image to Lab mode so you sharpen only the Lightness channel.

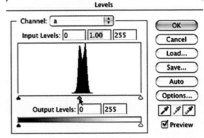

STEP 3: The a channel for the Everything But Green layer.

STEP 3: **Now choose the A channel. Moving the middle slider to the left makes the image more red, and moving it to the right makes the image more green. Try it and notice that moving this more than a small amount dramatically affects the color of the image.** That is because all the color information in this Lab image is squashed into that small area of the histogram, spanning only about 51 values in the A channel and 91 values in the B channel of this image. The Lab color space spans all the colors that the human eye can see. That makes this space so large that the rest of the histogram, outside the range of 51 used in this image, is reserved for other colors that are not in this image. **Moving the Input Highlight slider of the A channel to the left makes the highlights more red and the Input Shadow slider to the right makes the shadows more green. Moving the A channel's Output Highlight slider left makes the highlights more green, and moving the Output Shadow slider right reddens the shadows.**

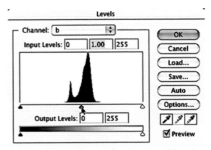

STEP 3: The b channel for the Everything But Green layer.

Now try out the B channel, where moving the middle slider to the left makes the image more yellow and moving it to the right makes it more blue. Try out the Input and Output Shadow and Highlight sliders to see what they do, too. Now hold down the Option key and choose Reset to put everything back where it started. Start with the Lightness channel, and adjust the brightness of the red and yellow parts of the image, actually everything but the greens. Then switch to the A and B channels and try to get the red and yellow colors the way you want them. You should realize that the controls are quite different than when working in RGB or CMYK. **To go back to my original layered Lab image, choose File/Revert. Some of the color adjustments in this image are subtle so turn your room lights down low to help see them.**

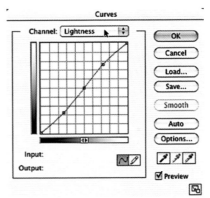

STEP 4: The Red Lightness S-Curve I used to add some contrast to everything but the greens.

STEP 4: I duplicated the layer structure I had used in my RGB image. Of course, the adjustments I made, especially in Levels, were quite different, and I was able to get a Lab image that looked somewhat similar, but it didn't seem to have the same amount of contrast and separation of colors. **The layers I had created so far were Green levels and Green Hue/Saturation to adjust the Greens and Selective Darken, Add Red and Yellow (my Red levels layer), as well as Saturate All & Reds and Pop Yellows for the Everything But Green layer.**

Things looked a bit flat and muddy, and I could not get this image to look as good as the RGB one. Then I thought maybe Curves would work better, instead of Levels, as the initial adjustment for a Lab image, so I created the layers Red S and Color Balance Curve for the Everything But Green layer and Green Curves for the Greens layer. As you can see, the S-Curve I used for the Lightness channel of the Everything But Green layer helped increase the contrast and in the A channel, I moved the curve up and to the left to add red and I did the same thing in the B channel to add

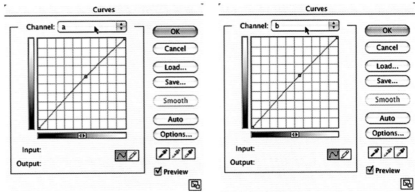

STEP 4: The Red a curve adds some red to the color balance. You want to be very subtle with your Lab a and b curve movements.

STEP 4: The Red b curve adds some yellow to the color balance.

Trying to Duplicate What I Did in RGB

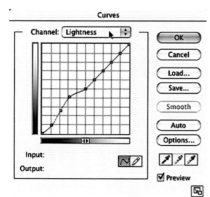

STEP 4: The Green Curves Lightness curve increases the slope of the curve, and thus the contrast, where most of the green values lie in the image.

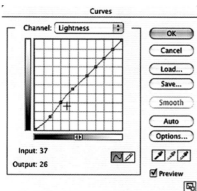

STEP 5: The Add Shadow contrast Curve helps the shadow areas in the Everything But Green layers of the image.

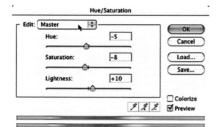

STEP 6: The Whiten Whites Hue/Saturation settings.

yellow. The Green Curves, as you can see, was mostly a move in the Lightness channel to lighten and brighten the greens by increasing the slope of the curve where most of the green values were sitting, to the bottom left half of the curve. I initially turned off the Eye icons for my Levels adjustments and replaced them with these Curves adjustments, leaving the Hue/Saturation layers as they were. At some point though, I accidentally turned on all the layers, by Option-clicking the Eye icon of a layer, and noticed that the image looked even better with both the Levels and Curves layers on at the same time. I tweaked each layer a little further and was becoming happier with this image, except the shadow areas in the reds and yellows, which looked a little flat, and the color balance on the greens was not what I wanted.

STEP 5: To solve this problem, I added the Add Shadow Contrast curve to the group of Everything But Green layers. This curve does a similar thing as the Green Curves to the top left by increasing the slope of the part of the Lightness curve that corresponds to the tonal range of the image we wanted to modify. I added a Color Balance adjustment layer at the top of the Greens layers to just pop the greens, especially the green highlights, a bit. I didn't modify the pixels in the Greens or Everything But Green layers, so you can always throw my adjustment layers away, or turn their Eye icons off, and try your own adjustments, making your own adjustment layers.

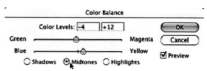

STEP 5: The Green Color Balance Adjustment layer. We also changed the Highlight and Shadows settings. You can check those out on your screen with my final BryceLAB image open.

FINE TUNING THE IMAGE

STEP 6: By editing the PopYellows layer mask, I created a mask for the Whiten Whites Hue/Saturation adjustment layer. Its job is to take the pinkish cast out of rocks that I wanted to be white in the final image. The effect was mostly created by lowering the Saturation and increasing the Lightness on the Edit Master part of this Hue/Saturation dialog. The Hue shift here takes a little yellow out of the whites.

STEP 7: If you turn off the Eye icon for the Fixing the Sky layer set, you'll notice that the sky in the top-left corner is badly blown out. There wasn't a whole lot of detail in the original image or scan here anyway, so I created the Fix Blown Out Sky and Sky Color Balance layers specifically to patch that blown-out corner. Fix Blown Out Sky is just part of the sky to the right copied and edited to make it appear as though it were raining in that top-left corner, as well. The color of this new sky area wasn't quite right, so I added a Grouped Color Balance adjustment layer just to tweak that sky part of the image. Remember that a Grouped adjustment layer is indented from the first real layer below it. It only affects the pixels in that real layer below it, and the Grouped layer also gets its transparency from that real layer below. To created a Grouped adjustment layer (now called a Clipping Mask in Photoshop CS), you need to turn on the "Use Previous Layer to Create a Clipping Mask" checkbox in the New Adjustment Layer dialog or Option-click the line between the already created adjustment layer and the real layer below it.

STEP 8: In the Final Adjustments layer set, the Burn and Dodge layer is a normal layer, not an Adjustment layer, filled with 50% Gray using Edit/Fill, with its Blend

Chapter 27: Bryce Stone Woman

mode set to Soft Light. Soft Light mode ignores 50% Gray but will darken the cumulative effect of all the layers underneath in areas that are darker than 50% Gray, and lighten those layers in areas that are lighter than 50% Gray. This allows you to burn and dodge the image using the Airbrush along with large, soft brushes having a low opacity. Before you start this type of work, type D to set the default colors of Black and White. Then you can type X, for eXchange, to toggle between painting on this Gray layer with either Black or White.

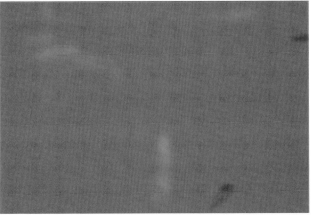

STEP 8: The Burn and Dodge layer. Areas that are darker than 50% gray will be darkened in the underlying layers, and areas that are lighter will be lightened.

STEP 9: **As yet another final adjustment, we created a mask and adjustment layer curve to very slightly darken the outer parts of the image. We then edited this by hand with the Airbrush to re-lighten some of those darkened areas. To stop accidental Move tool movement of layers, notice that the position is locked in all the real layers as well as adjustment layers that contain non-solid white masks.**

We know that this has been a whirlwind tour of color correcting and editing using Lab images. I have corrected quite a few of my fine art prints using Lab color since many of the original scans were done with a Lino Tango scanner in Lab color. Sometimes it is harder to correct in Lab color, and there are some filters in Photoshop that don't work with Lab images but only work in RGB. Now I sometimes correct in Lab color and sometimes in Adobe RGB, depending on the image in question and where I got its scan. It is usually easier to correct in Adobe RGB.

If you get your original scans as Lab at 16 bits per channel but want to correct in RGB, then do one 16-bit per channel conversion from Lab to Adobe RGB, before you

STEP 9: The mask for the Darken Edges curves adjustment layer. This was a very subtle darkening of the Lightness channel curve.

color correct. Lab is a larger gamut space than Adobe RGB, so if you color correct in Lab, you should leave the image in Lab until you print it. There is no reason to convert a final color corrected Lab image to Adobe RGB. The print driver will convert from Lab to the RGB space of your printer profile. When working with 8-bit per channel images, you especially want to avoid doing mode conversions when possible. See Chapter 16: "Image Resolution, Scanning Film, and Digital Cameras," for more information on the way to scan your images at 16 bits per channel, so you can work in Lab color or Adobe RGB.

The original Bryce image before we made any color corrections.

COMPOSITING MULTIPLE IMAGES WITH LAYERS, ADJUSTMENT LAYERS, AND LAYER MASKS

USE THE PEN TOOL TO CREATE MASKS

USE FREE TRANSFORM TO SCALE AND MATCH PERSPECTIVES

REPLACE AND COLOR MATCH FACES

LEARN ADVANCED COMPOSITING TECHNIQUES

CREATE COMPLEX COMPOSITE ADVERTISEMENTS

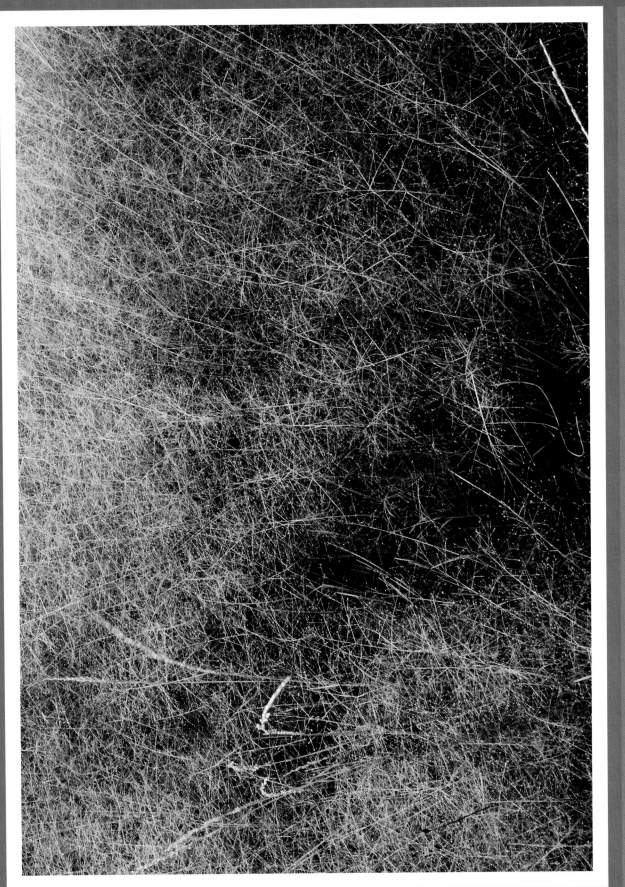

While teaching a Digital Printmaking and Photography workshop for the Ansel Adams Digital workshops in Mono Lake, I shot this wispy grass at sunrise one morning near the lake edge. Mono lake, near Yosemite, is a great area to shoot and take workshops. We learn new Photoshop techniques during the day, then have shooting sessions in the early mornings and evenings.

HANDS-ON SESSION: Rain in Costa Rica

Using the Pen tool and a variety of selection and masking techniques to create a composite of four images, giving us a rainy street scene in San Jose, Costa Rica.

In this session, we will use the Pen tool and other selection and masking techniques to create a composite of a rain scene with rain photographs from San Jose, Costa Rica. We want this scene to appear as though you are looking at it through the front window of a bus that is coming onto this street. The bus front window shot was taken going down the highway in Costa Rica between San Jose and San Isidro, a road where I didn't want to drive myself since many buses and trucks pass each other even around curves sometimes. Costa Rica is a friendly and beautiful country to visit; I've been there three times!

SETTING UP THE FOUR FILES

STEP 1: **Open the four PSD files in the RainInCostaRica folder on the *Photoshop CS Artistry* CD. Press the Tab key** to get rid of your palettes from the screen. **Click on the Blue Bus file to make it active, then type an F to put it in Full Screen mode followed by Command-0 to fill the screen with this file.** We are going to move all the other images into this file, each as a separate layer. **Switch to the Move tool (V) and activate the Red Car file from the Window/Documents menu.** You should now see the Blue Bus file behind in Full Screen mode and the Red Car file in front, but within a window. **Hold the Shift key down, click within the Red Car window, and drag the Red Car image until the cursor has moved on top of the Blue Bus image. Release the mouse and Shift key at that point, and you should have dragged and dropped the Red Car image as a new layer on top of the Blue Bus image.** Doing this with the Shift key down should have caused the Red Car image to be centered on top of the Blue Bus image within the Blue Bus file. **Now use the Window/Documents menu to make the Woman file active Shift-drag her image on top of the Blue Bus file in the same way you moved the Red Car over there. Use Window/Documents again to activate the Bus Window file and Shift-drag it onto the Blue Bus file. Use Window/Layers (F10 with ArtistKeys) to bring back the Layers palette.** Your Blue Bus file should now have a Layers palette with Blue Bus on the bottom, then Red Car, then Woman, and finally Bus Window on top. **Choose File/Save As and save this as RainInCostaRicaLayers.psd.**

STEP 2: The crop you should make on the Blue Bus layer. Don't crop more than this.

304

CROP AND COLOR CORRECT

STEP 2: **Turn off the Eye icons for the top three layers until you are just looking at the Blue Bus layer at the bottom of the Layers palette. Click on the words Blue Bus to activate that layer. Type a C to get the Crop tool and crop the black borders from the left, bottom, and right side.** Be careful not to crop off any more than is needed to remove the non-image black border from around the edge.

Choose Layer/New Adjustment Layer/Levels (Command-F2) to create the Levels adjustment layer and do Overall Color Correction on the Blue Bus image. Go through the process covered in Chapter 19: "Overall Color Correction," to do the Levels corrections on this image. With the highlights on this image, I actually left them as they were to keep the dull and rainy look the image has. **If you'd like, you can load my Levels adjustments, called BlueBusLevels, from the RainInCostaRica/Extra Info Files folder on the CD. Choose OK when you are happy with your Levels adjustments use Command-F3 to create a new Curves adjustment layer. I use an S-Curve, called Blue-BusCurves, to increase the contrast a bit. Choose OK on the S-Curve use Command-F4 to create a Hue/Saturation adjustment layer. What I did here is on the CD and is called BlueBusHueSat, so you can load that one and check it out, too.** This example is mostly about compositing, not color correction, so I'm not spending a lot of time on the color correction aspects. At any time, though, you can also open and look at my final version of this composite, called RainInCostaRicaFinalCC, from the Extra Info Files folder on the CD in the RainInCostaRica chapter.

Choose Layer/New/Layer Set and name the set Overall Color Correction. Drag the Layer thumbnail for each of the Levels, Curves, and Hue/Sat adjustment layers and drop it on the Overall Color Correction Layer Set thumbnail. Make sure they are still in the same order within the set with Levels on the bottom, Curves in the middle, and Hue/Sat on the top. You can then close this layer set to make your Layers palette smaller.

LEARNING ABOUT PATHS

STEP 3: **Click on the words Bus Window in the Layers palette to activate the Bus Window layer.** If you already know how to use the Pen tool and Paths, you can skip steps 3 and 4. The Pen tool allows you to make selections, called paths, by clicking to create points between either straight or curved lines. If you click a point and immediately release the mouse, you create an anchor point. If you click a point and drag before releasing the mouse, that point becomes a curve point. When you create or move a curve point, you get two lines coming out of the curve point; I call these handlebars. The handlebars control the shape of the curve. Try this out now! It's sort of like tracing—but more fun!

Type a P to get to the Pen tool. In the Options bar, click the Make Path icon, the middle one. Now, click anywhere in the Bus Window image with the Pen tool and immediately release to create an anchor point. Set four or five anchor points to create a box. When you put the last anchor point on top of the first, a little circle appears next to the arrow, indicating that you are closing the path. When you see the circle, click on top of the initial point again to close the path. If you're going to turn your path into a selection (as you are going to do here), you usually want the path to be closed. **After closing the first box path, move the cursor down below that box, and in a new area, click and drag to create a curve point. Where you click is the location of the point, and dragging out the handlebar beyond the point affects the shape of the line segment between that point and the previous point as well as**

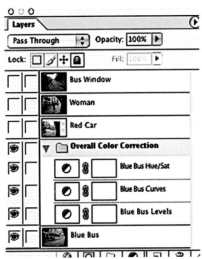

STEP 2: The Layers palette after doing the overall color correction on the Blue Bus image.

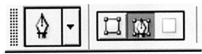

STEP 3: Use the middle icon to draw paths.

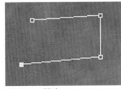

STEP 3: Click to enter corner points on a path.

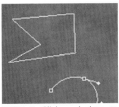

STEP 3: Click and drag to enter curve points on a path. The handlebars should be in tangent to the curve shape you are trying to draw.

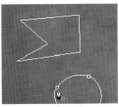

STEP 3: To close the curve, click the first point a second time when you see the small circle next to the Pen icon.

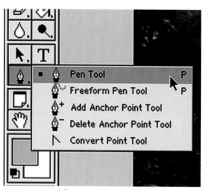

STEP 4: The Path Selection tool is for selecting and moving entire paths, and the Direct Selection tool is for selecting and moving parts of paths.

STEP 4: The different tools available from the pop-out menu for Pen in the Tools palette. The Pen tool and Freeform Pen tool are for entering points initially. To get the Magnetic Pen tool, first choose Freeform Pen Tool, then choose Magnetic Pen Tool from the Options bar at the top of the screen. The Pen+ and Pen– tools are for adding and deleting anchor points, and the Convert Point tool is for changing points between corners and curves and for decoupling the handlebars.

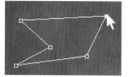

STEP 4: To move a corner point or a curve point, click it and drag.

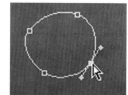

STEP 4: To adjust the shape of the curve, first click the point whose handlebars affect the part of the curve you want to change. Second, click the end of the handlebar and make it longer or shorter or change its angle. This changes the shape of the curve.

STEP 4: Moving a curve point to make the oval longer.

STEP 4: Changing the shape of a curve segment by dragging one end of a handlebar.

between that point and the next point. **Draw an oval shape by clicking and dragging four curve points. Close the path by clicking again on the original point. You now have a box path made up of anchor points and an oval path made up of curve points. If you bring up the Paths palette (Shift-F11), you can see them both in a new path called Work Path.** Work Path is a temporary place where you can create a path without naming it. Actually, each of these two disjointed paths is a subpath of Work Path. **Double-click Work Path and rename it Play Path.** After you name a path, any changes you make to it automatically save as part of that path.

STEP 4: **Now select the Path Selection tool in the Tools palette by typing an A or Shift-A, depending on how you have set your preferences.** See the diagrams on this page for the names of each of the Arrow and Pen tools. If you have Use Shift Key for Tool Switch on in General Preferences, you can switch between the two different Arrow tools by using Shift-A. You can switch between the two Pen editing tools by typing Shift-P. **Now try using the Path Selection tool, the black arrow, to edit the path. First click the box shape you made. When you click the box shape, its points become highlighted. If you click and drag anywhere on the box, the entire box shape moves. To move one of these points in the box shape, type Shift-A to switch to the white Direct Selection Tool, then click outside the box path to deselect the entire thing. Now to move a particular point, click back on that path to select it for point editing, and then click on the point you want to move, drag it to a new location, and let go.** This change updates automatically in your Play Path. **Click the oval subpath now, still using the white Direct Selection tool, and its points become highlighted. If you want to move one of these curve points to elongate the oval, just click and drag it like you would an anchor point with no handles. To adjust the shape of the curve, first click the point on one end of the curve segment that you want to change. This brings up the handlebars for that point. Now click the end of the handlebar next to the segment you want to change, and make it longer or shorter, or change its angle to change the shape of the curve. If you click, with this same white arrow tool, on a segment between two points, you can drag that segment to a new location or change the shape of a curved segment.**

You can also add points with the Pen+ tool (the Add Anchor Point tool) and delete points with the Pen– tool (the Delete Anchor Point tool). **To add a point, just click along the line segment where there currently isn't a point using the Pen+ tool. When over an existing point with the Pen+ tool, you will actually get the Direct Selection tool since you can't add a point where there already is one. When in the Pen– tool, you can click on any existing point to remove it, but you will be in the Direct Selection tool when you are not over an existing point.** When you add a point with the Pen+ tool, it is a curve point. You can then change the shape of the curve by adjusting that point's handlebars with the Direct Selection tool. When in the Pen+ tool, holding down the Option key will give you the Pen– tool when over a point, but otherwise it will show you the Direct Selection tool with a plus next to it. Clicking and dragging with that will make a copy of the entire path. When in the Pen– tool, holding down the Option key will give you the Pen+ tool unless you are over a point, in which case you get the Direct Selection+ tool mentioned in the last sentence for copying the entire path. **If you want to change a curve point to a corner point, or vice versa, click it with the Convert Point tool. To change an anchor point with no handlebars to a curve, you click and drag the corner point to define the**

length and angle of your handlebars. You also can use the Convert Point tool to decouple a curve point's handlebars. Clicking either handlebar and moving it slightly with this tool allows you to later use the Direct Selection tool to drag each end of the handlebar to change its curve segment shape without changing the one on the opposite side of the handlebar's point. This is a corner point where two curves meet but move out from the point in the same direction, causing a sharp angle. **To recouple the handlebars together again for a smooth curve, click and drag on the point between the handlebars using the Convert Point tool.** You can access the Convert Point tool from the Direct Selection (white arrow) tool by holding down the Command and Option keys and putting the cursor over an existing point or handlebar end. Access the Convert Point tool from the Pen tool using only the Option key. Using the Pen tool in Photoshop is a lot like using the Pen tool in Illustrator. **There are several ways to turn a path into a selection: Choose Make Selection from the pop-up menu in the Paths palette, drag the path to the Load Path as a Selection icon (the third one) on the bottom of the palette, highlight the name of the path and click the icon, or Command-click on the name of the path. Click on the Play Path you just created in the Paths palette and drag it to the trash at the bottom-right area of the Paths palette. If you made a selection, choose Command-D to deselect it.**

STEP 5: Start your path at the top left of the bigger bus window. Click to make the first point, then click and drag on each additional point to make the direction that you drag in parallel with the window edge at that point.

STEP 5: Here you can see the points we have placed at the bottom right of the large window. We are placing points as we work clockwise around the window.

KNOCKING OUT THE BUS WINDOW

STEP 5: Type a P to go back to the Pen tool. Click the pop-up arrow beside the Custom Shape icon and click the Rubber Band option. As you are drawing a curve, this option will show you the line segment between the current existing point and the next point on the curve. I think it helps to place the anchor points more accurately. **Now press Tab to get rid of all your palettes use Command-0 to zoom the image up and fill the screen. If Tab doesn't get rid of your palettes, try Return and then Tab a few times until the palettes disappear. The Bus Window layer should still be active and what you are seeing on your screen. Click down your first point at the top of the bigger window trace around the window clockwise placing points as you go.** When you place points on a shape that has subtle curves, you often want to click and drag, which places the curve points with handlebars, allowing you to make subtle changes in the shape of the line segment between the last point and the point you are currently placing. If there is a long straight section, place regular anchor points by just clicking within that section, but you always want to use curve points whenever there is a curve. Where a straight segment joins a curve you can click to finish the straight segment with a corner point, then hold down the Option key and drag from that point to create a single handlebar headed in the direction of the curve. See the illustrations on this page for comments about drawing this path. **When you**

STEP 5: Once you have worked your way all around the window, place the cursor back on top of the first point you clicked and you will see a small circle next to the arrow at the lower right. When you see this circle, click once to complete the path.

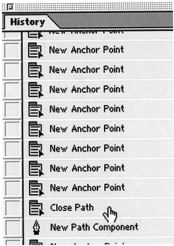

STEP 5: While working on a path in Photoshop, the History palette (F8) keeps track of each point that you enter. If you want to go back to redo several points, just click a few steps back in the History palette. The hand here is showing us the place where we closed the path on the big window and have just started the path on the smaller window to the left.

307

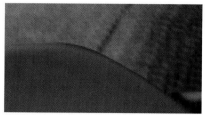

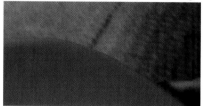

STEP 5: A window edge that has an ugly black line showing. Using the Paintbrush and painting in the mask with black along this edge, we removed it below. The trick is to click at one end of the part you want to remove, then Shift-click on the other end to paint in a straight line with the brush, and thus remove a straight piece of the window edge.

have traced all the way around, click again on the point that started the path, which completes and closes this path.

Now trace a similar path around the smaller window to the left side. When this second subpath is closed, use Shift-F11 to bring up your Paths palette and double-click on the Work Path and name it Bus Windows. Now choose Make Selection from the pop-up menu on the Paths palette with the Feather set to 0, Anti-Aliased turned on, and the New Selection choice active. This will turn your path into a selection. You are now going to choose Layer/Add Layer Mask/Hide Selection to remove the area of the window from view in this layer. Type B to get the Paintbrush and D for Default Colors, which gives you white when a mask is active. Select a small hard-edged brush, then zoom in to 200% and slowly look around the edge of the bus window for selection edges that don't look correct. Paint with black to remove more from the window frame edge and paint with white to bring some window edge back.

Notice when you do this that it also removes the windshield wipers from the bus windows. We'd probably like to keep them in and on since the bus is going out into the rain. We could have selected those with the Pen tool also, but just to give you some other selection skills, we'll select those using a Levels mask. **To temporarily turn off the mask you just created, Shift-click on the Layer mask thumbnail, the rightmost**

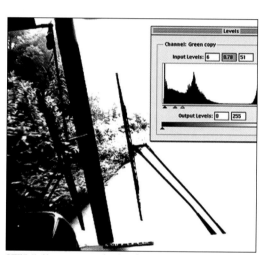

STEP 5: Here is the Layer and Channel setup for choosing the Green channel as the one to create our mask. Dragging it to the New Channel icon to the left of the Trash icon in the Channels palette will make a copy of this Green channel.

STEP 5: Here we are using Levels to separate the wipers from the rest of the image in this copy of the Green channel. These are the settings we used to separate the wipers.

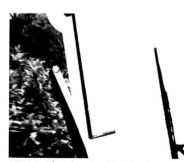

STEP 5: After choosing OK to Levels, we are painting using the Paintbrush with white in the Green copy channel to cleanly cut out the wipers.

one, for this Bus Window layer. Now use Shift-F10 to bring up the Channels palette. Click first on the word RGB, and then click each channel to look at each of the Red, Green, and Blue channels by themselves to find the one that has the most contrast between the wipers and the background street scene. I chose the Green channel. Drag the Green channel to the New Channel icon to the left of the Trash icon at the bottom of the Channels palette. Now choose Image/Adjust/Levels to go into levels on that channel. Move the Highlight and Shadow sliders in toward the center left as you try to separate the wipers from all the noise in the window scene. The right wiper separates easily, so zoom in on it and get the settings that separate it as exactly as possible. Turn the Preview button off and then on again in the Levels dialog to make sure the mask you are creating correctly gets the edges of the wiper. Move the Shadow, Brightness, and Highlight sliders of Levels as you are doing this to see what they do to the mask. Now look at the leftmost wiper and the metal bar that comes down into the window area on the left side. Select them as well as you can, but know that you will have to use the Paintbrush to clean up this mask. When the mask looks as good as you can get it, choose OK in Levels. Now type a B for the Paintbrush and a D for Default Colors, which will give you white as the foreground color. Paint with white at 100% to remove all the other parts of this mask that are not the wipers and that metal bar. Remember that you can get a straight line with the brush by clicking at one end of a line and then Shift-clicking at the other end, which draws the brush in a straight line between those two points. **When you are finished editing this mask, Command-click on this Green copy channel to load the white parts of it as a selection.** You are actually loading everything but the wipers since the wipers were black in this channel. **Choose Select/ Inverse to invert the selection so the wipers are actually selected. Click back on the word RGB in the Channels palette and you will again be working on the Bus Window layer. Shift-click on the Bus Window Layer Mask thumbnail to turn the mask on again. Choose Select/Save Selection and set the Channel pop-up in the Save Selection dialog to Bus Window Mask. Choose the Add to Channel option, then click on OK to add in the wipers. Click on the rightmost Bus Window Layer Mask thumbnail to make sure you are editing the Bus Window Mask, then use the Paintbrush again to do any final mask cleanup on the ends of the wipers where they connect to the bottom of the dashboard.** I had to paint a little more white in the layer mask so the wipers looked connected to the dashboard. **Click in the Lock Position checkbox to lock the position of the Bus Window layer so it can't be accidentally moved with the Move tool. Click on the words Blue Bus to activate that layer, then lock its position also.**

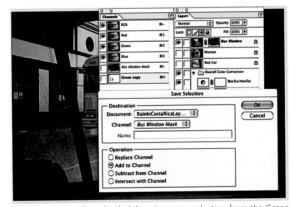

STEP 5: Here we have loaded the wipers as a selection from the Green copy channel, then we chose Select/Save Selection and are adding the wipers to the Bus Window mask using the Add to Channel option.

ADDING IN THE RED CAR

STEP 6: **Click on the name Red Car in the Red Car layer in the Layers palette.** This should turn on that layer and it will appear in place of the Blue Bus layer, which is now obscured underneath. **Type an L to switch to the Lasso tool, then type Return, type 3, and finally another Return. This will set the Feather of the Lasso to 3.** The first Return selects the Feather text box, the 3 sets the Feather, and the second Return deselects that feather text box so the next time you type a number it refers to the Opacity of the Red Car layer. **Now type a 5, which should set the Opacity of this Red Car layer to 50%. You will now see the red car and the blue bus superimposed on each other. Hold down the Command key while you click and drag the red car to the left so it looks like it is driving down the road in front of the bus.** While holding down the Command key, you activate the Move tool, which can inadvertently move a layer if you click and drag by accident. When in the correct position, you should see the red car within the left front window of the bus the viewer would be riding in. Getting the yellow curbs in the two images to line up is a good way to position the car on the road. Don't move the Blue Bus layer, though; it should already be in the correct position. **When the red car is approximately in the right place, type a 0 to set the Opacity of the Red Car layer back to 100%. Without the Command key down, you should still be in the Lasso tool, and with that tool make a very loose selection around the red car. Make sure you include all of the red car's splash. Now**

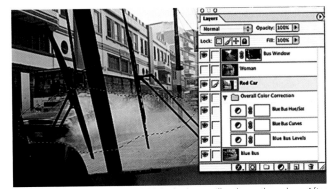

STEP 6: This is the approximate initial selection you'll make on the red car. After making the layer mask from this selection, you will paint white or black with the Paintbrush in that mask to add to or subtract from this selection.

STEP 6: Here is the red car in relationship to the blue bus before we scale the car.

STEP 6: Here is how they look after the car is scaled up by 145% and also moved to this new location further to the left and front.

STEP 6: The red car and blue bus after my final edits on the mask for the red car to tone down the splash a little. At this point, I have not yet added the Grouped Darken Car curve to the Red Car layer.

choose Layer/Add Layer Mask/Reveal Selection, or just click on the second icon from the left at the bottom of the Layers palette. This will add a layer mask that removes the rest of the Red Car layer from this composite.

You'll notice that the color correction on the Red Car layer doesn't match, but that can actually be an asset at this point to make it easier to see what is coming from each layer. **Turn the Eye icon off for the Bus Window layer so you can concentrate on cleanly integrating the red car. Use Command-K to bring up the General Preferences and set the History States to 99.** You'll be doing a lot of blending here, and if you don't like the direction it's going, you may want to back up a long way. It is amazing how quickly one can do more than 20 History States when retouching or blending a mask. **Use the Brush (B) to paint in the Red Car layer mask to blend the red car and its splash into the Blue Bus scene. You'll probably want to set the Opacity of your brush to about 30%.** If you're using a tablet, the splash is another good spot to use a brush with Shape Dynamics.

I'm assuming here that you have BarrysPhotoBrushes loaded as explained in Chapter 3: "Setting System and Photoshop Preferences." If not, you may want to load those brushes from the Preferences folder on the CD. Use one of the brushes from the middle set, which have 80% hardness, painting with black to cleanly remove the original background from behind the roof of the red car. In front of the red car, you want to keep most of the car's splash, but you want to use a soft brush, from the third set of brushes, to blend the splash and underside of the front of the car with the road in Blue Bus layer. When you have made some progress blending these, click on the Overall Color Correction Layer Set thumbnail and drag this up until the line above the Red Car layer is highlighted. Release the mouse at this point, and the color corrections you made to the Blue Bus layer are now applied to the Red Car layer as well. The two layers should now look good together, but if not, continue to work on the Red Car layer mask. If you are having trouble getting it to work, check out my version in the file called RainInCostRicaFinalCC.psd in the Extra Info Files folder for this chapter on your CD.

The red car may now look a little small because we have moved it in front of the blue bus and closer to your point of view, so it needs to be a bit bigger in its relationship to the bus. **Click on the Red Car Layer thumbnail to be sure that layer is active, then choose Edit/Free Transform (Command-T) so you can scale and move the red car.**

If you can't see the corner handlebars to do the transform, press the Escape key to get out of Free Transform while you close palettes, and put your window in Full Screen mode or whatever you need to do to have room to scale this layer. Once you are in Free Transform, you will want to hold down the Shift key while scaling the car so the scaling stays proportional. I held my Shift key down and then clicked and dragged the top-right handlebar up and to the right to increase the size of the car. **You can then release the mouse from the corner handlebar and move the red car's position by clicking and dragging in the center area of the scaling box. Scale the car and reposition it until you are happy with its size and location.** The Options bar at the top of the screen gives you the amount of scaling you have done so far, and you can change this amount by just typing a new value into either the horizontal or vertical scale text box. For a review of what Free Transform can do, see Chapter 9: "Transformation of Images." **When you are happy with the Free Transform, press Return to see it in full resolution. You will probably now want to click on the rightmost Layer Mask thumbnail in this Red Car layer so you can go back and edit this mask a bit more**

using black and white with the Paintbrush. To get my red car to look right, I actually scaled it up by 145% in width and height and also moved it further to the left and front until part of it was no longer visible. I also used Command-F3 at this point to add a Grouped Curves adjustment layer to the Red Car layer and then used this to darken the car a bit in relationship to the **Blue Bus scene.** You can load my Darken Car curve settings from the Extra Info Files folder for this chapter on the CD. **Lock the position of the Red Car layer when you finish it.**

STEP 7: The initial Lasso selection for the woman.

ADDING THE RUNNING WOMAN

STEP 7: **Click on the word Woman in the Layers palette to activate that layer. Type L to go back to your Lasso tool and make sure the Feather is still set to 3. Make a very loose selection around the edge of the woman and the reflection of her feet and legs on the pavement. Make sure this selection is wide enough to be considerably more than the 3-pixel feather away from the edges of the woman. Click on the Add a Mask icon, which is second from the left at the bottom of the Layers palette.** This just removes the parts of the Woman layer you are sure you won't be using. Now you are going to refine the mask, and then reposition and resize the woman if necessary. When you move or scale a layer that has a linked layer mask attached, the mask is also moved and scaled in the same ways. When you normally add a layer mask using the Add a Mask icon or the Layer/Add Layer Mask menu, that mask is linked to the layer. You can see the small Link icon between the layer's Layer thumbnail and its Layer Mask thumbnail.

STEP 7: The tighter selection of the woman made with the Wand and then the Lasso.

STEP 7: After saving the above selection to the Woman mask channel, and then deselecting that selection, we Gaussian Blur the mask by 1 to soften the edges. The final step is to blend the woman's hair and foot shadow with the Blue Bus layer's background.

Type a W to switch to the Magic Wand. Make sure the Tolerance is set to 32 and that Contiguous is checked. Click on the Layer thumbnail for the Woman layer and make a tighter selection on the woman by Shift-clicking several times in the black areas of her clothes. After selecting what you can this way with the Wand, type L to switch to the Lasso tool, then Return, 2 and Return again to set the Feather to 2. Now with the Shift key down, add in the areas that were not selected by the Wand. I've set the Feather to 2 because in the original image the woman is a bit soft along the edges since she is running. Choose Select/Save Selection and save to the Woman Mask channel using the Replace Selection option. Now choose Select/Deselect to get rid of your selection since it has been already saved to a mask and we now are going to want to blur that mask. Choose Filter/Blur/Gaussian Blur and do a blur of 1 to make her edges a bit softer than the Magic Wand did. Now type a B to bring back your brush, and click the Airbrush icon on the Options bar. Use soft brushes with a Flow of about 10% to blend the woman's flopping black hair and foot shadow into the Blue Bus layer's background. If you are using a tablet, select a brush with Shape Dynamics on, raise the Flow to about 20%, and turn off the Airbrush setting. As you can see from the illustration to the right, hair is a good place to use a pressure sensitive tablet and a pen for masking. **You should also drag the Overall Color Correction layer set up above the Woman layer so it is color corrected in the same way as the other two.** Since all three of the Blue Bus, Red Car, and Woman shots were taken at the same time with the same roll of film and only seconds apart, it is possible and even beneficial to use the

STEP 7: Here's the Woman layer mask as it is on the CD final version of this example.

STEP 7: Here's that same mask finessed with brushes that use Shape Dynamics.

STEP 7: Here we see the composite with the running woman added into the original Blue Bus scene.

same color corrections on all three layers. **Keep working on the Woman layer mask until she blends in well.**

FINISHING UP THE COMPOSITE

STEP 8: **Now you can turn the Eye icon back on for the top Bus Window layer and your composite should be almost complete. I liked the location of the woman where she was, but if you don't, you can click on the word Woman in the Woman layer to reactivate it, then use the Move tool to move that layer around. When the location is final, lock the position of the Woman layer as you did the other layers earlier. Go ahead and drag the Overall Color Correction layer set to the very top of the Layers palette and you should find the look is complete.**

For another compositing example that uses Photoshop's built-in Extract command, see Chapter 34: "HeartSinger CD Cover." Other great examples of compositing techniques are in Chapters 26, 27, 29, and 30.

STEP 8: This is the final composite with the Bus Window layer turned back on and the Overall Color Corrections layer set moved up to the top of the Layers palette so it corrects all these images in the same way. This has been a fun use of some of the pictures I took on my most recent trip to Costa Rica.

29 HANDS-ON SESSION: The McNamaras

Using adjustment layers, layer masks, retouching, and layer sets to color correct and composite the McNamaras' family portrait, where we need to move six smiling faces into the final image to create one where everyone is smiling.

I was an only child, so while growing up it was always more fun to go over to the McNamaras and play with their six kids. Now, as adults, we still get together a lot and I have had the joy of taking two of their five-year family portraits. Taking a family portrait of this many people, and especially this many kids along with their parents, is not the easiest task. I also wanted to use my 4x5 camera so there would be the maximum amount of detail in the image. All the kids were wiggling around, so it was hard to get them to smile at the camera, and then the parents often looked down and gave directions to their children at just that moment when all the children were actually looking at the camera. I knew this would be difficult to do with the 4x5, so I also brought along my trusty Canon F1 and shot two rolls of 35. With the 35mm stuff, I actually did get one picture where everyone was smiling and looking at the camera. That was the shot we used for the McNamara family. Still, though, I wanted to make a 4x5 version, because it would have so much more detail. Scans, with the Leaf 45 scanner, were made of enough of the 4x5 images that I had at least one smiling face of each person. Here we are going to composite all of them together to create the family portrait where everyone is smiling!

STEP 1: **Make sure that Photoshop is already running. Bring up the General Preferences (Command-K) and set History States to 40.** This will help you undo any mistakes made when retouching to blend the new images in. If you have not used the History palette before, read Chapter 8: "History Palette, History Brush, and Snapshots," because you will find the History palette very useful here. **Open each of the seven untagged jpeg files in the McNamaras folder on the *Photoshop CS Artistry* CD. Since these are old files, they were not tagged with a profile, but I know they were created in the ColorMatch RGB space. As you open these files, you will need to choose Assign Profile: ColorMatch RGB**

The original McNamaras image before color correction or the addition of the smiling faces.

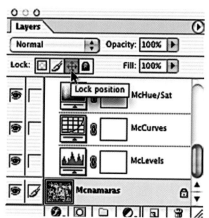

STEP 2: Locking the position of the McNamaras layer so it can't accidentally be moved.

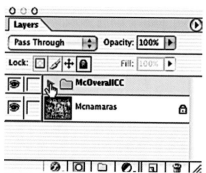

STEP 2: The Layers palette after the McOverallCC set is created and set up.

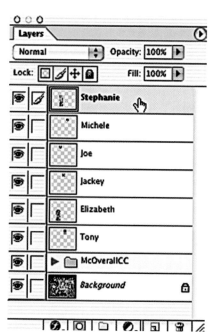

STEP 3: The Layers palette after moving all the smiling faces into the work file.

from the Missing Profile dialog and continue to work on them within the ColorMatch space. Choose the file McNamarasOrig.jpg from the Photoshop Window menu and put it in Full Screen mode by clicking on the middle icon at the bottom of the Tools palette or by pressing F. Press C to bring up the Cropping tool and crop out any black or white borders around the image. Choose File/Save As and save it in Photoshop format as McNamarasLayers.psd.

STEP 2: Choose Layer/New Adjustment Layer/Levels (Command-F2) to start the overall correction for the McNamarasLayers image, and call this first adjustment layer McLevels. Go through the basic levels adjustment, which you learned about in Chapter 19: "Overall Color Correction." You may want to review that chapter if you are not sure what to do here. I used the Highlight and Shadow Eyedroppers to set the highlight on Jackey's pants and the shadow in the darkest leaves along the top of the photo. If you want to check them out, you can look at my Levels settings and the Color Samplers I set for the highlights and shadows, in my McNamarasLayers file, from the Extra Info Files folder on the CD. When you are happy with the Levels color changes, press the Save button and save these as McLevels; then choose OK from your Levels adjustment layer. We'll use the saved version later when we are working on the new faces. We did this using an adjustment layer so that we would have the option of changing it later after we get all the faces composited in.

Now use Command-F3 to create a Curves adjustment layer and adjust the contrast of this image. It is sort of flat, especially for the people in the shadows in the back row. Use an S-Curve to increase the contrast a bit. Again, if you are having trouble, check my McCurves layer from my final version of this chapter in the Extra Info Files folder for this chapter on the CD. Save your Curve changes as McCurves; then choose OK to finish up this adjustment layer.

Now use Command-F4 to create another adjustment layer of type Hue/Saturation, and call it McHueSat. Do the overall Saturation adjustments for the McNamaras family like we did in Chapter 19. The contrast and saturation on this scan is flat with color casts. In fact, some of the separate face scans we are going to insert later look better, and you'll need to bring the McNamaras image up to their level. While the various photos were being taken, clouds were moving over, so some faces were in the sun and others in the shade. The people in the back all have dark, flat color casts over their faces. In the end they will all need to match and also make a pleasing color portrait. When you are happy with the added saturation and tonal changes, use the Save button to save your Hue/Sat changes as McHueSat; then choose OK in the Hue/Saturation dialog box. Because these are all adjustment layers, you can change them again later and you probably will before this example is finished.

Double-click on the *Background* layer at the bottom of the Layers palette and rename it McNamaras. Turn on the Lock Position icon to lock this layer against accidental movement. Now choose Layer/New/Layer Set and create a new layer set called McOverallCC. Drag that set to the top of the Layers palette and put the three adjustment layers inside it by dragging each layer's thumbnail and dropping it on top of the McOverallCC set's thumbnail. Make sure the order of the three layers stays the same inside this set. Now you can close the set to make more room in the Layers palette, which you will need.

ADDING THE SMILING FACES

STEP 3: Press V to switch to the Move tool. Now use the Window menu to switch, one at a time, to each of the smiling face images you opened in Step 1. For each

314

separate smiling face image, drag and drop it with the Move tool on top of the same person's face in your McNamarasLayers image. If you put the cursor on the nose in the smiling version, and then drag to the same person's nose in the McNamarasLayers file and release the mouse button at that point, you will have a good start on lining up the two heads. Go ahead and drag and drop each smiling person into his or her own layer; double-click on the layer name, and rename the layer name for the person. The names of the smiling people's files are the actual names of that particular person. After dragging each person into his or her own layer, you can choose File/Close (Command-W) to close

STEP 4: Here you see the two Jackeys before they are lined up. Pick an absolute position in the center of the image area (like her glasses' corner here) put the cursor on that position, and then drag the cursor to the same position in the other layer to move the Jackey layer and line them up. You can use the keyboard arrow keys to scroll by one pixel and fine-tune the positioning. After you adjust the position, you may have to rescale, readjust, and so on until you get it right.

the file for that person. When you have moved all six people into their approximate positions, go ahead and press Command-S to save the McNamarasLayers with all their layers. Your Layers palette should now look like the one on the previous page.

STEP 4: Some of the smiling layers will overlap each other, but don't worry about that now, because we are going to work on each one of them separately to integrate it into the image in a custom way. Turn off the Eye icons for all the smiling face layers except for Jackey. You still want the Eye icons on for the McNamaras layer and McOverallCC adjustment layer set. Click on the Jackey layer's name to make it active, and then type a 5 to set its Opacity to 50%. You can now see 50% of the Jackey layer and 50% of the original image of Jackey underneath. Use the Move tool (V) to move the Jackey layer around a bit until you figure out which 50% comes from this layer. The face in the Jackey layer is a bit bigger than the original face underneath. Use the Move tool to line up the glasses and lips on each layer as best you can. Remember that you can use the arrow keys to move the Jackey layer one pixel at a time in any direction. Now choose Edit/Free Transform (Command-T) and use the Free Transform command to scale this Jackey layer exactly and move it into the exact position above the original head below. Remember to hold down the Shift key while clicking and dragging in one of the corner handles to make your scaling proportional. To move the layer while in Free Transform, just click and drag in the middle of the box that defines the current image or use the arrow keys for fine adjustment. Press Return to end the Free Transform. For a review of the Free Transform options, see Chapter 9: "Transformation of Images, Layers, Paths, and Selections."

STEP 4: Here is how the two Jackeys look after they are lined up.

STEP 5: Press L to bring up the Lasso tool, and then press Return to highlight the Feather setting in the Options Bar. Now type a 2, and then press Return again to set the Feather at 2. Now make a selection around the inside of Jackey's face. This is the part of her face we are going to use from the Jackey layer. Now click on the Layer Mask icon (the second from the leftmost one at the bottom of the Layers palette) to add a layer mask, isolating this selected area as the new face and blending it with the old face. Type a zero (0) to set the Opacity of the Jackey layer back to 100%. You may notice a color difference between the skin and hair on the Jackey layer and the skin and hair in the original image. To fix this, add a Levels or Curves Adjustment

STEP 5: Make a Lasso selection (feather 2) of the inner area of Jackey's face; then click on the Layer Mask icon to create a layer mask only showing that part of the Jackey layer.

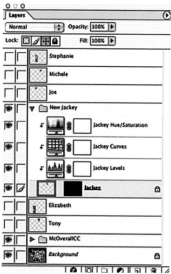

STEP 5: The Layers palette after blending Jackey's better smile into her previous head and creating the New Jackey layer set.

layer above the Jackey layer and grouped with the Jackey layer. I added grouped Levels, Curves, and Hue/Saturation adjustment layers above the Jackey layer and used them to match the color and contrast of Jackey's face and hair. I started by loading the McLevels, McCurves, and McHueSat settings into each of these so the adjustments I made to Jackey's face were the same as I had made to the old version of her face. Because the initial contrast on the new face is different than the original one, this only serves as a starting point and the colors have to be tweaked to match. I also tweaked the original McCurves adjustment layer, above the McNamaras layer, to add a little more contrast to the McNamaras layer to better match the new Jackey. We may have to modify all of these as we add other smiling faces to the composite. After you get the colors to match fairly well, press B to switch to the Paintbrush tool and then click on the Layer Mask thumbnail for the Jackey layer. Type a 0 (zero) to get 100% Opacity; then use a soft brush to paint in the layer mask to blend the two faces together even more. Paint with black to include more of the original Jackey face and paint with white to include more of the new face from the Jackey layer. Sometimes you might want to paint with 50% Opacity to blend the two images together. I also used the Rubber Stamp tool to clone away a little of Jackey's hair at the top of her head in the original McNamaras layer.

Once you are happy with the new Jackey face, choose Layer/New/Layer Set and add a set called New Jackey. Click on the Layer thumbnail for the Jackey layer and lock the position for this layer as you did for the McNamaras layer in step 2. That will prevent the Jackey layer, and those grouped with it, from being accidentally repositioned with the Move tool. Now drag and drop this Jackey layer on the thumbnail for the New Jackey layer set. This should move the Jackey layer and any adjustment layers grouped with the Jackey layer into this New Jackey layer set. You can then collapse this set to simplify your Layers palette before moving on to add more of the new smiling faces. Turning the Eye icon off and on for this New Jackey layer set will toggle the entire image between having the original Jackey face and the new, bigger smile Jackey face. Now might be a good time to save the file (Command-S).

STEP 7: Before Joe's, Jackey's, Tony's, and Michele's heads are replaced by smiling versions.

STEP 7: After the smiling heads are installed.

STEP 6: Joe was definitely not smiling very much in the original image. **Turn on the Eye icon for the Joe layer and you'll see that the new Joe definitely has a better smile. Now go through the sequence of adjustments you did for Jackey in steps 4 and 5, but this time do them for Joe and the Joe layer. You'll find that the area of each person's face that you have to change is different. Pull up the McNamarasLayers file from the Extra Info Files folder in the McNamaras example on the CD. This is my version of the final image. You can look at each of my layer masks and my adjustment layers to see what I did. Put all the Joe layers in a New Joe layer set as you did for Jackey's layers. Press Command-S to save your progressing McNamarasLayers file.**

Chapter 29: The McNamaras

STEP 7: Let's do Tony next because he's actually standing behind Jackey. Click on the Tony layer in the Layers palette and drag it below the Jackie layer in the Layers palette. Now do steps 4 and 5 for the Tony layer. Don't worry about any overlap between Tony and Jackey; that will go away when you create the layer mask for the Tony layer. To get Tony's head to look right in the composite, I ended up adding first a Levels, then a Curves, and finally a Hue/Saturation adjustment layer above Tony and grouped them with Tony's layer. Stick all of Tony's layers in a New Tony layer set. To the right of Tony is Michele, so turn on the Eye icon for her layer and work with her after Tony. To get Michele to look right, I had to include part of her neck as well as her head. You have to Clone stamp her collar and neck a bit on the right side. Turn the Eye icon on and off for the Michele layer, and Shift-click her Layer Mask thumbnail to turn the mask on and off in my final version of the McNamarasLayers to see what I did to make her look correct. Turning off the Eye icon for the Michele layer will let you see the original Michele; turning it on again allows you to compare the new version to the original to see if your composite is working. Shift-clicking on her Layer Mask thumbnail turns off the layer mask and shows you the entire new Michele layer. Toggling these back and forth can help you see what you need to do to solve any problems. If you make a mistake while Clone stamping, use the History palette (F8) to go back a few steps, or you can paint from an earlier state using the History Brush. See Chapter 8: "History Palette, History Brush, and Snapshots," for more info on how to do this. For the color correction on Michele, I just used a Levels and a Curves adjustment layer. In a similar way as you did Tony and Michele, now you should turn on the Eye icon for the Stephanie layer and blend in the slightly better expression for Stephanie. Do steps 4 and 5 for her. I had to add Levels, Curves, and Hue/Saturation adjustment layers to get her facial color to match the original. Each person's new layers should be put into a layer set for that person. Now might be a good time to save the file (Command-S).

STEP 8: You may notice that my final Layers palette, on the last page of this chapter, has two Curves adjustment layers on the top. One is called Open Up Parts, and the other is called Darken Parts. Although we didn't replace them, the faces of the three people at the top left of this family portrait are darker than many other faces in the image. Having these faces darker made it more difficult to match the new faces I was adding. I created the curve called Open Up Parts, which you see on this page, to allow me to brighten up those faces a bit. To make such a curve, just click on the topmost layer set in the Layers palette to make it active. Choose Command-F3 to create a new Curves adjustment layer. Click in the center of the curve and drag it up and to the left until the darkest face that you want to change is plenty bright enough. If you are not sure, make it a bit brighter than you would like. Don't worry about the faces that are already bright enough; they will return to normal in a moment. Click on OK in the Curves dialog; then choose Image/Adjustments/Invert (Command-I) to invert the mask for this layer causing it to now make no changes to the image. Type B for the PaintBrush, and then turn on Airbrush mode in the Options bar. Now set its Flow to about 7%, select a soft brush, and press D to make sure the foreground color is white. Paint over the areas of the faces that you want to brighten up. The longer you hold the Airbrush down, the more white is slowly applied until you get the degree of brightness that you want. If you overdo it, use Command-Z to Undo, or press X and paint with black to go back the other way. Using a similar technique, I also added the Darken Parts curve to fix the flat colors in the face of the woman to the top left with the red cloth belt. This curve is also used on several other faces to

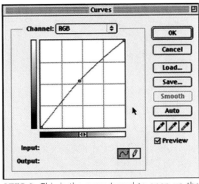

STEP 8: This is the curve I used to open up the dark faces a bit. It is only applied where the mask is not black.

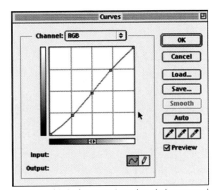

STEP 8: This is the curve I used to darken several faces. The S shape of the curve adds contrast, and moving the middle point down and to the right darkens the midtones as well. I also added some very minor color adjustments to this curve in the Green and Blue channels.

Adding the Smiling Faces

STEP 9: The initial Lasso selection for the Elizabeth layer with Opacity at 50%.

This example was in some previous versions of Photoshop Artistry, *although we did rework and improve the file and text for Photoshop CS Artistry.* Elizabeth's sister, Mary, was outside a Barnes and Noble bookstore one day, and she bet her friend $5 that her picture was in one of the books in the store. Her friend didn't believe her, so they went in and opened up a copy of Photoshop Artistry; then Mary made a quick $5. Pretty smart girl!

add some contrast where needed. Check these out along with their masks by looking at my final layers file on the book's CD.

ADDING THE SMILING ELIZABETH

STEP 9: **The last person who needs a better smile is Elizabeth. Because her feet were in sort of a strange position in the original and she was sitting in the front, I decided to replace her entire body. The best way I found to line up the two images of Elizabeth was to make the chair she is sitting in line up between the two shots. Because there is quite a bit of movement between the two images of her, my initial Lasso selection included more than just the new Elizabeth. It also included the old Elizabeth. We will need to get rid of all of her from the original photo, so we might as well start by seeing how the locations where she was in the original photo look if used from the new photo. After making your Lasso selection on the Elizabeth layer at 50% Opacity, click on the Layer Mask icon to add a layer mask that includes only the selected area; then set the Opacity on the Elizabeth layer back to 100%. Now you need to use the Paintbrush tool in the layer mask, painting in either black, to remove the Elizabeth layer, or in white, to add parts of the Elizabeth layer. Do this until you get the two layers to merge the best that you can.**

STEP 10: **You will find there are some fringe areas that won't work from either the Elizabeth layer or the original McNamaras layer. You will have to use the Clone Stamp tool (S) to clone some of what you need in those areas. Before you do this, though, go ahead and add a Grouped Levels adjustment layer and get the color of the Elizabeth layer to match the original photo. A good place to compare is the white chair that Stephanie is sitting on behind and to the right of Elizabeth. Part of the armrest for this chair will come from the original image and part of it will come from the Elizabeth layer. Get those whites to match, and you will have the color pretty close. I also added Curves and Hue/Saturation adjustment layers above the Levels and grouped them with Elizabeth to fix her contrast and saturate her colors a bit. Now that the colors match fairly well, use the Clone Stamp tool to clone the areas that won't work from either layer. For me, this was the top-right edge of the lower-left corner of Stephanie's dress, which came from the Elizabeth layer, and little sections of the pants on the boy to the left of Elizabeth. Remember, the Clone Stamp tool even lets you clone from all the layers onto a layer when Use All Layers is selected in the Options bar. To get the part of Stephanie's dress that I used from the Elizabeth layer to match, I lassoed that part of the dress, then added a Curves adjustment layer (again, grouped with the Elizabeth layer) and used it to match the two dresses. Because I had the dress area selected when I created the new adjustment layer, this automatically made a layer mask that applied the Curves adjustments only in that dress area. As you clone and paint in the layers and layer masks to get Elizabeth to look correct, it is easy to get confused and forget which layer or layer mask you are using or which tool you are using. It is even hard for me sometimes when I'm doing something like this. Slow down and concentrate; think twice and make sure you are using the right tool in the correct state. Sometimes it helps you get your bearings if you turn off the Eye icon of a layer or Shift-click a Layer Mask thumbnail to see the image without a layer or a mask. You will be switching between cloning on a layer and using the Paintbrush to edit a mask. Remember that you can always use the History palette or the History Brush to restore any layer, or just part of a layer, to a previous state.**

Chapter 29: The McNamaras

STEP 11: You now have all your smiling faces added and you have color corrected and masked them to match as best you can. Now it is time to look at the image as a whole and further tweak the color or contrast of any head that doesn't seem quite right. A particular person might seem slightly off color or have a different brightness or contrast than the rest. You might also decide to adjust the contrast or color balance of the entire McNamaras layer. Because you did all your color adjustments using adjustment layers, you can double-click on the Layer thumbnail of any of them and change the adjustment as many times as you like without degrading the original pixels in any of the layers. The final color changes to the pixels will not be made until you flatten the image; even better, use File/Save As to create a flattened version. When I zoomed out and looked at the image, I ended up changing the Joe and Jackey heads a little to make them fit in better with the rest of the faces. I used Joe's Levels adjustment layer to make his face a little darker and warmer, and I used Jackey's Curves adjustment layer to make her face a little warmer. My final version, called McNamarasLayers, is on the CD in the Extra Info Files folder for this chapter. If you're having a problem with anything, pull up my version and see how I did it. Press Command-S to save your file when you finish it. Before printing this in *Photoshop CS Artistry*, I did Image/Duplicate to create a merged version, and then Unsharp Mask to sharpen it—and of course I converted it to CMYK because it needed to be printed on a web press.

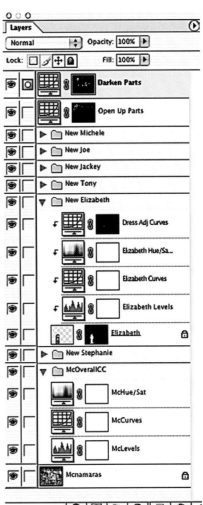

STEP 11: The final Layers palette after working on the new image of Elizabeth. This final McNamarasLayers file is in the Extra Info Files folder for the McNamaras chapter on the CD.

The final McNamaras' image after color correction and the addition of all the smiling faces. This was sharpened with Unsharp Mask set at an Amount of 150%, Radius of 1.5, and Threshold of 3.

30 HANDS-ON SESSION: The PowerBook Ad

*Create an image from components for a specified canvas size,
like a magazine ad; work with drop shadows, knock-outs, the
Pen tool, and linked layers for high-quality output. Use the Layer
Comps palette to show three versions of the ad.*

One of the final composite portable images. You
will produce three different comps in this example
using images on this page and the next.

STEP 1: The Banff Lake image that will be shown on the PowerBook
screen.

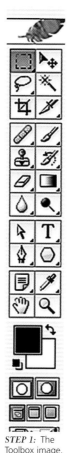

STEP 1: The
Toolbox image.

SETTING UP THE POWERBOOK IMAGE

Three years ago I purchased this 500 MHz Apple
PowerBook portable and it has been a big help in
writing these books, because I am able to work while
on the road and can also easily carry it to different
places within our home. This allows me to work late at
night while also listening to my eight-year-old son
sleep. I also have an Epson PhotoPC 3000Z 3.3
megapixel camera, which is very handy, and I was able
to photograph the PowerBook for this example, using
the camera mounted on a tripod. I originally photographed the PowerBook in color with the 3000Z,
then converted it to black-and-white for this example.

STEP 1: **Open the file PowerBook B&W.psd from the
CD folder called Ch30.The Power Book Ad.** Let's say
we want to use this to create an ad for a new computer brochure. The ad needs to be 4.3 inches wide
by 5 inches high for a 175-line screen print job. That
means we need to have an image that is at least 1,505
pixels wide by 1,750 pixels high, because we need 350
dpi to print at 175-line screen. The image we are
using is just slightly larger than that.

CREATING A NEW BACKGROUND FOR THE POWERBOOK

STEP 2: **We want this to be a color ad, so choose
Image/Mode/RGB to convert the PowerBook into an
RGB image.** We need to create an image to appear on the screen of
the PowerBook as well as a background for it to sit on. First, let's
work on creating a background. This black-and-white photo of the

Photoshop File Edit Image Layer Select Filter View Window Help   Wed 3:37 PM

STEP 1: The menu bar image.

320

STEP 1: The Roller Coaster image that will be an additional comp on the PowerBook screen.

STEP 1: The original PowerBook grayscale image taken with the Epson 3000Z.

PowerBook still contains shooting setup objects around the actual computer. **Double-click on the only layer in the Layers palette and name it My PowerBook. Use the Pen tool (P) to make a path around the outside edge of the PowerBook. Choose the middle Paths option at the top left of the Options bar. Start at the top-left edge of the PowerBook and click and drag curve points as you work your way around the computer, being careful to draw your path just a pixel or two inside the actual edge of the computer.** For more info about using the Pen tool and making paths, see the Pen tool part of Chapter 4: "The Tools Palette," or check out Chapter 28: "Rain in Costa Rica." **When you have drawn points all the way around the edge of the computer, click back on the original point to complete the path. Bring up the Paths palette (Shift-F11) and double-click on the Work Path, renaming it to Portable Outline. Click in the empty area of the Paths palette, toward the bottom of the palette, to deselect this path.**

STEP 2: Editing the clipping path with the white Arrow tool.

Choose Layer/New Fill Layer/Solid Color to create a solid color fill layer and name it Background Color Fill. Choose a brown color that is lighter and different from the color of the PowerBook when the Color Picker appears onscreen. Now drag that layer underneath the My PowerBook layer in the Layers palette. Bring up the Paths palette and click on your Portable Outline path to activate it. Now click back on the My PowerBook layer to activate it, and then choose Layer/Add Vector Mask/Current Path. This vector mask added to the My PowerBook layer should remove the background from around the PowerBook image. Type A to go to the Arrow tool, then Shift+A until you get the white Arrow tool, called the Direct Selection tool. Click once on the path with this tool to bring up the path points, and then to edit a point, click and drag it to a new position. After editing the path, you can choose Command-H to see the PowerBook against the background without the path lines there. If you see a white line on the edge of the PowerBook, then you need to move the path in a bit until the white edge is gone. To do this, use Command-H again to bring your path back. Then edit it and use another Command-H to see if it now looks correct. Scroll around the entire edge of the PowerBook, editing the path until you see no white borders and the path is smooth and clean. If you want to compare your work to mine, my final file, with all its layers, is called Power-BookAdLayers.psd and is in the the Extra Info Files folder for this chapter on the CD. Being able to edit a path as it is applied to a layer as a clipping path is a very useful feature. Notice that this edited path shows up in the Paths palette whenever

STEP 2: After using Command-H to hide the edges of the path so you can see any leftover white background around the edges of the PowerBook. If you do see some, Command-H again, then use the white Arrow tool to fine-tune the path.

Creating a New Background for the PowerBook

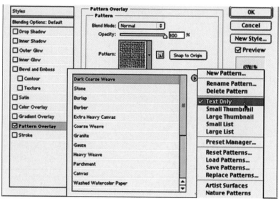

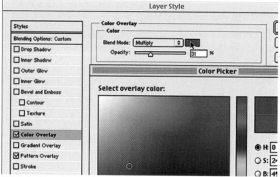

STEP 3: In the Layer Style dialog for the Background Color Fill layer, we clicked on Pattern Overlay to the left, then used the pop-up menu to set the display of patterns as Text Only. This allows you to pick the Dark Course Weave pattern, one of the Artist Surfaces patterns, without guessing which one it is from the Pattern icons.

STEP 3: Choosing a color with Color Overlay.

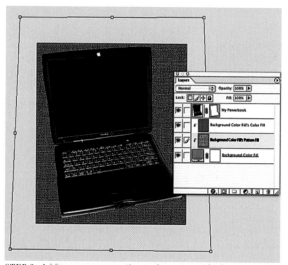

STEP 3: Adding some perspective to the pattern. I had you type H to switch to the Hand tool before going into Edit/Transform/Perspective because Perspective is not available while you are still using a vector tool.

this layer is active. **Use Command-Shift-S to save this file on your hard disk in Photoshop format as PowerBookLayers.**

ADDING EFFECTS TO YOUR BACKGROUND

STEP 3: **Shift-Option-double-click on the layer thumbnail for the Background Color Fill in the Layers palette to bring up the Layer Style palette for your Background Color Fill layer. You can also bring up this dialog by going to Blending Option from the Layers palette pop-up menu. First click on the words Pattern Overlay and choose the Dark Course Weave pattern, as shown to the left. Then click on the words Color Overlay and change the blend mode to Multiply. Experiment with Color and Opacity until you are happy with the color of your background with its Pattern Overlay. Choose OK in the Layer Style dialog and notice that the Course Weave pattern has no vanishing point.** If it were really sitting on a table and you were photographing it at an angle, as we are here, the pattern would seem closer together at the back of the table than it would at the front of the table. Notice that Edit/Free Transform is not currently an active option. **To add perspective to this pattern, you need to turn these effects into normal layers. Choose Layer/Layer Style/Create Layers, which will create a real layer to simulate each of your Layer Style effects. Click on the layer named Background Color Fill's Pattern Fill and zoom out so you can see the entire image plus some gray space around its edges. If not already in Full Screen mode with menu bar, type an F until you get there. You might also want to press Tab until all your palettes are removed from the screen. Press H to switch to the Hand tool. Choose Edit/Transform/Perspective, then click and drag on the handles at the top of the screen toward the center to give the pattern the perspective that seems right to you. If those handles are outside of the screen's area, use Spacebar-Option-click to zoom out until the handles are visible. After changing the perspective, you may need to use Spacebar-Command-click to zoom in so you can see the pattern in detail.**

MAKING THE LIGHTING MORE REALISTIC

STEP 4: **You might notice the bright highlight in the front-left corner of the PowerBook image. The light was coming from the front and above left. We want to make the background look as though it is lit in a similar way. Click back on the My PowerBook layer to activate it and choose Layer/New/Layer to create a new non-grouped layer named White. Choose Edit/Fill and fill this layer with 100% White. Now drag this layer down to the very bottom of the Layers palette. Click back on the Background Color Fill layer to activate it. Type G to switch to the Gradient tool and choose the gradient named "Black, White" by clicking on the gradient swatch in the Options bar at the top left of your screen. Because this is a Solid Color Fill layer, anything you do with the Gradient tool will happen to its layer mask. Zoom way out, then click your gradient way below the image and drag upwards and slightly to the right until you reach the top of**

Chapter 30: The PowerBook Ad

your background. When you release the mouse, this adds a gradient to the layer mask that is just a bit darker at the bottom than at the top. This reveals the White layer a bit toward the bottom of the image so you get the appearance of a light that is bright in front and fades toward the back. The brightness of the light in the front and how quickly it fades is determined by how you draw the gradient. To try different gradients, just keep drawing another one until you find the effect you like most.

ADDING A DROP SHADOW ON THE COMPUTER

STEP 5: **Click on the Layer thumbnail of the My PowerBook layer, then double-click to the right of the words My PowerBook to bring up the Layer Style dialog for this layer. Click on the word Drop Shadow toward the top left of the dialog to create a drop shadow.** When you are in Drop Shadow mode, you can move the cursor over the image and notice that it becomes the Move tool. If you click and drag on your drop shadow, you can easily move it to the position you want, relative to the object you are adding the shadow to. This will change the Distance and Angle values in the Drop Shadow sub-dialog. You can use the Opacity slider to change the darkness of the shadow, and you can use the Size slider to soften the edge of the shadow. The Spread controls how quickly the shadow blends into the background. You can also change the Blend mode of the shadow, although Multiply usually works quite well. Finally, if you click on the color box, you can bring up the Color Picker and change the hue of the shadow. **After adjusting your shadow as much as you can in the dialog, choose OK to add it to this layer as an effect. If you are not sure how dark to make it, it is better to make it darker than you think because you can always make it lighter later by lowering the opacity of the future Shadow layer. We need to turn this shadow into a regular layer because we want to use Edit/Free Transform to make it match the lighting of this image.**

Now choose Layer/Layer Style/Create Layer to turn this drop shadow effect into a real layer. If you get a message saying "Some Aspects of the Effects can not be Reproduced with Layers," just choose OK anyhow. Now you will have a new layer underneath your PowerBook layer named My PowerBook's Drop Shadow. Click on that new layer to make it active and choose Edit/Free Transform (Command-T). Zoom out so you can see the entire PowerBook and background. Holding

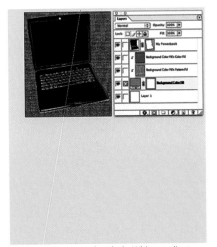

STEP 4: Here, using the Black, White gradient, we dragged the Gradient tool from way down at the bottom of the screen until it reached the top of the portable image. This makes a subtle gradient that is just a bit darker at the bottom than the top, so it brightens up the bottom of the background pattern by revealing a bit of the White layer underneath. If your gradient isn't quite right, another way to modify it after making it is to choose Command-L to go into Levels. Once in Levels, move the middle Brightness slider to the left and right to see how this adjusts the lighting effect of your gradient. Choose OK in Levels when you like what you've done.

STEP 5: Here we are using Edit/Free Transform with the Command key down to adjust the shape of the shadow layer. If you don't want to keep the Command key down, you can just choose Edit/Transform/Distort.

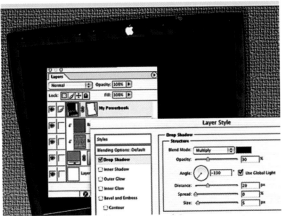

STEP 5: Here we see the setup for adding a drop shadow to the PowerBook using the Layer Style dialog. Notice the cursor at the top right of the screen where I can click and drag this shadow to whatever position I would like.

the Command key down allows you to click in a handle and drag it in any direction to make the shadow look the way you think it should to match the lighting on the PowerBook. When you are finished with this step, press Return to complete the Free Transform. Using the slider at the top of the Layers palette, you can still lower the opacity of this layer. To change the color of the shadow, use the Color Picker to pick a new Foreground color and choose Edit/Fill (Shift-Delete on the Mac and Shift-Backspace with Windows). Fill with the Preserve Transparency checkbox turned on in the Fill dialog, and after the Fill you may want to readjust the opacity again. Remember that you can also change the Blend mode of this layer, which will also affect the appearance of the shadow.

COLORIZING THE COMPUTER

STEP 6: **Click the Layer thumbnail of the My PowerBook layer so the next layer you add is above this one. Choose Layer/New Adjustment Layer/Hue/Saturation (Command-F4) and check the Use Previous Layer to Create Clipping Mask checkbox to cre-**

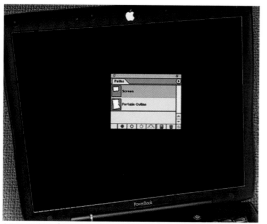

ate a grouped adjustment layer on top of the PowerBook layer. Turn on the Colorize checkbox to the right of the Hue/Saturation dialog. Now lower the Saturation considerably and move the Hue slider until you get the color that you want. After you click OK in this dialog box, double-click on the layer name to rename it Color Computer.** Because this adjustment layer is grouped with the PowerBook (and the mask on the PowerBook layer isolates it from the background), only the Hue of the computer will change. Having objects that are neutral gray, like this PowerBook, make it easy to colorize them using a Hue/Saturation adjustment layer set to Colorize.

STEP 6: The Layers palette setup for colorizing the PowerBook.

MAKING A PATH FOR THE COMPUTER SCREEN

STEP 7: **Type P to switch to the Pen tool and create a path around the edge of the screen area on the PowerBook. Be careful to make the path accurately around the edge of the PowerBook's viewing area. Bring up the Paths palette (Shift-F11) and double-click on Work Path, naming it Screen.**

ASSEMBLING THE SCREEN'S IMAGES

STEP 8: **Choose File/Open four times and open the following files from the folder named Ch30.The Power Book Ad on the *Photoshop CS Artistry* CD. Open the files named BanfLake.psd, RollerCoaster.psd, Toolbox.tif, and MenuBar.tif. Use the Window menu to bring the RollerCoaster image to the front, and then type F to put this file into Full Screen mode. Now use the Window menu to bring the BanfLake image to the front inside a normal window. Move the BanfLake window to the side so you can see part of the RollerCoaster image underneath. Type V to switch to the Move tool, then, while holding the Shift key down, drag and drop the BanfLake image on top of the RollerCoaster image. Having the Shift key down will center the BanfLake image on top of the RollerCoaster image. See the illustration of this process on the next page. Double-click on each layer in the Layers palette and name them with the correct names for each image. The bottom layer will be named RollerCoaster, and the next layer BanfLake.**

STEP 7: Use the Pen tool to create a path around the edge of the computer screen, then name it Screen in the Paths palette.

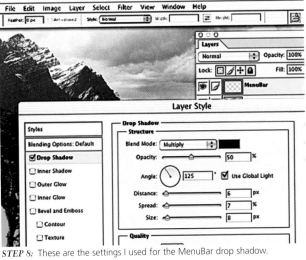

STEP 8: Using the Move tool with the Shift key down, click in the BanfLake window, then drag the cursor over on top of the RollerCoaster window where you should then release the Mouse button, which will drop the BanfLake image as a new layer on top of the RollerCoaster image.

STEP 8: These are the settings I used for the MenuBar drop shadow.

Use the Window menu to choose the MenuBar image, then drag and drop it so it is the layer on top of the BanfLake image. You'll get a message noting that the MenuBar image was created in the ColorMatch RGB color space, whereas the other two images are in Adobe RGB. Go ahead and choose OK to convert the MenuBar from ColorMatch RGB to Adobe RGB color space. Double-click on this layer and name it MenuBar. You'll notice that the MenuBar image is wider than the canvas width of the RollerCoaster and BanfLake images. Use Free Transform (Command-T) to scale the MenuBar layer until it spans the image. Somewhere between 55% and 56% should work. Because we're working on a Mac image and a Mac Powerbook, we're going to make the MenuBar look more like it does under OS X by adding a drop shadow. Double-click the MenuBar layer thumbnail to bring up the Layer Style dialog, then click the words Drop Shadow on the left of the dialog. This not only turns on the effect (which is what happens when you click the checkbox), but also brings up the settings for the effect so you can modify the default settings. In this instance, the default settings do a pretty good job; I made only minor changes that you can see in the illustration above.

Use the Window menu to switch to the Toolbox image then drag and drop it on top of the others. Use the Move tool to line up the Toolbox below the MenuBar and along the left edge of the screen. Double-click on the Toolbox layer and name it Toolbox. This layer is also too large and needs to be scaled using Free Transform. However, I only scaled this image to 60%. That seemed to maintain more of the actual relationship. Once again, you need to add a drop shadow to this layer. Instead of using the process that we used for the MenuBar, we'll simply copy the effect from the MenuBar layer and see how it works. To do this, click and drag the Drop Shadow sublayer in the Layers palette up to below the Toolbox layer. When you see the double black line, you can release the mouse and drop the effect. This is the easy way to copy the effect from layer to layer. Unfortunately, I didn't think the shadow looked right for this layer, so double-click the Drop Shadow sublayer itself to bring up the Layer Style dialog open to the Drop Shadow effect settings. I lowered the Opacity setting to 40% and made the Spread value 14. All the other settings I left the same. Once you have completed editing the shadow, type Command-A to select the area of the image window, then choose Image/Crop. This will trim any edges of layers

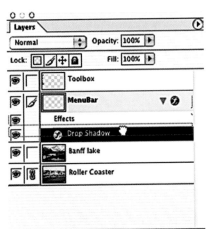

STEP 8: Click and drag the Drop Shadow effect from the MenuBar layer to the Toolbox layer. Release the mouse when you see the double black line.

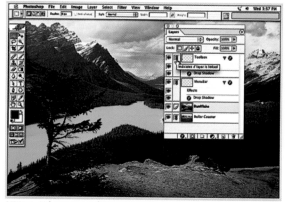

STEP 8: When you are finished with the ScreenLayers file, it should look like this with the Layers palette shown here. Notice that the middle linking column of the Layers palette is pointed out here.

STEP 9: This is how things will look after adding the ScreenLayers layers to the Screen Simulation layer set.

STEP 10: After you first go to Edit/Transform Distort, you'll see an outline of the entire ScreenLayers canvas area with handles on the corners.

that are wider than the image window. Type Command-D to get rid of the selection marquee.

Now click on the BanfLake layer to activate it, then click in the middle linking column for the other three layers in the Layers palette to link these other three layers to this BanfLake layer. Your Layers palette should now look like the one shown here. Choose File/Save As and save this file as ScreenLayers. You can now use the Window menu to switch to each of the BanfLake, Toolbox, and MenuBar images and close them. Your PowerBookLayers and ScreenLayers files should still be open.

MOVING THE SCREEN IMAGES TO THE POWERBOOK FILE

STEP 9: The active layer on the PowerBookLayers file should be the top Color Computer layer, and this file should be in Full Screen mode. Choose Layer/New/Layer Set and call this set Screen Simulation. Use the Window menu to activate the ScreenLayers file and type F until it is no longer in Full Screen mode. The active layer in this file should be BanfLake. Move this window over to the left until you can see the PowerBookLayers file underneath. With the Move tool (V), click on the BanfLake image, inside the ScreenLayers file window, and drag and drop it on top of the PowerBookLayers file. All four layers of the ScreenLayers image should move over to the PowerBookLayers file and into the Screen Simulation layer set. Click on the words Screen Simulation to activate the layer set, and then use the Window menu or Shift-F11 to bring up the Paths palette. Click on the Screen path you made earlier to bring it up on your screen. From the pop-up menu of the Paths palette, choose Make Selection to turn this path into a selection with a Feather value of zero and Anti-Aliased turned on. Now choose Layer/Add Layer Mask/Reveal Selection to add this selection to the Screen Simulation layer set as a layer mask. You'll notice that this entire ScreenLayers composite now appears as though it is inside the screen of the PowerBook computer. The only problem is the image is not lined up properly with the perspective of this PowerBook computer, whose screen is rotated back somewhat with the entire computer not directly facing the camera angle. There are various approaches to getting this image to look correct within the computer's screen area, and most of them won't work that well. The method I eventually discovered for doing this, pointed out to me by a student of mine who also worked at Adobe at the time, is actually very simple and works better than anything else I had thought of.

GETTING THE IMAGES TO LOOK CORRECT WITHIN THE POWERBOOK'S SCREEN AREA

STEP 10: The first thing you want to do is choose Filter/Blur/Gaussian Blur and put a 2-pixel blur on the layer mask you just added to the Screen Simulation layer set. This will soften the transition between the edge of the screen and the images that will be displayed inside it. This will look like a shadow you might see around the edge of a computer screen. **Now click back on the BanfLake layer to make it active. Use the Tab key to get rid of your palettes, and then use Option-Spacebar-click to zoom out so you can see the entire image on the screen. Now choose Edit/Transform/Distort, which will bring up a frame around the edges of the canvas for your four screen layers. The cursor will have changed into a gray arrow, which you can use to click and drag the four corner handles to distort this image. What you want to do is drag each of the four corner handles until they line up with the four corners of the actual computer screen. While zoomed out so you can see the entire top of the computer, move each of the corner handles to its respective corner of the computer screen.**

Now use Command-Option-0 to zoom to 100% and look more closely at the top-left corner. Move the handle for that corner inward for a moment so you can clearly see the top-left corner of the PowerBook's screen area. Now move the handle back so the corner of the image will be slightly to the left and above the corner of the PowerBook screen. This will allow the blurred edge mask to softly trim a little from the image and give the appearance of a slight shadow at the edge of the PowerBook screen area. Now move to the top-right handle and do the same thing. Move it down and to the left of the actual corner and give the computer time to refresh the screen so you can actually see the corner. Now move the handle back into place getting it exactly where you want it so the mask gives it a slightly softer edge appearance, simulating a shadow there. As you work on each corner at 100% zoom factor, you can hold the Spacebar down to get the Hand tool, and then click and drag when you want to scroll the image inside Photoshop.

While within Transform/Distort, you can move each of these corners as many times as you want until you are happy with the results. After getting all four corners where you want them, press Return to complete the distort. You will notice that the image details are sharper now than with the preview you saw using the Distort tool. **If you need to, you can use the Move tool (V) to move the image around within the Screen Simulation mask area. Once you are in the Move tool, you can use the Arrow keys to move this**

STEP 10: The first step is to click on each of these corner handles and move it to a corner of the actual computer screen area.

STEP 10: While zoomed to 100%, line up the top-left corner so you can see the blurred mask acting like a shadow along the edge of your ScreenLayers image. You can also use Command-H to hide the edges of the transform, which lets you see the composite without their interference. Another Command-H will bring those edges back.

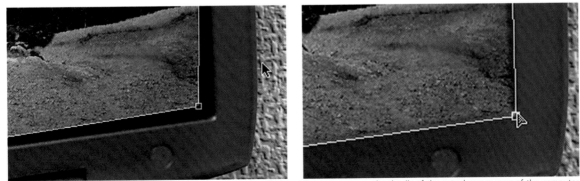

STEP 10: While zoomed into 100%, you can move a corner handle in a bit so you can see the details of the actual corner area of the computer screen. When you can clearly see those details, then you can move that corner back to exactly where you want it, as shown on the right.

Getting the Images to Look Correct Within the PowerBook's Screen Area

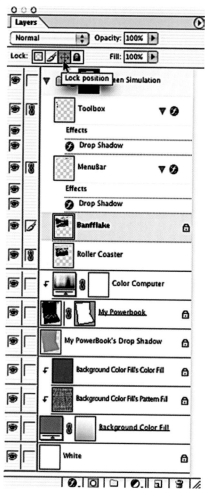

STEP 10: Here we see the final Layers palette for the first composite image. It is a good idea to use the Lock Position icon at the top of the Layers palette to lock each layer that has a mask or some other element that you don't want to accidentally move. In the top five layers, we only had to lock the BanfLake layer, because linking the other four to it also stops them from being moved. Although you can't lock just movement on the Screen Simulation set, you can lock the entire set using the rightmost locking icon while the set's layer is active. This will stop you from making further modifications to any layer within the set, including the mask that defines the screen area.

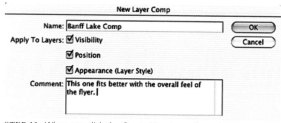

STEP 11: When you click the Create New Layer Comp button, you can name the comp and choose the options you need.

image one pixel at a time. When you are happy with its location, you should lock one of the layers, such as the BanfLake layer. Because all four of these layers are linked together, locking one of them will lock them all. Photoshop does not give you the option of locking just movement on the Screen Simulation layer set (with its attached layer mask) that you would not want accidentally moved. You can, however, activate the BanfLake layer and turn on the link column of the Screen Simulation layer set to link it to the four layers inside that set. This will stop it from being accidentally moved. You should also lock any of the other layers in this image that have pixel data or a mask in them. If you are not happy with the way the corners look on the PowerBook screen, you can change their shape by painting black with a soft brush in the corners of the MyPowerBook layer's layer mask.

USING THE LAYER COMPS PALETTE

Photoshop CS introduced the Layer Comps palette, a feature that has been requested by many of us for a long time. At the end of a project, when everything you need has been added to the file, it would be nice to save versions to show the client with different layers visible, in slightly altered positions, or with different blend modes and effects. Before Photoshop CS you had to save each different version of the file. If you were working with a large image, this took quite a bit of disk space. If you saved flattened versions to save disk space, any minor adjustments to a proof would require you to go back and remember exactly what you had in the version you needed to work with. With the Layer Comps palette you simply save a comp for each version and turn on that comp to quickly switch between versions. You can even make changes to a comp and update it. Let's see how it works in action.

STEP 11: Go to Window/Layer Comps to bring up the palette. You've just adjusted the image to have Banff Lake showing on the screen and it looks really good, so you definitely want to save this version of your file as a comp. Click the Create New Layer Comp button on the bottom of the palette. It's the one next to the Trash icon. A dialog box gives you the opportunity to name your layer comp as well as choose which options you need to remain in place for this particular comp. You may need only the layer visibility to remain the same if you are not planning to add or change any effects or reposition the layers. For maximum safety, check all three boxes. This will bring you back (as closely as possible) to the version that you are saving now. I say "as closely as possible" because the Layer Comps palette has its limitations. If you rearrange the stacking order of the layers in the Layers palette, the Layer Comps palette will not take you back to the previous arrangement. If you delete a layer, the Layer Comps palette will not bring it back. If you run a filter on a layer after you have created a comp, the Layer Comps palette will always show the filtered state and not the version you started with. For this reason, you want to have your image as complete as possible before you begin saving layer comps. It is a tool for final approval more than a tool for creating neat effects. **Name this comp Banff Lake Comp and check all three boxes.** The Comment area is a place for you to make notes that will explain to your associates, boss, or client any issues about the comp. I've typed in information here to illustrate using the dialog; **you don't need to type anything in the Comment area for the exercise.**

STEP 12: Next, click the Eye icon for the BanfLake layer to turn this layer off. The RollerCoaster image is now visible with the Toolbox and MenuBar. **Click the Create New Layer Comp button again and name this comp Santa Cruz.**

STEP 13: If you look at my version of this image in the file called PowerBookAdLayers.psd inside the Extra Info Files folder for this chapter, you'll see that I added a note to this comp as well. The note says, "John likes the Toolbox with less shadow." And really, when you look at the difference between the Banff Lake comp and the Santa Cruz comp, the shadow does seem to look heavier on the Santa Cruz image even though you haven't made any changes. Luckily, you can edit the layer effect, then update the Santa Cruz comp.

Double-click the Drop Shadow effect for the Toolbox layer. This brings up the settings that you originally used for the shadow. Click the Use Global Light checkbox to turn it off. You can type in the numbers you see in the illustration here, or you can click and drag the shadow so it looks right to you. If you're on the Mac, just look at your own screen and try to match it. **Once you're happy with the shadow, click OK. As soon as you have done this, click the name of the Santa Cruz comp (not the icon). Now click the Update Layer Comp button that looks like two arrows in a circle.** This changes the state of the comp to match the last edits you made. If you mistakenly click the icon for the Santa Cruz comp and not the name, you go back to the state of the comp without the edits you just made. If this happens, click on the icon for the Last Document State, then click the name Santa Cruz and make your update. The Last Document State comp can also be used when editing to judge which version you like best, then if you want to make a new comp from it or update a comp, you can.

STEP 14: **Finally, make a third comp by turning off the Toolbox and MenuBar layers and showing a full screen version of the Santa Cruz roller coaster. Name this comp Santa Cruz No Menu.** Now you can click the icons for each state to see which one you like best, or use the Apply Previous or Apply Next Selected Layer Comp buttons on the bottom of the palette to scroll through the comps. These buttons do not show you the Last Document State, so you'll have to click that icon if you've made adjustments that you want to check. It's fun to watch the Layers palette change as you scroll through the comps. Photoshop is an incredibly powerful compositing tool and the Layer Comps palette is one more addition to your digital tool set. Have fun!

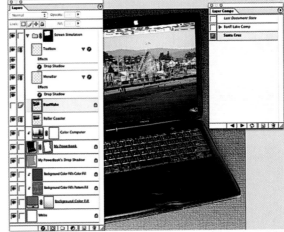

STEP 12: Here's the setup for the Santa Cruz comp. All I've done at this point is turn off the BanfLake layer Eye icon.

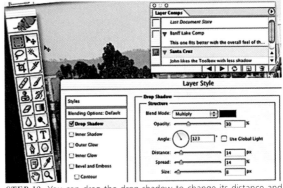

STEP 13: You can drag the drop shadow to change its distance and angle. I also lowered the Opacity to 30%.

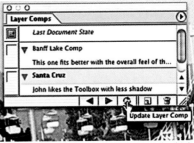

STEP 13: The Update button changes the high-lighted comp to match the most recent state of the document.

Using the Layer Comps Palette

CALCULATIONS, PATTERNS, FILTERS, COMPOSITING, AND EFFECTS

USE THE TYPE TOOL AND LAYER STYLES

WORK WITH FILTERS, TEXTURES, PATTERNS, AND BITMAPS

PAINT WITH BRUSH OPTIONS AND TOOL PRESETS

UNDERSTAND THE BLEND MODES AND USE THEIR POWER

USING CALCULATIONS AND APPLY IMAGE

LEARN LAYER VECTOR MASKS AND SHAPE LAYERS

Fernwood Pier on Salt Spring Island, BC, is a beautiful place to go for the sunset and even well after the sunset when I took this with my Pentax 6x7 and 45mm lens using Fuji Velvia film. Getting the blues in the foreground to print correctly in CMYK will not be easy! Scanned with the Polaroid Sprintscan 120, this makes a great print on my Epson 7600. We may be holding workshops here soon.

3 BLEND MODES, CALCULATIONS, AND APPLY IMAGE

How each of the Blend modes work; the subtleties of using them in Calculations, Apply Image, Layers, Layer Styles, Layer Sets, Fill, and the painting tools; when and how to use Calculations versus Apply Image versus Layers.

The Blend modes are used to determine how two sets of image information combine. The two sets of image information can be of various types within Photoshop. The first type might be a photographic image, called the *base color* in the Adobe Photoshop manual, and the second a solid color, which Adobe calls the *blend color*, that can be painted or filled on top of the first image. You can do this using one of the painting tools or the Fill command. If you create a layer that is a solid color, the *blend color*, then you can combine this layer with a photographic image on an underlying layer (or layers) by using a Blend mode in that solid color layer via the Layers palette. The cumulative effect of all underlying layers before the addition of the solid color layer would then be the *base color*. Blend modes also appear in a variety of places within the Photoshop Layer Styles palette. There they are usually affecting the way a shadow or effect will look. You can use the Apply Image command with different Blend modes to combine two-color photographic images that are in separate documents and have the exact same pixel dimensions. Finally, you can use the Calculations command with Blend modes to combine two images of the same size when you want a black-and-white mask channel as a result. The Blend modes appear in the painting tools, the Fill tool, the Layers palette, the Layer Styles palette, the Apply Image command, the Calculations command, and the Stroke command. Not all of the Blend mode options are offered in each of these areas. As we explain each Blend mode, you'll see why some of them make more sense in one area or another. Many of these options also offer you a way to use a mask as you combine the two groups of image information. The mask will affect the parts of the two groups that are combined.

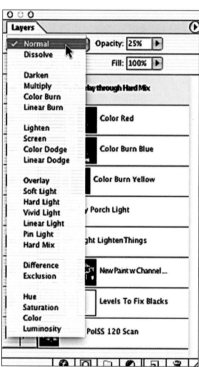

The Blend modes for the Layers palette, which I will call the standard set of Blend modes. These are also the Blend modes that appear in Layer Styles. The organization for the Blend modes has to do with neutral colors. The Darken, Multiply, Color Burn, and Linear Burn group all have white as their neutral color. The Lighten, Screen, Color Dodge and Linear Dodge group all have black as their neutral color. The group starting with Overlay and ending with Pin Light all have 50% gray as their neutral color. Though Hard Mix is grouped here, it has no true neutral color. 50% is the most neutral color with this mode. The neutral color is the color which causes a particular Blend mode to have no effect on underlying layers.

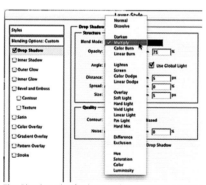

The Blend modes for layer styles appear in various places within the Layer Styles dialog but are usually the same set of Blend modes that you get in the Layers palette.

THE TOOLS FOR BLENDING

First, we discuss the different tools and methods for blending and when it makes the most sense to use each of them. Later, we discuss each of the Blend modes and its unique applications within each of the different blending tools. You can find many of the images we use in this chapter in the Blend Modes Cals & Apl Im folder on the CD.

Although this is not entirely a step-by-step hands-on session, we encourage you to play and explore these techniques with the images. By experimenting on your own, you learn new things, and you can have a lot of fun, too.

THE FILL COMMAND

The Edit/Fill command (Shift-Delete) is used to fill a selection, or the entire layer if there is no selection, with color (the foreground or background color, or a color you choose from the Color Picker), black, white, 50% gray, a pattern, or with information from the History Brush location. The Blend mode and Opacity in the Fill tool just determine how this filling image will combine with what was there before. Normal, at 100% Opacity, completely covers what was there before with the new color, pattern, or image. I mention image because you can change the "Use" pop-up to fill from the current History Brush setting or from a pattern. An Opacity of 50% will give half what was there before and half the new filled image or color. We usually use Fill to completely cover a selection or the entire image with a solid color or a tint. We also use Fill a lot to revert the selected area to a Snapshot or other location in the History palette. When you use Fill, you need to pick a Source, Opacity, and Blend mode before you do the operation, and then you have to undo it if you want to change it. If you need to prototype the opacity or mode of your Fill, use the layer techniques we show you in this book because it is quicker to make variations in the Layers palette.

THE PAINTING TOOLS

You use a painting tool when you want to apply an effect by hand and softly blend it in and out, like you would do with an airbrush or paintbrush. These tools in Photoshop have a lot more power, however, due to the magic of digital imaging and the blending modes. Go through Chapter 4: "The Tool Palette" and Chapter 35: "Painting in Photoshop" to learn about the subtleties of each painting tool. With the Blend Mode options in the painting tools, you don't just lay down paint, or even a previous version of the image. Instead, you can control how this paint or image combines with what is already there. Add the Photoshop History palette and the ability to use the History Brush to paint from any step in the last 1000 steps, and you have super power and flexibility. This History Brush also allows you to use the Blend modes. See Chapter 8: "History Palette, History Brush, and Snapshots," for more information and painting from history.

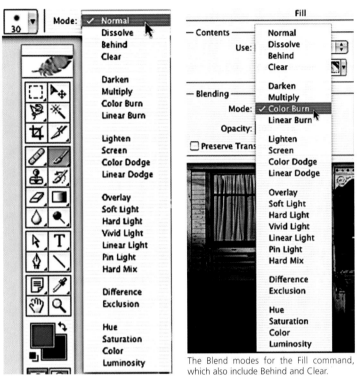

The Blend modes for the painting tools. Notice the addition of Behind, which paints only in the transparent areas, and Clear, which paints only in the non-transparent areas.

The Blend modes for the Fill command, which also include Behind and Clear.

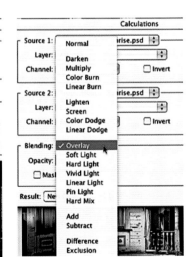

The Blend modes for the Apply Image command, which additionally have Add and Subtract and don't have Hue, Saturation, Color, or Luminosity.

The Blend modes for Calculations, which also include Add and Subtract but don't have Dissolve or Hue through Luminosity.

The Heartsinger CD Cover image produced using many layers and blend modes.

The Century Plant image.

The Las Vegas Night image.

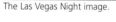

The Vegas Lights mask channel.

COMBINING IMAGES USING LAYERS AND BLEND MODES

Layers and Adjustment layers are the most powerful ways to combine two or more images while keeping the most options open for further variations and many versions of your composite. Sometimes we use layers even when we are dealing with a pattern or solid color. The reason is that with layers, you can always go back and change something, move something, and change the opacity or Blend mode without having to totally redo your image. Unlike the contents of the History palette, which go away when you close the file, layers stay around as long as you want. You can try an effect and be able to turn it on and off at will. Layers gives you the most sophisticated control of the Blend modes as well as many other abilities at the same time. If you don't understand layers, and if you haven't read Chapter 7: "Layers, Layer Masks, and Adjustment Layers," you should read it now before you continue. When you use layers, your files may get much bigger because many layers add at least the original size of the file in that layer to your document size. Adjustment layers allow you to do color changes and some types of fills with a new layer without adding all the extra file size. Layered documents have to be saved in Photoshop, TIFF, or PDF format to maintain the flexible layer information. Still, layers are WAY COOL!

COMBINING IMAGES, LAYERS, AND CHANNELS USING APPLY IMAGE

The basic function of Apply Image is to copy one image, layer, or channel, called the Source, and use it to replace the Target, which is another image, layer, or channel of exactly the same pixel resolution. To combine two items with Apply Image, they must be exactly the same width and height in pixels. The two images are combined using a blending mode and opacity that are chosen from the Apply Image dialog box. You can optionally choose a mask, which will combine the images only where the mask is white. Apply Image is useful when copying a channel or layer from one place to another, especially when you want to put it on top of an existing channel or layer and combine the two with a Blend mode.

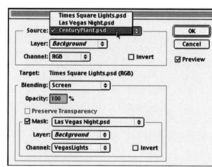

Here we see most of the possible options of Apply Image. Before we entered Image/Apply Image, we made Times Square Lights the active document in Photoshop. The active document or layer is always selected as the Target of Apply Image, so you will be changing that document, channel, or layer. The Source pop-up window shows you only open documents that are the same pixel size and dimensions as the target document. Here, we chose the Century Plant as the Source. The Blending pop-up is where you choose the Blend mode. There is an optional mask, selected here, that causes the blending to happen only within the areas of the mask that are white. If the Preview button is on, you see the results of the Apply Image in the Target window. This lets you try different options and see what they do.

The results of the Apply Image settings shown to the left. The Century Plant image is brought into the Times Square Lights image, shown on the next page, where the Las Vegas Night mask was white. In that area, it is blended using the Screen Blending mode.

Chapter 31: Blend Modes, Calculations, and Apply Image

Before you enter Apply Image, the image, layer, or channel you want to target should be active. This will be modified when you leave Apply Image by choosing OK, so you may want to first make a copy of that target item.

If the Preview button is on, you can see the results of the operation in the Target window. In choosing the source, you can pick any open document, layer, or channel, as long as it's the same exact pixel dimensions as the target. Like the source, the mask can be any open document, layer, or channel that is the same pixel dimensions as the target. The Preserve Transparency option, which is enabled if the target has transparent areas, will stop the Apply Image command from changing any transparent areas within a layer. Both the source and the mask have an Invert checkbox that you can check to turn that channel or layer to its negative.

In this chapter, we use three images that we have cropped to be exactly the same pixel size. They are the Las Vegas Night image, the Century Plant image, and the Times Square Lights image. The Las Vegas Night image has a mask, called VegasLights,

The Times Square Lights image.

The Las Vegas Night image.

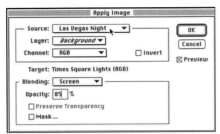

Here we see a more simple application of Apply Image. The source, target, and resulting images are shown here. The Screen Blend mode is analogous to taking transparencies of the two images and projecting them onto the same screen from two different slide projectors. The light areas of the images are emphasized. Setting the Opacity to 85% made the Las Vegas Lights a little less bright in the composite image below.

The composite image from the above Apply Image settings, which looks different than the example on the previous page because that example used a different source image and also used a mask to decide which areas were to be composited.

that is white where the neon lights are. There are no particular masks in the Century Plant image. Here are several examples using Apply Image, with the same three images, so you can get an idea what the command does. If you want to get a result that is color rather than black-and-white, you need to use Apply Image instead of Calculations. The effects you can create with Apply Image can also be achieved with layers, by first copying each different document into a separate layer within the same document. Layers give you more flexibility because the different layers don't have to start out being the exact same size, and you can move them around side-to-side as well as above-and-below in relationship to each other. Effects within layers can also be tried and undone in multiple combinations by turning the Eye icons on and off.

You should use Apply Image mostly in cases where you already know the spatial relationship between the objects being combined, and you have to do the operation quickly for some production purpose. Motion picture and multimedia work (where you are compositing many frames of two sequences together that have been preshot in registration, to be lined up exactly) is a good example of how you would use Apply Image. This process could be automated over hundreds of frames by using actions with a batch or by using another application automation tool like AppleScript.

COMBINING CHANNELS USING CALCULATIONS

The main purpose of the Calculations command is to use the Blend modes to combine images, layers, or channels and end up with a single black-and-white channel as the result. When you need a color result, use Layers or Apply Image; when you need a channel result, use Calculations. Calculations provides for two source files, Source 1 and Source 2, and a Result that can be either a New Document, New

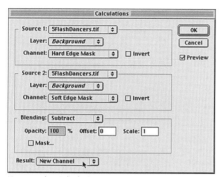

Here are the Calculations settings to produce the mask of the glow without the sign. When doing a Subtract, the item that you want to subtract should be in Source 1. The item you are subtracting from should be in Source 2. In this case, the result was a new channel. Depending on the choice we make for the Result, it could be a new channel in the existing file, a new file itself, or a selection in the existing file.

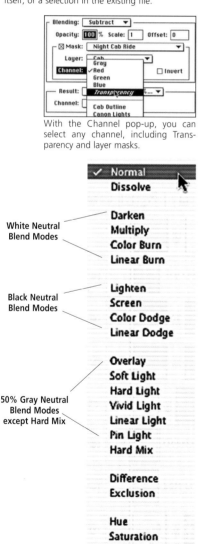

With the Channel pop-up, you can select any channel, including Transparency and layer masks.

White Neutral Blend Modes

Black Neutral Blend Modes

50% Gray Neutral Blend Modes except Hard Mix

The Flashdancers sign, where we want to make a mask of just the glow without the sign so we can have separate control over each.

We have a hard-edge mask of just the sign. We put this into Source 1.

We have a soft-edge mask of the glow, including the area of the sign. We put this into Source 2.

Here is the resulting glow mask where we subtracted the hard-edge mask from the soft-edge mask.

To move the sign to another background, we used the hard-edge mask to copy the text into one layer and the glow mask to copy the glow into another layer. We then had separate color, blending, and blur control over each item in the sign that allowed us to get the result we wanted on the new background.

Channel, or a Selection. When you enter Calculations, the two source files are set to the active window within Photoshop. You can use the pop-up menus to change any of these source files to any other open file that has the same pixel dimensions. The source files are the two that will be combined using the Blend mode that you choose. The Layer pop-up on each of these files is available for layered documents and allows you to choose the merged layer, which is the composite of all layers that currently have their Eye icons on or any other layer in the document.

The Channel pop-up allows you to choose any channel in the chosen file or layer. To access a layer mask channel, you need to first choose the layer that owns that layer mask. You can also choose the Transparency channel, which is a mask of any transparent areas in the chosen layer. This interface allows you to blend any two documents, layers, or channels that are open by using the Blending modes, and to then put the result into a new channel, document, or selection. These open items must have the same pixel dimensions as the active window. The blending interface also allows an optional mask, which will force the blending to happen only in the areas that are white in the mask. Both source items and the mask have an Invert checkbox to optionally invert any of them before doing the composite. You will learn more about Apply Image and Calculations as you go through each of the Blend modes next.

UNDERSTANDING EACH BLEND MODE

We'll go through the Blend modes that you see in the Layers palette Blend mode pop-up in order and by the way they are grouped. The five Blend modes that occur in other parts of Photoshop (Behind, Clear, Add, Subtract, and Pass Through) will be covered at the end of this chapter.

When you use the Fill command, you fill a selected area. You can fill with the foreground or background colors as well as from the History palette or from a pattern.

Chapter 31: Blend Modes, Calculations, and Apply Image

All these options are available to paint from by using different painting tools. When you paint, you select your "fill area" as you paint instead of by filling a selection or an entire layer. In either case, the modes work in the same way. These Blend modes also apply to layers, the Calculations and Apply Image commands, and the many other functions within Photoshop that can use Blend modes.

NORMAL

When painting or filling in Normal mode, you are filling the selected or painted area with the foreground or background color, a History state, or a pattern. Normal mode at 100% Opacity and 100% Fill for a top layer, or any layer, in the Layers palette means that that layer will be opaque. You will not see any of the layers below through a layer set up that way. You use Normal mode and 100% Opacity in Calculations or Apply Image to copy the source layer or channel to the target, or destination layer, or channel without any blending. This totally replaces the target, or destination, with the source. In the Layers Palette, or Layer Styles dialog, the Opacity controls both the visibility of the pixels within that layer as well as the Layer Effects applied to that layer whereas the Fill controls the visibility of just the pixels within a layer. Consider a layer containing an object surrounded by transparency where you used Layer Styles to add a drop shadow to that layer. If the regular Opacity was set to 100% and you then set the Fill to 0%, you would no longer see the object but you'd still see the drop shadow. You could change the appearance of that drop shadow by changing its Blend mode within the Layer Styles dialog.

I added an Outer Glow effect to the type layer, then lowered the Fill opacity to 0%. At this point, changing the blend mode of the layer will have no effect on the appearance of the image. If you want to change the way the glow interacts with the rest of the image, you have to do that in the Outer Glow Layer Styles dialog.

DISSOLVE

Depending on the opacity of the dissolve, this mode appears to take the opacity as a percentage of the pixels from the *blend color* and place them on top of the *base color*. The *base color* is the color or image that was there before the dissolve. The *blend color* is the color or image that is being dissolved on top of the *base color* or image. Try this with two layers, setting the mode between them to Dissolve. If you set the Opacity to 100%, you get all of the top layer and don't see the bottom layer. The same thing happens if you use a Fill of 100% or paint at 100% in Dissolve mode. When you set the Opacity to 50% and look at the pixels up close, you will see that there are about 50% pixels from the top layer and 50% from the bottom. If you set the Opacity to 10%, only 10% of the pixels are from the top layer or *blend color*.

With Dissolve, the pixels seem to be entirely from one image or the other; there don't seem to be any blended pixels. If you want to achieve this type of look between two images but have more control over the pattern used to create the dissolve, create a layer mask on the top layer filled with solid white. Now, go into Filter/Noise/Add Noise and add Gaussian noise to the layer mask. Where the noise is black, the bottom layer will show through and you will get an effect similar to Dissolve. This way you can use Levels or Curves or even a filter to change the pattern in the layer mask and thus change how the two images are combined. The more noise you add, the more you will see of the bottom layer. Also, in this case, some of the pixels can actually be blends between the layers, especially if you use Gaussian Blur to blur your layer mask, too. Dissolve is not an option with Apply Image or Calculations, but you can get a similar effect here by using a Gaussian noise mask as you combine images, layers, and channels.

The Las Vegas Lights layer at 30% opacity in Dissolve mode on top of the Century Plant image.

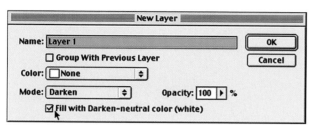

When creating a new layer with a Blend mode that has a neutral color, you can fill the layer with the neutral color for that mode. The layer will then start out with the chosen Blend mode and also be filled with the correct neutral color.

THE WHITE NEUTRAL BLEND MODES

The Blend modes in the first group, right below Dissolve, all have white as their neutral color. This means that wherever the blend color is white, these particular Blend modes will have no effect on the base color. When you choose Layer/New/Layer and select a Blend mode from this group in the New Layer dialog, you will be asked if you want to fill that layer with the white neutral color. You can then paint in this area with colors or patterns that are darker than white to influence what this layer will do to your overall composite. Depending on the Blend mode chosen from this group, your results will be different.

DARKEN

The Darken Blend mode is easy to understand. In the Darken mode, each of the corresponding pixels from the original image and the *blend color*, pattern, or image are compared, and the darker of the two is chosen for the result. If the *blend color* is white, this Blend mode's neutral color, you can easily see that the *base color*

The shoes and the glasses have each been placed here separately.

You have one mask for the shoes.

will then always be darker or the same so nothing will change. This Blend mode and Lighten, its opposite, are most useful in combining masks to create new masks. An example of this, shown here, would be the situation in which you have pasted two objects into a composite scene, and for each object you have a mask. When you paste in Photoshop, you always have a mask of the object, which is the transparency of the object's layer. You have a mask of each separate object, and now you need one mask that contains both objects at the same time.

Using Calculations to set the Blend mode to Lighten between the two masks will create the mask of both the objects. You can then use the inverse of this mask to give you a mask of the background. To do this in one step, select the Invert checkboxes on both the Source channels in Calculations. Because both Source masks have now been inverted, you would have to use Darken to combine the two masks and get the final inverted mask with the white background.

Another mask for the glasses.

These Calculations settings using Lighten will create the new mask below to the left.

MULTIPLY

Multiply is a very useful Blend mode that is available within all the Blend mode pop-ups. When you multiply two images together, it is analogous to what you would see if both the images were transparencies and you sandwiched them together and placed them on a light table or projected them onto the same screen. Anything that was black in either image would be black in the resulting composite image. Anything that was white or clear in either image would let you see through it to what was in the

This mask of both shoes and glasses was created with Calculations using Lighten.

To create this background mask with a single calculation, invert both the source masks and use Darken instead of Lighten.

The original Glow mask we want to drop a gradient into.

Doing a Load Selection on the glow, left, and dropping the gradient into the selected area, produces the halo around the glow at the right side.

Unwanted halo effect

Create the gradient in a separate mask channel and use Calculations to Multiply for the effect at right.

A Calculations Multiply of the Gradient and Glow mask channels drops the gradient into the glow area without a halo.

A powerful use for Multiply is to seamlessly add a gradient to an existing selection. Let's say we wanted to use the Glow mask to create a glow that was bright at the left side and fading toward the right. To do this, we would want to drop a gradient into this mask. If you do a Load Selection on the mask and then create the gradient within that selection, you will get a light halo around the edge of the gradient toward the right side. This is caused by the loaded selection. To avoid getting this halo, just create the gradient in a separate channel and then multiply the two channels together, giving you a better fade.

other image in that area. When you multiply two images together, the 0–255 values of the corresponding pixels in each image are actually multiplied together using the following formula:

(Source 1) x (Source 2) / 255 = destination

Just like multiplication in mathematics, the order of the Source 1 and Source 2 images doesn't matter. Dividing by 255 at the end forces all the values to be in the 0–255 range. You can see that when either Source value is 0, black, you are going to get 0 as the result. When either Source value is 255, white, you are going to get the other Source value as the result, because 255/255 = 1, so you end up multiplying the other Source value by 1. Multiply is used as the default Blend mode for many of the blend mode pop-ups that occur in the Layer Styles palette. Its sister Blend mode, Screen, also shows up there as the default in some cases.

COLOR BURN

Color Burn darkens and adds contrast to the original image, the *base color*, as the *blend color* goes further towards black. A Color Burn with white does nothing; then as the *blend color* gets darker, the original image picks up darkness and color more and more from the *blend color*. See the examples of using Color Burn here and also later in this chapter.

A Multiply of the Century Plant and Las Vegas Night images, shown earlier in this chapter, emphasizes the darker areas of each image. Notice the differences in the illustration on the next page, showing a Screen of the same two images.

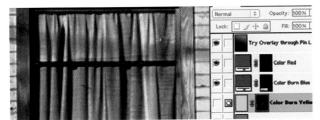

This is the original window frame without the Color Burn effect on.

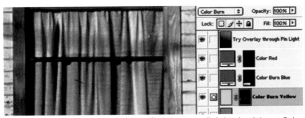

In this window frame, we have intensified the warm lighting by doing a Color Burn of the solid yellow color. Notice that the Blend mode of the active layer is set to Color Burn. Its layer mask is painted white in the window frame areas where I wanted the warm color effect.

LINEAR BURN

With Linear Burn, the *base color* will be darkened as the *blend color* gets darker and darker. White is the neutral color for this Blend mode and black will completely blacken the *base color*. Linear Burn appears to pick up less of the *blend color* and more of the blend lightness values than Color Burn does where Color Burn will change the contrast. We have another fun alternative to play with!

THE BLACK NEUTRAL BLEND MODES

The Blend modes in the second group, starting with Lighten, all have black as their neutral color. This means that wherever the blend color is black, these particular Blend modes will have no effect on the base color. When you choose Layer/New/Layer and select a Blend mode from this second group in the New Layer dialog, you will be asked if you want to fill that layer with the black neutral color. You can then paint in this area with colors or patterns that are lighter than black to influence what this layer will do to your overall composite. Depending on the Blend mode chosen from this group, your results will be different.

LIGHTEN

In the Lighten mode, each of the corresponding pixels from the original image and the blend color, pattern, or image are compared, and the lighter of the two is chosen for the result. This Blend mode is most useful in combining masks to create new masks. See the example of doing this, using Lighten and Darken, earlier in this chapter. Comparing Lighten to Screen, if you use Screen the two images will appear to be blended together more. Screen often looks better, because of this blending effect, when you are working with photographs. Lighten is more useful when you are dealing with masks.

SCREEN

Screen is sort of the opposite of Multiply, in that when you do a Screen between two images, anything that is white in either of the images will be white in the resulting image. Anything that is black in either image will show the other image in that black area. Screen, like Multiply, is also available in all the different Blend mode pop-ups. When you Screen two images together, it is analogous to what you would see if both the images were projected from two different slide projectors onto the same screen. Here is the formula for Screen:

$$255 - ((255 - Source\ 1) \times (255 - Source\ 2) / 255) = Destination$$

You can simulate the Screen command using the Multiply command if you first invert both of the Source images and then multiply them together, and finally, invert

A screen of the Century Plant and Las Vegas Night images emphasizes the lighter areas of each image. Compare this to the Multiply of the two shown on the previous page.

The positive version of the image in the examples on the next page.

The Black to White layer by itself.

The Spectrum layer by itself.

the result of that multiply. That is exactly what this formula for Screen does: (255 - Source1) does an Invert of Source 1. With the Screen formula then: The Invert of Source 1 is multiplied by the Invert of Source 2 and then is divided by 255. That part of the formula does the multiply of the two inverted images. Finally, subtracting that result from 255 at the end does the Invert of the result of that multiply, giving you a Screen. The important thing to remember between Screen and Multiply is that a Screen of two images will emphasize the lighter areas and a Multiply will emphasize the darker areas.

COLOR DODGE

Color Dodge brightens the original image, changing its contrast as the blending color goes further toward white. A Color Dodge with black does nothing; then as the blending color gets lighter, the original image picks up brightness and color more and more from the blending color. Creation of the Positive image here is explained in the "Hue, Saturation, Color, and Luminosity" section later in this chapter.

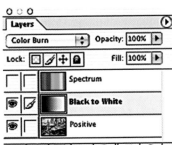

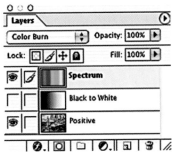

Layer setup for Black to White Color Burn and Dodge below left.

Layer setup for Spectrum Color Burn and Dodge below right.

Color Burn of the top Black blending to White layer with the positive image in the layer below.

Color Burn of the top Spectrum layer with the positive image in the layer below.

Color Dodge of the top Black blending to White layer with the positive image in the layer below.

Color Dodge of the top Spectrum layer with the positive image in the layer below.

Linear Dodge

With Linear Dodge, the *base color* will be lightened as the *blend color* gets lighter and lighter. Black is the neutral color for this Blend mode and white will completely whiten the *base color*. Linear Dodge appears to pick up less of the *blend color* and more of the blend lightness values than Color Dodge, which will change the contrast more.

The 50% Gray Neutral Blend Modes

The Blend modes in the third group, starting with Overlay and ending with Pin Light, all have 50% Gray as their neutral color. This means that wherever the blend color is 50% Gray, these particular Blend modes will have no affect on the base color. (Hard Mix is included in this grouping although it actually has no neutral color, possibly because 50% is the most neutral color for this Blend mode.) When you choose Layer/New/Layer and select a Blend mode from this group in the New Layer dialog, you will be asked if you want to fill that layer with the 50% Gray neutral color. You can then paint in this area with colors or patterns that are lighter than 50% Gray and your image, your base colors, will be lightened or brightened in some way. Painting or blending with colors that are darker than 50% Gray will darken your image in some way. Depending on the Blend mode chosen from this group, the appearance and mood of your composite will change.

Open the images named ParisDogLyrsToTryBlendModes.psd and Trophy-HouseatSunrise from the Ch31.Blend Modes, Calcs, etc folder on your hard disk and try out various Blend modes from this group, and the other groups, on the layers in these files. Don't forget you can use Shift-+ and Shift- – to cycle through the different Blend modes. I believe this will help you to get a feel for what each of the modes actually does. These effects can be somewhat described with words, but this is certainly a case where a picture is worth a thousand words, and this book is long enough!

The original Victorian before any effects are applied.

The mask showing where effects will be applied.

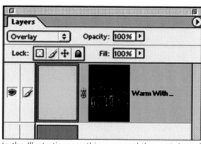
In the Illustrations on this page and the next, I used a layer filled with a solid color that has a layer mask which is white where I want to apply that color as a warming effect. Changing the Blend mode of this layer modifies the mood and intensity of the effect. This could have also been done using a Solid Color Fill layer instead of a regular layer.

Overlay

Overlay does a combination of Multiply and Screen modes. The dark areas of an original image are multiplied and the light areas are screened. The highlights and shadows are somewhat preserved, because dark areas of the image will not be as dark as if you were doing a Multiply and light areas will not be as bright as if you were doing a Screen. The tonal values and details of the original are preserved to some extent, but this is a more contrasty transition than Soft Light, just not as radical as Hard Light.

Soft Light

In Soft Light mode, the original image is blended with the blend color, pattern, or image by making the original image either lighter or darker, depending on the blend image. If the blend image is lighter than 50% gray, the original image is lightened in a subtle way. Even where the *blend color* is pure white, the resulting image will just be lighter than before, not pure white. If the *blend color*

Applying the warming using Overlay.

Applying the warming using Soft Light.

Chapter 31: Blend Modes, Calculations, and Apply Image

is darker than 50% gray, the original image is darkened in a subtle way. Even where the blend image is pure black, the resulting image will just be darker than before, not pure black. The tonal values and details of the original are fairly well preserved, just subtly modified by the blend image. If you add a 50% gray layer above an original image and set the Blend mode to Soft Light, you can then use a soft brush and paint or airbrush with white or black to dodge or burn the image by lightening or darkening this gray layer. Use less than 100% Opacity on your brush to get more subtle effects. This is better than using the dodging or burning tool because it's infinitely adjustable since you're not actually changing the original image, though you are increasing file size more than with an adjustment layer.

HARD LIGHT

In Hard Light mode, the original image is blended with the blend color, pattern, or image by making the original image either lighter or darker depending on the blend image. If the blend image is lighter than 50% gray, the original image is lightened and this lightening is a contrast effect. If the blend image is pure white, the resulting image will be pure white. If the blend image is darker than 50% gray, the original image is darkened and this darkening is a contrasty effect. If the blend image is pure black, the resulting image will be pure black. In Hard Light mode, the resulting image seems to take its lightness value from the blend color, pattern, or image. Because the tonal values of the original are not preserved very well, the adjustment is a radical one. This will produce a radical, contrasty dodge and burn. Use less than 100% Opacity on your brush or you will get pure white or black. If you find the effect you create using this Blend mode too harsh, try lowering the opacity of its layer or switching the Blend mode to Overlay or Soft Light.

VIVID LIGHT

This burns or dodges the image by changing the contrast depending whether the blend color is lighter or darker. In general, this tends to have a much more contrasty and radical effect than most of the other blend modes in this group. It is similar to doing a Color Burn in the areas darker than 50% gray and a Color Dodge in the areas lighter than 50% gray, but it may not be quite as radical a move on either extreme. Play with this comparing it to Color Dodge and Color Burn using the left to right gradient layer only on top of just the Dog layer in the ParisDogLyrsToTry-BlendModes.psd image.

LINEAR LIGHT

This is similar to Vivid Light except this changes the *base color* brightness, instead of the contrast, depending on the how different the *blend color* is from 50% gray in either the light or dark direction. This is like doing both a Linear Burn and a Linear Dodge on either side of 50% gray.

PIN LIGHT

Pin light is like doing a Lighten when the blend colors are lighter than 50% gray and doing a Darken when the blend colors are darker than 50% gray. This may be useful in some mask and effects operations.

HARD MIX

Hard Mix gives you a posterized effect. A pure white layer will return white, pure black returns black. At 100% opacity, all other colors are forced to pure values and will therefore be Red, Green, Blue, Cyan, Magenta, or Yellow.

Applying the warming using Hard Light.

Applying the warming using Vivid Light.

Applying the warming using Linear Light.

Applying the warming using Pin Light. Color Burn is another Blend mode that looks good with this image and is the one I used in the final version.

The 50% Gray Neutral Blend Modes

This is the effect of using a 50% gray layer in Hard Mix mode on the Trophy House image with its color correction layers turned on.

THE REST OF THE BLEND MODES

Of the remaining Blend modes, Difference and Exclusion appear in most of the Blend mode Menus; Hue, Saturation, Color, and Luminosity do not appear in Apply Image or Calculations; Behind and Clear only appear in the PaintBrush, Fill, and Stroke Blend Mode menus; Add and Subtract are exclusively in Apply Image and Calculations; and Pass Through is a Blend mode that is used only in Layer Sets. Here we go!

DIFFERENCE AND EXCLUSION

Difference is one of the most useful blending modes. Difference compares two images and gives you a mask that is black where each of the two images are exactly the same and is nonblack and closer to white the more the images are different from each other. Here is the formula for Difference:

| Source 1 - Source 2 | = Destination

Difference is similar to Subtract but the results are never inverted; they are always positive because the two vertical bars stand for absolute value and therefore make the result positive. With a little photographic planning, you can use Difference to automatically separate an image from its background. Pick a background that is quite different in color and brightness from the objects to be shot. First, place the objects, adjust your lighting, and shoot them. Without moving the tripod or changing the lighting, shoot the background without the objects. If these two photographs are scanned in register, doing a Difference between them can often automatically give you a mask of just the objects. The two objects in the example here were shot on a tripod using a Kodak DCS digital camera. When using a digital camera, scanning the images in register is no problem because they are sent directly from the camera to the computer. In this case, we had the computer in the studio, so we could try Difference between the two images and then adjust the lighting and exposure to make sure we'd get the best knock-out. Actually, to create the final mask of the objects in this case, we used Calculations first to do a Difference between the Red channels of the two images; then we used Calculations again to Screen the results of the Difference with itself. Screening an image (or mask) with itself brings out the brighter parts of the image. We then brought this Screened mask into Levels and increased its brightness and contrast slightly again to darken the blacks

The objects as originally shot with the Kodak DCS system.

The background shot with the same lighting and camera position.

Difference between the Red channels of the background and the object shots. Try each channel and see which does the best job.

These Calculations settings using Difference will create the mask to the left.

Above mask after some quick edits and a brightness adjustment with Levels. Sometimes using Calculations to Screen a mask with itself will bring out the bright values even more. After that, Levels can by used to redarken the shadows, adjust the shadow midtones, and further brighten the highlights that represent the objects you are knocking out.

New background placed behind the objects using an inverted version of the mask to the left. Check out these images on the CD for this chapter in a folder named "Still, StillBk Difference Stuff." The Channels palette in the Still.psd file has these channels along with hints about how I made them. Try it yourself and have some fun!

and brighten the whites. Finally we did some quick editing of the masks of the actual objects. Still, this process was faster using Difference and Screen than if we had done the knock-out by hand. Using Difference to do knock-outs works even better for objects that have no shadows or where the shadow is not needed in the knock-out.

Chapter 31: Blend Modes, Calculations, and Apply Image

A digital camera hooked up to a computer is a reality for more and more photographers today, especially those who do a lot of repetitive catalog work. Also, consider the motion picture industry or multimedia applications where artists or technicians might have to knock out hundreds or even thousands of frames to composite two sequences together. With Difference and a little computer-controlled camera work, this situation can also be automated. Say you're shooting some guys on horses riding across a field that you will later want to superimpose on another scene. Have a computer remember all the frame-by-frame motion of the camera while shooting the scene. Now immediately, while the lighting hasn't changed, use the computer to move the camera back to the original position at the beginning of the scene. With computer control, reshoot all those frames without the horses to get just the backgrounds. Now, using Difference and an Actions Batch, to automate hundreds of frames, you can quickly create a knock-out of all those frames.

The positive version of the image.

A negative version of the image.

Exclusion is similar to Difference but not as intense. Both an Exclusion and a Difference with black will do nothing to the image. An Exclusion or Difference with white will invert the image completely. An Exclusion with 50% gray leaves you with 50% gray, whereas a Difference with 50% gray still changes the image to make it appear partially negative. A Difference from black blending toward white is a slow transition from a positive image to a negative image with no gray section in the middle. In an Exclusion from black blending toward white, the portion from black to 50% gray is actually a transition from the positive image toward 50% gray. From 50% gray, the image turns more negative as we proceed toward white, where the image is totally negative.

HUE, SATURATION, COLOR, AND LUMINOSITY

These blending modes will affect the original image by using either the hue, saturation, color, or luminosity of the *blend color*, pattern, or image as the hue, saturation, color, or luminosity of the original image, the *base color*. In the examples on the next page, combining the two sides of the desert (the original desert Century Plant and Las Vegas), you can see how the Century Plant scene is modified by the hue, saturation, color, and luminosity of the Las Vegas Night scene. The Las Vegas scene has very intense hues that are also very saturated, so it is easy to see what happens with these two images. To get these different effects, we placed the Las Vegas scene as a layer on top of the Century Plant layer and just changed the layer Blend mode of the Las Vegas layer. In Hue mode, you see the hues from the Las Vegas scene, but the saturation and the intensity of those hues, and all the details, come from the Century Plant scene. In Saturation mode, the highly saturated values from the bright neon lights intensify the more subtle hues and details from the Century Plant scene. Color mode combines the hue and saturation from Las Vegas with the details, or luminosity, of the Century Plant. When you put the Las Vegas scene in Luminosity mode, then you are seeing all the details from that Las Vegas scene but the more subtle hue and saturation values from the Century Plant. In the Las Vegas scene, there are large black areas. These have no hue or saturation values, which is why they show up as gray when in Hue, Saturation, or Color modes.

A more interesting way to combine these two images is to double-click on the Las Vegas layer thumbnail to bring up the Layer Style dialog. Moving the left, Shadow, slider to the right in the This Layer part at the bottom of the Advanced Blending area of Layer Style removes the black part of the Las Vegas scene from the composite. In the final example of this image, we have used the Move tool to move the Las Vegas layer up a little bit. Now Las Vegas is at the end of the trail

Exclusion of the top Black to White gradient layer with the positive image in the layer below.

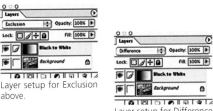
Layer setup for Exclusion above.

Layer setup for Difference below.

Difference of the top Black blending to White layer with the positive image in the layer below.

The Rest of the Blend Modes

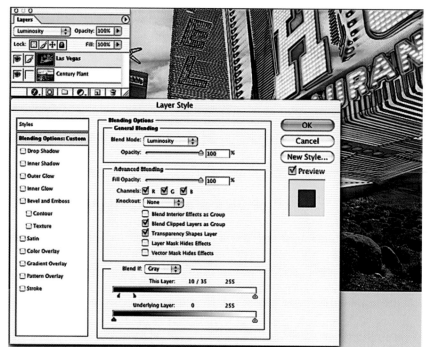

The Las Vegas Night image.

The Century Plant image.

Here we see the results of using This Layer within Layer Style in Luminosity mode to completely remove the black values in the 0–10 range and to blend out the black values in the 11–35 range from the composite of Las Vegas and the Century Plant. We double-clicked on the Las Vegas layer thumbnail to get the Layer Style dialog box.

The Las Vegas Hue with the Century Plant saturation and luminosity.

The Las Vegas Saturation with the Century Plant hue and luminosity.

The Las Vegas Color (hue and saturation), with the Century Plant luminosity.

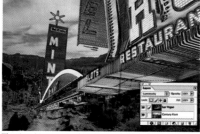

The Las Vegas Luminosity with the Century Plant hue and saturation.

in the desert. We are in Luminosity mode, but the colors of the Century Plant image show through in the black areas of Las Vegas because we have moved the Shadow sliders of This Layer over to the right.

First, we moved the Shadow slider of the This Layer slider to the right to 10. That removed all the digital values from 0 to 10 from the composite, allowing the Century Plant to show through. This produces jaggy edges on the transition between Las Vegas and the Century Plant backgrounds. By holding down the Option key and sliding the rightmost part of the Shadow slider further to the right, the Shadow slider has now split. We moved the rightmost part of this slider to 35. The meaning of this is that the black values in Las Vegas from 0 to 10 are completely removed, and the values from 11 to 35 are blended out making a softer edge between these two images. The Luminosity values in Las Vegas from 36 to 255 are still retained within this composite. For more information on this powerful Layer Style dialog box, see Chapter 32: "Vector Masks, Shape Layers and Layer Styles," which is on the CD and Chapter 34: "Heartsinger CD Cover."

BEHIND

This Blend mode is used to paint into the transparent part of a layer. It is available only from Fill and the painting tools, and only if the layer has a transparent area. It is not available if Lock Transparent Pixels is on for that layer. Behind allows you to paint a shadow or color behind an object (like a circle) in the layer, using a painting tool or the Fill command. The existing pixels in the layer won't be affected because Behind only paints into the transparent area. Once you have laid down paint, however, it becomes a permanent part of the layer and cannot be turned off like a layer style. Painting in Behind mode is like painting on the back of the acetate. Here we see a glow that was added to a circle using the Brush tool in Behind mode with a large soft brush.

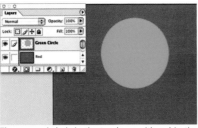
The green circle is in the top layer with red in the bottom layer. Now both layers' Eye icons are on.

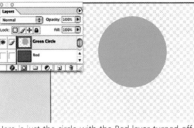
Here is just the circle with the Red layer turned off. The transparent area shows up as a checkered pattern.

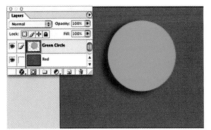
We have painted black into this transparent area using Behind mode with a large soft brush.

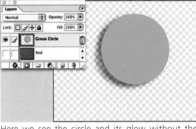
Here we see the circle and its glow without the background color. When painting in Behind mode, we didn't have to worry about painting on top of the green. It is automatically masked out because it is not transparent.

CLEAR

The Clear mode is available only when in a layered document from the Fill command, the Paint Bucket, the Brush, and the Pencil tool. It will fill the selected area with transparency. This is the little checkerboard pattern that means you can see the layers below through the transparent areas. Clear is also available as a menu item from the Edit menu, although Edit/Clear behaves a little differently depending on whether you are in a normal layer or a *Background* layer. When in a normal layer, Edit/Clear fills the selected area with transparency. When in a *Background* layer, Edit/Clear fills the selected area with the background color.

This brings up an interesting thing about Photoshop and how it deals with layers and the special layer called the *Background* layer. When you open a TIFF file or some other file that doesn't contain layers into Photoshop and then go into the Layers palette, you will notice that these files contain a single layer called *Background*. This isn't really a layer in the true sense of the word, because it is locked, can't have any transparent areas, and can't be moved with the Move tool. You can paint on it, though, and if you make a selection in a *Background* layer of an image and then choose Edit/Clear, the selected area will be filled with the background color. You will notice that Clear does not show up as an available option for a *Background* layer within Fill or the Paint Bucket tools. If you double-click on this special *Background* layer within the Layers palette and rename it something else, it will turn into a normal layer. Now, Edit/Clear will fill a selection with transparency, and Clear is available in the Fill and Paint Bucket tools. You can also now move this newly created real layer with the Move tool. Until you rename the *Background* layer and make it a real layer, you can't interchange its order in the Layers palette with other layers.

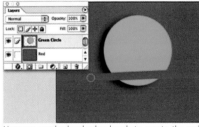
Here we used a hard edge brush to create the red line going across the circle by painting the line in Clear mode.

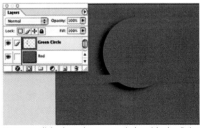
Here we clicked on the green circle with the Paint Bucket in Clear mode leaving only the shadow with this nice effect.

Here, I've superimposed the Las Vegas Night image on top of the Century Plant image using Apply Image with the settings shown below. Note that I'm only using one Channel, Blue, in Add mode, which gives a ghostly effect.

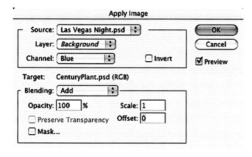

This uses the same settings as the image above only with Subtract as the Blend mode.

ADD AND SUBTRACT

Add and Subtract are available only in Apply Image and Calculations. Add takes the corresponding pixels of the original and the blend image and adds them together using the following formula:

Add = (Source 2 + Source 1) / Scale) + Offset = Destination

Subtract takes the corresponding pixels of the original and the blend image and subtracts them using this formula:

Subtract = (Source 2 - Source 1) / Scale) + Offset = Destination

Scale and Offset are additional parameters that you use with these blending modes in Apply Image or Calculations. The normal values for Scale and Offset for both Add and Subtract are 1 and 0. The order of the Source 1 and Source 2 parameters doesn't matter with Add, but it definitely does with Subtract. The Source 1 parameter is always subtracted from the Source 2 parameter, and the result has to be in the 0–255 range. When Source 1 is white, 255, which represents a selection, the result of the Subtract will always be black. The effect of the Subtract is then to remove the selected areas of the Source 1 mask from the selected areas of the Source 2 mask. This is a very useful function. Of the two, Subtract is the Blend mode I use more often, and I usually do Subtracts between masks. See the example of Subtract with Calculations earlier in this chapter.

When doing either an Add or a Subtract, the Offset value will make the resulting mask lighter if the offset is positive, and darker if the offset is negative. The offset is a number, in the 0-255 range, that will be added to the result of each corresponding pixel's calculations. If we do an Add of two images and set the scale to 2, we are getting an average of the two. This would give us the same result having one image in a layer on top of the other with the top image having a Normal Blend mode and 50% Opacity.

PASS THROUGH

Pass Through is a Blend mode that was created to describe the behavior of layer sets. When you create a layer set, its default Blend mode is set to Pass Through. This means that the layers inside the set will appear in exactly the same way as they would if the set was not there. You can also set a layer set to a different Blend mode, but this may dramatically change the total image appearance since this will cause all the layers in the layer set to be composited with themselves almost as if they were a separate image. Once the layers in the layer set are composited with themselves, the result of that composite is then composited, using the chosen Blend mode for the layer set, with the rest of the image as though the layers in the layer set were just a single layer. Choosing a Blend mode other than Pass Through stops the Blend modes of any of the layers inside the layer set from influencing any layers outside the layer set, and it can make a big change.

Have fun with all the Photoshop Blend modes!

Chapter 31: Blend Modes, Calculations, and Apply Image

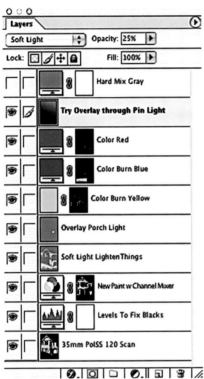

In the trophy house Victorian image, I used Blend modes in various ways to enhance the early morning light. Open the TrophyHouseatSunrise file from the Blend Modes folder on the *Photoshop CS Artistry* CD, click on each layer to activate it, then see how the Blend mode for that layer is affecting the results. Try some different Blend modes and learn what they do to the image.

I had fun creating with the Blend modes as I color corrected this Sunrise photograph of a Victorian with trophies in the window.

REMEMBER

Chapter 32: "Vector Masks, Shape Layers, and Layer Styles," is in PDF format on the Photoshop CS Artistry CD only.

33 HANDS-ON SESSION: Texture and Pattern

Create interesting texture effects using Fill layers along with adjustment layers and Blend modes, Texture channels, the Texturizer filter, and the Pattern Maker.

STEP 1: The original photo of the Packard.

STEP 1: Click the first grayscale pattern and change the mode to Soft Light when you create the Pattern Overlay. Make sure you have clicked on the name Pattern Overlay to see all the options available.

There are many ways to create and integrate patterns and texture in Photoshop. Once you start to play with some of the possibilities, you'll find it so much fun it's difficult to stop and get back to work. I'll take you through several of the options here, and don't forget to try out some of the layer styles that are described in Chapter 32: "Vector Masks, Shape Layers, and Layer Styles," which is a PDF chapter on the *Photoshop CS Artistry* CD. During this exercise, be sure you keep your History palette handy to check the state of your file as you make changes. It will help you determine which effects you really like.

USE A PATTERN OVERLAY EFFECT

STEP 1: The simplest and quickest way to add some texture to your file is to use a pattern overlay from the Layer Styles menu. **Open the Packard image in the Ch33.TexturePattern folder on the CD and bring up the Layers palette (F10 with ArtistKeys). Double-click on the *Background* layer and rename it Packard. Use the Crop tool (C) to crop off the copyright notice, then choose File/Save As and save this as PackardLayers. Click the Add Layer Style icon (the first one) on the bottom of the Layers palette and choose Pattern Overlay to apply this style to the layer. Choose the first grayscale pattern, then change the Blend mode pop-up to Soft Light.** The advantages to adding texture this way are speed and connection to the layer itself. If you move the layer the effect goes with it. On the disadvantage side, it's not as flexible or as editable as some of the other methods. **You can discard this effect now by dragging the word "Effects" to the Trash icon on the Layers palette.**

USE A PATTERN FILL LAYER

STEP 2: A Pattern Fill layer gives you the speed of a layer style, but with more flexibility. **Click the Create New Fill or Adjustment Layer icon (the fourth one) at the**

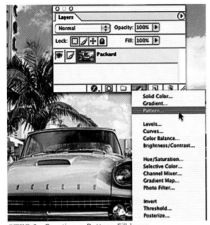

STEP 2: Creating a Pattern Fill layer.

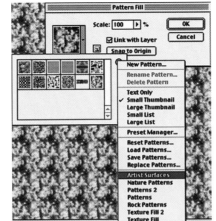

STEP 2: Load the Artist Surfaces textures by appending them to the default set.

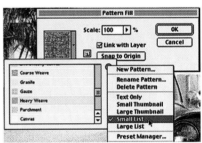

STEP 2: Using a Pattern Fill layer, you can quickly try out other patterns.

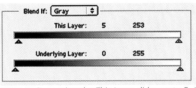

STEP 2: View the patterns as a list to choose one by name.

bottom of the Layers palette and choose Pattern from the menu to add a new fill layer above the Packard layer. When the Pattern Fill dialog appears, click the Option arrow beside the pattern swatch to bring up the Pattern presets, then click that Option pop-up and drag down to the Artist Surfaces presets. Load these by appending them to the current set. Use the Pattern Presets pop-up to view the patterns by Small List, which makes finding the correct one easier. Choose the Parchment texture and click OK to create the layer. Set the Opacity of the layer to 70% and choose Soft Light as the Blend mode. I find that when adding texture, the Blend modes that I use most often are Soft Light and Overlay, but don't feel that you have to stick with those choices. Multiply, Color Burn, and Darken may also be attractive, and if you are using a fill that has color as well, try all the modes to check their effects.

STEP 3: The advantage of using a Fill layer (as well as a layer style) is you can quickly preview and change the fill. Double-click on the Pattern Fill layer thumbnail to bring up the options and again click on the Presets pop-up to bring up the swatches. Make sure the dialog box is situated so you can see most of your image. Now, click a different pattern swatch and watch the image automatically update to show your choice. Try several different swatches, but choose the Heavy Weave pattern and click OK to close the dialog box. With Soft Light at 70% this pattern works well, but you may feel that the texture is a little too coarse to be realistic. So, Shift-Option-double-click the layer thumbnail or choose Blending Options from the Layer palette menu to bring up the Layer Style dialog and do some advanced blending. At the bottom of the Advanced Blending area of this dialog is a powerful feature that has been in Photoshop for a long time. There are two sets of slider bars that are very cool—This Layer, which allows you to remove some of the pixels in the 0–255 range from the active layer, and Underlying Layer, which allows you to specify the pixels from the composite of all the layers that lie below this layer that will definitely be in the composite. In the Blend If section of the dialog box, use the This Layer slider and move the left triangle to the right until it's at about 5. This subtly takes out the darkest pixels of the Pattern Fill layer and softens the effect. Zoom to 100% to see more clearly which pixels are blended away here. Click OK in the Layer Style dialog, then double-click the layer name and rename this layer Heavy Weave.

STEP 3: By moving the This Layer slider up to 5, I took out the very darkest pixels from the Pattern Fill layer.

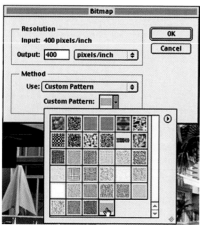

STEP 5: Choose the MezzoTint pattern you just created from the Custom Pattern pop-up.

STEP 6: Here's a section of the file with the Mezzo Pattern layer at 40% Opacity.

STEP 7: Your long, skinny selection on the left edge should look something like this.

When you use Edit/Fill on a blank layer, be sure Preserve Transparency is not checked, so the layer can accept paint.

DIFFUSION DITHER BITMAPS AND MEZZOTINT PATTERNS

STEP 4: **Turn off the Heavy Weave layer by clicking its Eye icon. Use Image/Duplicate (F5 with ArtistKeys) and click the Merged Layers Only box to duplicate only the Packard layer. Now choose Image/Mode/Grayscale and then Image/Mode/Bitmap, and click OK to the Flatten Layers question if you get it. You will get a dialog box that has a pop-up with several options. Choose Diffusion Dither and click OK. Zoom the image in to 100% because diffusion dithers don't look right unless the image is seen at 100% or closer.** A diffusion dither bitmap is an image made up of only black and white dots; there are no grays. The Bitmap mode contains one bit of information for each pixel; it is either on or off, black or white. These images are very compact, which is useful for the Web and multimedia. A regular grayscale image contains 8 bits per pixel, so each pixel can have 256 different gray values. Diffusion dithers are very universal because you can display them on any computer monitor and print them on any printer that can print black dots. **Now choose Command-Z to undo the diffusion dither.**

STEP 5: Next we'll create a bitmap file, but this time using a custom pattern the same size as the file. **Choose Select All (Command-A), then Edit/Copy, and finally File/New (Command-N) to get a grayscale file the same size as the other Packard files. Before clicking on the OK button in the New dialog box, name the file MezzoTint and make sure that the Background Contents pop-up is set to White to fill this new file with white. Choose Filter/Noise/Add Noise and add 100 of Gaussian noise. This is sort of a mezzotint pattern. Press Command-A again to select all of the grayscale pattern. Now choose Edit/Define Pattern to make this a new pattern Photoshop can use. The pattern should be named MezzoTint. Go back to the PackardLayers copy and choose Mode/Bitmap again. This time pick the Custom Pattern option in the pop-up, click the pattern swatch, and then choose the new pattern in the bottom of the menu. That will be the MezzoTint pattern you just defined. Press Return to get out of the dialog and you will see the image with this MezzoTint pattern. Choose Select/All, go to Edit/Copy, and then use the Window menu to switch to your color PackardLayers image. Turn on the Eye icon for the Heavy Weave layer and do an Edit/Paste to create a new layer. Double-click on the name of this new layer to rename it MezzoPattern. Zoom in to 100%.**

STEP 6: **With the MezzoPattern layer active and the Eye icons on for all three layers, change the Opacity to 40%. Change the Blend mode of the MezzoPattern layer in the Layers palette to Multiply to make the black dots more black and drop out the white parts of the pattern.** It will also bring out better color saturation in the non-black areas, and you will see better colors from the original Packard. **Choose File/Save to update your file.** Using the custom pattern the same size as the file means that the pattern did not have to tile and there are no seams or annoying repetitions in the pattern. The disadvantage to a bitmap is that it is only black and white, therefore adjusting tonal values is not an option except for changing the opacity.

STREAKED PATTERNS

STEP 7: Now we will create another pattern and add some more layers to give you other options with this image. **At this point, you may find it easier to work in Full Screen mode, so type F now if you are not already using the full screen. Remember to use the Window menu if you need to switch images. When we add the next layer,** we want it to be added above the MezzoPattern layer, so click on the MezzoPattern layer to make it the active layer, but turn off the Eye icon for this layer and the Heavy Weave layer. Click the New Layer icon to make a new blank layer, and then use Edit/Fill (Shift-Delete brings up this dialog) and use Pattern. Choose the MezzoTint pattern you created and fill at 100% Opacity in Normal mode. Use the Rectangular Marquee tool (M) to make a long, skinny selection on the left edge of this layer the full height of the file. This rectangle should be about ¼ inch wide. Now use Edit/Transform/Scale and grab the middle-right handle and drag it across the screen to the right side of the window. This stretches out the dots within this ¼-inch selection and gives you a streaking pattern. Press Enter or Return to finish the scale process and Command-D to deselect the area. Double-click the layer name and rename the layer Streaks. Press Command-Option-0 to zoom to 100%. Change the Blend mode of this layer to Linear Burn to remove all the white pixels. Now change the Opacity to 40%, and the black steaks turn gray. Save your file (Command-S).

THE TEXTURIZER FILTER

STEP 8: Another built-in texture feature of Photoshop is the Texturizer filter. **For this part of the exercise we'll use a copy of the Packard itself so drag the Packard layer to the New Layer icon to make a copy of it. Double-click the layer name to name this layer Texturizer, and turn off the Eye icons for all the other layers. Now go to Filter/Texture/Texturizer. Use the Textures pop-up to try the four default textures, then press the Option pop-up and go to Load Texture. Navigate to the Photoshop CS Presets folder and find the Textures presets. Any .psd file within that folder will now be available for you to use**

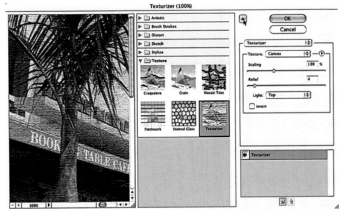

STEP 8: The Photoshop CS Filter Gallery dialog gives you options to combine several filters at one time. This is what the dialog looks like when you run a single filter.

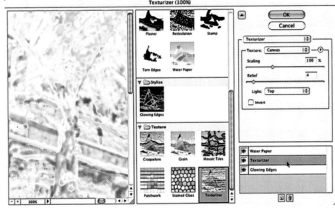

STEP 8: While still in the filter window, I've run three filters and changed their order.

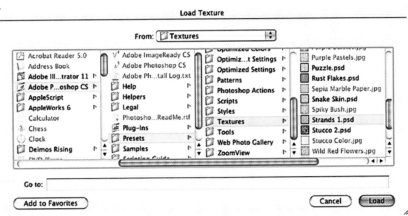

STEP 8: Check the Presets/Textures folder for other .psd files to use with the Texturizer filter.

STEP 8: Here's the result of using a Zebra pattern I found in the Presets/Patterns/ImageReady folder.

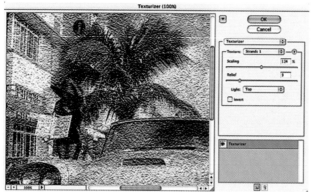

STEP 8: You can open the preview of the image by clicking the blue triangle at the top of the dialog box. Click again to view the Filter Gallery.

STEP 8: An unexpected and interesting effect using a color photo of a small boy in a cape with the Texturizer filter.

with the filter. I used the Strands file, but you don't have to end your search for texture with the files in this folder. A .psd file is all you need, and it doesn't matter where it's located. If you've run art filters in previous versions of Photoshop, you'll see the dialog has changed. The art filters are all accessible from this one dialog, which is called the Filter Gallery. Now, instead of only being able to run one filter at time on a layer, you can run a combination of filters, then change their stacking order, settings, and Eye icon states while still in the dialog. You'll see more of this in our next example.

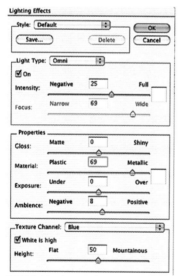

STEP 9: Use these settings...

STEP 9: ...to create this effect.

LIGHTING EFFECTS

STEP 9: **We'll talk more about the Lighting Effects filter in the next chapter, but for now drag the Packard layer to the New Layer icon to duplicate the layer, then double-click the name and rename this one Lighting Effects. Turn off the Eye icons for any layers that are above this layer. Now go to Filter/Render/Lighting Effects. Use the default settings, but change the type of light from Spotlight to Omni and widen its spread a bit by pulling out on the handles of the circle surrounding the light.** Lighting Effects can be great for enlivening a section of your photo or for adding special effects, but when you add a texture channel it's also great for creating an impasto or embossed look. **Choose the Blue channel for the texture channel and click OK.** You may need to play with this filter awhile before you feel comfortable with all its many options, but it's a great addition to your effects arsenal. Here again, you are not limited to only the RGB channels to use as textures, but you can use any Alpha channel that you have created for that document.

To create a pattern preview, select a sample

STEP 10: This area with the chair legs gave me interesting angles and negative space for patterns.

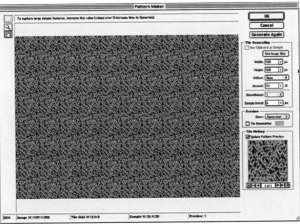

STEP 10: Though the Pattern Maker dialog box is big, the options are easy to understand and use.

THE PATTERN MAKER

For this part of the exercise we're going to work with the Pattern Maker feature introduced in Photoshop 7. I think this feature will be used most by Web designers, but it's so much fun to use that, whether you need to create patterns or not, you may find yourself spending hours like a kid with crayons. There are two different ways to create your patterns, and we'll do it both ways here.

CREATE TILES USING AN IMAGE

STEP 10: **Once again, drag the Packard layer to the New Layer icon on the Layers palette to duplicate it and name this layer My Pattern. Turn off the Eye icon for the Lighting Effects layer, and then go to Filter/Pattern Maker.** You'll get another of those very large dialog boxes with lots of confusing options. Don't worry, this one's really quite simple. On the upper-left side are three familiar tools: the Marquee, the Zoom tool, and the Hand tool. **Use the Marquee and drag a small rectangle in the area that you want to use as a pattern. I chose the legs of the folding chairs. Now click the Generate button.** The layer is filled with the pattern you just created and a pattern tile appears at the bottom-right of the Pattern Maker window to show you what a single tile looks like. The default settings work well for most tiles. **If you think the edges are too prominent and noticeable, you can raise the Smoothness setting, and then press Generate Again or Command-G. If you are not seeing details you wanted from the sample you used, increase the Sample Detail setting.** Changing these settings causes Photoshop to need more time to generate the pattern, so **don't use the higher settings unless you really need them. Another tactic you can try is changing the tile size. You can type in any number for the width and height of the tile, or click the Use Image Size button to create one tile that is the size of the current image. This also may take a bit of time to generate, but it ensures that there will be no seams in your layer. After you have generated several tiles, go to the Preview area of the dialog box and choose Show Original rather than Show Generated.** Your original image reappears and you can select a different area to use as a tile.

STEP 10: Going back and previewing the image again gives you a chance to make new selections.

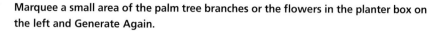

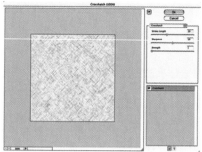

STEP 12: Use these settings for the Crosshatch filter: Stroke Length, 20; Sharpness, 10; and Strength, 1.

Marquee a small area of the palm tree branches or the flowers in the planter box on the left and Generate Again.

REVIEW, PREVIEW, AND SAVE PATTERNS

STEP 11: In the Tile History area, you'll notice a little control bar that tells you the number of the current tile and how many tiles you have created during this use of the Pattern Maker. You can click the forward and back arrows to review the patterns you've generated one by one. You can jump to the beginning of the list using the second icon in the control bar or jump to the end of the list using the next to the last icon. As you switch between the patterns, the large window will preview the tiled pattern in the image if Update Pattern Preview is selected. For faster scrolling you can uncheck this box. **If you come across a pattern that you're sure you don't want, you can click the Trash icon to delete it, and if you come to one that you might want to use for other purposes, click the Presets icon on the far left of the control bar to name your pattern and add it to the current presets.** Remember to resave the presets from the Presets Manager if you want to keep your patterns permanently. **When you've created and saved all the patterns you want, choose one to fill this layer by clicking OK.**

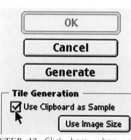

STEP 12: Click here when you want to use the contents of the Clipboard to build your patterns. This way, you can make a selection from any interesting file and use it in your current image.

PATTERNS WITH TRANSPARENCY

You aren't limited to creating patterns that completely cover the layer. If you make a selection from a layer with locked transparency, your pattern will also have transparent regions. Very cool.

CREATE PATTERNS FROM THE CLIPBOARD

STEP 12: The second way to create a pattern using the Pattern Maker is to use a selection from the clipboard. In this instance, we're going to create a small file with texture and color that might work and use it for our pattern. **Turn off the Eye icon for the My Pattern layer, and then go to File/New and create a new RGB file 400 pixels by 400 pixels. Choose a nice, warm ivory color for your foreground color and use Option-Delete to fill with this color. Go to Filter/ Noise/Add Noise and use Gaussian and Monochromatic of about 10%. Next go to Filter/Brush Strokes/Crosshatch and use 20 as the Stoke Length, 10 for Sharpness, and 1 for the Strength. When you have run both filters, use Command-A to select all of the file and Command-C to copy. Switch back to the PackardLayers file, click the Packard layer to activate it, and then click the New Layer icon on the bottom of the palette to create a new, blank layer. Name this layer Crosshatch, then use Command-Option-Shift-X to invoke the Pattern Maker once more. You may be asked if you want to convert the source data. Click OK to this dialog or you will not be able to use the contents of the clipboard when the Pattern Maker opens. The preview will be blank until you click Use Clipboard as Sample and generate the new pattern. If you feel the preview shows seams, click Use Image Size and generate again. Click OK when you are happy with the pattern to fill the layer. Set the Blend mode of the Crosshatch layer to Color Burn.**

FIBERS

STEP 13: Photoshop CS added a new filter called Fibers that creates textures using the foreground and background colors. Low settings give you a sort of gently creased fabric look, higher settings look like wood or marble. I've found these to be interesting as backgrounds for pieces, a little trickier when adding texture over existing images. For this image, I suggest you work with fairly subtle colors (I used a tan foreground and a gold background). **Turn off the Eye icons for all layers except the**

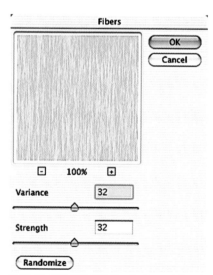

STEP 13: Start your pattern with these middle values, but move the sliders to discover other looks. The Randomize button uses these values but shifts the pattern each time you click.

Packard. Click the Create a New Layer icon on the bottom of the Layers palette, then use Option-Delete to fill that layer with the foreground color. It doesn't matter what color the layer starts out, the filter will fill any existing pixels with the pattern. **Make sure you have chosen the color swatches you want, then use Filter/Render/Fibers. Move the sliders until you have a look you like, then click OK. Now double-click the layer name and rename this layer Fibers.** Depending on the colors you chose to work with, you may find Multiply, Color Burn, Soft Light, or Overlay work for your blend mode. You might also want to reduce the opacity a bit.

TIME TO PLAY WITH LAYERS AND OPTIONS

STEP 14: Now you have several layers and effects that you can adjust until you get the final image you want. Remember that you can turn off any layer by clicking on its Eye icon. **Show the Layer Comps palette, then use the Layers palette to play with Opacity, Blend mode, This Layer slider, and the Underlying Layer slider in the Layer Style dialog for the layers until you get a combined effect you like. Remember, the Underlying Layer slider bar in the Layer Style dialog forces pixels of lower layers into the composite. Once you find a version that pleases you, click the Create New Layer Comp button on the bottom of the Layer Comps palette.** I've created several that are saved in the PackardFinal file in the Extra Info folder for this example on the CD. In a job like this where you are prototyping effects and have lots of possibilities, the Layer Comps palette is invaluable.

Before Photoshop had the Layer Style dialog and before it even had built-in layer effects, it had the ability to create millions of interesting effects using this type of technique of stacking layers, and then running filters and changing the Blend modes of each layer to create many of the effects that the current Layer Style dialog does in a more automatic way. Play with these features of Photoshop to prototype future effects that become the latest in your set of Photoshop surprises. I'm sure you can come up with something that looks great and nobody has ever tried before. The number of effect combinations you can create is unlimited. HAVE FUN!

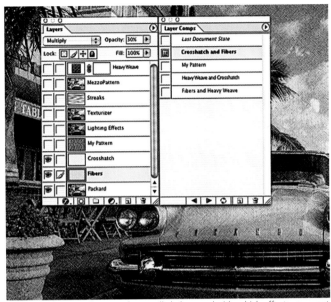

STEP 14: The Layer Comps palette really helps you decide which effects you want to keep and also what you did to achieve the effect. Here my Fibers layer is set to Multiply blend mode.

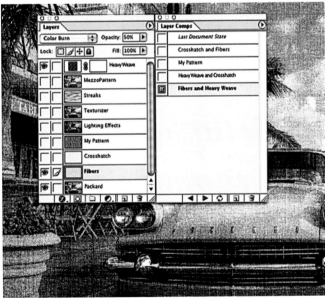

STEP 14: For this comp, some of the same layers are visible, but the Blend mode for the Fibers layer has changed. Glad I didn't have to remember that all by myself.

34 HANDS-ON SESSION: Heartsinger CD Cover

*A tour of some of the more versatile Photoshop filters
as well as many useful layer and blending techniques
for getting the most out of all the filters.*

The best way to learn the simple filters is to play with them. Try out their features and compare different settings on the same image. Understand the range of possible things you can do with each filter. This is fun and easy, although you do need to give yourself a bit of time, as there are quite a few filters and lots of choices to make. There are many other Photoshop books, including the Photoshop manual, that have charts of each filter and what it looks like during one particular iteration. Photoshop comes with a set of more than 75 filters, and with them and the rest of Photoshop, you can do millions of different effects. There are hundreds of other third-party filters on the market; some of them are really unique, but a lot of them just give you a slightly easier way to do something that could already be done with the standard Photoshop filters by combining them with the other features of Photoshop.

In the rest of *Photoshop CS Artistry*, we show you how to use the workhorse retouching filters in a lot of real-world examples. In this chapter, we are going to concentrate on how to use layers and masks to combine filters in interesting ways. We are also going to talk about some of the more complicated filters and how to understand them and make the best use of them. You need to play with all the filters and options because the possibilities for effects and combinations are in the millions; using the techniques we show you here, you can discover your own entirely new effects.

GETTING MARGEE READY

STEP 1: **Open the file MargeeOrig.psd. Double-click on the Background layer to name it Layer 0.** We first have to knock Margee out of the garden background and do a bit of cleanup on a rather dirty scan. First, the cleanup. We start by using Dust & Scratches, which is useful for a quick cleanup of this file because we are not going to be using a realistic version of the image. Then, we'll use Unsharp Mask, a filter that's explained in detail in Chapter 20: "Correcting a Problem Image."

Use Filter/Noise/Dust & Scratches and scroll around the picture to see areas that are dirty. I noticed areas in the hair and the lower-right side of the blue scarf that were particularly noticeable. You want to set your filter high enough to rid the file of most of the noise, but not so high that you ruin details. In this case, **I used a Radius of 1 and a Threshold setting of 25**. This rids the file of all but the largest pieces of dust, yet doesn't soften the facial features too drastically. Remember that you can use keyboard shortcuts to zoom in or out on the main window. By turning the Preview button on and off, you can see the effect your filter will have on the overall file. **For spots that weren't erased with the filter, type J for the Healing**

STEP 1: Use Filter/Noise/Dust & Scratches to do an overall cleanup of the file.

Brush, choose a 9-pixel brush and click the Sampled button on the Options bar. Option-click an area near the dust or scratch you want to correct, then release the Option key and brush over the scratch. The Healing Brush tool matches the texture from the sampled area while keeping the brightness and color from the area being corrected.

STEP 2: **Next, use Filter/Sharpen/Unsharp Mask** to bring back a bit of the detail in the photo. We're not going to do much. **Use between 115 and 125 for the Amount, 1 pixel for the Radius, and 7 levels for the Threshold value.**

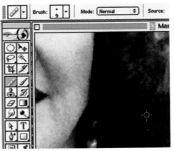

STEP 1: Option-click near the area you are correcting to set the sample point for the new Healing Brush tool.

STEP 2: After removing the dust, you'll need to resharpen the file to keep it from being too soft.

KNOCKING OUT THE BACKGROUND

STEP 3: Like most compositing jobs, we need to knock the figure out of its background before we start compositing. Photoshop offers many ways to make a knockout, but we're going to use the Extract command for this job.

First, you'll need to make a copy of Layer 0 by dragging the layer name to the New Layer icon at the bottom of the Layers palette. Double-click the words Layer 0 copy, then change the name of the layer to Extracted. Please remember to always make a copy of the layer when you use the Extract command, as the command clears all the pixels that are not defined to be retained. **Go to Filter/Extract to bring up the Extract window and choose the top tool on the window's Tool palette, the High-lighter.**

Choose a width for your brush that allows you to cover the edge of Margee's body and hair with some overlap on both the body and the background. I used 20. Also, change your highlight color from green to red (or some custom color) to be able to see your highlight better against the primarily green background of the picture. Now you're simply going to paint around the edges of the area that you want to extract from the background; in this case, Margee. There's no need to paint around the bottom of the dress, but you do need to make sure your outline is solid—any gaps will cause the Fill tool to fill the entire file. Zoom in if you need to check that you're covering the edge well. Once you've made your outline, choose the Fill tool from the window's Tool palette and click inside the red highlighted area to fill the area of the extraction with blue fill. Click the Preview button when you're done with these steps.

STEP 4: **In the Preview section of the dialog, set your Display Preview to White Matte and check the edges of your selection mask.** Chances are, you need to do some touch-up work. This is where the Extract command comes in very handy. **First, we'll be working with the Cleanup tool. Zoom in to see the edges better as you work. Select the tool by clicking the fifth**

STEP 3: Highlight the edges of Margee's body and hair, making sure to overlap both the areas that you want extracted and the areas that you want to remove.

STEP 3: Your file should look like this when you've completed highlighting.

STEP 3: If the blue fill spills over into the background, check your highlighted edges for gaps. When you use the Fill tool, Margee should be completely covered.

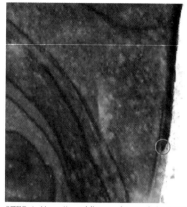

STEP 4: Here, I'm adding to the mask (making the deep blue edge more complete) by using Option with the Cleanup tool. Without the Option key, I can erase the errant blue pixels that you see in the white area.

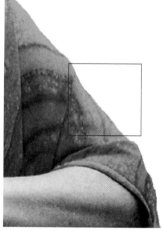

STEP 4: This is the edge before using the Edge touch-up tool. It's a bit soft.

STEP 4: After using the tool, the edge is more well-defined.

icon on the Tool palette, or by typing C when you're in this dialog box (all of the tools have keyboard shortcuts). **Use the tool to continue to delete unwanted areas by brushing over them, or use the Option key with the tool to bring back portions of the image that you want to keep. You can change to opacity or brush size using the same keyboard shortcuts that you use with the regular painting tools. Once you've completed correcting the mask, click the sixth tool in the palette to work with the Edge Touchup tool and sharpen the edges for a nice knock-out. Switch to Black Matte in the Display Preview to check your edges against a black background. When you're happy with the preview, click the OK button to make the knock-out.** Once you have this version on a separate layer, it can be used as it is, or to create a layer mask, as we will see later in this example.

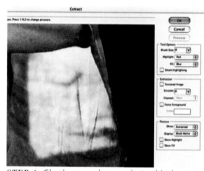

STEP 4: Check your edges against a black matte, as well. You might be surprised at the pixels you missed using no matte or the white matte.

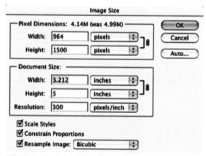

STEP 5: Resizing the file is a two-step process involving both Image Size (this dialog) and Canvas Size.

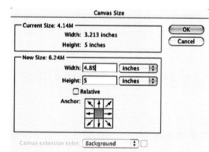

STEP 5: Make sure you keep the image in the center when you add extra space to the Canvas.

STEP 5: At this point, we're going to set up the file for print size. This is the cover art and will bleed on three sides. **Go to Image/Image Size, turn on Resample Image and Constrain Proportions, and then make the Height 5 inches. Now go to Image/Canvas Size and make the Width of the canvas 4.85 inches. Make sure that Relative is not checked. This gives you some space on both sides of Margee.**

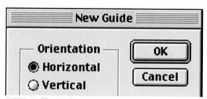

STEP 6: The easiest way to set a new guide when you know the exact location you want is to use View/New Guide.

STEP 6: Now we need to set ruler guides for the edge of the CD cover and the text safety area. **Go to View/New Guide and set the first horizontal guide at .125 inches. If your Ruler preference is set to pixels, you can type the abbreviation "in" after the number to specify inches. Set a second horizontal guide at .25 inches, a third at 4.625 inches, and a forth at 4.75 inches.** Unfortunately, the View/New Guide command always defaults to a vertical guide (I suppose you do use those more than horizontal), so you have to **make sure you click the Horizontal button each time. Now**

Chapter 34: Heartsinger CD Cover

set vertical guides the same way, but you only need guides on the right side at 4.625 and 4.75 inches. Save this file as MargeeCDsize in Photoshop format.

THE FILTER GALLERY

If you read the last chapter, "Texture and Pattern," you were introduced to the Filter Gallery. Margee has requested that the photograph look more like a piece of artwork and, because time is limited, filtering is where we start to achieve that result. But many of the built-in filters in Photoshop give you less than spectacular results if you rely on the default settings. One of the keys to successful filtering is experimentation; change the options and see what happens. The Filter Gallery permits experimentation with multiple filters without having to commit. You can run several filters each appearing as a sort of ersatz layer in the Filter Gallery. These layers can be turned on and off via Eye icons, and you can rearrange their stacking order. The settings used for each filter can be changed at any time until you say OK to the dialog. Because the effect of the filters is cumulative, this allows you to refine your results. This can be a great way to prototype effects. However, the Filter Gallery does have its limitations. There's no Save button that records all the different filters into one replicable effect, and there are no opacity sliders or Blend mode pop up to modify any single effect. So, it helps to keep a notebook handy to record which filters and which settings give you results that are worth using—you don't want to endlessly repeat the process—and sometimes you want the filters to each be on a layer so you can modify how they affect each other.

The Photoshop filters are arranged in groups that give you clues as to the function of the filters. In addition, the filters have names that sometimes clue you in to the result you can expect—sometimes. In other cases, and the Artistic filters are a good example, if you go by name in choosing your filter, you'll most likely be disappointed. Does this mean that the filters are useless? No, it means that you'll probably have to combine some filters or filtered layers to get an effect that you like. And once again, don't forget to write it down. Or, name your layers with descriptive names that remind you what you did. I find that I most often use Overlay, Soft Light, or Hard Light as the Blend mode for a layer filtered with the Artistic filters.

Now, on to filtering.

STEP 7: **Make a copy of the Extracted layer and name it Dry Brush. Go to Filter/ Artistic/Dry Brush and use these settings: Brush Size, 2; Brush Detail, 8; and Texture, 1. Click OK to apply the filter.** This will give you somewhat of a dry brush look, but it certainly isn't where we want to stop. You could go ahead and run the next filter, Colored Pencil, while you are in the Filter Gallery dialog, but I found that down the line, I didn't like the look of the artwork I got using this technique as much as using separate layers that allowed me to change blend modes.

STEP 8: **Make a second copy of the Extracted layer, move it to the top of the Layers palette, and call this one Colored Pencil.** If you use the default settings with this filter, you get a gray overlay on areas of the file as if you were drawing on gray paper, which doesn't work well

STEP 7: The Dry Brush filter breaks up the photo but doesn't really give a spectacular look.

STEP 8: Even though I changed the settings of the Colored Pencil filter, I didn't get what I'd call a true colored pencil effect.

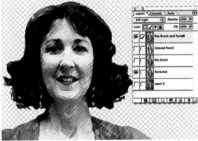

STEP 8: If you run both filters on one layer, you get this result when you switch to Soft Light mode.

STEP 8: If you run both filters on separate layers, and set the Blend mode of both to Soft Light, this is the result you get.

STEP 8: If you run the filters on separate layers, and leave the Blend mode of the Dry Brush layer as Normal but change just the Colored Pencil mode to Soft Light, this is the result you get. This is the version we will use for the example.

361

STEP 9: This is the result of the Find Edges filter.

here. **For this layer, go to Filter/Artistic/Colored Pencil and use a Pencil Width of 3, a Stroke Pressure of 12, and a Paper Brightness of 50 and click OK. This still doesn't give you what I'd call a true colored pencil effect, but now change the Blend mode of the Colored Pencil layer to Soft Light.** This is a much nicer effect than either filter by itself.

MORE FILTERS

STEP 9: **Make another copy of the Extracted layer. Move it to the top and call it Find Edges.** Now, I have to confess, the Find Edges filter is one of my favorites. Still, it's a filter that's generally better used in conjunction with some changes in levels or Blend modes, than by itself. **Go to Filter/Stylize/Find Edges, and change the Blend mode to Overlay. Next, change the Opacity of the layer to 80%. Open the History palette and click Blending Change (the state before the Opacity Change), and then click back on Opacity Change to see which effect you like the best. I left mine at 80%.**

STEP 9: Using the Find Edges layer in Overlay mode at 80% gives interesting detail and color to the artwork.

STEP 10: The Accented Edges layer in Soft Light mode at 60% adds yet another level of interest.

STEP 10: One final filter in this step, and yes, you need to **make an additional copy of the Extracted layer and move it to the top. Call this layer Accented Edges. Go to Filter/Brush Strokes/Accented Edges and use: Edge Width, 5; Edge Brightness, 35; and Smoothness, 3. Change the Blend mode to Soft Light and make the Opacity 60%. Save your artwork.**

ADDING THE POSTER ARTWORK

STEP 11: Not only is Margee an excellent singer, she's also an accomplished artist. Because the songs on the CD are associated with the seven chakras, she wants to use a poster that she did a few years back as part of the CD cover. **Open the file, PosterOrig.psd. Go to Image/Image Size and make the Height of the image 2.5 inches. Keep on Constrain Proportions and Resample Image.** This step is not absolutely necessary, but for me it's a bit easier than trying to do the entire resize with the Free Transform command. **Next, use the Move tool and move the entire layer over to the Margee file. Hold down the Shift key as you move the layer to have it placed directly in the center of the window. Before you continue working on the CD cover, return to the PosterOrig.psd file and use File/Revert to bring it back to its original size. You'll need it again later. Now return to the Margee file.**

STEP 12: This is how the Poster Resize layer looks after you change its opacity.

STEP 12: Move only the bottom-middle handle during the Free Transform to make the fourth heart fit at Margee's hands and the top heart fit at her shoulders.

STEP 12: This step is probably the hardest part of making this cover. The poster artwork has to fit a certain way over the body and hands. But the proportions of the poster are all wrong, so we're going to have to do some finagling to make things work. Be patient with this step. It's one of those things production artists have to do from time to time and it's not elegant work. Luckily, we'll add some effects later that will disguise some of the problems.

Change the name of the layer to Poster Resize and change the Opacity to 60%. If the large heart at Margee's throat is not centered,

Chapter 34: Heartsinger CD Cover

use the Move tool with arrow keys to nudge this layer into place. Here's where the fun begins. You have to resize the poster so the fourth heart from the bottom fits over the porcelain heart that Margee is holding, but at the same time, you have to make the large heart at the top fit right at Margee's shoulders and throat. So this is not going to be a uniform scale. Go to Edit/Free Transform and use only the bottom-middle handle to make the scale. Press Enter to accept the transformation.

STEP 13: **Drag a selection marquee around the bottom portion of the poster under Margee's hands and use Edit/Free Transform and the bottom-middle handle to resize that portion to about 1 inch from the bottom of the window. You don't need to cover the bottom of Margee's blue scarf, as we're going to fade the poster out before reaching the bottom of the scarf. Press Enter to accept this transformation.**

STEP 14: **Select the section of the poster to the right of the hearts and use Edit/Free Transform to extend the poster to the edge of Margee's scarf. Be especially careful not to select any of the large heart at Margee's throat. Use only the right-middle handle to avoid skewing the picture. Select the left section and repeat the process, extending the artwork to the other elbow.**

STEP 15: **Bring the Opacity of the Poster Resize layer to 100%. Now Command-click on the Extracted layer to load the silhouette as a selection. Make the Poster Resize layer the active layer and click the Add Layer Mask icon on the bottom of the Layers palette to make a layer mask. Once again, save your file.**

STEP 16: Now we'll get rid of the lightest areas of the poster and leave only the color overlaying the dress and scarf. **Double-click the Poster Resize layer thumbnail to bring up the Layer Style dialog. Start blending the gray levels by moving the top Blend If white slider down to 240.** This gets rid of the majority of the light areas. **Hold down the Option key to split the slider and move the left half of the slider down to about 200.** This gives you a softer blend between the colored areas and the rest of the file.

CORRECTING THE POSTER LAYER MASK

STEP 17: You probably noticed that the poster artwork ends rather abruptly before the bottom of the file. What we want is a gradual fade-out instead. **Command-click the Extracted layer to load that layer as a selection. Now Option-click the Layer Mask thumbnail of the Poster Resize layer to see only that mask.** We need to select the bottom portion of Margee's silhouette and add a gradient from white at the top to black at the bottom, in order to fade out the poster artwork. **Type M (or Shift-M) until you have the Rectangular Marquee tool. Option-drag around the upper portion of**

STEP 13: Select only the part of the poster under Margee's hands for the next resize.

STEP 13: You don't need to extend the poster to the bottom of the blue scarf. It will fade out before then.

STEP 14: Select the right side of the poster for resizing.

STEP 14: Extend the artwork to Margee's elbow.

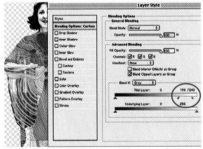

STEP 16: Using just the Gray This Layer slider, you can remove most of the white pixels from the poster artwork without having to create a mask.

363

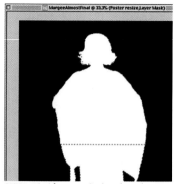

STEP 17: After you Option-drag the marquee, your selection looks like this. This is the section in which we will build the gradient.

STEP 17: If you have any gradient besides white to black here, click the gradient to get to the Gradient Editor. Note the Linear Gradient type is selected.

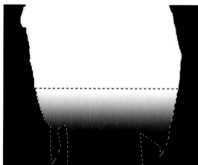

STEP 17: Make sure that you are using the default colors and the Foreground to Background gradient.

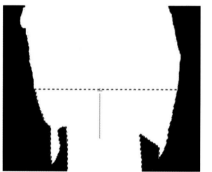

STEP 17: Drag only halfway down the selected area.

STEP 17: This is the resulting blend of the previous drag.

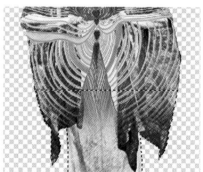

STEP 17: This is how the artwork looks when the blended mask is applied.

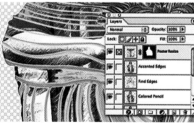

STEP 18: Make sure you are correcting the layer mask for the Poster Resize layer and not painting on the layer itself.

the selection to delete it from the selected area. You should leave only about one-third of the silhouette selected. **Type D to get the default colors and type G to get the Gradient tool.** Make sure you check the Tool Options bar for the current gradient before you start your blend. **If you are not currently showing white to black, click the gradient to bring up the Gradient Editor and select the Foreground to Background gradient. Be sure you are using the Linear Gradient. Start at the top of the selected area and drag about halfway down to fade the poster artwork out completely before you reach the bottom of Margee's scarf. Click back on the Layer thumbnail to check the placement of your blend. If you are not happy, you can click back on the Layer Mask thumbnail and immediately redraw the blend to shorten or lengthen the exposed poster artwork. Deselect the bottom portion of the layer mask when you are happy with how the blend looks.**

STEP 18: There are a couple of other issues about the layer mask for the Poster Resize layer that need to be addressed. The yellow band under Margee's right arm is distracting and needs to be removed. Also, the top edge of the poster artwork above the largest heart is very

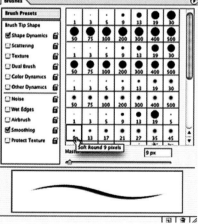

STEP 18: If you are using a pressure-sensitive tablet, use a soft 9-pixel brush with Shape Dynamics turned on.

straight-edged and rather artificial. We'll remove both by painting on the layer mask. **Use the Paintbrush tool (B or Shift-B) and click the Brush icon on the Tool Options bar to bring up the Brushes palette. Choose a Soft Round 9-pixel brush.** Because I use a Wacom tablet, I most often use brushes with Shape Dynamics turned on. If you are using a mouse, remember that Photoshop increases or decreases your brush by 1 pixel when you use the Left and Right Bracket keys until you reach 10 pixels, then it increases by 10. (To move to the next brush to the right in the current palette, type period; to move to the left, type comma.) **Click the Layer Mask thumbnail for the Poster Resize layer so you work on the mask, but make sure you are still viewing the artwork and not the mask. Set your Opacity on your brush to 100% by typing 0. Type X to exchange the foreground and background colors and gently brush away the yellow band under the arm. Increase or decrease the size of the brush as needed by using the keyboard shortcuts, and type X to paint the mask with white if you delete too much of the artwork.**

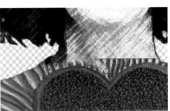

STEP 18: The soft-edged brush helps you paint away the yellow band without harsh edges. Decrease the brush size with the keyboard shortcut as you get closer to the center of the poster.

STEP 19: Use the same brush as before to remove the sharp edge at the neckline.

STEP 19: The finished product should look something like this.

STEP 19: **Scroll to the top of the poster artwork and look at the straight edge at Margee's neck. Use the same brush with black to gently remove the edge. Come in close to the heart and take away a bit on the shoulders to preserve a natural curve. Now save your file again.**

MOVE THE LAYERS AND MAKE A LAYER SET

STEP 20: Remember that this CD cover bleeds on three sides. Right now we have Margee positioned in the center of the window, but that area includes .125 inches of bleed. She needs to be moved to the left a bit. The actual area of the front of the CD is 4.75 inches. **Use View/ New Guide to place a vertical guide at 2.375 inches. Link Margee's filtered layers, the Extracted layer, the Original layer, and the Poster Resize layer. Type Command-T for Free Transform, then click the Delta (triangle) icon on the Tool Options bar to use a relative number to move your artwork. Type .05in for the X value to move all the layers to the right .05 inches. The hearts on the poster should be centered on the guide you just made. Use the arrow keys to move right or left until the hearts line up, then press Enter to apply the transformation. Click on the Accented Edges layer and then unlink Layer 0 (the original layer), Extracted, and Poster Resize. The other four layers are going to become a layer set. Rather than creating a set and then dragging the layers to it, use the Layers palette Options menu**

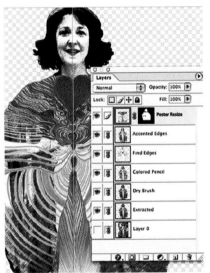

STEP 20: Link all the layers to move them as a group.

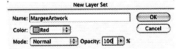

STEP 20: Even though my default unit of measure is pixels on this job, I can type in any number and specify the type of unit.

STEP 20: Unlink the three layers that are not filtered versions of Margee and create a layer set of the layers that are.

STEP 20: Once you've created a layer set, you can assign a Blend mode and Opacity for the set as well as for each individual layer in the set.

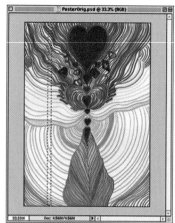

STEP 21: Select a portion that has the full range of colors.

STEP 21: Use Free Transform to stretch the color across the file.

STEP 21: Free Transform will give you an approximate preview until you hit Enter.

and use New Set from Linked (Shift-F12 with ArtistKeys). Name the new set MargeeArtwork, make the Blend mode Normal, and assign red as the color for the group. We used Normal rather than Pass Through because we do not want the Margee Artwork to interact with the other layers of the file. Save the file.

CREATE THE BACKGROUND ARTWORK

There is still more work to be done with Margee, but we're going to take a break from working with her to work on the background.

STEP 21: Reopen the PosterOrig.psd artwork, if you closed it earlier, and use Image/Image Size (F7 with ArtistKeys) to make the height of the poster 5 inches. Keep on Resample Image. Now make a selection using the Rectangular Marquee tool. Your selection should be about 20-30 pixels wide and should extend the entire height of the artwork. Choose an area that has a wide range of colors, as we will use this to create the background for the CD cover. But, don't include any of the heart art toward the center of the poster. Switch to the Move tool (type V) and Shift-drag this section over to the Margee file.

STEP 22: The band will now be in the center of the Margee file. Use the Move tool to place the band on the left edge of the window. Use Edit/Free Transform (Command-T) and drag the middle handle to the right to completely fill the window with color. You may find that you have to drag the handle a bit past the actual window's edge on the right to keep the color from fading away before the edge. When you have resized the artwork to fit, press Enter to accept the transformation. Double-click the layer name to rename it Background Lines, and move it to the bottom of the Layers palette.

STEP 23: This looks okay, but it would be nice to have something a bit more fluid to harmonize with the curves of the poster artwork. So let's filter a bit. First, make a copy of Background Lines by dragging it to the New Layer icon on the bottom of the Layers palette. Next, choose Filter/Distort/Pinch and set the amount to 100%. Say OK and you have a really nice effect that gives you a sense of energy radiating from the center. Name this layer, Pinch Filter.

(Note: If you are following the bolded steps to create this example and you want to finish the necessary steps only, you can skip to Step 37 and continue.)

FILTERS AND BLEND MODES FOR FURTHER EFFECTS

STEP 24: Maybe you want something a little wilder. Turn off the Eye icon for the Pinch layer, and then switch back to the Background Lines layer

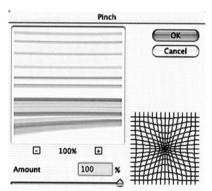

STEP 23: Set the Pinch filter to its maximum for the Pinch Filter layer.

to play a bit with the Wave filter. Use Filter/Distort/Wave and input the settings shown in the illustration. We're going to try the filter three different ways. First use Sine as the Wave type. By reducing the Number of Generators down to 1, you get a clearer picture of what the filter is actually doing to your file. Say OK to this filter and view the results in the file. Your results in this section may look slightly different, depending on the initial selection you made from the poster. If it helps, you can turn of the Eye icons for all layers except the Background Lines layer. Now, Undo (Command-Z) the filter to try another setting.

STEP 24: The result of the Wave filter using Sine as the Wave type.

STEP 25: **Make a copy of this layer and name it Triangle Wave. Return to the Wave filter (you can use Command-Option-F to run the same filter with different settings), use 75 as the maximum for both Wavelength and Amplitude, but use Triangle as the Wave type.** Once again, view the result in the file window.

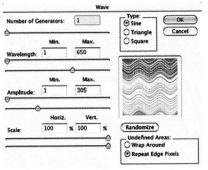

STEP 24: Set your filter options this way and get ready to run the filter several times.

STEP 26: **Return to the Background Lines layer and run the filter once again using Square as the Wave type. This time set the maximum Wavelength to 650 and Amplitude to 250 Minimum and 500 Maximum. Rename the layer Square Wave.** We'll keep this version, as well, and do some further experimentation.

STEP 27: **Turn on the Eye icons for the Pinch Filter and Square Wave layers only. Make sure the Square Wave layer is on top of the Pinch Filter layer. Now change the Blend mode of the Square Wave layer to Multiply.**

STEP 25: The result of the Wave filter using Triangle as the Wave type. Don't adjust that dial!

STEP 26: The result of the Wave filter using Square as the Wave type with adjusted settings.

STEP 28: **Double-click the Square Wave layer thumbnail to bring up the Layer Style dialog.** We are once again going to use the Blend If section, but this time we are going to use only Color channels rather than the gray level for our blends. **Use the Channel pop-up and switch to the Red channel. Use the This Layer Highlight slider and move the slider left to 184. Now hold down the Option key and split the slider, moving the left side down to 152. Switch to the Blue channel and use the This Layer Shadow slider. Move the slider right to 95, then hold down Option and move the right side of the slider to 118.** Again, if you tried to do this with a layer mask,

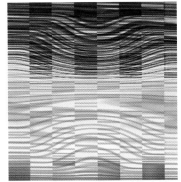

STEP 27: The Square Wave and Pinch Filter layers together with the Square Wave layer set to Multiply.

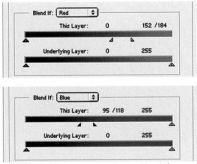

STEP 28: Use these settings in the Blend If area of the Square Wave layer blending options.

Filters and Blend Modes for Further Effects

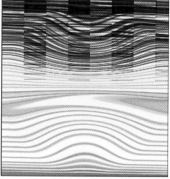

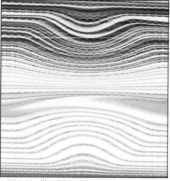

STEP 28: The result of the blending.

STEP 29: The Triangle Wave layer is above the Pinch Filter layer and set to Soft Light at 100%.

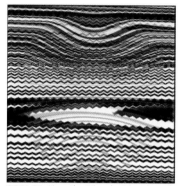

STEP 29: Here the Triangle Wave layer is set to Difference at 100%.

STEP 29: Here the Triangle Wave layer is set to Difference at 100%, but the Blend If Blue Highlight slider is set to 127 and 200.

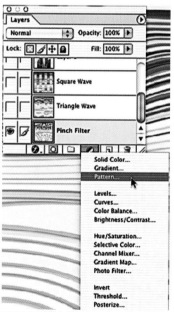

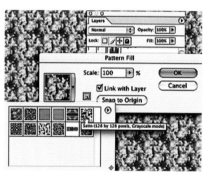

STEP 30: The currently loaded patterns appear when you click the pattern swatch. Choose the pattern you want, then click back on the Pattern Fill dialog box to close the swatches.

STEP 30: Click this icon to add a fill or adjustment layer. Option-click to bring up a dialog that allows you to group this layer with the one beneath it.

you'd make yourself crazy. I rely on Blend If a lot when I'm doing compositing.

STEP 29: **Turn off the Square Wave layer and turn on the Triangle Wave layer. Make sure that it is above the Pinch Filter layer. Set the Blend mode on this layer to Soft Light.** This gives you some nice textural effect. **Now set the Blend mode to Difference.** When I'm compositing, I generally try several of the Blend modes, usually Multiply, Overlay, Soft Light, Hard Light, Color Burn, and Difference. I love Difference, just because you can end up with such funky colors. When you are not in a painting tool, you can use Shift-+ or Shift-– to cycle through the Blend modes for the currently active layer. With each Blend mode, try the Blend If command if you are looking for a special effect. **You can now throw away the Triangle Wave and Square Wave layers unless you want to experiment more.**

ADDING TEXTURE WITH LAYERS, FILTERS, AND LIGHTING EFFECTS

STEP 30: Photoshop has Pattern layers, which can be used to quickly generate a texture and Gradient Map layers (which can give you unexpected and sometimes delightful color variations on a photo or layer). **Click the Pinch Filter layer to make it active and use the Layers palette New Fill Layer icon to create a new Pattern layer. Click the pattern swatch to show the currently loaded patterns. And, you can add pattern swatches, as we will see later in this example. For now, click the right-most swatch on the top row if you are using the default patterns. This is the Satin pattern. Say OK to this layer and set the Blend mode to Soft Light or Color Burn.** Both give you interesting texture. **Now set the mode to Difference. This is pretty jumbled, but if you do some blending of the gray levels, you can get some cool effects. Another possibility is to add a Hue/Saturation layer above the Pattern layer, grouped with the Pattern layer. Use the Colorize option to change to hue of the Pattern layer and see how it affects the Blend mode. Throw this Pattern layer away when you finish playing.**

STEP 31: Now let's use some filters to produce layers for texture. **Click the New Layer icon on the Layers palette to make a new, transparent layer. Use the Eyedropper to**

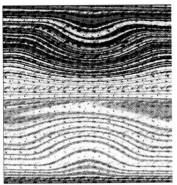

STEP 30: The Satin Pattern layer over the Pinch Filter layer in Color Burn mode.

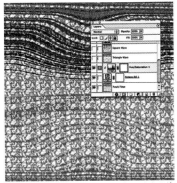

STEP 30: Though the Pattern layer is in Difference mode, I've blended out the highest gray values of the Pattern layer and added a Colorized Hue/Saturation layer on top.

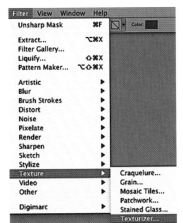

STEP 31: The Texturizer filter can add texture to any layer or selection quickly. You can use a single layer file as a pattern.

sample a medium blue color from the Pinch Filter layer. Now Option-Delete to fill the layer with that foreground color. Go to Filters/Texture/Texturizer and choose Burlap from the pop-up menu. When you use the Texturizer, you can load textures from other places (such as the Presets/Textures folder that ships with Photoshop), and you can create your own. Basically, any single-layer Photoshop file can be used as a texture, but the tiling will look better if you use files created with use as a pattern or texture in mind. **Experiment with different Blend modes but come back to Normal.**

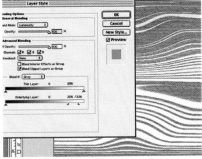

STEP 31: My Burlap layer in Luminosity mode with some blending of the gray values.

STEP 32: **Use the same blue foreground color that you chose before and Option-click with the Eyedropper tool to select a light orange background color. Now go to Filter/Render/Clouds to create a Clouds layer. If you hold down the Option key as you create this effect, you get a more contrasty version of the filter. For this layer, I liked Exclusion for the Blend mode with some heavy blending of the underlying layer to push the color stripes back through.** Darken, Difference, and Luminosity also gave interesting results.

STEP 32: The Clouds layer is set to Exclusion and the Blend If Underlying Layer Shadow slider settings are 165 and 215.

STEP 33: In the same group is a filter you might not have considered for creating texture. But, if you use Render/Lighting Effects with a texture channel, you can create both texture and focus at the same time. First you'll need to create the channel.

Open the Channels palette and click the New Channel icon at the bottom of the palette to create a new channel. It will be completely black. Now press Shift-Delete to bring up the Fill dialog box. Choose Pattern from the Use: pop-up, then click the Custom Pattern pop-up. Use the pop-up menu from this subwindow to load the preset called Patterns. Switch to the Small List view to help find the correct texture. Scroll down the list until you find the Metallic Snakeskin texture. Click OK to fill the channel, and then double-click the Alpha channel and name it Metallic Snakeskin.

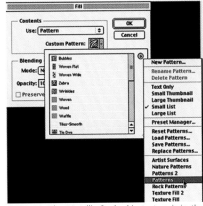

STEP 33: The Metallic Snakeskin texture is in the Patterns presets.

Adding Texture with Layers, Filters, and Lighting Effects

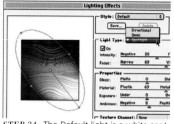

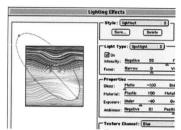

STEP 34: The Default light is a white spotlight with white ambient light and no texture channel chosen.

STEP 34: You can set up your own lighting situation and save it for later use.

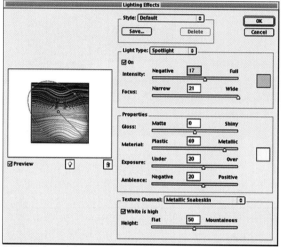

STEP 35: I used these settings and the Metallic Snakeskin texture…

STEP 35: …to achieve this effect.

STEP 34: **Make a copy of your Pinch Filter layer, name it Lighting Effects, and go to Filter/Render/Lighting Effects.** This is an enormous dialog box, but don't let it intimidate you. Like most things in Photoshop, if you work with one option at a time, you'll get the hang of it. First, notice the area named Light Type. There are three light types for you to choose from, and you can have any or all of them in any lighting situation that you set up. The Omni light is always round and shines from directly above the image. Directional lights shine from a distance, so the light is diffused and hits the entire image from the same direction. Spotlights are elliptical. The shape of the ellipses can vary from completely round to elongated, and is controlled via handles that appear when you click on the light source in the Preview window. The straight line defines the light direction and angle. The Focus slider (which only appears for this light type) controls how far toward the edges of the ellipses the beam is spread. The front edge is always at the gray circle at the end of the straight line. At its widest, the beam will spread so that it touches the middle handles of the ellipses. In all three light types, the color square in this area of the dialog defines the color of the current light, and you can change that color by clicking the square to bring up the Color Picker. Each light in a setup can have its own color (but all lights in a setup have the same ambient color). The Intensity slider controls the brightness of the light with Full being 100% of the light color, and Negative being 100% of the complementary color.

The Properties area controls the ambient light (chosen by clicking on the color square) and the reflective properties of the image. These controls remain the same for every light in a particular setup. Gloss controls how bright the highlights will be. Material controls the reflection with Metallic reflecting more than Plastic. The Exposure slider controls the overall brightness of the image itself. Ambience controls how much of the light beam and the image are affected by the ambient light source, moving from Positive where the entire image is affected, to Zero where all ambient light is blocked out and only the color of the lights themselves shine on the image, into the Negative area where the light sources draw inward until they become only spots of color.

The Texture channel area is where you add texture, but unlike many of the other areas of Photoshop, where you can search for a file, you must have the texture available as a channel in the current file. If you use one of the color channels of the current document, you can achieve some impasto effects. If you use a Texture channel that you've created, you can simulate just about any texture imaginable.

STEP 35: **Choose the Metallic Snakeskin channel as the Texture channel and either use the settings shown in the illustration or create your own. Click OK.** Try the same settings with a different Texture channel that you create and also with one of the Color channels of the document (Blue gives you a nice result).

LIQUIFY

STEP 36: And now for something completely different—Liquify. This modal dialog gives you many of the capabilities of Painter's liquid brushes, plus additional functionality. **Make a copy of the Pinch Filter layer and rename it Liquify; then go to Filter/ Liquify.** This command, which was new in Photoshop 6, allows you to move the pixels of your image as if it were a pool of viscous liquid. If you make alterations that you really like, you can freeze areas that you want to leave undisturbed, continue working, and thaw those areas later when you are ready to change them. You can reconstruct your file choosing different algorithms to give different effects. It's all pretty neat.

All the tools in the palette can use different size brushes and pressure. If you have a pressure-sensitive tablet, you can also click a button to use pressure to change the brush size. However, I didn't find the tools particularly responsive and had better results setting the exact pressure I wanted to use. You can Shift-click with the tools, as you would regular painting tools, to make straight-line editing passes on the image, and you can select an area of the image with any selection tool or a mask before entering the Liquify dialog to edit a smaller area of the file. If you make an irregular shaped selection, Photoshop will give you a rectangular area in the dialog, but the area outside your selection will be frozen, so as not to be affected by your edits. You can also choose an alpha channel to use as a freeze mask and perform Boolean operations on masks.

You'll probably use the Warp and Turbulence tools most often. The Warp tool pushes the pixels as you drag, a sort of heavy-duty Smudge effect. The Turbulence tool is similar at first glance, but if you hold each tool stationary over your image, you'll see a big difference. The Warp tool has no effect when not moving; the Turbulence tool scrambles the pixels of the image using a sort of fractal pattern. When you move the tool, it pushes the pixels but in a softer way than the Warp tool.

The Twirl Clockwise tool rotates pixels to the right. You might not notice a lot happening as you drag, but if you hold the mouse button down in one area, you'll see the pixels rotate around the center of your brush. Hold down the Option button to twirl Counterclockwise.

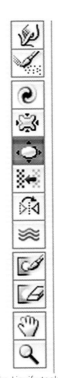

STEP 35: Before the adjustments.

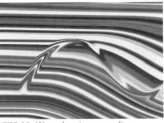

STEP 36: Warp drag in a wavy line.

STEP 36: Warp Shift-click horizontally.

STEP 36: The Liquify tools and their keyboard shortcuts from top to bottom are: Warp (W), Reconstruct (R), Twirl Clockwise (C), Pucker (S), Bloat (B), Push Left (O), Mirror (M), Turbulence (T), Freeze (F), Thaw (D), Hand (H), and Zoom (Z).

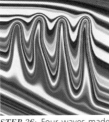

STEP 36: Four waves made with the Warp tool.

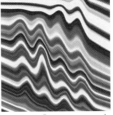

STEP 36: Four waves made with the Turbulence tool.

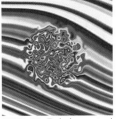

STEP 36: Turbulence tool held in one position.

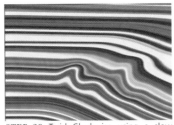

STEP 36: Twirl Clockwise using a slow drag.

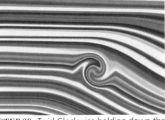

STEP 36: Twirl Clockwise holding down the mouse in one spot.

STEP 36: Margee as she looks in the original photograph.

The Pucker tool pulls the artwork toward the center of the brush, and the Bloat tool pushes away from the center of the brush. You want to play a little with both Pucker and Bloat to get a feel for how to paint with them. Although I started using both tools only in stationary positions, after a while I became pretty adept at moving the pixels while dragging. Once again, though, I set a specific pressure, rather than using pressure sensitivity. These two tools can come in very handy in retouching, using pucker to make a nose or chin slightly smaller, and bloat to open eyes that are a bit squinted. I've illustrated those techniques to the left with Margee's face.

Push Left is a bit difficult to understand at first. When you drag using this tool, pixels move perpendicular to the stroke direction. If you simply drag, pixels move to the left. If you Option-drag, pixels move to the right. Here's a place where I felt Shift-clicking worked better than dragging.

STEP 36: Here, the nose has been narrowed using the Pucker tool.

STEP 36: Here, the eyes have been opened a bit using the Bloat tool.

The most difficult tool to work with is the Mirror tool. This tool takes pixels to the left of the brush area of a downward stroke and copies those pixels to the brush area. An upward stroke takes pixels to the right of the brush area to copy. A left-to-right stroke uses pixels below the brush for the copy. A right-to-left stroke uses pixels above the brush. Confused yet? Option-dragging takes pixels from the opposite direction. If you freeze the area that contains the pixels to be copied, you get a more controlled reflection of that area. Once again, I've used Margee's face to show you how this works. Hopefully the illustrations below-left will help you get an inkling of how to use the tool. It may be one of those things you just have to try until you get the "Aha!" response. Overlapping strokes creates a watery reflection, but it may be easier to use one of Photoshop's other filters.

The Reconstruction tool allows you to either revert or reconstruct the file. This tool works in conjunction with the Reconstruction area of the dialog. If you choose Revert as the mode, the brush takes your artwork back to its original state as you stroke an area. But choose the other methods, and you can get some very interesting results.

STEP 36: Here I've frozen the right half of Margee's face using the Freeze tool. After two passes from top to bottom with the Mirror tool, I've basically brought the right half of her face to the left side.

STEP 36: Here I've thawed the area so you can better see the result.

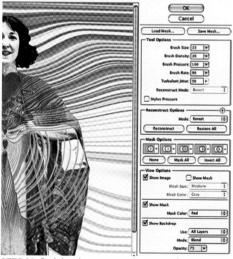

STEP 36: Backdrop lets you see other parts of your artwork against the liquified layer. All Layers shows you all visible layers, or choose a specific layer.

Chapter 34: Heartsinger CD Cover

STEP 36: I created a mesh working with the Extracted layer and then saved the mesh.

STEP 36: Next, I switched to the Dry Brush layer. This is how it looks before editing.

STEP 36: When I loaded the saved mesh, this was the result.

The Reconstruct button does the same thing to all unfrozen areas of the artwork. Choose the method you want (see the Photoshop Help file for a description of what each does), click Reconstruct, and watch your image change. If subtle changes are what you're looking for, use the Reconstruct tool rather than the button. You also have a Revert button, which can take all of the artwork back to its original form in one click.

Liquify also has the capability to save and load a mesh. If you turn on the mesh and use one of the tools, you'll see how the pixel grid is being manipulated. This will be old hat for those of you who have worked in 3D. Once you have the mesh contorted the way you want, click the Save Mesh button to save it and name it. Then, when you open the next file or work on the next layer, you can quickly load the same changes that you made. This could speed production of special effects and should prove very useful for some of you.

If you're an illustrator, you're going to absolutely love the Liquify command. It's worth the time it will take you to learn to use it. Certainly, for retouchers as well, there are some tricks worth learning. For the rest of us, we can finally do what we'd really like to do to the client's job and not have the damage be permanent. **Play with this command and its tools.** Enjoy!

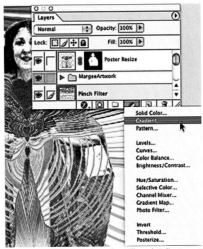

STEP 37: Click and drag the Fill and Adjustment Layer icon to the Gradient layer.

ADD A GRADIENT LAYER

STEP 37: **Turn on the Margee Artwork set by clicking the Eye icon beside that folder. Return to the Pinch Filter layer. We want to give a little color punch to this background, so click the Fill and Adjustment layer button on the Layers palette and choose Gradient to add a Gradient Fill layer above the Pinch Filter layer. Click the gradient swatch to bring up the Gradient Editor and choose the Blue, Red, Yellow gradient. Say OK to both areas of this command. Now lower the Opacity of this layer to 45%.** This is a good start, but we want the color to follow the spectrum of colors of the poster better, so we'll need to do a bit of editing.

STEP 38: **Double-click the thumbnail for the Gradient Fill layer, and then click the gradient swatch. Move the Color Stop icons until Red is on the left, Yellow in the middle, and Blue on the right. Remember, if you inadvertently add an extra color stop, you can remove it by dragging it off the palette. If you need to get back to your last saved gradient, you can hold down Option and the Cancel button becomes Reset. Say OK to both areas of this change.**

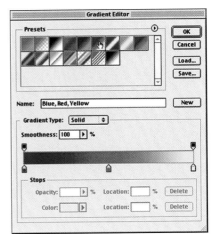

STEP 37: Once you choose a Gradient layer, click the gradient swatch to go to the Gradient Editor and choose a gradient.

373

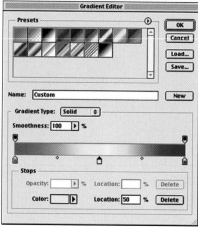

STEP 38: At any time you can edit the gradient you are using for your Gradient layer. Here, I've moved the color stops to create more of a natural spectrum for this file.

ADD A GRADIENT MASK TO THE GRADIENT LAYER

STEP 39: Now the color is basically correct and in the right areas, but the yellow in the center is a bit too intense and we want to take it out. We could edit the gradient again, maybe even add some transparency to the gradient. But because everything is pretty good the way it is, we'll elect to add a layer mask to the Gradient layer. **Make sure the Gradient Fill layer is active. Type D for the default colors, and then X to swap the foreground and background colors. Now type G for the Gradient tool and choose the Reflected gradient type (it's the fourth icon on the Options bar). Click and drag from the heart second from the bottom to about the tip of Margee's nose, while holding the Shift key to keep the blend straight up and down.** Because the blend is foreground (black) to background (white), the mask will be black in the center and white from the point you finished your drag. And as you are using the Reflected gradient, that pattern is reflected from the point of origin to the other side of the mask. This removes the yellow color in the center but leaves the gradient intact on both the top and bottom. Just right. **Save your file.**

STEP 39: The new gradient is good but too yellow in the center.

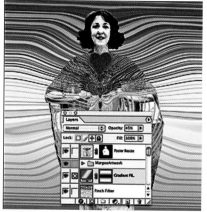

STEP 39: Adding a Gradient mask to the Gradient layer allows me to remove certain areas of the blend in a gentle way.

STEP 40: Here I've made a selection, which I'll define as a pattern.

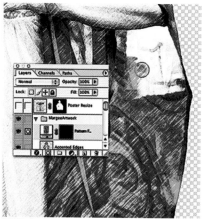

STEP 41: The new Pattern layer should be part of the Margee Artwork set.

ADD A PATTERN LAYER

STEP 40: The original photo of Margee was taken outside and the light shining through the blue scarf now looks awkward. We need to "add scarf" to the image. For this, we'll use a Pattern layer. When you define a pattern, you make a rectangular selection. All the layers that are turned on when you invoke the Define Pattern command will be part of the pattern. **So, turn on only the layers in the Margee Artwork set. Now make a rectangular Marquee selection in the blue scarf area under Margee's left arm. Try not to take the darker blue vertical area, as that will make the pattern more noticeable when it tiles. When you are happy with your selection, go to Edit/Define Pattern. The selected area will show in the swatch area. Name this Blue Scarf and press Command-D to deselect the area.**

STEP 41: **Open the layer set and click the Accented Edges layer to make it active. Now click the Fill and Adjustment Layer icon on the Layers palette and choose Pattern to add a new Pattern layer. When the dialog box comes up, you should see the pattern that you just created. If not, click the pattern swatch and find the Blue Scarf pattern in the swatches area. Say OK to fill this layer** with the Pattern tile. The Pattern layer automatically has a layer mask attached to it, and the layer mask will be active. If black is still your foreground color, Option-Delete to fill the layer mask with black. You are now looking at the Margee Artwork, but we're going to paint on the Pattern layer mask.

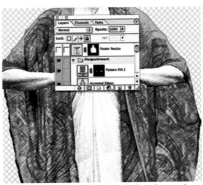

STEP 42: Type B to get the Brush tool and choose the Soft Round 45-pixel brush to start with. Type D to get the default colors and 7 to paint at 70% Opacity. Now paint over the areas of the artwork where the back light shines through the scarf, and the Pattern layer will reappear where you paint out the mask. Use smaller brushes and less opacity when needed, and don't forget to switch colors and paint with black if you make mistakes that need correction.

STEP 42: When you finish painting the mask on the Pattern layer, the large white areas should be gone and the pattern of the scarf should look natural. It's not necessary that it be perfect because overlying artwork will mask a lot of problems.

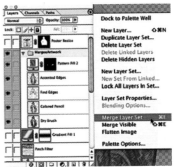

STEP 43: Merge Layer Set collapses all the layers in the group into one layer.

ADD HANDS FROM MERGED LAYER SET

STEP 43: **Click the Margee Artwork layer set icon on the Layers palette.** When you are on a layer set layer, you have an additional Layer command, namely Merge Layer Set. The keyboard shortcut, Command-E, is shared by three commands: Merge Down, Merge Linked, and Merge Layer Set. The setup of the Layers palette determines which command is currently available. **Use the Layers palette Options pop-up to choose Merge Layer Set.** The set becomes a layer with the name Margee Artwork. Convenient, huh?

STEP 44: Make a selection about this size to copy to a new layer.

STEP 44: **Make a rectangular selection of the arms and hands of the Margee Artwork layer and use Layer/New/Layer via Copy (Command-J) to copy those pixels to a new layer in exactly the same position. Double-click the layer name and rename it Hands. Turn the Eye icon on for the Poster Resize layer, then move the Hands layer to the top of the Layers palette. Make a selection of the hands and arms only, using whatever method is most comfortable and quickest for you.** It doesn't have to be perfect,

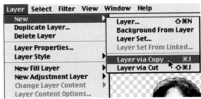

STEP 44: The great thing about using Layer/New Layer via Copy or via Cut is they put the material on the new layer in exactly the same position as the old layer. This can be indispensible for compositing.

as you are going to have to do some painting on the layer mask anyway. But the better your selection, the less work later. I'm pretty handy with the Pen tool, so I made my selection that way. The Magnetic Lasso also made a decent selection without much trouble. **When you have a good, basic selection, click the Layer Mask icon to add a layer mask.**

STEP 44: Move the Hands layer to the top of the palette.

STEP 44: This was my initial Pen Tool path.

STEP 45: **Use a soft-edge brush to clean up your layer mask for the Hands layer.** It should look like the arms are coming out of the poster artwork, and like that artwork is printed on the blue scarf. I brought the Extracted layer to the top of my Layers palette and turned the Eye

STEP 44: The Pen tool selection made a pretty good start at the layer mask.

STEP 45: I moved the Extracted layer to the top and turned it on and off to help me decide how to clean the Hands layer mask. Notice that I've painted out the red heart just under Margee's thumbs.

375

icon for that layer on and off to help me discern where the edges of the hands should be. You could also make that layer's opacity low and keep it on to guide you. **You should see the poster artwork around the heart, and you also want to paint out the partial red heart just under Margee's thumbs. Save your work.**

ADD HEART FROM ANOTHER FILE

STEP 46: The porcelain heart is an important element in this piece, so we have a separate file from which to place an unaltered version. **Open the file HandsSmall and open the Channels palette. Command-click the Heart Mask channel to load it as a selection. Now use the Move tool (V) and Shift-drag a copy of the heart to the Margee file. Double-click the layer; name it Heart, and move it to the top of the Layers palette. Change the Opacity of this layer to 60% and use Edit/Free Transform (Command-T) to resize the heart to slightly larger than the one in the Margee Artwork layer. When you are happy with the size and placement of the heart, hit Enter to accept the transformation. Return the Opacity to 100% after the transform.**

STEP 47: **There's a shadow on the edge of the heart that makes it look like a composited item, so add a layer mask to the Heart layer, use a soft-edge brush, about 5 pixels at 30% Opacity, and gently brush away any annoying edges by painting the layer mask.**

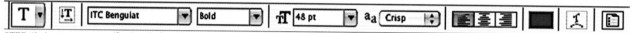

STEP 48: I set my type specifications before I began typing the new layer, but you can type first, then highlight the text and change the specs.

STEP 48: When you begin typing, a new layer appears with a generic name, Layer #. As soon as you switch tools or layers, the word you typed becomes the layer name.

ADD TEXT AND LAYER EFFECTS

STEP 48: Now we're ready to use Photoshop text handling ability. **Type T to access the Type tool, click the foreground color swatch on the Tools palette, and choose a deep green for the first word: Heartsinger.** I set my Type specs before I started typing, but you could as easily type the word, highlight the letters, and then change the specs. **I used ITC Benguiat Bold at 48 points. You'll need to find an appropriate typeface in what you have loaded on your machine. Once you have typed the word, you'll notice that the Tool Options bar changes slightly to make Warp Text an option.** Although we won't use Warped Text for this illustration, it's a neat technology and you should know how to use it. If you've used "envelope" type extensions for Illustrator, you'll immediately recognize what's going on here. Unfortunately, unlike those

STEP 49: The Bulge Style with Horizontal Bend only looks like this.

STEP 49: The Bulge Style with Vertical Bend, Horizontal Distortion, and Vertical Distortion.

STEP 49: The Bulge Style with Vertical Bend only.

376

extensions, or even Painter's type on a curve option, you cannot edit the Bezier curves by using anchor points or handles.

STEP 49: **Make sure you are currently on the Heartsinger layer and in the Type tool. Click the Warp Text icon on the Tool Options bar. A dialog appears with a pop-up where you choose the type of "envelope" you want to use. Make sure you can see the type as you choose different envelopes and study their effects. In my illustration, I chose the Bulge effect**. The three sliders appear for each effect, as well as the Horizontal and Vertical buttons. The Bend slider controls where the effect will be most prominent—top or bottom, right or left—depending on the particular envelope you've chosen. The Horizontal slider controls which side of the envelope will be larger, with left being the left side of the type and right being the right. The Vertical slider controls whether the top or bottom of the text will be spread wider. Left is the top of the text, right is the bottom. The two buttons control whether the primary effect is Horizontal or Vertical, and the change is sometimes radical. Depending on which buttons and sliders you choose, you can bend, twist, and flip the type over itself. This is an area you really want to explore if type effects are important to you. After you play with the effects, make sure you **Cancel or Undo (Command-Z) to bring the type back to its original shape.**

STEP 50: We're going to add a layer effect for the Heartsinger layer to make the text stand out from the background. **Option-double-click the Heartsinger layer or double-click to the right of the layer name in the Layers palette to bring up the Layer Style dialog box. On the left side of this dialog is a list of default styles that ship with Photoshop. Start styling this text by applying the Outer Glow style.** If you click the checkbox to the left of Outer Glow, you apply that style to the layer, but you do not see the controls for the style. Click the style name and the rest of the dialog box changes to show you the controls available for that style. **Situate the Layer Styles window so you can see the effect on the Heartsinger layer as you work.**

STEP 51: Using the default settings, you can just see a little yellow line around the type. It really doesn't stand out from the background. **The first change we'll make is the size of the glow in number of pixels. Use the Size slider or type 27 in the entry area to make the actual glow larger. This makes the glow larger, but it's also blurred so much that it looks puny. So, use the Spread slider or type 15 to expand the Type mask before the blurring happens.** Now the text is starting to stand out, but maybe more than we need on this already busy cover.

STEP 52: **Now, click the Contour pop-up in the Quality area.** This is a really mind-boggling feature of Photoshop. The effects you achieve can range from subtle to very dramatic, depending on how you combine the contour you use with other settings in the dialog box. **If you are using the default contours, click the leftmost contour on the second row, the Half-Round contour. This further spreads the glow. Now lower the Opacity to 55% and click the small yellow color swatch to open the Color Picker and warm the color toward orange. If you'd like to continue to experiment, do so. If not, click OK and you're finished with this effect.**

STEP 53: **Type T to return to the Type tool and click in the image below the word Heartsinger. Click the color swatch on the Tool Options bar and choose a deep blue color for**

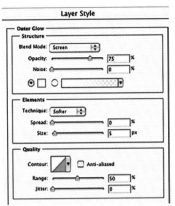

STEP 50: These are the default settings for the Outer Glow layer style.

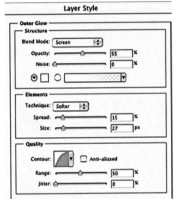

STEP 50: These are the settings I used for the Outer Glow on the Heartsinger layer.

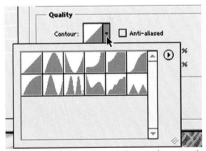

STEP 52: Click the pop-up to give you the currently loaded contours. You can edit a contour by clicking on the Contour icon after you close the Contour Picker.

STEP 52: After changing the contour, color, and opacity, the text is softly differentiated from the background.

Add Text and Layer Effects

STEP 53: Make sure all the text is highlighted as you change the size of the characters.

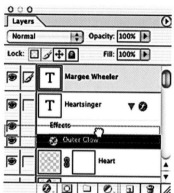

STEP 54: You can simply drag and drop to copy the layer effect from one layer to another.

the text. **Type the words Margee Wheeler**. You will be using the same type specs that you used for the Heartsinger layer, so the text will be too large. **Double-click the Text icon (not the name) for this layer in the Layers palette to highlight all of the text and use the keyboard shortcut (Command-shift-<) to resize the type until it almost fits under the word Heartsinger. This should now be 36-point text. There is no keyboard shortcut to scale the type one point at a time, so you'll have to type 35 in the entry area for size on the Tool Options bar.**

STEP 54: The first thing you'll notice is that the type blends in with the bottom of the blue scarf. **In the Layers palette, click and drag the Outer Glow effect sublayer from the Heartsinger layer to the Margee Wheeler layer**. The entire effect is copied to the layer. You can even drag an effect from one file to another. You can also use Layer/ Layer Style/Copy Layer Style from the menu bar. Though this may seem to be more work, it gives you the advantage of being able to link several layers and then use Layer/Layer Style/Paste Layer Style to Linked to apply that style to several layers at once. **Turn on the guidelines (Command-') if they are not currently showing and position both text layers so they fit within the safety area.**

ADD HEARTS AND LAYER EFFECTS

STEP 55: To complete the Seven Chakras motif, we need to add a couple more hearts to the image—one at the third eye and one at the crown chakra. Luckily, Photoshop makes this an absolute snap with the Custom Shapes tool. **First, click the Eyedropper tool and make sure it is set to 3 by 3 Average in the Tool Options bar. Now sample the colors of the large heart at Margee's throat and shoulders until you find a deep red that you like. Next, type U for the Shape tool. In the Tool Options bar, make sure you have chosen the icon for a new shape layer, then click the icon for the Custom Shapes tool** (or you can type Shift-U until you get there). **You can click either the Shape icon or the pop-up arrow to get the palette of currently loaded shapes. Load the Shapes presets to find the correct heart. Draw a small heart between and slightly above Margee's eyes.** Remember, you can use the Option key to draw from the center out, and the Shift key to keep the drawing proportional, but hold down the keys after you start your drag. When you are happy with the size of the heart, you can go to the next step if the Make New Shape icon is highlighted in the selection interaction area of the Options bar. If it's not the highlighted icon, switch to it now then go to Step 56.

STEP 55: Click the New Shape Layer icon on the left of the Options bar, then choose the Custom Shapes icon.

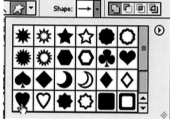

STEP 55: Load the Shapes collection of presets from this pop-up. Click the second heart to use this as the custom shape to draw.

STEP 55: As you click and drag, you see the path that forms the shape.

STEP 55: When you release the mouse after the drag, the shape becomes filled with the current foreground color and a vector mask is applied to the layer in the shape that you just built.

STEP 56: **Draw another heart above Margee's head. It should be slightly larger than the one for the third eye.** We drew these two hearts on different layers, even though they are the same color, because we want to add an effect to this heart and not the one at the third eye. **Once again, drag the Outer Glow effect from the Heartsinger layer (or the Margee Wheeler layer) to the Shape 2 layer.** The effect is pretty good, but a little too bright for this area. **Double-click the Outer Glow sublayer to bring up the Layer Styles dialog box. Click the Contour pop-up to choose the Linear contour.** This pulls the glow in and makes the effect more suitable to this heart.

STEP 56: This glow uses the Half Round contour.

STEP 56: This glow uses the Linear contour.

STEP 56: Align both hearts on the center guide.

ADD LAYER STYLES TO THE MARGEE ARTWORK LAYER

STEP 57: You're almost done! We only need to add a couple of layer styles to the Margee Artwork layer to make that layer stand apart from the background. **First, click the Margee Artwork layer to activate it, then double-click the layer thumbnail to bring up the Layer Styles dialog. Click on Drop Shadow (remember to click the name to bring up the options for that style). First, change the angle to 90° so the shadow will be on all sides of the artwork. Now use the following settings for the shadow itself: Distance, 23 pixels; Spread, 23%; Size, 46 pixels. Lower the Opacity to 55% and click the color swatch to make the shadow color a deep indigo blue rather than black. At the bottom of the dialog, you can add Noise to the shadow, and I used 4%—just a touch. I also felt the Half Round contour was a softer shadow than the Linear contour, but experiment with both, or click the contour swatch itself to edit the contour. Choose the contour you prefer.**

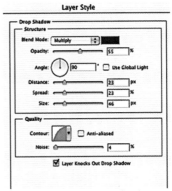

STEP 57: These are settings for the Drop Shadow style.

STEP 58: **Now, rather than say OK and leave the dialog, click the Outer Glow style name to switch to those options. Bring the Opacity back up to 60% and click the color swatch to use the original color for Outer Glow. The RGB numbers for this yellow are 255, 255, 190. We want this yellow to be brighter than the glows on the other layers. Bring the Spread slider in to 0 and the Size slider to 16. And finally, use the Linear contour (the first one in the Contour Swatch palette) to keep this glow sharper than the glows on the text or hearts. Say OK to this dialog and check your work. You might want to turn the Eye icon for this particular effect on and off to see whether you like the effect or think the artwork is more natural without it. We printed the CD cover with the glow.** So, you're finished with the CD cover. Now all you need to do to make this a real-world product is design the back cover of the four-page brochure, the inside spread, the tray card, and the CD itself. After this example, that should be a snap.

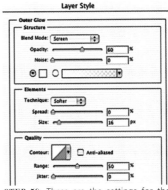

STEP 58: These are the settings for the Outer Glow style.

A WORD ABOUT THE EDIT/FADE COMMAND

When you run a filter in Photoshop, you have the option of Edit/Fade after running the filter to change the effect of the filter before it is made permanent. Using Fade is sort of like running a filter on the image in a separate layer above the image. If you do that, you can always go back and change the Opacity or Blend mode of that layer to blend the filter with the original image underneath. Doing this

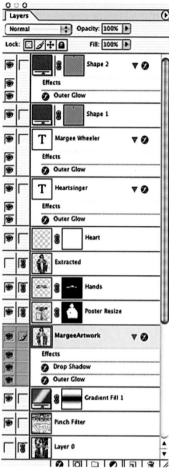

Your final layers palette will look something like this depending on which filter layers you chose to keep.

with layers is a great approach, and we used it a lot earlier in this chapter. The Edit/Fade command is like running the filter in this other layer, but if you don't adjust it before you do something else, it gets merged with the layer below. The feature says: "Let's give them one more chance to tweak this filter by changing the Opacity or Blend mode; then we'll make the effect permanent on the layer that was active when they ran the filter."

To use Edit/Fade, select it after running a filter and you will get the Fade dialog box. You can switch the Blend mode or Opacity, but you have no layer options or layer mask. You can then Undo and Redo the Fade, but when you do anything else that changes the Undo buffer, the ability to further change the Fade goes away, except by using the History Brush or Fill from History.

If you really want flexibility, just make a copy of the layer you were going to run the filter on, put that copy on top of the current layer, and run the filter on the copy. Because this is a separate layer, you have all the capabilities of Fade, plus you have layer options, plus you can change it or undo it at any time just by changing the Eye icon, Opacity, Blend mode, or layer options. Even when you save the file and quit, you will later have these same options upon reopening the file.

You've built the front cover, now you can do the back cover, tray card, and inside pages of the brochure.

Chapter 34: Heartsinger CD Cover

35 HANDS-ON SESSION: Digital Paint

An exploration of the brush capabilities in Photoshop CS.
How to build, use, and save custom brushes. A few
techniques to get you started.

Okay, it's confession time. When I first wrote this chapter for the last version of *Photoshop Artistry*, I was petrified. I've been a very good production artist for many years; give me a comp and I can make your project look the way you want it. But, Art, personal creativity?

I've learned a lot in the past 18 months, not the least of which has been to share the process as well as the results. If you've come to this chapter to explore a personal impulse to say something other than the strictly photographic, you are in the right place. Although, I cannot, in one chapter, tell you all there is to know about digital paint, I can begin to point the way for some of you. And, I encourage you, whether you consider yourself an artist or not, to explore what's available to you in Photoshop and other applications to stretch you creatively.

I've always been told to write what you know. In drawing, you must forget what you know about objects and simply draw what's there, what your eyes report to you. Painting, I believe, is the point where you must do both. You must use everything you know about value, light and shadow, color; and you must let go of all you know and be guided by internal impulse and by the paint itself. Only through exploration of the medium will you begin to know what you have to say.

We'll be re-painting a couple of different photographs in this chapter. It's not necessary to work from a photograph if you want to simply pick up your pen and paint. I did say "pen" and by that I mean you'll need a pressure-sensitive tablet to really make use of and control the brush capacities. I'll be using the Wacom Intuos tablet with the stylus to illustrate some of those capabilities.

I'll also show you some of the things that you can do with procreate ™ Painter that are beyond what Photoshop can do. If you really get the painting bug, you might want to try that application as well. Using the two in conjunction with each other gives you the most power and control as each application has strengths the other does not have.

We'll be repainting this image later in the chapter.

One of the two painted versions of the Red Mountain image.

WHY PAINT DIGITALLY?

I'm not a purist or a technocrat. I don't think everything is better digitally, but there are some very good reasons to work digitally:

1. No fumes, no mess.
2. No drying time. No "fat over lean" colors.
3. Mix media difficult or impossible to mix traditionally. Experiment freely.
4. Work in layers allowing for changes in composition.

For commercial illustrators, the reasons are clear. Increasingly short deadlines and computer-savvy (at least partially) clients require faster turnaround than ever. Digital has the advantage, here. But for artists? Well, my feeling is that digital is neither the greatest nor worst that art has to offer. It's simply another tool. In the hands of an artist, great art is possible. And for some of us, it is the perfect venue to begin to explore our artistic leanings. We already have the computer, an imaging program, maybe even a pressure-sensitive tablet. Really, we're ready to begin to paint.

But, before we begin to paint, we need to explore Photoshop's brushes.

PHOTOSHOP BRUSHES

To get the most out of the brushes, you need to use a pressure-sensitive tablet. Barry and I have a running disagreement about tablet use. He feels they are generally a nuisance. I've used a Wacom tablet for about ten years and absolutely refuse to work without it. Not only is it more ergonomic than using a mouse, the feel is more natural, the strokes you make more realistic, and the finished product more polished. And, if you've used a traditional airbrush, you owe it to yourself to try the Intuos Airbrush—it's amazing. Though Photoshop's brushes are limited in the their ability to move underlying layers of paint as Painter's can do, they are nonetheless amazing. Here's the basics of how they work.

THE BRUSHES PALETTE

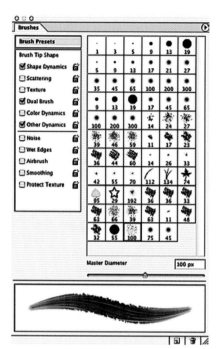

STEP 1: Here's the default Photoshop CS brushes in Small Thumbnail view. We'll be working with a smaller set than this for painting.

STEP 1: I'm going to assume that you have Barry's Photo Brushes loaded from the CD. Barry set these up for work with realistic photography, but there are too many to really be effective for use in painting. We'll be loading a special set of tool presets for this painting part of this exercise and bypass the brushes palette for the most part, but you may want to modify brushes that I use in this chapter, so it's important to know your options. Also you'll notice in most of the book, we show you the Brushes palette in Small Thumbnail view, as shown in the illustration above, but in this chapter we will switch between thumbnail and Small List view. You'll want to reload Barry's Photo Brushes when you finish this chapter to continue work on other exercises, but first, let's take a look at the default brushes that Adobe ships with Photoshop CS. **Type B to access the Paintbrush tool (make sure you're in the Paintbrush and not the Pencil or all your brushes will be hard edged) and press Shift-F12 to bring up the Brushes palette.** I generally don't dock my Brushes palette in the Palette Well because the pop-up covers so much of the palette when the Brushes palette is so far to the right of the screen. Shift-F12 or clicking the Palette button on the Options bar makes it very easy to access the entire palette, so use one of these two methods. **Use the palette pop-up to Reset the brushes to the default brushes. Say OK to completely replace the brushes instead of appending them.** This is a big palette (far more than we need), but we're going to start with it because it has some nice brush tips to work with. **Click the pop-up again and switch to the Small List View.**

STEP 2: **Make sure you have the Brush Presets area highlighted, and hold your cursor still over one of the brushes. The Stroke Thumbnail at the bottom of the palette updates as you move over each brush to preview the stroke it makes. Now, hold down the Option key as you move your cursor over the brush names. You'll see a pair of scissors. Like all the other palettes with swatches, you can cut any brush from the palette using the Option key. We're going to work with the six brushes pictured**

STEP 2: When you see the Scissors, you can click to delete a brush from the presets.

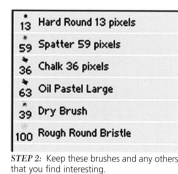

STEP 2: Keep these brushes and any others that you find interesting.

382

Chapter 35: Digital Paint

in the illustration to the previous page. You can delete others if you like or simply scroll until you find the right brush.

Next, click on the Brush Tip Shape tab of the palette. This will look very familiar to those of you who have worked in Photoshop versions previous to Photoshop 7. The Diameter, Angle, Roundness, Hardness, and Spacing options are here. A quick explanation for those of you new to Photoshop: Diameter is the size of the brush in pixels; Angle controls the angle of the brush (meaningless when the brush is 100% round, but important otherwise); Roundness controls whether the brush is "squeezed" or used at full size; Hardness is the amount of blur applied to the edge of the brush with 100% being sharply defined and 0% being soft and blurry; Spacing is how often a dab of paint is placed along a stroke—at 100% each dab will be tangent or just touching the next, at 25% they overlap to create a relatively smooth stroke depending on the brush tip.

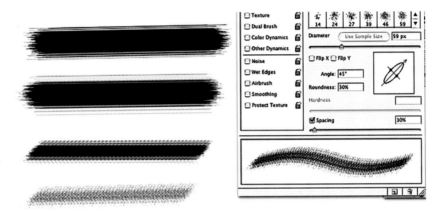

STEP 3: The top stroke is the default 59-pixel Spatter brush. In the second stroke, only the angle has changed. In the third stroke, Angle and Roundness have changed, and in the fourth stroke, Spacing has also changed.

STEP 3: **Go to File/New and click the Preset Sizes pop-up for a 5x7 document with a white background. Type Command-Option-0 to make sure you view your document at 100%.** This will help you see more clearly exactly what each stroke is doing. **Click the icon for the 59-pixel Spatter brush and notice that the default Angle on this brush is 0°, the Roundness is 100%, and the Spacing is 2%. Type D for the default colors, and type 0 to make sure the Opacity of the brush is 100%. Type Shift-3 to set the Flow to 30%.** Get used to typing the keyboard shortcuts to adjust Opacity and Flow; they are not the same thing and how you set the two does make a difference. Think of Opacity as the transparency of the medium itself. You'll find that thick oil paint is very opaque and a water color wash may have only 10-20% Opacity. Flow is more analogous to the amount of paint on the brush, with 0% being a dry brush and 100% being fully loaded.

Now, make a stroke on your new, blank canvas. Next, grab the Arrowhead in the square to the right of the Angle and Roundness settings. This controls the Angle of the brush. Drag it to the left to see the Preview change. Because of the way the pixels are arranged in the Custom Brush, changing only this one option does make a difference in the way the stroke appears. **Bring the arrow to the left until the Angle is 45° and make another stroke. See the difference? Now, grab one of the dots on the circle and push toward the center until the Roundness is 30%. If you have trouble doing this manually, you can double-click on any of the input areas to type in a value. Once again, paint a stroke on the canvas. Finally, change the Spacing to 10%**

STEP 4: Shape Dynamic controls.

STEP 4: Angle has directional controls as well as the controls found on most other options.

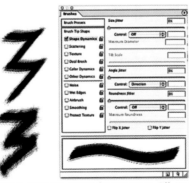

STEP 4: With the control for Size set to Off, I've made the first stroke using Initial Direction as the Angle control. The second stroke is made using Direction as the control.

and lay down a stroke. All this variation in a single brush, and you're only getting started.

STEP 4: **Change the Spacing back to 2% and turn Shape Dynamics on by clicking the checkbox.** Just as in the Layer Styles dialog that is the model for this dialog, clicking the checkbox will turn on the options, but to actually see what options you have you need to click on the words themselves. **So, if you haven't already, click the words, Shape Dynamics.**

You'll see here several words that will be repeated over and over in different options in this dialog—Jitter, Control, and Minimum. Though each option is relatively simple, when you put all of them together, the number of iterations are overwhelming, so take it slow.

First, we'll talk about Control. This means how does Photoshop know what you want it to do? If you turn the Control Off, Photoshop makes the decisions for you. Use Fade if you want the effect or jitter to fade out at a certain number of dabs. With Pen Pressure, less pressure results in a smaller value, heavy pressure gives you the higher values. Pen Tilt is only available on tablets that support tilt, and when you use it, you have an additional slider for Tilt Scale or how far from the pen nib the paint will spray out. Stylus Wheel works when you have an Airbrush device with a wheel. If you look at the controls for Angle, you'll see that there are two extra, Initial Direction and Direction. These are very important if you are using a flat brush. Initial Direction means that the angle of the brush will be consistent with the   stroke of the stylus. Start a flat stroke horizontally and it will be large in the horizontal direction and thin in the vertical. Direction, on the other hand, will rotate the angle of the brush as the direction of painting changes.

Jitter means amount of randomness. You are able to change the Jitter value for Size, Angle, and Roundness in this one little area of the Brush Options palette. In other areas, you can change jitter for Hue, Saturation, Lightness, Opacity, and Flow, among others.

This is a good brush to demonstrate what Jitter means. **Turn the control for Angle jitter off and turn the control for Size back to Pen Pressure. Set the Minimum Diameter for the brush all the way to 0%, then move the Size Jitter slider to the right and watch the brush preview. Bring the Size Jitter slider up to 50% and make a stroke with the brush.** This gives you a really nice grainy sort of pastel look that is great, but let's go a few steps further to really see what's happening here. **Once again turn the Control for Size Off. Now click back on the Brush Tip shape area of this palette and set the Spacing of this brush to 100%. This means that the dabs of paint set down by the brush do not overlap. You can now see that there is a variation in the size of the dabs. If you move the Size Jitter slider to 100%, Photoshop will apply maximum randomness to the size of the dab during the course of the stroke.** Turning the Control to Off means that Photoshop makes the decision of how the jitter will be applied to the stroke. When you choose Pen Pressure (the default on many brushes), the pressure of the stroke will control the amount of jitter. In this case, a light touch will produce small dabs, and more pressure will produce the larger dabs.

There's one more setting that contributes to the size dab that your brush lays down, the Minimum Diameter setting. In this case we're talking minimum size of the dab. With the slider all the way to the left, the dab can be so small as to be barely visible. The higher the value, the larger the dab must be. To see this clearly, **go back to Brush Tips and change the Spacing setting to 1. Return to the Shape Dynamics area, use Pen Pressure as the Control method, and set Size Jitter to 0. Notice how the beginning and end of the stroke preview are pointed? Now move the Minimum**

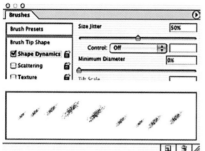

STEP 4: By setting the Spacing of the brush (in the Brush Tip Shape area) to 100%, the Size Jitter to 50%, and the Minimum Diameter to 0%, you can see the different size dabs that the brush will make.

PAINTBRUSH TOOL TIP

If you use Brush Size as your Painting tool cursor preview (as we most often do) and you find that the stroke of your brush does not always line up with the cursor, try changing your display to Precise Cursor under Edit/Preferences/Display and Cursors. The cursor and the stroke will now track together as they should.

Chapter 35: Digital Paint

Diameter slider to the right and you see that the beginning and end of the strokes enlarge. This setting can make a big difference when you are building brushes that behave like bristle brushes. With a watercolor brush, you'll want to be able to make a fine point; a flat hard-bristle brush will always have more width and splay very little.

STEP 5: **To experiment with the Roundness Jitter setting, you'll want to bring the Roundness of the brush in the Brush Tips area back to 100% because the roundness percentage in the Shape Dynamics section is based on the current roundness of the brush in the Brush Tips. At only 30% Roundness, your brush doesn't have a lot of jitter space available to it. Set the Roundness Jitter to 100%.** This also gives you a nicely textured brush, but very different from the brush using the Angle jitter. Are you starting to see how much you can manipulate these brushes? And this is only the first two sections of this palette. **In the Brush tips area, set the Roundness back to 30%.**

SAVE A BRUSH PRESET

STEP 6: **Let's review the brush that we've built so far. First, in the Brush Tips section, you can see the brush is 59 pixels and uses a custom brush tip. The Angle is 45°, the Roundness is 30%, and the Spacing is 1%. In the Shape Dynamic tab, turn off the Size Jitter by setting the Control to Off. The Angle Jitter is set to 0% and its Control is Off. The Roundness Jitter is set to 100% and its Control is also Off.** We've set several different options from the original preset and it might be difficult to remember exactly what we set if we wanted to get back to this brush (and the minute you click back on a different brush preset, you will lose these changes). **So save this brush as a new preset by clicking the pop-up on the top right of the palette and selecting New Brush Preset from the menu.** By default, you will get the name of the preset that you used to create the brush with a number appended. To me, this is not particularly helpful, so **I always try to give my brush a name that means something to me. For this brush, type in the name, Powdery Pastel, and click OK. Now click on the Brush Presets tab, view by Small Thumbnails** (use the pop-up to do this) and you will see that there is a 59-pixel brush in the last spot on the palette. This is your current brush. Notice also that if you move your cursor over an empty area of the palette, you get a paint bucket that allows you to "pour" your brush into a new preset. Use either method to save your preset, but save your presets. You'll see as we explore more of the capabilities of the brushes how frustrating it is to lose settings.

STEP 7: **To see the effects of the next section of the palette, Scattering, click back on the Brush Presets tab and choose the Hard Round 13-pixel brush. In the Brush Tip Shape section, make the spacing 100% so you can see each individual dab of paint. Turn off Shape Dynamics by simply clicking on the checkbox beside those words—no need to change any settings if you're not using them at all. Now click the word, Scattering, to access that section of the palette. Set the Scattering Control to Off and raise the amount to 200%.** This scatters the dabs of paint away from the stroke—vertically for a horizontal stroke, horizontally if the stroke itself is vertical. When you click Both Axis, the dabs scatter in both directions. **Uncheck the Both Axis box if you checked it and move the Count slider up to 2**. Notice that instead of one dab at each location, you now have two. You can move this slider all the way up to sixteen, but at

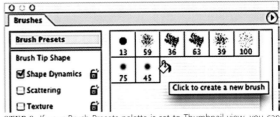

STEP 6: When you select New Brush from the Brushes Palette pop-up, you are prompted to name your new brush preset. The default name will use the name of the original preset and append a number, but it's better to give your brushes more meaningful names.

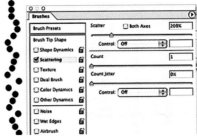

STEP 6: If your Brush Presets palette is set to Thumbnail view, you can change settings on a brush, and then "pour" your new brush into the palette. When you click an empty space, you get the Brush Name dialog box in the above illustration.

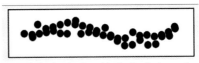

STEP 7: The dabs are scattered across the stroke.

STEP 7: Setting the Count in the Scattering section to 2 gives me two dabs of paint at every location. You can see both because the Scatter value allows very little overlap.

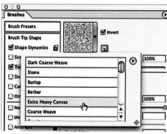

STEP 8: Choose the Extra Heavy Canvas texture from the Artistic Textures presets.

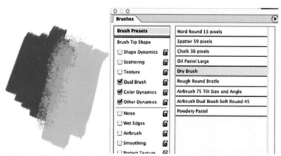

STEP 8: Using the same texture with different Blend modes can give you very different looks.

some point you'll see the dots overlap. You can also set a Jitter value here, which means that you could have 1 dot in some locations with up to 16 in others.

STEP 8: For Texture, let's use the brush preset that we created in Step 6. **Click on the Brush Presets tab and click on Powdery Pastel (or the last icon if you are in Small Thumbnail view). Now click the word Texture on the Brushes palette to access this section. The first decision you have to make is which texture to use. Click the texture icon pop-up and load the Artist Surfaces if you do not have them already loaded. Use the pop-up to view by Small List and choose the Extra Heavy Canvas texture. Turn on Invert if it is not already on. Make a stroke using each of the eight blend modes.** The Blend modes control how the brush tip and the texture interact with each other. If you find a look you want to use again, save a preset for it. The Texture Each Tip checkbox will cause the texture to interact with each dab of the brush rather than the stroke as a whole. If you try these out using the same settings, you won't notice much difference in the Blend modes. However, if you lower the Depth setting to about 50%, you'll see that there are differences. The Depth setting controls how much paint is laid down on the texture. At 100%, no paint permeates the low points of the texture. As you lower the Depth setting, less paint is applied to the high sections of the texture until at 0% no paint is laid down at all. If you want to vary the depth, you can set a jitter value and Minimum Depth (these settings are only available when you texture each tip). The Invert checkbox inverts the texture. Without it, the light parts of a texture receive the most paint. When Invert is on, the dark parts of the texture are high and receive the most paint.

STEP 9: **Photoshop allows you to use two brush tips together to create effects and texture. To explore, go back to the Brush Presets, and click on the Oil Pastel Large brush** (it's the first 63-pixel brush if you are viewing by thumbnail). I've chosen this brush because Dual Brush is the only option that is currently turned on for this brush. **Click on the words Dual Brush and take a look at this portion of the palette.** Don't let it scare you; basically, it's controls for the second brush. At the top, Mode is how the second brush tip will blend with the first, or primary, brush tip. Next are the icons for the secondary brush tips—in this case, the brush preset uses a 90-pixel sampled brush for its second tip. The controls below the icon allow you to change the characteristics of the second tip: its size, spacing, scatter, and count. **Change the Blend mode of this tip to Linear Burn and increase the Spacing to 125%. Now move the sliders on the controls to get a better idea of how the two tips interact with each other.** This is another area where there are too many options to imagine all the possibilities. If you find a look you like (or even think you like), save a preset.

STEP 10: **The next area is Color Dynamics. To set up this step, choose two contrasting colors as your foreground and background (I chose blue and orange), and then go back to the Brush Presets tab and choose the 36-pixel Chalk brush. Paint an area with one color, then paint an adjacent area with the second color (use X to switch foreground and background color). Now choose the Dry Brush and color an area that overlaps both colors.** What exactly is happening here? Click the Color Dynamics area to see the settings. There is a Jitter set to switch between the background and foreground colors as you paint. Currently the Control is set to Off, so Photoshop makes the decision for you. For more control, you can set this to Fade, Pen Pressure (although I tend to touch down with a light

STEP 10: The Dry Brush preset uses Color Dynamics to blend between the current foreground and background colors.

touch when I begin a stroke), Tilt, or Stylus Wheel. By the way, this Dry Brush preset (and variations of it) is one way to blend colors on artwork that you've built with texture and still maintain some texture. It requires a lot of choosing colors and is not nearly as useful as blending methods in Painter. Photoshop's primary blending tool, the Smudge tool, is not particularly useful for blending when texture is involved. Even at very low strengths, it tends to obliterate whatever texture you have created.

In this same area of the palette, you have sliders for Hue, Saturation, and Brightness Jitter. The jitter setting creates variation from the foreground color, and I haven't found these sliders to be particularly useful when trying to mimic most traditional media. If you use them, I recommend keeping the values low unless you are trying to achieve some special effect. There's also a Purity slider, which really should be renamed Saturation because that's what it does. Zero is completely desaturated; 100% completely saturated.

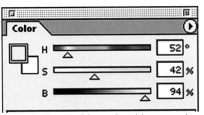

STEP 11: The HSB sliders make mixing your colors easier.

STEP 11: Finally, in the middle of the Brush Presets options are the Other Dynamics, which control the Opacity and Flow jitter of brushes. I'll introduce you to another brush I like here. **Click the Brush Presets area and choose the Rough Round Bristle brush. While you are still in this tab, click off the Shape Dynamics. The brush is no longer highlighted in the list. This is one of the reasons it's hard to remember all the settings that you've used for a brush; you often can't remember which preset you started with. Turn off the Dual Brush settings as well. What you have left is just the Brush Tip shape and Other Dynamics. Click Other Dynamics to view the current settings. Both Opacity and Flow have a Jitter setting and both Controls are Off. This means that the opacity and flow will both change over the course of a stroke, but Photoshop will control how the change occurs. Set your Option Bar Opacity to 100% by pressing 0 (zero) and your Flow to 100% by pressing Shift-0. Click the Brush Presets area again and use the Master Diameter slider to make the diameter 50 pixels.** We're going to paint a bit with this brush and experiment with the Opacity and Flow settings, as well as the Other Dynamics settings. **Choose a nice bright yellow and make some strokes.** I like the feathery edge of this brush.

Now, choose a yellow orange and make some strokes on top of the ones you just made. I generally switch my Color palette to HSB mode when I'm choosing color for painting. You can click in any of the input areas and then use the up- and down-arrow keys to bring the values up and down. So if I've chosen yellow and I want to warm it up by moving it toward red, I click in the H input area and use the down arrow to move one degree at a time. Once I have a hue I like, I can do the same thing with saturation and brightness.

When the Options bar settings are at 100% for both Opacity and Flow, this brush has nice edges, but other than that its strokes are not very interesting. **Lower the Flow to 50% by typing Shift-5, choose a nice red, and paint a few more strokes.** Now portions of the underlying paint show through and the color is richer. **Lower the Flow to 20% and there is even more of the underlying color mixed in. Finally, lower the Opacity to 50% and make a few more strokes. If you want to simulate a drier brush, raise the Opacity and Flow Jitter values.** This brush is very

STEP 11: Using the Rough Round Bristle brush at 100% Opacity and 100% Flow gives you a nice stroke but very little depth.

STEP 11: Lower the Flow setting to 50% and the look is much more interesting.

STEP 11: The second set of red strokes is the same color as above, but the Flow has been lowered to 20%.

STEP 11: The third set of red strokes were made using 50% Opacity and 20% Flow.

delicate and allows quite a bit of underlying color to show through. Once again, you have even more control of how the color is laid down if you change the Control setting for Opacity and/or Flow Jitter to Pressure, Tilt, or Wheel.

SAVE A TOOL PRESET

STEP 12: If we save this brush as a Brush Preset now, it will save the size of the brush, the Brush tip shape, and the settings for the Opacity and Flow Jitter set in the Other Dynamics. Unfortunately, it will not save the Opacity and Flow settings in the Options Bar. To save those options along with the brush style, you need to set a tool preset. **Click the Tool Preset pop-up on the far left of the Options Bar and select New Tool Preset from the menu. Name this brush Acrylic blend brush. Do not include the Brush Color.**

STEP 12: To save the Options Bar settings, you need a Tool preset rather than just a Brush preset.

STEP 12: A bunch of flowers is sometimes just a single flower with adjustments.

STEP 12: All of these strokes were made using the Acrylic Blend brush tool preset. I continued to lower to Opacity as I blended.

When you save a tool preset with the correct blend mode, opacity, and flow, you have a much more complete brush. The caveat is that when you change the Options Bar settings, choosing a mere Brush preset does not clear the Options Bar but maintains the last settings that were used. You'll find yourself switching between Tool Presets that you've saved and the Brushes palette, where you finesse the brush tips and dynamic settings to extend the versatility of a brush. Before you make a bunch of strokes, check the Options Bar so you don't have to redo a lot of work because you're in a bad blend mode. And keep that History palette handy (with a lot more than the default 20 steps available).

I used the brush to complete the flower petals, adding a tiny bit of Hue Jitter in the Color Dynamics section. I lowered the opacity as I blended in more color to keep the blend smooth. I made a selection of the flower, duplicated it twice, added stems, and did a couple of minor free transforms and a hue/sat adjustment. Quick bouquet.

OTHER BRUSH SETTINGS

In the lower section of the Brush Options are five additional checkboxes that have no settings associated with them. You can either click them on or off, but there are no sliders to slide or numbers to input. The first three—Noise, Wet Edges, and Airbrush—turn on or off depending on the preset you use.

Noise adds a bit more randomness to a brush and (according to the Photoshop manual) is primarily useful for brushes that are built with gray values. It's certainly a good idea, but really needs a slider. Try it out with the Rough Round Bristle preset. Bring the opacity of the brush down to about 50 and make strokes with Noise on and off. You may need to zoom in to see what's actually happening.

Wet Edges has been around for a long time. It causes the color of the stroke to be weighted to the outside of the stroke, which gives you a watercolor effect. The Water Color Small Round Tip and Wet Sponge presets both use this option.

Next is the Airbrush option, which also appears on the Options bar. You can turn this on for any of the presets, and what it will do is continue to build up the application of paint in one location if you hold the mouse or stylus down up to the maximum opacity you have set in the Options Bar.

The lower two options, Smoothing and Protect Texture, do not change from preset to preset but remain on or off until you manually change them. Smoothing helps to create a smoother stroke if you are using a stylus, but the computation sometimes lags behind the actual completion of the stroke. Protect Texture will use the texture that was active when you turned on the option for all brushes that use Texture. This is great because if you've built a brush using the Burlap texture and you've got a portion of your painting done with that texture, you don't want to switch brush presets to a brush that uses Granite.

Now, let's paint.

LANDSCAPE VERSION 1

We're going to repaint a photo Barry took with a 3.3 megapixel digital camera when he was in Aspen teaching at Andersen Ranch. He's concerned that I didn't use his color corrected version of the file, but this worked just fine for me. You are not constrained to using the techniques or tools that I present to you here, but I've created a set of tools for use in this part of the exercise. You can use these as the start of your artistic exploration.

STEP 1: The original Red Mountain image.

CREATE THE INITIAL SKETCH

STEP 1: **Click the Tool Preset icon on the Options bar, then click the pop-up menu and choose Load Tool Presets. Choose the Tools for Red Mountain preset from the *Photoshop CS Artistry* CD. Open the Red Mountain file from the CD. Bring up the Layers palette (F10 with ArtistKeys) and make a new blank layer. Type D for the default colors and then Command-delete to fill the layer with white. Double-click the layer name and rename this layer, Sketch layer.**

STEP 2: Use as much or as little detail as you need to decide where to block in colors.

STEP 2: **Lock the position of this layer by clicking the third lock icon on the top of the Layers palette. Every subsequent layer that you create should also be locked this way to prevent accidentally moving the layer as you draw or paint. Now lower the opacity of the Sketch layer to about 50%. Type B to access the Brush tool. From the Tool Presets, choose the Pencil Soft 20px brush. This is a very soft large pencil, but notice that it has a low flow and moderately low opacity setting. Trace over the major shapes and areas that you want to block in color in the next step. You may need to move the Opacity slider on the Sketch layer up and down to check your work.** If you are used to sketching on paper, you may find this step disconcerting because the feel of the stylus on the tablet is very smooth; the surface has no bite as paper would. Some artists tape a sheet of paper over the tablet at this step to make the feel more familiar.

STEP 2: Bring the opacity of the Sketch layer down to about 50% so you can see the underlying image as you draw.

ROUGH IN THE COLOR

STEP 3: **Set your Color palette to HSB if you have not already done so.** This allows you to choose a basic hue for your colors, then move the sliders to warm or cool the color (Hue), change the tint (Saturation), or the tone (Brightness). **Build a color palette that contains the basic colors you want to use. You can choose colors from the Background layer, if you like, or use the Color palette to mix your own. Choose all your colors first or add as you paint. I've created a basic palette for this step that you can load from the CD called RedMountain.aco. Show the Swatches palette, then use the pop-up to load this swatch set if you want to use it. Drag the Sketch layer to the new layer icon at the bottom of the Layers palette to make a copy of this layer and rename the layer, Block in Color. Turn off the Eye icon for the Sketch layer.**

STEP 4: Here is my blocked-in color version of the image. In some areas I've used large chunks of unbroken colors; in other areas, such as the rocks on the hill on the right, I've been more specific.

STEP 4: **Block color into the shapes you've drawn.** You can be very precise with your edges, or you can be very loose. I found that I liked leaving white canvas showing through in the sky and mountain where the added luminosity works well. In the darker areas of the painting, I was more particular about covering the canvas. **I used the Oil Pastel CS brush for much of my work here, using the bracket keys to change the size of the brush as needed. I began by choosing colors from the Background layer and adding them to the palette, but quickly found that turning the Eye icon on and off for the Block in Color layer and merely using the Background layer as a reference was preferable for me. This allowed me to interpret the color I was seeing rather than being completely literal. You don't need to strictly adhere to the color that's in the photograph; in fact, if you do, you'll probably end up with something stilted and lifeless. This is a good place to start to move away from the photo and paint what you feel, what comes to you. Remember, this is digital, so you can undo what you've done, or (like many a great painter) paint over your mistakes. Continue to add color to your palette and build tool presets as you experiment with brushes. Save your file.**

ADD DETAIL

At this point, you need to decide what direction you're headed with this piece. For the look of flat acrylics with opaque colors, you can continue to work with the same brush you've been using to block in the color. Simply change the size of the brush as you become more detailed in your painting. I personally like to build many layers of color. I'm fascinated (yes, and sometimes horrified) at the way colors combine. You may work differently, preferring to use very clean and precise areas of pure color.

What technique do you want to mimic? Dry or wet? We're going to work on a Dry Brush version, which will add texture as we paint with a brush tool preset. If you want to try a wet into wet version, you'll need to use the Smudge tool to blend your colors. With the Smudge tool, you'll want to block the initial colors in fairly completely over the canvas, unless you want to smudge the white of the canvas along with the paint colors. And if you really want to work wet into wet, Painter offers you better tools and more options. I'll talk more about that at the end of the chapter.

For now, it's on to Dry Brush.

STEP 5: The Dry Brush 70% hue jitter brush has a bit of variation in the hue of the paint. There are places like the sky where I liked this effect. Other areas did not work as well.

STEP 5: In the areas where I was sometimes layering a light color over a darker color, I increased the opacity of the brush to 100%.

STEP 5: **Drag the Block in Color layer to the New Layer icon to make a copy of the layer. Rename the layer, Dry Brush. Click the Tool Preset icon on the Options bar to choose the Dry Brush 70% hue jitter brush. Begin to use the Option key to pick up colors from the roughed-in version and spread paint into adjacent areas. This is a very back-and-forth process, choosing color in first one area then another. Notice that the brush you are using has only a 70% opacity and 40% flow. You may decide to raise or lower the opacity to have more or less coverage in certain areas. Also this brush has a bit of Hue jitter, which will give you some variation in the color of the paint. If you don't like this for part or all of the painting, click the Color Dynamics checkbox on the Brushes palette to turn Hue jitter off. Also, there may be times when you want to choose a color fresh from the Color palette rather than from the painting if you are working over an area that has become muddied from the mixture of paint.**

I found there were areas such as the trees where I was working with a lot of very dark colors that I needed to increase the opacity all the way to 100% to get the coverage that I wanted at this stage. I decreased the brush size as well several times to use almost a pencil effect. I have another Dry Brush preset that I used on occasion, the Dry Brush Scattered 200% preset. I narrowed this down to about 9 pixels, again for small detail at 100% opacity. And for the trunks of trees and sharp edges of rocks or logs, I used the #2 pencil preset.

Chapter 35: Digital Paint

This brings me to an important issue about digital paint. To create this piece, I used five brush presets and could have used only three. You don't need a lot of brushes to paint. Use three or four and explore what their capabilities are. Get to know them well. Start with something that you think will work for you, then refine your brushes until they work the way you do. Don't get bogged down in the thousands of choices available to you.

LANDSCAPE VERSION 2

I wanted to give you another possibility of working with a photo, cloning. We'll use the Clone Stamp with a special preset to create a pastel version of this same image. You can do just the first three steps, or use the result as the basis for doing more extensive work with a different Brush preset. Instructions here are minimal. You'll figure it out quickly.

STEP 5: Here's my final dry brushed version of the image. This version of the image can be found in the RedMountainFinal.psd file on the *Photoshop CS Artistry* CD.

CREATE THE GROUND

STEP 1: **Turn off the Eye icons for all layers but the Background. Create a new, blank layer above the Background layer and name it Pastel. Rather than working on a white canvas or ground, this time fill the layer with color. The color you choose depends on the effect you want. I chose a light gray, but you could try a warm ivory, a cool blue, lavender, or even a darker gray or brown tone. Remember, this color is going to show through in places because we are using a lot of texture here.**

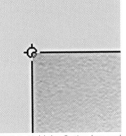

STEP 2: Hold the Option key and click the upper-left corner of the Background layer.

STEP 2: Click the upper-left corner of the Pastel layer without the Option key to establish the clone relationship.

SET UP THE CLONE RELATIONSHIP

STEP 2: I've created a Clone Stamp tool preset for you to use for this version. The Large Chalk Dissolve 20% stamp uses dissolve mode to clone color from the image, in this case the Background layer. The Opacity setting controls how dense the application of color will be, but the setting must be below 100% for the colored ground to show through. Before you use the Clone stamp, you have to tell Photoshop the pickup location for the art you want to use. **If you are not already in Full Screen mode, type F now to do so. Turn off the Eye Icon for the Pastel layer. Type S to use the Clone Stamp tool, then click the Tool Preset icon on the Options bar to choose the Large Chalk Dissolve 20% preset. Hold down th e Option key and click on the upper-left corner of the Background layer. This sets the pick-up location for the tool. Now, turn the Eye icon back on for the Pastel layer and, without the Option key, click on the upper-left corner of this layer. This sets the put-down location for the stamp.** Now, whenever you paint, the Clone Stamp will pick up the color from the Background layer directly below the spot where the cursor is on the Pastel layer. NOTE: If you do not finish your painting in one Photoshop session and return to cloning

STEP 3: Here, I've begun to clone the underlying image. The opacity is quite low here, but every time I move over an area again, the paint builds up, and builds up very quickly. In my original try at this technique, I didn't follow the natural patterns of the image; that is, horizontal strokes for the sky and diagonal strokes for the mountains which gave me a very unnatural look. Though you can cover a lot with pure pigment later on, every step is important. I also found that after I had applied color with the brush tool, there were a few spots where I wanted to bring back a bit of the underlying image, so I re-established the clone relationship and used the Clone stamp over the Brush tool work.

STEP 4: My final pastel version is on the *Photoshop CS Artistry* CD.

after you have quit, you will have to re-establish this relationship to continue to clone in the right place. That is why it is best to establish one place that you always start your clone; in this case, the upper-left corner.

STEP 3: **Follow the basic flow of the scene. As you go over an area with the stamp, the color will build up. Keep your touch light if you want a lot of the gray ground to show through. When you get as much of the underlying picture showing as you want, stop. You can be done at this point, or you can use the Brush tool to fill in color where you want.**

STEP 4: **If you want to add color, you might try the Brush tool using the Oil pastel light small dissolve preset. This is currently set to a very low opacity; I switched freely from 40 to 70 or 90% also changing the size of my brush when necessary to make fine marks. I used mostly colors from the image or the palette, but now and then I chose pure black to add detail and depth.** Still this image was completed using only two brushes. You don't need a complex set of tools.

A DIGITAL PORTRAIT

Rich Harris, Creative Director at Wacom, showed me this quick technique for producing a watercolor or colored pencil drawing, and I loved it so much I immediately had to try it on numerous photos of family and friends. Hope you enjoy it as much as I did.

STEP 1: **Open Alison.tif from the CD. Go to Image/Mode and choose Grayscale from the menu. Click OK if Photoshop asks whether you want to discard the color information.** By the way, if you don't like the grayscale version that Photoshop gives you automatically, try creating your own using Image/Adjust/Channel Mixer and clicking the Monochrome checkbox. Photoshop does a nice job here, but I hardly ever create a grayscale image these days without checking the Channel Mixer.

STEP 1: The original RGB version of Alison.

STEP 1: Photoshop's default grayscale version.

STEP 3: The two layers together after the Gaussian blur.

Chapter 35: Digital Paint

STEP 4: Here's Alison after I finished painting in the color.

STEP 5: Placing the underlying layer of color unifies and warms the portrait.

Painter can smear underlying color as you work, even on a bristle-by-bristle basis. The Resaturation and Bleed settings let you control how much paint is picked up by your brush as you stroke.

You can build a brush that blends the colors together in Painter without destroying the underlying texture.

Here are some of Painter's watercolor brushes. I've painted strokes with just a few so you can see the variety.

STEP 2: **Double-click the name of the layer to rename it Alison. Make a copy of the layer by dragging it to the Make New Layer icon at the bottom of the Layers palette. Now invert this layer (Command-I) and change the Blend mode to Color Dodge.** The image will almost completely disappear, but don't be worried—we're going to bring it back.

STEP 3: **Go to Filter/Blur/Gaussian Blur and use about 10 pixels on this layer.** The details will come out again. You can use a different value for more or less detail. **Merge these two layers together using the Layers palette pop-up and change the Blend mode to Multiply.**

STEP 4: **Go back to Image/Mode and once again make the file RGB. Now Command-click the Make New Layer icon to create a layer beneath the Alison layer.** This is the paint layer. **You can now choose a brush to lay down the color of the portrait, letting the upper layer supply the detail.** Many of the presets you have currently loaded are interesting. Try different layers of color that use different brushes, some textured, some softer. **Don't forget to experiment with Opacity and Flow as you paint.** I used mostly a Soft Round 13-pixel brush for this version, changing the size of the brush to work in different areas.

STEP 5: Finally for this picture, **I added a new layer at the bottom of the stacking order and filled it with color a bit lighter and similar to the flesh tones of Alison's skin.** This simulates starting the portrait on colored paper rather than white.

PHOTOSHOP'S LIMITATIONS

Photoshop made a giant leap toward working naturalistically with version 7, but it still has limitations when you compare it to Painter, or ask it to do some things that you could do with real paint.

Photoshop can do a pretty good job of simulating wet on dry methods of painting or dry media such as chalk or pastel. You cannot get realistic wet on wet results. There is no way to ask underlying colors to spread or bleed as you paint a new color on top. Painter can do this, and it's one of the major reasons you might choose Painter over Photoshop.

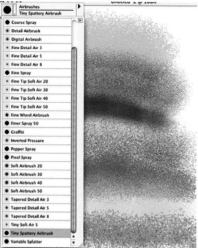

I've airbrushed with five of the default variants in Painter. The sprays from these brushes behave much more like a real airbrush than Photoshop.

Painter also works with paper grain better than Photoshop. In Painter, you choose a texture for your canvas, and any brush that uses texture will know to use that paper grain. You can ask Photoshop's brushes to remember a texture by turning on Protect Texture in the Brushes palette, and that's good. But when you switch to the Smudge tool to blend your colors, your texture is quickly obliterated. In Painter, you can build tools that smudge the colors together but recognize the underlying texture.

If you work in Watercolor or Airbrush, Painter is also a better choice for you. The tools in Painter are far superior to Photoshop, and really, all the brushes are more responsive in Painter.

And finally, there's Impasto. Painter allows you to paint a brushstroke that has depth. If it's the look of thick oils or acrylics you're after, Photoshop will only frustrate you.

So, if you merely need a painterly effect, Photoshop probably has all the power and flexibility that you will need. If you want to feel like you're actually using paint, try out Painter now, or watch for future versions of Photoshop.

AND FINALLY

Don't expect to whip out a painting in an hour or two. Painting (not just achieving painterly effects) takes time. Give yourself the time and you'll find the rewards are very great. Painting is meditation and connection. Once you begin to paint, you see the world differently, reveling in beauty you never noticed before. You become aware of the intricacies of this amazing planet and all it's creatures. Paint for peace.

Painter's Impasto brushes simulate depth.

This version of Red Mountain was painted using Painter and the Smeary Bristle Cloner brush. Where either of the two Photoshop versions took about eight hours to complete in a way that I liked, this version was accomplished in just half an hour. It has the look and feel of alla prima painting, with colors worked quickly and pigments mixing on the canvas. It was a lot of fun.

This is the original version of Maria Ferrari's gorgeous Gerbera Bouquet. Maria, a professional photographer from New York City, took Barry's class and is now teaching Photoshop in the city. Her Web site is mariaferrari.com. Look her up if you need a great teacher or photographer.

Here, I created a duplicate of the original layer, added a layer mask to it, and created a new background layer under the duplicate of the flowers. The flowers layer has been filtered with both the Dry Brush and Watercolor filters. It's a fairly nice effect, but I wouldn't say it really looks painted.

Here, I took the filtered version and used the Smudge tool with different brush tips and at different opacities to manipulate the color. This gave me more of the feeling I was looking for than the filtered version or simply smudging the original.

IMAGES FOR THE WEB AND MULTIMEDIA

PHOTOSHOP CS WEB FEATURES

BUILD YOUR PHOTOGRAPHY WEB SITE WITH PHOTOSHOP

WHEN TO CHOOSE GIF, JPEG, OR PNG

4-UP DIALOGS TO OPTIMIZE WEB IMAGES

WEB IMAGE GALLERIES, CONTACT SHEETS, AND PICTURE PACKAGES

While scoping out good shooting locations for our Advanced Oregon Coast photography workshops, Wendy took this in Newport, Oregon, with our Epson 3.2 megapixel point and shoot. We like the fog, it's so quiet, peaceful, fresh, and soothing!

HANDS-ON SESSION: Optimizing Images for the Web

Using the 4-Up Dialogs , Master Color Palettes, and
Weighted Optimization to create gif, jpeg, and png files.

WEB OPTIMIZATION WITH PHOTOSHOP & IMAGEREADY

In this chapter we'll take an in-depth look at all of the many options and settings for optimizing images for Web and multimedia use. As we explore the extensive functionality for this, we'll be looking not only at Photoshop, but also at ImageReady. Although Photoshop has more than enough Web optimization options for most people's needs, ImageReady differs in certain crucial aspects, and for some projects, it may make more sense to handle Web optimization in ImageReady. We'll cover those differences in great detail in this chapter, as well as point out times when ImageReady may be a better choice. Our coverage of ImageReady here is limited to preparing Web or multimedia versions of your images that look great and download fast. We won't be talking about how to use the program to actually create a Web page, or more specialized Web graphics.

FILE NAMING CONVENTIONS

When you are creating images to use on the Web or in multimedia, it's a good idea to use filenames that will work on most computer systems. In the past, we recommended naming such files using the 8.3 ("8-dot-3") naming convention, which meant that you had a filename of no more than eight characters and a three-letter file format extension. The 8.3 rule was mainly to accommodate older DOS Windows systems that would truncate any filenames longer than 8 characters (if you're burning CDs using ISO 9660 formatting, then you definitely want to use the 8.3 naming format or your filenames will be truncated). In today's Web world of the early 21st century, strict adherence to the 8.3 naming convention is not as critical as it once was, because most servers are now running more modern OS's that can handle longer filenames. It's still a good idea, however, to keep your filenames from getting too long and to use lowercase letters with a three-character extension indicating the file format. Make sure that any reference to the file in the HTML code of your Web page uses the same naming conventions, and never use spaces between words in filenames. If you must have a space, use the underscore character or a dash. On UNIX systems, it can be even more complicated, because they see a difference between upper- and lowercase letters in filenames. As we explore the various features that Photoshop has to offer for optimizing images, we will be working on the files gc.psd, redac.psd, and macn.psd within the gif jpeg and Color Palettes folder on your CD. The names of

STEP 2: In the Save As dialog, choose JPEG from the format menu, and click the As a Copy option to save the new JPEG to disk and leave your PSD file open and unaltered. Give your file a name that indicates the JPEG quality level. Here, we used "med" for medium.

these files use the 8.3 convention and are abbreviations for Grand Canyon, Red Acura, and McNamaras. The .psd indicates that they are in Photoshop format.

CREATING JPEGS IN PHOTOSHOP CS VIA THE SAVE AS DIALOG

There are two routes within Photoshop to creating compressed images in the jpeg and gif formats, and we'll cover both of them in this chapter. The method with the most functionality and options is the Save for Web dialog. This is a great part of the program that made its debut in version 5.5, and you may find that, once you become familiar with it, it's the best way to create gifs and jpegs. The other way to do this is how Photoshop users have been doing it for years, through the regular Save As dialog. Even though Save for Web has many more features available, if you just need to make a quick jpeg, then the "old fashioned" way is still perfectly valid.

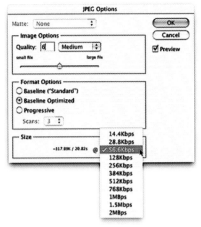

STEP 2: The Photoshop CS JPEG Options dialog box. These options will appear after you have chosen the JPEG format and then pressed Save in the Save As dialog.

STEP 1: If you're primarily interested in how to optimize images for the Web, you could skip ahead a few pages to learn about creating Web images in the very useful 4-Up dialogs found in Photoshop CS. You probably should read the next four pages anyway, though, as they contain plenty of useful information, especially concerning the creation of custom color palettes for multimedia projects. **Open the files gc.psd, redac.psd, and macn.psd from within their respective folders located within the Ch. 36 folder on your CD.**

STEP 2: **Make the redac.psd file active and go to File/Save As (Command-Shift-S). In the Save As dialog, choose jpeg from the drop-down format menu and click in the As a Copy checkbox. We're going to save a medium quality version of the file, so choose a name that reflects what you are doing. This is helpful for identification purposes when you're comparing different quality versions of the same image. For example, we used redacmed.jpg for the redac file to indicate that its quality is medium. Make sure you have the "As a Copy" box checked and press the Save button. In the jpeg Options dialog that appears, experiment with different quality settings.** With the preview turned on, you can see how the different levels of compression affect the image quality. Because viewers of a Web site or a multimedia presentation are going to be seeing the images at 100%, be sure that you're zoomed in to 100% so you can accurately judge the compression/quality trade-offs. At the bottom of the dialog box you can see how large the final jpeg will be when compressed, and also what the download time will be for various connection speeds (this information only appears if the preview is turned on). You can also choose from three different format options, Baseline Standard, Baseline Optimized, and Progressive. For most uses, Baseline Optimized will give you the best result and do a good job at compressing the image. The only very minor caveat with Baseline Optimized is that it may not be readable by some older browsers, but I've never ran into any problems with this. **If you want an image that appears in the browser gradually, looking chunky and pixilated at first and then getting better as more of it loads, choose Progressive. Choose a Medium setting of 6 and click the OK button.**

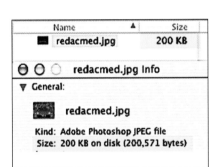

STEP 3: In the JPEG Options dialog, the size of our compressed file was forecast at about 118k, but in reality it turns out to be 200k because image previews and icons that were saved with the file have dramatically increased its size.

STEP 3: **Next, take a look at the file in the Finder on a Mac, or in Windows Explorer on the PC, and see what the file size is.** In the jpeg Options dialog the previewed compressed size for a level 6 jpeg of the red Acura was about 118k, but our final result is a surprisingly large 200k. The reason for the larger size is that image previews and icons were saved along with the file, making the final compressed size larger than expected. Having said that, let me just add that the file size with previews

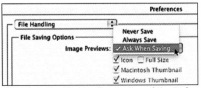

STEP 3: In the File Handling section of the Preferences, you can control the saving of image previews and icons. These add file size to your image and should not be saved with web images.

Save As

Save As: redacmed_nopreview.jpg

Format: JPEG

Where: test jpegs

Save: ☑ As a Copy   ☐ Annotations
      ☐ Alpha Channels   ☐ Spot Colors
      ☐ Layers

Color: ☐ Use Proof Setup: Working CMYK
       ☐ Embed Color Profile: ColorMatch RGB

Image Previews: ☐ Icon   ☐ Macintosh Thumbnail
                ☐ Full Size   ☐ Windows Thumbnail

STEP 3: If you have chosen Ask When Saving for image previews and icons in the Preferences, the Save As dialog will include checkboxes where you decide whether or not to include them when saving an image. In Windows Thumbnail is the only checkbox option.

Name		Size
📄 redacmed_nopreview.jpg		116 KB
📄 redacmed.jpg		200 KB

⊖ ○ ○   redacmed_nopreview.jpg In

▼ General:

📄 redacmed_nopreview.jpg

Kind: Adobe Photoshop JPEG file
Size: 116 KB on disk (118,581 bytes)

STEP 3: By eliminating the preview and icon from the second file shown above, I was able to save 84k, making the file about 42% smaller than if the preview and icon had been included.

Name	Size ▼
🖼 macnmed_nopreview.jpg	144 KB
🖼 redacmed_nopreview.jpg	116 KB
🖼 gcmed_nopreview.jpg	92 KB

STEP 4: The actual amount of jpeg compression you get will vary, depending on the complexity of each image. All of these images were the same pixel dimension (640x480), and were all saved with the same, medium quality jpeg settings and no previews, yet each one is a different size.

is much larger with Photoshop CS than when this same image was saved with the same settings in Photoshop 7. It seems excessive that the previews would add more than 75k to the size of the file. These extras are only seen when you are browsing your hard drive, or opening a file into an application that recognizes the thumbnail previews. For Web images or on a multimedia CD, they just take up extra space and make your file larger (and in this case, ridiculously larger) than it needs to be. If you're preparing images that will be viewed on a Web site, or you want to trim some kilobytes from a file that you're emailing, don't save the previews. Let's save another version and see how to turn the preview option off.

First, go to the Preferences, Photoshop/Preferences/ File Handling (on PCs the Preferences are under the Edit menu), and in the options for Image Previews, choose either Never Save, or Ask When Saving, and click OK. Next, choose Save As again (Command-Shift-S) and save the image as a jpeg with the same settings as in Step 2. For identification purposes, we'll call it "redacmed_nopreview". If you chose Ask When Saving for the image previews, make sure that the checkboxes at the bottom of the Save As dialog are all unchecked. In the jpeg Options dialog, choose a Level 6 quality setting, Baseline Optimized. After you save your file, compare the file size of the no preview image with the first jpeg you made. On my Mac system running OS 10.2.6, the file with no preview was reduced from 200k down to 116k, a savings of 84k or about 42%! When this same file was saved in Photoshop 7, the addition of the previews and icons added only 13% to the final file size. Although having the previews and icons is very helpful for images that reside on your computer, or that you archive to a CD or DVD, leaving them off of Web images will keep them as small and fast-loading as possible.

STEP 4: With jpeg compression, just because you use the identical settings on images that share the same pixel dimensions, it doesn't mean you'll end up with the same file size. The amount of compression you get depends on the visual complexity of each individual image. The more complex it is, the less compression you get; the more areas of flat color or repeated patterns, the better the compression. **Try this out for yourself by saving copies of the Grand Canyon and McNamara files with the same medium quality jpeg settings we used for the Red Acura image.** These three images each started out with a pixel resolution of exactly 640x480, but they will yield different final jpeg file sizes. When you open them back up from jpeg compression, they will still be 640x480 pixels; their file size just gets compressed for saving on disk and transmitting over a network.

A Cautionary Note: Because the jpeg format achieves it compression by discarding unnecessary image data, you should never use it as a file format for working on images you care about. If you start out with a jpeg, such as from your digital camera, and then do some editing and save it repeatedly every time you save in jpeg format, more data is being deleted, degrading image quality. The jpeg format should be used only as a format for emailing, Web images, or for original captures from a digital camera. Save your image in Photoshop format if you're going to be working on them.

Saving gifs and Working With Color Palettes

As with jpegs, a more full-featured way of creating a gif is to use the Save for Web dialog in Photoshop, or the 2-up and 4-up optimized tabs in ImageReady. We're definitely headed in that direction, but before we indulge ourselves there, we'll go over the other way you make a gif, and also talk a bit about the color tables that are created with these files.

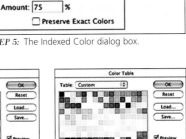

STEP 5: **Make sure you have the original psd versions open of the three files from the jpeg session we just finished. We are going to create gif versions of all these images and take a look at their Color Tables. For each one, choose Image/Duplicate to make an onscreen copy of the image, then choose Image/Mode/Index Color. In the Indexed Color dialog box, select the Local (Adaptive) Palette, 256 Colors, Forced Black and White, no Transparency, and a Diffusion Dither of 75%. Now**

STEP 5: The Indexed Color dialog box.

choose File/Save As and save each file with the Format set to CompuServe gif. Give it a filename that identifies its color depth; for the Red Acura, we used redac256.gif. Redac tells us it's the Red Acura, and 256 tells us it has 256 colors. Make sure you are saving it with no previews, and when the option for Row Order appears, choose Normal.

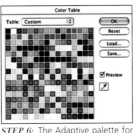

STEP 6: The Adaptive palette for the Red Acura image.

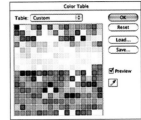

STEP 6: The Adaptive palette for the McNamaras image.

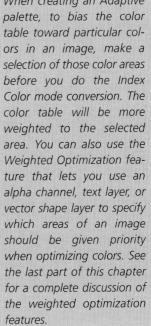

STEP 6: The Adaptive palette for the Grand Canyon image.

STEP 6: **Now make the redac256.gif image the active one by clicking its title bar, and from the main menu, choose Image/Mode/Color Table.** The color table is the exact collection of 256 colors that were used to describe this image. Because we chose an Adaptive color palette, the 256 colors you see here were adapted from actual colors in the image. The first two pixels in the upper left are a result of choosing Forced Black and White, ensuring that the color table will have an absolute black and white included. **Now, switch to the other images and examine their color tables to see how a different set of 256 colors was used for each one.**

Compare each color table with the actual image, and you'll see that Photoshop did a very good job at choosing the 256 colors that best represent all of the colors in the image. For the Red Acura, there are lots of rich, saturated reds, as well as the purples, greens, and blues that make up the streaked background. The Grand Canyon's color table has soft pastel blues, subtle greens, and a range of reddish-brown earth tones. In the color table for the McNamaras image, a wide range of colors is used to describe the varying skin tones, clothing colors, and background vegetation. When creating gifs from photographic images, an Adaptive palette will usually give you the best results, because it is built from colors contained in the actual image.

You've probably noticed that, in addition to Adaptive, there are two other Local palette choices in the same section of the popup menu in the Indexed Color dialog. Perceptual creates a palette from colors in the image, but it gives priority to choosing those colors for which the human eye has greater sensitivity. Selective is similar to Perceptual, but it works better for images with broad areas of color and it favors the preservation of Web-safe colors. If you're making a gif from an image that is not photographic, like a logo, or a graphic, then using the Selective palette will generally produce a better result.

When creating an Adaptive palette, to bias the color table toward particular colors in an image, make a selection of those color areas before you do the Index Color mode conversion. The color table will be more weighted to the selected area. You can also use the Weighted Optimization feature that lets you use an alpha channel, text layer, or vector shape layer to specify which areas of an image should be given priority when optimizing colors. See the last part of this chapter for a complete discussion of the weighted optimization features.

THE SYSTEM PALETTES AND WEB PALETTE

STEP 7: The System palette was created to deal with the differences between Adaptive palettes of images that need to be displayed on the same page on an 8-bit monitor. A System palette contains a broad range of colors from all over the spectrum so that you can display any image and it will look reasonably okay. It won't usually look near as good as it would with its own Adaptive palette, but by using the System palette, you can display many different gif images at the same time with reasonable results. The problem for Web developers is that the Mac and Windows OS each have

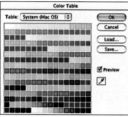

STEP 7: The Mac System palette.

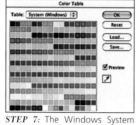

STEP 7: The Windows System palette.

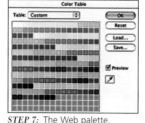

STEP 7: The Web palette.

different colors in their System palettes. Fortunately, there are 216 colors in common between the two palettes. The palette with these common colors is called the Web palette or Web-safe colors. Photoshop CS allows you to choose any of these palettes when creating 8-bit images. **Creating images using the Web palette allows them to display well on an 8-bit color monitor on the Mac and on the PC when using Netscape or Internet Explorer to browse your images. Having said that, you should still evaluate how much using these palettes will affect the color quality of your image, and also take into account your target audience.** Desktop and laptop computers being sold today have the ability to display at least thousands of colors, so **preparing images for 8-bit color display is not as crucial an issue as it once was.** Where 8-bit color will probably continue to be important is in the color displays of hand held computers and other PDA devices. If you're creating a Web presentation of your photographs, then you're probably going to be more concerned about those viewers who have monitors that can display a quality image, rather than a hand-held device. Besides, **for some images, using the Web or System palettes can make them look really bad, and the best choice would still be an Adaptive palette.**

CREATING A MASTER PALETTE FOR MULTIMEDIA USE

STEP 8: **When creating images for a multimedia CD where you have absolute control over your palettes, you can also create a custom palette for each group of images that would be on the screen at one time. To do this from Photoshop CS, make sure that the three original 24-bit psd images are all open and choose one of them (it doesn't really matter which one you activate, but we'll do the Grand Canyon).**

STEP 8: The Photoshop CS palette choices in the Indexed Color dialog. The Master palette options are only available when you have more than one image open, and are used to create a common palette from colors in all of the open images.

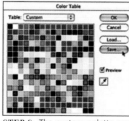

STEP 8: The custom palette created from all three of the open images, using the Master (Adaptive) setting. Click the Save button to save this palette for future use and call it "_all3.act".

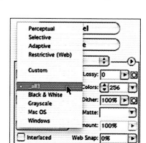

STEP 8: When you save a custom palette in the Presets/Optimized Colors folder (left), it will be available in Photoshop's Save for Web dialog (right).

Choose Image/Mode/Index Color and from the popup Palettes menu, pick Master (Adaptive). The last time we used this dialog, we chose Local (Adaptive), which built a color table based on colors in the active image. With Master (Adaptive) selected, Photoshop will build a palette based on colors in all of the open images. **For the remaining settings in the Indexed Color dialog, choose 256 Colors, Forced Black and White, and 75% Diffusion Dither. Choose OK to convert to 8-bit color and then from the File menu,**

choose Save As and name the file gcall3.gif, to denote that we've used the color palette created from all three images. Now that this custom table has been created, we can easily select it for the remaining two images. **Switch to one of the other two original 24-bit images and choose Image/Mode/Index Color, but this time, set the Palette type to Previous. This will use the same palette that was used for the previous image. Save this with another appropriate "all3" name like mcnall3.gif and then do the same thing with the third image.** You now have these images created with the same adaptive palette that was customized for just these three images. **With one of these new gifs active, go into Image/Mode/Color Table and look at this common palette. It is a mixture of the three you saw on the last page. Click the Save button and save this palette as "_all3.act".** Now you can load this palette from the Color Table dialog box and also from the Save for Web dialog. If you need to make a lot of common palette images, you can create an action to do it to all the files in a folder and save yourself some time.

ImageReady also lets you create a master palette from multiple images, but the procedure is different than in Photoshop. Because the ImageReady process involves dealing with its optimized dialogs, we'll cover that first.

THE 4-UP DIALOGS IN PHOTOSHOP CS AND IMAGEREADY CS

STEP 1: **In Photoshop, open the file redac.psd from the gif jpeg and Color Palettes folder on your CD. Choose Image/Duplicate and name the duplicate file redac_ir.psd. With the new duplicate as the active image, click on the Jump To button at the very bottom of the Tools Palette to jump over to ImageReady CS with the redac_ir file.** With the same image open in each program, we'll explore the different ways to make gif and jpeg files with Photoshop or ImageReady.

In Photoshop, make the first redac file the active image and choose File/Save for Web (Command-Option-Shift-S) to open the Save for Web dialog. Click on the 4-Up tab to choose the 4-Up view. This allows you to look at the original image and 3 different previews of the optimized Web file at the same time. Now, using either the task bar (Windows) or the Dock (Mac), switch to ImageReady and you will notice that the different optimize options (Original, Optimized, 2-Up, 4-Up) are available all the time at the top-left of the document window without going into the Save for Web modal dialog. This gives ImageReady the flexibility of saving any version of an optimized image at any time without entering and then leaving the Save for Web modal dialog. In Photoshop, you have to enter this dialog each time you want to access the Save for Web features.

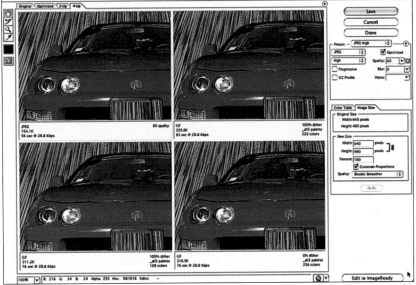

STEP 1: The Photoshop CS Save for Web dialog is a modal dialog box containing the different Web file types and optimize options in the upper-right corner, the Image Size and Color Table information below that to the right side, and the four views when looking at it in 4-Up mode. In Photoshop, you can only save one image at a time without re-entering this dialog and you can only see one Photoshop image within this dialog at a time.

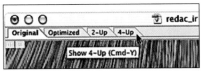

STEP 1: Unlike Photoshop, where you have to enter the Save for Web dialog, in ImageReady CS, the Optimized, 2-Up, and 4-Up views are always available as tabs at the top-left of the document window.

The 4-Up Dialogs in Photoshop CS and ImageReady CS

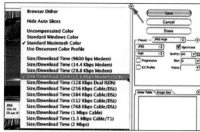

STEP 2: The Preview menu in Photoshop's Save for Web dialog allows you to choose the color space used for image display within the dialog and also the speed of the Internet connection used to calculate Web file download times.

ORIGINAL, OPTIMIZED, 2-UP, 4-UP

STEP 2: In either application, clicking on the Original tab will allow you to use the entire window space to look at the original image without any Web optimizations. Clicking on the Optimized tab allows you to use the entire window to look at the one Optimized version. The 2-Up view allows you to compare the Original to one optimization or to look at two optimizations at a time. The 4-Up view gives you the most options because it allows you to compare four versions of an image at a time, so we will start there. **Click on the 4-Up option in ImageReady; then click on the top-left version of the red Acura image. Now switch back to Photoshop and click on the top-left version of the red Acura image. Choose Original from the Preset pop-up in the top-right of the window. This will continue to show you the original image in the top-left window. Now click in the top, right window and change the settings to jpeg High to look at a jpeg version of the image.** Photoshop will now create the jpeg version with the High quality setting and display it on the screen. Notice that below this top-right subwindow on the left you also see the file size of this version and how long it will take to transfer over the Web using a given connection speed. You can use the Preview pop-up menu at the top-right of this Save for Web dialog to change the speed of the internet connection for these calculations and to also change the way Web images are displayed in Photoshop. We will explain the other settings in this Preview pop-up later. **To change the Internet connection speed display calculations in ImageReady, you use the pop-up menus on the bottom-left of the window.**

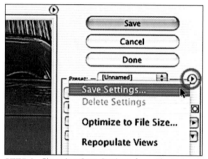

STEP 3: Choosing Save Settings from Photoshop's Save for Web dialog to save a particular set of file optimization options. You need to save these settings within the "Adobe Photoshop CS / Presets / Optimized Settings" folder on your hard disk.

MAKING YOUR OWN OPTIMIZE SETTINGS

STEP 3: When you pick one of the Settings choices in either application, you are just selecting a preset for creating the Web image in this window. You can then customize that choice by changing any of the options like Quality, Blur, and Matte that you see here. Photoshop and ImageReady come with several predefined settings choices, but you can also create your own settings once you have discovered which Save for Web options work best for your most common images. **To create your own settings file, just modify some of the default settings and choose Save Settings from the Opti-**

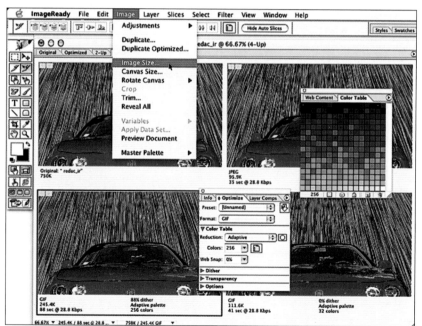

This is the ImageReady 4-Up view of the current file. In ImageReady, to see a 4-Up view of any file, all you have to do is switch to that file and then click on the 4-Up tab. Here you can save as many variations as you want from any open file because the 4-Up choice is always there. The Optimize and Color Table options are palettes in ImageReady. If they are not visible, choose Window/Optimize or Window/Color Table. To change the Image Size in ImageReady, you need to choose Image/Image Size, which is really a better way to do it than using the built-in Image Size option in Photoshop's Save for Web dialog because you will probably want to sharpen the image after resizing it and before saving it in a Web format.

Chapter 36: Optimizing Images for the Web

mize Pop-up menu to the right of the Settings menu. In order for your new setting to be available within the Save for Web setting menu, you need to save it within the Adobe Photoshop CS/Presets/Optimized Settings folder on your hard disk. Now click in the bottom-left window; then change the Quality slider to 51. Choose the Save Settings pop-up and save this as "jpeg-51" within the above mentioned folder. This setting will now be available in Photoshop's Save for Web Presets menu.

PHOTOSHOP VS. IMAGEREADY WEB-OPTIMIZE LAYOUT

STEP 4: **Notice that in the Photoshop Save for Web dialog, you have all the Optimize settings options built into the top-right corner, and then below that there is an Image Size section and a Color Table section.** You can use the Image Size section, while in Save for Web, to actually resample the file and make a smaller (or larger) Web image. That may seem convenient, but actually **it works better if you sharpen an image after it is resampled and before converting it to jpeg or gif. Doing the resample within the Save for Web dialog doesn't give you that option.** In ImageReady, on the other hand, you have to use the Image/Image Size command to resample each image before you optimize it. This is probably better because you can then sharpen it before converting it to jpeg or gif. You can do it the same way in Photoshop; you just need to remember to resample and sharpen the image before applying optimization settings and exporting as a jpeg or a gif. This means that for the sharpest Web images, you probably shouldn't use the Image Size section of the Save for Web dialog in Photoshop. The Color Table section of Save for Web is only used when you are making gif or png-8 files that will be using a color table. In ImageReady, the Color Table is a free floating palette that you can access by choosing Window/Color Table.

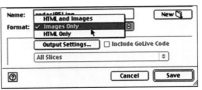

STEP 4: When saving the optimized image in this step, make sure that the Images Only option is selected in the Format menu below the Name field.

Switch to ImageReady, and here you will need use Window/Optimize to bring up the Optimize palette. Click on the top-left image panel and choose Original from preset menu so that this view of the image shows you the original Red Acura (this is the default choice, so it may already be showing the original view). Click on the top-right view and choose jpeg-High from the Optimize palette's preset menu to set it to the High quality jpeg option. Now change the Quality slider to 51, which I think is the best jpeg compromise for this image between image size and image quality. Choose File/Save Optimized As and save this file as rdacIR51.jpg so you can look at it later. In the Format/Save As Type menu just below the Name field, be sure that Images Only is selected. This will only export the jpeg file and not an accompanying HTML file. To save the optimized image from the Photoshop Save for Web dialog, you would have to choose OK at the top-right of the dialog while an optimized preview window with these options was selected. That would then take you out of Save for Web without the option of trying and saving further optimizations. To do more, you would have to then re-enter Save for Web, which takes extra time.

COMPARING GIF TO JPEG

For continuos tone photographic images, jpeg will be the best format to use in most situations. Because a gif file can have no more than 256 colors in it, subtle tonal transitions are not handled very well and images will often exhibit posterized banding or a speckled dithering pattern. Plus, unless you reduce the colors quite a lot, a gif file will almost always be larger than a jpeg. Still, there may be some cases, such as for graphic titles, or Web site buttons and banners, where gif is the better choice. To get a sense of how gif settings will affect not only file size but image quality, read on.

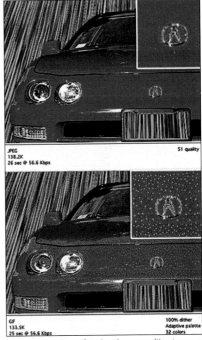

In order to get a gif to be the same file size as a quality 51 jpeg, I had to reduce the colors down to 32, which resulted in a considerable amount of dithering throughout the image. The insets show 200% detail views of jpeg artifacts and gif dithering near the Acura emblem. For continuous tone photographic images, jpeg is generally a much better choice that will give you smaller images and better image quality if used carefully.

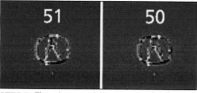

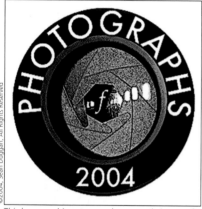

STEP 5: There is a surprising amount of difference, both in file size and image quality, between jpeg level 51 and 50. At a quality setting of 50, the Acura emblem begins to fall apart (right), whereas it still looks pretty good at quality 51 (left). Be sure to inspect the fine details when choosing your optimization settings.

This logo combines type and a grayscale image of a camera lens. Because there are very few colors and no subtle tonal transitions in this image to begin with, it is an ideal candidate for the gif format. This 300x300 pixel image was saved as a gif using only 8 colors and a perceptual color palette The final file size was 11K. To get a jpeg version that small, I had to use a quality level of 15, and the edges of the type and the bladed iris in the lens became too soft and mushy.

STEP 5: **You should still be viewing the 4-up display of the red car photo in ImageReady. Click in the bottom-left view for the red Acura. Choose gif 128 Dithered from the Settings menu in the Optimize dialog. You are now comparing the Original to a jpeg at quality 51 to a 128-color gif file.** Notice that the gif file is very sharp, but the fine color transitions in the hood of the car look pixilated. **Use the Command-Spacebar-click shortcut to zoom into the Acura emblem and the color transitions on the hood of the car.** Change the Palette options in the Optimize palette between Perceptual, Adaptive, and Selective, and notice how the Color Table changes, within the Color Table palette. Notice how the Acura's pixilated hood changes, too. You can use this to get the best palette for each image. I think the Adaptive looks the best here. If you need to scroll, just hold the Spacebar down; then scroll with the mouse just as you would within Photoshop. **Change the Colors pop-up to 64 and notice that the gif file is still bigger than the 51 quality jpeg; you have to go down to 32 colors to make the gif smaller, and by then it doesn't look that good. Choose File/Save Optimized As to save this 32-color gif just for fun. Now go up to the full 256 colors and the gif looks great but it is now more than twice as big as the 51 jpeg, too big for an actual Web image (actually, if this image were really being placed on the Web I would choose a smaller image size, which would in turn reduce the final file size at these settings). Change the Colors back to 32. Click on the bottom-right window, choose jpeg and set the Quality to 25. Now this jpeg is much smaller than the 32-color gif in the bottom-left window.** With the exception of what happens to the Acura emblem when you go below the 51 quality setting, jpeg does a much better job than gif in size versus quality with this image.

WHEN TO USE GIF OVER JPEG

Anytime you have an image that can be classified more as a graphic than a photograph, then you should certainly explore the gif and the png-8 formats. Each of these formats can have a maximum of only 256 colors to describe an image, and you can also choose fewer colors if the image can handle it, such as in the example of the camera lens logo on this page. **Images containing solid colors, straight lines, text and graphics are a great place to use the gif and png-8 formats even when these 8-bit files will be displayed on a 24-bit, full-color display.** The advantages of using gif or png-8 is that hard edges will be more crisp and defined. This is especially important if there is type in the image. If the type is small to begin with and you need to make the image a certain file size, the jpeg format will often make the edges of type soft and blurred.

By now you should be getting some idea about the power of using the 4-Up dialog within ImageReady and Photoshop to compare how different formats, color palettes, and compression levels affect your image. It's a great tool for helping you

STEP 6: The Optimize to File Size option in the Save for Web dialog.

STEP 6: In ImageReady, you can find Optimize to File Size in the Optimize palette's popout menu.

Chapter 36: Optimizing Images for the Web

decide just how to optimize your files. ImageReady just has the edge of letting you do multiple saves while you are working. If you only save one image most of the time, then you can probably do all of your optimizing work within Photoshop and you don't need ImageReady to make jpeg, gif, or png files.

OPTIMIZE TO FILE SIZE

STEP 6: Another feature you might find useful sometimes is the Optimize to File Size command that is found in the Optimize palette pop-up in ImageReady and within the Optimize pop-up menu to the right of the Settings menu in Photoshop's Save for Web dialog. **With this feature you choose a desired file size and the application will use either jpeg or gif to create a file with that size**. You can force it to choose one or the other format by being in that format when you enter the Optimize to File Size menu option, and choosing Current Settings when you get there. If you don't care whether a gif or jpeg is used, then choose Auto Select gif/jpeg.

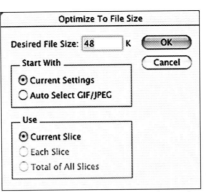

STEP 6: Choose Optimize to File Size from either Photoshop or ImageReady to get this dialog and have the application choose the gif or jpeg settings to get the file size you need.

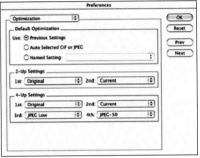

STEP 7: In ImageReady, you can set Optimization Preferences to determine the settings you want for Default Optimization, the 2-Up and 4-Up views. If you set the 1st setting (the top-left in the Optimize 2-Up and 4-Up views) to Original, then the next one has to be set to Current. In 4-Up view, you can set the 3rd and 4th to whatever you want.

SETTING PREFERENCES FOR THE 4-UP DIALOGS

STEP 7: **With ImageReady you can use the Preferences to set up your Optimization defaults to determine which choices you initially get when you enter the different Optimization dialogs.** You can see the dialog here with the preferences set to show different levels of jpeg quality. I use something like this as a starting point for a jpeg image; then I tweak the quality slider until I get the quality I want at the size I need. You have to be careful not to completely rely on the optimization preferences because the current settings within the Optimize palette may override the preference settings for the preview window that is currently active. If that happens, just use the Presets menu to put that window back where you want it. **In Photoshop if you set the top-right optimize view to a certain setting, like jpeg High, quality 60, and choose the Repopulate Views option from the popout menu next to the presets, Photoshop will automatically update the bottom-left and bottom-right views with jpeg settings that are 1/2 that quality, 30, and 1/4 that quality, 15.** By default, Photoshop uses the last settings you had in the Optimize part of the Save for Web dialog as the settings for the top-right view and then repopulates the lower views with settings that are 1/2 and 1/4 of that top-right setting. As this is the default behavior for the Photoshop 4-Up window, you don't have the same amount of control here as in ImageReady, where you can set this in the Preferences. **In the Save for Web dialog, the Done button will remember the current settings and close the dialog without exporting any image. If you hold down the Option key (Alt on PC), the Done button changes to a Remember button, which remembers the current settings for a preview but does not close the dialog. This is useful if you find a group of settings that you like but want to explore other configurations and then return to the remembered settings quickly using the Reset button. Holding down the Option key changes Cancel to Reset, which will reset a preview to either that last settings used to save an image, or the last remembered settings.**

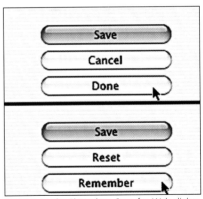

STEP 7: In the Photoshop Save for Web dialog, holding down the Option key (Alt on PC) will change the Done button to Remember and the Cancel button to Reset. The Done button remembers the current settings and closes the dialog without exporting an image. Remember will remember the current settings but leave the dialog open. Reset will restore either the settings last used to save an image, or the previous remembered settings.

The 4-Up Dialogs in Photoshop CS and ImageReady CS

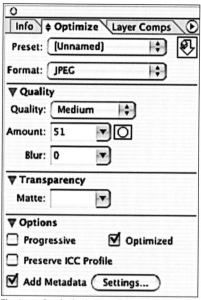

The ImageReady Optimize palette with all of the jpeg options visible.

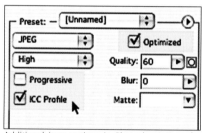

Additional jpeg options in Photoshop's Save for Web dialog that affect how the file is saved.

The bottom part of ImageReady's Optimize palette lets you include an image's metadata in the final, optimized file.

UNDERSTANDING THE OTHER OPTIONS FOR OPTIMIZING WEB IMAGES

There are various options available for jpeg, gif, or png that have some similarities and also some very important differences. To see all the options within the ImageReady Optimize palette, choose Show Options from the palette's pop-up menu. The same section of the Save for Web dialog in Photoshop always shows you all options. We will now explain the other jpeg options (Optimized, Progressive, ICC Profile, Blur, and Matte) and the other gif Options (Lossy, Color Reduction Algorithm, Dither, Transparency, Interlaced, Matte, and Web Snap). png-8 files have the same options as gif but there is no Lossy option. Using the Lossy option can allow you to make a gif file smaller than the corresponding png-8, but also of lower quality.We'll also cover how to create a Master Palette in ImageReady and the Weighted Optimization features that let you use an alpha channel, text layer, or vector shape layer to influence factors such as compression quality, dithering, and color palettes.

THE OTHER JPEG OPTIONS

OPTIMIZED, PROGRESSIVE, ICC PROFILE, AND METADATA

STEP 8: One of the other jpeg options here that we have not explored is Optimized, which creates a jpeg image with a little better compression than when Optimized is off. I have been using Optimized for quite a while with my jpegs of photographs, and I'm very happy with the results. This is the same as choosing Baseline Optimized when you create a jpeg through Photoshop's Save As dialog. Progressive gives you a jpeg file that appears quickly on a Web page as a low-quality image that progressively gets better and sharper over time as the rest of the data downloads. **Make sure you are in ImageReady and then choose File/Open to open the file macn.psd on the CD within the McNamaras folder within the Ch. 36 folder on the CD. Set the top-right view to jpeg quality 60, the bottom-left view to jpeg quality 51, and the bottom-right view to jpeg quality 25. Notice for each of these jpeg versions that when you turn Progressive off, the file size actually gets a little bigger; when you also turn Optimized off, it gets bigger still.** Having Progressive on doesn't usually make the file much larger and, as you can see here, it can sometimes actually make the file smaller. Your choice of having Progressive on for an image should be based on the overall design of the Web page that the image appears on. You should also consider the time it will take for the full quality image to load. I personally don't like the initially blurry progressive images and would only use them when I expected a blank image box to sit there for a long time while the full image loaded onto the page. I always choose Optimized, though.

The ICC Profile choice, if on, will embed in the jpeg file an ICC profile for the color space the image was created in. This may make the file a very small amount larger but is a good choice if you really care about the way images look on a viewer's screen. In my tests with the images we've been using in this chapter, the file size only increased by a couple of kilobytes at most. **For an embedded ICC Profile to be of any use, of course, the person viewing the image needs to be using an ICC-aware application and, hopefully, a calibrated monitor.** If I were going to use a jpeg as a comp to send to an art director or an art dealer, I would turn ICC profile on. If you think there will be enough people looking at your site with calibrated monitors and browsers that make use of profiles, or if they are proofing an image directly in Photoshop or another ICC-aware application, then turn ICC profile on.

Chapter 36: Optimizing Images for the Web

In ImageReady you can choose to add an image's metadata to the exported file. This is certainly something to consider, especially if you embed copyright and usage information, keywords, camera data, or other information in the file that you want to be preserved in the optimized version. A settings button next to this choice in the ImageReady optimization palette gives you further control over what metadata is included. Keep in mind that, depending on how much metadata you have associated with a file, this option could significantly increase the file size. **For photographers who make use of the expanded metadata capabilities of Photoshop CS, this is one reason why you might want to use ImageReady to prep your Web images.**

BLUR AND MATTE

STEP 9: The Blur option blurs the file with a Gaussian Blur of between 0 and 2 to minimize the artifacts caused by the lower-quality jpeg settings. This also blurs the entire image, however, so I usually don't use this option much for photographs. You might try it on problem text or graphics, like the Acura emblem in the redac image, to see if it can help the result. Blur settings below .5 are probably what you will want. **Use the Window menu in ImageReady to switch back to the redac image and set the quality slider on both the top and bottom-right views to 25. Make sure all the settings are the same. Now change the Blur setting on the bottom-right image to 0.4, and you will notice as you compare the blurred bottom-right to the unblurred top-right that the size of the final jpeg gets smaller**. This is another possible use of Blur. The noise around the Acura emblem lessens somewhat, but the entire image also blurs a bit, too. **One thing to be aware of is that the blur settings are sticky and don't reset to 0 when you're finished saving an image!** When I was working on this example, the blur value of 0.4 was still in place when I went to optimize another jpeg image. It was also still lurking around on the following day. This could be a bug, or it could also be designed that way, but just be on the lookout for it or you might inadvertently be blurring your jpegs when you don't mean to.

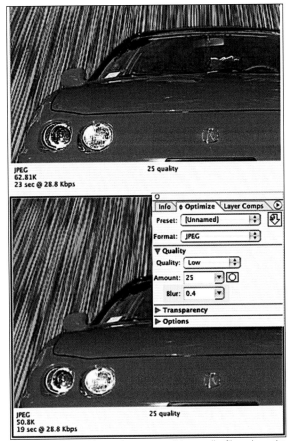

JPEG
62.81K
23 sec @ 28.8 Kbps   25 quality

JPEG
50.8K
19 sec @ 28.8 Kbps   25 quality

STEP 9: Applying a Blur to a jpeg can result in a smaller file and can also smooth obvious compression artifacts. In the lower image, a blur of 0.4 reduces the file size by nearly 20% and also helps with the jpeg artifacts around the Acura emblem. The problem with this approach, of course, is that it blurs the entire image (note the reduced sharpness in the headlights) which is generally not an acceptable trade-off for most photographers who are concerned about their images looking their best.

The Matte option allows you to choose a Matte color to fill transparent areas of an image. You would only use this option if the image you were trying to compress had a transparent area that you wanted to fill with the background color of a Web page. The jpeg format, unlike gif or png, doesn't allow for a transparent area that will later be filled with a Web site's background. With jpeg, however, you can choose a Matte color and then fill a transparent area with it when you save the optimized image. You need to know the Web site's background color ahead of time to do this. The jpeg matte will even give you soft shadows and nice things that you can't get with gif transparency, but the catch is that if you later change the site's background color, you will have to re-create your jpeg files. That might be fine if you are generating your Web pages and their jpeg files automatically from a database using scripts and actions, like we often do. For more info about Transparency and Matte, see the discussion about these issues in a few pages at the end of the next gif Options section.

The jpeg option for Weighted Optimization using alpha channels, text layers, and vector shape layers is covered at the end of this chapter.

THE GIF OPTIONS

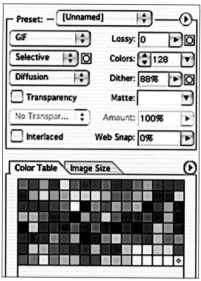

STEP 10: Here are the gif options from within the Photoshop Save for Web dialog. In this dialog you always see all the options for each format.

The ImageReady Optimize palette with all of the gif options visible.

STEP 10: **In ImageReady, use the Window menu to switch back to the macn.psd file and use the Preset menu in the Optimize palette to set the top-left view to Original, the top-right view to jpeg Medium, the bottom-left view to gif 128 Dithered, and the bottom-right view to gif 64 Dithered.** One of the advantages of ImageReady over Photoshop is that you can look at 4-Up versions of more than one image at a time and just switch between them using the Window menu. Because Photoshop's 4-Up capabilities are within the Save for Web modal dialog, you don't have this capability in Photoshop. When you are in Photoshop CS's Save for Web modal dialog, you can't do anything else within Photoshop until you either exit the dialog using Cancel or Done, or export an optimized image and exit the dialog using the Save button. That's why we'll play with the gif options using ImageReady.

Notice that for this file, the Medium 30 quality jpeg looks pretty good because it doesn't have a graphic like the Acura emblem in the redac image. Let's play with the gif Options and see if we can use them to reduce the size. **For this image, the gif 64 Dithered version in the bottom-right view doesn't look that bad. Click on the bottom-left view and also set it to gif 64 Dithered. Now click back into the bottom-right view, and we'll play with the options and see how the file gets smaller and the quality degrades as we work.** When you convert an image into gif (or png-8) format, it goes from having potentially millions of possible colors down to having 256 or fewer colors. In this case we have chosen 64 colors to reduce the size of the file. When you do the conversion to 256 or fewer colors, you sacrifice color information, but the gif (or png-8) format will give you the best rendition of the image with that number of colors; either format will compress a reduced color image, and their file compression, which is essentially based on color reduction, is lossless. The initial information loss occurs by reducing the number of colors to 256 or less.

LOSSY AND COLOR REDUCTION

With the gif format, you have the additional option of turning on the Lossy option, which allows some further loss in image quality with the aim of making the image smaller. **Changing the Lossy factor here to 80 will actually make this gif version of the image about the same size as the jpeg 30, but it looks pretty bad. Setting the Lossy option to 40 here doesn't appear to do too much damage to the image, and it does reduce its size from 188.1k down to 123.6k, which represents a significant reduction.** In the end, it all comes down to what still looks acceptable to you and meets your file size requirements. As with many things in life, and certainly digital imaging, it's a big trade-off. The Lossy setting can also be influenced by the Weighted Optimization feature, which is covered at the end of this chapter.

As you are making these adjustments, you'll notice that if you use Spacebar-Command-Click to zoom into 200%, that many Web images look bad at that zoom factor. When I'm working on a high-quality art image that is not for the Web, I often zoom into 200% or higher to see all the details of what I'm doing. With Web images, it's best to do your final comparisons at 100% because that is what the user will see on the Web page.

In the Color Table section of the Optimize palette, you can choose the Reduction algorithm that controls how the image is converted from 24-bit into 8-bit color and specifically how the palette is made. The default option for the gif 64 Dithered setting is Selective, which is what the bottom-left view should be using. Try Perceptual and Adaptive in the bottom-right view to see which one of the three works best. Perceptual gives priority to the colors the human eye is more sensitive to, Selective favors large areas of color and including more Web colors and it is the default, and Adaptive gives priority to the colors appearing most within the image. For this image, it is hard for me to tell the difference between them, but if you zoom into 200%, you can see pixels change as you switch between them. Adaptive seems to add a couple of extra kilobytes to the file size, but somehow, maybe just because I'm used to using it, I like it better here. If you choose Custom at this point, from this same pop-up menu, that option will preserve the current Selective, Perceptual, or Adaptive color table as a fixed palette, and that palette will not change after you make further changes to the image. This may allow you to preserve a higher quality set of colors in the palette as you then go on and further refine the image to make it smaller. Choosing Mac OS gives you the standard Mac OS palette, Windows gives you the default Windows palette, and Web gives you the Web palette, which contains the 216 colors that are common to both the Mac OS and Windows palette. None of these three palettes are recommended for photographs. Black & White will simply make a color table of just those two colors and create a dithered bitmap rendition of your image, and Grayscale will turn it into a grayscale version.

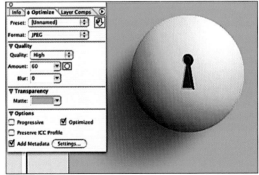

STEP 10: The Color Reduction Algorithm choices in ImageReady. Selective is the default setting. In the bottom section the _all3 palette is a custom master palette that I created in Photoshop.

THE DITHERING OPTIONS

Leave the Color Reduction Algorithm set to Adaptive and immediately underneath that menu is the Dither Algorithm pop-up. The file seems to be the smallest with the setting on Diffusion. Both the Pattern and Noise choices make a much bigger file without a noticeable difference at 100% viewing. Setting Dither Algorithm to No Dither does shave about 10k off the file size, but it also makes color transitions, especially on some of the shirts, clump up a bit. If you choose any of the dither types, you can also change the numeric Dither box to the right of this pop-up from the default 88% setting to a lesser amount of dithering. I tried turning Diffusion Dither back on and found that I needed a setting of about 50% before I noticed a difference between that and No Dither. **I've just decided to choose No Dither with this image in the quest for a smaller file. Try these same settings with the redac image and notice how bad the subtle color gradations on the car hood look when you switch from 88% Diffusion Dither to No Dither.**

TRANSPARENCY AND MATTE

STEP 11: The Transparency and Matte options control what will happen to images that contain transparent areas within their original RGB format. You'll notice that turning either option on or off while working on this macn image makes no difference in the size or appearance because this image contains no transparent areas. **For images that contain no transparent areas, just leave Transparency off and leave Matte set to None.**

To learn more about Transparency and Matte, make sure you're in ImageReady and open the file Spherical Lock.psd from the Transparency and Matte folder inside the Ch.36 folder on your CD. We will use this file to explore the Transparency and Matte options within all the file formats.

STEP 12: **Turn off the white background layer by clicking it's eye icon. Type D to get the default colors and F for Full Screen mode; then Tab to hide all the palettes. Use Window/Optimize to bring up the Optimize palette. Make sure you can see all the options in this palette by choosing Show Options from the Optimize palette menu. In this same menu, make sure that Auto Regenerate is also turned on with a check mark next to it. Click on the 4-Up tab and then click on the top-left view and set it to**

STEP 12: Here is the jpeg version of the spherical lock after we have set the Matte color to #339966.

411

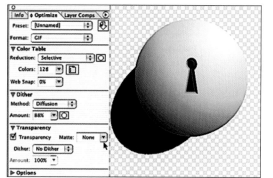

STEP 12: How our sphere's shadow looks as a gif with Transparency on and Matte set to None.

Original using the Preset menu within the Optimize palette. **Now click on the top-right view and set the Settings to jpeg High.** Notice that the default for jpeg is to fill the transparent area, the checkerboard pattern, with the background color, white. jpeg format doesn't have a Transparency option, but it does allow you to fill the transparent parts of an image with a Matte color. If you choose the background color of your Web site as the Matte color, shadows within the jpeg file will look great, like they have 256 levels of transparency. You would have to re-create your jpeg file, however, each time you changed the background color on your Web page. **Click in the white box next to word Matte in the Transparency section of the Optimize palette. This will allow you to choose a color for the jpeg Matte. Type in #339966 at the bottom-right of the Color Picker dialog to insert this green color as your Matte color. This is what we would do to create a jpeg version of this image to sit on a Web page that had this green background color.**

STEP 13: **Now click in the bottom-left view area and change the Settings for that view to gif 128 Dithered. This setting starts out with the Matte color set to white and Transparency on. When Transparency is on with a gif file and a Matte color is chosen, only the pixels that are 100% transparent will show the background of your Web page. Areas that are partially opaque, like the ball's shadow, will be blended with the Matte color, which is now white. Click on the pop-up menu to the right of the Matte option and set the Matte to None.** Now, with the Matte option off, opaque areas that are less than 50% opaque show up as transparent, and you will see your Web site's background in those areas. Areas that are more than 50% opaque, the darker shadow areas, now show up as black, which doesn't look convincing at all. There is no blending with gif transparency.

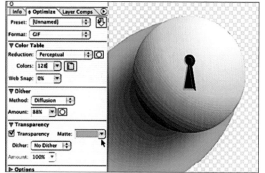

STEP 14: With Transparency on and Matte set to #339966, this is the result when creating a gif file. With only 128 colors to work with, note how the addition of the extra green colors has created banding in the shadowed side of the sphere

STEP 14: **Now turn Transparency off and you will get an even bigger black area. With Transparency off and no Matte color, areas that are totally transparent in the original are filled with white and areas that are partially opaque are filled with black. This is also of no use for our hypothetical Web page. Turn Transparency back on; then click in the white box next to Matte and in the lower right of the color picker, set the Matte color to #339966.** With these settings, the totally transparent areas of the image will be replaced by your site's background color or pattern, and the partially opaque areas will be blended with the Matte color. **If we now turn Transparency off,** the Matte color will blend with the shadow to give a natural look, but as with jpeg, you will need this Matte color to be the same as the background color of your Web page. **To lessen the banding of the sphere's gradations and of the shadow as it blends into the green background, set Colors to 256 and set the Color Reduction Algorithm to Adaptive. You might also want to set the Dither percentage up to 100%.** Now your gif file is almost three times as big as the jpeg version. If you want any random background pattern or color on your Web site to seamlessly blend with a soft shadow in your optimized image, neither gif, png-8 nor jpeg format will work for you. As you'll see in the next step, however, the png-24 format works great for this purpose.

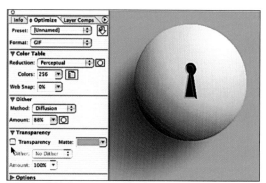

STEP 14: With Transparency off and Matte set to #339966, this is the result when creating a gif file. Increasing the colors to 256 has helped reduce the banding seen in the previous example.

Chapter 36: Optimizing Images for the Web

STEP 15: **Click in the bottom-right view and choose png-24 from the Settings menu. With Transparency on, the png-24 format will correctly show your 256 levels of shadow transparency onto any Web background color or pattern**. Notice that the size of this file is twice as big as the gif and about 6 times bigger than the jpeg. The advantage of this extra size, though, is that the ball and its shadow will be decompressed losslessly onto your Web page. The problem with using png-24, besides the larger file size, is that not all older browsers support the format and especially not its 256 levels of transparency. Though this is not a problem with modern Web browsers, you should check out the support for png-24 images within the default versions of browsers and platforms you care about before you assume this file format will work for your site.

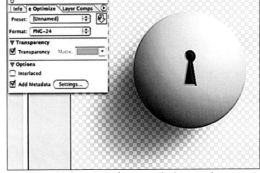

STEP 15: With the png-24 format, and a browser that supports this format, the shadow will correctly blend with any color or pattern background on your Web site.

TRANSPARENCY DITHERING

If you want to have a transparent shadow but need smaller file sizes than png-24s, you can try out the Transparency Dithering feature in Photoshop's Save for Web, or ImageReady's Optimize palette. As you have seen from the previous examples there is no gradual blending with gif transparency. While this is not a problem if you are matting the image to a solid color, it can be an issue once you change the background color of your Web page. Then you have to go back to your design files and export new versions of the gif with the transparency matted to that new background color. It also is a problem if you want your image to be placed on a multi-colored background As a possible way around this, you can try the Transparency Dithering setting in ImageReady's Optimize palette and Photoshop's Save for Web dialog. Transparency Dithering uses the same dither algorithms that are found in the color dithering menu to try and fake the appearance of semi-transparent areas with a dither. We have not been impressed with this option, however, as the effects are not very smooth and it still looks more like an obvious dither than a natural, soft shadow. If you must have realistic 24-bit transparency in your Web images and you don't mind the extra overhead of a larger file size, then png-24 is the way to achieve this.

STEP 15: This is a screengrab from Internet Explorer 5.2 (Mac) showing the png-24 transparent image blending perfectly with a Web page's multi-colored background.

INTERLACED AND WEB SNAP

STEP 16: **Use the Window menu to switch back to the macn image within ImageReady. If you're not currently viewing it in one of the Optimized panels, choose the 4-Up Optimized tab. Activate the top-right panel and choose gif 64 Dithered from the Settings**

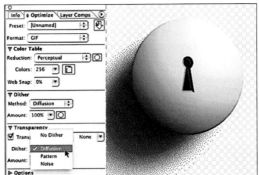

Choosing a Transparency Dither in ImageReady.

menu. In the lower part of the Optimized palette, turning on the Interlaced option will make the gif image download in multiple passes from a poorer, low-res version to a final, higher quality version. This behavior is similar to the Progressive jpeg setting. Unlike the Progressive jpeg option, however, turning on Interlaced with gif increases the file size by about 7k, so I'm leaving it off here. Again, if you feel it's really important for some sort of image to show up immediately when the page loads, then you can use the Interlaced option.

This is a screengrab from Internet Explorer 5.2 (Mac) showing the how the drop shadow looks with a Diffusion Transparency Dither of 100% when placed over a multicolored Web page background. The effect creates a shadow that looks more like a dither than a true. soft shadow. The png-24 format definitely comes out on top in this comparison.

STEP 16: Here we see the Color Table portion of ImageReady's Optimize options with Web Snap set to 0.(top); and with Web Snap set to 50% (bottom). The colors in the Color Table (right) that have been converted to Web colors are marked with small white diamonds.

In the Color Table section of the Optimize palette are the Web Snap controls. **Changing the Web Snap option doesn't change the file size, but it does switch colors in your current color palette to colors within the Web palette based on the tolerance factor you choose. Open the Color Table palette from the Window menu so you can see the changes. With Web Snap set to 0, you'll notice here that none of the colors in the palette for this image are common to the Web palette. When we change Web Snap to 50%, you'll see that some of the palette's colors have been changed to match similar Web palette colors (Web-safe colors are denoted by the small, white diamond shape in the center of the swatch).** The purpose for doing this is to make the image look better on 256-color systems where the browser is currently using the viewer's system palette. For this image I found that increasing the Web Snap to above 50% degraded the appearance of the image too much for my taste. One would be more likely use the Web Snap option for a site whose target audience are users who only have 8-bit systems. These days that is less likely to be desktop Web surfers and is probably more of an issue with PDAs or public internet kiosks. Even then, **if optimum image fidelity is your paramount concern, then photographic images are usually not good candidates for using Web Snap.**

ADDITIONAL COLOR TABLE FEATURES

STEP 17: Because we have the Color Table palette already open, this is a good opportunity to point out some additional features that can be very useful. **First, press "i" on the keyboard to select the Eyedropper tool and click on a color in the optimized image. In the Color Table, you'll see that one of the colors is now highlighted by a light box. If you want to select multiple colors, hold down the Shift key as you click to add more colors into the selected group. You can even hold the Shift key down and drag through the image to quickly select a range of colors. If you click and hold on a color swatch in the Color Table, that color will be temporarily inverted in the optimized image, showing you where that particular color appears. Clicking and holding on a bright red swatch, for example, will turn parts of the red sweater in the center a cyan color.** Two out of three of these tricks will work in Photoshop's Save for Web dialog. The one that is left out in the cold is the last one, clicking and holding on a swatch to see that color highlighted in the image. This is another instance of the occasional interface inconsistencies that still exist between the two programs.

STEP 17: If you click in the optimized image, that color is highlighted in the Color Table.

STEP 17: Shift-click on additional colors in the image, or shift drag through the image, to add more colors to your selection.

Once you have a color or group of colors selected in the Color Table, you can shift them to Web-safe colors by clicking on the cube icon in the bottom of the palette. Web-safe colors are denoted by the small, white diamond shape in the swatch. Clicking on the padlock icon will lock or unlock selected colors so that they are protected against change or deletion if you want to try further experimentation while preserving the integrity of an important group of colors. Locked colors are indicated by a small white square with a dot in the center in the lower-right corner of the swatch. Both the locking and shifting to Web-safe colors behavior is the same in the Photoshop Save for Web dialog.

STEP 18: Another useful feature of the Color Table is the ability to select a color, or a range of colors and map them to transparency. **To map a color, or colors, to transparency, use the eyedropper**

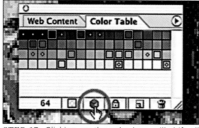

STEP 17: Click and hold on a swatch in the Color Table to see that color highlighted in the optimized image. The highlighted color is inverted; in this case, the red of the sweater is temporarily turned cyan.

STEP 17: Clicking on the cube icon will shift all selected colors to their closest Web-safe equivalents.

to click on a color in the image; we used the red in the woman's sweater. **Shift-click and drag around to pick up more than one shade of red in the sweater. Next, in the color palette, click on the transparency icon at the bottom of the palette. The selected colors are remapped to transparent pixels and the optimized preview is updated.** The swatches for the colors change to half colored and half transparent. Because they retain a record of what the original color was, you can always select the colors again and click on the transparency icon to return them to their original state. The behavior of this operation is the same in Photoshop's Save for Web dialog.

THE PNG-8 AND PNG-24 FORMAT

The png-8 format can be used in place of gif when you have a graphic that can be saved with a maximum of 256 colors. Like gif, you can also reduce the colors further if the image will tolerate it. Sometimes you can get slightly smaller file sizes on certain images with png-8. If you do use the png-8 format, be sure to check that all browser versions your Web site is built for support this format. As we stated previously, this is more likely to be an issue if you are still trying to accommodate older browsers.

The png-24 format creates a lossless, 24-bit compressed image and has the capability to create an image with 256 levels of transparency, like you can have with a Photoshop mask channel. Using 256 transparency levels allows transitions, like subtle soft shadows, to seamlessly blend into any Web background, as we saw earlier with the png-24 transparent version of the spherical lock image. png-24 images are generally a lot larger than jpeg images, which are also in 24 bit, so usually the only reason you would create a png-24 image would be if you need a lossless 24-bit image or if you need to have 256 levels of transparency. If you don't need one of those features, then you'll probably want to use jpeg, gif, or png-8. As with png-8, double-check that the versions of each browser you care about support it and the features you are using.

CREATING A MASTER PALETTE IN IMAGEREADY FOR MULTIMEDIA USE

Earlier in this chapter, we showed you how to use Photoshop's Indexed Color dialog box to create a Master color palette from all open images. This is useful for multimedia projects, where you have control over the color palette that is used to display the images. ImageReady also allows you to do this, but it goes about it in a completely different way.

STEP 1: **Open the redac.psd, gc.psd, and macn.psd files from the Ch.36 folder on the CD. Click the Optimized tab for each image and choose gif 128 Dithered from the Settings menu. Next, increase the colors to 256 for each image.** The exact gif or dithering options you use here are important only in that they will determine how the color palette for each image is calculated. Because that information is then used to create the Master palette, you should first set up the individual images like you would if you were just creating a single optimized image.

STEP 2: **Make the Grand Canyon image active and from the main menu, select Image/Master Palette/Clear Master Palette if it is available. If there is nothing to clear, then this option will be grayed out. Clearing the Master palette ensures that you're only using colors from the current images. Next, go back into that same menu, but this time, choose Add to Master Palette. Switch over to the Red Acura**

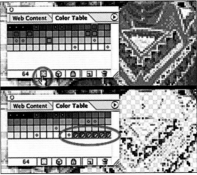

STEP 18: Select a color, or several colors, in the image and then click on the transparency icon. This will remap the selected colors to transparent pixels. Colors that have been remapped to transparency have a swatch in the color table that is half their original color and half transparent. Click on the icon again to return selected colors to their original state.

STEP 2: In ImageReady, adding colors from an optimized image to a Master palette.

Creating a Master Palette in ImageReady for Multimedia Use

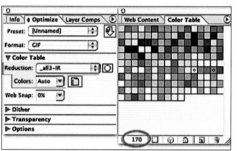

STEP 3: After all color information from the three images has been added, the Master palette is built.

STEP 3: Before the new Master palette can be used, it must be saved first.

image and, using the same menu command, add its colors to the Master palette. Finally, do the same for the McNamaras image. The color information for all three images has now been added to the data that will be used to create the Master palette.

STEP 3: **Next, go back to the Image/Master Palette menu and choose Build Master Palette.** The Master palette has now been built based on the color information in our three images, although, somewhat frustratingly, there's no indication that anything has happened. To make it available to us, we first need to save it. **Return to the Image/Master Palette menu and select Save Master Palette. I called mine "_all3-IR.act". The IR tells me that it was made in ImageReady and distinguishes it from the earlier all3 palette I created in Photoshop. In order for this custom palette to show up automatically in ImageReady's menu, you need to save it in the following location on your hard drive: Adobe Photoshop CS/Presets/Optimized Colors.**

STEP 4: When the "_all3-IR" Master palette is used for the Grand Canyon image and the number of colors is set to Auto, ImageReady will only use a subset of the available colors to describe the image. At the bottom of the Color Table, it shows that for this image it is using only 170 colors of the 256 available in the master palette. The same palette used with the red Acura or McNamaras image will display a different subset of colors for each image when the colors are set to Auto.

STEP 4: **Now, go back to the Grand Canyon image and from the Color Reduction Algorithm drop-down menu in Optimized palette, you should see the Master palette you just created. Select it and from the Colors menu, choose Auto.** If you study the Color Table, it probably seems that many of the very bright colors from the other two images are not represented here. This is kind of confusing at first, especially because it's not very well documented. What's happening is that **ImageReady is only using a subset of the Master palette's colors because it doesn't need to use all of them to describe this particular image. At the bottom of the Color Table, you'll see a number that represents exactly how many of the 256 colors in the master palette are being used in the image; in the case of the Grand Canyon image, only 170 are being used.** If you switch over to the McNamaras or the Red Acura image and set their Color Reduction to the newly created Master palette and the Colors to Auto, you'll see that more colors are being used in each image's Color Table.

WEIGHTED OPTIMIZATION

Weighted Optimization allows you to use an existing alpha channel, text layer, or vector shape layer in your image to customize settings such as jpeg quality, gif lossiness, dither, and color reduction. For those who want to have the most control in the quest for the smallest, yet best-looking Web images, weighted optimization is one way to accomplish this.

JPEG QUALITY MODIFICATION

STEP 1: **Switch to Photoshop and open the file, Bodie Relic.psd from the Weighted Optimization folder in the Ch.36 folder on the *Photoshop CS Artistry CD.*** Bodie is a fascinating ghost town in California's eastern Sierra high desert that has been preserved as a state park and left much the way it was when it was abandoned. It's a bit of a drive off the beaten path and literally out in the middle of nowhere, but well worth the time if you ever get the chance to visit.

Click on the car Channel in the Channels palette, and you'll see that the foreground area, including the car, is white, and the background is black. We'll use this

STEP 1: We can use the car channel to apply different optimization settings based on the areas that are white and black.

STEP 1: Click on the car channel for the Bodie Relic image.

channel, and later the text layers, to explore different ways of using weighted optimization.

STEP 2: **Click back on the RGB composite channel to return the image view to normal and choose Save for Web from the File menu. Activate the 4-Up tab to see four different views of the image. In the top-right view, select jpeg High from the drop-down Preset menu. Next, activate the lower-right view and set it to jpeg High as well. Just to the right of the Quality field, click on the small channel icon to bring up the weighted optimization settings for jpeg. This icon/button is only enabled if the image you are working with has an alpha channel, text layer, or shape layer.**

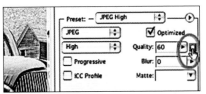

STEP 2: If the image you are optimizing has an alpha channel, text layer, or vector shape layer, the channel button is enabled in Photoshop's Save for Web, and in ImageReady's Optimize palette. Click on it to open the weighted optimization dialog.

STEP 3: **In the Modify Quality Setting dialog that appears, select car from the pop-up Channel menu. Now move the sliders to specify a minimum and maximum quality range. Notice that for the minimum setting, the slider is black, corresponding to the black areas in the channel, and the maximum slider is white, representing the white areas of the channel. In my first try with this image, I set the minimum to 8 and I left the maximum set to 60, which was determined when I initially chose the jpeg High setting.** The sliders control the quality settings for areas of the mask channel that are black, white, or some level of gray. In this case, areas of the image represented by black in the channel, the background, will be given a jpeg quality setting of 8, and areas where the channel is white will be compressed with a higher setting of 60. Any areas of gray (the transition between foreground grass and background on either side of the car) will receive some setting between 8 and 60 depending on their actual gray value.

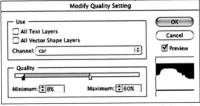

STEP 3: In the Modify Quality Setting dialog, the sliders determine the jpeg quality for the areas in the image represented by black and white in the mask channel. In this case, black areas receive a quality setting of 8 (low) and white areas are set to 60 (high).

As you move the sliders, you can see a preview of how the different quality values are affecting the image. Notice that the car and foreground always look pretty good because they are receiving a quality setting of 60. **Enter a setting of 8 for minimum, leave maximum at 60, and click OK.**

STEP 4: **Now, evaluate the quality trade-offs that our minimum setting produced.** When I zoomed in to 200% in the Save for Web 4-up views, it became apparent to me that 8 was too low and resulted in some serious edge pixilation in the houses in the background. **Click on the channel icon in the jpeg settings (it's dark now, indicating that a channel is being used) to open up the Modify Quality dialog and change the minimum value to 35 and the maximum value to 50.** You should see a significant improvement in how the background looks, and the file size will be reduced

STEP 3: A 200% view of how my initial settings affected the image (lower view). Although I did shave almost 5k off the file size, the minimum quality level of 8 was a bit too rough on the background, causing severe edge pixilation on the houses.

STEP 4: After changing the minimum setting to 35 and the maximum to 50, the jpeg artifacts in the background are greatly reduced and the file size was reduced to 78k. The progressive option is turned on here as it seems to be very effective with weighted optimization images. In this case, with Progressive on, the file size is nearly 10k smaller than with it off, for a final file size of just over 70k.

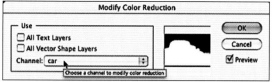

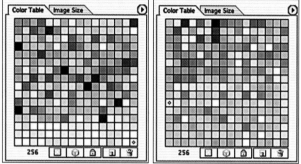

STEP 5: In the Modify Color Reduction dialog, you specify a mask channel and the resulting color table will be weighted toward colors that occur within the white areas of the mask.

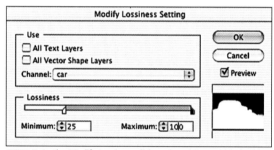

STEP 5: The color table on the left was made from the entire Bodie image. The Color Table on the right was created by using the car mask to give priority to colors in the white areas of the mask.

Modify Lossiness Setting

STEP 6: In the Modify Lossiness dialog, the white and black sliders are the exact opposite from the jpeg settings. White and maximum quality (no lossiness) is on the left; and black, representing minimum quality (more lossiness), is on the right.

STEP 6: The background of the image is very grainy because it is receiving a Lossy setting of 100, whereas the car and foreground are set to a Lossy value of 25.

by about 15k. **Using the Progressive option seems to help reduce the file sizes when using this procedure with jpegS. For this image, with my final weighted optimization settings of minimum 35 and maximum 50, turning the Progressive option on reduced the file size by another 8k, making my total file size reduction from the regular high quality jpeg over 20k.**

WEIGHTED OPTIMIZATION WITH GIF, PNG-8, AND WBMP FILES

STEP 5: **In the Save for Web dialog, click on the upper-right image to make it active and from the drop-down Preset menu, select gif 128 dithered.** For gifs, you can use weighted optimization in three areas, Color Reduction, Lossiness, and Dithering. png-8 files behave the same as gifs with the exception that they have no Lossy setting.

Click on the mask channel icon next to the Color Reduction drop-down menu. For this setting, there are no sliders to adjust. You simply specify a channel and Photoshop or ImageReady will weight the resulting color table more toward colors that appear within the white areas of the mask. **Move the Modify dialog so that you can see both the Color Table and the optimized view of the image and turn the preview on and off.** The differences are subtle, but when you specify the car channel, the buildings in the background lose some of their reddish brown color. They actually take on a slight greenish tone due to the fact that all of the grasses in front of the car are influencing the colors that are being selected for the image. Watch how the Color Table changes as well. This particular image doesn't necessarily benefit from weighted color reduction, but for some images this technique would work very well for favoring a certain range of colors in an image. **Click Cancel in the Modify Color Reduction dialog to return to the Save for Web controls.**

STEP 6: **Next, in the Settings menu, select gif-32 Dithered and then click on the mask channel icon next to the Lossy settings to bring up its Modify dialog box. As in the previous step, from the drop-down Channel menu select the car channel. The Lossy Modifier controls can be a little tricky at first because the white and black sliders, and their corresponding numerical values, are the exact opposite of the jpeg sliders.** On the left is the white slider and a value of 0, which represents no loss of quality. On the right is the black slider and a value of 100, which is the highest lossy setting. Remember that the color of the sliders corresponds to the colors in your mask channel. **So, if we set the white slider to a value of 25 and leave the black slider at 100, it means that the white areas of the masked image will receive a lossy setting of 25 and the black areas will receive the highest setting of 100.** With these settings the result is actually kind of interesting for this particular image, with a very grainy background and only a slightly grainy foreground.

Weighted Optimization Using Text Layers and Vector Shape Layers

STEP 7: With Photoshop CS and ImageReady CS you can also use text layers or vector shape layers to control jpeg quality, and settings such as color reduction, dithering, and lossiness in gif and png-8 files. Let's try out a few of these options using the text layers in the Bodie file. **Make sure the text layers are visible and choose File/Save for Web. In the Save for Web dialog, click on the 4-Up tab and then click on the lower right preview and set it to jpeg Medium. Now click on the upper right preview and give it the same settings. Zoom in to 200% and scroll the image so you can see both the large and small type. Just to the right of the Quality setting, click on the channel icon to bring up the Modify Quality dialog. Click the Use All Text Layers box. Set the black slider to 10% and the white slider to 50%.**

STEP 8: As you can see from the thumbnail in the Modify Quality dialog, the text is being treated as a mask, with the type showing up as white and all other areas showing up as black. **The areas of the image that contain type are receiving the 50% quality setting, while the rest of the image is being compressed at 10%. Compare the top-right preview image to the lower right.** You can see that the wiggly jpeg artifacts around the small text are not as noticeable in the version that is receiving text priority optimization. **With the dialog still open, select the car channel from the Channel menu. The mask thumbnail updates to add the car mask to the existing type mask. Now the car is receiving the same quality settings as the type. If you wanted to give priority to an area that had a vector layer (like a company logo, for example) you would just select the Vector Shape Layers checkbox. Click Cancel when you're done experimenting.**

STEP 9: **From the Settings menu, choose gif-128-Dithered. Click on the mask icon next to the Lossy setting. In the Modify Lossiness dialog, select Use All Text Layers and experiment with the settings. I** found that a maximum setting of 75 reduced the file size from 164k to 60k and added a worn and distressed look that worked very well for an image of a ghost town. The text was protected from the lossy setting and remained crisp and smooth.

Batch Optimization Using Droplets

Once you have established the perfect optimization settings that would work well for several images in a project, ImageReady provides a convenient way to save a particular group of optimization settings as a Droplet and quickly run those settings on several images at once, or even an entire folder. Droplets are easy to create and use and for those times when you have to process a lot of images that all have the same settings, this is a great productivity booster. Lets take a quick look at how Droplets work.

STEP 1: **Make sure that you are working in ImageReady. Open the file called button1.psd from the Global Navs folder inside the Ch36**

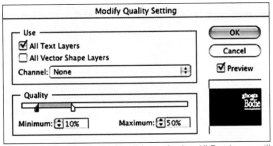
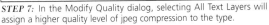

STEP 7: In the Modify Quality dialog, selecting All Text Layers will assign a higher quality level of jpeg compression to the type.

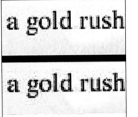

STEP 8: The type in the top preview is receiving 50% quality using its type layer to give priority to the text. The bottom preview is receiving an overall 30% quality setting.

STEP 8: In the Modify dialogs, you can combine text layers with an alpha channel to give priority to different areas in the image. Notice how the thumbnail has changed to add the car mask to the text mask.

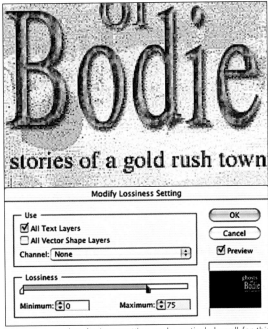

STEP 9: Increasing the Lossy setting works particularly well for this image, giving it a worn and weathered look (not to mention making it a much smaller file!). By using the text layers to protect the type, we can prevent the lossiness from affecting that part of the image.

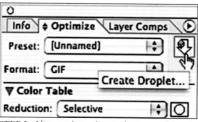

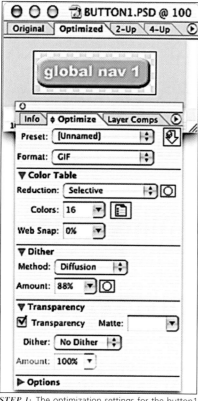

STEP 1: The optimization settings for the button1 file.

STEP 2: After you have chosen the appropriate settings, click on the droplet icon to create a droplet.

folder on the *Photoshop CS Artistry* CD. **Click on the Optimize tab and use these settings: gif, 16 colors, Selective, Diffusion Dither of 88%, Transparency with a Matte to white. You can also refer to the screen shot on the following page to see how the Optimize palette should look.**

STEP 2: **In the top-right corner of the Optimize palette there is the droplet icon that looks like a small cube and a downward arrow. Click on this icon and save the settings to your desktop.** By default the name will automatically give a brief description of what the settings are, but you can choose another name if you want to.

STEP 3: **To try another way of saving a droplet, simply drag the droplet icon from the Optimize palette onto your desktop. You can also select the Create Droplet option from the popout menu on the Optimize palette.**

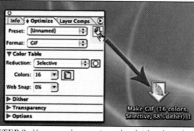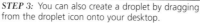

STEP 3: You can also create a droplet by dragging from the droplet icon onto your desktop.

STEP 4: Dragging the global navs folder onto the droplet.

STEP 4: **Close the button1.psd file. Now, copy the global navs folder from the CD to your computer. Place it in on the desktop, which is where you saved the droplet.** The reason to do this is that by default the droplet will try to save the new optimized files in the same folder and because the CD is locked, this would generate an error. **Once the folder has been copied onto your desktop, drag the folder onto the droplet icon and ImageReady will quickly process all the button files and generate a gif for each one.** If you open the folder when the batch process is done, you should see eight gifs in addition to the eight original psd files. If you had folders with many images that all required the same optimization settings, I think you'll agree that this method would save you a lot of time!

BATCH OPTIONS FOR DROPLETS

STEP 5: **To customize the droplet you created in the previous steps, double-click on its icon to open the Droplet palette and double-click on Batch Options.** Here you can specify additional settings for how the optimized images are handled by the droplet, such as where the new files are saved and how duplicate file names are dealt with. In the Playback options you can choose Run in Background so that you can continue working on other files in ImageReady while the batch process is churning away in the background. **Click Cancel after you are finished checking out all the options here.**

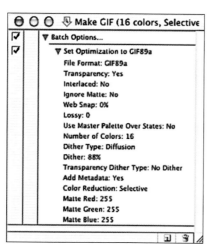

STEP 5: After a Droplet has been created, you can double-click on it to see the settings in detail. Double-click on Batch Options to further refine how the droplet functions.

Chapter 36: Optimizing Images for the Web

Adding Optimization Settings to ImageReady Actions

For some projects you may be using Actions to process images prior to optimizing them. An example of this might be several steps that would be applied to all the images of people on a company's Web site, such as cropping them to a specific size, sharpening, and then adding a sepia tone look. If you have an existing action that you want to add optimization settings to, all you have to do is drag the droplet icon in the ImageReady Optimize palette onto the action in the Actions palette. As you drag, try and position your mouse cursor where you want the settings to be placed within the hierarchy of steps for that action and then let go of the mouse button. If the optimization settings don't land in the right place, you may have to move them into the correct position after the drag operation. You can also select the place in the action where you want to add the optimization settings and choose that option from the ImageReady Actions palette popout menu.

In the ImageReady Actions popout palette menu, you'll also see the word Droplet down at the bottom. In this location of the program, the term refers to saving an action as a droplet, whereas before we were simply saving optimization settings as a droplet. Both work the same way, by dragging a folder of images onto the droplet, but an actions droplet can contain more general editing operations. Optimization droplets can only contain optimization settings.

Unfortunately, actions that you create in Photoshop cannot be loaded into the ImageReady Actions palette. So, if there are final preparations that you need to apply to a group of Web images, such as resizing, converting to black and white, adding a sepia tone, etc., you will need to create that action within ImageReady if you also want to add the optimization settings from a droplet, or from ImageReady's Optimize palette. From a workflow standpoint, if you have already created such an action in Photoshop, then it would be better to process the images as a batch within Photoshop and then drag the folder of processed images onto the ImageReady droplet.

To learn more about the ins and outs of creating and working with Actions, see Chapter 11: "Automating Photoshop."

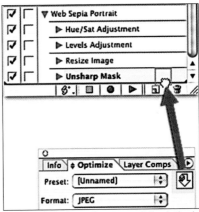

To add optimization settings to an existing Action in ImageReady, choose the desired settings and drag the droplet icon in the Optimize palette into the action you want to add them to. You may need to reposition the optimize step within the action after you drag it.

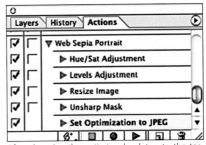

After dragging the optimize droplet onto the targeted action, it will appear as a step in the action.

You can also insert the current optimization settings into an existing action by selecting this option from the ImageReady Actions popout menu.

37 HANDS-ON SESSION: Web Photo Galleries, Contact Sheets, and Picture Packages

Using Photoshop's Automated Features to Make a Web Photo Gallery, Contact Sheets, and Picture Packages.

CREATING WEB PHOTO GALLERIES

Photoshop CS features several improvements and functionality enhancements to the Web Photo Gallery feature. The choice of built-in gallery styles is holding steady at eleven, but they are becoming more sophisticated in terms of the ability of the user (i.e., your clients) to interact with the galleries of images you post. In addition to a gallery style that automatically plays a slide show of your images, there are now galleries that will include image metadata, as well as offer a place for the viewer to post feedback or approval notes that will be automatically emailed to you. You can use captions, copyright notices, and other items from the File Info dialog in the Web pages that display your images, and an option exists to preserve all image metadata. For those who know how to tweak the code, there is the possibility of creating your own custom HTML templates that can be accessed from the gallery style menu.

Let's take the Web Gallery feature for a spin and check it out. To do this exercise, all you need is a collection of images gathered into a single folder. They can be your own images, or you can use the twelve files we prepared for you in the Web Gallery Images folder on the *Photoshop CS Artistry CD*. If you're using your own files, eight to twelve images is a good number to start with. We're going to create a simple gallery and use the existing automation options so that the images will look like matted photographs on a gallery wall.

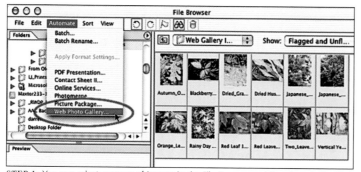

The Centered Frame 1- Feedback gallery places the thumbnails in a scrolling frame on the left and the main image on the right. A popup feedback area can be accessed by the viewer to approve images, enter comments, and email the feedback to the photographer.

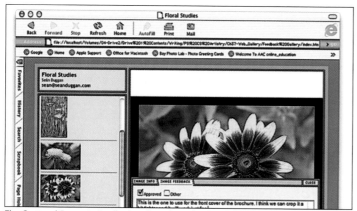

STEP 1: You can select a group of images in the File Browser and then launch the Web Gallery feature, as well as Photoshop's other automations, from the File Browser's Automate menu.

STEP 1: For your own images, collect them together into a single folder on your hard drive. The files on the CD are already in a folder. **In Photoshop, use the File Browser to locate the folder of images. Select all of the thumbnails by using the Command-A shortcut, or by dragging to select them. From the File Browser's Automate menu, choose Web Photo Gallery. In the initial dialog that appears, there are several settings we can make that will influence the appearance of our gallery. In the middle of the dialog there is a section for Source Images. Since we entered the Web**

Photo gallery feature through the File Browser, the source images will be specified as "Selected Images from File Browser." If you entered the dialog through the main File/Automate menu, "Folder" will show in the popup menu under Source Images. In that case, you need to click on the Choose button to open a dialog from where you can locate the target folder of your images, highlight it, and click the Choose button. Once the source images have been identified, click on the Destination button and specify a location for Photoshop to place all the finished gallery files. It's best if you create a new folder for this, and there is a button for that purpose. Once you have specified your destination folder, highlight it and click the Choose button.

STEP 2: Now we can select the different options for the Web Gallery. **Under the Style drop-down menu, there are eleven different styles to choose from.** If you select each one in turn, you can see a small preview of the basic format of that style. **For this tutorial, choose Simple. If you want your email address to be available as a link on the Web pages, enter that information. Below the Source Images section are the General Options. Extension refers to the file format extension on the Web pages. If you already have an existing site that you're going to add the gallery to, then you should use the same extension that is already in use on your site.** In general, Windows systems use the three-letter extension and on Mac it really doesn't matter. If this is your first foray into making a Web site, either one is fine, but try and stay consistent if you add more pages to the site. A link to "mypage.html" will not be able to find a file called "mypage.htm". The "Add Width and Height Attributes for Images" will add that information to the page's HTML code, which can speed the loading of the page. We usually recommend choosing to Preserve all metadata in any images we upload as this often includes copyright or usage information.

STEP 3: **Open the popup menu for the Options and choose Banner. Enter a title for your gallery, your name, and contact information such as a phone number (your email address will already be a clickable link at the top of the page). I usually leave the date blank (the default behavior is for the current date to be in the date field whenever you enter the dialog) unless it is important that the gallery have the date added. For the Font, choose Arial, and for the Font Size, enter a 4.**

STEP 4: **Click in the Options drop-down menu and select Large Images.** These settings will affect the larger versions of your images, which will each appear on their own individual pages. **The Border setting allows you to specify a border around your images. The color of this border is based on the text color which we'll be setting shortly. For now, enter a value of 30 for the Border. This will make the images look like a matted photograph. Click in the Resize Images check box. If you had already prepared your images to be a specific size for your Web gallery, then you would leave this unchecked. For Image Size choose Custom and enter a value of 475 pixels.** This will make the longest dimension of the image 475 pixels. If we have a horizontal picture, it will be 475 pixels wide, and if we have a vertical image, it will be 475 pixels tall. **For JPEG quality, choose 7.**

If you're using the images from the CD, for Titles click in the Titles checkbox. This will take information from the title section in the File Info dialog box to generate the titles. If you want to check this out, it's found in the main Photoshop menu under File/File Info. If you're using your own images and they don't have any file info attached to them, just use the filename for the title. The font and font size should be Arial and 3.

STEP 2: The options for gallery style, email address, and location of source and destination folders. For this exercise, choose Simple for the style.

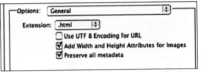

STEP 2: The General Options for the Web Photo Gallery dialog.

STEP 3: The Banner is the section at the top of the page that contains your name, the title of the gallery, your contact information, and the date.

STEP 4: These are the settings I used for the Large Images.

Creating Web Photo Galleries

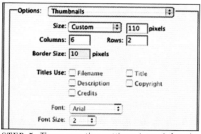

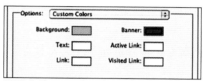

STEP 5: These are the settings I used for the Thumbnails. If options are grayed out it means they are not available in the style you are using.

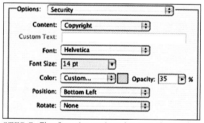

STEP 6: These are the color settings I used for the pages, and also to create the "matted photograph" look or the thumbnails and larger images.

STEP 5: **In the Options menu, move on to the next choice, Thumbnails. Set the size of the thumbnails to Custom, 110 pixels. As with the images, this makes the longest dimension of the thumbnail 110 pixels in length. Choose a column and row arrangement that is suitable for the number of images you have.** In the example I created here, I had twelve images, so I chose 6 columns and 2 rows. **For the Border, enter a value of 10. As with the large images, this will give the thumbnails the appearance of matted photos.**

STEP 6: **From the Options menu, choose Custom Colors.** Although the actual colors you end up using for your own Web galleries are up to you, it's wise to follow a few common rules. You should choose colors that are subtle and do not get in the way of the prime purpose of your gallery, which is showing your images. Ideally, neutral colors such as white, black, or grays are the best for viewing photographs. For this exercise, use the same settings that I have here. **Click in the Background swatch and in the Color Picker, select Only Web Colors in the lower left, and in the lower right, enter a hexadecimal value of #999999, and click OK. Follow the same procedure for the Banner color, except set it to be #333333. The Text, Link, Visited, and Active Link colors should all be set to white.** A standard convention used by many Web pages is to use different colors to indicate links and visited links, but the way this automation works, this setting will also change the border color of the thumbnails. If my visited link color was green, for instance, then the thumbnails would have green mattes around them if a person had already been to that page! Since that's not the effect I'm looking for, I'll leave them set to white. If I were creating text links on a Web site, however, I might use different colors for the various stages of a link in order to provide a clear road map for the user of the site.

The Horizontal Slideshow gallery style will automatically switch the main image every 5 seconds.

STEP 7: The Security options let you place information from the File Info dialog, or custom text, over your image like a watermark. For this example I'm accessing the copyright notice from the File Info dialog.

STEP 7: **From the Options menu, choose Security.** You can use these options to place information from the File Info dialog, or custom text, over the large versions of your image like a watermark. **For this example, I am using the copyright notice from the File Info dialog. I've set this to be a turquoise color at 35% opacity so it will be faint but still noticeable.** If you're concerned about unauthorized usage of images you're posting to a Web

The thumbnails for the Table 1 gallery have frames that are reminiscent of slide mounts.

A large image in the Table 1 gallery style. On the right, information from the photo's File Info dialog can be displayed. Below the image are numeric links to jump to other photos in this series.

The Horizontal-Feedback gallery style with a custom background color to match the subject matter of autumn leaves. On the right, file information can be displayed and there is an area for client feedback and approval that can be emailed to you.

Chapter 37: Web Photo Galleries, Contact Sheets, and Picture Packages

site, this may be of interest to you. If you find that the result ruins the look of your images, try using smaller text, less opacity, or just turn it off altogether. **Now click the OK button and let Photoshop make a Web gallery for you! After it's done it will automatically open up the new gallery in a browser.**

ARRANGING GALLERY THUMBNAILS

The one thing that the Web Gallery feature doesn't allow you to do from within the controls that it provides is arrange the thumbnails in a specific order. In the first gallery I created using the settings in this tutorial, the vertical and horizontal thumbnails were all mixed up and it looked a bit jumbled. Fortunately, there is a way to control the arrangement of the thumbnails. The secret lies in understanding that by default Photoshop arranges the thumbnails numerically or alphabetically by file name. So, to create a thumbnail arrangement that you like, all you have to do is rename the files by adding numbers onto the front of the name. In the File Browser I reviewed the images and added 01, 02, 03, etc., to the beginning of each file name, creating an arrangement that separated the verticals and horizontals into different rows. I also looked at the colors in the photographs and placed images with strong red tones at the beginning and end of each row.

WEB GALLERIES AND RAW FILES

If you shoot with a digital camera that saves RAW files that are supported by Photoshop, you can create a Web gallery directly from the RAW files without having to process each one through the Adobe Camera Raw interface. The two methods for selecting files that were discussed previously work with RAW files as well. Either specify a folder from within the Web Photo Gallery dialog, or simply select images in the File Browser (use command-click to select noncontiguous groups of images) and then choose Web Photo Gallery from the File Browser's Automate menu. The images will be opened using the Camera Raw default settings and no changes will be made. If an image looks too underexposed or the color temperature is wrong in the File Browser view, however, then it will look this way in the finished gallery. For quick approvals from a client, this is certainly a great timesaver, but if you want the images to look their best, we recommend first processing them individually through Camera Raw and then targeting a folder of color-corrected duplicates for the Web gallery.

USING ACTIONS TO IMPROVE IMAGE SHARPNESS

The one thing that this automated Web gallery feature does not do is sharpen your images, and images that are made smaller for the Web always need careful sharpening to make them look their best. Unfortunately, we cannot really go back and sharpen the JPEGs that Photoshop created to make this gallery because then we would be compressing them as JPEGs a second time, which is not advisable for good-looking images. The solution to this situation is to go back and create a new set

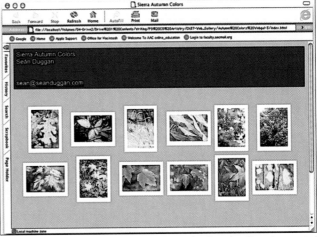

The finished index page of the Autumn Colors web gallery that Photoshop created using the settings in these steps.

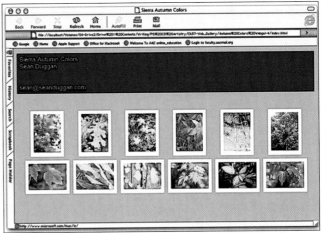

By adding numbers to the front of each file name (i.e., 01, 02, 03, etc.), you can control the ordering of the thumbnails. The images here are grouped according to whether they were vertical or horizontal, and also for color; each row begins and ends with an image that has strong red tones.

On the top is how the the blackberry bramble image looks after Web Gallery automation treated it...not very sharp. On the bottom is the same image after some custom sharpening with the unsharp mask filter.

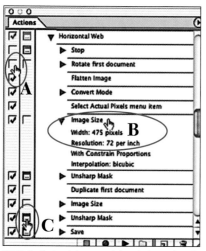

STEP 8: Customizing an existing Action script: To turn off a particular step, click in the leftmost column (A) until the checkmark is hidden. With an image open, double-click on a step (B) to change its settings; the action will record your changes and then stop. To pause the action with a dialog box open so you can adjust settings as the action is running, click in the second left column (C) to turn on the dialog icon.

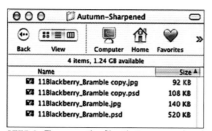

STEP 9: These are the files that were produced when I ran the Horizontal Web action on the Black-berry Bramble image. The two top ones are the thumbnail-sized versions. The bottom ones are the larger gallery images. The JPEGs here will need to be renamed to the exact same file names as those produced by the Web Gallery command. Once that is done, you can replace the first set of web image files with the new sharpened versions.

STEP 9: This is the folder structure created by Pho-toshop's Web Gallery automation.

of images and thumbnails from the original files that are the same pixel dimensions as those that Photoshop produced, and run the Unsharp Mask filter on them. Doing this manually for each image would be pretty tedious. To make it go a bit faster, I created two special Actions for creating sharpened Web images and their thumbnails at the sizes that we used in the previous tutorial. If you have the ArtistKeys loaded into the Photoshop Actions palette, you can find them listed as Horizontal Web and Vertical Web.

STEP 8: **In your original images folder that you used for the Web gallery, create another folder and separate your horizontal and vertical images.** The fastest way to create a new set of images with Actions would be to run a batch process on an entire folder. You might want to open up a single image first, however, and run the action on it to become familiar with what it's doing. **Start with a horizontal image, go to the Actions palette menu, and highlight button mode setting until it shows the Actions as a named list. Find the Horizontal Web action (it's about 28th in the list) and click the triangle handle next to it to display all the steps for that action. Click the check box next to Rotate First Document to hide the checkmark and turn off that step.** This action was originally created for images that had already been rotated to vertical in preparation for making inkjet prints, so if your images are already horizontal, they won't need rotating.

The Horizontal and Vertical Web actions include steps for flattening layers and converting to RGB, so you don't need to do any special preparation to your files. **Click the Play button to run the action.** It will resize the file to 475 pixels wide (or tall if using the Vertical Web action), allow you to choose a sharpening value (or you can use the ones that I have already entered, they're pretty good for Web images), dupli-cate it, resize it to a thumbnail 117 pixels wide, then run the unsharp mask filter on the thumbnail. Finally, it will save a Photoshop format of the thumbnail (for gener-ating future JPEGs), and then a final JPEG version. Then it will switch back to the larger image, save a PSD and JPEG versions of it, and close the file when it's done. If you're using the Vertical Web action, there is no step for rotating that you have to turn off. When you apply these Actions using a batch process, it's best to save them into a new folder. I also let the action give the file the default names, and then I renamed them after it was finished. For more detailed information on working with Actions and batch processing, refer to Chapter 11, "Automating Photoshop."

STEP 9: Once you've created the sharp-ened versions of the images and thumb-nails, you need to give them the same names as the files that were produced by the Web Gallery automation, and then replace those files with the newer, sharp-ened files. **Find the folder where Photo-shop placed your Web gallery files. Inside it is a folder called images and another called thumbnails. Open up these folders so you can see what the file names are. Rename the new sharp-ened files with exactly the same names. Once that is done, you can drag the new**

Chapter 37: *Web Photo Galleries, Contact Sheets, and Picture Packages*

files into the appropriate gallery folders and replace the versions that were created by the automation. Just make sure you're putting thumbnails into the thumbnails folder and the larger versions into the images folder. **After you've replaced all the images and thumbnails, return to the browser page displaying your gallery and hit the reload or refresh button.** You should see a definite improvement in the sharpness of your images!

GETTING BETTER TITLES

If you're using file names as titles, you're probably less than thrilled with image titles or captions that have a 3-letter file format extension. Try opening up each of your original images and going to File/File Info and entering in the title of the image in the Document Title box. Then you can redo the Web gallery automation and check the "Title" checkbox in the Large Images and Thumbnails title options. Before you redo the entire gallery, however, make backup copies of the images and thumbnail folders that have the sharpened files, so you can replace the unsharpened images again. The automation will overwrite your sharpened versions each time you redo the gallery.

Even if you do get great captions using the File Info feature, however, the actual file name, minus the extension, still shows up as the image title in the banner on the individual image pages and in the top of the browser window. If you have a file name with underscores between the words and a number before the name as in my example here, it looks a bit odd (note: file names with no spaces between words is actually recommended for the Web – see the illustration below). This is somewhat aggravating, especially since you can make sure you have the "Titles:Use File Name" option unchecked and it still shows up in these two places. To fix this involves a quick edit of the actual HTML code. Fortunately, it's not complicated and you can do it with a basic text editor such as Text Edit on the Mac or WordPad on the PC. If you use Microsoft Word to make these edits, you can change the title in the banner in the layout view, but you'll have to choose View/HTML Source in order to change the title that appears in the browser window. To modify my file, I opened up the page titled "06Japanese_Maple-2..html" in Text Edit, found the two lines of code with the title, removed the "06" and replaced the underscore with a space between the two words and then saved and closed the file. You can refer to the screenshot on the previous page to see the places in the code where I modified the text.

Located under File/File Info, the File Info dialog gives you several ways to add information to your file. This data is saved with the image and can be accessed by the Web Gallery automation for the creation of titles, captions, and copyright notices. For the best looking image titles, use this feature instead of the file names (unless you need to use file names for cataloging purposes).

Even though "Use File Name" for captions was not checked, it still appears in the banner on the individual image pages, and also in the page title at the top of the browser window. In this case it's a problem since my file name has an underscore between the two words, as well as the number in front that I used to arrange the thumbnails.

File names for the HTML gallery pages are derived from the image file names. One potential problem with the way Photoshop handles this is that it preserves the spaces between words in the file names. Files destined for the web should always use an underscore or dash character between words instead of a space, as this can sometimes cause problems. To play it safe, we recommend that you avoid spaces in your image file names that are used for web galleries. If you need your title on the web page to look nice, use the File/File Info dialog to enter a title prior to creating your web gallery.

Here is the HTML source code for the Japanese Maple-2 page opened up in Text Edit. I've highlighted two instances where I would go in and change the title. The top one is the title that appears in the top bar of the browser window, and the second one is where the title shows up in the banner on the actual web page. Fortunately, these web pages have minimal display text, so finding what you need to edit in the code is pretty easy.

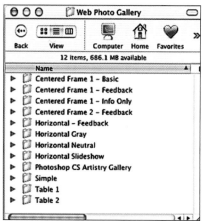

The presets for the web galleries can be found in the Photoshop application folder on your hard drive under Presets/Web Photo Gallery. Each gallery style is located in its own folder. The name of the folder is what shows up in the drop down-menu inside the Web Gallery dialog box. Here, you can see the **Photoshop CS Artistry** Gallery that I created.

CREATING CUSTOM WEB GALLERIES

If you're experienced at editing HTML, you can create your own custom Web gallery styles by duplicating one of the existing preset styles and modifying it to suit your needs. This is very useful if you want to create a gallery for your studio that always has the same unified look. The preset files can be found in the Adobe Photoshop CS/Presets/Web Photo Gallery folder on your hard drive. Any new style you create will show up in the Web gallery styles menu as long as it remains in this folder. I have created a custom gallery for Photoshop Artistry images to try this out, so let's go over some of the main points. As the focus of this book is not HTML, this is not meant to be a step-by-step tutorial, but some general guidelines to help get you started. If you are not familiar with editing HTML, either in a Web editor such as Adobe GoLive or Macromedia Dreamweaver, or straight in the code with a text editor, then you might want to skip ahead to the next section on Contact Sheets.

I began by duplicating the Simple gallery folder in the Web Photo Gallery presets. If you take a look at the HTML code for the IndexPage.htm file, you see that there are several places where there are bits of code with a percent symbol on either end. These represent values that are replaced by entries in the Web Gallery dialog box when the automation generates the final code.

The first thing I did was to change the %TITLE% value to something more absolute. By removing the %TITLE% from the code, I could make the title whatever I chose to enter here. Next, I moved on and changed the body tag values to ones that would work better for the gallery style I was planning.

After those basic changes, I moved on to more drastic alterations. First I created some graphics and an HTML table for the top banner portion of the page. I then replaced a large chunk of the default code with my new code containing my custom header graphics.

As I worked with this I found that I usually wanted to replace the generated values with ones that worked with the design I was creating. If you are creating a custom gallery, either for your own studio, or for a company intranet or extranet, then you probably want to maintain control over how it looks, and using absolute values is the way to do this, especially for things such as background, text, and link colors. If there are some things that you do want to remain editable via the Web gallery controls, then you should leave the default values in place. These are the ones in caps enclosed by two percent symbols. I left the creation of the thumbnail index alone, for example, since I wanted to be able to control the layout arrangement of

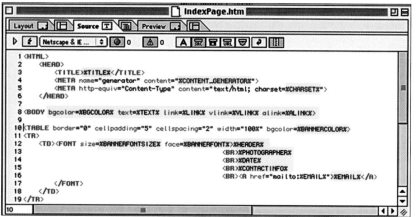

Here is the HTML for the IndexPage.htm file from the Simple style gallery template. Highlighted areas show values encased in percent symbols that are replaced by whatever is entered in the corresponding places in the Web Gallery dialog box.

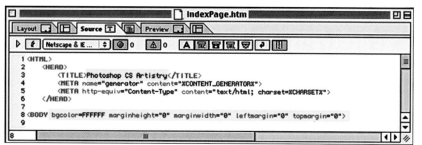

Here is the HTML for the IndexPage.htm file from the PS Artistry Gallery. Highlighted areas show places where I modified the default code. These areas will now be unavailable in the Web Gallery dialog. The title for this gallery will always be "Photoshop CS Artistry" because I have replaced %TITLE% with an absolute value.

Chapter 37: Web Photo Galleries, Contact Sheets, and Picture Packages

the thumbnails based on the number of images I was placing in the gallery.

After some testing and tweaking I finally had something that was working pretty good for my index page. I also modified the subpage where the larger images are displayed and created some new Previous, Next, and Home buttons. The files for this custom gallery are on the CD, so if you want to check them out, just drag the folder "Photoshop CS Artistry Gallery" and place it in the Web Photo Gallery Sheets folder within the Presets folder. That gallery style will then show up in the Web Photo Gallery Style menu.

For those who know how to wrangle HTML, you can come up with your own design pretty easily. This is a great feature for photographers who want to present a professional and consistent look when showing their images online.

CONTACT SHEETS

Photoshop can also automate the creation of Contact Sheets, which is a great time-saver that any photographer will appreciate. All you need to do is gather the images for your contact sheet together in a folder, or select a group of images in the File Browser. From the File menu, choose Automate/Contact Sheet II. In the contact sheet dialog box

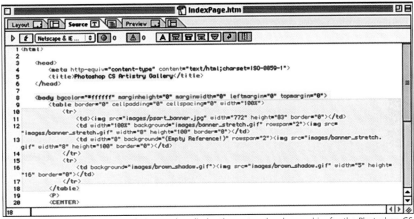

In the default source code for the Simple gallery's index page, the highlighted code shows where the banner would be created using values from the Web Gallery dialog box. I replaced this code with custom code as seen in the next illustration.

Highlighted in blue is the new code I created to display the custom header graphics for the Photoshop CS Artistry gallery. This new HTML table replaced the default code that normally contained the banner information. The code that is shown in yellow was changed to specify a fixed title for the page, as well as a background color and page margins.

This is the custom Index page for the Photoshop CS Artistry gallery.

The level 2 page for the Photoshop CS Artistry gallery.

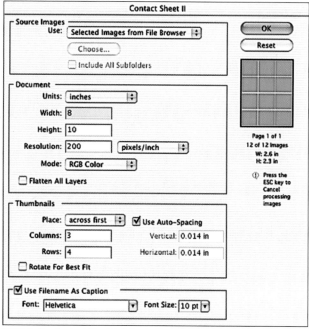

STEP 1: The Contact Sheet II dialog in Photoshop CS.

A finished contact sheet generated from the settings used here. The numbers that I added to the file names to control the arrangement of thumbnails in the Web Photo Gallery have also affected the arrangement of images on the contact sheet.

you specify the source folder, or files that are selected in the File Browser, the size and resolution of the finished sheet, and choose from four image modes (Grayscale, RGB, CMYK, Lab). In the Thumbnails section, you decide how many rows and columns of thumbnails you want and Photoshop will calculate the approximate size of the thumbnails for you based on the overall page size of your sheet. If you have too many images to fit on a page using the settings you've chosen, Photoshop will continue making as many sheets as it takes to deal with all the images. Clicking "Use Filename as Caption" will do just that, and you can choose from a short list of utilitarian typefaces. Using the file name as the caption is very useful if you want to create a printed reference catalog of your images. Unlike Web galleries, however, you cannot use the File Info dialog as a source for labeling the thumbnails. Hopefully that will be added in a future version as it is a very useful feature.

The Flatten All Layers check box will merge all the layers together when the automation is finished, leaving you with a single layer and the background. If you uncheck this, however, all of the layers, including the type layers, are preserved. This is useful if you want to further customize things like the captions, or even rearrange the thumbnails in a way that is not provided by the program.

Two options that are new to Photoshop CS are the Use Auto Spacing and Rotate for Best Fit options. Use Auto Spacing lets the program make the decision as to the spacing between the thumbnail images on the contact sheet. We recommend leaving this on as the automation usually does a pretty good job. If you turn it off, then you have to enter in your own spacing values, and it takes a lot of trial and error to get them correct. The Rotate for Best fit option will rotate all images so that they appear in the same orientation on the sheet, similar to how real 35mm contact sheets look. While this certainly looks neat and tidy, I usually leave this off, since I don't want to have to rotate the contact sheet to view vertical images in their correct orientation.

STEP 1: If you want to give the contact sheet feature a test drive, you can either use a folder of your own images, or just use the same folder you used earlier to create the Web gallery. You can also find the folder in the File Browser and select all of the thumbnails (Command-A). **Go to File/Automate/Contact Sheet II, or if you're starting from the File Browser, use the Browser's Automate menu and choose Contact Sheet II. In the Contact Sheet dialog, choose your settings and enjoy the ride!**

One thing to note if you are using selected images in the File Browser for a contact sheet, is that the images will be arranged according to how you have sorted them in the

Chapter 37: Web Photo Galleries, Contact Sheets, and Picture Packages

File Browser. So, if you have a group images sorted by Date Created, that's how they will appear on the contact sheet.

PICTURE PACKAGES

The most noteworthy improvement to the Picture Package feature in Photoshop CS is that you can now create your own custom package layouts. For photographers or labs using this feature in a production workflow, the ability to customize layouts as well as make up packages from different images will save time and materials by allowing for more flexible image layouts. To explore Photoshop's Picture Package feature, we'll use the same folder of autumn images as in the previous tutorials.

If Rotate for Best Fit is turned on, all the thumbnails will be rotated to the same orientation, much like a traditional contact sheet made from 35mm negative strips.

STEP 1: **Open any image from the Web Gallery Images folder on the CD (you can also choose one of your own images if you want to). We chose the Red Leaf 1 file. From the File menu, select Automate/Picture Package, and from the top section choose Frontmost Document for the Source. As with the Web Photo Gallery and Contact Sheet features, you can also enter Picture Package directly from the File Browser by selecting a thumbnail and choosing Picture Package from the File Browser's Automate menu.** You may see an apparent duplication of the file in the background as you enter the dialog, or when you choose the source. Photoshop is creating a low-res copy that it is using to generate the package previews. In addition to using an image that you already have open or one from the File Browser, you can select a file on disk, or even use an entire folder of images. **From the Document section in the middle of the dialog, select 8x10 inches for page size and (4) 4x5s for the layout. Set the resolution to 200 and the mode to RGB.** For most proof type prints, or small snapshot images, I have found that 200 ppi generally works just fine. As with everything, however, you should test out different resolutions to identify where your own quality threshold lies.

STEP 2: Photoshop CS lets you use different images on a single layout. **To add a new image, move your mouse over one of the thumbnails and click to select a new file for that spot of the layout. Navigate to the picture you want to use. We decided to put the Autumn Oak in that place. Next, move your mouse over the top right image in the layout and click down to select another image. We used the Dried Grasses picture.**

STEP 3: **Uncheck the Flatten Layers check box.** This will keep all the layers separate in the final layout file. In many cases, you'll probably want to just leave this checked, but this option is useful if you decide that the color of text you chose

STEP 1: The Picture Package dialog in Photoshop CS. If you have an image open when you enter the dialog, the Source is specified as the Frontmost Document.

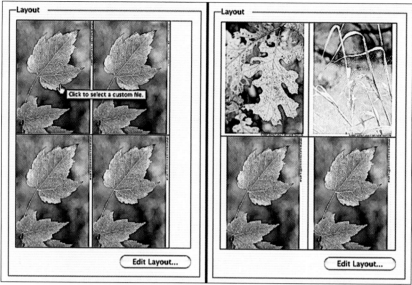

STEP 2: Move your mouse cursor over a photo on the package layout, and you can click to select a new image for that position.

for a label or copyright watermark does not work on all of the images. Having the text layers preserved lets you easily change the color or font before flattening the layout and making a print.

STEP 4: **For the Label settings, choose Title from the drop-down Content menu. This will use existing information from the File Info dialog. For the rest of the label settings that we used, refer to the screen shot on the previous page.** The position setting controls where on the image the text will appear. If you wanted to use the text as a PROOF notice, you could choose a lower opacity and rotate it so it was placed diagonally across the image. **Click OK to start the picture package automation.**

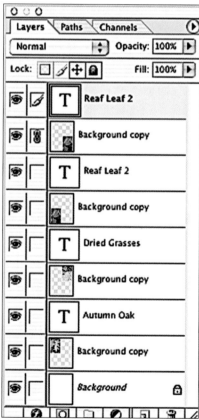

STEP 5: The Layers palette of the finished Picture Package. Note that the active text layer is linked to its respective image layer.

STEP 5: When the package is finished, check out how the titles have been added. They are rotated in the correct placement, even if a landscape image has been rotated to a portrait orientation in order for it to fit on the sheet. **One potential problem with the titles, however, is that the color and opacity you choose may not work on all images if your package is made up of different photos. If you left the Flatten All Layers option unchecked, however, you can easily change the text color and opacity to something that will show up better on each image.** If you are doing packages of multiple images, we recommend that you don't flatten the layers until you can decide if a label's color needs to be changed. If your package is of a single image, this is not as critical since you can choose a text color that you know will show up well depending on how you place it on the image.

If you decide to try this on a folder of images, Photoshop will use the chosen layout to create a picture package sheet of every image in the folder. If you have a lot of images in the folder, this could take a while and start to gobble up RAM as Photoshop leaves each of the finished packages open while it starts on the next one. If you want to cancel the operation at any time after it's begun, just press the Escape key.

CREATING CUSTOM PICTURE PACKAGE LAYOUTS

The major difference between the Picture Package feature in Photoshop CS and Photoshop 7 is the ability to easily edit an existing layout and create your own custom layouts. The capability to do this existed in version 7, but it required a complicated procedure that involved altering the actual code that Photoshop used to create the packages. Fortunately, that workaround is a thing of the past and editing a package layout is now pretty easy.

One print size that is still missing from the list of default package layouts is one that is very common to anyone who has ever had their photos processed at a 1-hour lab, a 4x6. Since many photo albums, frames and even greeting cards are formatted to fit 4x6 prints, it remains a mystery why Adobe has not added this most common of print sizes to the list of available packages. Now that we can easily edit the existing layouts, however, we'll fix this and explore how the editor works.

Chapter 37: Web Photo Galleries, Contact Sheets, and Picture Packages

STEP 1: **Open the Picture Package feature and choose a package layout that is the closest to what you want to create. Since our goal is 4x6 prints, we'll start off by selecting the (4)4x5 layout. In the lower-right corner of the dialog, press the Edit Layout button. In the Page Size popup menu, choose 8.5 x 11 inches to take advantage of the standard letter size paper. From the Units popup, choose inches.**

STEP 2: **Click on the top left image position. Photoshop refers to each image position as a zone. You can edit an image zone visually by dragging on the handles around the image, or numerically by typing in values in the fields on the left side of the dialog. We'll give both methods a try. First, change the height of the upper-left zone to 6.0 inches. Next, so we can see what we're doing, click on the lower-left image and then press the Delete Zone button to remove that zone. Click on the lower-right image, and delete that zone, too. Now click on the upper-right zone and drag down while watching the value for the height. Stop when you reach 6.0 inches. If you can't get it to be exactly 6 inches, just get it as close as you can and then type in the correct value.**

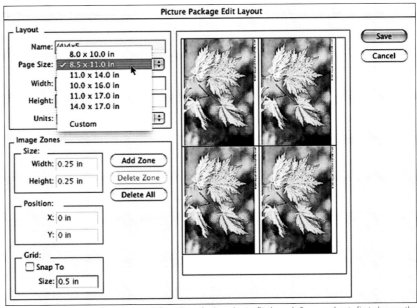

STEP 1: The Picture Package Layout Editor. To make it easier to fit three 4x6s on a sheet, first change the page size to 8.5 x 11 inches.

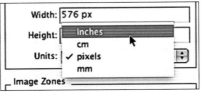

STEP 1: Unless you're particularly adept at calculating how many pixels make up a 4x6 inch print, change the Units to inches.

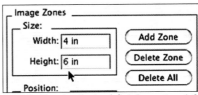

STEP 2: Changing the top left 4x5 zone to a 4x6.

STEP 3: **To add the third zone, Option-click on the top-right zone and choose Duplicate from the contextual menu. The duplicate zone appears in the top-left corner by default, so click and drag on that area to move the copy down to the lower part of the layout. Type in 6.0 inches for the width and 4.0 inches for the height to convert this zone to a horizontal orientation. Carefully place this so that it butts up against the lower edge of the top two zones. In the top of the dialog, click in the Name field and rename this new layout (3)4x6. Now click the Save button to save the edited layout. Be sure that you rename any layout before you save it so you don't replace one of the default layouts.**

STEP 3: The duplicate zone after resizing to 6 inches wide and 4 inches high.

BIBLIOGRAPHY

PUBLICATIONS

Adams, Ansel. *Examples: The Making of 40 Photographs*. Bullfinch Press.

Adams, Ansel with Mary Street Alinder. *Ansel Adams: An Autobiography*. Boston, MA: New York Graphic Society Books, 1985.

Adams, Ansel with Robert Baker. *Ansel Adams: The Camera*. Boston, MA: New York Graphic Society Books, 1980.

Adams, Ansel with Robert Baker. *Ansel Adams: The Negative*. Boston, MA: New York Graphic Society Books, 1981.

Adams, Ansel with Robert Baker. *Ansel Adams: The Print*. Boston, MA: New York Graphic Society Books, 1983.

Blatner, David, and Bruce Fraser. *Real World Photoshop 7: Industrial Strength Production Techniques*. Berkeley, CA: Peachpit Press, 2001.

Blatner, David, *Real World QuarkXPress 6*. Berkeley, CA: Peachpit Press, 2004.

Booth, Sara, ed. *Step-by-Step Electronic Design*. Peoria, IL: Step-by-Step Publishing.

Crumpler, Wendy. *Photoshop, Painter and Illustrator Side-by-Side, 2nd Edition*. Alameda, CA: Sybex, Inc., 2001.

Eismann, Katrin, Sean Duggan and Tim Grey. *Real World Digital Photography*. Berkeley, CA: Peachpit Press, 2004.

Johnson, Harald. *Mastering Digital Printing*. Cincinnati, Ohio: Muska & Lipman, 2003.

Margulis, Dan. *Professional Photoshop 7, The Classic Guide to Color Correction*. New York, NY: John Wiley & Sons, Inc., 2002.

McClelland, Deke. *Macworld Photoshop 7 Bible*. Foster City, CA: IDG Books Worldwide, 2001.

Rich, Jim. *Photoshop 6 Color Companion*. Pittsburg, PA: GATF Press, 2001.

Sammon, Rick. *Complete Guide to Digital Photography*. London: W. W. Norton & Co., 2004.

Threinen-Pendarvis, Cher. *The Painter 8 Wow! Book*. Berkeley, CA: Peachpit Press, 2004.

Weinman, Lynda. *Creative HTML Design.2*. Indianapolis, IN: New Riders Publishing, 2001.

Weinman, Lynda, and John Warren Lentz. *Deconstructing Web Graphics.2*. Indianapolis, IN: New Riders Publishing, 1998.

Weinman, Lynda. *Designing Web Graphics.3*. Indianapolis, IN: New Riders Publishing, 1999.

Weinman, Lynda, and Bruce Heavin. *Coloring Web Graphics*. Indianapolis, IN: New Riders Publishing, 1996.

Wilhelm, Henry with Carol Brower. *The Permanence and Care of Color Photographs: Traditional and Digital Color Prints, Color Negatives, Slides, and Motion Pictures*. Grinnell, IA: Preservation Publishing Company, 1993.

WEB SITES (SEE WWW.BARRYHAYNES.COM FOR INFO RELATING TO *Photoshop CS Artistry*)

Atkinson,Bill. *www.billatkinson.com*. Bill Atkinson Photography.

Cramer, Charles. *www.charlescramer.com*. Charles Cramer Photography.

Ferrari, Maria. *www.mariaferrari.com*. Maria teaches Photoshop in New York City and is a wonderful photographer.

Haynes, Barry and Wendy Crumpler. *www.Maxart.com, www.barryhaynes.com*. Photographers, Imaging consultants, and *Photoshop CS Artistry* authors. See our site for Workshops, Art Gallery, Print Sales, and free Latest Tips.

Matthews, Brett. *www.sublimelight.com*. Wonderful photographs of light on water.

Ross, Denise W. *www.dwrphotos.com*. Great hand colored black-and-white prints.

Sammon, Rick. *www.ricksammon.com*. Graphic Arts Consultant.

Velandria, Ed. *www.tarantula.com*. Award-winning Web designer and creative director at Tarantula.

Weinman, Lynda. *www.Lynda.com*. Web books and information.

Wilhelm, Henry. *www.wilhelm-research.com*. Color permanence information.

INDEX

Please note that page references with pages that are in the format CD:5 refer to chapter 32, which is on the Photoshop CS Artistry CD in PDF format.

454

COLOPHON

This book was produced almost entirely by the authors on two machines: first, a Mac Power G4 with two 450MHz processors, a 30GB internal hard disk + 200 Gigs firewire external, 1.25GB RAM, built-in video with a LaCie electron 19 blue display, ZIP transportable drive; and second, an eMac 700MHz G4 with 60GB internal, 750MB RAM, built-in 17" monitor, ZIP transportable drive. CD & DVD backups were burned using a third eMac with CD/DVD burner.

Each chapter of this book was set up as a separate document in QuarkXPress. The text was input directly into Quark using a template document with Master pages and style sheets. Charts were done in Adobe Illustrator and color correction and separation was done, of course, from Photoshop CS using the methods and settings described in this book.

Screen captures were done with Snapz Pro X. Low-res RGB captures were placed in the original documents and sized in Quark. After design decisions were made as to final size and position, Wendy's script automatically resampled them to 350 dpi, sharpened, separated, and saved as CMYK TIFFs in Photoshop. They were then reimported into Quark at 100% using Wendy's very cool sript.

Most photographs in this book are from the Polaroid SprintScan 120 scanner. There are also Imacon scans, UMax Powerlook 3000 scans, and Photo CD or Pro Photo CD scans from 35mm slides done primarily by Palmer Photographic in Mountain View, CA.

Most pages were output at 2400 dpi using a 175-line screen. Critical color proofing was done using Spectrum Digital Match Print proofs and less critical color was proofed with Fuji First Look proofs. We used the techniques explained in this book, as well as our GTI Soft-View D5000 Transparency/Print Viewer, to calibrate Photoshop CS separations on our LaCie electron 19 blue display and our eMac monitors to color proofs for critical color pages and the cover.

Transfer of files was done primarily using CDs, which were sent via UPS between the authors and the printer. Files were sent as Quark documents with high-res photos in position. Film was set in signatures of 16 pages starting with the most color-critical signatures first. In time critical instances, images and Quark files were sent via internet between the authors and the publisher.

Printing was done by CDS Publications in Medford, Oregon, direct to plate with a Creo platesetter, then printed on a Mitsubishi L-750 4 color heat set web press. The book is printed on 70lb Opus Dull and the cover is 12pt C1s with a lay-flat gloss laminate.

Typefaces are New Caledonia, New Caledonia SC&OSF, and Frutiger from Adobe and, on the cover, ITC Orbon from International Typeface Corporation.

PHOTO AND ILLUSTRATION CREDITS

The first and/or most prominent occurance of each art piece is listed. Most photos not listed here are by Barry Haynes

Wendy Crumpler *(541-754-2219)*
© 2004, Wendy Crumpler, All Rights Reserved
Peruvian Lady, Toadstools: 6
Rosehips: 8
Pumpkin: 41
Fish Art, Tree: 42
Manhattan Sunrise: 130
Mary, LuAnn: 133
Ceiling Lights: 134
Riot Grrl: 135
Delphinium: 199
Heartsinger CD Cover: 381
Brushed Red Mountain: 391
Pastel Red Mountain: 392
Painter Red Mountain: 394
Alison: 100, 392, 393
Where I'm Going: Sec Div 397

Sean Duggan *(530-477-8494)*
© 2004 Sean Duggan, All Rights Reserved
Man Sitting: 95
Jacks Internet Cafe: Chap 32 PDF
Spherical Lock: 411
Bodie Relic: 417
Miami Lifeguard Tower: 424
Fencing Series 2003: 424
Red Leaf Cluster: 424

Autumn Oak, Blackberry Bramble, Dried Grasses, Dried Husks, Japanese Maple-1, Japanese Maple-2, Orange Leaves, Rainy Day Leaves, Red Leaf-1, Red Leaves Cluster, Two Leaves, Vertical Yellow: 425-433
Photographs 2004: 406

Maria Ferrari *(212-924-1241)*
©2004, Maria Ferrari, All Rights Reserved
Gerbera Bouquett: Back Cover, 395

Barry Haynes *(541-754-2219)*
©2004, Barry Haynes, All Rights Reserved
Ship Rock Sunset: Cover
Sea Foam: Sec Div xxxv
Paris Cafe: Sec Div 125
Garribaldi Harbor: Sec Div 215
Metal Table Top: Sec Div 267
Mono Lake Grass: Sec Div 303
FernWood Pier: Sec Div 331
Golden Gate: 7
Yosemite Lake: 8
7A: 43
Wendy: 48
Paris Dog: 72
School Bus: 103
Flowers and Fence: 113
Yellow Wall, Window & Trees: 115

Aspens & Wildflowers, House: 134
The Doc and the Dummy: 135
The Selma: 159
Florida Swamp Scenes: 186
British Columbia Parliament: 194
Bandon Harbor: 197
Colony Hotel: 198
Banff, Peyto Lake: 224, 243
Kansas: 244, 255
Yellow Flowers: 256
Burnley Graveyard: 268
Al: 277
Bryce Stone Woman: 296
Costa Rica Scenes: 77, 312
McNamaras: 313, 319
Astoria Victorian: 349
The Packard: 350
Red Mountain: 381

Adams Collection *(561-694-2000)*
© 2001, Adams Collection, All Rights Reserved
Cochrane Train Station by Arthur F. Lynch, Jr.

Margee Wheeler
© 2001, Margee Wheeler, All Rights Reserved
Self Portrait: 359
Poster Artwork: 366

informIT

www.informit.com

YOUR GUIDE TO IT REFERENCE

New Riders has partnered with **InformIT.com** to bring technical information to your desktop. Drawing from New Riders authors and reviewers to provide additional information on topics of interest to you, **InformIT.com** provides free, in-depth information you won't find anywhere else.

Articles

Keep your edge with thousands of free articles, in-depth features, interviews, and IT reference recommendations—all written by experts you know and trust.

Online Books

Answers in an instant from **InformIT Online Books'** 600+ fully searchable online books.

POWERED BY

Catalog

Review online sample chapters, author biographies, and customer rankings and choose exactly the right book from a selection of more than 5,000 titles.

New Riders

www.newriders.com

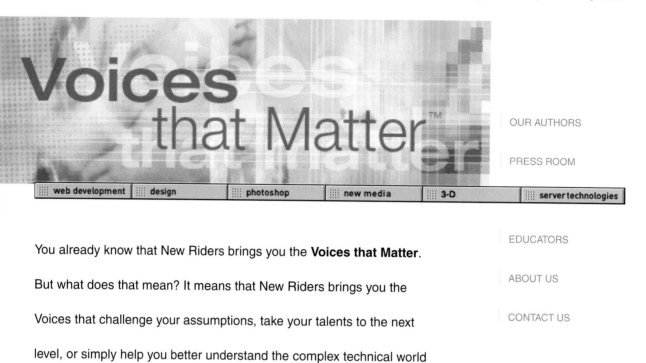

OUR AUTHORS

PRESS ROOM

| web development | design | photoshop | new media | 3-D | server technologies |

EDUCATORS

ABOUT US

CONTACT US

You already know that New Riders brings you the **Voices that Matter**.

But what does that mean? It means that New Riders brings you the

Voices that challenge your assumptions, take your talents to the next

level, or simply help you better understand the complex technical world

we're all navigating.

Visit **www.newriders.com** to find:

▸ *Discounts* on specific book purchases

▸ Never before published chapters

▸ Sample chapters and excerpts

▸ Author bios and interviews

▸ Contests and enter-to-wins

▸ Up-to-date industry event information

▸ Book reviews

▸ Special offers from our friends and partners

▸ Info on how to join our User Group program

▸ Ways to have your Voice heard

New Riders

W W W . N E W R I D E R S . C O M

VISIT OUR WEB SITE

WWW.NEWRIDERS.COM

On our Web site you'll find information about our other books, authors, tables of contents, indexes, and book errata. You will also find information about book registration and how to purchase our books.

EMAIL US

Contact us at this address: **nrfeedback@newriders.com**

- If you have comments or questions about this book
- To report errors that you have found in this book
- If you have a book proposal to submit or are interested in writing for New Riders
- If you would like to have an author kit sent to you
- If you are an expert in a computer topic or technology and are interested in being a technical editor who reviews manuscripts for technical accuracy

- To find a distributor in your area, please contact our international department at this address. **nrmedia@newriders.com**

- For instructors from educational institutions who want to preview New Riders books for classroom use. Email should include your name, title, school, department, address, phone number, office days/hours, text in use, and enrollment, along with your request for desk/examination copies and/or additional information.
- For members of the media who are interested in reviewing copies of New Riders books. Send your name, mailing address, and email address, along with the name of the publication or Web site you work for.

BULK PURCHASES/CORPORATE SALES

The publisher offers discounts on this book when ordered in quantity for bulk purchases and special sales. For sales within the U.S., please contact: Corporate and Government Sales (800) 382-3419 or **corpsales@pearsontechgroup.com**.
Outside of the U.S., please contact: International Sales (317) 428-3341 or **international@pearsontechgroup.com**.

WRITE TO US

New Riders Publishing
800 East 96th Street, 3rd Floor
Indianapolis, IN 46240

CALL US

Toll-free (800) 571-5840. Ask for New Riders.
If outside U.S. (317) 428-3000. Ask for New Riders.

FAX US

(317) 428-3280

**Commercial Photoshop
with Bert Monroy**
Bert Monroy
073571388X
$45.00

**Photoshop CS Book for
Digital Photographers**
Scott Kelby
0735714118
$39.99

**Photoshop Restoration
and Retouching, Second Edition**
Katrin Eisemann
0735713502
$49.99

**The Glitterguru on
Photoshop**
Suzette Troché-Stapp
073571133X
$39.99

**Photoshop CS
Down & Dirty Tricks**
Scott Kelby
0735713537
$39.99

**Photoshop Type Effects
Visual Encyclopedia**
Roger Pring
0735711909
$45.00

VOICES
THAT MATTER™

Our next book and/or training DVD is:

Making The Digital Print There are many steps in achieving a great digital print—having to do with properly calibrating the scanner, monitor & printer, making the scan, color correcting and sharpening the file, as well as setting it up for the printer—that are common with almost all digital printers. You'll learn how to get the best results on the latest models of the most popular printers available for photographs. For the first edition of this book, printers like the Epson Stylus Photo 1280, 2200, 4,000, 7600, 9600, and the Lightjet 5000 will be covered. The book/training DVDs will also go through many new color correction and sharpening examples showing you how to solve a range of more advanced Photoshop color correction problems. Hybrid digital printing methods, like outputting to an imagesetter and making black and white darkroom contact prints, will also be discussed. This book/DVD will also point you toward the 3 or 4 best desktop film scanners and show you how to use each one to get the highest quality scans. See www.barryhaynes.com for updates on this advanced material.

GET ON OUR E-MAIL LIST FOR COURSES AND TIPS!

Please copy this format and e-mail this information to barry@maxart.com, then we will add you to our e-mail list so we can let you know about new books, workshops, and new technical information postings on our Web site.

☐ LET US KNOW WHEN MAKING THE DIGITAL PRINT SHIPS

Actually, I'm more interested in a book about _____

_____

and I'd like to be on you information and course mailing list. Here's my important information:

Name _____

Address _____

City _____*State* _____*Zip* _____

Phone _____*E-mail* _____

See the next page for information about our workshops for Photographers and Artists

Quotes from Photoshop Instructors:

"I teach online for The New School University in New York City so my students come from all over the States and all over the world. It's critical that I have a "text book" that students can follow easily. The *Artistry* book is the best book I have found to teach the intermediate to advanced courses. Students find the examples useful because they are "real-life" problems they will have to solve. An excellent book by authors who are willing to spend time answering your questions and emails afterwards!"

Marion Suro

"Hi, Barry and Wendy. We are using *Photoshop 5 Artistry* for our digital class here at Northern Kentucky University. It is a fountain of information that will serve students well long after the class is finished... I basically learned Photoshop via your first book; I don't think it's an exaggeration to say I couldn't have done it without you. Thanks."

Barry Andersen, Professor of Art, Northern Kentucky University

I always look forward to tech editing *Photoshop Artistry*. As a contributing author for 7 books on Photoshop, a technical editor for over 12 books on Photoshop, a teacher of Photoshop, and a Photoshop user for over 10 years, I always learn a lot from Barry and Wendy. Artistry takes nothing about Photoshop at face value and reveals features and techniques that are not documented elsewhere.

Gary Kubicek
Author, Editor, Teacher
Westminster, Maryland

"Barry, we are anxiously awaiting *Photoshop 5 Artistry*! When will it be available? We use it as the primary text in our Intro to Digital Imaging course and love it. When I began using Photoshop 5, I went through each chapter to see if we would need to make any changes from procedures in the *Artistry 4* book....Thanx again to you and Wendy for the great book."

Stan Shire, Chair, Department of Photographic Imaging, Community College of Philadelphia

Quotes from Photographers:

"Simply, *Photoshop Artistry* is a book that will open the full potential of Photoshop to the user. There are theoretical sections, but the book is mainly concerned with a series of hands-on tutorials that will take you right around Photoshop and make you a competent user; the book is always there for reference if you should need it!"

With Regards, Ahmno "Himalaya CyberLink"

"Barry, Just wanted to say how much I've enjoyed your *Photoshop Artistry* books—and how much I've learned from them. I started with the Version 4 book, then bought each successive book when I upgraded to Photoshop 5 and then 6.01. At all my nature photography seminars and workshops I recommend your books as the best of all, the "must have" one if you're serious about making good prints."

John Shaw

"Barry, yours is by far the best of the Photoshop adjunct books... Wish I could come to your workshops. I continue to use your book to refresh basics... We missed meeting in Camden, Maine. Kodak invited me as an artist-in-residence and suggested that I take your Photoshop offering. I was using an Amiga at the time. Had a one-person show at the Neikrug with some of those images. Am really a photojournalist (past stringer for *Life*, *People*, *Time*, etc.) ... Look forward to many of your future books."

Judith Gefter, a few credentials: Life member of ASMP, listed in 15 Who's Who's including WW in American Art.

More Quotes from Photographers:

"Did you ever pick up a book and hear the author's voice behind your ear and know you know the voice? Well that about describes how I met you two. I've started reading, and I just needed to say how pleased I am. I'm a computer professional, system architect, and have been doing serious nature photography for five years. I recently decided to extend my photo activities through a digital darkroom. I greatly enjoyed visiting your site; it transpires the same warmth and good feeling I found in your book."

Milicska Jalbert, Montreal, Quebec

"Barry-
Thank you and your co-authors for writing *Photoshop 7 Artistry*. I'm having a ball with *Matering the Digital Image*. It is giving new life to the 10,000 35mm chromes I've taken over the last 27 years. I now seem to have an almost inexhaustable library of image components."

Nick Dantona

"As a nature photographer I am particularly concerned with enhancing my photos without making artifical manipulations; this book has shown me the exquisite subtleties of photoshop that allow me to make the best print possible without altering the content of my image. My classmates at the Digital Darkroom class taught at Corcoran College for the Arts in Washington, D.C. range from graphic designers to art students, and we all agree that *Photoshop 6 Artistry* is truly a must-have book for photoshop users of all levels."

Cristina Mittermeier

"I've just discovered *Photoshop 7 Artistry*, highly recommended by my tutor. I'm a newbie, also trying to use my right brain for a change. I have all the equipment: I just need to use my mind and heart. Many thanks. I am in awe of what you are doing and find your "voice" in *Photoshop 7 Artistry* to be delightful."

Stephen P. Herman, M.D.

"I have both your 5.5 & PS 7 Artistry books and am now using PS 7 exclusively for my landscape and wildlife photography business. Your PS 7 book is by far the best and most used resource I own. Bravo!!"

Chuck Klingsporn

Quotes About Our Workshops:

"Barry Haynes and Wendy Crumpler's book and workshop have accelerated my exploration of the "digital darkroom." In-depth instruction and thorough workshop experience in scanning film, Photoshop technique, and printing have vastly shortened my learning curve and leveraged my abilities closer to the professional level that I seek. I heartily recommend that every serious photographer devour Barry and Wendy's book and enroll in their workshop."

Berle Stratton

"A very pleasant, thorough, and intensive yet diverse workshop that is taught with each participant's individual and unique needs in mind. Barry helped me to approach digital printing on a more technical level without compromising creativity."

Dominic Abbatiello

Check our Web site at www.barryhaynes.com for more quotes from workshop students and *Photoshop Artistry* readers.